TOURISM

TOURISM

second edition

a modern synthesis

STEPHEN J. PAGE AND JOANNE CONNELL

THOMSON ™

Australia · Canada · Mexico · Singapore · Spain · United Kingdom · United States

Tourism: A Modern Synthesis, Second Edition
Stephen J. Page and Joanne Connell

Publishing Director John Yates	**Publisher** Jennifer Pegg	**Development Editor** Natalie Aguilera
Production Editor Alissa Chappell	**Manufacturing Manager** Helen Mason	**Marketing Manager** Leo Stanley
Typesetter Saxon Graphics, Derby	**Production Controller** Maeve Healy	**Cover Design** Land-Sky Ltd
Text Design Design Delux, Bath, UK	**Printer** C&C Printing Press, China	

Copyright © 2006
Thomson Learning

The Thomson logo is a registered trademark used herein under licence.

For more information, contact
Thomson Learning
High Holborn House
50-51 Bedford Row
London WC1R 4LR

or visit us on the World Wide Web at:
http://www.thomsonlearning.co.uk

ISBN-13: 978-1-84480-198-5
ISBN-10: 1-84480-198-5

This edition published 2006 by
Thomson Learning.

British Library Cataloguing-in-Publication Data
A catalogue record for this book is available from the British Library.

Brief contents

 V **Trends and themes in the use of tourist resources** 405

 VI **Managing tourism activities** 473

Contents

Understanding tourism 1

Understanding the tourism industry 87

6 Information communication technologies and e-tourism 108

7 Travel intermediaries – tour operators and travel agents 124

Managing tourist operations and communicating with the visitor 225

11 Human resource management in tourism 227

12 Financing tourism operations 244
(John Pinfold and Stephen J. Page)

16 Marketing tourism destinations 319

The impact of tourism 341

IV

17 Economic impacts 342

xiv

Contents

Trends and themes in the use of tourist resources 405

Managing tourism activities 473

27 The future of tourism 515

Preface

Welcome to the second edition of *Tourism: A Modern Synthesis*, which has been completely revised, rewritten and redesigned to meet the needs of the reader after extensive feedback from readers, adopters, students and reviewers. This new edition, builds upon the embryonic book published in 2001, and as tourism has continued to develop as a subject of study, the book has evolved to incorporate many of the new themes and debates which now impact upon the study of tourism.

The features of this book

The changes which have occurred in international and domestic tourism globally since 2001 have been massive. Events such as 9/11, SARS, the 2004 Asian Tsunami to name but a few have led commentators to depict tourism as operating in a turbulent times. But underpinning the current thinking associated with the highly volatile nature of tourism, is over 30 years of academic endeavour in the study of tourism, which has built up a large collection of concepts, theoretical debates and industry examples. This new edition seeks to embody many of these new methods of thinking about the development, management and operation of tourism as a global activity, embracing many of the classic and popular concepts and approaches that have become firmly embedded in the subject. Above all the book, sets out to link the conceptual issues with practical real world examples in a cohesive and concise framework that is both logical, topical and interesting for the reader.

The first edition evolved from the efforts of four authors but in this edition, a cohesive approach has been adopted, to present a seamless transition through the book with new material to show how current thinking has moved on since the first edition. The features of the book have also expanded to bring the subject more to life than the first edition. The book has seen new material added in every chapter, particularly in the tourism industry section which has seen massive change, notably with the e-travel revolution, new methods of management and massive changes in the way tourism operates globally as well as with new forms of supply such as low cost airlines.

This book is an invaluable global resource for any student or teacher of tourism, as a concise resource for classroom and independent study, given the additional features of the book which make it highly desirable as a resource:

Chapter Learning Outcomes are used at the beginning of each chapter to focus the reader on the expected outcome they should derive after reading the chapter, which is helpful in identifying the key features a lecture or tutorial might seek to develop;

Discussion Questions and Exercises are included at the end of every chapter so that the reader can self-review the subject they have studied and see how the knowledge they have accessed on tourism can be applied to current themes in tourism;

Tourism Insights have been introduced in this edition, as opposed to large unwieldy case studies. These are short in-depth discussions of a contemporary theme or issue in tourism. In some cases, they focus on problems posed by tourism, in other cases, they highlight good practice or current thinking on a theme;

Web-based Case Studies are also included on the website to provide more detailed analysis of key issues and to avoid diverting the reader's attention from the main flow of the book and important issues and concepts. They are a supplementary learning aid;

Further Reading is identified at the end of every chapter to identify current thinking and literature which might help the reader to begin further research on the subject. As the tourism literature is growing at an exponential rate, this simple signpost to a key study is a starting point and a self-help feature;

References are included at the end of each chapter. Whilst the first edition minimized the number of references in each chapter, this edition introduces many classic and contemporary studies appearing in the academic literature. They act as a starting point for further research when writing essays, undertaking assignments or beginning extended projects and dissertations;

Web-Based Sources are used throughout the text to highlight industry examples, good practice and additional sources of material to help with assignments and in-class discussion, since tourism is a commercial business subject and so a blend of industry material was seen as essential;

Tables are used to provide illustrations of the current scale, impact and as ways of summarizing key features of a tourism phenomenon. Current commercial data is also presented, together with snapshots of recent research studies on contemporary tourism themes;

Figures are used to explain key concepts, simplify complex issues and to identify the context of tourism (i.e. locations, localities and places) as well as providing a road map of key issues for topics.

Photographs have been sourced from various tourism organizations and bodies to bring key elements of tourism to life, expanding upon specific themes discussed in the text;

A **Glossary of Key Terms** has been included to help guide the reader through the jargon, complex terminology and concepts introduced throughout the book.

The structure of the book

The principal feature of each chapter is that it is intended to cover the breadth and scope needed at an introductory level. It introduces basic principles and concepts which an introductory lecture on the topic might want to cover in an up-to-date and discursive way. The book is not a simple compendium of facts and figures. Instead, it is a balance of much-needed concepts associated with the analysis of tourism. Above all, the sub-title *Modern Synthesis* is exactly that: it introduces current thinking on many of the key themes in each chapter along with the essential concepts and issues in an unambiguous manner.

It is intended that this book will help students to have a thorough understanding of:

- the concepts and characteristics of tourism as an area of academic and applied study;
- the structure of and interactions in the tourism industry;
- the place of tourism in the communities and environments that it affects;
- the nature and characteristics of tourists.

The book adopts a fairly straightforward approach to tourism as Figure 0.1 shows. It has a series of integrated sections and chapters and their rationale is outlined in the following section:

Part One: Understanding Tourism

Part One of the book provides the wide range of concepts and approaches developed over the last forty years to understand the nature of tourism and characteristics of tourists. The underpinning concept of globalization is introduced as a theme running throughout the book, given the global nature of tourism. The volatility of tourism is outlined, with an Insight focused on the impact of SARS and effect on tourism. This leads to a wide-ranging review of how to conceptualize and understand tourism. The historical evolution of tourism demand, and its measurement and analysis are also presented. The growing interest in tourists as consumers is also discussed, highlighting the growing recognition of tourism as a global consumer product.

Part Two: Understanding the Tourism Industry

Part Two of the book is essentially focused upon the concept of supply in tourism, and the tools which have evolved to analyse and manage it. The global expansion of new trends using technology, notably the e-travel revolution is discussed which provides a benchmark for further debate in subsequent chapters. This theme is apparent in the different components of supply (tourism intermediaries, transport, attractions and accommodation/hospitality services).

Part Three: Managing Tourist Operations and Communicating with the Visitor

Part Three of the book builds upon Parts One and Two, identifying the tools, techniques and concepts associated with the management of supply and demand. As a people business, the first chapter discusses human resource issues which is followed by the often neglected area of financing tourism businesses. The role of entrepreneurship in creating innovation, forcing businesses to adapt, develop and accommodate change is presented, with examples of how entrepreneurs established individual businesses. One consequence of change in tourism, is the need for management of private sector activity in tourism, which leads to an in-depth discussion of the public sector's role in tourism. This also provides a basis for the subsequent chapters on tourism marketing concepts and how destinations are created and marketed by different agencies to explain how the tourism sector communicates with consumers.

Part Four: The Impact of Tourism

In Part Four, the natural outcome of tourism activity, resulting from the supply and demand issues, is examined in terms of tourism impacts. The scope of economic, sociocultural and environmental impacts are presented, along with the tools used by researchers to understand and measure tourism impacts. This provides a background for the in-depth analysis of the concept of sustainability and its development as a tool for the planning and development of tourism as well as current challenges to sustainable tourism such as global warming.

Part Five: Trends and Themes in the Use of Tourist Resources

In Part Five, the impact of tourism is examined in relation to the different resources and environments consumed by tourism. The examples of urban, rural, coastal and resort tourism and the less developed world provides topical and insightful perspectives on different types of tourism destination.

Part Six: Managing Tourism Activities

In Part Six, the culmination of tourism in different environments raises the issue of how we need to plan and manage tourist activity. The role of tourism planning and its implementation is reviewed, and the current thinking on the concept of the tourist experience, the principles of service quality and how to enhance the visitor experience are discussed. The highly contentious and volatile nature of tourist health and safety, as impinging upon tourist decision-making and tourist development is outlined in detail, as a current theme affecting global tourism. The book then concludes with a series of debates associated with how to conceptualize, analyse and measure future change in tourism.

Companion website

The book is also accompanied by a companion website available at http://www.thomsonlearning. co.uk/page2 which contains:

- self-evaluation questions
- web case studies with self-evaluation questions
- web resource links
- PowerPoint slides with a facility to download the main figures from the book.

Publisher acknowledgements

Many people have contributed directly to the book with case studies: Eric Laws and Grace Wen; Paul McCafferty and indirectly, two of the former authors of the first edition, whose former chapters were consulted. At the University of Stirling, a number of people provided help with the typing and figures: Neil McLaren, Sharon Martin and Lynne McCulloch. At Thomson Learning, Jennifer who steered the second edition through to the finished product. John Pinfold, Massey University, New Zealand, co-authored Chapter 12.

The publishers would like to thank the following academics who gave their time and advice by reviewing the second edition of this text at the proposal and manuscript stages:

Shirley Barrett, University of Ulster, Magee College, Londonderry
Brandon Crimes, University of Hertfordshire, Hatfield
Patrick De Groote, Hasselt University, Hasselt/Diepenbeek
Arnaud Frapin-Beaugé, International Hotel Management Institute, Kastanienbaum
Joan Henderson, Nanyang Technological University, Singapore
Howard Hughes, The Manchester Metropolitan University, Manchester
Anna Leask, Napier University, Edinburgh
Richard Lewis, Sheffield Hallam University, Sheffield
Ian Rodwell, Grimsby Institute for Further & Higher Education, Grimsby
Gaye Walsh, Buckinghamshire Chilterns University College, High Wycombe.

Walk-through tour

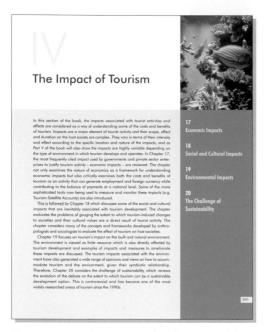

Part opener An overview of each section of the book and how the chapters link together.

Chapter opener Bullet points at the start of each chapter highlight the concepts, each referenced in terms of expected learning outcomes.

Glossary terms On the companion website key terms are explained in more detail.

Photographs The text is illustrated with relevant visual material from different tourism environments to highlight key points from across the globe.

Tables Tables provide a range of tourism data, summaries of key themes and snapshots of key research data published on tourism.

Insight box Insights provide more in-depth analysis of key and relevant themes discussed in each chapter.

Numbered list Key points are listed as bullet points or numbered lists to highlight key findings.

Book structure

The tourist and the tourism sector
(Chapter 1)

Demand

- The evolution of tourism (Chapter 2)
- Understanding tourism demand (Chapter 3)
- Understanding the tourist as a consumer (Chapter 4)

Supply

- Understanding and managing tourism supply: an introductory framework. Tourism as a business (Chapter 5)
- Information communication technology and eTourism (Chapter 6)
- Travel intermediaries: tour operators and travel agents (Chapter 7)
- Transporting the tourist (Chapter 8)
- Attractions (Chapter 9)
- Tourist accommodation and hospitality services (Chapter 1)

The integration of demand and supply

Managing tourism business

- Human resource management in tourism (Chapter 11)
- Financing tourism operations (Chapter 12)
- Tourism and entrepreneurship (Chapter 13)
- The role of the public sector in tourism (Chapter 14)
- The marketing of tourism in the public and private sector: concepts and destination marketing (Chapter 15 and 16)

The impact of tourist activity

- The economic impact (Chapter 17)
- The social and cultural impact (Chapter 18)
- The environmental impact (Chapter 19)
- Tourism and sustainability (Chapter 20)

Dimensions of tourist activity

- Urban tourism (Chapter 21)
- Rural tourism (Chapter 22)
- Coastal and resort tourism (Chapter 23)
- Tourism in the less developed world (Chapter 24)

The tourist experience

- Planning and managing the tourist experience (Chapter 25)
- Tourist health and safety: global challenges for tourism (Chapter 26)

The future of tourism

- The future of tourism (Chapter 27)

About the website

TOURISM: A Modern Synthesis Second Edition

Stephen J. Page and Joanne Connell

Visit the *Tourism: A Modern Synthesis* companion website at
www.thomsonlearning.co.uk/page2
to find valuable teaching and learning material including:

- An Instructors' Manual that includes exercises and the answers to the questions at the end of each chapter

- PowerPoint slides

- Test bank

- Weblinks

- Articles for further reading

Case matrix

Insight = Mini case in the chapter
W = Web based case accessed from www.thomsonlearning.co.uk/page2

Insight	Web Case	Case Title	Destination/ Location	Page Number
1.1		The impact of SARS on tourism in Asia – the effect of crises on tourism growth	South East Asia	5
1.2		Globalization and tourism: South Korean tourism activity in New Zealand – Kyung-Sik Woo and Stephen J. Page	New Zealand	17
	1.1W	An expanding niche market for youth travel – the student gap year and tourism	UK	
2.1		The evolution of tourism in Monaco as a high-class tourism destination	Monaco	26
2.2		The history of the Thomas Cook Company: Milestones in its development	UK and global	27
2.3		Holidays in inter-war Scandinavia	Scandinavia	29
	2.1W	A typical oral history of a visitor to a UK seaside resort in the 1960s	UK	
	2.2W	Literary tourism development – the Trossachs, Scotland: Evolution, continuity and change	Scotland	
	2.3W	The establishment of the first National Tourism Organization, the New Zealand Tourist and Health Resorts (THR) in 1901	New Zealand	
3.1		Examples of tourism statistics for five countries	Global	52
3.2		The United Kingdom's international passenger survey	UK	58
3.3		The United Kingdom Tourism Survey (UKTS)	UK	59
	3.1W	The Chinese outbound boom, Grace Wen Pan and Eric Laws	China	
4.1		Tourist motivation – adventure tourism as a global growth market	Global	81
	4.1W	Motivations for visiting gardens in Great Britain	Great Britain	
5.1		easyJet's growth as a tourist supply firm – a major success story of growth and competition	Europe	100
5.2		Managing costs as a tool to stay competitive: the case of the airline sector	Global	103
6.1		The scale of e-travel in the USA and Europe	USA and Europe	111
6.2		The development of GDS	Global	113
	6.1W	e-tourism, the tourism industry and e-business in Europe	Europe	
7.1		The Cendant Corporation – and travel distribution	Global/USA	127
7.2		TUI AG – the world's largest integrated tour operator	Europe	132
7.3		Travel agencies in Australia	Australia	144
	8.1W	International aviation cooperation – the Association of Asia Pacific Airlines	Asia-Pacific	
	8.2W	Yield management in budget airlines: The case of easyJet	Europe	

Understanding Tourism

Tourism is a global phenomenon that has experienced rapid growth in the post-1945 period, particularly in the developed countries of the world. To help explain how, where and why tourism has developed through the ages, its importance and significance in modern society, the first four chapters in this book set the scene so that we can begin by defining and understanding the global phenomenon called 'tourism'.

The first chapter discusses the various problems of defining tourism and the ways in which the study of tourism helps us understand the scale and extent of the growth in tourism globally. The field of study known as tourism is also introduced to the reader to understand how different people from different disciplines study tourism. These issues having been presented, the next chapter expands on the concept of the historical development of tourism, examining some of the factors that have promoted the growth, expansion and decline of tourism in different places and through distinct periods of time. Indeed, an historic perspective stresses the dynamic and ever-changing nature of tourism activity, highlighting the time frames over which tourism can grow and subsequently decline and reflecting changes in consumer preferences, available modes of travel and the emergence of competing destinations. It also highlights the theme of continuity and change in tourism activity and demand. The issues relating to demand are further explored in Chapter 3; in particular how changes in tourism development can be affected by the diversity of social, economic and political factors that shape tourism demand. Understanding tourism demand inevitably involves some discussion of tourism statistics and the various measures used by organizations such as the World Tourism Organization in documenting and monitoring the global changes in tourism. In Chapter 4, the focus shifts to unravelling how the individual tourist or group of tourists decide to pursue a tourism experience, focusing on the perennial problem facing tourism researchers and marketers: what motivates a tourist to travel to a specific destination or place? Central to this discussion about why people go on holiday and why they choose certain types of holiday activities are the different concepts and theories put forward by researchers in an attempt to explain the range of factors and situations which shape tourist motivation.

So, in summary, this grouping of chapters begins with a wide-ranging review of the field of tourism and tourism demand, followed by an examination of the development of places promoted by growth in tourism demand, the tourist as source of demand and the factors which shape specific forms of demand.

1

Introduction to Tourism: Themes, Concepts and Issues

Learning outcomes

In this chapter, we explore the nature of tourism as a subject area and the problems of defining the terminology of tourism. After reading the chapter and answering the questions, you should be able to understand:

- why tourism is an important subject to study

- how different definitions of tourism have been developed and the frameworks used to study tourism

- the different forms of tourism

- the difference between domestic and international tourism

- the changing nature of global tourism.

Overview

This chapter presents an introduction to the study of tourism and the concepts with which students need to be acquainted, including the meaning of 'tourism' and what is meant by the terms 'tourist', 'traveller', 'visitor' and 'excursionist'. Some of the leading studies in the growing field of tourism studies are reviewed in the chapter to provide an overview of the evolution of tourism as an area of study. Some of the basic patterns of international tourism are examined and the issues relating to tourism development in the wider environment of global change are recognized.

Introduction

Tourism is not a new phenomenon: Smith (2004: 25) noted: 'tourism and travel have been part of the human experience for millennia', describing it as a form of nomadism that characterizes *Homo sapiens*, which is both normal and, under the right conditions, pleasurable. However, in the last thirty years, most certainly with the rise of the jet aircraft, tourism has grown in significance and emerged as a global phenomenon, affecting an increasing range of environments and attracting new markets as opportunities for travel have widened. Although the latter part of this chapter will examine in detail what we mean by the terms 'tourism' and 'tourist', it is useful to outline a number of the essential ideas which are associated with tourism. In essence, tourism is associated with the following issues:

- travelling away from one's home for 24 hours
- using one's leisure time to travel and take holidays
- travelling for business.

Whilst these three issues are a simplification of what is meant by 'tourism', this book aims to address many of the questions and themes which are important in developing an understanding of tourism, which is a convenient catch-all term often used without a clear understanding of its meaning, scope and extent. This book assumes no prior knowledge of the subject area, progressively developing the reader's understanding of the scope, complexity and range of issues that the tourism phenomenon poses for anyone who is serious about the study of the subject.

The late twentieth century and the new millennium have witnessed the sustained growth of the leisure society in which people place value on holidays, travel and the experience of visiting new places and societies. The growth of this consumer-focused society in the developed world since the 1950s, with its emphasis on **discretionary spending** on leisure activities, reflects greater disposable income and the increased availability of time to engage in leisure pursuits and holidays. Although this **leisure society** has its roots in the Western developed world, trends that emerged in the 1990s indicated an expansion in the global propensity to travel and engage in holidays. As a result of major economic, political, social and cultural changes, demand is escalating in countries formerly not engaged in international tourism activity such as **post-Communist countries** and in new world regions such as Asia, China and the Indian subcontinent.

Tourism: A global activity

Most existing tourism textbooks have failed to adopt a truly global perspective to embody the speed of change in tourism on a world scale. Tourism is part of a global process of change and development (known as **globalization**) which is no longer confined to the developed countries that traditionally provided the demand for world travel. In this respect, understanding the pace of change in tourism is more complex as the forces of change are diverse and not homogeneous. Increasingly, the development of tourism throughout the world is a function of complex factors that coalesce to generate dynamic processes that one must understand in a local context, while recognizing the national and international factors affecting change. Therefore, understanding how and why changes in tourism activity occur, what motivates people to travel and how their patterns of tourism affect tourism destinations and destination communities are pervasive challenges now facing tourism organizations, researchers and students. Increasingly, governments are recognizing the importance of tourism, in particular to national economies, but they are also recognizing the problems arising from tourism activity as a route to national economic development. As an example of a government boosting a tourism economy, in July 2004, the UK Culture Secretary launched the strategy *Tomorrow's Tourism Today* for England, with a vision of increasing the annual turnover of tourism from £76 billion in the UK in 2002 to £100 billion in 2010 (www.culture.gov.uk). This example demonstrates the growing importance which a national government attaches to increasing the economic development potential of the sector and the need to reduce the UK's balance-of-payments travel deficit due to outbound travel, which rose from £2 billion in 1990 to £15 billion in 2002.

It is easy to underestimate the global significance of tourism. However, as the following statistics suggest, tourism is one of the most important global industries. In 1991, the international tourism industry employed 112 million people worldwide and generated over US$2.5 trillion at 1989 prices. By 2003, this had reached 214 million people employed, according to the World Travel and Tourism Council. In 2003, the World Tourism Organization estimated that tourism was worth US$474 billion. In 1996, 593 million tourists travelled abroad. In 2003, 694 million tourists travelled worldwide. In global terms, the expansion of international tourism continues to generate an insatiable demand for overseas travel as the following statistics show:

- Europe remains the most visited of all regions of the world, with 401 million arrivals in 2003.

- The Americas had 112 million arrivals in 2003, a 19.8 per cent share of the total market.

- The fastest growing region (up to 2002 and excluding the effect of SARS) was the East Asia Pacific region with 119 million arrivals in 2003.

- Africa received 30 million arrivals in 2003 as did the Middle East.

Therefore, it is not surprising that many analysts at the World Travel and Tourism Council argue that tourism is the world's largest industry. Seeking evidence to substantiate this claim was particularly difficult until an accounting process known as **Tourism Satellite Accounts** (TSAs) was developed to provide more reliable and comparable data generated by individual nations (see Chapter 17 on economic impacts), as it has been easy for governments to underestimate the real value tourism has in different countries. However, there is growing evidence that tourism is a volatile economic activity that can be subject to shock waves, such as the oil crisis in the 1970s, Gulf War, the **Asian economic crisis** in 1997 and 1998, the effect of 9/11 and the impact of **SARS** (see Insight 1.1). Such events rapidly changed the economic fortunes of the tourism industry in specific countries and heightened public consciousness about global travel and the associated risks. They illustrate how consumer confidence can be damaged by media reporting, resulting in changes in consumer behaviour, propensity to travel and choice of destinations.

INSIGHT 1.1

The impact of SARS on tourism in Asia – the effect of crises on tourism growth

SARS (Severe Acute Respiratory Syndrome) was first observed in China and Hong Kong in November 2002 (Table 1.1), having been identified as a new type of virus – a novel corona-type virus which produces flu-like symptoms and can prove fatal. The distribution of the virus by a number of super-carriers (i.e. travellers who were unaware they were carriers) meant that it was subsequently passed on as those carriers travelled across the world, particularly in the case of trips to Vietnam, Canada and Singapore. What is apparent from this is the rapid geographical diffusion by air travel, highlighting the globalized nature of tourism, and the regional to global spread. Initially, the infection spread from Guangdong province in China to Hong Kong; subsequently, a super-carrier in Hong Kong infected 12 other people who then travelled by air to Canada, the USA, Vietnam and Singapore. The global nature of the health crisis meant that by April 2003 there were 3000 cases in 27 countries. The effects of this crisis on the region included hotel occupancy rates in Hong Kong's tourism sector dropping from 85 per cent to 10–20 per cent in

some cases. In the UK, travel insurers in late April withdrew cover for travel to SARS-affected areas whilst airlines continued to reduce capacity.

According to APEC (2003), the SARS outbreak could have reduced GDP growth in the Asia Pacific region in 2003 by 0.5–1 per cent. Some of the impacts on tourist arrivals by air in Asia 2003 observed by APEC (2003) were:

- Air Canada air travel to Asia dropped 18 per cent in March 2003.

- Visitor arrivals in Hong Kong dropped 65 per cent in April and 68 per cent in May 2003.

- Visitor arrivals to Bali in Indonesia dropped 35 per cent in March 2003.

- In Malaysia, visitor arrivals dropped 58.6 per cent in April 2003.

- In Japan, Asia's largest outbound travel market, sales of overseas travel in 13 major travel agencies dropped

47 per cent in April 2003, 59 per cent in May 2003 and 59 per cent in June 2003.

- Arrivals in the Philippines April–June 2003 from East Asia dropped 25 per cent.
- In April 2003, visitor arrivals in Singapore fell 67 per cent.
- Taiwan experienced an 82 per cent drop in arrivals in May and 67 per cent drop in June 2003.
- Thailand saw a drop of 35 per cent in visitor arrivals in April 2003.
- Vietnam experienced a 50 per cent drop in arrivals in April and a 75 per cent drop in May 2003.

In fact the World Travel and Tourism Council (www.wttc.org) reports on SARS identified the overall expected direct impact in Hong Kong in 2003 as:

- US$3.6 billion in lost revenue
- 27 340 jobs lost
- US$1.2 billion of GDP lost

while the wider impact on the travel and tourism economy could be as much as 41 270 jobs lost, US$3.6 billion of GDP lost, US$0.3 billion lost in exports, services and merchandise and US$0.3 billion lost in personal and business travel by residents and other companies.

To restore passenger confidence, Singapore Airlines instituted a website setting out health tips for passengers, the distribution of health kits on board their aeroplanes, thermal scanning of passengers at arrival gates for signs of

SARS, links to the World Health Organization website and a press release and diagram explaining air quality on board its aircraft along with the press release from Association of Asia Pacific Airlines to dispel many of the myths on air quality. It also reassured passengers with an explanation of the health checks it was undertaking on ground staff and the measures taken at check-in to identify passengers with signs of SARS. Given the international media coverage of SARS and the media attention cycle which continued to feature it for a number of months, a local issue was amplified to a global concern. However, powerful images and messages were portrayed by the global media that certainly compounded the impact of SARS on Asian and Canadian tourism; some reports even suggested that tourists should not visit Toronto, where an outbreak occurred. Given the general public's poor knowledge and understanding of the disease, this style of media reporting made the short-term effects more serious for affected tourism destinations. A number of good studies exist for further reading on the SARS epidemic, including those by Henderson (2003) and Dombey (2003) who focus on Singapore and China respectively and their respective tourism industries. These studies reinforce the point that tourism can be severely and suddenly affected by crises such as health problems and terrorism (e.g. 9/11) as well as through media reporting which forms and shapes tourist's perceptions of destinations and their relative safety. However, the ability of tourism to bounce back from a crisis must be recognized: recovery rates after severe events are generally two to three years (or even sooner as in the case of SARS).

This chapter now examines some of the key concepts that underpin the study of tourism, including:

- the scope of tourism as an area of study
- tourism as an integrated system
- definitions of tourism
- international and domestic tourism patterns
- tourism as a global activity and the implications of globalization.

In the process, several contemporary themes and issues that highlight the difficulties and nuances of both understanding and managing tourism as an activity are explored.

Tourism as an area of study

Tourism is now embraced as a subject for serious academic study but it has not always been this way. Prior to the 1980s, the study of tourism as an intellectual pursuit was viewed by many academics and analysts as superficial and not really worthy of academic respect in the same way that established disciplines, such as history, economics and politics, were. Indeed, tourism was often perceived as a practitioner subject taught at craft level. This changed considerably in the 1990s. Yet tourism does have a much longer history of study, as Hall and Page (2005) chart, with

TABLE 1.1 Summary of probable SARS cases with onset of illness from 1 November 2002 to 31 July 2003

Areas	Cumulative numbers	Number of deaths	Date of onset of 1st probable case	Date of onset of last probable case
Australia	6	0	26.2.03	1.4.03
Canada	251	43	23.2.03	12.6.03
China	5327	349	16.11.02	3.6.03
China SAR	1755	299	15.2.03	31.5.03
China Macao	1	0	5.5.03	5.5.03
Taiwan	346	37	25.2.03	15.6.03
France	7	1	21.3.03	3.5.03
Germany	9	0	9.3.03	6.5.03
India	3	0	25.4.03	6.5.03
Indonesia	2	0	6.4.03	17.4.03
Italy	4	0	12.3.03	20.4.03
Kuwait	1	0	9.4.03	9.4.03
Malaysia	5	2	14.3.03	22.4.03
Mongolia	9	0	31.3.03	6.5.03
New Zealand	1	0	20.4.03	20.4.03
Philippines	14	2	25.2.03	5.5.03
Ireland	1	0	27.2.03	27.2.03
South Korea	3	0	25.4.03	10.5.03
Romania	1	0	19.3.03	19.3.03
Russian Federation	1	0	5.5.03	5.5.03
Singapore	238	33	25.2.03	5.5.03
South Africa	1	1	3.4.03	3.4.03
Spain	1	0	26.3.03	26.3.03
Sweden	5	0	28.3.03	23.4.03
Switzerland	1	0	9.3.03	9.3.03
Thailand	9	2	11.3.03	27.5.03
UK	4	0	1.3.03	1.4.03
USA	27	0	24.2.03	13.7.03
Vietnam	63	5	23.2.03	14.4.03
TOTAL	**8096**	**774**		

Source: World Health Organization (www.who.int)

reference to the work of geographers dating back to the 1920s. Today, many schools, colleges, polytechnics and universities around the world offer courses in tourism-related studies, with qualifications offered from certificate level through to PhD level (see Figure 1.1), and it is now maturing as a subject area in its own right.

The majority of influential tourism textbooks which have popularized the study of tourism are a product of the 1980s and early 1990s, despite some notable exceptions in the 1970s (e.g. Burkart and Medlik 1974, 1975) and a rapid profusion of specialist texts have also emerged in the new millennium. The rapid expansion in the number of tourism textbooks and **academic journal** articles published in top journals such as *Annals of Tourism Research, Tourism Management* and the *Journal of Travel Research* are one indication of the emergence of the subject as a serious area of study at vocational, degree and postgraduate level throughout the world. As Hall, Williams and Lew (2004: 9) indicate,

> in terms of the advancement of knowledge, there is now a substantial body of tourism literature as evidenced in journals, books, conference proceedings and electronic publications ... some 77 journals, published in English either in full or in part, are identified as having had a substantial academic component devoted to tourism research.

This literature base is supplemented by trade publications such as *Travel Trade Gazette* and electronic newswires such as TravelMole (www.travelmole.com) where research findings are also reported. However, as Ryan (2005) notes, textbooks are an important medium of communication, offering a synthesis of existing knowledge and opportunities to debate tourism, its concepts and development more fully than is possible in academic journals. The available textbooks on tourism have generally been written from a North American (e.g. Mathieson and Wall 1982; Mill and Morrison 1985; Murphy 1985), European (e.g. Foster 1985; Lavery 1989; Cooper *et al.* 2005) or Australasian perspective (e.g. Pearce 1995; Hall 2003), with few widely available student texts written from an Asian perspective (see Hall and Page 2000 for an exception to this) or an indigenous or less developed world perspective (e.g. see Hall and Page 1996).

Difficulties in studying tourism

As a subject area, tourism is fraught by a number of problems which any student and researcher needs to be aware of. Some of the principal problems are:

1 *Recognition:* Tourism is not easily recognized as a subject because some analysts view it as an industry, while others view it as a subject or as a process. Consequently, there is no universal agreement on how to approach it.

2 *Conceptualization:* Academics argue that tourism is a subject that is conceptually weak, which means that there are no universally agreed sets of laws or principles that all researchers adopt as the starting point for the discussion of tourism. To add to the difficulties, tourism is a **multidisciplinary** subject (see Table 1.2) and different disciplines examine tourism from their own standpoints rather than from a universally agreed tourism perspective. In this respect, the different subject areas that inform tourism use concepts and modes of analysis that have been developed in their own disciplines. This means that, as a multidisciplinary subject area, tourism is not integrated between the different disciplines studying it and this severely limits the intellectual development of the area as there is no cross-fertilization of ideas across disciplines.

TABLE 1.2	Disciplines contributing to the study of tourism
Discipline	*Example of contribution to tourism studies*
Geography	Spatial analysis of where tourism develops and why
Ecology	The impact of tourism on the natural environment
Agricultural studies	The significance of rural tourism to rural diversification
Parks and recreation	Recreation management techniques in natural areas such as national parks used by tourists
Urban and regional planning	The planning and development of tourism
Marketing	The marketing of tourism
Law	The legal framework and implications for tourists and tourism operators
Business and management science	The management of tourism organizations
Transport studies	The provision of tourist transport services
Hotel and restaurant administration	The provision of hospitality services and accommodation for tourists
Educational studies	Tourism curriculum design and development
Sociology	Sociological analyses and frameworks to understand tourism as an element of people's leisure time
Economics	The economic impact of tourism
Psychology	Tourist motivation to explain why people travel
Anthropology	The host–guest relationship
Safety management and ergonomics	The design and development of environments and activities which are safe for tourists

3 *Terminology:* There is a wide range of jargon used (e.g. 'ecotourism', 'alternative', 'responsible' and 'sustainable') that refers to facets of the same issue, which is perplexing for students and researchers because of the semantic complexity, the lack of universally agreed definitions of phenomena being studied.

4 *Data sources:* The data sources available to tourism researchers are weak compared with those available for other subjects.

5 *Reductionism:* The different approaches used by researchers from different disciplines and industry backgrounds have led to what Cooper *et al.* (1998) call reductionism. This means that tourism is reduced to a series of activities or economic transactions and is not seen in terms of a wider series of concepts and overarching analytical frameworks that would help in the understanding and interpretation of tourism. One example is that sociologists often use the **postmodern** paradigm to explain tourist behaviour.

6 *Rigour:* In academic environments, there is still suspicion about the intellectual rigour with which tourism researchers approach their subject. This is made more difficult by the tendency for non-specialists to dabble in this area of research, which is perceived by some as easy to understand and associated with 'fun' aspects, such as travel and leisure.

7 *Theory:* To date no theoretical constructs or theory which explain the development and internal dynamics of tourism as a process of global economic and social change have been developed. Most academics argue that a subject will not advance learning and understanding until theories are developed which can be tested, modified and rejected or redeveloped. Thus, tourism remains theoretically devoid as a subject area. In other words, much of the research in tourism has tended to be descriptive, lacking in contributions to the development of tourism knowledge and using established techniques and methodologies. Although there is evidence that this situation is changing slowly (see Ryan and Page 2000), the absence of theoretically derived research remains a major weakness for students and researchers. More insightful studies such as Urry's *The Tourist Gaze* (1990), with its attendant postmodernist and sociological analysis of modern-day tourism, are the exception rather than the rule in tourism.

8 *Academic/practitioner divide:* There are inherent tensions in tourism research between the pursuit of knowledge by academics to advance their subject area and the practical and applied needs of the tourism industry and public sector policymakers who wish to influence the research agenda by seeking usable results from academics.

As a consequence of these problems, one is forced to look around for a conceptual or organizing framework which helps the student of tourism to understand the holistic nature of tourism and how the main components of tourism can be integrated. One **methodology** used by researchers to understand the nature of tourism phenomena is a **systems** approach (Leiper 1990). The main purpose of such an approach is to rationalize and simplify the real-world complexity of tourism into a number of constructs and components that highlight the inter-related nature of tourism.

Tourism as an integrated system

Since tourism is a multidisciplinary area of study (Gilbert 1990), a systems approach can accommodate a variety of different perspectives because it does not assume a predetermined view of tourism. Instead, it enables one to understand the broader issues and factors which affect tourism, together with the interrelationships between different components in the system. According to Leiper (1990), a 'system' can be defined as a set of elements or parts that are connected to each other by at least one distinguishing principle. In this case, tourism is the distinguishing principle which connects the different components in the system around a common theme. Laws (1991: 7) developed this idea a stage further by providing a systems model of the tourism industry in which the key components were the inputs, outputs and external factors conditioning the system, for example the external business environment, consumer preferences, political factors and economic issues. As external factors are important influences upon tourism

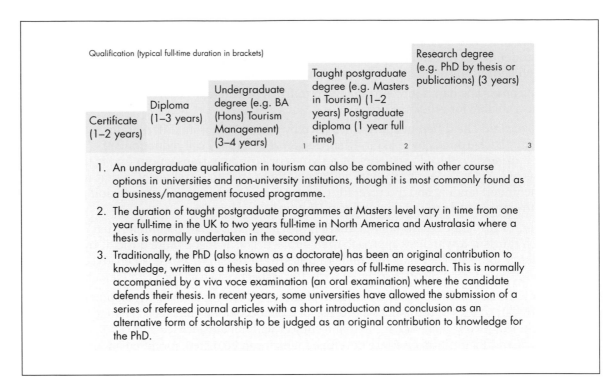

Qualification (typical full-time duration in brackets)

Certificate (1–2 years)

Diploma (1–3 years)

Undergraduate degree (e.g. BA (Hons) Tourism Management) (3–4 years)

Taught postgraduate degree (e.g. Masters in Tourism) (1–2 years) Postgraduate diploma (1 year full time)

Research degree (e.g. PhD by thesis or publications) (3 years)

1. An undergraduate qualification in tourism can also be combined with other course options in universities and non-university institutions, though it is most commonly found as a business/management focused programme.

2. The duration of taught postgraduate programmes at Masters level vary in time from one year full-time in the UK to two years full-time in North America and Australasia where a thesis is normally undertaken in the second year.

3. Traditionally, the PhD (also known as a doctorate) has been an original contribution to knowledge, written as a thesis based on three years of full-time research. This is normally accompanied by a viva voce examination (an oral examination) where the candidate defends their thesis. In recent years, some universities have allowed the submission of a series of refereed journal articles with a short introduction and conclusion as an alternative form of scholarship to be judged as an original contribution to knowledge for the PhD.

FIGURE 1.1   The staircase of tourism qualifications

systems, the system can be termed 'open', which means that it is influenced by factors aside from the main inputs. The links within the system can be examined in terms of flows between components and these flows may highlight the existence of certain types of relationships between different components (see Figure 1.2). For example:

- What effect does an increase in the cost of travel have on the demand for travel?
- How does this have repercussions for other components in the system?
- Will it reduce the number of tourists travelling?

A systems approach has the advantage of allowing the researcher to consider the effect of such changes to the **tourism system** to assess the likely impact on other components. Leiper (1990) identified the following elements of a tourism system: a tourist; a traveller-generating region; tourism destination regions; transit routes for tourists travelling between generating destination area and the travel and tourism industry (e.g. accommodation, transport, the firms and organizations supplying services and products to tourists). In this analysis, transport forms an integral part of the tourism system, connecting the tourist generating and destination regions, represented in terms of the volume of travel. Thus, a tourism system is a framework which embodies the entire **tourist experience** of travelling. The analytical value of such an approach is that it enables one to understand the overall process of tourist travel from both the supplier's and the purchaser's (tourist's) perspectives (supply and demand) while identifying the organizations which influence and regulate tourism. This approach highlights the importance of:

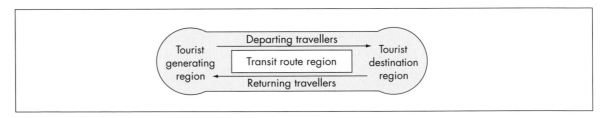

Departing travellers

Tourist generating region

Transit route region

Tourist destination region

Returning travellers

FIGURE 1.2   Leiper's tourism system

- the tourist
- the integral relationships in the overall tourist experience
- the effect of transportation problems on travellers' perceptions
- the tourist's requirement for safe, reliable and efficient modes of transport and service provision
- the destination.

Defining tourism

As Williams and Shaw (1988: 2) observed, 'the definition of tourism is a particularly arid pursuit' but important if one is to understand the nature, scope, impact and magnitude of global tourism. The terms 'travel' and 'tourism' are often interchanged within the published literature on tourism, but they are normally meant to encompass the field of research on human and business activities associated with one or more aspects of the temporary movement of persons away from their immediate home communities and daily work environments for business, pleasure or personal reasons (Chadwick 1994: 65). These two terms tend to be used in differing contexts to mean similar things, although there is a tendency for the United States to continue to use the term 'travel' when in fact 'tourism' is meant. Despite this inherent problem that may be little more than an exercise in semantics (how to define things), it is widely acknowledged that the two terms are used in isolation or in unison to describe three concepts:

- the movement of people
- a sector of the economy or an industry
- a broad system of interacting relationships of people, their needs [sic] to travel outside their communities and services that attempt to respond to these needs by supplying products (after Chadwick 1994: 65).

From this initial starting point, one can begin to explore some of the complex issues in arriving at a working definition of the terms 'tourism' and 'tourist'. In a historical context, Burkart and Medlik (1981: 41) identify the development of the term 'tourism'. They also point to the problems of separating and differentiating between technical definitions of tourism by organizations and more abstract conceptualizations of the term 'tourism'.

The *concept* of tourism refers to the broad notional framework that identifies tourism's essential characteristics and distinguishes tourism from similar, often related but different phenomena. In contrast, *technical definitions* have evolved through time as researchers modify and develop appropriate measures for statistical, legislative and operational reasons; this implies that there may be various technical definitions to meet particular purposes. However, the concept of tourism and its identification for research purposes are important considerations in this instance for tourism statistics, so that users are familiar with the context of their derivation. While most tourism books, articles and **monographs** now assume either a standard definition or interpretation of the concept of tourism, which is usually influenced by a social science perspective (e.g. a geographical, economic, political or sociological approach), Burkart and Medlik's (1981) approach to the concept of tourism continues to offer a valid assessment of the situation, highlighting five main characteristics (see Table 1.3). Furthermore, Burkart and Medlik's (1981) conceptualization of tourism is invaluable because it rightly recognizes that much tourism is a leisure activity, which involves a discretionary use of time and money, and recreation is often the main purpose for participation in tourism. But this is no reason for restricting the total concept in this way and the essential characteristics of tourism can best be interpreted within a wider concept. All tourism includes some travel but not all travel is tourism, while the temporary and short-term nature of most tourist trips distinguishes them from migration.

However, there is a growing body of knowledge in tourism which is beginning to look at the relationship between tourism and migration. Migration patterns can influence the nature and scale or tourism patterns especially where migration is related to ethnic populations who travel back to their family in their native country. Attention now turns to the technical definitions of tourism (also see Leiper 1990 for a further discussion).

TABLE 1.3 Conceptualizing tourism

- Tourism arises from the movement of people to, and their stay in, various destinations.
- There are two elements in all tourism: the journey to the destination and the stay, including activities, at the destination.
- The journey and the stay take place outside the normal place of residence and work, so that tourism gives rise to activities which are distinct from those of the resident and working populations of the places through which tourists travel and in which they stay.
- The movement to destinations is of a temporary, short-term character, with the intention to return home within a few days, weeks or months.
- Destinations are visited for purposes other than taking up permanent residence or employment remunerated from within the places visited.

Source: Adapted from Burkart and Medlik (1981: 42)

Technical definitions of tourism

Technical definitions of tourism are commonly used by organizations seeking to define the population to be measured and there are three principal features which normally have to be defined, as Table 1.4 shows (see BarOn 1984 for a detailed discussion). As Smith (2004) discusses, attempts to define tourism are not new. The first attempt was by the Committee of Statistical Experts of the League of Nations in 1937, with other bodies progressing this work in the 1950s including the International Union of Official Travel Organizers (IUOTO), the United Nations and more recently the **World Tourism Organization** (hereafter WTO). Among the most recent attempts to recommend appropriate definitions of tourism was the WTO International Conference of Travel and Tourism in Ottawa in 1991, which reviewed, expanded and developed technical definitions and stated that tourism comprises:

> *the activities of a person travelling outside his or her usual environment for less than a specified period of time and whose main purpose of travel is other than [the] exercise of an activity remunerated from the place visited. (WTO 1991)*

Here 'usual environment' is intended to exclude trips within the areas of usual residence, frequent and regular trips between the domicile and the workplace and other community trips of a routine character. 'Less than a specified period of time' is intended to exclude long-term migration, and 'exercise of an activity remunerated from the place visited' is intended to exclude migration for temporary work.

The definitions in Table 1.5 were developed by the WTO. Such definitions can best be thought of as how the majority define these terms and Table 1.6, compiled by Lumsdon (1997), summarizes most of the key terms used to define tourism. There are, however, different interpretations in some countries where tourism statistics are gathered. Clearly, how the various terms are

TABLE 1.4 Key technical issues in defining tourism

- Purpose of travel (e.g. the type of traveller, be he or she a business traveller, holiday-maker, someone visiting friends and relatives or someone visiting for other reasons).
- The time dimension involved in the tourism visit, which requires a minimum and a maximum period of time spent away from the home area and the time spent at the destination. In most cases, this would involve a minimum stay of more than 24 hours away from home and a maximum of less than a year.
- Those situations where tourists may or may not be included as tourists, such as cruise-ship passengers, those tourists in transit at a particular point of embarkation/departure and excursionists who stay less than 24 hours at a destination (e.g. the European duty-free cross-Channel day-trip market).

TABLE 1.5 Definitions of tourism developed by the WTO

International tourism:	Consists of inbound tourism, visits to a country by non-residents, and outbound tourism, residents of a country visiting another country.
Internal tourism:	Residents of a country visiting their own country.
Domestic tourism:	Internal tourism plus inbound tourism (the tourism market of accommodation facilities and attractions within a country).
National tourism:	Internal tourism plus outbound tourism (the resident tourism market for travel agents and airlines).

Source: WTO cited in Chadwick (1994: 66)

TABLE 1.6 Technical definitions: Tourism

Traveller, visitor or tourist	Terms used to describe a person travelling to and staying in a place away from their usual environment for more than one night but less than one year, for leisure, business and other purposes
International tourism	Travel between countries by various modes of travel for the purpose of tourism. This can be subdivided as follows:
Long haul	Travel which involves long distances (e.g. over 1000 miles) for example, between continents
Short haul	Travel between countries which involves shorter distances or travel time (e.g. 250–1000 miles)
Inbound	Visits to a country by non-residents (importation of overseas currency)
Outbound	Visits by residents of one country to another country (exporting currency to other countries)
Internal tourism	Travel by residents in their own country
Domestic tourism	Internal travel and inbound tourism in total
National tourism	Internal travel and outbound tourism
Excursionist or same-day visitors	Visitors who begin and end their visit from the same base (home or holiday base) within the same 24-hour period

Source: Lumsdon (1997: 6)

defined is crucial to the measurement of tourism demand (see Chapter 3). International comparisons on an equal basis can only be made if like for like is defined, collected and analysed in a similar fashion. Goeldner, Ritchie and McIntosh (2000: 17) note that the National Travel Survey conducted by the Travel Industry Association of America's US Travel Data Center reports on all trips, whatever the purpose, which are in excess of 100 miles and all trips involving an overnight stay whatever the distance. In the UK, the United Kingdom Tourism Survey (UKTS) distinguishes between short holidays (one to three nights) and long holidays (more than four nights' duration). In order to improve statistical collection and improve understanding of tourism, the United Nations (UN) (WTO and UN 1994) and the WTO (1991) also recommended differentiating between visitors, tourists and excursionists.

From this classification of travellers, the distinction between international and domestic tourism needs to be made:

- **'Domestic tourism'** usually refers to tourists travelling from their normal domicile to other areas within a country.

- In contrast, '**international tourism**' normally involves a tourist leaving their country of origin to cross into another country, which involves documentation, administrative formalities and movement to a foreign environment.

The WTO (1991) recommended that an international tourist be defined as:

a visitor who travels to a country other than that in which he/she has his/her usual residence for at least one night but not more than one year, and whose main purpose of visit is other than the exercise of an activity remunerated from within the country visited.

and that an international excursionist, e.g. a cruise-ship visitor, be defined as:

a visitor residing in a country who travels the same day to a country other than that in which he/she has his/her usual environment for less than 24 hours without spending the night in the country visited and whose main purpose of visit is other than the exercise of an activity remunerated from within the country visited.

Similar definitions were also developed for domestic tourists, with a domestic tourist's visit having a time limit of not more than six months (WTO 1991; WTO and UN 1994). The WTO (1983) suggested the following working definition of a domestic tourist:

any person, regardless of nationality, resident in a country and who travels to a place in the same country for not more than one year and whose main purpose of visit is other than following an occupation remunerated from within the place visited. Such a definition includes domestic tourists where an overnight stay is involved and domestic excursionists who visit an area for less than 24 hours and do not stay overnight.

Interestingly, the inclusion of a same-day travel, excursionist category in UN/WTO technical definitions of 'tourism', makes the division between 'recreation' and 'tourism' even more arbitrary and there is increasing international agreement that 'tourism' refers to all activities of visitors, including both overnight and same-day visitors (WTO and UN 1994: 5). Given improvements in transport technology, same-day travel is becoming increasingly important to some countries, with the UN (WTO and UN 1994: 9) observing, 'day visits are important to consumers and to many providers, especially tourist attractions, transport operators and caterers'. Chadwick (1994) moves the definition of tourists a stage further by offering a typology of travellers (tourists) which highlights the distinction between tourist (travellers) and non-travellers (non-tourists) which is summarized in Figure 1.3. Figure 1.3 is distinctive because it highlights all sections of society which are involved in travel of some kind but also looks at the motivation to travel. It is also useful because it illustrates where technical problems may occur in deciding which groups to include in tourism and those to exclude. As Figure 1.4 suggests, when operationalizing the typology of travellers, there are other key considerations: notably, the time spent as a tourist and travelling, evolving forms of tourism (e.g. **gap years** and **second home** ownership) and the geographical dimension (where, when and the form or forms of tourism engaged in), as travellers can engage in different forms of tourism. As Image 1.1 shows, one area of growth in tourism-related travel is the student gap year. Certain companies have developed this as a product, and different forms of travel and experiences can be developed with different rewards and risks for the participants. This concept has also begun to have some influence upon young professionals aged 25–40 who have careers but seek spiritual refreshment.

Image 1.1: Global Vision International website. Source: Global Vision International

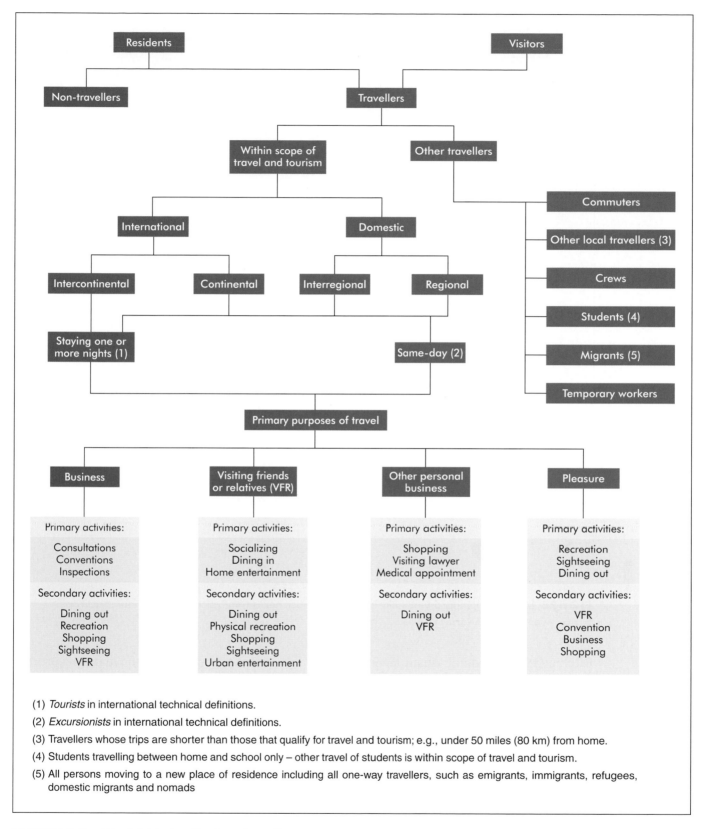

FIGURE 1.3 Chadwick's classification of travellers. Source: *Travel, Tourism and Hospitality Research, Second Edition,* Ritchie and Goeldner, copyright © (1994) John Wiley and Sons, Inc. This material is used by permission of John Wiley and Sons, Inc.

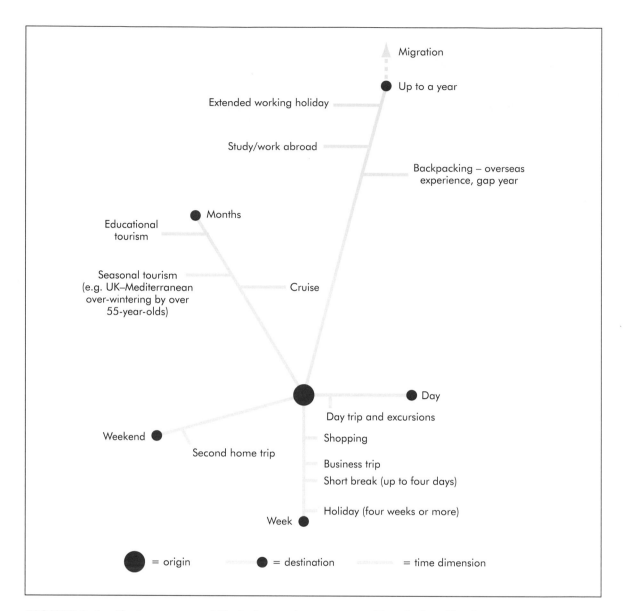

FIGURE 1.4 The temporary mobility in time and space nexus with typical profile of tourist activity.
Source: Adapted from C.M. Hall (2005)

Ritchie (1975, cited in Latham 1989: 55) argued that an important part of the maturing process for any science is the development or adaptation of consistent and well-tested measurement techniques and methodologies that are well-suited to the types of problems encountered in practice. There is a need for a classification of tourism which can evolve and accommodate more complex forms of tourism, as Figure 1.4 suggests. A robust system is required to not only classify what we mean by 'tourism', 'tourist' and a 'trip', but how we measure these interactions between origin, destination and travel routes. In this context, the measurement of tourists, tourism activity and the effects on the economy and society in different environments is crucial to the development of tourism as an established area of study within the confines of social science and management disciplines. In relation to establishing demand, tourism statistics and the associated challenges and issues in measuring tourism are explored in Chapter 3. Yet one of the most enduring themes throughout this book and one which is affecting all forms of tourism in the way they are produced and consumed by tourists in the twenty-first century is the process of globalization.

Globalization and the production and consumption of tourism

This chapter has established that tourism is a global economic activity and as such is part of a much wider process of globalization. Meethan (2004) describes the growing importance of the term 'globalization' in everyday language, based upon the principles of a new economic order, with global markets, and as a process, shaping our purchases and preferences as consumers. While our daily lives are largely fixed to the localities we live, work and play in, globalization is an international process which transcends local and national boundaries, representing an international geographical entity which has eroded the autonomy of the **nation state**. The process of globalization has many facets, but its development since the 1980s has been aided by financial deregulation in many countries and the lifting of barriers to capital and private enterprise. An example of this in the tourism sector is the growth of multinational enterprises in tourism (e.g. **transnational hotel chains** with head offices outside the country/region of operation, to where profits are repatriated). The impact of information technology has also made the world a more interconnected place compressing time and place and intensifying connections, with enterprises able to access and do business with global consumers via the internet. However, globalization is much more than the **internationalization** of business.

To understand tourism and globalization in terms of the service sector it is helpful to introduce two terms: **production** and **consumption**. In the global economy, tourism has increasingly become commodified (i.e. portrayed as a commodity to be traded, which as a service is consumed) so that consumers (the tourists) consume the destination as a product. This process requires a complex range of organizations involved in the supply of tourism to combine in order to 'produce' tourism experiences that the tourist consumes. For the tourist, globalization means that increasingly a global **bundle of services** and commodities are purchased. In this respect, 'globalization' is an umbrella term to describe a number of converging trends, particularly the ability of larger global companies to achieve economies of scale and to control the supply of products to consume. Researchers have also described circuits of production and consumption in tourism as a function of globalization where these bundles of services and products are purchased and consumed across the world from the point of origin (e.g. purchase of travel) to the destination. Part of the globalization process is leading to global standards and expectations of standards. However, unlike global manufacturing and production, the production and consumption of tourism is not **placeless**, nor can it be located in the cheapest location, like call centres. Instead tourism is place-specific (i.e. the destination is the point of consumption) and production is fragmented across many sectors of the economy (e.g. accommodation, tour operators, transport, destinations).

Global **investment flows** are creating global forms of tourism production (i.e. hotel chains and integrated tourism companies) as tourism flows are now reaching all parts of the globe and intensifying activity at specific locations. As Shaw and Williams (2004) argue, this is manifest in the pivotal role of world tourism cities like London, Paris, New York and Rome where global control of capital flows is often located. Similarly, at a regional level, tourism activity is intensifying in the three main regions that dominate global patterns: Europe, North America and East Asia Pacific. This globalization process, as they argue, is bringing cultures into contact with each other, highlighting inequities between the developed and the developing worlds. Underlying this culture contact is a growing dependency between the developed and the developing worlds.

Image 1.2: World cities are a key resource for tourism in locations such as New York City

Where global capital exploits tourism destinations, the local communities and resource base to profit from tourists, the inequalities are reinforced. As a result, Shaw and Williams (2004) point to globalization as part of a process of tightening interconnections which cut across national boundaries. Networks are based on the production–consumption exchange process in tourism manifest in terms of:

- economic interconnections – global flows of capital, activities of transnational companies like multinational hotel corporations
- global consumerism
- global mobility of people for tourism or migration (after Shaw and Williams 2004: 42).

Some of the dimensions of globalization in tourism discussed by Shaw and Williams (2004) include:

- globalization of media images by satellite television and the internet which has assisted in the promotion of places to a global audience
- dynamic forms of place promotion by tourism agencies through advertising, especially via the internet
- travel promotion by tour operators and transport
- the globalization of business
- the globalization of migration and the recognition of the linkage between homeland and new area of settlement, generating a demand for travel to visit friends and relatives
- the 'McDonaldization' of tourism experiences – the standardization of the provision of hotel and restaurant experiences worldwide
- investment flows from tourist-generating areas following the tourist to the destination area, such as the Japanese investment in Australia's Gold Coast since the 1980s and Korean investment in Rotorua, New Zealand's tour companies, retail shops and retail outlets (see Insight 1.2).

INSIGHT 1.2

Globalization and tourism: South Korean tourism activity in New Zealand – Kyung-Sik Woo and Stephen J. Page

South Korea is a major source market for New Zealand, the fifth largest overseas market in 2004 and a high spending and yielding market. In a study by Woo (1996) a time-budget survey (i.e. how visitors spent their time and where they went) of inbound South Korean tourists travelling on package tours found that they followed three itineraries:

- Auckland to Rotorua and return to Auckland
- Auckland to Rotorua and Waitomo Caves and return to Auckland
- Auckland to Rotorua and Waitamo Caves and Taupo and return to Auckland (Figure 1.5).

What is interesting from the study is that South Koreans travelled by South Korean airlines, using a Korean-owned inbound tour operator and ate at Korean-owned restaurants; they followed a regimented pattern of tourist travel, visiting and spending money in Korean owned souvenir and gift shops. They even spent the limited free time available in Korean owned pubs in Rotorua. This example not only illustrates the control of the tourism process by Korean-based owners or Korean owners in New Zealand, but the pattern of investment focused on a very lucrative niche market. Here production and consumption are closely linked and the same nationality-owned businesses 'provide a form of culturally-specific economic mediation between the tourists and the host communities' (Shaw and Williams 2004: 45).

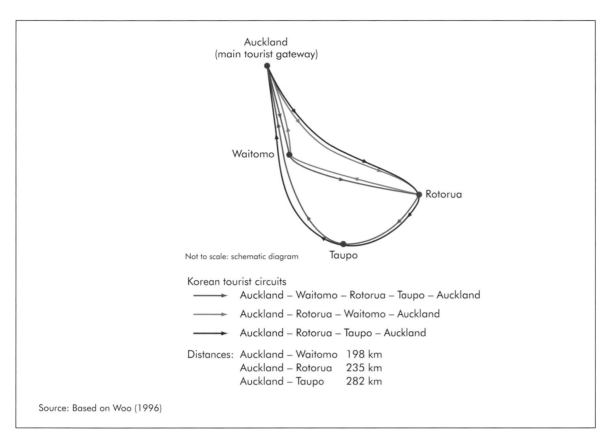

Auckland
(main tourist gateway)

Waitomo

Rotorua

Not to scale: schematic diagram

Taupo

Korean tourist circuits
Auckland – Waitomo – Rotorua – Taupo – Auckland
Auckland – Rotorua – Waitomo – Auckland
Auckland – Rotorua – Taupo – Auckland

Distances: Auckland – Waitomo 198 km
Auckland – Rotorua 235 km
Auckland – Taupo 282 km

Source: Based on Woo (1996)

FIGURE 1.5 Korean tourist itineraries in New Zealand

Conclusion

This chapter has introduced the conceptual issues associated with the study of tourism, highlighting the development of the subject area and some of the principal difficulties which students and researchers need to be aware of when attempting to define the subject. It has distinguished between the terms:

- a tourist
- domestic tourism
- international tourism

and acknowledged that tourism is a multidisciplinary subject rather than a discipline in its own right because other subjects study and contribute to it. It has no core body of knowledge that is distinct, unique and not modified from other disciplines such as geography, marketing or economics; a feature debated by Hall *et al.* (2004). The lack of any theoretical core of knowledge has also impeded the intellectual development of tourism from making major leaps forward in understanding although, as Hall *et al.* (2004)

acknowledge, the subject is in good health if a high level of research activity is a measure. But others still criticize tourism for being eclectic, disparate and under-theorized (e.g. Meethan 2001: 2). Intellectually, other disciplines have viewed tourism as a descriptive subject but the recent scale and significance of tourism as a global activity and process, with economic implications for governments, has elevated the subject's acceptability as an academic area worthy of study. Crises such as 9/11 and SARS have reinforced that public awareness of tourism as an academic subject, as the volatile nature of an economic sector which many countries depend upon has reached centre stage. One of the most interesting changes in the status of tourism as a subject area worthy of pursuit is the demand for students and skilled workers who have a grasp of the dynamic and ever-changing nature of tourism and an ability to manage the detrimental impacts of tourism on the total population and natural environment. A review by Ryan and Page (2000) acknowledged that this was by far one of the major growth areas of research activity in the period 1990–9, as analysts have started to recognize how all-embracing tourism-induced change can be on the natural environment. This remains true in the new millennium.

Although this chapter has addressed a host of technical and semantic issues associated with the measurement and definition of tourists and tourism, which may appear dull and uninteresting, a fundamental understanding of these seemingly tedious issues is fundamental when wider issues of tourism impacts and effects are evaluated: without a baseline or an agreement on what one is observing or measuring, the results and recommendations will have little meaning – especially if the wrong assumptions or features are measured. One continued problem which tourism researchers consistently make is that they fail to agree clear parameters of what is being observed, measured and evaluated and rarely refer to the technical issues necessary to precisely delimit what they are studying

Discussion questions

1 What are the different subjects which contribute to the area known as tourism studies?

2 What are the main components of Leiper's tourism system?

3 What are the problems in trying to calculate the number of tourists which arrive in a country in a given time period?

4 How will the process of globalization continue to affect tourism?

References

APEC (2003) 2003 APEC Economic Outlook. Singapore: APEC.

BarOn, R. (1984) 'Tourism terminology and standard definitions', Tourist Review, 39 (1): 2 4.

Burkart, A. and Medlik, S. (1974) Tourism, Past, Present and Future. Oxford: Heinemann.

Burkart, A. and Medlik, R. (eds) (1975) The Management of Tourism. Oxford: Heinemann.

Burkart, A. and Medlik, R. (1981) Tourism, Past, Present and Future, Second Edition, London: Heinemann.

Chadwick, R. (1994) 'Concepts, definitions and measurement used in travel and tourism research, in J. R. Brent Ritchie and C. Goeldner (eds) Travel, Tourism and Hospitality Research: A Handbook for Managers and Researchers, Second Edition. New York: Wiley.

Cooper, C.P., Fletcher, J., Gilbert, D.G. and Wanhill, S. (1998) Tourism: Principles and Practice, Second Edition. London: Pitman.

Cooper, C., Fletcher, J., Fyall, A., Gilbert, D. and Wanhill, S. (2005) Tourism: Principles and Practice, Third Edition. Harlow: Prentice Hall.

Dombey, O. (2003) 'The effects of SARS on the Chinese tourism industry', Journal of Vacation Marketing 10 (1): 4–10.

Foster, D. (1985) Travel and Tourism Management. London: Macmillan.

Gilbert, D.C. (1990) 'Conceptual issues in the meaning of tourism', in C.P. Cooper (ed.) Progress in Tourism, Recreation and Hospitality Management Volume 2. London: Belhaven.

Goeldner, C.R., Ritchie, J.R.B. and McIntosh, R.W. (2000) Tourism: Principles, Practices and Philosophies. New York: John Wiley and Sons Inc.

Hall, C.M. (2003) Introduction to Tourism: dimensions and Issues, Third Edition. French, NSW: Hospitality Press.

Hall, C.M. (2005) Tourism: Rethinking the Social Science of Mobility. Prentice Hall: Harlow.

Hall, C.M. and Page, S.J. (eds) (1996) Tourism in the Pacific: Issues and Cases. London: Thomson Learning.

Hall, C.M. and Page, S.J. (eds) (2000) Tourism in South and South East Asia: Issues and Cases. Oxford: Butterworth-Heinemann.

Hall, C.M. and Page, S.J. (2005) The Geography of Tourism and Recreation, Third Edition. London: Routledge.

Hall, C.M., Williams, A. and Lew, A. (eds) (2004) 'Tourism conceptualisation, institutions and issues, in A. Lew, C.M. Hall and A. Williams (eds) A Companion to Tourism. Oxford: Blackwell.

Henderson, J. (2003) 'Managing a health-related crisis – SARS in Singapore', Journal of Vacation Marketing, 10 (1): 67–77.

Latham, J. (1989) 'The statistical measurement of tourism', in C.P. Cooper (ed.) Progress in Tourism, Recreation and Hospitality Management, Volume 1. London: Belhaven.

Lavery, P. (1989) Travel and Tourism. Huntingdon: Elm Publications.

Laws, E. (1991) *Tourism Marketing*. Cheltenham: Stanley Thornes.

Leiper, N. (1990) *Tourism Systems: An Interdisciplinary Perspective*, Palmerston North, New Zealand: Department of Management Systems, Occasional Paper 2, Massey University.

Lumsdon, L. (1997) *Tourism Marketing*. London: Thomson Learning.

Mathieson, A. and Wall, G. (1982) *Tourism: Economic, Physical and Social Impacts*. Harlow: Longman.

Meethan, K. (2001) *Tourism in a Global Society*. Palgrave: London.

Meethan, K. (2004) 'Transnational corporations, globalisation and tourism', in A. Lew, C.M. Hall and A. Williams (eds) *A Companion to Tourism*. Oxford: Blackwell.

Mill, R.C. and Morrison, A. M. (1985) *The Tourism System: An Introductory Text*. New Jersey: Prentice Hall.

Murphy, P.E. (1985) *Tourism: A Community Approach*. London: Routledge.

Pearce, D.G. (1995) *Tourism Today: A Geographical Approach, Second Edition*. Harlow: Longman.

Ryan, C. (2005) 'The Ranking and Rating of Academics and Journals in Tourism Research', *Tourism Management*. 26(5):657–62.

Ryan, C. and Page, S.J. (eds) (2000) *Tourism Management: Towards the New Millennium*. Oxford: Pergamon.

Shaw, G. and Williams, A. (2004) *Tourism and Tourism Spaces*. London: Sage.

Smith, S.L.J. (2004) 'The measurement of global tourism: Old debates, new consensus and continuing challenges', in A. Lew, C.M. Hall and A. Williams (eds) *A Companion to Tourism*. Oxford: Blackwell.

Urry, J. (1990) *The Tourist Gaze: Leisure and Travel in Contemporary Societies*. London: Sage.

Weiler, B. and Hall, C.M. (eds) (1992) *Special Interest Tourism*. London: Belhaven Press.

Williams, A. and Shaw, G. (1988) 'Tourism and economic development: introduction', in A. Williams and G. Shaw (eds) *Tourism and Economic Development: Western European Experiences*. London: Belhaven Press.

Woo, K.-S. (1996) *Korean Tourists Urban Activity Patterns in New Zealand*. Research report. Auckland: Masters of Business Studies, Massey University of Albany.

Woo, K.-S. and Page, S.J. (1999) 'Tourism demand in East Asia Pacific – the case of the South Korean outbound market and activity patterns in New Zealand', in C.M. Hall and S.J. Page (eds) *The Geography of Tourism and Recreation: Environment, Place and Space, First Edition*. London: Routledge.

WTO (World Tourism Organization) (1983) *Definitions Concerning Tourism Statistics*. Madrid: WTO.

WTO (World Tourism Organization) (1991) *Resolutions of International Conference on Travel and Tourism, Ottawa, Canada*. Madrid: World Tourism Organization.

WTO and UNSTAT (1994) *Recommendations on Tourism Statistics*. Madrid and New York: WTO and UN.

Further reading

A good introduction to tourism as a global activity can be found in:

Hall, C.M. and Page, S.J. (2005) *The Geography of Tourism and Recreation: Environment, Place and Space, Third Edition*. London: Routledge.

2

The Evolution and Development of Tourism

Learning outcomes

After reading this chapter and answering the questions, you should be able to:

- understand the principal factors that have influenced the development of tourism through time and space

- recognize the theme of continuity and change as a central feature of tourism development

- understand that the development of tourism globally, in a given location or at a certain time, is explained by a combination of political, economic, social and technological influences.

Overview

Throughout history people have travelled for many different reasons and so tourism is as old as human activity, though its development from antiquities highlights its critical link – that one had to have the means by which to consume tourism. Travel for pleasure purposes is essentially a more recent phenomenon which has grown rapidly in the last 200 years. From the end of the eighteenth century, when only the wealthy few could indulge, tourism has developed into something that many ordinary people now consider as a necessity.

Introduction

Tourism is by no means a new phenomenon, with its historical origins in the ancient cultures of the Greek and Roman **social elite**. While we may consider the seaside resort to be a feature of modern times, there were many seaside **resort**s in the Roman Empire where the upper classes and the masses flocked each summer to get away from the overcrowded and unhealthy conditions in Rome. In the respect that these early 'tourists' pursued pleasure and relaxation in regions away from the main towns and cities, they epitomize modern-day tourism: the pursuit of pleasure in a location away from everyday life and the use of one's **leisure time** for non-work purposes. However, the root of modern-day tourism is to be found much later. As Inglis (2000: 1) observes, 'Vacation-taking and holiday-making turn up...at more or less the same moment as the consumer... From some time early in the second half of the eighteenth century when consumers begin to take holidays as a fashionable activity.' This trend-driven element of tourism is a considerable force in the pursuit of pleasure through history, as the status and recognition which are still afforded to travel experiences are considerable in Western society. However, as Table 2.1 shows, throughout history tourism has been dependent upon several factors which have facilitated its growth and development, particularly transport and access, along with the leisure time and means by which to afford to travel (in other words, disposable income and wealth). Turning to a different perspective on historical associations, the late twentieth century saw the rise of the **heritage industry** as a core interest within tourism, with a dramatic rise in, demand for and supply of heritage-based attractions. This meshing of tourism and history and the associated issues of **interpretation**, **management** and ownership provide some interesting debate in contemporary studies of tourism (see Urry 1990).

TABLE 2.1 Illustrations of the development of tourism: A range of historical forms of tourism and factors promoting their development

Era	Typical form of tourism	Facilitating factors	Main participants/tourists
Greeks	Olympic Games	Leisure and sport ethic	Leisured classes staying in tented encampments
Romans	Coliseums for events and leisure/tourism Business travel Seaside and inland spa tourism Urban and rural tourism	Expansion of the Roman empire Construction of Roman roads Road/sea travel 200 holidays a year for leisured classes Demand for business travel due to imperial expansion	Urban leisured elite construct second homes in rural locations away from main cities Imperial civil servants for business travel Middle classes – travel to seaside resorts and spas for health and spiritual reasons
Middle Ages	Festival and event tourism linked to religious events Jousting tournaments Pilgrimages Limited business travel	General population as day-trippers in immediate locality related to holy days	Knights and landed classes Religious orders for pilgrimages and the nobility
Renaissance and Reformation	Continuity with fairs and events/festivals Second home ownership	Holy days Dissolution of the monastries and creation of landed estates with confiscated lands used to stimulate country estate development and rural tourism Improved road access	Nobility

TABLE 2.1 continued

Era	Typical form of tourism	Facilitating factors	Main participants/tourists
Sixteenth and seventeenth centuries	Continuity with festivals Grand Tour Spa tourism	Improved transportation – sea and rivers/land to allow touring and access to spas and inland resorts Rise of international travel New Protestant work ethic emerging to differentiate between classes and work/leisure.	Nobility and pursuit of the Classical antiquities initially as part of an educational experience followed by the pursuit of the picturesque
Eighteenth century	Continuity with previous forms of tourism (spas, Grand Tour and festivals) New forms of tourism – the rise of the seaside/coast	Royal patronage of bathing Improved road access by stagecoach to the coast Changing attitudes towards use of leisure time and willingness to explore the coast in Christian doctrines Fashion and taste promote the coast	Nobility
Nineteenth century	Spas Coastal tourism Urban tourism Rise of interest in wilderness areas Development of international business travel – imperial expansion in European countries Pleasure cruising	New technology, the steamship making urban areas and the coast more accessible to a mass market from the 1840s Reducing costs of travel Rise in holidays for industrial workforce	Growing social differentiation (upper, middle and working classes) with distinct forms of tourism and holiday-taking. Tourism becoming a mass consumer product later in Victorian period
Twentieth century	All forms for Victorian period and expansion of sea travel	Reducing cost of sea and land-based travel and greater prestige and status associated with foreign travel Rise of the car and charabanc in the 1930s making a wider range of areas accessible The rise of the aircraft and jet aeroplane post-1950	As for Victorian period but faster pace of diffusion of former upper/middle class forms of tourism becoming more widely available to the population Innovations in the 1930s such as the holiday camp idea Emergence of mass tourism in the 1950s at the coast and then via package holidays

Tourism, history and the past: Its significance and analysis

How should we study a subject such as the historical development of tourism when it is as vast and broad as human civilization itself? The historian has adopted different techniques towards the study of tourism in past times, notably from the emergence of social history in the 1970s and 1980s, although many examples of the study of tourism can be dated to earlier periods, particularly the rise of seaside resorts in the 1930s. The historian's analysis of tourism is dominated by two complementary and yet divergent themes: the development of tourism and its *continuity* as a phenomenon through time, which is often running parallel to and sometimes in opposition with the process of *change*, where tourism is constantly evolving and changing. Perhaps one of the central features driving continuity and change in tourism was summed up by Löfgren (2002: 282).

If today's tourists are no longer satisfied with sun and tour guides, history teaches us tourists never seem to be satisfied, whether in 1799 or 1999. Restlessness, frustration, and boredom are part of that great personal experience. A strange and often insatiable longing for transcendence gives tourism an element of secular religion, a quest for that fulfilment waiting out there somewhere – in the elsewherelands. As soon as our vacation is over we start to fantasise about the next one: the perfect holiday.

If this holds true through history, then the constant demands among tourists for places to visit and different experiences helps to keep the phenomenon of tourism growing. This is perhaps best illustrated by the example of Blackpool, one of Britain's most popular seaside resorts. Blackpool developed as a major day-excursion market, promoted by its main railway company and as a working-class domestic tourism holiday resort in the **Victorian** period. The resort continued to grow through to the 1950s (despite the impact of the first and second world wars, in 1914–18 and 1939–1945 respectively) and then started to decline in the 1970s as overseas holidays became more fashionable. Despite attempts to attract conferences and conventions to Blackpool, the resort has changed and declined since its Victorian, Edwardian and inter-war heyday. Yet the plans by the UK government to relax the gambling laws in 2005 may pave the way for the development of resort-style casinos in Blackpool similar to those in Las Vegas. As the chief executive of one company seeking to develop a casino in Blackpool states:

> *Leisure Parcs Limited believes that the modernization of the UK gambling laws offers the opportunity to bring about the development of Las Vegas-style resort casino hotels to act as a catalyst for regional economic regeneration and for the creation of one or more tourism destinations of international quality.*
> (Marc W. Etches, Managing Director, Leisure Parcs Ltd [www.blackpoolcasinos.com])

Such a statement illustrates the economic development objectives associated with tourism. This simple example also shows that tourism never stays static: it may continue to exist in a locality but it is in a constant state of flux, evolution, development and change. In the case of Blackpool such change may be a massive economic transformation to reposition itself once again as a major tourism destination, although it does still have a large day-trip market with 6.2 million visitors to Blackpool Pleasure Beach, the top free attraction in the UK in 2002. Therefore, in any analysis of tourism the historical dimension has a great deal to offer the student of tourism. Yet as Durie (2003) notes, in spite of several good studies by historians (e.g. Walton 1983) and geographers (e.g. Towner 1996), the historical study of tourism remains a comparatively new field of study. Any historical analysis of tourism will reveal a great deal of attention to empirical research (i.e. a concern for facts and figures) as well as interest in the factors promoting tourism development (e.g. transport) and the role of leading entrepreneurs as agents of change in developing places from non-tourism locations to tourism locations (see Insight 2.1 and the critical factors stimulating the development of tourism in Monaco).

A more in-depth review of some of the ways historians analyse tourism reveals a wide range of themes which have begun to attract attention, including (but not exclusively) some of the following themes:

- The emergence of pleasure travel as a distinct activity.
- The rise and continuing role of the seaside resort (e.g. Walton 1983, 2000).
- The **cultural history** of tourism and holiday-making (e.g. Inglis 2000; Löfgren 2002), particularly the role of the beach and coast and its use for tourism.
- The rise of tourism in specific countries (e.g. Durie 2003) and on entire continents (e.g. Towner 1996).
- The rise of the **package holiday** and **mass tourism** (Bray and Raitz 2001).
- The rise of commercialized leisure and tourism in the American city (Hannigan 1998) such as the development of Coney Island Amusement Parks as leisure attractions.
- The development of urban tourism locations, such as **spa**s and resorts inland, and towns as service centres for visitors; this also provided development opportunities for individual entrepreneurs such as Billy Butlin in the 1930s in the UK.
- The emergence and role of heritage as part of the contemporary tourism product.

The evolution of tourism in Monaco as a high-class tourism destination

Monaco is an independent Mediterranean state which saw its sovereign state status granted in 1861, and it comprises 485 acres in size, a proportion of which has been reclaimed from the sea in the last two decades. The state is adjacent to France and has a Mediterranean coastline, running along 2.5 miles with an extremely mild climate and over 1500 hours of sunshine a year. Despite its small size, it has been associated with the most chic and upmarket tourism sector. The stimulus to tourism development can be traced to the period after 1863 when a monopoly was granted to establish a tourism company – The Sea Bathing and Circle of Foreigners Company – to develop and promote the area. This saw the construction of accommodation, promotion of

the location and the development of its world-famous casino which has provided substantial revenue for the state. After 1867, scheduled land and sea links were established with a rail link to Nice, France. This opened the area up to a much wider circle of visitors and the area now known as Monte Carlo. In that area upmarket villas and residences were constructed. To add to the cultural infrastructure, the Monte Carlo orchestra was established in 1869, which also acts as venue for opera and ballet, assisting in the development of an image as the French Riviera, described by www.tourism-monaco.com as 'A riviera gem – an international cultural centre', adding to the image as a playground of the rich, the famous and chic and an upmarket destination.

- The way in which the private and public sectors set about attracting and developing tourism in specific locations using public sector finance, such as rates.
- The role of private transport providers, such as railway companies, and the imagery and promotional material developed to promote the localities.
- The historian and techniques for analysing tourism.

These themes also reveal two approaches used in historical research: the analysis of how changes have come about and the formative influences on the contemporary era, and the in-depth study of specific eras and phenomena in past times; this latter approach is described as taking a cross-section of a specific era. Some of the key questions which historians ask when examining the evolution and development of tourism include:

- When did the **development process** begin?
- How did the sequence of change induced by tourism development in the location, society, economy, built and natural environment and landscape occur?
- Why did development occur when and where it did?
- What were the formative influences on the development process (i.e. agents of change)?
- What was the scale of change induced by and contributed to by tourism?
- What role did the private and public sector play in initiating, managing and promoting tourism development?

To address these questions, historical researchers focus on specific themes and issues dependent upon their interest or specialism (i.e. economic, social, cultural and political dimensions and the geographers' concern with place and localities in past times). This leads them to the all-important issue of how does one reconstruct past experiences of tourism? Walton's (1983, 2000) seminal studies of the English seaside resort outlined a number of important source materials available to reconstruct the history of tourism, including:

- The **Census** to illustrate the population composition, growth and impact of tourism on employment and the demand for migrant labour.
- Visitors' use of **guide book**s in resorts and diaries of experiences of touring.
- Records of resort development by builders and entrepreneurs and the records of municipal corporations and their involvement in tourism.

- Records of tourist-related businesses (e.g. the Thomas Cook archive) where these records exist and are available for consultation.

While this chapter cannot present a comprehensive review of tourism through history, nor the separate tourism histories of the world's regions, it is hoped that some of these principal features of the historical analysis of tourism will be portrayed. For example, historical analysis of tourism is being used by the public sector through oral history and a living tradition of tourism. This is the recording of past histories, of how people remembered their experiences of tourism, to understand both the cultural meaning of tourism to people in past times and how the tourism system developed and functioned in the areas these people visited (see Insight 2.2).

INSIGHT 2.2

The history of the Thomas Cook Company: Milestones in its development

1841	Thomas Cook organizes Leicester to Loughborough rail journey for 500 travellers
1845	Thomas Cook organizes tour to Liverpool with an extension to Caernarvon and Snowdon
1846	First tour of Scotland, 800 miles for a guinea, with 500 passengers. Sightseeing in Stirling, Ayrshire and on Loch Lomond. Initial bankruptcy but restarts business
1847	Two further trips to Scotland. Excursions to the Lake District, Fleetwood, Blackpool, Liverpool, Isle of Man and Belfast
1849	No excursions by rail; rail companies are trying to run their own and will not negotiate. Offers coach trips to areas of local interest
1851	First edition of *The Excursionist*
1855	First European tour
1862	Rail companies refuse to issue more tourist tickets to Scotland
1866	First North American tour
1869	First river cruise on the River Nile
1870	Opening of offices in four European cities
1872	Cairo office opened
1873	*Cook's Continental Timetable* issued
1874	Introduction of Thomas Cook Credit Note
1879	Publication of *The Excursionist* to promote travel products overseas
1881	French edition of *The Excursionist* published; Eiffel Tower opened
1919	Sale of first airline ticket
1928	Company sold to Wagon-Lits, its main competitor
1948	State ownership of Thomas Cook as part of the British Transport Holding Company
1972	Sale to private sector consortium of Midland Bank, Trust House Forte and the AA
1977	Midland Bank becomes sole owner
1990	Purchase of foreign exchange company to become the largest foreign exchange retailer
1992	Sold to LTU Group
1995	Company website launched and sale of products online
1999	John Mason Cook (JMC) brand launched. Pressaug AG buys the company
2001	C&N Touristic AG takes over the company and is renamed Thomas Cook AG

Cook is widely acknowledged for his early role in the marketing and promotion of domestic and international travel, initially printing handbills. In 1851 he published Cook's *Exhibition Herald and Excursion Advertiser* which survived until 1939. This brochure promoted company products and services including excursions, special events, to encourage travel and included advertisements from hotels, transport companies. *The Excursionist* highlighted the power of advertising (see Image 2.1) to generate travel business, selling 100 000 copies a month in the 1880s in English and foreign editions. For example, in 1881 the company took 200 000 visitors to Paris to see the Eiffel Tower (Image 2.2) making a record profit of £22 819. By 1891, the company was emerging as a truly global operation, with 84 offices, 85 agencies, 2692 staff (of which almost 1000 were in Egypt, Image 2.3) branching out into steamer tours to the West Indies in 1893 and conducted cycling tours of Europe in 1896. By 1899, the more adventurous tourists were travelling on the new Trans-Siberian Express and it was a record year in which seven million travelling tickets were issued, double its volume of the previous decade.

Further reading

Brendon, P. (1991) *Thomas Cook: 150 Years of Popular Tourism*. London: Secker and Warburg.

Withey, L. (1998) *Grand Tours and Cook's Tours: A History of Leisure Travel, 1750–1915*. London: Arun.

However, only limited evidence survives to reconstruct tourism prior to the eighteenth century (as we saw in Table 2.1). The period after 1700 is often acknowledged as the beginning of the rise of domestic travel through to mass travel in the Victorian years in Europe.

The origins of modern tourism

It is impossible to pinpoint a precise point in time when tourism as we understand it today began. Rather, it evolved through time building on the needs, compunctions and desires of society and the opportunities that were presented. Pilgrimages in medieval Britain (and brought to life for a modern audience by Chaucer's *Canterbury Tales*), show that both the supply and demand for what might be loosely termed 'tourism products and services' (such as accommodation and transport) was operating as far back as the fifteenth century. In the wider context, the sixteenth-century Elizabethan mansion became a social and cultural centre, and the early origins of the VFR (**visiting friends and relatives**) sector are easily identified in this period (Girouard 1978). From the seventeenth century, a form of tourism known as 'polite visiting' emerged: those in the upper classes travelled on circuits of the country or took day trips, visiting the country estates of associates or society figures to view the architecture, garden, parkland and works of arts. Such occupations are reflected in the literature of the time, perhaps the most well known example being Jane Austen's *Pride and Prejudice* (1813), in which the protagonist's visit to Darcy's country estate is documented. Publications by respected writers stimulated travel to unknown and remote places from the late eighteenth century onwards. A good example is the Hebridean Islands off Scotland's west coast which, prior to the 1770s, were not visited for pleasure purposes. As Cooper (1979) states, after the publication and success of Johnson's *A Journey to the Hebrides* (1775) and Boswell's *Journal of a Tour to the Hebrides* (1785), the islands became a magnet for travellers, most notably poets, artists and composers, who further popularized the region to others through their works. These early visits required special preparations and a degree of discomfort in terms of accommodation, travel and food was to be expected. However, visits remained confined to a small number of academics and intellectuals until the introduction of regular steamship services from Glasgow around 1840 (Cooper 1979).

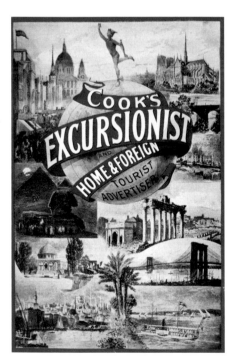

Image 2.1: Thomas Cook's The Excursionist. Source: © Thomas Cook

A form of tourism based on social and cultural experiences and education for young aristocrats became particularly prominent during the eighteenth century; it was known as the **Grand Tour**. Historical evidence shows that several nationalities undertook Grand Tours, including the British, French, Germans and Russians, but most research on the subject concerns British outbound travellers. Towner (1985) suggests that the number of Britons undertaking Grand Tours per year was 15 000–20 000 at the peak in the mid-eighteenth century, from the landed and, as they grew in wealth, the middle classes. Towner (1996) presents a comprehensive review of the Grand Tour and notes some of the reasons for travel, which included a shift away from the increasingly unfashionable society and culture of Britain and the perception that travel would broaden the mind. Grand Tour itineraries were often influenced by travel literature, and in particular, Nugent's Grand Tour guide book, published in 1756 in four volumes and covering France, Germany, Italy and the Netherlands. Tourists visited Classical antiquities, principal works of art and architecture, picturesque landscapes, gardens and natural curiosities, as well as mixing with fashionable society on their travels. Similar to modern-day tourism, the Grand Tour was typified by distinct seasonal patterns of travel. As Towner (1996) notes, tourists wished to see particular places at particular times of the year: Venice was popular around May and June for the Ascensiontide, while Rome was favoured at Christmas, both for the renowned festivities. Other places were rarely visited when the climate was less hospitable: the heat of Rome and Naples in August, or the poor winter travel conditions in the Alps were usually avoided. The length of a Grand Tour varied from around three years in the seventeenth century to about six months or less in the nineteenth century. Stays of around three months were common in the cultural centres such as Paris and many of the Italian cities, while other locations were sometimes visited overnight or only for a short stay (Towner 1996).

The examples in this section have emphasized the importance of the continuity and change theme within tourism. In terms of the influence of literature and culture on travel behaviour, historically this was significant yet it is equally so in the twenty-first century, where media influences, such as travel writing, literature, film and television play a crucial role in stimulating interest in visiting certain locations. Similarly, while the Grand Tour itself died out, the same patterns of travel are identifiable in contemporary forms of travel, such as the student gap year (see Chapter 1) or backpacking.

The rise of mass domestic tourism and the seaside resort

At the same time as the aristocracy and upper classes undertook their Grand Tours of Europe and beyond, within the United Kingdom and northern Europe those who could afford to visited seaside resorts and spa towns. Accordingly, domestic travel for pleasure purposes, akin to what we could recognize today, became popular in the eighteenth century. The major form of tourism at this time might be more accurately described as health tourism, as the drinking and bathing in mineral and sea water was purported to contain health-giving properties. Many inland spa resorts grew up in the eighteenth century across Europe, and later extended to resorts located at the sea. In the UK, the first spa was in Scarborough (North Yorkshire), which developed very early, in the mid-seventeenth century, as a result of Dr Robert Wittie's treatise on the curative powers of the Scarborough sea water in 1667. Indeed, Scarborough was to become Britain's first seaside resort too and was well-established as a fashionable spa resort by the 1730s.

By the end of the eighteenth century sea bathing had become popular among the upper classes. Visits to the seaside and 'taking the waters' were often stimulated by royal patronage, with George IV visiting places such as Brighton (where Dr Richard Russell had promoted the therapeutic qualities in 1750) and Weymouth in the 1780s. The Royal Sea-Bathing Infirmary opened at Margate in 1796. According to Walton (1983: 216), referring to the writer William Hutton, who remarked in 1788 that 'wherever people in the high life take the lead, the next class eagerly follow', tourism began a process of democratization. This pattern, where either the elite or the adventurous first visit a destination or make an activity fashionable and are subsequently followed by others, is one that was to continue for the next 200 years, as we saw illustrated in Table 2.1.

However, in the eighteenth century, it was only the money- and time-rich in society who possessed the resources required for travel outside their own immediate area. Another historical theme emerges here: as technological advances take place within a society, the impact on the

INSIGHT 2.3

Holidays in inter-war Scandinavia

In the study by Rowntree and Lavers (1951), *English and Labour: A Social Study*, evidence was collated on leisure-time pursuits in Scandinavia, observing the 1938 legislation enacted in Denmark, Norway, Sweden and Finland providing for paid holidays. In each country (excluding Finland), 12 days' paid holiday was provided for employees who typically worked 47-hour weeks, while in Finland three weeks' paid holiday was accrued by those who had been employed by a company for five years, two weeks after one year's service and one week after six months' service, plus one compulsory paid state public holiday and ten days' unpaid

holiday which was available. In each country, workers' organizations set up by the trade unions promoted holidays similar to those in the Soviet Union, such as the Danske Folk-Ferier in Denmark, Norsk Folk Ferie in Norway and Reso in Sweden, which provided holiday camps and accommodation to promote domestic (and in some cases overseas) holidays. For example, in 1948, the Holiday Union in Finland had the capacity for 28 000 people a season in accommodation at camps (the population was 4.1 million) complemented by some employers who provided holiday accommodation.

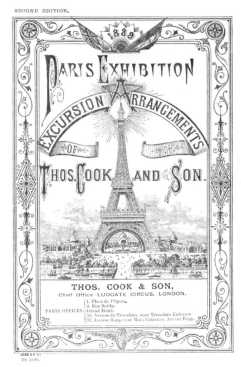

Image 2.2: Thomas Cook advertisement for the Paris Exhibition and Eiffel Tower. Source: © Thomas Cook

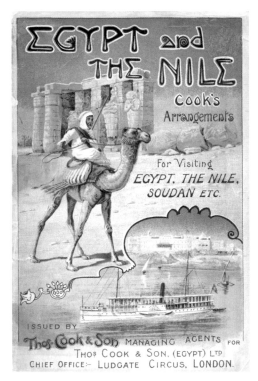

Image 2.3: Thomas Cook advertisement for a tour of Egypt. Source: © Thomas Cook

economy is such that a wider section of the society can take advantage of greater levels of disposable income and free time for leisure purposes. Certainly, the Industrial Revolution in northern Europe in the late eighteenth and nineteenth centuries saw the value of money increase, and the middle and upper classes found they could afford to 'taste the delights of a week by the briny' (Hern 1967: 151).

The fact that some in society had the financial means to participate in leisure travel is only a partial explanation of the factors that initiated tourism. Time free from work or other responsibilities is also a key determinant. Working structures became more highly organized and rationalized in the later nineteenth century and working hours were reduced (Urry 1990). In the UK, legislation to create public or bank holidays came in 1871 (establishing four days per year) and led to the emergence of the week's holiday. Walton (1983) states that longer, week-long breaks were pioneered in the north of England's textile regions, where total shutdown of factories would take place to enable workers to enjoy a holiday *en masse* as a community and giving all workers the same holiday entitlement. These 'Wakes weeks', as they were known, were favoured by employers in the hope that it would promote morale and thereby efficiency and regular attendance at work. This mass exodus meant that many workers travelled at the same time to similar destinations. Cotton workers in Lancashire, with their relatively high incomes and stable employment, often saved for their holidays through 'going off clubs' for 51 weeks of the year. Holidays taken by the working class were common by the 1890s (Walton 2000).

As well as money and time, the supply of services such as accommodation in facilitating tourism is equally important in generating tourism demand. In the USA's first **National Park**, Yosemite National Park, demand for quality hotel accommodation outstripped supply in the late nineteenth century, and the park authority acknowledged the need for a new hotel to meet the needs of visitors. The Fountain Hotel, built in 1891, helped to popularize visits to the Park by offering luxury alongside easy access to wild land (Whittlesey 2003). As well as accommodation, the means of travel is a crucial factor in stimulating tourism. In the period from 1900, railways had a significant effect on leisure travel. According to Hern (1967: 8) it was the railway that brought an even bigger change in attitudes, for it changed the class structure of the English seaside holiday. Thomas Cook is widely credited with using railways for leisure travel with guided tours from the early 1840s, expanding to European and Far East tours by the 1860s (see Insight 2.2). As an example of the level of leisure travel in the mid-Victorian period, there were some 5000 miles of railway and Brighton received some 132,000 visitors by train in a single day in 1862. The coming of the railway enabled people to travel further, faster and at a relatively affordable price. Indeed as Walton (1983: 218) observed:

In the railway age … transport and distance from population centres came to have only secondary importance except on the remoter coastlines. The early arrival of a railway could give a resort a head start over actual and potential rivals … but communications arteries between population concentrations and coastlines tended to create wide areas of potential development … without determining the pace and character of that development in any particular place.

In line with growing affluence, free time and improved transport systems, seaside resorts developed quickly toward the end of the nineteenth century and firmly established themselves in the late Victorian years as sites of mass consumption. In England and Wales the number of rail travellers increased twenty-fold between 1840 and 1870 and the resorts accounted for their full share of this traffic (Walton 1983: 4). As more and more people were able to travel, so a resort hierarchy developed where certain places (such as Southend) were seen as embodiments of mass tourism to be despised and ridiculed (Urry 1990: 16), while others were held in high esteem (such as Bournemouth). It is certainly the case that some places consolidated their position as premier seaside resorts (e.g. Brighton and Blackpool), while other locations were still at an earlier stage in their development. Walton (1983: 3) aptly summarizes:

> The Victorian and Edwardian seaside resort was important not only as a repository for investment, consumer spending and social emulation, but also as a crucible of conflict between classes and lifestyles, as wealthy and status conscious visitors and residents competed with plebeian locals and roistering excursions for access to and enjoyment of amenities.

The seaside brought mutually incompatible modes of recreation and enjoyment into close proximity in ways that seldom happened inland (see also Chapter 23 and coastal tourism).

Understanding the development of resorts in time and space: The resort lifecycle model

Butler (1980) devised a model to show how tourism destinations develop over time (Figure 2.1) which helps us to understand how resorts and tourist destinations have developed through time. The model depicted resorts moving from the initial stage of being found *exploration*, through the *involvement* and *development* stages to a *stagnation* stage. Beyond this a number of options are possible from *decline* to *rejuvenation* (regeneration). The model in essence depicts the development process and if a geographical dimension is added, it is also possible to illustrate the pattern of development through time. In the case of British seaside resorts, the period 1750–1911 shows an initial growth of elite resorts focused on Kent and Sussex (and Weymouth); *c.*1750 saw a wider spread around England and Wales (as well as in Scotland) as shown in Figure 2.2. Figure 2.2 also shows that during the nineteenth century many seaside resorts in the UK were in the involvement or development stages and were not to peak until well into the twentieth century. However, such growth was not uniform. Even locations in close proximity grew at different rates.

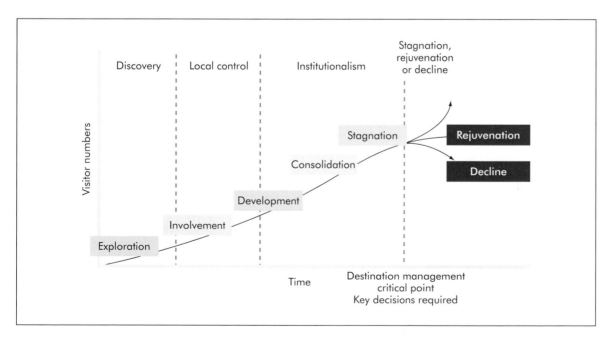

FIGURE 2.1   Destination lifecycle model. Source: Howie (2003: 2) adapted from Butler (1980)

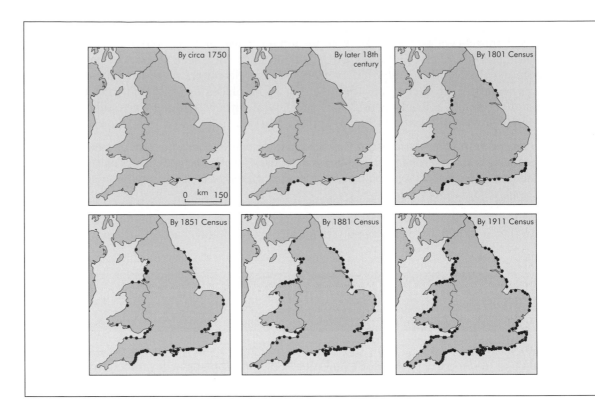

FIGURE 2.2   The pattern of seaside resort growth in England and Wales 1750–1911. Source: *An Historical Geography of Recreation and Tourism in the Western World 1540–1940*, Towner, copyright © (1996) John Wiley and Sons Ltd. This material is used by permission of John Wiley and Sons Ltd.

Tourism in the twentieth century: c.1900–1939

The growing demand for leisure travel among the working population began as day trips initially in the late eighteenth century and increasingly throughout the nineteenth century. It was this form of tourism that was to develop further in the twentieth century. The development of tourism in the early part of the twentieth century displays numerous themes and exogenous factors. Particularly important are the economic, social and political climates as well as aspects discussed in the previous section such as affluence, holiday entitlement and technological advances.

In the early part of the twentieth century, travel was expanding due to growing affluence and continued improvements in transport systems, as depicted in Image 2.4 in the 1901 Holiday Brochure in which different destinations and modes of transport are highlighted. War, however, was to have a marked effect on many nations and in many ways in 1914 and again in 1939. Following World War I (1914–18) there was fluctuating prosperity, depression and recovery. Although there was a worldwide economic depression in the period between 1929 and 1931, such effects were not evenly distributed. Severe unemployment in the UK in some regions (in unskilled occupations) was offset to some extent by other areas and occupational groups where the economy was making people more wealthy than before (Constantine 1983).

Image 2.4: Thomas Cook Edwardian holiday tour brochure, c. 1901. Source: © Thomas Cook

In terms of free time, there was a growing recognition of the value of a holiday. Whereas the UK's Bank Holidays Act of 1871 had ensured not only crowded trains, but crowded beaches, longer holidays were to become more typical. Similar experiences have also been recorded in the USA in the late nineteenth century, with Philadelphians crowding onto trains on Sunday mornings to visit Atlantic City and Cape May (Lenček and Bosker 1998). The similarities in European and North American experiences of coastal tourism led Lenček and Bosker (1998: 140) to argue that:

> At the turn of the [nineteenth] century, seaside life at the [New] Jersey shore was a burlesque for the masses. Everyone was welcome, and the price of admission was the cost of a bathing suit – frequently, even that was not necessary. For Americans, as much as for Europeans, resort and public beach were very much about status, social climbing and health. And about vanity and fashion.

As they also noted, at the southern tip of New Jersey Cape May (which was in the 1880s a hundred-mile stretch of coastline and 54 seaside cities) was pioneer of American seaside resorts, with coastal towns receiving US$150 million in revenue and tourist spending each season. By 1900, Atlantic City had 400 hotels, some able to accommodate up to 1000 guests. In the USA, Newport, Rhode Island also developed as the elite mecca of the American millionaire. Much of the development was based on second homes/villas, funded by industrial wealth, which led to a demand for summer houses after the 1860s to meet the needs of the rich in the north-east seaboard. In Australia, coastal resorts developed in the late nineteenth century in Queensland, South Australia and Victoria. However, here, as in New Zealand, daylight bathing was banned until the early years of the twentieth century. Hall (2003) noted that it was not until 1903 that it became legally permitted to swim at Sydney's Manly Beach and the emergence of the Australian beach culture was stimulated. In terms of the interior, Australia Railways made Australia's rural hinterland accessible to its metropolitan population, such as the Sydney–Blue Mountains railway after the 1850s which led to the development of inland tourist towns at locations such as Katoomba (Hall 2003).

Before the outbreak of World War II the Amulree Report in the UK led to the Holidays with Pay Act 1938. Similar legislation was also enacted in Scandinavia and other countries (see Insight 2.3). While this only established voluntary agreements with employers, between 1931 and 1939 the number of workers entitled to paid holidays increased from 1.5 million to 11 million (Constantine 1983). This, coupled with a shorter working week (reduced from 54 hours in 1919 to 48 hours by 1939) (Haywood, Kew and Bramham 1989) and a doubling of average weekly wages over the same period (Constantine 1983), all contributed to the development of tourism, particularly in the form of the seaside holiday.

By the 1930s holidays had become an expected part of life by many in employment rather than a luxury preserved for the elite. Improvements elsewhere fuelled the demand for leisure travel. While the masses may have taken a short annual holiday by the sea, wealthier individuals took advantage of technological advances in transportation systems and took more exotic holidays by ocean-liner, aeroplane or motor car. The freedom offered by the car was quickly recognized. In 1920 there were 200 000 cars on British roads, rising to one million by 1930 and two million by 1939. In addition to private cars, long-distance bus services in the form or charabancs began to challenge the railways for speed, comfort and convenience. For example, 37 million passengers were carried on long-distance services and tours in 1939. In continental Europe coach travel for holiday purposes was also widely used in France, Switzerland and Italy.

In an international context, Douglas and Douglas (2000) examined the growth of the P&O steamer routes and their impact on tourist travel from the UK and Europe to the Far East, especially the greater expansion of cruises after the opening of the Suez Canal in 1869. P&O's association with Thomas Cook and Sons having rendered most of Europe safe for British travellers undertook their first world tour in 1872–3 (20 days at one pound a day), not surprisingly using P&O ships for the main sea travel. The Thomas Cook company ensured that greater numbers of visitors to India, Malaysia and often beyond were in the hands of British travel entrepreneurs. By 1886, Cook and P&O were organizing trips from Bombay to Jeddah for Muslim pilgrims, an activity for which the shipping company later built a special vessel (Douglas and Douglas 2000: 32–3) and the promotion of this form of travel is depicted in Image 2.5. In the case of the **South Pacific**, similar developments associated with cruising have also been documented by Douglas and Douglas (1996) where they observed the impact of the Canadian Australian Royal Mail Steamship

Image 2.5: Thomas Cook steamship and cruise advertisement. Source: © Thomas Cook

Line and the New Zealand Union Steamship Line in developing tourism in Fiji (with stopover traffic at Suva) after 1893. By 1930, monthly services provided by steamships had acted as a catalyst for international tourism and they formed the precursor of the modern-day luxury liners that called at South Pacific ports. Douglas and Douglas (1996) examined the process in other parts of the South Pacific including Melanesia and Hawaii as well as the emergence of the South Pacific as the playground of European and American tourists. There is also a degree of continuity in the decline and subsequent rebirth of the South Pacific as a cruise ship destination, with vessels calling at many of the ports which had developed in the nineteenth century.

In terms of other forms of long-distance travel, transatlantic crossings between Europe and North America had been possible since 1838; the following year Samuel Cunard founded the Cunard Line after winning the lucrative North Atlantic mail contract. By the 1930s, however, sea travel had expanded considerably and cruising was a popular form of travel among those who could afford to travel this way. Air travel had become a novel form of travel for the elite following, for example, Louis Bleriot flying from France to England in 1909, and the tour operator Thomas Cook offering Ariel Travel for Business or Pleasure from 1909. As Coltman (1989) notes, Britain began to subsidize air travel in the 1920s and from this national airlines emerged, while in the USA their growth and development has been linked to the growth of US mail contracts. In fact many of these routes laid the foundations of modern-day air travel routes. In the early twentieth century there were many economic and social changes, particularly during the **Edwardian** years (1901–14) in the UK, Europe and North America. These changes impacted upon the recreation and leisure behaviour of the population, with some further expansion of tourism opportunities for the middle and working classes (Clarke and Crichter 1985). In fact, there is evidence of public sector involvement in promoting tourism at a local level (i.e. place-marketing by seaside resorts) (Ward 1998) and some countries seizing the lead as shown in Case Study 2.3W and Image 2.6.

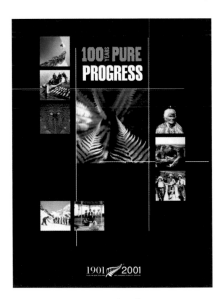

Image 2.6: New Zealand Tourism Board anniversary publication of 100 years of public service to tourism, reproduced courtesy of New Zealand Tourism Board

Increased leisure time, paid holidays and developments in transport inspired and enabled many to travel, expanding the geographical extent of domestic tourism in many countries dependent upon the transport infrastructure available and its cost. At the same time, following the Edwardian period and aftermath of World War I, a period of economic fragility ensued. The historical development of tourism was directly affected by economic austerity, unemployment and financial hardship followed which suppressed many of the initial opportunities made available in the Edwardian period. Alternative forms of tourist activity began to appeal to a larger number of participants, particularly those that could be enjoyed at relatively little cost in times of economic depression. In Britain, the inter-war period saw an enormous growth in the demand for outdoor recreation, such as rambling and cycling, and the accommodation favoured was either camping or the Youth Hostel. In England and Wales, the Youth Hostel Association had 300 establishments in the 1930s with a membership of 225 000 people walking or cycling. In Australia in the inter-war period, the growth of coastal resorts also gave way to the bush-walking movement. This led to the rise of the conservation movement (Hall 2003) and the formation in 1932 of the National Parks and Primitive Areas Council (NPPAC) in New South Wales.

Lower cost forms of domestic tourism, particularly the rise of holiday homes on the fringe of urban areas such as London's green belt (Hall and Page 2002), provided a substitute for holidays in times of austerity. So too did working holidays among the working classes whose families engaged in traditional activities such as hop-picking in Kent, living in often cramped conditions. What is apparent is that the development of mass tourism opportunities for the population in specific countries is very much a cyclical process linked to the economy and the availability of disposable income in households. When income is in short supply, cheaper alternatives are often selected (see Image 2.7).

Tourism in the twentieth century: c.1945–1970

In most developed Western countries, there was rapid growth in tourism after World War II. In the case of Australia, Hall (2003: 52) confirmed that:

> The period after the Second World War witnessed an unparalleled development in leisure services for the Australian population. A new period of prosperity following the depression of the 1930s and the war years meant that people had greater disposable income and more leisure time in which to enjoy the prosperity, particularly as three weeks of annual holidays became standard. One of the greatest impacts was the growth in personal mobility through car ownership

also mirrored in the USA on a much larger scale. One consequence in Australia and North America was the development of motels to meet the routeway demand for travellers. Many aspects, such as holiday entitlements and growing affluence, which affected growth in the previous period, continue in the period after 1945, illustrating the continuity as well as change in the way these processes and factors impact upon tourism behaviour. The immediate post-war period was one of continued and rapid growth and recognition of the tourism industry in the UK.

The 1950s and 1960s saw great changes in the nature of tourist travel with the introduction of package holidays by air using charter aircraft, and also in the development of home-centred forms of leisure. Radio and television in the home challenged the cinema as a major form of leisure entertainment. Television advertising was gradually introduced by tour operators to promote domestic and overseas tourism. At the same time, growing affluence meant that overseas travel truly came within the grasp of the working classes, having previously been a luxury enjoyed by the upper and middle classes. In contrast to outbound and domestic tourism in the UK, and despite restrictions on overseas currency available for travel, visitors to the UK also became a valuable invisible export for the economy. One of the major features of tourism in Britain during the inter-war years and through to the 1950s and 1960s was the development of the **holiday camp**. Ward and Hardy (1986) provide a detailed history of the development of holiday camps in the UK, showing that they date back to 1897, with a camp for young men on the Isle of Man. The entrepreneur Billy Butlin is often credited with the concept and development of holiday camps after developing amusement parks in the UK 1925–1937, and certainly Butlin's skill was important in its

development in the UK. In 1936, the first Butlin's opened in Skegness with a capacity of 1000 followed in 1938 by Clacton with a 2000 capacity. By 1948, it was estimated that 1 in 20 of all holiday-makers in the UK stayed at a Butlin's holiday camp each year (Ward and Hardy 1986: 75). However, from the 1960s the popularity of holiday camps diminished and many closures took place. The company then focused on three sites – Minehead, Skegness and Bognor Regis in developing a new style of holiday resort (www.butlinsonline.co.uk). In 2001, it also entered the conference and event market to extend its markets. Holiday camps as a type of holiday are not restricted to the UK and, following the theme of continuity and change, have been refocused and reborn not just in the new Butlin's resorts but in the shape of ventures such as Center Parcs and the Disney theme parks.

Image 2.7: National Parks in the USA have a long history of hosting visitors

Tourism in the twentieth century: Post-1970

In the last 35 years, tourism activity has developed many of the features established in the earlier periods of the twentieth century, while new trends have altered the nature of demand and supply. The theme of continued expansion remains applicable into new millennium. Some of the themes that are particularly significant in this period, many of which are interrelated, include:

- greater internationalization and globalization of tourism
- changes in technology
- the legislative environment
- increasing political recognition of tourism's economic impacts
- a rise in consumer spending
- emergence of new consumers
- changes in products
- development of marketing, research and information.

The discussion of tourism history is somewhat Western-centric as, for many countries and areas, tourism development is a very recent phenomenon. Some of the most well-known and loved holiday destinations have only a recent history in terms of tourism. For example, tourism in the Maldives began in the early 1970s, with the arrival of the first tour group in 1972 and the first resort, Kurumba Village, completed in the same year. However, such destinations are still subject to the wider global changes: in many cases, they have evolved as tourism destinations as a direct result of these changes.

A greater internationalization and globalization of tourism

As Figure 2.3 shows, global tourism expanded significantly in the 1970s (excluding the effect of the oil crisis) and at much faster rate after 1984, though the annual change in visitor arrivals worldwide has fluctuated between 1.5 per cent and 16 per cent depending on a wide range of factors. What is indisputable is the growing global reach of tourism, aided by declining relative costs of travel, increased consumerism in tourism and constant innovation in products and provision. The number of domestic trips (i.e. UK residents holidaying in the UK) has remained relatively constant, however.

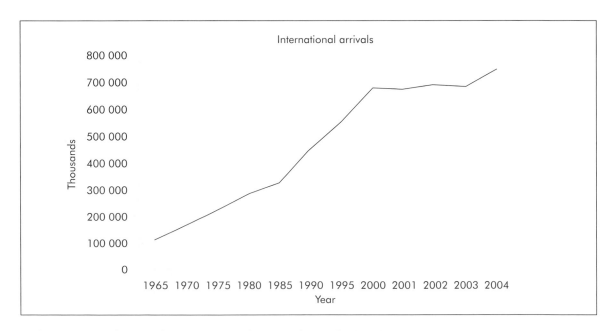

FIGURE 2.3   The growth in international tourism demand 1950–2004. Source: Based on WTO data

Travellers are now becoming more adventurous with long-haul travel to Australasia and Asia Pacific growing, even though North America and Europe have remained the dominant destinations in terms of international arrivals. Accompanying this growth, an increasingly wide geographic range of destinations emerged in this period, not just in the more traditional holiday countries but including areas as diverse in product offering as Africa, East Asia Pacific and Antarctica. In addition to the growth of international travel, there have also been significant increases in intra-regional travel, particularly in regions where tourism is a relatively new activity in which to engage. For example, tourism in East Asia Pacific is dominated by demand generated from within the region.

A final area of change has been in the growth of the short-break market, initially within domestic markets but increasingly intra-regional and international destinations are competing for the short-break traveller. Cities such as New York, Paris and Brussels have traditionally been popular for Europeans taking a short break but an increasingly wide choice of further-flung destinations, such as New Orleans, Reykjavik, Prague and Las Vegas, have begun to compete in the marketplace. A number of factors have boosted the short-break market, including greater disposable income, political changes allowing travel into Eastern European countries and vast improvements in travel technology.

Changes in technology

Improvements in transport have been an enduring theme in the history of tourism, and have heavily influenced tourism development during more contemporary times. The underpinning explanation for the internationalization of tourism is the introduction of new technology in the airline industry. The year 1970 brought a technological breakthrough in air transport, with the introduction of the DC-10 and the much bigger Boeing 747 on a global scale: the first wide-bodied jets. The earliest 747 (747-100), the first flight of which was a Pan-Am service from New York to London, had a cruising speed of 600 mph, a range of 6000 miles and capacity for 370 passengers (later to increase). One of the implications of the new era aircraft were the economies of scale generated, meaning more people could travel more cheaply, more quickly and more easily, covering greater distances, than before. In addition to air travel, changing technology and developments leading to high-speed rail links and improvements in road travel have assisted land-based tourism. Other technological advances include the opening of the Channel Tunnel transport system, linking France and the UK, in 1994, although financial problems associated with its capital/debt problem continue to affect it.

The legislative environment

Since the late 1960s, a growing political recognition of tourism as a significant part of a nation's economy has developed in many countries or, in the case of countries where tourism activity has a longer tradition, has remained important as a strategic objective. In some countries, government policy has been set out within a legislative structure during this period. For example, the 1969 Development of Tourism Act laid down a public sector structure in the UK, establishing a formal structure of tourist boards and financial mechanisms for stimulating tourism capital projects. Other legislation has also affected the private sector; for example, from 1970, tour operators were required to have an Air Travel Organizers Licence (**ATOL**) (see Chapter 7 for a more detailed discussion).

Throughout Europe, legislation for the tourism industry has been a feature of developments from the 1980s. State subsidies for tourism have been replaced with **EU**-funded regional incentives for development in areas of decline and high socioeconomic deprivation, so that new employment opportunities can be created in peripheral regions. European legislation has also introduced measures to liberalize air and road transport, the harmonization of hotel classifications, the relaxing of frontier controls and efforts to balance VAT and duty-free regulations in a bid to ease the flow of tourism at a transnational level, so that barriers to tourism are removed.

Political and economic events

The explanation of why certain events affect the tourism industry often lies within a combination of factors rather than a single influence. Political issues affecting the industry are difficult to explain without reference to economic factors. As tourism is demand-inelastic (see Chapter 17), variations in the economy have a direct impact on tourism demand (see Chapter 3). Particular factors that impact on tourism demand include high unemployment, high interest rates and high levels of inflation. When such conditions prevail, tourism demand can be suppressed. In the UK, economic recession in 1980 was the deepest since the 1930s and some aspects of tourism demand were affected. Further recession in the early 1990s, while impacting some parts of the tourism industry, had beneficial effects on others. Economic uncertainty due to high interest rates and fear of redundancy may have caused many consumers to abandon plans for expensive overseas holidays. As a result domestic tourism within the UK grew by 4.5 per cent in 1991 (ONS 1999).

Politics can influence the tourism industry in other ways too. Disputes can seriously impede travel, especially when conditions escalate. During the 1990s, ethnic conflict in the former **Yugoslavia** decimated the country's tourism industry. Statistics show that arrivals from the UK to Yugoslavia peaked at 656 000 in 1990, after which they fell to 22 000 by 1992. In 1991, the Gulf War led to US$2 billion of lost traffic to Europe which was a contributory factor in the downfall of the International Leisure Group (ILG) in the UK. At the time ILG was the UK's second largest tour operator (with brands such as Intasun, Select and Club 18–30) and operated an airline (Air Europe). While financial difficulties with one of ILG's major shareholders was instrumental, the fact that in the early part of 1991 bookings were seriously down because of people's wariness of travelling (in addition to economic factors) played a part in the ultimate bankruptcy of the company. More recently, the 9/11 attacks and subsequent terrorist alerts have undoubtedly affected tourism demand on a global scale not seen before. The threats over travel along with economic recession in many generating countries have led to a decrease in world tourism figures. International arrivals dropped by 8 million in 2002 to 689 million, with the last four months of 2001 seeing an 11 per cent fall globally, with a decrease in every region. Many tourists chose domestic holidays over overseas trips, and many chose to avoid air travel. In turn, several airlines went into administration or suffered severe losses due to falling passenger numbers.

The rise of a consumer society

In the period since 1970 there has been a general rise in affluence of many people in employment. In the UK, between 1971 and 1997, real household disposable income per head nearly doubled, with an equivalent average annual growth rate of 2.6 per cent (ONS 1999). Other exogenous factors affecting society as a whole also influence the tourism industry. As with other developed countries, the UK has seen a declining birth rate and ageing population. Data from the Office for National Statistics (ONS 1999) show that births have decreased from 963 000 in 1971 to 745 000 in 1997, while the proportion of people aged over 75 years has increased from 5 per cent to 7 per cent in the same time period. While at one time it may have been possible to consider those who were retired and the elderly as a single group, increasing life expectancy and retirement at a younger age means this is no longer possible. Assuming the financial means are available, early retirement is often now synonymous with a higher propensity to travel. Smaller family sizes may mean that a larger proportion of family income is available for holidays. All of these factors point towards an explanation for the increase in the volume of tourism, domestically, in international terms and within the short-break market.

Changing products

The impact of new technology aircraft resulted in greater accessibility of a wider range of destinations to a greater number of people. Consequently, the period from the 1970s is typified by a growth in tourism destinations and activity. Such growth was not entirely positive for domestic tourism in the mid-1970s and 1980s, particularly in countries such as the UK where seaside holidays were the mainstay of the tourism product. Many domestic resorts declined due to their lack of cost competitiveness and lack of attraction compared to cheap overseas package holidays. The changes led to a legacy of landscape decline in the built environment of resorts. However, tourism is not just concerned with seaside resorts. Increasingly in the last 30 years, niche products have emerged and developed, some have even become mainstream. Examples include ecotourism, film tourism, adventure tourism and heritage tourism, and many others which will be discussed in various parts of this book. Such product developments reflect the trend away from a product-led (**Fordist**) tourism industry to a more consumer-focused approach (**post-Fordist**), which is able to respond to, stimulate and predict consumer needs and wants. What is also important in this transition from what Poon (1993) describes as old to new tourism is an increasing demand for quality, service, flexibility and differentiation, very different from the standardized packages that dominated post-1945 tourism. Many tour operators and travel agents are now realizing that package holidays may be on the decline, with an increasingly empowered consumer able to book online or take independent holidays.

The period from the 1970s is an interesting one as supply of and demand for tourism has grown rapidly at an international level. The period also saw the development of powerful tour operators with a high degree of vertical and horizontal integration, able to shape the tourism industry. The segmentation of the tourist market and differentiation of products has resulted in a huge variety of tourism products, services and experiences.

Linking history and tourism: The rise of heritage tourism

Tourism has a long and fascinating history, the surface of which has only been briefly scratched in this chapter. The link between tourism and history does not end there, however, as history itself is one of the essential components of the contemporary tourism industry. Throughout the world, the commercialization of history and culture as part of the process of developing tourism products is a recurrent theme. Indeed, historic buildings and places and those with cultural and religious significance, such as the Acropolis, the Pyramids, the Taj Mahal and the city of Nazareth, act as the focal point for many holiday excursions and a backdrop for many city breaks. In the UK, visits to National Trust historic house and garden properties continue to grow, with membership at around three million people.

Even recent history can quickly become integrated into tourism. For example, in South Africa, the end of racial segregation has stimulated the growth of tourism attractions based on the apartheid theme. Indeed, since 1997 the Robben Island prison, where Nelson Mandela was in captivity, has been open to visitors as a museum, attracting just over 300 000 visitors in 2002. Industrial heritage is often reflected in tourism products, particularly in the UK, where six such sites have attained World Heritage Site status. These include Ironbridge, New Lanark, Blaenavon, Saltaire, Derwent Valley Mills and, in 2004, the maritime mercantile City of Liverpool, one of the world's major trading centres in the eighteenth and nineteenth centuries was added to the list (see whc.unesco.org for more information). Historic resources play an important role in tourism. However, the operation of historic and cultural sites for visitor use raises many competing and conflicting challenges for the planning and management of both tourism promotion and conservation of the historic environment. Such management-related issues will be discussed later in this book.

Conclusion

This chapter has shown that the development of tourism in the last 200 years has been inextricably linked to political, economic, social and technological influences. While the general theme has been one of growth there are some exceptions and conditions which should be borne in mind. First, tourism is not and never has been a universal activity for all. Throughout history those without the financial means or time available have not been able to participate. While the proportion of those in this category has decreased it has not been eliminated and in recent years the proportion of those not taking a holiday has remained fairly constant.

As Crouch (1999) notes, even those in work are finding it increasingly difficult to take time from work and holidays in the future may become more frequent, shorter, spread throughout the year and more intensive. This leads to a second conclusion, that of the development of the tourism product itself. This chapter has shown that destinations move through a cycle of development which lead to a stage of consolidation (at least) or decline (at worst) and where a catalyst for change can be mobilized, **rejuvenation** may occur to try and find a new economic rationale for such areas. Social changes in fashion and a theme of 'been there, done that' means that new types of holiday and activities are needed. A feature of the development of tourism in some locations is the obsolescence of the once popular accommodation stock, now being put to alternative uses or pulled down. A third feature of the development of tourism that should be considered is the volatility of the market. Again, it is a combination of factors sometimes operating at a macro level that can have far-reaching effects on the industry. Aspects such as political and economic stability in the generating area and destination are crucial. At any time specific changes in tax policies, the value of currency and controls on tourist spending can affect the number of tourists travelling from a country. Similarly, price, competition and the quality or popularity of the product can influence the destination area. History has shown that such aspects can be susceptible to rapid change and greatly alter the tourism industry. When all of these are added to changing consumer tastes and fashion it can be seen why tourism may be volatile. Yet, as shown in Chapter 1, globalization and a greater competition for tourism mean places need to stay ahead of the game through reinvestment, to try and anticipate trends and to avoid areas losing their economic rationale once they lose popular appeal. Once tourism has become a mainstay of many communities, often over a long time frame, adaptation and change can be a difficult process. What a historical perspective shows is that adaptation, innovation (see Chapter 13) and understanding the tourist as a consumer are all critical to maintaining the tourism development process. For this reason, the next chapter focuses upon the tourist as a consumer to understand what motivates him or her to visit different places.

Discussion questions

1 Suggest how employment changes have affected tourism.

2 Suggest how economic changes have affected tourism in the last 100 years.

3 Show how changes in fashion have affected the popularity of selected destinations.

4 What different types of tourist go on holiday in the UK and why?

References

Bray, R. and Raitz, V. (2001) *Flight to the Sun: The Story of the Holiday Revolution*. London: Continuum.

Butler, R.W. (1980) 'The concept of the tourist area cycle of evolution: implications for management of resources', *Canadian Geographer*, 24 (1): 5–12.

Clarke, J. and Critcher, C. (1985) *The Devil Makes Work: Leisure in Capitalist Britain*. Basingstoke: Macmillan.

Coltman, M. (1989) *Introduction to Travel and Tourism: An International Approach*. New York: Van Nostrand Reinhold.

Constantine, S. (1983) *Social Conditions in Britain 1918–39*. London: Methuen.

Cooper, D. (1979) *The Road to the Isles: Travellers in the Hebrides 1770–1914*. London: Routledge and Kegan Paul.

Crouch, S. (1999) 'Relationship marketing', *Tourism – The Journal of the Tourism Society*, 99: 13–15.

Douglas, N. and Douglas, N. (1996) 'Tourism in the Pacific: Historical factors', in C.M. Hall and S.J. Page (eds) (1996) *Tourism in the Pacific: Issues and Cases*. London: Thomson Learning.

Douglas, N. and Douglas, N. (2000) 'Tourism in South East and South Asia: Historical dimensions', in C.M. Hall and S.J. Page (eds) *Tourism in South and South East Asia: Issues and Cases*. Oxford: Butterworth-Heinemann.

Durie, A.J. (2003) *Scotland for the Holidays: A History of Tourism in Scotland 1780–1939*. East Linton: Tuckwell Press.

Girouard, M. (1978) *Life in the English Country House*. London: Yale University Press.

Hall, C.M. (2003) *Introduction to Tourism: Dimensions and Issues*. Frenchs Forest: Pearson Education Australia.

Hall, C.M. and Page, S.J. (2002) *The Geography of Tourism and Recreation: Environment, Place and Space, Second Edition*. London: Routledge.

Hannigan, J. (1998) *Fantasy City: Pleasure and Profit in the Postmodern Metropolis*. London: Routledge.

Haywood, L., Kew, F. and Bramham, P. (1989) *Understanding Leisure*. Cheltenham: Stanley Thornes.

Hern, A. (1967) *The Seaside Holiday: The History of the English Seaside Report*. London: Crescent Press.

Howie, F. (2003) *Managing the Tourist Destination*. London: Continuum.

Inglis, F. (2000) *The Delicious History of the Holiday*. London: Routledge.

Lenček, L. and Bosker, G. (1998) *The Beach: The History of Paradise on Earth*. London: Pimlico.

Löfgren, O. (2002) *On Holiday: A History of Vacationing*. Berkeley and Los Angeles: California University Press.

ONS (Office for National Statistics) (1999) *Social Trends 29*. London: HMSO.

Poon, A. (1993) *Tourism, Technology and Competitive Strategies*. Wallingford, Oxon: CABI.

Rowntree, S. and Lavers, G. (1951) *English Life and Leisure: A Social Study*. London: Longmans, Green & Co.

Towner, J. (1985) The Grand Tour: A key phase in the history of tourism. *Annals of Tourism Research*, 15 (1): 47–62.

Towner, J. (1996) *An Historical Geography of Recreation and Tourism in the Western World, 1540–1940*. Chichester: Wiley.

Urry, J. (1990) *The Tourist Gaze: Leisure and Traditional Contemporary Societies*. London: Sage.

Walton, J.K. (1983) *The English Seaside Resort: A Social History, 1750–1914*. Leicester: Leicester University Press.

Walton, J.K. (2000) *The British Seaside: Holidays and Resorts in the Twentieth Century*. Manchester: Manchester University Press.

Ward, C. and Hardy, D. (1986) *Goodnight Campers: History of the British Holiday Camp*. London: Mansell.

Ward, S.V. (1998) *Selling Places: The Marketing and Promotion of Towns and Cities 1850–2000*. London: E&FN Spon.

Whittlesey, L. (2003) 'Music, song and laughter: Yellowstone National Park's Fountain Hotel, 1891–1916', *Montana*, 53 (4): 63–5.

Further reading

A good range of texts exists on the historical development of tourism, but the following provide a good overview:

Towner, J. (1996) *An Historical Geography of Recreation and Tourism in the Western World, 1540–1940*. Chichester: Wiley.

Walton, J.K. (1983) *The English Seaside Resort: A Social History, 1750–1914*. Leicester: Leicester University Press.

Walton, J.K. (2000) *The British Seaside: Holidays and Resorts in the Twentieth Century*. Manchester: Manchester University Press.

3

Understanding Tourism Demand

Learning outcomes

After reading this chapter and answering the questions, you should be able to:

- recognize the different forms of tourism demand

- understand the range of factors influencing tourism demand including particular factors at the destination and in generating areas

- be aware of those influences on tourism demand which the tourism industry can affect and those which are beyond its control

- recognize the procedures for measuring tourism demand

- understand the challenges and problems of collecting tourism statistics.

Overview

Demand is the basis upon which researchers conceptualize how visitors choose and pursue a range of opportunities in their leisure time. Thus, a consideration of demand in relation to tourism can assist in understanding **motivation**, needs and experiences, as well as being a useful indicator of changing trends. Hall and Page (2002: 60) state that, 'an understanding of tourism demand is a starting point for the analysis of why tourism develops, who patronizes specific destinations and what appeals to the client market'. Quite simply, as Song and Witt (2000: 1) argue, 'tourism demand is the foundation on which all tourism-related business decisions ultimately rest'.

Attempting to define 'demand' as a concept is a complex task and often depends on the disciplinary perspective adopted by the researcher. For example, the geographer is pre-eminently concerned with 'the total number of persons who travel, or wish to travel, to use tourist facilities and services at places away from their place of work or residence' (Mathieson and Wall 1982: 1). The **geographer** examines these issues in a spatial context to assess the impact on domestic and international tourism destinations (Image 3.1). In contrast, the **economist** examines the tourist propensity to purchase tourism products or services at a specific price during a given period of time. Different again, psychologists approach tourism demand with a particular focus on motivation and behaviour, while anthropologists and sociologists also focus on the impact of tourism on the societies hosting tourists and the social dimensions of the tourists visiting. Attempting to explain what demand means in simple terms is probably expressed most clearly by Pearce (1995) as the relationship between individuals' motivation to travel and their ability to do so. This means that a range of factors influence tourism demand in both the **tourist generating** and **destination areas**. However, before examining the factors influencing demand, it is first necessary to consider more closely the different types of demand.

Based on Smith's (1995) observations, demand occurs at four different levels, including:

- the amount of products that will be consumed at various prices
- actual levels of participation
- the unsatisfied component of participation
- the desire for emotional and psychologically based experiences.

Burkart and Medlik (1981) divided the influences on the tourism market into two components:

- 'Determinants' refer to the exogenous or external factors that shape the general demand for tourism within society or a specific population. Such factors tend to be common to all world regions, although are likely to show a different emphasis in every country (e.g. the economy in each country will have a greater or lesser effect on outbound tourism).
- 'Motivations' refer to the personal factors that directly affect the individual and are expressed as tourism desires and choices. Motivations can be influenced by internal (e.g. perceptions and personality) and external (e.g. culture, age and gender) aspects.

Essentially, leisure demand results from a variety of social, economic, **demographic** and **psychological** factors peculiar to the individual (Argyle 1996; Ryan 1997; Hall and Page 2002). Models of **tourist motivation** which explore the effect of these diverse influences are examined in the next chapter. However, extrinsic factors or determinants, such as government policy, media communications, marketing, societal norms and pressures, knowledge, information on and images of destinations, technological change and wider socioeconomic determinants have an equally important role to play in shaping tourism destination **demand** (see Figure 3.1). These particular issues will form the focus of this chapter.

The term 'demand' is sometimes ambiguous in its use and meaning, often referring to different measures of tourism participation and behaviour. Subsequently, the study of tourism demand can be approached from differing perspectives. It is therefore important to understand the elements of tourism demand and how researchers and analysts use the term.

Image 3.1: Countries like Brazil have emerged as long-haul destinations in the last decade

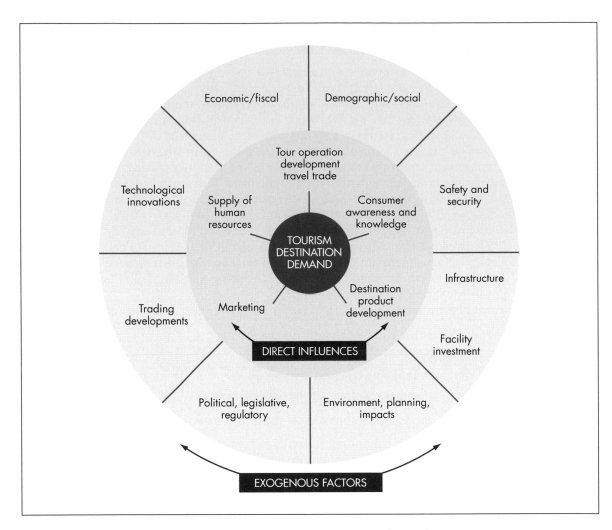

FIGURE 3.1   Factors shaping development of tourism destination demand. Source: Adapted from WTO (1995)

The elements of tourism demand

Aggregate/effective/actual demand

The term 'demand' is often used to specify actual or observed tourism participation and activity. This type of demand is known as 'effective' or 'actual' demand and refers to the aggregate number of tourists recorded in a given location or at a particular point in time. It is most easily visualized by reference to tourism statistical sources, where the total numbers of people are shown, travelling from one country to another or by purpose of visit. Clearly tourism suppliers require demand for their products, but too much effective demand poses the problem of exceeding the supply of products, such as overbooking of airline seats. Effective tourism demand within a population can be measured by means of gross **travel propensity**, which yields the total number of tourism trips as a percentage of the population. Gross travel propensity often exceeds 100 per cent in western European countries, where individuals take more than one tourism trip. Net travel propensity incorporates suppressed and no-demand categories and refers to the percentage of the population that takes one or more tourism trips in a given period of time. This figure is unlikely to exceed 80 per cent even in countries where the highest levels of tourism activity occur. Dividing gross travel propensity by net travel propensity gives travel frequency or the average number of trips taken by those participating in tourism in a given period (Cooper *et al.* 1998). Table 3.1 outlines how travel propensity is calculated.

TABLE 3.1	Measures of effective demand: Worked example of travel propensity

The population of an unspecified country is 30 million. Of that 30 million:
8 million take 1 holiday of 1 night or more = 8 × 1 = 8 million trips
4 million take 2 holidays of 1 night or more = 4 × 2 = 8 million trips
2 million take 3 holidays of 1 night or more = 2 × 3 = 6 million trips
1 million take 4 holidays of 1 night or more = 1 × 4 = 4 million trips
TOTAL: 15 million take at least 1 holiday = 26 million trips

Percentage of the population taking a holiday
Net travel propensity =
number of population taking one or more holiday / total population × 100
= 15 / 30 × 100 = 50%
Total number of tourism trips taken as a percentage of the population
Gross travel propensity =
number of total trips / total population × 100 =
= 26 / 30 × 100 = 87%

Average number of trips taken by tourists
Travel frequency =
gross travel propensity / net travel propensity = 87% / 50% = 1.74

Source: Adapted from Cooper *et al.* 1998

Suppressed demand

It is often suggested that suppressed demand can be subdivided into 'potential' and 'deferred' demand (Cooper *et al.* 1998). Both refer to those who do not travel for some reason, the nature of that reason being the distinguishing factor. Those who might be classified as potential demand are more likely to become actual demand in the future when circumstances allow. It may well be that waiting for additional income or holiday entitlement is needed for that suppressed, but potential, demand to become actual or effective. It can be seen that the reason behind potential demand relates more specifically to factors associated directly with the individual (Image 3.2).

With deferred demand, the reasons for the 'suppression' are down to problems on the supply side, with perhaps accommodation shortages, transport difficulties or the weather prevent people from travelling to their chosen destination. Again, though, once such problems are overcome those in this category move upwards and become effective or actual demand. For the tourism industry, ensuring that those classified within either of the suppressed demand categories turn into effective demand is crucial, as such individuals represent potential new customers.

No demand

Generally, there is a proportion of the population that does not participate in tourism. Reasons for this may be a lack of money (which may be resolved later in life), an unwillingness or inability to find the time necessary or a desire to enjoy holiday time at home rather than away from it. Whether the reasons are through choice or otherwise, those in this category represent 'no demand'.

Other aspects of demand

There are other ways of viewing demand in addition to the three elements discussed above, which build on these basic concepts. Cooper *et al.* (1998) refer to 'substitution of demand'

Image 3.2: The pull of natural environments such as the French Alps has been a key influence on tourism demand

when demand for an activity is replaced by another form of activity, for example staying in a hotel rather than self-catering. In addition, redirection of demand occurs when the geographical holiday location is changed, perhaps as a result of over-booking in one destination.

Having established the parameters of tourism demand, it is now appropriate to conduct an analysis of the ways in which demand is influenced by exogenous factors. Such externally driven influences can be divided into two forms: those affecting demand in the tourist-generating region and those affecting demand in the tourist destination.

Factors influencing demand in the tourist-generating area

There are numerous factors influencing demand from the tourist-generating area, which in simple terms can be grouped as:

- economic determinants
- social determinants
- political determinants.

These determinants act as significant enabling or constraining variables on individuals within a tourist-generating region.

Economic determinants

Personal incomes The availability of the necessary finance is perhaps the most obvious variable influencing tourism demand. Incomes and tourism expenditure are closely linked, and it is possible to examine this relationship through statistics on economic trends and tourism activity in any country. In the UK, for example, household disposable income rose in real terms one and a quarter times between 1971 and 2002 (ONS 2004) and, as such, it is not surprising that a consequential rise in tourism purchases also occurred. As a product, tourism has traditionally been considered as 'demand elastic' (see Chapter 17), which means that consumers tend to be sensitive to a price rise. Put simply, as prices rise, demand reduces; similarly, if incomes rise and prices remain the same, then demand increases.

Distribution of incomes Within a tourist-generating nation, income distribution is likely to affect tourism demand. A skewed income distribution, for example where there are relatively few wealthy and many poor households, is likely to limit the proportion of people who can afford to travel internationally. In wealthier developed countries, a more equal income distribution may result in a high overall level of tourism demand. Clearly there must also be a willingness to spend on tourism products. According to the **Office for National Statistics** (ONS 1999), in 1995, four in ten households in the UK felt that they could not afford a week's holiday, compared to six in ten in Portugal and one in ten in Germany. This is a point often overlooked by tourism researchers who naturally assume that such barriers do not exist when looking at the tourism-generating propensity of the population in individual countries.

What is apparent is that the propensity for holiday-making, especially multiple trips to different destinations, is greater among higher occupational and income groups. Those not taking a holiday are more numerous among the lower income groups. Added to this are differences in the patterns of domestic and outbound demand within countries. As with other aspects in society (e.g. unemployment), tourism activity is not evenly distributed across all social groups or geographically within countries. In the UK for example, higher income and socioeconomic groups are overrepresented as are those living in the more prosperous areas of the south east, and these groups show a higher propensity towards taking holidays (ONS 2004).

Value of currency/exchange rates A destination's exchange rate has a far-reaching influence on tourism demand from a generating area and international tourism is highly susceptible to exchange rate fluctuations that can alter the cost of a holiday considerably. The potential consequences of changes in exchange rates are immediately acted upon by the tourism industry and travellers alike. Crouch (1994) identified the impact of an unfavourable exchange rate to include less travel abroad, a reduction in expenditure of length of stay, changes in the method or length of travel time and a reduction in spending by **business travel**lers. A movement in exchange rates of at least 10 per cent is necessary before a consequential correlation in visitor movement can be traced, according to some studies, and for some destinations (with high international appeal or very strong economies) movements of 20 per cent have been necessary to seriously change tourism demand.

Social determinants

Demographic variables Although Chapter 4 examines the demographic variables in more detail in terms of tourist motivation to travel, it is evident that a range of demographic variables affects demand. For example, the age of a traveller will often exert an influence on the type of travel product and destination they choose, particularly as research on youth tourism and the backpacker market indicates how influential age is on the selection of this type of experience. The impact of education can also be a major determinant of both employment type and income-earning potential and therefore the type of tourism experience one seeks. Similarly, stage in the family lifecycle has a bearing on the availability of time and disposable income available for tourism. Other factors such as home ownership, occupation and ethnic group are increasingly being recognized as major determinants of tourism demand.

Holiday entitlements The growth of leisure time over the last two centuries has greatly increased the amount of time available for tourism, especially in the developed world, but since the 1980s there has been some reversal. In Germany and Italy typical holiday entitlement amounts to 28 days, in addition to 12 or 14 public holidays, whereas 10 days is normal in Japan. Increases in holiday entitlement are likely to result in increases in tourism demand, as the extra time may allow trips to more distant destinations or longer stays.

The patterns of public and school holiday periods give rise to seasonal patterns of tourism demand in developed countries. One result of this is the growth of supplementary, shorter holidays in addition to the main holiday, often referred to as 'short breaks'. Low levels of holiday entitlements do act as a real obstacle upon the opportunities for recreational travel, while a high entitlement encourages such travel.

Political determinants

Government tax policies and controls on tourist spending Approaches taken by governments can greatly influence tourism demand. Examples include exchange control, currency export prohibition, taxation of tourists and residents and visa regulations. Bull (1995) shows that government **fiscal** and control policies can change tourist flows and specific destinations can gain or lose potential profitability. According to Pearce (1989) more than 100 countries used to have certain restrictions which limited the amount of currency citizens could obtain for foreign travel.

Many governments have used tourism as a source of tax revenue, and Bull (1995) notes three specific types:

- taxes on commercial tourism products
- taxes imposed on consumers in the act of being tourists
- user-pays charges.

Some countries also impose exit or travel taxes on their residents who wish to travel overseas.

Factors influencing demand in the tourist destination area

In a similar vein, the level of demand at a tourist destination is influenced by economic and political factors, but tourism products and services also have a role to play here. Dominant among these are the **price** of the tourism products, the supply of tourism products and services and their overall quality. Moreover, the government of the destination area can affect the trading operations of suppliers or the way tourists purchase goods and services and thereby influence demand.

Economic

Price Tourism suppliers, such as in the accommodation and transport sectors, may well price their goods or services independently, but a close watch on the behaviour of their competitors is clearly necessary (Burkart and Medlik 1981). The relationship between price and demand is an inverse one. Higher prices result in lower demand and vice versa. Low prices in Spain and the Balearic Islands caused huge demand from UK tourists in the 1960s, 1970s and 1980s. However, in a volatile market, fashion and environmental damage have combined to cause a downturn in the region's popularity. In addition to the price of what might be thought of as the central part of the tourist product (accommodation and transport), the demand for tourism is also influenced by other forms of expenditure associated with the holiday. In this respect, the influence of price is not straightforward. While tourists are sensitive to the cost of a holiday and changes in the price, a reduction may result in the perception of a lower quality product.

Supply-related

Competition If the number of suppliers providing goods and services in the destination increases with demand, the level of **competition** among suppliers also increases, as will be discussed in Chapter 5. The extent of this form of supply competition will relate to both the number and size of the suppliers involved. Price competitiveness between countries is also an issue (see Chapter 17) and Han, Durbarry and Sinclair (2006) identified that the US outbound market to mainland Europe showed a propensity to substitute one country for another depending on price.

Political

Government controls at the destination Just as governments in the generating area can influence demand, so can those at destinations. Regulation can directly limit the number of tourists, through visa restrictions, and a case in point are those in force in Bhutan. Other countries restrict the opportunity for charter flights to enter, again influencing demand, but possibly more as an attempt to promote the national airline. It is possible for countries to control the amount of tourist expenditure (e.g. Egypt) or restrict the amount of currency that can be exchanged. Moreover, governments at tourist destinations can manage capacity through planning regulations and thereby restrict competition.

Other factors influencing tourism demand

While there are some factors which mainly influence tourism demand at the destination or from the generating area there are others which fall between these categories but are nevertheless important determinants. Among these are the promotional efforts of the destination and the time/cost of travel.

Promotional efforts of the destination

While it could be argued that the promotional efforts of a destination are largely due to the destination itself, aspects of imagery and how such efforts are received make this influence distinctive. As a product, tourism is intangible which means that it is impossible for the consumer to 'test' the product before purchase (see Chapter 15). As such, tourism promotion is different to promotion in other industries. When contemplating a visit to a new destination the consumer must use various means to secure information that will enable them to make a decision. Brochures once dominated the range of promotional tools but the internet has quickly proved to be one of the most valuable marketing tools for tourism suppliers, with customers able to check availability and book online without the need for a third party. The success of promotional efforts can influence tourism demand; however, such efforts are beyond the control of some suppliers at a destination, especially when media images of negative issues (see Chapter 26) portray the destination in poor light.

Health, safety and security issues

Reductions in tourism demand at both regional and international levels has been a marked pattern in tourism activity in the new millennium as the 9/11 attacks on the US affected tourism demand dramatically (also see Chapter 26) and political, war-related and terrorist activity have long featured as a constraint on the freedom for tourism travel. Other events, such as SARS and the outbreak of foot-and-mouth disease in the UK in 2001, had short-term effects on tourism demand in these regions. That these issues and their implications for the tourism sector are of great contemporary significance is now being recognized by politicians, decision-makers and the tourism industry in terms of destination development and tourists' willingness to change travel plans when a crisis occurs or to seek places 'off the beaten track' (Image 3.3).

Time and cost considerations

The cost and time involved in the travel component itself is important. While some distance is needed the time and cost of travel over very long distances may be prohibitive and influence demand. As such, it is likely that the faster people can travel to destinations, the more popular the tourism product will be. Time and cost considerations also have a significant role in countries with large land borders such as in the EU and along the US–Canada border which amount to some of the largest tourist flows at a global scale, due to convenience and opportunities for ease of travel.

Seasonal variations

Seasonality is a well-documented aspect of tourism demand, and an important determining factor in relation to providing the motivation for tourists to escape to warmer climes or experience different climatic regions: Antarctica, for example. In the case of urban tourism, Butler and Mao (1997) identified three types of seasonality in destinations:

- one-peak seasonality, with a distinct summer season
- two-peak seasonality, with a summer and winter season
- non-peak seasonality, mainly occuring in urban areas where the urban centre has all-year-round use, but seasonal demand from different domestic and international visitors.

Among the factors influencing seasonality of different markets are the interaction of temperature, rainfall and daylight in the origin and destination areas, pricing policies of tourist operators and airlines, the different holiday habits of travellers and importance of fashion, tastes and provision of events and attractions in the destination. An inclement climate, such as the winter in Canada, may lead to the development of indoor facilities, like West Edmonton Mall, to create a demand for leisure shopping.

Seasonally distorted patterns of holiday-taking occur as a result of institutionally driven holiday periods, such as school holidays and calendar-related events, such as Thanksgiving and Christmas. In the Balearic Islands, more than 80 per cent of arrivals fall in the May–September period, and this is typical of many holiday resorts.

Image 3.3: Tourists are constantly seeking new experiences 'off the beaten track'

Many destinations seek to reduce patterns of seasonality that show marked peaks by creating interest and promoting off-peak short breaks, sometimes based around event strategies.

So far, this chapter has identified the main determinants of tourism demand. However, an essential aspect of understanding demand for tourism is an appreciation of how tourism activity is measured, evaluated and reported; these are central to the appropriate planning and management of tourism activity in destinations.

Measuring tourism demand: Tourism statistics

Smith (2004: 29) recognizes that 'the fundamental concept in measuring tourism is, of course, tourism:

> *Tourism is the set of activities engaged in by persons temporarily away from their usual environment, for a period of not more than one year, and for a broad range of leisure, business, religions, health, and personal reasons, excluding the pursuit of remuneration from within the place visited or long-term change of residence*

which highlights the scope of what we might measure – the scale of tourism as an economic activity, the reasons for becoming a tourist, where one goes on holiday, through to an endless range of possible issues. Accordingly, measurement of such a diverse activity poses many methodological problems. Such issues will be explored later, but first, why is it important to measure tourism activity?

What do tourism statistics measure and how are they used?

Burkart and Medlik (1981) provide a useful insight into the development of measurements of tourism phenomena by governments during the 1960s and their subsequent development through to the late 1970s. While it is readily acknowledged by most tourism researchers that statistics are a necessary feature to establish effective demand for tourism, Burkart and Medlik (1981: 74) identify the principal reasons for statistical measurement in tourism:

- to evaluate the magnitude and significance of tourism to a destination area or region
- to quantify the contribution to the economy or society, especially the effect on the balance of payments
- to assist in the planning and development of tourism infrastructure and the effect of different volumes of tourists with specific needs to assist in the evaluation and implementation of marketing and promotion activities where the tourism marketer requires information on the actual and potential markets and their characteristics.

Consequently, tourism statistics are essential to the measurement of demand in terms of the volume, scale, impact and value of tourism at different geographical scales from the global to the country level down to the individual destination. In order to assist in activities such as the planning and development of tourism, impact assessments and to inform promotional campaigns and market research, tourism statistics crucially provides data on the:

- **volume of tourism**
- **value of tourism**.

These are typically measured by:

- **frontier arrivals**
- accommodation arrivals
- nights spent
- **tourist receipts**.

We will now examine the organizations that measure tourism activity and methodologies used, with some discussion of the inherent problems in data collection. In addition, insights on international and domestic tourism activity are now presented.

International and domestic tourism: Statistics and insights

The two principal organizations that collate data on international tourism are the World Tourism Organization (WTO) and the Organization for Economic Co-operation and Development (**OECD**). The WTO provides the main source of data, collated from a survey of major government agencies responsible for data collection and the trend in international arrivals since 1950 is shown in Figure 2.3, p.36. This shows an almost constant growth in arrivals despite temporary setbacks due to crises (e.g. the oil crisis in the 1970s, Gulf War in the 1980s and SARS). While most international tourists are expressed as frontier arrivals (i.e. arrivals determined by means of a frontier check), the use of arrival/departure cards (where used) provides additional detail to the profile of international tourists and where they are not used periodic tourism surveys often are. WTO statistics are mainly confined to all categories of travellers and in some cases geographical disaggregation of the data may be limited by the collecting agencies use of descriptions and categories for aid of simplicity (e.g. rest of the world) rather than listing all categories of arrivals.

The major publications of the WTO and OECD in relation to international tourism, are:

- the WTO's *Yearbook of Tourism Statistics,* which contains a summary of the most salient tourism statistics for almost 150 countries and territories
- the OECD's *Tourism Policy and International Tourism,* referred to as the Blue Book; this is less comprehensive, covering only 25 countries, but it does contain most of the main generating and receiving areas. While the main thrust of the publication is government policy and the obstacles to international tourism, it does expand on certain areas not covered in the WTO publication.

In addition, international regional tourism organizations such as the Pacific Asia Travel Association, the **ASEAN** Tourism Working Group, **APEC** and the EU (Europa) also collect international tourism statistics (Hall 2003). National Tourism Organizations (**NTO**s) also collect data on international arrivals and Insight 3.1 outlines the statistics collected by a selection of NTOs, giving an indication of the range of measures in place to record tourism activity and Web Exercise 3.1 helps expand this theme. What is apparent from Web Exercise 3.1 and the WTO website is that one of the remarkable developments in the last decade has been the growth in significance of certain outbound markets such as China (see Case Study 3.1W).

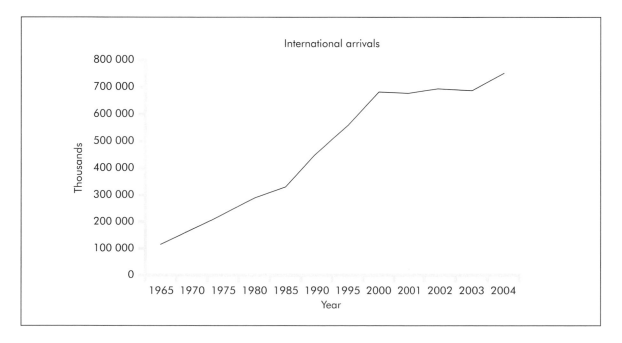

FIGURE 3.2 The growth in international tourism demand 1950–2004. Source: Based on WTO data

INSIGHT 3.1

Examples of tourism statistics for five countries

By selecting five contrasting countries from the developed and developing world, it is possible to illustrate the problems of data availability for students and researchers. Examining Table 3.2, it is evident that the range of tourism statistics available in each country varies considerably, with a combination of national tourism organizations and national statistics offices responsible for organizing and managing the gathering of tourism data. What is more notable is the variations in what can be accessed online in summary form, and the different elements measured (i.e. visitor numbers, accommodation use and the various approaches to measuring domestic tourism and the leisure day-trip market). In the case of Malta, their online *Manual of Tourism Statistics* (Malta

Tourism Authority 2003) examines the differences between international visitor survey results, Air Malta passenger data and airport arrival/departure data, which highlights the problems of consistency and, in some cases, the impossibility of comparing data. Table 3.2 also indicates a problem with tourism in less developed countries where the cost of data collection over and above simple arrival/departure cards and a visitor survey is prohibitively expensive in relation to the budgets available to tourism authorities.

Student exercise

Examine the websites for each country listed in Table 3.2 and see how up to date the data are for each organization.

Domestic tourism statistics

Data on domestic tourism volume, expenditure and patterns are normally coordinated by national tourism organizations, often with the assistance of regional tourism bodies. Tourism data are also collected by commercial organizations and those requiring the results can subscribe to or purchase reports from a range of bodies, such as Mintel (www.mintel.com), the Economist Intelligence Unit (www.eiu.com) and the European Union's statistical agency – Eurostat (www.europa.eu.int). Moreover, consultants can be commissioned to specifically collect the data required. However, in both cases the expense is such that most turn to national government organizations for tourism data.

According to the WTO, domestic tourism is estimated to be up to *ten times greater* in volume than international tourism and yet comparatively little research has been undertaken on this neglected area of tourism activity. Pearce (1995: 67) argues that this may be attributed to the less visible nature of much domestic tourism, which is often more informal and less structured than international tourism, and a subsequent tendency by many government agencies, researchers and others to regard it as insignificant. This problem of neglect is compounded by a paucity of data, since it is not a straightforward matter of recording arrivals and departures. Instead, an analysis of tourism patterns and flows at different geographical scales is required, to consider geographical interaction of tourists between a multitude of possible origin and destination areas within a country, as well as a detailed understanding of inter-regional flows. Where government agencies and other public sector organizations undertake data collection on domestic tourism, the results are not often directly comparable, limiting the identification of general patterns and trends (Pearce 1995: 67). Yet one of the enduring problems in tourism research is that organizations that collect data are often beset with methodological difficulties, which must be clearly identified and understood when interpreting statistics. These, and associated problems, will now be explored.

Measuring demand: Problems and challenges

Despite the clear need for statistical inputs, an information gap exists between the types of statistics provided by organizations and the needs of users. The compilation of tourism statistics provided by organizations associated with the measurement of tourism have established methods and processes to collect, collate and analyse tourism statistics (Lennon 2001), yet these have only been understood by a small number of researchers and practitioners. A commonly misunderstood

TABLE 3.2 A selection of tourism statistics collected by four NTOs and from data accessible online

Country	Organization	Statistics and surveys undertaken on tourism	Volume of International tourism	Domestic tourism	Volume of tourism to country
England	English Tourism Council (www.staruk.com)	United Kingdom Tourism Survey (UKTS) International Passenger Survey (IPS) United Kingdom Occupancy Survey (Accommodation) Visitor Attraction Monitor	24.2 million (2002)	167.3 million (2002)	£38 million
New Zealand	Tourism Research Council (www.trc.govt.nz) and Statistics New Zealand (www.stats.govt.nz)	International Visitor Survey Domestic Travel Survey Accommodation Survey Tourism Satellite Account (economic impact) Arrivals (arrival cards) Departures (departure cards) New Zealand Tourism Forecasts 2003–2009	2.2 million (year ending May 2004)	38.9 million day trips 16.5 million overnight trips 50.5 million visitor nights (year ending May 2001)	NZ$ 16.8 billion
Germany	German National Tourism Board (www.germany-tourism.de) and Federal Statistics Office	International Visitor Arrivals Overnight stays by foreign and domestic visitors Accommodation statistics German Travel Monitor (domestic tourism)	17.2 million (2003) 37.7 million overnight stays (2002) in hotels with 9 rooms or more	296.8 million overnight stays (2003)	8% of GDP (2002) National GDP 2129.8 billion euros (2002)
Malta	Malta Tourism Authority (www.tourism.org.mt) National Statistics Office (www.nso.gov.mt) Malta International Airport	Disembarkation cards Visitor arrivals Inbound Tourism Survey (Tourstat) Malta Hotels and Restaurants Association Survey Cruise Passengers Passenger Movements – Malta International Airport	1.12 million (2003)	–	265 million euros (1998)
Fiji	Fiji Visitors Bureau (www.fiji.com) Fiji Islands Bureau of Statistics (www.stats.fiji.gov.fj)	International Visitor Arrivals Tourism Earnings	430800 (2003)	–	F$ 622.1 million (2003)

feature which is associated with tourism statistics is that they are a complete and authoritative source of information (i.e. they answer all the questions posed by the researcher and are completely reliable). Other associated problems are that tourism data are subject to considerable time lag in their generation, analysis, presentation and dissemination to interested parties. Accordingly, available statistics are not always recent and may not relate to the previous year or season (see Web Exercise 3.2), as shown in Tables 3.3 and 3.4.

TABLE 3.3 International tourist arrivals

| | International tourism receipts | | | | | International tourist arrivals | | |
| | Change Local currencies, constant prices (%) | | US$ (billion) | Receipts per arrival | Market share (%) | (million) | Change (%) | Market share (%) |
	02/01	03/02	2002	2003	2003	2003	03/02	2003
World	0.3	−2.2	474.2	514.4	100	694.0	1.2	100
Europe	−1.8	−2.8	240.5	2819	54.8	4015	0.4	57.8
Northern Europe	4.1	−1.5	35.5	40.7	7.9	47.1	1.5	6.8
Western Europe	−0.6	−2.7	87.1	102.8	20.0	139.1	−1.4	20.0
Central Eastern Europe	−4.4	−4.3	23.5	25.5	5.0	68.3	4.7	9.8
Southern/ Mediterranean Europe	−4.5	−3.0	94.4	113.0	22.0	147.0	0.0	21.2
Asia and the Pacific	5.1	14.5	94.7	88.6	77.2	119.1	−9.3	17.2
North East Asia	11.1	−10.2	47.9	43.7	8.5	67.2	−8.8	9.7
South East Asia	−1.5	−13.2	27.4	24.9	4.8	35.7	−15.4	5.1
Oceania	1.2	−14.7	14.3	14.5	2.8	9.4	−1.9	1.4
South Asia	−2.6	1.2	5.1	5.4	1.1	6.8	16.5	1.0
Americas	−4.8	−0.3	114.3	115.8	22.5	112.4	−2.1	16.2
North America	−8.0	−3.9	85.1	83.8	16.3	76.1	−6.7	11.0
Caribbean	−3.2	12.3	16.6	17.8	3.5	17.3	7.6	2.5
Central America	12.3	8.1	3.4	3.7	0.7	4.9	3.4	0.7
South America	14.2	7.4	9.2	10.5	2.0	14.2	13.5	2.0
Africa	2.0	−2.6	11.8	4.0	2.7	30.5	4.9	4.4
North Africa	−16.2	−7.1	3.8	4.0	0.8	10.8	4.8	1.6
Sub-saharan Africa	11.8	−0.1	8.0	10.0	1.9	19.8	4.9	2.8
Middle East	11.6	17.1	13.0	14.1	2.7	30.4	70.3	4.4

Source: World Tourism Organization (WTO) © (Data as collected by WTO June 2004)

In fact, most tourism statistics are typically measurements of arrivals (Table 3.3), trips, **tourist nights** and **tourist expenditure**, and these often appear in total or split into categories such as business or leisure travel (Latham and Edwards 2003). Furthermore, the majority of published tourism statistics are derived from sample surveys with the results being weighted or statistically manipulated to derive a measure which is supposedly representative of the real-world situation. In reality, this often means that tourism statistics are subject to significant errors depending on the size of the sample (see MacLeay 2001 for an example in the UK) so may not effectively represent actual demand.

Latham and Edwards (2003) identify a number of distinctive and peculiar problems associated with the tourist population as Table 3.5 shows. Even where sampling and survey-related problems can be minimized, one has to treat tourism statistics with a degree of caution because of additional methodological issues that can affect results. For example, Table 3.6 shows that tourism research typically comprises a range of approaches towards tourist populations which can be grouped into four categories.

TABLE 3.4 World's top tourism destinations and international tourist receipts, 2002 and 2003 compared

International tourist arrivals		million		Change (%)		International tourism receipts	US$ billion		Change (% 02/01)	Change (% 03/02)	Local currencies (% change)	
Rank	Series	2002	2003	02/01	03/02	Rank	2002	2003			02/01	03/02
1 France	TF	77.0	75.0	2.4	−2.6	1 US	66.5	65.1	−7.4	−2.2	−7.4	−2.2
2 Spain	TF	52.3	52.5	4.5	0.3	2 Spain	33.6	41.7	2.2	24.1	−3.2	3.7
3 US	TF	41.9	40.4	−6.7	−3.6	3 France	32.3	36.6	7.8	13.2	2.1	−5.4
4 Italy	TF	39.8	39.6	0.6	−0.5	4 Italy	26.9	31.3	4.3	16.2	−1.2	−2.8
5 China	TF	36.8	33.0	11.0	−10.3	5 Germany	19.2	23.0	4.0	20.0	−1.5	0.3
6 UK	VF	24.2	24.8	5.9	2.6	6 UK	17.6	19.4	8.1	10.5	3.8	1.4
7 Austria	TCE	18.6	19.1	2.4	2.6	7 China	20.4	17.4	14.6	−14.6	14.6	−14.6
8 Mexico	TF	19.7	18.7	4.6	−4.9	8 Austria	11.2	13.6	11.1	21.0	5.2	1.2
9 Germany	TCE	18.0	18.4	0.6	2.4	9 Turkey	11.9	13.2	18.2	10.9	45.4	10.5
10 Canada	TF	20.1	17.5	1.9	−12.7	10 Greece	9.7	10.7	3.1	9.9	−2.3	−8.2

Source: World Tourism Organization (WTO) © (Data as collected by WTO June 2004)
Note: Series = World Tourism Organization Statistical Series

TABLE 3.5 Problems associated with the statistical measurement of tourist populations

- Tourists are a transient and highly mobile population making statistical sampling procedures difficult when trying to ensure statistical accuracy and rigour in methodological terms.
- Stopping and sampling respondents often have practical problems due to accompanying passengers and the time required.
- Some people avoid interviewers and interviews.
- The environment in which interviews are often conducted (i.e. airports, seaports and points of entry and departure) are problematic, with many distractions of large numbers of people, sometimes leading respondents to curtail long interviews.

Other variables, such as the weather, may affect the responses.
Source: Adapted from Latham and Edwards (2003: 56) with authors' additions

TABLE 3.6 The scope of research on tourist populations

- Pre-travel studies of tourists' intended travel habits and likely choice of destination (intentional studies).
- Studies of tourists in transit to provide information on their actual behaviour and plans for the remainder of their holiday or journey (actual and intended studies).
- Studies of tourists at the destination or at specific tourist attractions and sites, to provide information on their actual behaviour, levels of satisfaction, impacts and future intentions (actual and intended studies).
- Post-travel studies of tourists on their return journey from their destination or on-site experience or once they have returned to their place of residence (post-travel measures).

Source: Adapted from Latham (1989)

In an ideal world, where resource constraints are not a limiting factor on the generation of statistics, each of the aforementioned approaches should be used to provide a broad spectrum of research information on tourism. In reality, organizations and government agencies select a form of research that meets their own particular needs. In practice, most tourism statistics are generated with practical uses in mind and they usually, though not exclusively, can be categorized as shown in Table 3.7. The tourism industry requires reliable statistical data to inform decision-making in the public and private sector organizations alike. Many countries attach a high priority to the collection and analysis of tourism data. Despite this, national and international tourism data sources are often criticized for lacking consistency and coherence.

The effectiveness of the national organizations as providers of related tourism data depends on a variety of factors. These include the scope and frequency of the data collection as well as the methods used in the data collection and analysis. Here, aspects such as sampling techniques and sample size will greatly influence data reliability. Even in large-scale surveys, such as the UK's International Passenger Survey in which some 250 000 plus travellers are interviewed, sampling error for particular countries varies. Countries with low visitation rates from and to the UK have high sampling errors, whereas popular generating and destination nations have low sampling errors in the survey. Many commentators in recent years have noted the shortcomings of published tourism statistics (e.g. Chadwick 1994; Ryan 1995; Smith 1995). Both the **World Travel and Tourism Council (WTTC)** and the International Monetary Fund (**IMF**) have recommended that governments effectively collect and analyse tourism data and represent them in the country's national accounts and there is evidence that these recommendations are being adopted.

Establishing international tourism demand

In contrast to domestic tourism, statistics on international tourism are normally collected to assess the impact of tourism on a country's **balance of payments**. However, as Withyman (1985: 69) argued:

> Outward visitors seem to attract less attention from the pollsters and the enumerators. Of course, one country's outward visitor is another country's (perhaps several countries') inward visitor, and a much more welcome sort of visitor, too, being both a source of revenue and an emblem of the destination country's appeal in the international market. This has meant that governments have tended to be generally more keen to measure inward than outward tourism, or at any rate, having done so, to publish the results.

This statement indicates that governments are more concerned with the direct effect of tourism on their balance of payments. Indeed, outbound travel can assume a greater significance for the receiving countries, as Web Case 3.1, the case of the Chinese outbound boom demonstrates. However, it is the inbound, or 'arrivals', which are statistics of significance for marketing arms of national tourism organizations to base their decisions on who to target in international campaigns. The wider tourism industry also makes use of such data as part of their **strategic planning** and for more immediate purposes where **niche market**s exist. However, it is increasingly the case that only when the economic benefits of **data collection** can be justified will national governments continue to compile tourism statistics. Where resource constraints exist, the collection and

---

TABLE 3.7 Categorizing tourism statistics

- Measurement of tourist volume, enumerating arrivals, departures and the number of visits and stays.

- Expenditure-based surveys which quantify the value of tourist spending at the destination and during the journey.

- The characteristics and features of tourists to construct a profile of the different markets and segments visiting a destination.

- Tourism Satellite Accounts.

compilation of tourism statistics may be impeded. This also raises important methodological issues related to what exactly is being measured. As Withyman (1985: 61) argued:

In the jungle of international travel and tourism statistics, it behoves the explorer to step warily; on all sides there is luxuriant growth. Not all data sources are what they appear to be; after close scrutiny they show themselves to be inconsistent and often unsuitable for the industry researcher and planner.

The key point Withyman recognizes is the lack of comparability in tourism data in relation to what is measured (i.e. is it visitor days or visitor nights?) and the procedures and methodology used to measure international tourism. Yet the principal difficulty which confronts tourism researchers is whether business travel should continue to be considered as a discrete part of tourism. Chadwick (1994: 75) notes that the consensus of North American opinion seems to be that, despite certain arguments to the contrary, business travel should be considered part of travel and tourism. Latham (1989: 59) suggests that the main types of international tourism statistics collated relate to:

- volume of tourists
- expenditure by tourists
- the profile of the tourist and their trip characteristics.

As is true of domestic tourism, estimates form the basis for most statistics on international tourism since the method of data collection does not generate exact data. For example, volume statistics are often generated from counts of tourists at entry/exit points (i.e. **gateway**s such as airports and ports) or at accommodation. But such data relate to numbers of trips rather than individual tourists, since one tourist may make more than one trip a year and each trip is counted separately. In the case of expenditure statistics, 'tourist expenditure' normally refers to tourist spending within a country and excludes payments to tourist transport operators. Yet deriving such statistics is often an indirect measure based on foreign currency estimates derived from bank records, from data provided by tourism service providers or, more commonly, from social surveys undertaken directly with tourists. **Tourist statistics** are usually collected in one of five ways (see Table 3.8).

The last area of data collection is profile statistics, which examine the characteristics and travel habits of visitors. For example, the UK's International Passenger Survey (IPS) is one survey that incorporates volume, expenditure and profile data on international tourism (see Insight 3.2).

TABLE 3.8 How international tourism statistics are collected

- Counts of all individuals entering or leaving the country at all recognized frontier crossings, often using arrival/departure cards where high volume arrivals/departures are the norm. Where particularly large volumes of tourist traffic exist, a 10 per cent sampling framework is normally used (i.e. every tenth arrival/departure card). Countries such as New Zealand actually match the arrival/departure cards, or a sample, to examine the length of stay.

- Interviews carried out at frontiers with a sample of arriving and/or departing passengers to obtain a more detailed profile of visitors and their activities within the country. This will often require a careful sample design to gain a sufficiently large sample with the detail required from visitors on a wide range of tourism data including places visited, expenditure, accommodation usage and related items.

- Selecting a sample of arrivals and providing them with a self-completion questionnaire to be handed in or posted. This method is used in Canada but it fails to incorporate those visitors travelling by road via the United States.

- Sample surveys of the entire population of a country, including travellers and non-travellers, though the cost of obtaining a representative sample is often prohibitive.

- Accommodation arrivals and nights spent are recorded by hoteliers and owners of the accommodation types covered. The difficulty with this type of data collection is that accommodation owners have no incentive to record accurate details, particularly where the tax regime is based on the turnover of bed nights.

INSIGHT 3.2

The United Kingdom's international passenger survey

As a government-sponsored survey, which began in 1961, the International Passenger Survey now covers all ports of entry/exit to the UK. The International Passenger Survey (IPS) is a survey of people travelling into and out of the UK (ONS 1999). A sample of travellers are interviewed using a face-to-face method of data collection. The UK's Office for National Statistics (ONS) commissions the work, together with other government departments, and data collection and survey analysis are performed. The results of the IPS are available in various formats: a travel pack with CDs or disks in dataset form to allow the user to perform their own analysis; *MQ6 Overseas Travel and Tourism* is published on a quarterly basis giving the latest information; *Overseas Travel and Tourism* does the same but on a monthly basis and *Travel Trends* is published on an annual basis reporting the results of the IPS. In the 1997 IPS survey, 258 000 respondents were randomly selected for interview, representing approximately 0.2 per cent of all who were eligible. The main questions asked concerned nationality, residence, country of visit (for UK residents travelling abroad), purpose of visit, flight or ferry information, earnings, expenditure and demographic characteristics. The survey had an 83 per cent response rate. A system of stratified random sampling is used, based on the seven principal airports in the UK together with other regional airports, ferry ports and the Channel Tunnel. The IPS provides information on international tourism, outbound and inbound to the UK. Information on the number of visits, length of stay and value are provided as well as other aspects which include method of travel, purpose of visit, age and gender. According to Latham (1989: 64), IPS's four principal aims are:

1 To collect data for the travel account (which acts to compare expenditure by overseas visitors to the UK with expenditure overseas by visitors from the UK) of the balance of payments.

2 To provide detailed information on foreign visitors to the UK and on outgoing visitors travelling overseas.

3 To provide data on international migration.

4 To provide information on routes used by passengers as an aid to aviation and shipping.

According to MacLeay (2001: 29), standard variables in the UK IPS (which would seem to be broadly in line with international visitor surveys in other countries) include:

● mode – main method of travel

● quarter of travel (i.e. Jan–Mar, Apr–Jun, Jul–Sept, Oct–Dec)

● whether or not on a package trip

● country of residence for overseas visitors

● spending on visit

● age group

● nights spent on visit

● country of visit for UK residents

● nationality of traveller

● UK port of entry

● overseas port used

● vehicle used

● flight type

● class of travel.

Establishing demand for domestic tourism

Pearce (1995) acknowledges that the scale and volume of domestic tourism worldwide exceed that of international tourism, though it is often viewed as the poorer partner in the compilation of statistics. So, it is difficult to understand demand in a domestic context because most domestic tourism statistics tend to underestimate the scale and volume of flows, certain aspects of domestic tourist movements being sometimes ignored in official sources. The visits to friends and relatives, the use of forms of accommodation other than hotels (for example, second homes, camp sites and caravan sites) and travel by large segments of a population from towns to the countryside are not for the most part included (Latham 1989: 65). This is supported by the WTO, which argues that there are relatively few countries that collect domestic travel and tourism statistics especially visits to attractions (Image 3.4).

Moreover, some countries rely exclusively on the traditional hotel sector, thereby leaving out of the account the many travellers staying in supplementary accommodation establishments or with friends and relatives (see Web Exercise 3.3 for the situation in Europe). Therefore, the collection of domestic tourism statistics requires the use of different data sources aside from the more traditional sources such as hotel records, which identify the origin and duration of a visitor's stay. Insight 3.3 shows the example of the United Kingdom Tourism Survey (UKTS), which records domestic tourism in the UK.

WTO (1981) identified four uses of domestic tourism statistics as Table 3.9 shows. Many countries also collate supplementary information beyond the minimum standards identified by WTO, where the socioeconomic characteristics of tourists are identified, together with their use of tourist transport and purpose of visit, although the

Image 3.4: Heritage attractions often comprise a key feature of demand for a country's tourism product

cost of such data collection does mean that the statistical basis of domestic tourism in many less developed countries remains poor. The methods used to generate domestic tourism statistics are normally based on the estimates of volume, value and scale derived from sample surveys due to the cost of undertaking large-scale surveys of tourist activities. The immediate problem facing the user of such material is the type of errors and degree of accuracy which can be attached to such data.

INSIGHT 3.3

The United Kingdom Tourism Survey (UKTS)

According to the UKTS, in 2002 UK residents spent 531.9 million nights away from home in the UK, equivalent to 167.3 million trips, and spent £26.6 million. The majority of trips were for holidays, to visit friends and relatives and for business and other purposes (www.staruk.com). The average expenditure was £160 per visit, with an average spend of £50 a night, with accommodation comprising 30 per cent of spending, followed by 21 per cent on eating out, 17 per cent on shopping and 19 per cent on travel. Some 57 per cent of trips were one or two nights' in duration with 15 per cent of trips taken by 16–24-year-olds, 21 per cent by 25–34-year-olds, 23 per cent by 35–44-year-olds and 17 per cent by 45–54-year-olds and 24 per cent aged 55 years or over.

But how does the UKTS derive these statistics? The UK national tourism organizations (Visit Britian, VisitScotland, Northern Ireland Tourist Board and Wales Tourist Board) contract a market research agency (in 2003 it was BRMB) to undertake an annual survey – the UKTS). As Hay and Rogers (2001: 269) observe, the main objective of the UKTS is to provide measurements of tourism by residents of the UK, in terms of both volume (trips taken, nights spent away from home) and value (expenditure on those trips and nights).

The UKTS continuously interviews adults aged 15 years or more every month, using a random sample and the method of sampling, its accuracy and issues of question style can be found in Hay and Rogers (2001).

Further reading

Hay, B. and Rogers, M. (2001) 'Practical solutions to impossible problems? Lessons from ten years of managing the United Kingdom Tourism Survey', in J. Lennon (ed.) *Tourism Statistics: International Perspectives and Current Issues*. London: Continuum.

Ford, H. and Wright, I. (2001) 'The future of the United Kingdom Tourism Survey', in J. Lennon (ed.) *Tourism Statistics: International Perspectives and Current Issues*. London: Continuum.

Also, see the other country studies in:

Lennon, J. (ed.) (2001) *Tourism Statistics: International Perspectives and Current Issues*. London: Continuum.

TABLE 3.9 Uses of domestic tourism statistics

- To calculate the contribution of tourism to the country's economy, whereby estimates of tourism's value to the gross domestic product is estimated due to the complexity of identifying the scope of tourism's contribution.

- To assist in the marketing and promotion of tourism, where government-sponsored tourism organizations seek to encourage its population to take domestic holidays rather than to travel.

- To aid with the regional development policies of governments which harness tourism as a tool for area development where domestic tourists in congested environments are encouraged to travel to less developed areas and to improve the quality of tourism in different environments.

- To achieve social objectives, where socially oriented tourism policies may be developed for the underprivileged; this requires a detailed understanding of the holiday-taking habits of a country's nationals.

Source: WTO (1981)

Conclusion

The demand for tourism products is clearly crucial to the survival of the tourism industry. Recognition of the barriers to demand is, in part, for marketers particularly important in terms of pricing products and promotional efforts. In some countries, there are growing moves by employers to recognize that a holiday is essential to the health and well-being of the workforce and leave entitlements are accordingly being improved. In other cases, there are growing concerns in Europe that hours of work are increasing overall in countries like the UK while in other countries they are declining, providing more leisure time. Whatever the situation, this chapter has shown that a complex array of factors affects the demand for tourism. There are numerous factors that influence demands which are beyond the control of those within the tourism industry. While exogenous factors such as terrorist acts or economic stability are obvious examples of where tourism demand can be suppressed, attitudes of governments in the generating or destination areas have also been shown to be influential.

The chapter also recognized that tourism is measured and evaluated by governments and agencies in different and sometimes conflicting ways, often making data sources little more than an indication of the order of magnitude of tourism rather than a precise delineation of its scale and volume. Official statistics and data sources have to be treated with caution, as tourism statisticians observe, since problems of accuracy, methodology and consistency confront researchers and students. Much of the research which the private sector commissions to examine tourism-related problems is kept confidential from clients even though it sometimes uncritically uses public data sources supplemented with face-to-face interviews with decision-makers where tourism structure plans are being developed for governments. Classifying and enumerating tourists remains a complex problem, not least because the population is highly mobile and they are consuming an experience rather than a tangible product. As a result, any analysis of tourism is highly dependent upon the tools and methods of analysis one employs.

Discussion questions

1 Define the different types of tourism demand.
2 What are the main economic-related determinants influencing tourism demand?
3 To what extent is price important in influencing tourism demand?
4 What are the main factors influencing demand at the tourist destination area?

References

Argyle, M. (1996) *The Social Psychology of Leisure.* Harmondsworth: Penguin.

Bull, A. (1995) *The Economics of Travel and Tourism, Second Edition.* Melbourne: Pitman.

Burkart, A. and Medlik, S. (1981) *Tourism: Past, Present and Future, Second Edition.* London: Heinemann.

Butler, L. and Mao, B. (1997) 'Seasonality in tourism: Problems and measurement', in P. Murphy (ed.) *Quality Management in Urban Tourism.* Chichester: Wiley.

Chadwick, R. (1994) 'Concepts, definitions and measures used in travel and tourism research', in J.R. Brent Ritchie and C. Goeldner (eds) *Travel, Tourism and Hospitality Research: A Handbook for Managers and Researchers, Second Edition.* New York: Wiley.

Cooper, C.P., Fletcher, J., Gilbert, D., Wanhill, S. and Shepherd, R. (1998) *Tourism Principles and Practice, Second Edition.* London: Longman.

Crouch, G. (1994) 'The study of tourism demand: A review of findings', *Journal of Travel Research,* 33 (1): 2–21.

Hall, C.M. (2003) *Tourism in Australia: Dimensions and Issues.* Frenchs Forest, NSW: Hospitality Press.

Hall, C.M. and Page, S.J. (2002) *The Geography of Tourism and Recreation: Environment, Place and Space, Second Edition.* London: Routledge.

Han, Z., Durbarry, R. and Sinclair, M.T. (2006) 'Modelling US tourism demand for European tourism destinations', *Tourism Management.* 27(1):1–10.

Hay, B. and Rogers, M. (2001) 'Practical solutions to impossible problems? Lessons from ten years of managing the United Kingdom Tourism Survey', in J. Lennon (ed.) *Tourism Statistics: International Perspectives and Current Issues.* London: Continuum.

Latham, J. (1989) 'The statistical measurement of tourism', in C.P. Cooper (ed.) *Progress in Tourism, Recreation and Hospitality Management Volume 1.* London: Belhaven.

Latham, J. and Edwards, C. (2003) 'The statistical measurement of tourism', in C. Cooper (ed.) *Classic Reviews in Tourism.* Clevedon: Channel View Publications.

Lennon, J. (ed.) (2001) *Tourism Statistics: International Perspectives and Current Issues.* London: Continuum.

MacLeay, I. (2001) 'Disseminating the results from the UK International Passenger Survey (IPS)', in Lennon, J. (ed.) *Tourism Statistics: International Perspectives and Current Issues.* London: Continuum.

Mathieson, A. and Wall, G. (1982) *Tourism: Economic, Physical and Social Impacts.* Harlow: Longman.

ONS (Office for National Statistics) (1999) *Social Trends 29.* London: ONS.

ONS (Office for National Statistics) (2004) *Social Trends 34.* London: ONS.

Pearce, D.G. (1989) *Tourist Development, Second Edition.* Harlow: Longman.

Pearce, D. (1995) *Tourism Today: A Geographical Analysis, Second edition.* Harlow: Longman.

Ryan, C. (1995) *Researching Tourist Satisfaction: Issues, Concepts and Problems.* London: Routledge.

Ryan, C. (ed.) (1997) *The Tourist Experience.* London: Cassell.

Song, H. and Witt, S. (2000) *Tourism Demand Modelling and Forecasting: Modern Econometric Approaches.* Oxford: Pergamon.

Smith, S.L. (1995) *Tourism Analysis: A Handbook, Second Edition.* Harlow: Longman.

Smith, S.L. (2004) 'The measurement of global tourism: Old debates, new consensus and continuing challenges', in A. Lew, C.M. Hall and A. Williams (eds) *A Companion to Tourism.* Oxford: Blackwell.

Withyman, W. (1985) 'The ins and outs of international travel and tourism data', *International Tourism Quarterly,* Special Report No. 55.

WTO (World Tourism Organization) (1981) *Guidelines for the Collection and Presentation of Domestic and International Tourism Statistics.* Madrid: World Tourism Organization.

WTO (World Trade Organization) (1995) *Global Tourist Forecasts to the Year 2000 and Beyond.* Madrid: WTO.

Further reading

One of the best sources to introduce tourism demand is:

Hall, C.M. and Page, S.J. (2005) *The Geography of Tourism and Recreation: Environmental, Place and Space, Third Edition.* London: Routledge.

A comprehensive discussion of tourism statistics can be found in:

Latham, J. and Edwards, C. (2003) 'The statistical measurement of tourism', in C.P. Cooper (ed.) *Classic Reviews in Tourism.* Clevedon: Channel View.

4

Understanding the Tourist as a Consumer

Learning outcomes

After reading this chapter and answering the questions, you should be able to:

- recognize the role of consumption in tourism

- understand theories and models relevant to the explanation of tourist motivation

- recognize the importance of those factors that influence motivation

- identify the factors that affect the tourism decision-making process in selecting tourism products.

Overview

The question of why people go on holiday is fundamental to the study of tourism. What motivates people to participate in different forms of behaviour has concerned researchers and academics long before it was applied to the field of tourism. This chapter sets out to explain contemporary patterns of tourism activity as they relate to the individual. It contends that tourism activity is not merely an outcome of people's freedom to choose where they go on holiday; there are many factors at work which initiate the desire to travel and then influence the ultimate selection of destination.

Introduction

According to Hall and Page (2002: 60) 'one of the fundamental questions tourism researchers consistently seek to answer is: why do tourists travel? This seemingly simple proposition remains one of the principal challenges facing tourism research. This area of tourism research is more firmly bedded in **social psychology**. At one level people may choose where they wish to travel to, so the patterns of tourism activity could be explained in terms of individual choice. Clearly, though, as individuals we do not have limitless choice and our actions are inevitably influenced by a combination of opportunities and constraints, including available finance and time. A number of social divisions may also circumscribe choice in tourism. Just as there are inequalities in many countries in terms of education, employment, housing and income, so there are inequalities in tourism. Argyle (1996) acknowledges the significance of gender, age, social class, retirement, unemployment, social relationships, personality and socialization in affecting leisure behaviour. So, while choice is an important factor in tourism decision-making, individuals are rarely 'free' to make those choices, being constrained and influenced by personal and situational circumstances. While there is no universally accepted theory of tourist motivation, several researchers have developed frameworks to use in the understanding of why people go on holiday (e.g. Pearce 2005).

This chapter identifies and explains some of the critical arguments in understanding the less than straightforward questions of why people go on holiday and what influences certain holiday choices.

Motivation and decision-making in tourism

Moutinho (1987: 16) argued that motivation is 'a state of need, a condition that exerts a push on the individual towards certain types of action that are seen as likely to bring satisfaction'. Essentially, in relation to tourism, motivation is a part of the consumption process and is stimulated by a complex mixture of economic, social, psychological, cultural, political, industry-related and wider environmental influences. Motivation as a subject is an integral part of the study of **consumer behaviour** in tourism. Motivation acts as a trigger which stimulates the chain of events in the tourism process.

Understanding tourist motivation and decision-making is important for two main reasons:

- *Planning considerations*: All destinations require some form of planning and management, and control of negative impacts, where it may be appropriate to divert tourists or particular activities away from vulnerable areas.

- *Economic considerations*: Growth and development of the tourism industry in a region or corporate growth are dependent on understanding consumer behaviour, particularly through market segmentation strategies.

The term 'motivation' is open to interpretation and is often used to merely describe the purpose of a holiday, such as visiting friends and relatives (which is really a motive rather than a motivation). However, the study of motivation is really concerned with more deeply rooted psychological needs and desires. Accordingly, it is a very complex area of research. Researchers are charged not just with explaining behaviour but with understanding it too (Walmsley 2004).

Hall and Page (2002: 61) note that 'the factors which shape the tourist decision-making process to select and participate in specific forms of tourism is [sic] largely within the field of consumer behaviour and motivation'. As Mill and Morrison (1992: 17) argued, 'The key to understanding tourist motivation is to see vacation travel as a satisfier of needs and wants...it is the difference between those travel agents who see themselves as sellers of airline seats and those who view themselves as dealers in dreams', and a useful starting point for understanding motivation is to study the decision-making process in tourism that affects what products a tourist purchases (a theme also discussed in Chapters 15 and 16).

The decision-making process in tourism is viewed in two ways by researchers. First, it may be likened to the basic decision-making process aligned with all product purchasers, where the consumer identifies a need, looks for information on the product, its cost and where it might be purchased, weighs up the alternative products and suppliers, makes a choice, consumes and finally makes a judgement on the experience of that product which may then influence future purchasing decisions. Most models of consumer behaviour reflect this basic outline (see Figure 4.1); however, many other factors influence this process, some of which the consumer is barely conscious of (see Figure 4.2). Imagery, advertising, word of mouth recommendation and peer pressure are just a few examples of the more obvious influences, but other more intrinsic factors should not be underestimated. The tourism decision-making process is affected by personal, behavioural and destination-specific qualities, as well as the exogenous factors influencing demand illustrated in the last chapter. Based on Ryan (1997), these include:

- social and personal interactions, such as the needs of others with whom the individual is travelling, whether there are children in the group, likely contact with service staff and host community

- travel experience, expectation of delays, comfort and ease of travel to destination

- destination-specific factors, such as the quality of the accommodation and facilities, and historical or other interests, which may act as a particular draw for tourists

- personal factors, such as self-confidence, personality, experience, lifestyle and life-stage

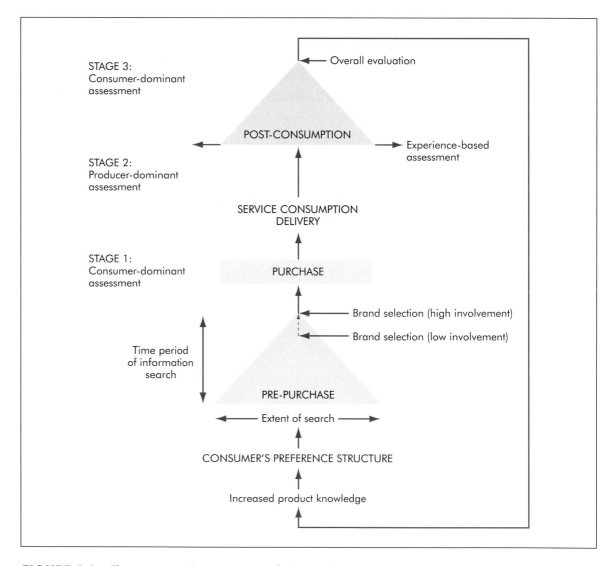

FIGURE 4.1 The consumer decision process for hospitality services. Source: Adapted from Teare, R., Moutinho, L. and Morgan, N. (eds) (1994), *Managing and Marketing Services in the 1990s*, Cassell, London, p.239

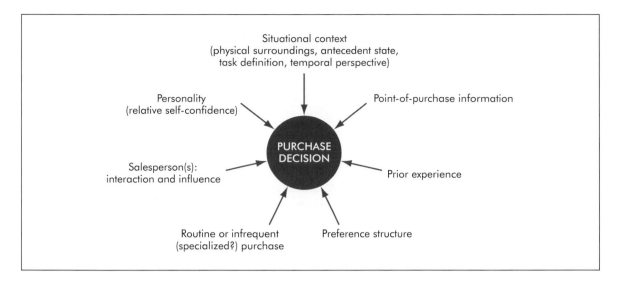

FIGURE 4.2 Factors influencing the purchase decision. Source: Teare et al. (1994: 27)

- behaviour patterns, which may dictate an individual's propensity to experience new places and activities, or to search for holiday information pre-booking
- responsive mechanisms, desire for authentic experiences, social skills and feeling at ease in a strange environment.

Post-holiday, all of these aspects will combine to influence future holiday choices. But not all tourism consumers are intricate planners who will compare brochures, destinations, packages and prices. Some make impulse purchases, many attracted by imminent departures at discounted cost. The internet has made such purchases even more easy to obtain from the comfort of home. Despite this, the consumer will still be motivated but will demonstrate a more minimal decision-making process.

The theme of **constraints** and opportunities then, is one that dominates this area of tourism. As Patmore (1975: 7) remarked, 'there are three broad constraints, including *desire, ability* and *mobility*…desire has first to be aroused; the wish to participate – so often an imitative wish, the desire to imitate something at least of the lifestyle of those ranked higher'. These issues will form an important focus later in the chapter but prior to a more detailed exploration of the concepts of tourism motivation, it is first important to establish what is meant by the term 'consumer', why it is important to understand tourism behaviour and how the consumer has changed in contemporary times.

The tourist as a consumer

A consumer is an individual who, through a process of decision-making, obtains goods and services for personal consumption. In basic terms, such a process involves a 'purchase', but in tourism, the importance of *experiencing* a destination environment must also be recognized where the tourist becomes a consumer of place or culture, as well as a purchaser of tourism products. Figure 4.3 illustrates the changes that have occurred in tourism activity since 1945, clearly indicating that tourism has evolved from a product-led industry dominated by standardized and limited holiday choices, where consumers were inexperienced as purchasers of the new tourism packages. Through the latter part of the twentieth-century and into the new millennium, as part of the growth of consumer culture, tourists have become more experienced, aware, discerning and demanding in relation to holiday experiences. No longer are the basic sun, sand and sea ('3S') holidays sufficient to meet the demands of the modern tourist, but a more individualized quality product, that the tourist is more ready to put together without the assistance of a travel agent, is emerging. The contemporary tourism industry has had little choice but to become more consumer oriented in order to meet and where possible exceed the increasingly sophisticated needs of the market.

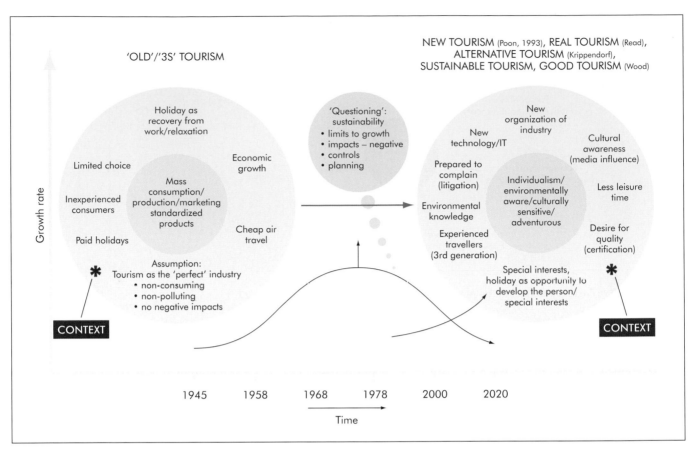

FIGURE 4.3 A re-examination of the tourism lifecycle. Source: Howie (2003: 63) Adapted (in part) from Poon (2003)

Hogg (2003) outlines the various changes that have occurred and paved the way for the new consumer in the twenty-first century, and states that consumers have become more knowledgeable, demanding and thinking. Middleton and Clarke (2001) argue that the rise of a more demanding tourism consumer has occurred globally over the last 20 years and has arisen due to a number of factors, some of which include:

- increased affluence
- better education
- more experience of travel, including international travel
- more culturally diverse travelling population
- greater exposure to the media and other forms of information.

Tourist motives

Demand for tourism is highly segmented and is distinguished through a number of different markets. For example, day visitors whilst not strictly tourists are a major component of the market for many destinations motivated by the access to the area and availability of activities to undertake (e.g. shopping) within the confines of one day. Conversely, other forms of travel due to business may have a different set of motivating factors according to the purpose of the business trip (i.e. to attend a meeting or conference at home or overseas; to attend a training course; to attend an exhibition or trade show where the audience is informed about a new product or service; as 'incentive travel', a reward for employees for good performance). In its broadest form, Swarbrooke and Horner (2001) indicate that in Europe business travel may be worth up to

US$380 billion by 2009, and so is a significant activity. Each of these forms of tourist travel has different motives. Motives for travel are not the same as motivations, as we have already pointed out, but are useful categorizations of tourists whose main reason for travel is to participate in a particular niche interest. Some of the major motives for travel include a desire to participate in one or more of a number of activities while on holiday, such as:

- culture/heritage
- sport (active and passive or spectator forms)
- events
- food and wine
- visiting friends and relatives/social forms of activity
- business travel
- religious
- health-related
- educational.

Such motives may be given by tourists in visitor surveys when asked 'for what reason did you visit here today?', which to some extent is useful, but the deeper motivation is often veiled. That is why an understanding of needs, desires and personal goals in a tourism context is necessary.

Theoretical and conceptual approaches to tourist motivation

Maslow's hierarchy of needs

Maslow (1943) is acknowledged as the best-known work on motivation. Although originally related to the field of clinical psychology, his work has been more widely applied and often cited in tourism studies. Maslow argued that our individual needs fall into five broad categories, as shown in Table 4.1. Maslow suggested that that these five categories formed a hierarchy, beginning with lower order physiological needs moving through to higher order self-actualization needs. This is based on the premise that each of the needs expressed in a category should be satisfied before the individual sought motivation from the next category of need. It can be seen that once the basic human requirements of thirst and hunger have been met, the need for these to motivate the behaviour and actions of an individual may no longer apply. At this point the individual may be motivated by higher order classification rising to self-actualization. Several tourism researchers have applied Maslow's model in the context of tourism motivation (for example, Pearce and Caltabianco 1983; Cooper *et al.* 1998). For example, tourists visiting friends and relatives may show needs for belongingness and love, while those choosing a holiday out of a need to keep up with their friends and neighbours demonstrate esteem needs. The framework is easy to apply, although tourists are often motivated by more than one factor, which limits the application of the theory.

TABLE 4.1 Maslow's hierarchy of needs

1	Physiological needs	Hunger, thirst, rest, sex, activity	Lower
2	Safety needs	Freedom from threat, fear anxiety; feeling secure	
3	Belonging and love (social) needs	Receiving and giving affection and love, friendships	
4	Esteem needs	Self-esteem, esteem for others; self-confidence, reputation, prestige	
5	Self-actualization needs	Personal self-fulfilment	Higher

Push and pull factors

Maslow's hierarchy of needs can be useful in demonstrating the source of our initial needs and wants, where the satisfaction of these needs may ultimately lead to the purchase of a holiday. Another way of considering this process is, as Dann (1977) described, **push factors** and **pull factors**. Push factors are those that propel a desire to travel; pull factors are those that influence which destination is selected, given the initial push, and arise from on a desire to travel. As Sharpley (1994: 99) states 'the motivation to satisfy needs, combined with personal preferences, pushes the tourist into considering alternative products; the final choice depends on the pull of alternative holidays or destinations'. The themes of push and pull, or escaping and seeking, were commonly applied in early tourism motivation studies (see Crompton 1979; Krippendorf 1987; Mannell and Iso-Ahola 1987).

Gilbert (1991) acknowledges the push and pull factors influencing the tourism consumer decision process, and suggests that the process has four distinct stages:

1 *Energizers of demand*: These are the various forces, including motivation, which initiate the decision to visit an attraction or go on holiday at the outset.

2 *Effectors of demand*: Information about a destination will have been received by various means (brochures and media). The consumer will have developed their own ideas and perceptions about the destination and this perception may enhance or reduce the likelihood of a visit.

3 *Roles and decision-making*: The role of the tourist as a consumer will influence the final choice of holiday. For example, different members of a family will have a varying impact on where and when the family will take the holiday and what they will do there.

4 *Filterers of demand*: The decision to travel is heavily influenced by a series of demographic and socioeconomic constraints and opportunities. While there may be a strong 'push', demand is filtered through such constraining factors.

Dann's perspectives on tourism motivation

To this point, our investigation of tourist motivation could, perhaps, be most easily related to what might be termed a 'leisure' holiday. However, tourism takes many forms and visiting friends and relatives or business travel may result from different motives or even be more related to the actual purpose of the visit (for example a family reunion) than the needs and wants of the tourist. Dann (1981), in a study of tourist motivation, identified seven perspectives (Table 4.2), which provides a more in-depth attempt to identify the principal elements of tourist motivation.

In terms of Dann's sixth point, tourism experiences, or rather the anticipation and expectations of a holiday, can act as strong motivators in relation to push factors. A useful way of thinking about this is what the sociologist Urry (1990) terms the **tourist gaze**.

The tourist gaze

Tourism demand as a form of consumption has emerged as a theme in the literature on the sociology and geography of tourism (Meethan 2001). Most notably, the work of Urry (1990, 1995) on the notion of the tourist gaze has gained wide recognition. Developing Foucault's idea (1976) of the medical gaze and MacCannell's (1976) earlier work on sightseeing as consumption, Urry (1990: 1) suggests that tourists observe the environment with 'interest and curiosity...in other words, we gaze at what we encounter'. So, the gaze is one way of understanding the experiential elements of tourism motivation as it relates to expectation. Viewed as 'visual consumption of the environment', five forms of the tourist gaze are outlined by Urry (1995: 191) (see Table 4.3). While the idea of the tourist gaze is not concerned solely with motivation, it is valuable to the process of understanding why people visit certain environments and assists in attaching meanings to tourist settings. Thus, the tourist gaze provides an interesting introduction to the consumer of the tourism.

A range of factors are involved in producing the tourist gaze, but the main premise rests on the identification of differences from everyday/ordinary experiences. According to Urry (1990),

TABLE 4.2	Seven perspectives on tourist motivation based on Dann 1981
Travel as a response to what is lacking yet desired	Tourist motivation may result from a desire for something new or different and cannot be provided in the individual's home environment
Destination pull in response to motivational push	The distinction between the needs, wants and desires (push factors) of the individual and how these are shaped by perceptions of the destination (pull factors)
Motivation as fantasy	Tourists may be motivated to travel to engage in forms of behaviour or activities that are not culturally acceptable in their home environment. One context of this is travel to enable deviant behaviour such as gambling, drugs or prostitution where, because such activities may be illegal in the home country but not in others, this creates the desire to travel
Motivation as classified purpose	Some are motivated to travel or 'caused' to travel by the nature or purpose of the trip. Visiting friends and relatives is one example, the opportunity to undertake specific leisure activities another
Motivational typologies	Different types of tourist may influence the motivation to travel
Motivation and tourist experiences	Tourism often involves travel to places not visited previously. As such, some are motivated to travel by what they expect to experience in contrast to their home area and other holiday experiences
Motivation as auto-definition and meaning	The ways in which tourists define their situations and respond to them may provide a better understanding of tourist motivation. Such an approach is seen in contrast to simply observing behaviour as a means to explain tourist motivation

TABLE 4.3	Forms of the tourist gaze
Romantic	Object of vision or awe consumed in solitude, involving a prolonged immersion, e.g. the early tourists to the Trossachs or the Lake District, whose gaze resulted in works of art and literature
Collective	Social activity involving a series of shared encounters based around familiar objects, e.g. a domestic coach tour
Spectatorial	Again, a social activity based on a series of brief encounters, which encompass collecting symbols of the visit, e.g. sightseeing tour with much photography and souvenir purchase
Environmental	Collective organization of a sustained and multifaceted nature, involving study and inspection of the environment, e.g. rainforest conservation holiday
Anthropological	A solitary pursuit, involving a prolonged contact with the object of the gaze and involving study and interpretation, e.g. backpacker trip where tourist lives as a local resident

Source: Adapted from Urry (1995: 191)

objects suitable for the tourist gaze include a unique object, a particular sign, an unfamiliar aspect of what was previously considered ordinary, an ordinary aspect of life undertaken by people in unusual contexts, a sign which indicate that a certain object is extraordinary, and familiar tasks being carried out in unusual environments (see Web Case Study 4.1 on Visiting Gardens). The gaze concept, like most attempts to conceptualize the more nebulous aspects of tourism motivation and the tourism experience, has gained some criticism. For example, Meethan (2001: 83) argues that the notion of the gaze is problematic and that it 'cannot adequately account for multiple, different, conflicting interpretations…'. While the gaze notion may not be universally accepted, the concept does give a functional framework for appreciating the way in which demand is constructed. It is their visual distinctiveness which sets many destinations apart and which is instrumental in attracting visitors. Accordingly, the consumption idea is a central tenet.

Tourist roles

One of Dann's perspectives (motivational typologies) (see Table 4.2) suggests that tourist types, the personality traits of tourists that enable us to classify them, could provide an explanation for why some travel to certain destinations. In the 1970s, several studies attempted to classify tourists according to observable behaviour. One of the first researchers to do this was Cohen (1972), who established four categories of tourist:

1   *The organized mass tourist* takes a highly organized package holiday and has minimal contact with the host community, holidaying within an 'environmental bubble'.

2   *The independent mass tourist* uses similar facilities to the organized mass tourist but also wants to break away from the norm and to visit other sights not covered on organized tours in the destination.

3   *The explorer* arranges their travel independently and wishes to experience the social and cultural lifestyle of the destination.

4   *The drifter* does not seek any contact with other tourists or the organized tourism industry, preferring to live with the host community.

This type of classification is problematic, since it does not take into account the increasing diversity of holidays undertaken and the different locations chosen. Along these lines, one of the best-known theories was developed by Plog (1974) based on the US population. Plog identified two opposite types of tourist each at the end of a continuum (Table 4.4). Allocentrics are tourists who seek adventure on their holidays and are prepared to take risks. As such, they prefer holidays in more exotic locations and prefer to travel independently. At the other extreme are psychocentrics. These tourists look rather inwardly and concentrate their thoughts on the small problems in life. On holiday they are not adventurous, but prefer locations that are similar to their home environment. Such tourists may repeatedly return to the same destination where they have experienced a satisfying experience, safe in the knowledge of the familiar. In between these two extremes other categories exist such as near-allocentric, mid-centric and near-psychocentric.

While Plog's typology provides a simple model that can explain, to some extent, aspects of tourist motivation, there are some difficulties in its application. One aspect, for example is that both tourists and destinations change over time. A young adult may well be allocentric at certain stages in their lifecycle and more mid-centric at other stages: when children are present, for example.

TABLE 4.4	Plog's tourist types
Type	*Characteristics*
Allocentric	Enjoy travelling independently, cultural exploration, often in above-average income groups, seek adventurous experiences on holiday
Mid-centric	The majority of the population go to known destinations, but do not go for exploration and adventure. May travel to destinations previously 'found' and made popular by allocentrics
Psychocentric	Tend to be rather unsure and insecure about travel. Go to places similar to their home environment

Tourism researchers have developed other systems for defining tourists, but much of this early work was based on non-empirical research and it was not until the 1980s that researchers began to undertake quantitative studies of tourist motivation. Pearce (1982) developed 15 **tourist role**s (tourist, traveller, holiday-maker, jet-setter, businessman, migrant, conservationist, explorer, missionary, overseas student, anthropologist, hippie, international athlete, overseas journalist and religious pilgrim) and by using statistical techniques, identified five major tourist types:

- environmental
- high contact
- spiritual
- pleasure first
- exploitative travel

but this classification did not distinguish solely leisure-based roles.

The travel career ladder

Researchers recognize that tourist motivation changes over time and tourists may have several 'motives' to travel. Pearce (1993) suggested that that individuals exhibit a 'career' in terms of tourism behaviour. Individuals thus start out at different levels and are likely to change levels as they progress through the various lifecycle stages and can be constrained from progressing by money, health and other people. The model also recognizes that tourist can 'retire' from their **travel career**, or by not taking holidays at all they are not a part of the system' (Pearce 1993: 125). Pearce's model builds on the pyramidal system conceptualized by Maslow, with five motivational levels and suggests that tourist motivation is an ever-changing process and individuals move up the 'ladder' now modified to Trend Career Patterns (Pearce 2005).

Current thinking on tourist roles

Building on Pearce's (1982) work, Yiannakis and Gibson (1992) derived a comprehensive classification of leisure tourists, and more recent work has added two more roles to this original typology (Foo, McGuiggan and Yiannakis 2004) (Figure 4.4). Yiannakis and Gibson (1992: 287) suggested that individuals 'enact preferred tourist roles in destinations which provide an optimal balance of familiarity-strangeness, stimulation-tranquility, and structure-independence'. In other words, some types of tourist on holiday seek unusual environments where others seek familiar ones, some want peace and quiet where others want activity, and some require an organized holiday or itinerary and others do not. Each tourist role seeks something different. Yiannakis and Gibson (1992) found that, in terms of strangeness-familiarity, the archaeologist and the seeker prefer strange environments, while the sport tourists prefers a familiar environment. The organized mass tourist prefers a tranquil environment, and those seeking a high degree of structure include the jetsetter, drifter and action seeker, while the sun lover and escapist prefer low-structured environments. In more recent research, Gibson and Yiannakis (2002) investigated the relationship between tourist role preferences according to gender and adult life-course and psychological needs. This research showed that there are three trends in tourist role preferences over the course of adult life. These are:

- Roles where preferences mostly *decrease* through life-course, which include certain roles that people are less likely to assume as they grow older. Such roles are the action seeker, the active sport tourist, the thrill seeker, the explorer, the drifter and the sun lover. Needs driving these roles vary but, to take the example of the active sport tourist, for males the push to participate include a combination of unsatisfied and satisfied needs: unsatisfied needs for play, sexual needs, the home and family, and satisfied needs for setting goals and control over their life.
- Roles where preferences mostly *increase* through life-course, which include roles that people are more likely to adopt as they grow older. These include the anthropologist, the high-class tourist, the educational tourist and the organized mass tourist.
- Roles where preferences *vary* through life-course include the seeker, the jetsetter, the independent mass tourist and the escapist.

Sun lover: Interested in relaxing and sunbathing in warm places with lots of sun, sand and ocean

Action seeker: Mostly interested in partying, going to night clubs and meeting the opposite sex for uncomplicated romantic experiences

Anthropologist: Mostly interested in meeting local people, trying the food and speaking the language

Archaeologist: Mostly interested in archaeological sites and ruins; enjoys studying history of ancient civilizations

Organized mass tourist: Mostly interested in organised vacations, package tours, taking pictures and buying lots of souvenirs

Thrill seeker: Interested in risky, exhilarating activities which provide emotional highs, such as sky diving

Explorer: Prefers adventure travel, exploring out-of-the way places and enjoys challenges involved in getting there

Jetsetter: Vacations in elite world-class resorts, goes to exclusive night clubs and socializes with celebrities

Seeker: Seeker of spiritual and/or personal knowledge to better understand self and meaning of life

Independent mass tourist: Visits regular tourist attractions but makes own travel arrangements and often 'plays it by ear'

High-class tourist: Travels first class, stays in the best hotels, goes to shows and dines at the best restaurants

Drifter: Drifts from place to place living a hippie-style existence

Escapist: Enjoys taking it easy and getting away from it all in quiet and peaceful places

Sport tourist: Primary emphasis while on vacation is to remain active, engaging in favourite sports

Educational tourist: Participates in planned study programmes or education-oriented vacations, primarily for study and/or acquiring new skills and knowledge

FIGURE 4.4 A typology of 15 leisure-based tourist roles. Source: Reprinted from *Annals of Tourism Research*, vol.31, Foo, McGuiggan and Yiannakis, 'Roles tourist play', 408–27, copyright (2004), with permission from Elsevier

The findings of this research indicate that tourist roles serve as a medium for tourists to satisfy their needs and wants at various stages of the life-course.

So, it can be seen that there are several ways in which we can explain the push factors in tourism motivation. Once the motivation to embark on a holiday has been determined numerous pull factors effectively influence our choice of destination. Within this, aspects such as the purpose of the holiday and tourist typologies may well be particularly influential. However, the circumstances that affect us as individuals, both personal and wider external influences, greatly affect the nature of the holiday and the final selection of a particular destination. These influences on tourist motivation will now be investigated.

Factors influencing tourist motivation

While we have seen that the decision to go on holiday is an outcome of personal motivation, the selection of a destination/type of holiday is set against a series of constraints of which individuals are aware. The choice of the final holiday is limited because some holidays are too expensive, are not suited to the time we have available, are too far away, or may even involve activities that are beyond our capabilities. There are numerous ways that such constraints could be organized, but the ensuing discussion will focus on two broad categories:

- *personal and family influences*, including age, stage in the family life-cycle, and gender issues
- *social and situational influences*, including the tourism and work relationship, social class and income issues.

Age

Variations in tourism participation are strongly related to age, and this is evident in the style of which many tour operators segment their holiday products by age (Club 18–30, Saga). There are many inequalities in terms of age and tourism. In the UK, statistics indicate that those aged 16–24 and over 65 are more likely to not have a holiday than other age groups, and one of the main constraints for both groups is limited income. Overseas holidays are more likely to be taken by those aged 35–54, while the retired population generates the largest proportion of domestic holidays.

Typically, young adults are shown in advertising as backpackers, or else attracted to fun-seeker package holidays aimed specifically at the age group in destinations such as Ibiza. To some extent, tourism participation could be seen as a wage-earning symbol of adulthood for young people. Young adulthood is a time to experiment, to develop confidence in one's own identity, to establish independence, to broaden horizons and to experience sexuality and relationships, and tourism can provide a useful outlet for such needs. By the time of old age there is an inevitable reduction in an individual's physical and mental facilities and as such a reduction in the more active holiday pursuits. Disincentives for travel include falling ill, availability of medical services, personal security, safety and hygiene, whereas motivations include health and well-being, socializing, companionship and opportunity to participate in activities. In Great Britain, people aged over 70 make fewer trips and travel considerably less distance than younger people. In addition, car use for domestic travel declines with age (ONS 2004). However, it is clearly incorrect to equate retirement with old age. In the Western world, there is an ageing population which includes the 'baby boomer' generation, who contrary to traditional analyses, have both the time and the budget for travel. People for whom retirement has come in their fifties represent an attractive 'target' for tourism operators. Often the over-fifties are free from family commitments but may still have limited free time and an attractive pension. Thus, such individuals may approach early retirement as a welcome gift. Opportunities may well expand as the individual enters retirement, and only retract when the individual becomes elderly. Some tourism markets benefit substantially from the more mature population, such as the coach travel market (see Chapter 8). For some, retirement stimulates a move to a favoured holiday destination and the holiday experience is therefore recreated on a permanent basis, linking tourism and migration within a domestic and sometimes overseas context.

Family lifecycle

Closely overlapping with age, the family lifecycle, or lifecycle, groups people not only by their age but also by their marital status and whether they have children. Numerous classifications have been developed over time and reflect the societal structure and dynamic of the time. To give an example, the framework set out by Rapoport and Rapoport in 1975 defined four stages:

1 Adolescence (15–19 years old).
2 Young adult (to late 20s).
3 Family establishment (25–55).
4 Later years (55+).

More recently, a European/North American model outlining eight stages has superseded the earlier basic formats of lifecycles (Table 4.5). Such classifications, while useful, need constant updating. Looking at the two examples it can be seen that little account is made of single-parent families, gay people and extended families. Such models imply the stages to be the 'norm' and pay little attention to those choosing not to have children or cultural differences in families by ethnic

TABLE 4.5   The family lifecycle (European/North American model)

Stage	Characteristics	Tourism behaviour
1. Early childhood	Entirely dependent on parent or guardian. Classic sea and sand holidays	Seeking seaside or inland resorts with entertainment facilities for children
2. Early teenager	More influence on decision-making process but still dependent on parent	Resort based holidays with nightlife. Also youth hostels and semi-independent activity holidays. Group based holidays
3. Young person	Young, single, not living at home	Holiday-taking dependent on time and resources, therefore wide ranging – 'sunlust' to activities. High on adventure, backpacking and experiences
4. Partnership stage	Couples living together with busier lifestyles. Time is a major barrier to travel	Wide ranging, more short breaks to fit in with dual careers
5. Family stage – early	Includes single parent or separated partners. Financial and school constraints are key factors. Seeking family-centred holidays	Key interest in main holidays, or visiting VFR at other times
6. Family stage – late	Still major constraints regarding education. Holiday-taking patterns breaking up	Mix of holidays and children seeking semi-independence
7. Empty nest	Children leave home and parent or parents have increased freedom and spending power	Wide ranging but higher prosperity to take more expensive explorer holidays and second breaks
8. Retired	One person or partners retired; income fixed but time available	Continued search for quality. As age increases seeking more passive holidays. Old age no longer a barrier to travel

Notes: This generalized model does not include the increasing number of people who remain single or do not have a family. It does, however, recognize different family structures, particularly single-parent families

Source: Lumsdon (1997: 44)

class. Despite these concerns, it is fair to say that different stages in a lifecycle are characterized by different interests, activities and opinions. These translate to different holiday requirements at each stage, and some companies can effectively 'capture' loyalty at an early stage and maintain this throughout the lifecycle, the Disney Corporation for example.

Since the 1950s, it has been considered that women made holiday decisions. However, more recent research has indicated that the holiday choice of a heterosexual couple is made jointly, particularly in the case of high-income households. Women tend to dominate the information-search stage. It is in reality very difficult to judge how decisions are made as tourism decisions often involve a string of choices, including travel, time, accommodation, activities, destination and duration.

The presence of children in a household has a significant influence on tourism participation and patterns, and can often create a substantive diversion from the type of pre-family holidays taken by a couple. Households with children tend to have a more limited choice in terms of travel date and duration, dominated by school holidays. People with very young children are constrained by the abilities and tolerances of their children, in terms of travel time and accommodation flexibility. Couples without children tend to take more short breaks throughout the year and some very long trips (more than two weeks) (Dellaert, Ettema and Lindh 1998). Children are an important determining factor of parental holiday satisfaction and can often play a role in the decision-making process, in terms of identifying a holiday desire and negotiating activities. Thornton, Shaw and Williams (1997) observed that children certainly have an effect on tourism behaviour, and Connell (2005) highlights the emergence of **toddler tourism**, where young children's pester power has played an important role in choice of destination: as is the case of the film location of the children's TV programme *Balamory*. It has also been shown that grandparents play a role in taking younger children on trips, particularly day trips and short breaks, as well as within the VFR sector.

Gender

Gender as an influence in tourism decision-making is not widely researched or discussed. Much gender-related tourism research concentrates on employment patterns and sex tourism, focusing on women as producers rather than consumers (Pritchard 2004). Yet one of the primary relations between individuals in any society is based on gender. Clarke and Critcher (1985) argue, in the context of leisure participation that women have less leisure time than men, undertake fewer leisure activities and spend a higher proportion of their time in and around the home and family. If this is accepted, then there are also clear implications for gender to be an issue in tourism participation and motivation. One illustration may well be that for those women who have primary responsibility for household organization and child care, a self-catering holiday may not fully provide a means of escape from the home environment when this is an important motivator. However, if tourism is part of a family ritual, then all members participate. So, it is not necessarily participation in tourism that is an issue for women with primary care roles, but the type and quality of that participation. Women's caring roles do not just relate to children, since around 70–80 per cent of those caring for an elderly or infirm relative or partner are women, so a holiday may be a rest from caring or caring in a different location (Gladwell and Bedini 2004).

Contemporary tourism, reflecting wider societal changes, has witnessed the empowerment of women and the rise of the lone female traveller. As Kinnaird and Hall (1994) argue, women's travel is often associated with high, mystical destinations (e.g. Tibet, Bhutan) or voluntary environmental work, with tracing routes (such as backpacker routes) or just getting away from being a carer (e.g. going to a spa or on a pampering short break). In addition, female group travel is much in evidence in the European youth market. The industry tends to negate against the lone traveller, male or female, and tourism tends to be promoted as a couple or family pursuit. Packages are sold on double occupancy basis, and single-room supplements can be exorbitant. Indeed, as Pritchard (2004) contends, the tourism industry is failing to meet the needs of female consumers, particularly business travellers and lone travellers.

Men and women tend to be viewed differently by society in terms of being travellers. For example, men who travel alone might be considered as seeking adventurous activity, expedition or sex tourism. Women may be thought of as brave, vulnerable or even abnormal (Kinnaird and Hall 1994). Some women decide not to travel independently or to avoid certain countries for safety reasons. Many women recognize increased vulnerability in an unfamiliar destination but will take calculated risks although, as Carr (2001) argues, personality as well as gender affects perception of risk. Kinnaird and Hall (1994) note that the differing socialization process in leisure experience seems to affect tourism behaviour, but as Foo *et al.* (2004) illustrates, motivation is a function of the role of the tourist (e.g. sun lover, jetsetter). Foo *et al.* (2004) found that women are more likely to take a passive role in strange environments than men and that men pursue a wider range of leisure opportunities in unfamiliar environments.

Disability

Some of the barriers to tourism participation faced by the less-able are outlined in Table 4.6. Murray and Sproats (1990) identified financial constraints as a major issue for disabled tourists, and it is true that some disabled persons live on modest incomes if they are reliant on state benefits. However, as a group of travellers, this is a large and growing sector, often with more money to spend than most would acknowledge (Ray and Ryder 2003). Mobility-challenged consumers tend to form the focus of much of the development work in the tourism sector, although they form only about 5 per cent of the total disabled population. In tourism, there is little research on visual, hearing and mental impairments.

TABLE 4.6 Barriers to tourism participation faced by persons with a disability

Internal Intrinsic barriers	Economic barriers	Exogenous Environmental barriers	Interactive barriers
Lack of knowledge	Affordability	Architectural/accessibility of accommodation etc.	Skills challenges and incongruities
Ineffective social skills	Income disparities	Ecological, paths, trails, hills etc.	Communication challenges
Health-related barriers	Need for travel companions/special facilities	Transport	Lack of encouragement to participate
Physical or psychologically related barriers		Rules and regulations	Attitudes of travel and hospitality industry workers
Is travel seen as a right?		Safety	Availability and accuracy of information

Source: Reprinted from Tourism Management, vol.24, McKercher, Packer, Yau and Lam, 'Travel agents as facilitators or inhibitors of travel: perceptions of people with disabilities', 465–74, copyright (2003), with permission from Elsevier

Increasingly, the tourism industry is able to offer improved products and services to the disabled market. Airlines are particularly good at accommodating wheelchair users; they provide allocated seats and special narrow wheelchairs that can be used to move along aisles, although other forms of transport are often more problematic. Tourism operators often do not know what sort of modifications are required to meet the needs of a range of disabled people, and often do not achieve the right standards. However, this is changing. In many countries, there are strict legal requirements placed on businesses to provide accessibility and the tourism industry is not exempt. In the UK, Visit Britain operate the National Accessible Scheme, which assists accommodation operators in making their products more accessible with standards for visual and physical impairments. The Disability Discrimination Act (1995) in the UK places a responsibility on all public and private organizations to make services fully accessible to disabled persons.

A growing number of specialist organizations and tour operators now offer both domestic and overseas tourism experiences. One good example is Access Africa, which has established wheelchair-accessible lodge accommodation in South Africa, with adapted safari vehicles and personal carers available in a tailor made itinerary. Gladwell and Bedini (2004) state that the internet is a favoured mechanism for planning holidays for disabled people. Websites such as disabilityworld.com assist the disabled tourist to find accessible attractions and accommodation and allow informed choices to be made for planning day trips and holidays. The disabled tourist is often quite a loyal one to destinations that are sensitive to needs (Burnett and Baker 2001).

A further issue relates to carers. Gladwell and Bedini's (2004) research identified that those able-bodied individuals who act as full-time carers to a disabled, infirm or elderly relative or partner suffer from 'leisure loss', in that carers have less time and energy to devote to leisure and tourism and may be more prone to illnesses themselves. Some tour operators take such issues into consideration, offering a personal assistant while on holiday to relieve the carer. Other carers take holidays alone while the patient takes respite care.

Nationality and national identity

Leisure participation rates vary with **ethnicity** and **nationality**. However, these patterns are complicated by socioeconomic and lifecycle influences. Early work on tourism patterns and race was conducted in North America, and this shows evidence of differences between non-white and white Americans, although there were many variations and no real conclusive findings (Shaw and Williams 1994). In general, there is a lack of research evidence as to whether tourism motives and destination choices vary between nationalities, although several recent studies indicate that differences exist. For example, Foo *et al.* (2004) identified some differences in motivation between American and Australian tourists, Kozak (2002) found differences between English and German tourists to Mallorca and Turkey, and some of this research suggests that different nationalities perceive destinations slightly differently. Tourists from cultures that are viewed as extrovert are more likely to adopt adventurous forms of tourist behaviour and tourists who are culturally dissimilar to the destination are less likely to visit lots of attractions and different areas within the destination (McKercher and Lew 2004).

Pizam and Sussman (1995) examined the behaviour of Japanese, American, French and Italian tourists, and identified differenced in five behavioural characteristics, including:

- social interaction (e.g. Japanese tend to stay within their own group)
- commercial transaction (e.g. Americans buy the most)
- preference for activities (e.g. Italians and French are the most adventurous)
- bargaining and trip planning (e.g. Japanese plan the most, Italians the least)
- knowledge of destination (e.g. French, Italians and Americans are interested in authentic experiences)

For overseas travel, language barriers may act as a disincentive to travel, although in many cases, legal requirements for **visa**s prove to be most problematic. In recent times, certain nationalities have been deterred from visiting certain countries due to the threat of terrorism and other safety concerns (see Chapter 26). Accordingly, there is a need for tourism marketers to understand each nationality and develop strategies appropriate to the needs and aspirations of each of the major markets for a country. The role of nationality and cultural characteristics is fully recognized by NTOs charged with marketing to overseas tourists. They prepare market reports on the key overseas segments according to market research, profiling each nationality, and examining their needs and expectations. Such work assists individual operators to cater for each nationality that they are likely to encounter, as well as in the wider marketing effort (see Web Exercise 4.1).

Tourism and work

Work provides a means for tourism and, often, escaping from work provides the motivation for tourism. Whatever the balance, leisure, tourism and work are inseparable. However, leisure and work both compete for an individual's time. If one increases then the other decreases. The nature of work, however, is an important influence on tourism not just in terms of competition for time. Where an individual's work is boring, arduous or monotonous, tourism may well represent an escape. Opposing this, some are fortunate to find their work exciting, enjoyable and possibly difficult to disassociate from their leisure. Here a holiday may be seen as a means to extend one's work interests. Zuzanek and Mannel (1983) identified four hypotheses in terms of a work/leisure relationship:

1 *The Trade-off* **Hypothesis**: Work and leisure are competitors for time and an individual chooses between them.

2 *The Compensation Hypothesis*: Leisure and holidays compensate for the boredom and troubles associated with work and everyday life.

3 *The Spin-off Hypothesis*: The nature of an individual's work produces a similar pattern of leisure activities.

4 *The Neutralist Hypothesis*: There is no discernible relationship between leisure and work.

What can be seen here is that in the vast majority of cases different types of work produce different levels of satisfaction, which in turn influence individual needs and wants and hence leisure and tourism motivations.

Social class and income

Lumsdon (1997: 42) suggests that **social class** be 'considered to be one of the most important external factors, assessed primarily by occupation and level of income'. However, social class is an awkward concept in that there are numerous dimensions associated with power, money, prestige, culture and background. Nevertheless, social class is used throughout social research and as a means of segmenting the population (along with gender and age) for the purposes of surveys and opinion polls, although class is now more commonly established by occupational grading schemes.

So what is social class and how might it be an influence in terms of tourism motivation? Social class was defined for the UK population census in 1911 to facilitate the analysis by arranging the large number of occupational groups. This initial system took no account of differences between individuals in the same occupation groups (e.g. in terms of remuneration) and over the years other systems have been introduced. For example, in 1951 (amended 1961) the seven social class groups were replaced by 17 socio-economic classes for the UK Census. Here the aim was to bring together people with jobs of similar social and economic status. In common use is a system devised by the Market Research Society, where:

Class

A   Professional/senior managerial

B   Middle managers/executives

C1   Junior managers/non-manual

C2   Skilled manual

D   Semi-skilled/unskilled

E   Unemployed/state dependants

The implications for leisure and tourism participation are that, moving from the professional occupational grouping to the unskilled, there is an increase in television viewing, a decline in membership of library membership and book reading, and a decline in holiday-making, sports participation and countryside recreation (ONS 2004). The statistical data suggest that professional occupations enjoy a more active and varied range of leisure activities. As tourism is price elastic (i.e. small price increases may result in many people seeking cheaper alternatives) and as incomes are generally synonymous with occupational groups, these classifications have an influence on the tourism patterns.

While it is fair to accept that aspects of occupational grouping do influence tourism, such assumptions should be approached with caution. The categories do not relate to lifecycle, hence a young professional worker with four children may have less disposable income than a working couple in the skilled manual class who have no dependants.

It is also pertinent to note that there are other more subjective dimensions of social class, more associated with class imagery. An individual's accent, style of speech, residence, social network, job, educational background, dress, car, income, race, family background and leisure activities may be more influential than their occupation. The subjective judgements associated with the upper, middle or working classes may also affect the nature and type of holiday as well as other aspects of life. Tourism destinations have traditionally been associated with certain social groupings, and marketers are often charged with repositioning a destination as part of a wider tourism strategy. English seaside resorts provide a good example of this and the illustrations of the marketing literature for Eastbourne in 1961 and 2004 show clear shifts in the product as a new focus is developed for the next decade (Images 4.1 and 4.2).

Image 4.1: 1961 Eastbourne Borough Council Holiday Guide which targeted family holidays with a coastal theme, reproduced with permission from Eastbourne Borough Council

Image 4.2: 2004–2005 advertising campaign by Eastbourne Borough Council which targets the 35+ market as part of its tourism strategy around four themes: Traditional Seaside, Cultural Pursuits, Sports & Activities and Coast & Countryside (incorporating the South Downs and working with neighbouring authorities). The image appeared in a London Underground advertising campaign and also in postcard mailings. Reproduced with permission from Eastbourne Borough Council

Inequalities in tourism among occupational groups are more evident in the type of holiday taken than the participation rates. The AB groups are more likely to take overseas holidays than the DE groups, despite the existence of cheap package deals which have 'democratized' foreign travel (Shaw and Williams 1994: 49). Higher-status consumers tend to travel independently more often and the short-break market is dominated by the AB groups. Attempts to make tourism and leisure more socially inclusive abound, most notably in the **social tourism** movements of northern Europe (see the example of the North Yorkshire Moors Bus, www.northyorkmoors-npa.gov.uk).

Tourist motivation and segmentation

So far this chapter has shown that people are motivated to travel for a variety of reasons. However, understanding the tourist and their motivations is far from easy. For instance Laws (1991) argued that however convenient it is to categorize travellers, not all individuals fall neatly into behavioural models or typological classifications. Moreover, it is not realistic to assume that the accurate descriptions of tourists through their reasons for travel that were gained at the time of purchase will remain constant throughout the travel experience. Despite such concerns, by identifying types of customers and classifying them into groups or market segments, a process called **segmentation**, tourism suppliers may be able to deliver their products more effectively. Through segmentation marketers can establish common reasons behind the purchase of tourism products within a market segment. For example, Image 4.3 highlights the importance of children as one market segment which some holiday companies have seen as an important component of the family holiday market and worthy of investment; thus they target markets with family-friendly products. Through an understanding of this common purchasing behaviour by market segment, it

Image 4.3: In recent years Butlin's have made multi-million pound investment in three resorts at Minehead, Bognor and Skegness to develop the family holiday market, diversifying into a wide range of new experiences for the market which can be found at http://www.butlinsonline.com

becomes possible to target market segments with particular products. Clearly, different groups of tourists will make varying economic contributions as a result of their activities. For example, in Canada, the Canadian Tourism Commission has estimated the scale of spending on outbound travel is likely to rise from C$18.6 billion in 2003 to C$26.6 billion in 2009. This spending is likely to result in a maturing of the traditional destinations (although they expect the dominant flows to the USA – New York City, Las Vegas, Florida and Hawaii to continue) and more exotic destinations to grow in popularity. Wealthier tourists may be more valuable to destinations than other tourist types, thus efforts may be specifically made to target such groups and, to do this, marketers use segmentation techniques ranging from the simple to the more complex, as we shall now examine.

Segmentation by purpose of travel

The purpose of a trip is used to divide groups of tourists. Commonly, business travellers are separated from those on a leisure holiday, with those visiting friends and relatives making a third group. Occasionally, the leisure holiday might be further subdivided into groups reflecting sun, sea and sand or sunlust holidays from a sightseeing or wanderlust tour. Travel for health and for sport may be additional subdivisions both of which are growth areas internationally.

Psychographic segmentation

Segmentation based on lifestyle factors or activities, interests, attitudes and opinions is known as 'psychographic segmentation'. Such behavioural characteristics can help to build a picture of common purchasing behaviour. This enables tourism suppliers to target certain types of individual with their products in the knowledge that such groups may be more receptive than the population at large. One example is the **adventure tourism** market, where operators aim to target thrill seekers and adventurous people and some of the principal motivations are outlined in Insight 4.1.

What Insight 4.1 shows is that the segmenter can identify specific traits in terms of motivators which will appeal to different elements of the adventure tourism market, including those who have never undertaken the activity before, those seeking to develop their skills in particular activity and those who may be undertaking an adventure activity as part of a corporate training exercise (team building).

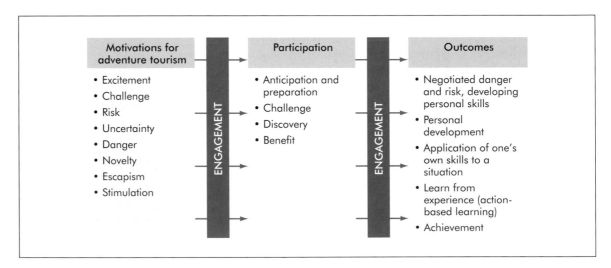

FIGURE 4.5 *Motivation for undertaking adventure tourism. Source: Reprinted from Tourism Management, vol.26, Page, Bentley and Walker, 'Scoping the nature of adventure tourism in Scotland, 381–97, copyright (2005), with permission from Elsevier*

INSIGHT 4.1

Tourist motivation – adventure tourism as a global growth market

There is a growing interest globally in the pursuit of more adventurous forms of tourism, ranging from the entire holiday experience based on a sense of adventure, such as trekking through the Andes or a land-based expedition across the Sahara, to high-risk activities such as parasailing and white-water rafting. The motivations for such travel include an interest in exploring, in meeting indigenous people, and in competing with nature, the weather and difficult terrains. Many specialist travel companies have developed to cater to small group, luxury and more budget forms of adventure travel at a global scale. Many of the consumers who pursue these experiences are part of the explorer type identified by Cohen and other researchers, although the growing affluence of former mass tourists seeking something different also feature among key motivations. But these forms of travel may also be grouped under the more affluent and experiential forms of tourism: luxury or high-cost travel experiences such as ecotours to Antarctica and excursions on the Orient Express. In contrast, more mass-market products have been developed which meet different needs of the more adventurous traveller who seeks the thrill, challenge, adrenaline rush and experience of adventure sports, as shown in Figure 4.5.

The motivations for engaging in adventure sports, which include a wide range of activities (see Table 4.7) include a continuum from the more passive, organized activities such as horse riding through to the ultimate challenge of extreme sports such as white-water rafting, bungee jumping and other physically challenging activities. Many tourist destinations have added these activities to complement the traditional ski holiday market that appealed to the adventure tourist, thereby diversifying the market appeal (Image 4.4). Yet there are inherent complexities in analysing the motivations of individuals and groups who consume these products, as noted by a recent market research study undertaken for Perthshire Tourist Board in Scotland. One of the main problems is in identifying

the multiple motivations associated with engaging in adventure activities and in then seeking to classify people into convenient groupings based on common attributes. The study identified many of the conventional labels used to segment this market, who were typically aged 24–39 years of age, including the avid professional (enthusiasts), those who were sampling the experience for the first time, those wishing to learn a new sport, dabblers who had acquired the skill level necessary but undertook the activity infrequently and the corporate groups who were using it for team-building purposes. When examining the motivations of these adventure tourists (Table 4.8) it is evident that many of the wider motivational features in Figure 4.5 are reiterated through the use of series of statements which the participants were asked to rate. On the basis of these ratings for each statement, it is possible to segment the market according to the prevailing typologies used to describe the diversity of participants in this market.

Image 4.4: Imagery used to promote adventure tourism by the former Perthshire Tourist Board, Source: VisitScotland

Behaviourist segmentation

This form of segmentation is multifaceted and aims to group consumers according to their relationship with a product (Swarbrooke and Horner 1999). Aspects that marketers consider include the benefits sought by the consumer (e.g. value for money with no frills on budget airlines), loyalty (e.g. frequent flyers schemes), purchase regularity, attitude to product and awareness of product.

In addition to these, there are a number of other techniques, such as geographic segmentation and socioeconomic segmentation, which rely on the delineation of occupational grouping and purchasing power. An example in the allocation of categories to residential areas where certain groups of people reside. The **ACORN** system is one of these classifications, and marketers can use this to target promotions to groupings of households that are likely to display certain socio-economic or sociocultural characteristics.

TABLE 4.7 Adventure tourism activities

Aviation-related	Marine	Land-based
Ballooning	Black-water rafting	Cross-country skiing
Hang gliding	Caving	Downhill skiing
Gliding	Charter sailing	Heli-skiing
Heli-bungy jumping	Diving/snorkelling	Ski-touring
Parachuting	Jet-biking	Trekking/tramping
Paragliding	Jet-boating	Vehicle safaris
Scenic aerial touring (small aircraft/helicopter)	Parasailing	Flying-fox operations
	Rafting	Bungy jumping
	River kayaking/sea kayaking	Mountain biking/cycling
	Canoeing	Guided glacier trekking
	River surfing/river-sledging	Horse-trekking
	Water skiiing	Hunting
	Wind surfing	Mountain-guiding
	Fishing	Rap-jumping/abseiling
		Rock climbing

Source: Page (1997)

TABLE 4.8 Motivations and attitudes towards adventure activities

(1 = strongly agree, 5 = strongly disagree)

From a survey of 216 adventure tourists in 2003, visitors were asked to rate the following statements to highlight their attitudes towards different aspects of adventure tourism. The results identify different attitudes towards different aspects of adventure tourism which combine to shape the motivation to engage in these activities which can also be used to segment the market into the different groupings of adventure tourist types.

	Rating						
Statement	1	2	3	4	5	Missing	Total
I enjoy outdoor activities which are safe with no uncertainty	45	88	42	18	3	20	216
Danger and controlled risk is exciting to me	34	82	50	22	6	22	216
I like novel activities I have not tried before	48	99	41	8	1	19	216
Outdoor activities allow me to escape from the routine of everyday life	68	104	24	0	1	19	216
Outdoor activities require a great deal of concentration	25	82	69	18	1	21	216
Outdoor activities require a high level of physical fitness I do not possess	4	21	53	82	37	19	216
I got a sense of personal achievement from undertaking outdoor activities	63	115	16	1	1	20	216
I like to feel an adrenaline rush sometimes from challenging activities	58	96	35	6	2	19	216

Source: Page (2003), © reproduced with permission from Perthshire Tourist Board

Conclusion

As Hogg (2003) argues, consumption now dominates our lives and not only does it mark social differences it has also come to represent how people relate to one another. No longer is a holiday just viewed as an opportunity to have a break away from everyday life, the tourist as consumer now demands to know 'what's in it for me?' In other words, a complex array of benefits and experiences combine to form the individual's motivation for tourism.

While the literature on tourism motivation is still at an early stage of development, the problems of determining tourist motivation may be summarized as follows:

- Tourism is a combination of products and experiences which meet a diverse range of individual needs.

- Tourists do not always articulate the deep psychological needs that motivate tourism behaviour because they are not fully conscious of these factors. Sometimes when individuals do know what they are, they may not reveal them.

- Tourism motives are multidimensional and sometimes contradictory, including a range of push and pull factors. Few travellers engage in single-purpose trips

and there may be many decision-makers in a tourist group.

- Motives may change over time. Understanding tourist motivation is not best served by using static models, but by recognizing the dynamic and changing elements of tourism motivation through time (e.g. travel career ladder and tourist roles).

This chapter set out with the question of 'why do people go on holiday'. At the outset it has been shown that a variety of push factors may motivate the desire to travel. Such factors may result from the particular relationship an individual has with their work or home environment. Alternatively, the motivation to travel may be driven by other forces as in the case of needing to visit relatives or go on a business trip. Other types of tourist may be motivated by higher order psychological needs such as for self-esteem.

While people are instrumental in their motivation, once a decision to travel has been made a variety of pull factors influence that decision. While in theory we may be free to choose our tourism activities, our choice is inevitably limited by an awareness of constraints which influence and circumscribe the range of opportunities.

Discussion questions

1 What models aid our understanding of tourist motivation?

2 Discuss the extent to which people are free to choose where they go on holiday.

3 How important is social class in understanding tourist motivation?

4 What are the main uses of tourist segmentation?

References

Argyle, M. (1996) *The Social Psychology of Leisure*. London: Penguin.

Burnett, J. and Baker, H. (2001) 'Assessing the travel-related behaviors of the mobility-disabled consumer'. *Journal of Travel Research*, 40 (1): 4–11.

Carr, N. (2001) 'An exploratory study of gendered differences in young tourists perception of danger within London', *Tourism Management*, 22: 565–70.

Clarke, J. and Critcher, C. (1985) *The Devil Makes Work*. Basingstoke: Macmillan.

Cohen, E. (1972) 'Towards a sociology of international tourism', *Social Research*, 39 (1): 64–82.

Connell, J. (2002) 'A critical analysis of gardens as a tourism and recreation resource in the UK', unpublished Ph.D thesis, Department of Geographical Sciences, University of Plymouth.

Connell, J. (2005) 'Toddlers, tourism and Tobermory: Destination marketing issues and television-induced tourism', *Tourism Management*, 26 (5): 763–76.

Cooper, C.P., Fletcher, J., Gilbert, D., Wanhill, S. and Shepherd, R. (1998) *Tourism Principles and Practice, Second Edition*. London: Longman.

Crompton, J. (1979) 'Motivations for pleasure vacation', *Annals of Tourism Research*, 6: 550–68.

Dann, G. (1977) 'Anomie to ego-enhancement and tourism', *Annals of Tourism Research,* 4: 184–94.

Dann, G. (1981) 'Tourist motivation: An appraisal', *Annals of Tourism Research,* 6 (4): 187–219.

Dellaert, B.G.C., Ettema, D.F. and Lindh, C. (1998) 'Multi-faceted tourist travel decisions: A constraint-based conceptual framework to describe tourists' sequential choices of travel components', *Tourism Management,* 19 (4): 313–20.

Foo, J., McGuiggan, R. and Yiannakis, A. (2004) 'Roles tourists play: An Australian perspective', *Annals of Tourism Research,* 31 (2): 408–27.

Foucault, M. (1976) *The Birth of the Clinic.* London: Tavistock.

Gibson, H. and Yiannakis, A. (2002) 'Tourist roles: Needs and the lifecourse', *Annals of Tourism Research,* 29 (2): 358–83.

Gilbert, D.C. (1991) 'An examination of the consumer decision process related to tourism', in C.P. Cooper (ed.) *Progress in Tourism, Recreation and Hospitality Management, Vol. III,* London: Belhaven.

Gladwell, N. and Bedini, L. (2004) 'In search of lost leisure: The impact of caregiving on leisure travel', *Tourism Management,* 25 (6): 685–94.

Hall, C.M. and Page, S.J. (2002) *The Geography of Tourism and Recreation: Environment, Place and Space, Second Edition.* London: Routledge.

Hogg, G. (2003) 'Consumer changes', in S. Hart (ed.) *Marketing Changes.* London: Thomson.

Howie, F. (2003) *Managing the Tourist Destination.* London: Continuum.

Kinnaird, V. and Hall, D. (Eds) (1994) *Tourism: A Gender Analysis.* Chichester: Wiley.

Kozak, M. (2002) 'Comparative analysis of tourist motivations by nationality and destinations', *Tourism Management,* 23: 221–32.

Krippendorf, J. (1987) *The Holidaymakers.* Oxford: Butterworth-Heinemann.

Laws, E. (1991) *Tourism Marketing, Services and Quality Management Perspectives.* Cheltenham: Stanley Thornes.

Lumsdon, L. (1997) *Tourism Marketing.* London: Thomson International Business Press.

MacCannell, D. (1976) *The Tourist: A New Theory of the Leisure Class.* London: Macmillan.

Mannell, R. and Iso-Ahola, S. (1987) 'Psychological nature of leisure and tourism experience', *Annals of Tourism Research,* 14: 314–41.

Maslow, A.H. (1943) 'A theory of human motivation', *Psychological Review,* 50: 370–96.

McKercher, B. and Lew, A. (2004) 'Tourist flows and the spatial distribution of tourists', in A. Lew, C.M. Hall and A. Williams (eds) *A Companion to Tourism.* Oxford: Blackwell.

McKercher, B., Packer, T., Yau, M.K. and Lam, P. (2003) 'Travel agents as facilitators or inhibitors of travel: Perceptions of people with disabilities', *Tourism Management,* 24 (4): 465–74.

Meethan, K. (2001) *Tourism in Global Society: Place, Culture, Consumption.* Basingstoke: Palgrave.

Middleton, V.T.C. and Clarke, J. (2001) *Marketing in Travel and Tourism, Third Edition.* Oxford: Butterworth-Heinemann.

Mill, R. and Morrison, A. (1992) *The Tourism System: An Introductory Text.* Harlow: Prentice Hall.

Moutinho, L. (1987) 'Consumer behaviour in tourism', *European Journal of Marketing,* 21 (10): 3–44.

Murray, M. and Sproats, J. (1990) 'The disabled traveller: Tourism and disability in Australia', *Journal of Tourism Studies,* 1 (1): 9–14.

North York Moors National Park Authority (2001) 'Social inclusion, North York Moors', *Tourism 2001* (4), www.northyorkmoors-npa.gov.uk/.

ONS (Office for National Statistics) (2004) *Social Trends 34.* London: ONS.

Page, S.J. (1997) 'The cost of accidents in the New Zealand adventure tourism industry', report for the Tourism Policy Group, Ministry of Commerce, Wellington.

Page, S.J., Bentley, T.A. and Walker, L. (2005) 'Scoping the nature and extent of adventure tourism operations, in Scotland: How safe are they?', *Tourism Management,* 26 (3): 381–97.

Page, S.J. (2003) *The Market for Adventure Tourism in Perthshire.* Dept of Marketing, University of Stirling.

Patmore, J.A. (1975) 'People, Place and Pleasure', inaugural lecture, University of Hull, UK, 30 April.

Pearce, P. (1982) *The Social Psychology of Tourist Behaviour.* Oxford: Pergamon.

Pearce, P. (1993) 'Fundamentals of tourist motivation', in D.G. Pearce and R.W. Butler (eds) *Tourism Research: Critiques and Challenges.* London: Routledge.

Pearce, P. (2005) *Tourist Behaviour: Themes and Conceptual Schemes.* Clevedon: Channel View.

Pearce, P. and Caltabiaco, M. (1983) 'Inferring travel motivation from travellers experiences', *Journal of Travel Research,* 22: 16–20.

Pizam, A. and Sussman, S. (1995) 'Does nationality affect tourism behavior?' *Annals of Tourism Research,* 22 (4): 901–17.

Plog, S. (1974) 'Why destination areas rise and fall in popularity', *Cornell Hotel and Restaurant Administration Quarterly,* February: 55–8.

Poon, A. (2003) 'Competitive strategies for a new tourism', in C. Cooper (ed.) *Classic Reviews in Tourism.* Clevedon: Channel View.

Pritchard, A. (2004) 'Gender and sexuality in tourism research', in A. Lew, C.M. Hall and A. Williams (eds) *A Companion to Tourism*. Oxford: Blackwell.

Rapoport, R. and Rapoport, R.N. (1975) *Leisure and the Family Life-cycle*. London: Routledge.

Ray, N. and Ryder, M. (2003) '"E-bilities" tourism: An exploratory discussion of the travel needs and motivations of the mobility-disabled', *Tourism Management*, 24 (1): 57–72.

Ryan, C. (ed.) (1997) *The Tourist Experience. A New Introduction*. London: Cassell.

Sharpley, R. (1994) *Tourism, Tourists and Society*. Huntingdon: Elm.

Shaw, G. and Williams, A. (1994) *Critical Issues in Tourism*. Oxford: Blackwell.

Swarbrooke, J. and Horner, S. (1999) *Consumer Behaviour in Tourism*. Oxford: Butterworth-Heinemann.

Swarbrooke, J. and Horner, S. (2001) *Business Travel and Tourism*. Oxford: Butterworth-Heinemann.

Teare, R., Moutinho, L. and Morgan, N. (eds) (1994) *Managing and Marketing Services in the 1990s*. London: Cassell.

Thornton, P., Shaw, G. and Williams, A. (1997) 'Tourist group holiday decision-making and behaviour: The influence of children', *Tourism Management*, 18 (5): 287–98.

Urry, J. (1990) *The Tourist Gaze. Leisure and Travel in Contemporary Societies*. London: Sage.

Urry, J. (1995) *Consuming Places*. London: Routledge.

Walmsley, D.J. (2004) 'Behavioural approaches in tourism research', in A. Lew, C.M. Hall and A. Williams (eds) *A Companion to Tourism*. Oxford: Blackwell.

Yiannakis, A. and Gibson, H. (1992) 'Roles tourists play', *Annals of Tourism Research*, 19: 287–303.

Zuzanek, J. and Mannell, R. (1983) 'Work leisure relationships from a sociological and social psychographical perspective', *Leisure Studies*, 2.

Further reading

Pearce, P. (2005) *Tourist Behaviour: Themes and Conceptual Schemes*. Clevedon: Channel View.

This book is the fundamental starting point to understand the study of tourist behaviour.

Connell, J. (2004) '"The purest of human pleasures": The characteristics and motivations of garden visitors in Great Britain', *Tourism Management*, 25 (2): 229–47.

This article outlines a little-researched area, visiting gardens, and the diverse motivations in seeking to enjoy such attractions.

Understanding the Tourism Industry

In the previous section, the focus was on the demand for tourism services and how the tourist affects the demand through individual factors, tastes and preferences. This recognizes the tourist as a consumer and this raises the question – how does the tourism industry fulfil this demand and, in some cases, how does it generate demand for the services and products it offers? This section addresses these issues by commencing with a review in Chapter 5 of the term 'tourism supply' and what the scope and nature of the tourism sector is. This should not be seen in isolation from tourism demand, but for the ease of explanation, the supply issues are explained separately. In the discussion of supply, the challenge of managing a tourism enterprise is highlighted along with some of the prevailing issues for tourism operators such as competition and the need to make costs savings to remain competitive. Having provided a broad overview of what exactly constitutes tourism supply, attention shifts to one of the most dramatic changes which has revolutionized the landscape of tourism supply – the introduction of new technology. The impact of this on the tourism sector, for both supply and demand, has been tremendous, with new forms of travel distribution emerging – e-tourism. Whilst the broad trends and themes which have impacted upon the management of tourism supply from a technology perspective are examined, the chapters which follow all return to this theme to discuss how recent developments and innovations using technology have affected the distribution of tourism supply. One of the most visible impacts has been the rise of the low-cost airlines with over 90 per cent of bookings made online, and the rise of the e-savvy traveller. For this reason, Chapters 5 and 6 should not be seen in isolation from the chapters that follow them, where we examine the processes of globalization and the impact of technology that are simultaneously occurring in time and space to create a truly globalized tourism industry, returning to one of the all-embracing themes of the book developed in Chapter 1.

More detailed analysis of each sector of the travel and tourism sector is presented in each of the subsequent chapters so that the reader can appreciate the wide range of suppliers and sectors which exist and interact to produce the tourism experience. In Chapter 7, the nature of travel and tourism intermediaries, which assemble and distribute tourism products to the consumer through various distribution channels is reviewed. This illustrates how intermediaries have to work with a wide range of suppliers to deliver the tourism experience and reviews the major suppliers of products and services. The transportation sector is discussed in Chapter 8 and the wide range of modes of transport which the tourist utilizes as well as the significance of transport as an integral part of the tourism experience are examined. This is followed by a discussion of the scope and nature of tourism attractions (Chapter 9) where the emphasis is on the ways in which they can be understood as a vital part of the visitor's experience at a destination. Last, the hospitality sector is introduced in Chapter 10. We focus largely on the accommodation sector, emphasizing the significance of processes such as globalization in the worldwide expansion and development of accommodation. The different types of accommodation which the tourist uses are discussed together with current developments in the accommodation sector and some of the principal developments in the hospitality sector are also reviewed.

5 Understanding and Managing Tourism Supply: An Introductory Framework

Learning outcomes

After reading this chapter and answering the questions, you should:

- be familiar with the concept of tourism supply

- understand how different sectors are involved in tourism supply

- be aware of issues relating to supply and the interconnections which exist in the tourism supply chain

- understand the significance of management as a tool to guide the development of supply in tourism enterprises.

Overview

The purpose of this chapter is to provide the reader with an appreciation of the many types of tourism supplier, providing key examples of organizations involved and the scale of operations together with some of the issues facing them, notably the management of tourism and strategy issues. The significance of the travel distribution sector, transport, visitor attractions, accommodation and hospitality sector as components of supply are introduced together with the challenges involved in ensuring the supply is able to meet demand.

Introduction

The study of tourism **supply** is often seen as an abstract economic concept and difficult to visualize and for that reason, this chapter presents an introductory framework which introduces supply and different approaches used to explain its significance. This chapter provides an overview of the various approaches and concepts related to tourism supply which are subsequently developed in the ensuing chapters on supply issues (Chapters 6–10). The analysis of the tourism sector by economists has traditionally distinguished between the demand for goods and services and the ways in which the demand is satisfied, as well as how this affects the *consumption* of tourism goods and services. Economists also examine how the supply of tourist services are produced (i.e. the *production* side). In the real world, the tourism industry consider supply in terms of three basic questions: 'what to produce?', 'how to produce it?' and 'when, where and how to produce it?' according to Bull (1991). Some analysts, however, argue that the tourism industry only really grapples fully with supply issues in conditions of oversupply that may occur in times of economic downturn when demand drops and surplus capacity occurs. Yet it is also argued that many examples of mismanaging tourism supply exists in the competitive environment. For example, the oversupply which exists on transport corridors such as the English Channel crossing by air, rail and sea has led to overprovision and deep discounting which has undermined the profitability of supply.

Despite this, the analysis of tourism supply is 'poorly researched within most conventional texts on tourism, [as] the issue of supply attracts comparatively little attention' (Hall and Page 1999: 92) and consequently it remains a neglected area of study, often based on simplistic descriptions of the tourism industry. Few studies provide a conceptual framework in which supply issues can be examined although geographical studies of tourism (e.g. Williams and Shaw 1994; Hall and Page 2002) have argued that the production of tourism services and experiences offer new directions for research. As Figure 5.1 shows, the scope and nature of tourism supply issues is vast given the scope of those businesses which are directly or indirectly involved in tourism production and this is a good reason for seeking to understand many of the conceptual issues in this chapter. This is followed by more in-depth studies in subsequent chapters. The difficulty is that the tourism industry remains sceptical of academic researchers and their ability to understand complex business issues which they do not face in centres of learning. This is compounded by a gap between the research needs of industry, the sensitive nature of much of their commercial data and the perspectives of academic researchers, who are often inexperienced in the business and managerial aspects of tourism (unless they have worked in industry). Despite this, the more able academic researchers who have industry experience and skills which industry seek do work as consultants to industry to try and address specific business problems.

What is supply?

Sessa (1983: 59) considers 'tourism supply is the result of those productive activities that involve the provision of goods and services required to meet tourism demand and which are expressed in tourism consumption'. Sinclair and Stabler 1992: 2) indicate that supply issues can be classified and divided into 'three main categories:

1 descriptions of the industry and its operation, management and marketing;
2 the spatial development [the geographical development] and interactions which characterize the industry on a local, national and international scale;
3 the effects which result from the development of the industry.'

Although the tourist is a mobile consumer at different geographical scales, much of what can be deemed tourism supply is geographically fixed at specific places. Yet there are also trends, which are examined in other chapters (e.g. Chapter 10 on accommodation and hospitality services), that show that transnational corporations are relocating capital and finance to a wider range of international locations to fulfil the demand for tourism services. As Meethan (2004) indicates, the

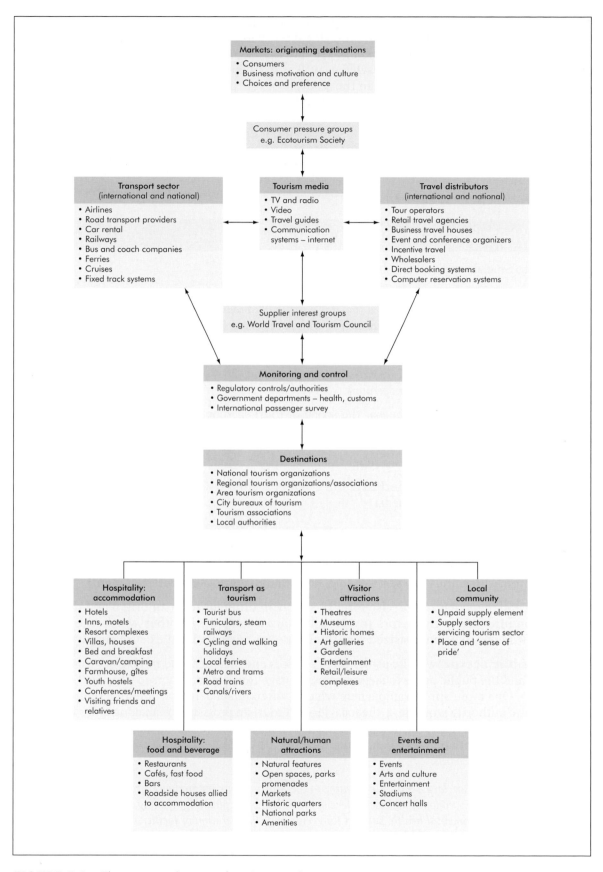

FIGURE 5.1 The scope and nature of tourism supply. Source: Lumsdon (1997:13).

development of production and consumption chains means that bundles of services can be purchased and consumed, highlighting the globalized nature of tourism activity. As part of this, both transport and information technology (IT) are key elements in forming inter-sector linkages and this is discussed in the case of easyJet, as well as in Chapters 6 and 8.

Tourism supply issues are critical in the analysis of tourism because they help to understand how the tourism industry is both organized and distributed geographically, particularly if one adopts a holistic perspective using the tourism system and the supply aspects as critical inputs to the system. Tourism supply issues also exist in an environment in which policy, planning, development issues and political factors impinge upon the regulatory framework and influence the extent to which the tourism industry operates in a regulated through to deregulated environment.

The determinants of tourism supply

According to Sinclair and Stabler (1997: 58):

*Tourism supply is a complex phenemenon because of both the nature of the product and the process of delivery. Principally, it cannot be stored (i.e. it is a perishable product), it is **intangible** in that it cannot be examined prior to purchase, it is necessary to travel to consume it, heavy reliance is placed on both natural and human-made resources and a number of components are required, which may be separately or jointly purchased and which are consumed in sequence. It is a composite product involving transport, accommodation, catering, natural resources, entertainment, and other facilities and services, such as shops and banks, travel agents and tour operators.*

What this quotation illustrates is that the scope of tourism supply issues is extremely broad and wide ranging and comprises many disparate suppliers, providing a combination of tangible and intangible products. For the purposes of this chapter (and which is discussed in more detail in other chapters) the key aspects of tourism supply are:

- tour operators and **intermediaries** (e.g. travel agents or service providers like internet travel agencies such as Expedia)
- attractions and activities
- accommodation
- transportation
- other tourist facilities and services (e.g. hospitality, catering and entertainment).

It is also apparent that the precise form of supply in different tourism origin and destination areas is conditioned by the actors involved in tourism supply, in other words the nature of provision. It needs to be emphasized that three types of business form exist in supply terms:

- *The **public sector**, with its provision of services and facilities, and infrastructure from taxes and the public purse to facilitate and manage tourism activity (see Chapter 14 for more detail). One interesting example here which is often misunderstood and underemphasized is the local authority working at the local level in tourism provision, managing and coordinating services which meet the needs of tourists and residents alike. The scale of provision in Scotland was recently identified by the COSLA report (2002, annex 1) Review of the Area Tourist Boards:*

  Local authorities are an essential contributor to the Scottish tourism product, through their responsibilities for economic and social development, licensing, planning, trading standards, roads and transport, environmental health, support for events and the operation of facilities such as museums, galleries, country parks and entertainment venues. This role is vital in ensuring that visitors have a satisfying and rewarding experience once they are in the area. This involves ensuring, among many other things, that:

  - *necessary infrastructure to support the tourism product is in place at the local level;*

- *visitor attractions are easily accessible, well signposted and well cared for;*
- *there is adequate, quality information available on local attractions and events that will enhance the visitor's experience;*
- *high standards of environmental care are maintained;*
- *there is particular attention to security and safety, for example through lighting, policing and inspection of premises;*
- *new and enhanced tourism products are developed and supported.*

- *The **private sector**, which dominates provision and is driven by profit motives in most cases (although lifestyle businesses which seek to maintain marginal profitability to meet family and social motives also exist). At a global scale, small businesses dominate the tourism sector, although much of the power and control of the tourism sector is a function of the growing role of transnational and global companies which control different aspects of supply (see Table 5.1).

- *The voluntary and **not-for-profit*** sector, which has more aesthetic and esoteric reasons for being involved in tourism, such as volunteering to help heritage bodies to maintain national historic assets. Some business interests in this sector receive public sector grants to act as custodians of state resources (e.g. the National Trust). This sector provides a counterbalance to organizations with profit-driven motives who may not necessarily have the long-term protection of natural and built assets as their main objective, especially if it affects profits and shareholder interests.

Collectively, these actors vary in their significance in different tourism supply situations but they do condition the mix of supply available to the tourism sector, with state **regulation** and private sector profitability often in a state of tension in many countries. There are also globalization processes at work which will impact upon tourism supply and that transcend individual countries.

TABLE 5.1   The advantages and disadvantages of transnational companies (TNCs)

Disadvantages of TNCs	Advantages of TNCs
Knowledge and skill transfer may be inappropriate and undermines competitive advantage of home country	Knowledge and skill transferred and industrialization promoted
Local jobs destroyed and inappropriate jobs supported	Jobs created in the TNC and stimulated in other economic sectors
Local competition eliminated, particularly small and medium-sized enterprises	Competition stimulated to improve standards – exposure to international hotel chains requires locally owned hotels to raise standards
Destroys local culture and imports management approaches – The Disney Corporation was criticized for imposing its culture on the French for example	Effective management and 'modern' attitudes promoted
Leakage of financial benefits to head office	Foreign exchange earned or saved by host nation
Demand distorted and social inequalities promoted	Demand stimulated locally in terms of domestic tourism
Interferes with host country politics creating a neocolonial relationship – for example in terms of tour operators and destinations	

Source: Knowles, Diamantis and El-Mourhabi (2004: 238)

The influence of global transnational companies

Research by Hall and Page (1996) in the South Pacific highlighted the interrelationships which exist between tourism and **international business**. For example, the way in which tourism is organized constitutes a form of international business, especially the way it is managed by global transnational companies (TNCs) where its organizational behaviour, methods of financing and approach to marketing and promotion comprise global activities in their own right. However, in tourism studies the link between these activities and international business remains weakly articulated as Hall and Page (1996) identified. Some more recent studies in economic geography (e.g. Ioannides and Debbage 1998) have broached this subject, but many of these issues are subsumed in more simplistic notions of the supply of tourism. Yet what remains clear is that tourism is inherently a form of international business which manifests itself in:

- tourists and host cultures interacting with each other

- the movement of capital and labour to facilitate international business, especially the international investment in the tourist infrastructure

- the formation of **supply chain**s which are organized internationally as the key function of TNCs, or where TNCs organize these elements of tourism to package and supply tourism.

What is interesting from a tourism perspective is the power and control which these key businesses now wield over the global supply, particularly in Europe with the rise of large TNCs such as TUI, MyTravel and Thomas Cook in Europe, discussed in Chapter 7. Whilst many national and international bodies, especially competition commissions, seek to control the power of TNCs because they attempt to merge and create large entities, the involvement of airlines in strategic alliances helps to overcome competition issues (see later in the chapter). Yet there are also larger entities that have developed, such as the integrated tourism companies like TUI (see Chapter 7) which operate globally and have a strong strategic vision of the market conditions they operate in and the way they need to respond to develop their products. For example, in 2005 Thomson, which is part of the TUI group, begun developing low-cost products and destinations such as Egypt in 2005 to combat the low-cost airline phenomenon which was impacting upon its traditional holiday business and leading to flight-only travel. It has also introduced other measures to allow holiday-makers to compile their own packages from a portfolio of products to respond the growth of online booking and launched a low-cost airline.

It is also important to recognize that the tourism industry and individual firms (Image 5.1) are directly influenced by the market conditions which affect the economic/business environment in which tourism and other economic activities operate. Although there is not space within this chapter to examine these issues in detail (see Sinclair and Stabler 1997 for more detail), four market situations normally prevail in the tourism sector.

Image 5.1: The hospitality sector, where it utilizes historic properties, can create a unique form of tourism supply

Perfect competition

Within economic models of perfect competition, economists make a number of assumptions related to tourism issues. These are that there is a large number of consumers and firms that exists so that neither can affect the price of the **undifferentiated product**; and that there is free entry to and exit from the market with no barriers to the market. However, in the real world few conditions exist where perfect competition can prevail.

Contestable markets

Contestable markets exist where there are 'insignificant entry and exit costs, so that there are negligible entry and exit barriers. Sunk costs [known more commonly as capital] which a firm incurs in order to produce and which would not be recoupable if the firm left the industry are not significant' (Sinclair and Stabler 1997: 61). What this means is that producers cannot react immediately, despite the onset of information technology and greater market intelligence, whereas consumers can react immediately. In other words, businesses compete with each other for the consumer by adopting different pricing strategies so that market segmentation can occur and operators can contest the price. Yet firms in contestable markets charge similar prices because it is frequently a mass market and little product differentiation may exist. In economic terms, this means that existing operators cannot charge more than the average cost because more competitors would enter the market to compete. This is due to the low sunk costs and low entry/exit barriers which rivals would have.

Oligopoly

Oligopoly exists where there are a limited number of suppliers who dominate the tourism sector. This is particularly the case where 'tourism has a dualistic industrial structure which is polarized between large numbers of small firms (typically in retailing, accommodation services) and a small number of large companies (for example in air transport)' (Williams 1995: 163). What this means is that in an oligopoly, a firm can control its price and output levels because there are entry and exit barriers. Many of the supply conditions are ultimately dependent upon the suppliers who determine the output and pricing level. Although in an ideal world, oligopolies set prices where profits are maximized and may even collude to establish a monopoly and increase profit levels, in the real world producers may alter prices and output without reference to competitors to gain market advantage. Sinclair and Stabler (1997: 81) argue in the case of the air transport market that:

> Although a domestic monopoly or oligopoly structure has been common, with a single state supported airline or a small number of competing airlines, deregulation has made some markets competitive in the short run. In the international market some routes are competitive, being served by many carriers. Most of the others are served by at least two carriers, indicating an oligopolist market, although a few routes are served by a single carrier which may be tempted to exercise monopoly powers.

Thus, where a large number of small firms operate in the tourism industry, a competitive market exists. However, where a limited number of operators or tourism businesses exist, an oligopolistic situation may also verge on the conditions akin to monopoly if the competition is limited.

Monopoly

This is probably easily described as the opposite of perfect competition, since it is where a company or firm can exercise a high degree of control over a product or level of output. This means that businesses can charge a price which is above the average cost of production, indicating that consumers pay a higher price than would be the case in a more competitive market situation. Quite often, **monopoly** situations exist which are detrimental to the interests of consumers, but in the transport sector, monopolies may exist where the state is the main provider of a service due to the lack of a viable service from the private sector. Even where governments have privatized monopolies on tourism provision (e.g. with air travel), the enterprises can react in a way where the free market leads to oligopolistic or monopolistic behaviour prevailing in specific areas, which has been the case in the airline industry in the USA (see Page 2005).

Therefore, in any analysis of tourism supply issues and market conditions, Sinclair and Stabler (1997: 83) argue that a number of factors need to be considered in evaluating tourism which include:

- the number and size of firms
- entry and exit barriers to specific tourism businesses
- the extent to which market concentration exists in a specific tourism sector (i.e. where a small number of large operators control the majority of the market such as the UK tour operator sector, which has a small number of large integrated operators controlling the business)
- economies and diseconomies of scale

- the costs of capital and operation
- the extent to which price discrimination exists and products are differentiated
- pricing policies.

Yet these factors do not occur in isolation and in many cases they can be understood in a more dynamic context by looking at the tourism supply chain to show how the businesses working in tourism fit together, and what is the type of relationships that exist between them.

The tourism supply chain

Tapper and Font (2004), in their *Tourism Supply Chains* study, described this concept as:

> *all the goods and services that go into the delivery of tourism products to consumers. It includes all suppliers of goods and services whether or not they are directly contracted by tour operators or by their agents...or suppliers (including accommodation providers): Tourism supply chains involve many components...bars and restaurants, handicrafts, food production, waste disposal, and the infrastructure that supports tourism in the destination. (p. 1)*

Many of these supply chains are managed by business-to-business relationships, using what is known as supply chain management to improve the performance and output in the chain. What Figure 5.2 shows is that these chains, which can often encompass a wide range of tourism and non-tourism sectors but determine the visitor's overall experience of the destination, in relation to those elements of the supply chain they interact with. The supply chain may also help operators to understand where efficiency gains, cost savings and investment may be needed to add value to the customer's experience of tourism.

This suggests that in any assessment of the supply of tourism, there are a wide range of factors that can affect the operation notwithstanding the wider market conditions and the supply chain is a critical element in the management and development of the tourism sector. In other words, the products and services that tourism businesses provide are a function of changing market conditions, and businesses need constantly to consider the market and adapt their business strategies to remain competitive. For this reason, it is useful to examine the relationship between management, tourism supply issues and the way businesses adapt through their use of management strategies.

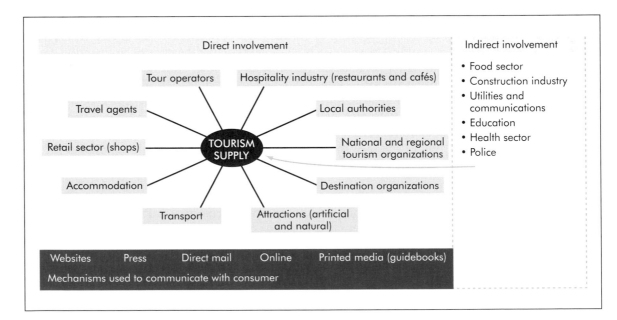

FIGURE 5.2 The supply of tourism – a production system

The management of tourism supply

Management normally occurs in the context of a formal environment – the organization (Handy 1989). Within **organization**s (small businesses through to multinational enterprises), people are among the elements which are managed. As a result, Inkson and Kolb (1995: 6) define management as 'getting things done in organizations through other people' which Leiper (2004) describes as the process of managing. In a business context, organizations exist as a complex interaction of people, goals and money to create and distribute the goods and services which people and other businesses consume or require (Image 5.2).

Organizations in tourism are characterized by their ability to work towards a set of common objectives (e.g. the sale of holidays to tourists for a profit). To achieve their objectives, organizations are often organized into specialized groupings or departments to achieve particular functions (e.g. sales, human resources management, accounts and finance). In addition, a hierarchy usually exists where the organization is horizontally divided into different levels of authority and status, and a manager often occupies a position in a particular department or division at a specific point in the hierarchy. Within organizations, managers are grouped by level in the organization from the:

- *Chief executive officer* (CEO) or *general manager* at the top who exercises responsibility over the entire organization and is accountable to a board of directors or other representatives for the ultimate performance of the organization.
- *Top managers* are one level down from the CEO and their role is usually confined to a specific function, such as marketing or sales. They may act as part of an executive team who work with other top managers and the CEO to provide advice on the relationship between different parts of the organization and contribute to corporate goals.
- *Middle managers* fill a niche in the middle of the hierarchy with a more specialized role than the top managers. Typically they may head sections or divisions and be responsible for performance in their area. In recent years, corporate restructuring has removed a large number of middle managers to cut costs and placed more responsibility on top managers or the level below – first-line managers.
- *First-line managers* are the lowest level of manager in an organization, but arguably perform one of the most critical roles – the supervision of other staff who have non-managerial roles and who affect the day-to-day running of the organization (after Page 2005).

Yet the existence of different theories of management (Leiper 2004) means that organizations may choose different structures to manage their businesses, as epitomized by the less hierarchical and team-based approach at Southwest Airlines which is discussed further in Chapter 11 along with the concept of empowerment and new styles of management in the digital age.

Managers can also be classified according to the function they perform (i.e. the activity for which they are responsible). As a result, three types can be discerned:

- *Functional managers* manage specialized functions such as accounting, research, sales and personnel. These functions may also be split up even further where the organization is large and there is scope to specialize even further.
- *Business unit, divisional or area managers* exercise management responsibilities at a general level lower down in an organization. Their responsibilities may cover a group of products or diverse geographical areas and combine a range of management tasks, requiring the coordination of various functions.
- *Project managers* manage specific projects which are typically short-term undertakings, and may require a team of staff to complete them. This requires the coordination of a range of different functions within a set time frame (after Page 2005).

The goals of managers within organizations are usually seen as profit driven, but as the following list suggests, they are more diverse and encompass:

Image 5.2: Historic properties are a key element of tourism supply and face many management challenges in attracting visitors.

- *Profitability*, which can be achieved through higher output, better service, attracting new customers and by cost minimization.
- In the public sector, other goals (e.g. *coordination, liaison, raising public awareness and undertaking activities for the wider public good*) dominate the agenda in organizations. Yet in many government departments in developed countries, private sector, profit-driven motives and greater accountability for the spending of public funds now feature high on the agenda and this has led to many public sector tourism organizations, like national tourism organizations (NTOs), being restructured.
- *Efficiency*, to reduce expenditure and inputs to a minimum to achieve more cost-effective outputs.
- *Effectiveness*, achieving the desired outcome; this is not necessarily a profit-driven motive.

Managers are therefore necessary to implement the management process and there are four commonly agreed sets of tasks. McLennan *et al.* (1987) describe these as:

- *Planning*, so that goals are set out and the means of achieving the goals are recognized.
- *Organizing*, whereby the work functions are broken down into a series of tasks and linked to some form of structure. These tasks then have to be assigned to individuals.
- *Leading*, which is the method of motivating and influencing staff so that they perform their tasks effectively. This is essential if organizational goals are to be achieved. Leadership is a critical role in the success of any enterprise, but has been attributed to the success of key low-cost airlines such as Southwest Airlines (Gittell 2003), Ryanair (Evans, Campbell and Stonehouse 2003) and Air Asia (Page 2004).
- *Controlling*, which is the method by which information is gathered about what has to be done.

Managing requires one to gather and analyse information on the stated organizational goals and, if necessary, take action to correct any deviations from the overall goals.

Above all the management process is associated with the need for managers to make decisions, which is an ongoing process. In terms of the levels of management, CEOs make major decisions which can affect everyone in the organization, whereas junior managers often have to make many routine and mundane decisions on a daily basis but may be interacting directly with tourists. In each case, decisions made have consequences for the organization. To make decisions, managers often have to balance the ability to use technical skills within their own particular area with the need to relate to people and to use 'human skills' to interact and manage people within the organization and clients, suppliers and other people external to the organization. Managers need these skills to communicate effectively to motivate and lead others. They also need cognitive and conceptual skills. Cognitive skills are those which enable managers to formulate solutions to problems. In contrast, conceptual skills are those which allow them to take a broader view, often characterized as 'being able to see the wood for the trees': the manager can understand the organization's activities, the interrelationships and goals and can develop an appropriate strategic response (Inkson and Kolb 1995).

In recent years, there has been a growing recognition that to perform a managerial task successfully, a range of competencies are needed. A 'competency', according to Inkson and Kolb (1995: 32) is 'an underlying trait of an individual – for example a motive pattern, a skill, a characteristic behaviour, a value, or a set of knowledge – which enables that person to perform successfully in his or her job'. The main motivation for organizational interest in competency is the desire to improve management through education and training. Competencies can be divided into three groups (Page, Wilson and Kolb 1994: 25) with some of the required competencies (in brackets):

- understanding what needs to be done (i.e. critical reasoning, strategic vision and business know-how)
- getting the job done (i.e. confidence, being proactive, control, flexibility, effectiveness)
- taking people with you (i.e. motivation, interpersonal skills, persuasion and influence).

One of the key skills here is the strategic ability of a tourism business to compete in the marketplace, and its ability to change to new conditions and the business strategies it adopts.

Tourism business strategies and supply issues

According to Evans *et al.* (2003: 9), **strategy** is one of the most important factors which determines the success or failure of tourism businesses in both the public and private sectors. They point to the use of the term 'strategy' by management theorists such as Mintzberg, who identified that it may constitute:

- a plan
- a ploy
- a pattern of behaviour
- a position in relation to someone else or a perspective.

This involves a range of strategic elements including identifying long-term objectives. In particular, this requires different courses of action – strategic alternatives to be recognized and planned for at different levels within the organization from the strategic level of the CEO or board through to the tactical level of middle managers or at the operational level of customer delivery. This very hierarchical approach does not, however, account for the success of strategic approaches by airlines such as Southwest, where the policy of empowering staff to work as teams and to work towards set corporate objectives around the company vision of the CEO has raised questions about many of the established approaches to managing organizations (see Chapter 11 for more detail).

Shaw and Williams (2004) discuss the strategic reactions of tourism companies to competition in the marketplace. Intermodal competition, for example, is a key element of transport (except in cases of monopoly provision or one mode of transport such as ferry to cross between two islands and no air access). Shaw and Williams (2004) show that where contestable markets exist, as in the airline sector in the USA, different strategies may result. Evans *et al.* (2003) point to the influential work of the strategic management theorist Porter (1980, 1985) (see also Chapter 15) in setting out the strategic reactions in maintaining a competitive advantage which could involve:

- differentiation (i.e. making your product look different and more attractive to the competitor)
- cost leadership
- the use of either approach to set out a narrow focus on the market such as one segment.

Shaw and Williams (2004) indicate that the most common response to competition is cost competition (i.e. reducing the price) which will require reducing the cost of production, typically labour inputs, although other options exist such as developing strategic alliances or takeovers. Knowles *et al.* (2004) highlight the various growth strategies and competitive models that tourism organizations use to gain competitive advantage, as shown in Table 5.2. These strategies are often combined in the most successful companies by innovation to maintain a competitive edge, as Insight 5.1 on easyJet shows.

TABLE 5.2 Growth strategies and competitive methods

Growth strategies	Competitive methods
Joint ventures	Technology based systems
Franchising	Brand development
Strategic alliances	Product quality
Management contracts	Sophisticated pricing
Conversions	Global marketing and advertising
Sale and leaseback	
Acquisition of small firms	

Source: Knowles *et al.* (2004: 162)

INSIGHT 5.1

easyJet's growth as a tourist supply firm – a major success story of growth and competition

easyJet is one of the great success stories of tourism in the late 1990s and new millennium, from its humble origins in 1995 to its dominance of the low-cost market in Europe in 2004, where it is one of Europe's largest online retailers. In 2004 it operated 180 routes to 55 EU airports. Its massive growth is shown in Table 5.3 which is based on passengers carried and its success is not dissimilar to that of other low-cost rivals such as Ryanair. Yet, as the marketplace shows, numerous low-cost rivals in the USA and Europe failed due to a lack of good management skills, strategic vision and a rigid concern for costs and consumer service. A number of notable failures exist among large carriers who responded to competition on full-service routes by developing low-cost offshoots (e.g. British Airway's Go and United Airlines' Shuttle). Many of the principles of success in the case of easyJet, aside from its visionary founder – Stelios Haji-Ioannou, whose family provided much of the start-up capital and are still the main shareholders – are discussed below.

In 2002, the company purchased one of its rivals – Go, with its Stansted airport base. The scale of success is illustrated in the company's financial results for the six months up to March 2004: despite the costs of incorporating Go into its business easyJet's revenue of £439.7m was up 18 per cent on the previous period in 2003 while passengers carried had risen by 15.9 per cent, reaching ten million. In developing the low-cost airline business, success really hinges upon cost control of operations, as shown in Table 5.4 which illustrates its appeal to consumers. One of easyJet's real selling points for consumers is the low cost, shown in Figure 5.3 which compares easyJet with conventional carriers. This is reflected in the £38 average one-way fare it received from passengers it carried in the six months to March 2004, with high loadings of 83 per cent and additional revenue derived of £2.52 per passenger. However, one of its principal competitive advantages, following the global trend towards low-cost airline operations based on

the highly successful US airline Southwest, is the way in which it has harnessed the use of technology.

As Page (2005) shows, the main advantages which easyJet along with other low cost airlines have derived relate to the development of much simpler products that consumers can understand and purchase without lots of caveats and restrictions. There is a one-class service and simple pricing of each flight segment. In supply terms, the creation of a simple mechanism by which to distribute the product has led to the establishment of both call centres and incentivized internet sales, with a discount over and above the call centre price. easyJet now receives over 93 per cent of its bookings from the internet. It has also made extensive use of incentivized newspaper promotions along with very aggressive media campaigns. This has led to a strong brand proposition, where the company's orange livery (see Image 5.3) is also very prominent on the internet even with part-nered products.

Behind the scenes, the basic principles of financial success with its passenger profitability relate to the use of yield management systems where seats are priced at different rates according to popularity of departure times and cost. In some cases, new routes are given an impetus by very low prices to establish a market demand in situations where this may not have existed before, since some relatively unknown secondary airports may be used with low landing and service costs. This is certainly the case with Ryanair, which has even offered free flights (customers pay the departure taxes and fees only) to create a new market, with massive media campaigns. Companies such as easyJet have also avoided the costs involved in large global distribution systems (see Chapter 6) by bypassing the travel agent and middleman.

In information technology terms, easyJet has also created what are termed **complementary services**, by offering additional services on their websites using independent suppliers and adding value to the purchasing experience, in many cases replacing the role of the travel agent. This is known in the trade as dynamic packaging, so that consumers can buy the total travel experience online rather than having to search various sources for products. Thus it offers hotel bookings via Octupustravel.com, car hire via Europcar, travel insurance via Mondial Assistance, airport parking, ski bookings via Snow Mango and airport transfers as well as ski hire via Ski Set Ski Hire.

Image 5.3: easyJet – a distinctive livery and brand presence for an airline in the low cost sector. Source: Reproduced with permission from easyjet.com

TABLE 5.3	easyJet passenger numbers 1995–2005					
Year	000s of passengers					
1995	30					
1996	420					
1997	1 140					
1998	1 880					
1999	3 670					
2000	5 996					
2001	7 664					
2002	11 400					
2003	20 300					
2004:	Jan	1 683 699		2005:	Jan	2 083 852
	Feb	1 864 970			Feb	2 168 988
	March	1 996 790			March	2 573 000
	April	1 947 675			April	2 438 194
	May	2 092 709			May	2 551 619
	June	2 241 252			June	2 586 889
	July	2 413 367			July	2 847 598
	Aug	2 459 735			Aug	2 903 404
	Sept	2 355 324			Sept	2 743 221
	Oct	2 405 703				
	Nov	2 120 948				
	Dec	2 134 787				

Source: easyJet (www.easyjet.com)

Given the nature of competition in the tourism sector, especially in the transport sector, one response among some airlines has been the development of strategic alliances. Evans (2001) highlights a range of motives, objectives and different outcomes. Evans summarized the strategic process by which airlines entered into collaborative arrangements in terms of:

- *internal drivers* (i.e. risk sharing, economies of scope and scale, accessing assets such as limited slots at airports and shaping the competition), and

- *external drivers* (i.e. the changes induced by information technology and turbulent economic climates, rapid product and market changes as well as global competition).

Although some alliances and **collaboration**s are successful, they can be very unstable and subject to what is called 'churn' (i.e. partners enter and leave as business needs and objectives change). This highlights what Evans *et al.* (2003) point to as 'strategic fit', the need for partnerships to be workable as well as able to offer compatability, commitment and a sense of partnership (Image 5.4).

Image 5.4: In a global tourism market heritage resources may provide a unique selling proposition when collaborating with other businesses

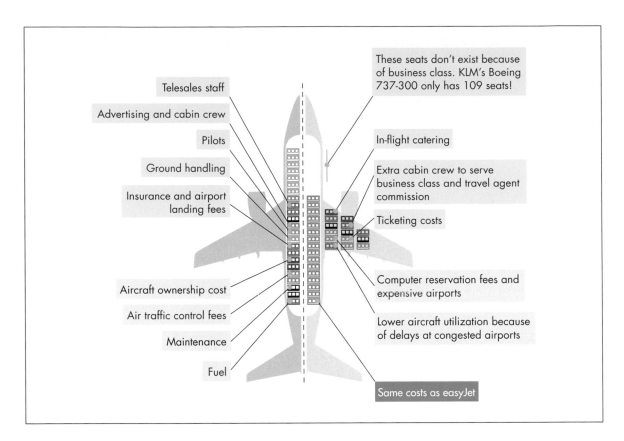

These seats don't exist because of business class. KLM's Boeing 737-300 only has 109 seats!

Telesales staff

Advertising and cabin crew

Pilots

Ground handling

Insurance and airport landing fees

In-flight catering

Extra cabin crew to serve business class and travel agent commission

Ticketing costs

Aircraft ownership cost

Air traffic control fees

Maintenance

Fuel

Computer reservation fees and expensive airports

Lower aircraft utilization because of delays at congested airports

Same costs as easyJet

FIGURE 5.3 easyJet costs

In the airline sector, Bennett (1997: 214) distinguished between the following:

- *Tactical partnerships*, comprising a loose form of collaboration designed to derive marketing benefits, characterized by code sharing among cooperating partners. This is reflected in the smaller feeder and regional airlines being aligned with key hub-based carriers.
- *Strategic partnerships*, where an investment or pooling of resources by partners aims to achieve a range of common objectives focused on the partners' strategic ambitions.

French (1997) by contrast, outlined the principal features which may be included in **strategic alliances** developed by airlines including equity stakes, code sharing, joint services, block seat booking or joint booking arrangements, joint marketing, joint fares, franchise agreements, wet-leasing (where one airline company hires the aircraft and crew to another company) and frequent flyer programmes. In the various studies of strategic alliances by Bennett (1997) and Evans (2001), it is apparent that some of the competitive reasons for adopting this business strategy include:

- gaining **economies of scale** to improve profitability and to gain from economies of scope (i.e. one purchasing cost for the alliance members)
- accessing other airlines' assets
- reducing risk by sharing it, given the highly volatile nature of the tourism business environment
- helping share the market, which may help reduce incapacity in mature markets and could reduce competition
- achieving a high degree of adaptability to the industry (e.g. deregulation and privatization), to stay ahead of the competition.

One other strategy actively pursued by most global and, to a lesser degree, small- and medium-scale enterprises is to control costs, as Insight 5.2 shows.

Managing costs as a tool to stay competitive: the case of the airline sector

As Insight 5.1 discussed, one of the main features which characterizes the success of low-cost airlines is their ability to control their costs (see Table 5.4). Even so, there are many examples of low-cost airlines which have collapsed in the USA and Europe due to underestimating the market and management challenges posed by developing a new venture and controlling costs. In the airline sector, Seristö and Vepsäläinen (1997) outlined many of the cost and revenue factors associated with airline operations and this helps to show where operational costs occur and how airlines might make savings, given the predictions of global airline losses discussed in Chapter 8. Seristö and Vepsäläinen (1997: 11) argue, 'for many a carrier ever more critical measures will be needed to achieve sustainable profitability' and they looked at 42 different airlines and their main costs. Among the main factors which contributed to operational costs were:

- the fleet composition of airlines
- personnel, particularly the number of flight crew per aircraft
- the route network
- the composition of traffic, route structure and salaries/remuneration levels

This led the researchers to build a model (Figure 5.4) to show how costs were related to the supply and demand for airlines services (i.e. what interdependencies and relationships exist) and they identified areas where cost reductions could be made. One strategy, as Figure 5.4 shows, is that airlines might choose to divest themselves of non-core activities by outsourcing the provision of services and activities to other companies. Contracting other companies to supply them would reduce the overheads and staff costs the airlines would incur from hosting them in-house. Seristö and Vepsäläinen (1997) then summarized the areas where cost savings could be made in terms of route structure, fleet composition and company policies, as shown in Table 5.5. One recent example of an airline pursuing a cost reduction strategy is British Airways (BA).

BA introduced its two-year 'Future Size and Shape Strategy' to restructure the company (www.ba.com). One goal was to reduce staffing by 13 000 from the 2001 staffing level of over 50 000 staff worldwide, whilst releasing capital to refocus attention on core activities. In its 2003/2004 Annual Report BA stated that it had made savings of £869 million against a target of £650 million with the target of 13 000 staff cuts exceeded at 13 082. It also made savings on distribution costs in 2003/2004 of £257 million against a £100 million target through greater use of technology and restructuring of travel agent commissions. The ultimate aim was to reach a ten per cent operating margin. The 'Future Size and Shape Strategy' also sought to cut costs by a gradual reduction in fleet types (standardizing where possible as the low-cost airlines have done, reducing engineering costs), and through the reduced costs of supplies by a procurement strategy and greater use of information technology as well as a low-cost fares strategy on its 180 short-haul routes to regain market share from the low-cost airlines. For BA, the 'Future Size and Shape Strategy' is also likely to be followed in 2005–2006 by further measures to control costs, such as modernizing labour practices and reducing overheads to compete in a global context. The follow-on to the 'Future Size and Shape Strategy' is the 'Fit for 5' strategy, as the company prepares to move to its own dedicated Terminal 5 at Heathrow Airport in 2008. This strategy also includes the pursuit of operational efficiencies along with investment in training for staff and new product development to enchance the company's reputation as a global airline.

TABLE 5.4 Key characteristics of low-cost carriers which make them more competitive than other carriers

- Some carriers have introduced single/one-way fares not requiring stopovers or Saturday night stays to get advanced purchase (APEX) prices

- No complimentary in-flight service (no frills) which often reduce operating costs six to seven per cent

- One-class cabins (in most cases)

- No pre-assigned seating (in most cases)

- Ticketless travel

- High-frequency routes to compete with other airlines on popular destinations and up to three flights a day on low-density routes

- Short turnarounds, often in less than half an hour, with higher aircraft rotations (i.e. the level of utilization is higher than other airlines) and less time charged on the airport apron and runway

- The use of secondary airports where feasible (including the provision of public transport where none exists)

- Point-to-point flights

- Lower staffing costs, with fewer cabin crew as there is no complimentary in-flight service; this also reduces turnaround times as there is no cleaning caused by food service

- Flexibility in staff rostering, a lack of overnight stays for staff at non-base locations and streamlined operations (e.g. on some airlines, toilets on domestic flights are only emptied at cabin crew request rather than at each turnaround to reduce costs)

- Many of the aircraft are leased, reducing the level of depreciation and standardizing costs

- Many airline functions are outsourced, such as ground staff and check-in, minimizing overheads and reducing overhead costs by 11–15 per cent

- Standardized aircraft types are used (i.e. Boeing 737s) to reduce maintenance costs and the range of spare parts which need to be held for repairs

- Limited office space at the airports

- Heavy emphasis on advertising, especially billboards, to offset the declining use of travel agents as the main source of bookings

- Heavy dependence upon the internet and telephone for bookings

- Small administrative staff, with many sales-related staff on commission to improve performance (as well as pilots in some cases)

Source: Page (2003)

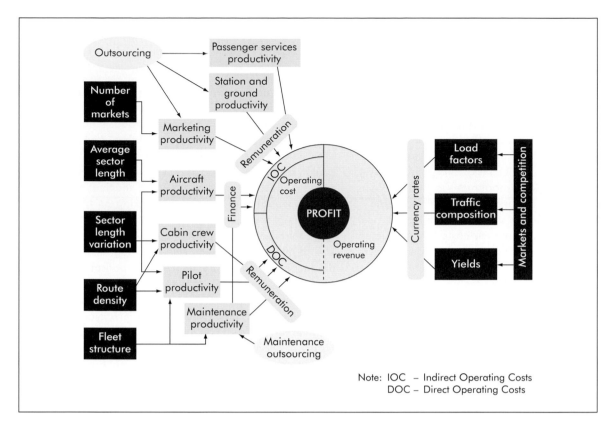

FIGURE 5.4 Interdependencies in the factors and variables affecting airline costs. Source: Seristö and Vepsäläinen (1997).

TABLE 5.5   The potential for cost reductions among airlines

| | Cost drivers | | |
Cost items	Route network	Fleet composition	Company policies
Aircraft crew costs	XXX	XXX	XXX
Engineering overheads	X	XXX	
Direct engineering costs	X	XXX	X
Marketing	XXX		X
Aircraft standing	XXX	X	
Station and ground services	X		X
Passenger services	X		X
General and administrative costs	X		X
Fuel		X	
Airport and en route costs	X		
Direct passenger service			X

Notes

XXX Significant cost reduction potential

X   Some cost implications

Source: Reprinted from *Journal of Air Transport Management*, 3 (1), Seristö and Vepsäläinen, 'Airline cost drivers: Cost implications of fleet, routes, and personnel policies', 11–22, copyright (1997), with permission from Elsevier

Conclusion

Tourism supply issues illustrate that the tourism sector operates in a dynamic business environment which is subject to constant change in both the tastes and trends which tourists pursue (i.e. consumption) and the regulatory environment in which tourism operates. The business environment is always in a state of constant flux, and effective, responsive and strategic management is vital for both private and public sector if tourism is to remain competitive and consumer-focused in the global marketplace. It must be combined with ways to reduce costs and to pursue growth strategies. One also has to have a clear understanding of what the competition is doing.

It is evident that attempts to conceptualize and develop frameworks and models of tourism supply have been limited within tourism studies, and largely descriptive sector-by-sector studies have prevailed. But the concepts of TNCs and supply chains help to overcome these weaknesses. As a result, the consumption of tourism services and goods are often emphasized by researchers to the neglect of the production of tourism goods and the complexity involved in decisions made by businesses in this context. What one often overlooks is that although tourism is a dynamic business activity based upon discretionary spending, especially within specific tourism businesses, it is the constraints upon production which inhibit a situation of perfect competition. The retailing of tourism goods and services is highly competitive in most countries where the formulation of tourism products based upon different elements (e.g. accommodation, transport and attractions) is increasingly subject to a greater degree of control by regulatory bodies. The increased competition is also manifest in the pressure which multinationals and large national corporations are placing on the existing suppliers of tourism services due to the financial leverage and control which they exert through increased concentration of their activities, particularly through integration in the tourism sector. At the same time, tourism businesses are being forced to re-examine their traditional methods of production because of reduced profit margins and competition from new entrants using technology such as the internet. Although the tourism sector has a chequered history of adopting successful technology to improve business processes, the internet is helping businesses to communicate with customers and to perform business processes more efficiently, as well as to communicate directly with new growth sectors such as the over-50 age group (the 'silver surfers'). For this reason, the next chapter examines the role of technology and the e-tourism revolution and the impact on tourism supply for consumer choice and competition.

Discussion questions

1 Why is an understanding of tourism supply fundamental to the analysis of how the tourism sector is organized and operates?

2 How do transnational tourism companies impact upon the organization and management of tourism supply?

3 What are the principal features of management relevant to the supply of tourism supply?

4 What types of business strategy have airlines pursued to address competition?

References

Bennett, M. (1997) 'Strategic alliances in the world airline industry', *Progress in Tourism and Hospitality Research*, 3: 213–23.

Bull, A. (1991) *The Economics of Travel and Tourism*. Melbourne: Pitman.

COSLA (2002) *Review of the Area Tourist Boards*. Edinburgh: COSLA.

Evans, N. (2001) 'Collaborative strategy: An analysis of the changing world of international airline alliances', *Tourism Management*, 22: 229–43.

Evans, N., Campbell, D. and Stonehouse, G. (2003) *Strategic Management for Travel and Tourism*. Oxford: Butterworth-Heinemann.

French, T. (1997) 'Global trends in airline alliances', *Travel and Tourism Analyst*, 4: 81–101.

Gittell, H. (2003) *The Southwest Airlines Way*, New York: McGraw Hill.

Hall, C.M. and Page, S.J. (1996) 'Australia and New Zealand's role in Pacific tourism: Aid, trade and travel', in C.M. Hall and S.J. Page (eds) *Tourism in the Pacific: Issues and Cases*. London: International Thomson Business Press.

Hall, C.M. and Page, S.J. (1999) *The Geography of Tourism and Recreation, First Edition*. London: Routledge.

Hall, C.M. and Page, S.J. (2002) *The Geography of Tourism and Recreation: Environment, Place and Space, Second Edition*. London: Routledge.

Handy, C. (1989) *The Age of Unreason*. London: Business Books Ltd.

Ioannides, D. and Debbage, K. (eds) (1998) *The Economic Geography of the Tourism Industry: A Supply Side Analysis*. London: Routledge.

Inkson, K. and Kolb, D. (1995) *Management: A New Zealand Perspective*. Auckland: Longman Paul.

Knowles, T., Diamantis, D. and El-Mourhabi, J. (2004) *The Globalisation of Tourism and Hospitality: A Strategic Perspective*. London: Thomson.

Leiper, N. (2004) *Tourism Management, Third Edition*. Frenchs Forest, NSW: Pearson.

McClennan, R., Inkson, K., Dakin, S., Dewe, P. and Elkin, G. (1987) *People and Enterprises: Human Behaviour in New Zealand Organisations*. Auckland: Rinehart and Winston.

Meethan, K. (2004) 'Transnational corporations, globalisation and tourism', in A. Lew, C.M. Hall and A. Williams (eds) *A Companion of Tourism*. Oxford: Blackwell.

Page, C., Wilson, M. and Kolb, D. (1994) *On the Inside Looking In: Management Competencies in New Zealand*. Wellington: Ministry of Commerce.

Page, S.J. (2003) *Tourism Management: Managing for Change*. Oxford: Butterworth.

Page, S.J. (2004) 'Air travel in Asia', *Travel and Tourism Analyst*, 3: 1–56.

Page, S.J. (2005) *Transport and Tourism: Global Perspectives, Second Edition*. Harlow: Prentice Hall.

Porter, M. (1980) *Competitive Strategy: Techniques for Analysing Industries and Competitors*. New York: The Free Press.

Porter, M. (1985) *Competitive Advantage: Creating and Sustaining Superior Performance*. New York: The Free Press.

Seristö, H. and Vepsäläinen, A (1997) 'Airline cost drivers: Cost implications of fleet, routes, and personnel policies', *Journal of Air Transport Management* 3 (1): 11–22.

Sessa, A. (1983) *Elements of Tourism*. Rome: Cantal.

Shaw, G. and Williams, A. (1994) *Critical Issues in Tourism: A Geographical Perspective, First Edition*. Oxford: Blackwell.

Shaw, G. and Williams, A. (2004) *Tourism and Tourism Spaces*. London: Sage.

Sinclair, M.T. and Stabler, M. (eds) (1992) *The Tourism Industry: An International Analysis*. Wallingford, Oxon: CAB International.

Sinclair, M.T. and Stabler, M. (1997) *Economics of Tourism*. London: Routledge.

Tapper, R. and Font, X. (2004) *Tourism Supply Chains, Report of a Desk Research Project for the Travel Foundation*. Leeds: Leeds Metropolitan University.

Williams, A. (1995) 'Capital and the transnationalism of tourism', in A. Montanari and A. Williams (eds) *European Tourism: Regions, Spaces and Restructuring*. Chichester: Wiley.

Williams, A. and Shaw, G. (1994) *Critical Issues in Tourism*. Oxford: Blackwell.

Further reading

Hall, C.M. and Page, S.J. (2005) *The Geography of Tourism and Recreation, Third Edition*. London: Routledge.

6

Information Communication Technologies and e-Tourism

Learning outcomes

After reading this chapter and answering the questions, the reader should be able to:

- understand the scope of information technology and its impact on the tourism sector

- distinguish between a computer reservation system and a global distribution system

- understand the scope of the internet, the e-travel revolution and the role of travel services it provides

- recognize what a destination management system is.

Overview

This chapter examines the interface between tourism and information technology. It introduces the concept of information technology, which is one of the major drivers of change in the way the tourism sector communicates and operates, and its impact on the industry.

Technology has revolutionised the pace, scale and nature of business processes in tourism, changing the parameters and scale of business operation. It is now possible for small businesses to operate globally through the use of technology (e.g. a website, email and web-based booking). Technology has also transformed the nature of tourism supply, questioning the role of intermediaries (Chapter 7) and providing the consumer with more autonomy and power in the decision to purchase and consume tourism products.

Introduction

The speed and pace of change in tourism during the 1990s and new millennium has been assisted from a business and consumer's perspective by the development and implementation of information technology (IT) defined by Poon (1993) as 'the collective term given to the most recent developments in the mode (electronic) and the mechanisms (computers and communications technologies) used for the acquisition, processing, analysis, storage, retrieval, dissemination and application of information'. This means that the use of a range of electronic, computer-based and communications-based technologies are increasingly being used to aid the operation and execution of business processes in tourism. One of the main tasks undertaken by these technologies is processing and facilitating the flow of information within and between organizations and to and from the consumer. This involves the use of a range of information technologies which comprise three basic elements: software, hardware and people who operate the IT systems. According to Cooper *et al.* (1998: 424) these ITs 'commonly involve the use of computers, videotext and teletext, telephones/faxes, management information systems (MISs), modems, multimedia kiosks, computer networks, the internet, satellites and wireless communication systems'. But the real revolution in IT has been what Buhalis (2003) termed the growth in **information and communication technologies** (ICTs) in tourism. ICTs have improved processing capability and the speed of computing, reduced equipment size and reduced costs of purchasing software and hardware. Now ICT-led business models have developed and demand and supply have become globalized, particularly in tourism (Buhalis 2003: 3). Yet what is current today is likely to be changed tomorrow given the pace of change in technology.

This has meant that those in the tourism industry can redevelop their mode of production and management practices using ICTs. But above all, as Buhalis (2003: 3) rightly identifies, ICTs increasingly empower and enable both tourism consumers and suppliers to communicate, enhance awareness of needs and offers, inform, negotiate and develop bridges to reduce distance and cultural and communication gaps. Above all, technology is revolutionizing the tourism sector and bringing new modes of communicating with consumers, although there are a number of current concerns associated with this development:

- many of the dot.com businesses which have revolutionized the supply of tourism services are still struggling with issues of profitability, given the high capital costs of investing in technology
- there is growing unease amongst some consumers over purchasing products online due to security issues of payment for these services and the rise of unsolicited web marketing which has heralded a new junk mail era
- consumers are being saturated with online information, some of which is questionable in terms of its derivation, origins and authenticity
- levels of customer loyalty for suppliers are declining due to the availability of low-cost options they can find by surfing the internet, which may filter through to lower rates of brand loyalty
- new forms of technology may quickly supercede existing modes of electronic delivery as are discussed in this chapter and Chapter 27.

Despite these concerns, technology has played a major role in the management of tourism supply as the next section shows.

The use of ICTs to manage tourism supply

ICTs have revolutionized the management of tourism supply functions, especially internet processes and the management of supply, via:

- helping companies to understand how to improve profitability and yields from products. This is most notable with airline reservation systems where the company can understand more precisely how to match supply to demand. This allows airlines to vary prices to match demand

- helping companies to understand what the tourist requires and to tailor the product to market demand

- allowing enhanced cooperation between partners in the supply chain (e.g. lastminute.com has over 19 500 suppliers).

- enabling operational practices in tourism management to help manage supply and demand in a more timely fashion and to react quickly to changes.

- completely reorienting the nature of tourism intermediation (the process of taking supplier's products and brokering them to clients), with the rise of **e-mediaries** and the **e-tourism** revolution

- extending the geographical scope of a company's reach and scale of operation,

all of which can be seen in Figure 6.1. Introducing ICT can require business re-engineering to implement technology so that organizations can achieve certain strategic benefits, namely 'establishing entry barriers; affecting switching costs; differentiating products/services; limiting access to **distribution channel**s; ensuring competitive pricing; decreasing supply costs and easing supply; increasing cost efficiency; using information as a product in itself; and building closer relationships with customers' (Buhalis 1998: 410). This has led to the development of electronic business via business to business (B2B), business to consumers (B2C) and business to government (B2G). In other words, in some situations, ICTs can offer new management opportunities and challenges. Buhalis (1998: 410) identifies four ways in which ICTs can be used strategically by businesses:

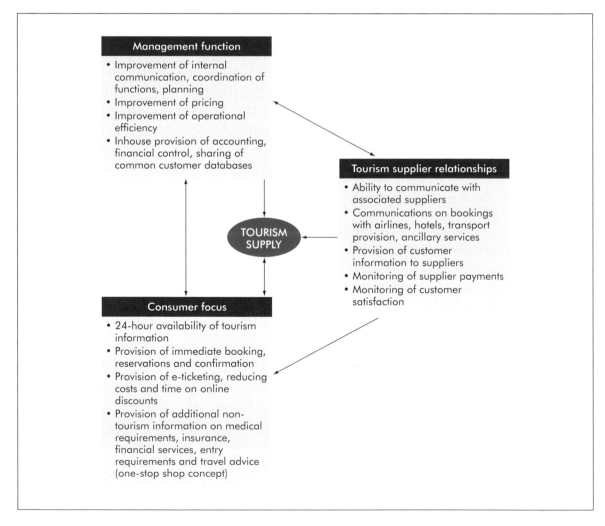

FIGURE 6.1   Examples of the impact of ICTs on tourism supply

- to gain a competitive edge
- to improve business performance and productivity, and to develop new businesses
- to facilitate new ways of managing and organizing business activities

One good illustration of the way ICTs have been harnessed to transform the supply of tourism products and their distribution is given in Insight 6.1. What Insight 6.1 shows is the scale and significance of e-tourism (i.e. travel booked and paid for electronically, typically involving paper-less ticketing, but to understand why this has emerged, the role of the consumer needs to be considered.

INSIGHT 6.1

The scale of e-tourism in the USA and Europe

The Travel Industry Association of America estimated that in 2003, 40 per cent of online travel bookers make all their travel purchases online. This is significant for a US population of 98.3 million who are estimated to be online. In Europe, Marcussen's (2004) report, 'The online travel market in Europe 1998–2006' (www.crt.dk/trends) found that the market for online travel was worth 11.2 billion euros in 2003. This had risen from 7.6 billion in 2002 and this was worth about 5.2 per cent of the European travel market. This is expected to rise to 20.5 billion euros in 2005, with the UK having the largest market share, Germany with 21 per cent, France 11 per cent, and Scandinavia, Finland and Iceland with 10 per cent. The Benelux countries, Austria, Switzerland and Ireland had an 11 per cent share and Italy, Spain, Portugal and Greece had a 7 per cent share.

The consumer and ICTs: The distribution channels

This chapter provides an overview of the principal areas where tourism and IT interact and highlights the e-tourism revolution. There is a growing literature on this expanding area of tourism research and publications by Sheldon (1997), Inkpen (1998), Buhalis (2003), O'Connor (2004) and Page (2004) are very worthwhile for further reading since they deal with many of the technical issues and recent developments. One of the easiest ways to begin any examination of ICTs in tourism is to consider the distribution channels in tourism, and how the tourism industry delivers their products and services to the consumer. Figure 6.2 shows that the consumer normally purchases the 'tourism product' in one of four ways: through a travel agent, via a tour operator, through a regional tourism organization (RTOs) or directly using an ICT technology to purchase the product(s). It is notable that in a climate of declining state financial resources, more innovative

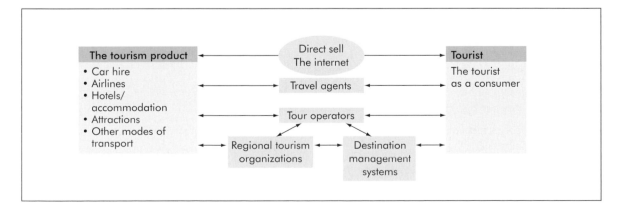

FIGURE 6.2 Distribution channels in tourism

RTOs such as Tourism Auckland are acting as an intermediary and raising funds through commissions on the sale of travel products. At each point of sale, the exchange of information is vital and for it to flow quickly, accurately and directly between the customer, intermediaries and the suppliers involved in Figure 6.2, ICTs are vital. Although ICTs are not a solution for poor business performance by individual enterprises or tourism organizations, the use of ICTs does raise a number of fundamental challenges for the tourism sector, namely a long-term vision for their strategic use of IT and the introduction and maintenance of the most appropriate technology for business processes, and ongoing training and staff development. ICTs also have another vital role to play given the nature of the tourism product, which is perishable and cannot be stored or resold at a later stage: they are useful in selling and filling capacity or trying to match supply with demand – the ultimate aim of managing tourism. In the tour operator sector, ICTs have enabled the sale of 'last-minute holidays' at a substantial discount to fill capacity. ICTs also enable retailers to provide up-to-date representations and descriptions of the products they are selling through the use of ICTs. In this respect, ICTs can assist in cooperation within the tourism industry through fast and accurate communication and may offer some of the tools to develop global strategies. For example, Table 6.1 illustrates how ICTs can be used by tourism organizations to develop their businesses.

One of the most profound changes which has occurred in tourism through the impact of ICTs is in the ability of the tourism industry to respond to the changing requirements of consumers seeking high quality and value for money. ICTs have offered many opportunities for the tourism industry to find new ways of meeting this demand, where the rapid expansion of the more sophisticated or 'new tourist' (Poon 1993) challenged the industry to address the demands for smaller market segments. This is reflected in the greater degree of interactivity which ICTs are offering the consumer, particularly in an age where accurate information and detail on the products and experiences being sold to consumers is increasingly demanded. This is heralding what marketers are calling the 'one-to-one' marketing approach, where gaining intelligence on customers through the use of loyalty schemes and integration of the customer's demands (e.g. automated check-out) and improved service provision are designed to enhance levels of customer satisfaction. This has also been extended through the use of the internet as a communication medium. In effect, ICTs have really revolutionized the marketing, distribution, operational functions of tourism in both the private and public sector. For example, the International Air Transport Association recently announced that by 2007 all airline tickets will be paperless.

To understand the impact and significance of ICTs on specific aspects of the tourism industry, especially the different sectors such as the airlines, hotels and retailers, it is useful to outline the major developments in ICTs during the 1980s and 1990s and their implications for tourism in the new millennium.

TABLE 6.1 How tourism organizations can use ICTs to develop their business

- *Cost leadership*, to drive the unit price of production down

- *Product differentiation*, where ICTs can be used to add value or differentiate a product from the competition

- *Improved customer focus*, with ICTs helping to establish more targeted and detailed micro or niche markets through better use of market intelligence and market research

- *Market leadership*, where ICTs help to set the market conditions and enhance the ability to innovate, since they can be used to communicate more quickly with consumers

- *Improved integration of the supply chain*, as ICTs can manage core business and outsource non-core activities; they can also be used to manage strategic alliances

- *Improved communication with consumers*, with one-to-one marketing by email and technology (i.e. mobile phone email alerts)

- *Better response to competition*, by using ICT as a barrier to entry, improving supplier–supplier and consumer–supplier relationships

- *Re-engineering of business processes*, to create more virtual relationships

From computer reservation systems to global distribution systems in tourism

According to Sheldon (1997) the current technology used in the tourism industry dates to the 1950s and the development of the early **computer reservation systems** (CRSs) pioneered by the airline industry. These CRSs grew rapidly in the 1970s and 1980s (see Knowles and Garland 1994 and Archdale 1991 for more detail). In a typical CRS one would find:

- a central site housing the computer systems driving the CRS
- the network hardware at the central site and computer staff required to maintain it
- a series of front-end communication processors to process information and online storage devices at the central site.

This is complemented by satellite communications to remote communications concentrators in key cities that relay data from the earth station. The data are then relayed to reservation terminals and airports, giving rapid communication. The major change in the 1990s was the move from CRSs, which contained largely airline information for the proprietary airline, to systems containing data for multiple airlines. Sheldon (1997) examines the shift from CRSs to **global distribution systems** (GDSs) and Insight 6.2 traces the development of GDSs in the fast growing period to 2001 when their role in tourism was significantly challenged by the internet (O'Connor 2003).

The value of GDSs in the USA according to Sheldon (1997) were enormous and they became the main booking mechanism for travel, since a CRS will only show one airline's schedule whereas a GDS can show multiple carriers including flight schedules, passenger information, fare quotes and rules for travel and ticketing details. This has also been accompanied by the airlines' move towards the internet. Yet ICTs are not just confined to the traditional distribution channels. More recently, ICTs has been used in baggage and cargo handling systems and cabin automation and in-flight entertainment (see Page 2005 on the leading edge technology used by Singapore Airlines), safety systems on tourist transport and gate management and control at airports. What Figure 6.3 shows is how the management of luggage loading/unloading and the passenger flows are managed through the use of ICTs so that all elements in the system interconnect and the flow of passengers and luggage are managed to optimize the throughput.

INSIGHT 6.2

The development of GDSs

1976　Three North American airlines began to offer their GDSs – Apollo (United Airlines), Sabre (American Airlines) and PARS (TransWorld Airlines) as well as offering US travel agents terminals to access their systems

1981　Eastern Airlines established System One Direct Access (SODA)

1982　Delta Airlines launched its DATAS II system

1987　In Europe, the systems Galileo and Amadeus were formed and offered to travel agents. In Asia, the Abacus system was formed and also offered to travel agents

1988　Japan Airlines formed axess

1989　System One was purchased by a non-airline company – EDS. The merger of

1990　PARS and DATAS II resulted in the formation of Worldspan. In Japan, All Nippon Airways and Abacus formed Infini

1993　Galileo and Apollo were merged to establish Galileo International

1994　System One merged with Amadeus

1994　The rise of the internet and competition with the GDSs

2001　The largest GDSs in terms of bookings are Amadeus, Galileo, Sabre and Worldspan

Source: Page (1999: 187), modified from Sheldon (1997: 24); O'Connor (2003)

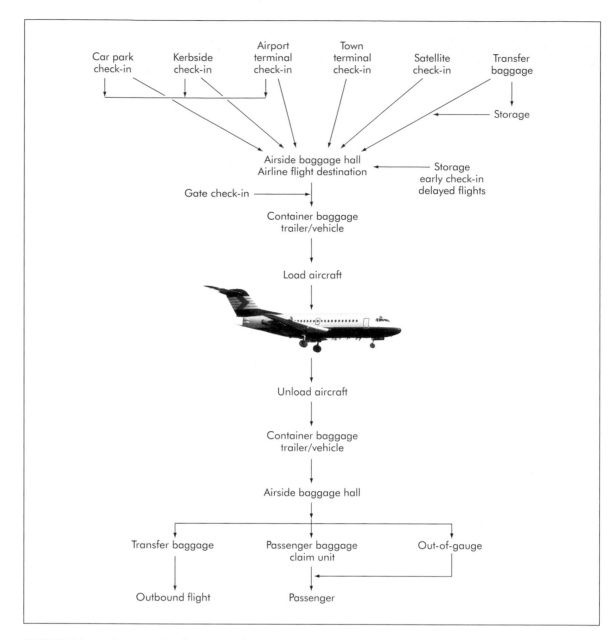

FIGURE 6.3 Luggage loading and unloading in the airport system. Source: Page (1999), adapted from Ashford and Moore (1992).

Denver International Airport opened five years late due to the problems with its automated baggage system (Goetz and Szyliowicz 1997). Similarly, the UK's air traffic control project at Swanwick found 15 000 errors in the computer software and is expected to be £100 million over budget. Therefore, one should not overestimate the problems of implementing new ICTs and the cost overruns which can be incurred in new projects with a large IT component. The cost of investment is also illustrated by Singapore Airlines Abacus GDS in Asia which has 12 500 terminals in 5000 travel agencies.

In fact commentators have argued that the introduction of GDSs is one of the single most important mechanisms for the globalization of the tourism industry. According to French (1998) the major tourism-generating markets of North America, Europe and Asia Pacific are fast approaching saturation with most travel agencies possessing reservation systems provided directly by or linked to one of the four leading GDSs (i.e. Amadeus, Galileo, Sabre and Worldspan). The market is saturated in that revenue growth in GDSs and profits are likely to stagnate. This is partly a function of the challenge posed by the internet and the rise of e-tourism.

Tourism and the internet: The e-tourism revolution

At the same time as the worldwide development of GDSs took place in the 1990s, a parallel development took place with the expansion of the role and influence of the internet and the **World Wide Web** (WWW). The **internet**, also known as the 'information superhighway', has revolutionized the potential relationship between the consumer and the suppliers in the tourism supply chain which poses a challenge for the traditional intermediaries (i.e. travel agents). The WWW provides instant access, interactive multimedia information and a greater degree of interactivity at the consumer's convenience. The WWW allows the fast distribution of multimedia information. It displays graphics, data, videos, images and sounds, opening up a new marketing communication channel for the tourism industry. The major change for the tourism industry is the shift from traditional advertising functions: the WWW requires a multidimensional content involving interactivity and the management of two-way information flows. Users are empowered (Buhalis 1998) as electronic commerce (e-commerce) becomes the byword of the new millennium.

Understanding the e-tourism revolution

Buhalis (2003: xix) defined **e-tourism** as:

> *the digitization of all the processes and value chains in tourism, travel and hospitality…industries that enable organizations to maximize their efficiency and effectiveness, where ICTs can allow businesses to communicate easier with its customers. A similar definition has also been used by the European Union's content funded Tourism Resource Centre Content Village (www.content-village.org), where etourism is about using internet technologies to transform the way tourism activities are conducted.*

Buhalis (2003) outlined the scope of e-tourism in terms of the supply distribution channel and ICTs creating intermediaries online (e.g. offline agencies which distribute online, e-tour operators, e-tourism agencies) and e-suppliers/principals including e-airlines and e-destinations. For example, many low-cost airlines now have more than 90 per cent of their bookings made online (see Chapter 8) and the low cost of processing such bookings reduces the company's operational costs while developing a new market – the online consumer interested in travel.

What makes the e-tourism revolution so distinctive is that whereas CRS and GDSs were airline controlled or supplier focused, the internet is not as closed and dependent upon supplier contracts. It is more open and competitive, also allowing suppliers to bypass intermediaries like travel agents and tour operators to reach the consumer directly if they choose to. Buhalis and Licata (2002) trace the evolution of the commerce era, from the GDS to the internet and the rise of **e-mediaries**, single suppliers and a complex pattern of e-tourism options as shown in Figure 6.4. Some single suppliers arose (i.e. British Airways.com) while multiple supplier sites evolved (called agency-killers!) and online travel agencies such as Expedia.com. A range of web-based travel agents have also arisen in Europe and internet portals like AltaVista and Yahoo have also set up online travel distribution. Last-minute agencies have also entered the market. In fact, a recent analysis of leading websites of online travel organizations highlighted the range of products they offer (Table 6.2), with many of the e-mediaries in tourism developed by non-tourism companies. Among the key development is the rise of software known as **dynamic packaging**.

Dynamic packaging allows consumers online to package products themselves, offering discounts and inducements for such multiple purchases and greater tailoring of products to meet individual needs as identified by Poon's (1989) 'new tourists' needs. Indeed, in February 2004 Lastminute.com announced that sales of dynamically

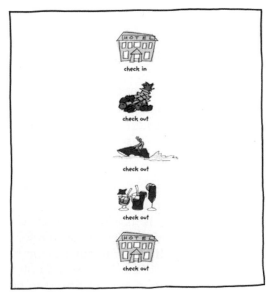

Image 6.1: The online travel agent market has grown rapidly since the late 1990s, such as the case of Expedia.com

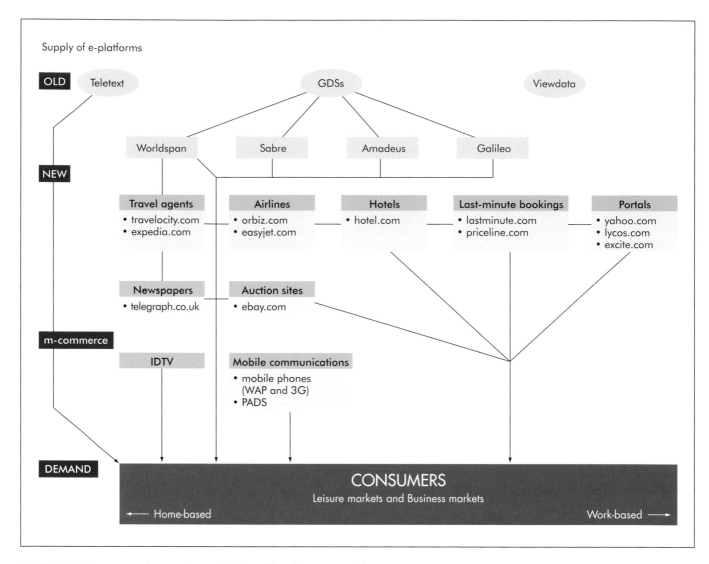

Supply of e-platforms

FIGURE 6.4   e-tourism and e-mediaries – The old, new and the consumer. Source: Buhalis and Licata (2002)

packaged products had exceeded £9 million, a dramatic increase on sales of £1.3 million in January 2003. Other operators are planning to follow this model of flexible 'build your own product' to incorporate more flexible demands from consumers as announced in 2005 by Thomson Holidays. Recent reports on this technology also suggests that, with the predicted growth in independent holidays for the next five years, travel agents who adopt this technology may be able to compete with tour operator packages, by offering significantly cheaper prices. The growing role of e-tourism across Europe among tourism businesses can be found in Case Study 6.1W.

To use the internet, users must use a browser (software that allows one to search and visit sites). Then to search for information on the web, one has to use a 'search engine' or 'directory', the most popular being Netscape and Yahoo. Other popular search engines are Excite, AltaVista and the Microsoft Corporation. Examining the role of travel and tourism and products on the internet is an almost impossible task because there is no easy way of identifying what constitutes a travel page. For this reason, the following exercise will help you to familiarize you with some of the ideas and arguments put forward so far on the growing interactivity which the internet offers travellers. Examine the following student exercise:

Student Exercise   Travel Sites on the Wide World Web

Using an internet connection, search the following site: www.yahoo.com
Once you are into the Yahoo! home page, search using the following term: 'travel'
How many categories of travel can you observe?
How many sites are there?
Now search for the following company and examine their home page: www.travelocity.com
What does this site allow you to do? How many categories of travel products and activities do they allow you to examine?
Does it replace the need for visiting a travel agent?
Last, search for the following site: www.lonelyplanet.com
What is the Lonely Planet site?
Look at their health site: What does it contain? How useful would it be for travellers going to destinations with significant health risks?

Yet consumers' use of the internet and adoption of new technology, as Case Study 6.1W suggests, is not a simple process as barriers exist to expanding business and consumer use of the internet.

TABLE 6.2   Leading websites by product

Products	Expedia	Travelocity	Priceline	Yahoo! Travel	Lastminute	Ebookers
Flights	X	X	X	X	X	X
Hotels	X	X	X	X	X	X
Car hire	X	X	X	X	X	X
Cruises	X	X		X	X	X
Packages: general	X	X	X	X	X	X
Packages: city breaks	X	X	X	X	X	X
Packages: sport and event holidays		X				X
Last-minute deals	X		X	X	X	X
Corporate travel						X
Destination information	X	X	X	X	X	X
Visa/health information	X	X	X	X	X	X
Event/attraction tickets	X				X	
Train*				X		
Insurance	X	X	X	X	X	X
Airport parking						X
Bureau de Change						X
Restaurants					X	
Other non-email modes of communicating with consumers:						
Voice recognition hotel bookings					X	
WAP phones	X				X	
NTL/digital TV					X	
Personal digital assistants					X	

Notes
X = Product provision in February 2004
* = Provision of the facility by Qjump on Yahoo! Travel and absence from other sites may be a function of the www.Thetrainline.com
Source: © Mintel (2003) *Online Intermediaries*, updated and developed by the author, February 2004

Barriers to increasing online tourism use by consumers

Among analysts, there is a growing awareness that the online population comprises of a wide range of users, but two types exist:

- 'lookers', who browse and use the internet for travel planning
- 'bookers', who browse and purchase.

Among recent studies of internet use for tourism purposes, a five-stage decision process has been identified when travellers make internet purchases, comprising:

- awareness of alternative retail options
- attitudes towards using the internet as a shopping method
- intention of using the internet as a shopping tool
- the decision to accept/reject the internet as a shopping medium
- evaluation post-purchase

which, in part, is affected by a consumer's experience of using the internet. This process has been compounded by a general consumer reluctance to buy online due to constraints and barriers (Card, Chen and Cole 2004; Heung 2003) and research indicates that there are four critical factors:

- credibility of the website/retailers
- accuracy of information
- the robustness and suitability of the technology
- security of payment

associated with internet use. Another concern for the tourism industry is the slow uptake of **e-commerce**, despite its overriding role as a market leader in the tourism field. This raises the critical issue of what make a good e-tourism website. A study on www.weblyzard.com identified three key success factors for website optimization:

- user friendliness, with good navigation, an ability to segment customers, rich media presentation, customer support and a high level of perceived customer relationship management
- a user-friendly web search engine, with embedded keywords, good quality copy and a clear title page
- booker friendliness, with trust-building elements, low-price guarantees, a good comfort level and special offers (Image 6.2).

Image 6.2: The lastminute.com boom since the late 1990s has crested turbulence in tourism distribution, particularly in terms of disintermediation

The same study noted that these elements were affected by the expectations of the user, their experience of use, the speed and operability of the site. For the website provider, measuring the success of the site could be achieved by examining revenue generated, level of inquiries generated, page views, visits and hits. What this study also highlighted was that in supply chain terms, the website could provide value improvements through enhancement of existing communication with more customers, integration of the value chain and reducing bookings costs as exemplified by **e-booking** run by low-cost airlines.

But converting lookers to bookers remains a perennial problem for the tourism sector (Gianforte 2003), since in travel planning, tourist information sites and airline sites are used widely. But in booking, airline sites dominate online purchasing. In fact, the time taken by many consumers from looking to booking may even reach a month (see Page 2004) and so one needs to consider this problem when monitoring sales. With the continued growth of the internet, it is not surprising to find other sectors of the travel and tourism industry seeking to adopt and harness its powerful impact in a marketing and sales role, which is why attention now turns to the concept of destination management systems.

Destination management systems

There is a growing recognition in the public sector (see Chapter 14) that to develop and enhance the tourist experience in a destination, the public organizations responsible for tourism also need to develop a presence on the WWW and to take a lead in helping **small- or medium-sized enterprises** (SMEs) to distribute their products electronically. This is reflected in the development of **destination management system**s (DMSs) which are used to coordinate, develop and facilitate the production and delivery of the destination's tourism product. The initiative is usually taken by **regional tourism organization**s (RTOs) and may be very helpful for SME tourism enterprises to promote and sell their products. As a form of tourism marketing, DMSs in their most advanced state allow the reservations, promotion and distribution of tourism to take place. However, in their crudest form, a DMS is a storage mechanism with information on tourism suppliers, visitor attractions and other activities in the destination region. Such DMSs have a distinct geographical focus as O'Connor (2004) observed, as they store and distribute information about tourism, supplies and a region's tourism industry. These basic DMSs are often a redevelopment of RTOs' databases which comprise:

- editorial content about products and services
- data on tourism in the region

with multimedia content (e.g. photographs, videos and graphics). A typical construction of a DMS, with its constituent parts and functional links, is shown in Figure 6.5.

More sophisticated systems have call centres, multimedia kiosks, tourist information centre connections and links to GDSs as well as services for members. This is the basic format now being developed by visitscotland.com to help sell tourism products and services online, with a DMS

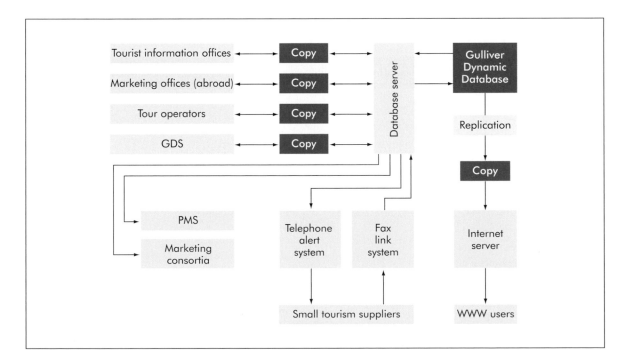

FIGURE 6.5 An example of a DMS: The Gulliver DMS. Source: O'Connor (2004: 182)

component. Some of the best examples of well-developed national DMSs according to O'Connor (2002) include:

- the Australian Tourism Commission
- Visit Britain
- the Canadian Tourism Commission
- the Finnish Tourism Board
- the Singapore Tourism Board.

As Figure 6.5 illustrates, a typical configuration of a DMS will achieve economies of scale by amalgamating a wide range of data sources and material in one place so that it only has to be maintained in one location (Table 6.3). As the WTO (1999) argue, the economies achieved by using ICTs are the creation and maintenance of one website which is only equivalent to the printing and distribution of a glossy brochure to a large audience. Much of this has evolved from the work of RTOs with background information on the region and data on individual products. Many RTOs make this information available through their tourist information centres. Although many RTOs' original function was not to sell products or to compete with tour operators, many recognize that simply distributing information on its own is not effective. A natural development for many RTOs has been the development of DMSs which allow customers to book products in the destination (pre-trip or after arrival). Not only does this bring extra revenue in commissions for RTOs but it also allows one port of call for all services where a wide range of tourism businesses are involved.

According to the WTO (1999), DMSs have been implemented on a piecemeal basis in the late 1980s and early 1990s but the new millennium has seen major growth in this area. The implementation of ICTs also led to calls for a programme of change management when DMSs and other marketing functions are radically changed. The outcome for RTOs is the opening up of a new marketplace on a much more global scale with the impact of the internet and implementation of DMSs. The chief function of the DMSs is communication with consumers, supplier and tourism stakeholders in the region (a stakeholder is a party who has an interest or involvement in tourism and can wield political influence and power). The challenge for the DMS is for it to be appealing, and exciting because of the sheer volume of competition. Despite the high cost of development, key success factors in DMS implementation include public sector involvement, high quality data on the region's tourism industry and products, and links to other external systems such as travel e-mediaries, as well as being strategically aligned to the marketing of the region.

TABLE 6.3   Some of the applications for which destination management systems are being used

- Design and production of printed material
- Tourist information centre – information and reservations
- Call centre services (information and reservations)
- Information and reservation kiosks
- Database marketing
- Interactive television – multimedia information
- Supply of data to third parties (e.g. the media and for public relations purposes)
- Conference marketing
- Project/event management
- Site interpretation for visitors
- Tourism supplier liaison
- Research design
- Administration and finance functions
- Performance management and evaluation

Source: Modified from WTO (1999)

Many of the analysts studies of e-tourism highlight the lack of development in the mature market, especially among the 55–65-year-old age group who have not embraced PCs. However, evidence from many EU countries and evidence from the USA indicate this market will continue to see its use of e-tourism rise in the next decade, which is important given the ageing of the population as a whole in most developed countries. Whilst some countries have seen specialist operators develop to target groups such as the mature market (e.g. Saga in the UK), the use of telephone sales still underpins the product base. Even so, in Europe analysts estimate that there are over 11 million internet users and this is rising annually, especially in the more developed western Europe regions. But e-tourism is not just being delivered through the internet.

Many tourism suppliers have started to harness the value of new technology available via WAP mobile telephones, the expanding availability of broadband access globally and, in some countries, interactive digital television. Figure 6.6 summarizes some of the principal areas of technology as noted by the European Commission in (2003) *Working Together for the Future of European Tourism: Mobile Services for Tourism* (and the wider significance of these changes can be accessed at www.digitalords.com, which looks at wireless applications in tourism).

As Figure 6.6 shows evolving technology now allows internet services to be transferred to mobile terminals as a more flexible form of provision. For example, a consumer can text a railway company to request the train times for their journey and purchase a ticket. This is also allowing for suppliers to rethink how they target consumers, reducing costly brochure production in some cases and providing new opportunities for **e-tailing**. Much of this market hangs upon the uptake and use of 3G (Third Generation) mobile phones and other technologies.

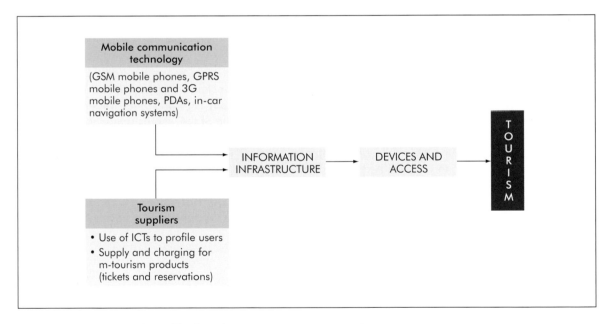

FIGURE 6.6   m-tourism – The key elements. Source: Developed from EU (2003)

Conclusion

ICTs have undoubtedly revolutionized the distribution and management of tourism supply issues. Buhalis (1998: 419) poignantly illustrates the effect of ICTs on the tourism industry:

> [it has] stimulated radical changes in the operation and distribution of the tourism industry...the most apparent example in tourism is the re-engineering of the booking process, which gradually becomes rationalized and enables both consumers and the industry to save considerable time in identifying, amalgamating, reserving and purchasing tourism products.

This has allowed tourists greater flexibility in their choice of holiday experience and a greater degree of autonomy in their mode of purchasing travel products. Not only have ICTs allowed the development of virtual enterprises, they have also applied more pressure to tourism companies to stay ahead of the game and ensure they can compete in the marketplace. Forrester Research (1999) identified the impact of the internet on customer loyalty: 69 per cent of internet bookers were found to be disloyal while a further 24 per cent were curious bookers and only 7 per cent were loyal bookers who stayed with the same site. In other words, the majority of travel consumers, if Forrester's research is typical of global consumer trends, are prone to use the internet to shop around to get the best value and are not concerned with which company or site they use. Time had not altered that radically: in this, the early development of online bankings, brand loyalty has not become a dominant feature, but it may do once the market matures. According to the WTO (1999) the real challenge for existing travel-related companies is to compete head on with the new intermediaries that have entered the market by building relationships and alliances as well as developing brand trust and adopting niche marketing strategies. The travel companies may gradually be able to nurture their clients on to online booking while keeping brand loyalty.

The greatest challenge has to be – the portal. A 'portal' is an online organization with potentially millions of clients using it as its main service – it might be a search engine or a software provider or television distributor. The portal is critical for tourism organizations as the portal is the site which one first sees when using web browser software – the default home page that appears when one first goes online. The most popular portals are providers such as AOL and compuserve, as well as search engines such as Yahoo, Excite and HotBot. These portals effectively control distribution and so any organization seeking to have a presence on the WWW must partner with a portal to distribute their products. As the WTO (1999) argue, currently portals view travel companies as providing information of interest to its users. With portals like Yahoo reporting millions of page views per day, it is going to be essential for tourism organizations to partner with these organizations to gain effective distribution. This does mean that the nature of travel and tourism marketing is dramatically changing alongside the impact of technology on sales functions. But a note of caution also needs to be added: there are many examples of areas of the tourism industry which have not embraced ICTs, especially in the small-scale bed-and-breakfast sector, which is partly the result of the low skill base of many staff. In contrast, tour operators have seized the value of the web as a management tool to harness and manage demand, especially in the tailoring of products. There is no doubt that ICTs have revolutionized the supply of tourism. Examples of their impact will be highlighted in the following chapters, which examine different aspects of supply in terms of tour operating and retailing, transport and accommodation and hospitality services.

Discussion questions

1 Why are ICTs important to the management of tourism operations?

2 How have ICTs evolved in the period since the 1970s?

3 What is a destination management system?

4 What future technological changes in ICTs may affect the tourism sector?

References

Archdale, G. (1991) 'Computer excavation systems – the international scene', *INSIGHTS*, November: D15–20.

Ashford, H. and Moore, C. (1992) *Airport Finance*, New York: Van Nostrand Reinhold.

Buhalis, D. (1998) 'Strategic use of information technologies in the tourism industry', *Tourism Management*, 19 (5): 409–23.

Buhalis, D. (2003) *eTourism*. Harlow: Prentice Hall.

Buhalis, D. and Licata, M.C. (2002) 'The future e-tourism intermediaries', *Tourism Management*, 23 (3): 207–20.

Card, J., Chen, C. and Cole, S. (2003) 'Online travel products shopping: Differences between shoppers and nonshoppers', *Journal of Travel Research*, 42 (2): 133–39.

Cooper, C., Fletcher, J., Gilbert, D., Shepherd, R. and Wanhill, S. (1998) *Tourism: Principles and Practice, Second Edition*. Harlow: Longman.

DTI (2003) *e-Commerce Impact Study of the Tourism Sector in the UK*. London: DTI.

Economist Intelligence Unit (2003) *e-Readiness Rankings*. London: Economist Intelligence Unit.

EU (2003) *Mobile Services for Tourism*. Brussels: EU.

European Commission (2003) *Working Together for the Future of European Tourism: Mobile Services for Tourism*. Brussels: EU.

Forrester Research (1999) *Travel Bookers Aren't Loyal*. Cambridge, MA: Forrester Research.

French, T. (1998) 'The future of global distribution systems', *Travel and Tourism Analyst*, 3: 1–17.

Gianforte, G. (2003) 'The world at our fingertips – how online companies can turn clicks into bookings', *Journal of Travel Research*, 10 (1): 79–86.

Goetz, A. and Szyliowicz, J. (1997) 'Revisiting transportation planning and decision making theory: The case of Denver International Airport', *Transportation Research A*, 31(4): 263–80.

Heung, V. (2003) 'Internet usage by international travelers: Reasons and barriers', *Contemporary Journal of Hospitality Management*, 15 (7): 370–78.

Inkpen, G. (1998) *Information Technology for Travel and Tourism, Second Edition*. Harlow: Longman.

Knowles, S.T. and Garland, M. (1994) 'The strategic importance of CRSs in the airline industry', *Travel and Tourism Analyst*, 4: 4–16.

Marcussen, C. (2004) Trends in European Internet Distribution of Travel and Tourism Services, crt.dk/uk/staff/chm/trends.htm

Mintel (2003) 'Online intermediaries – revolutionising travel distribution', *Travel and Tourism Analyst*, February, 1–42.

O'Connor, P. (2002) 'The changing face of European destination management systems', *Travel and Tourism Analyst*, April.

O'Connor, P. (2003) 'Online intermediaries – revolutionising travel distribution – global', *Travel and Tourism Analyst*, January.

O'Connor, P. (2004) *Using Computers in Hospitality, Third Edition*. London: Thomson.

Page, S.J. (1999) *Transport and Tourism*. Harlow: Addison Wesley Longman.

Page, S.J. (2004) 'eTravel in Europe', *Travel and Tourism Analyst*, May.

Page, S.J. (2005) *Transport and Tourism: Global Perspectives, Second Edition*. Harlow: Prentice Hall.

Poon, A. (1989) 'Competitive strategies for a new tourism', in C.P. Cooper (ed.) *Progress in Tourism, Recreation and Hospitality Management*, 1. London: Belhaven.

Poon, A. (1993) *Tourism, Technology and Competitive Strategies*. Wallingford, Oxon: CAB International.

Sheldon, P. (1997) *Tourism Information Technology*. Wallingford, Oxon: CAB Publishing.

WTO (World Tourism Organization) (1999) *Marketing Tourism Destinations Online: Strategies for the Information Age*. Madrid: World Tourism Organisation.

Further reading

These two books offer a good introduction to this subject.

Buhalis, D. (2003) *e-Tourism*. Harlow: Prentice Hall.

O' Connor, P. (1999) *Electronic Information Distribution in Tourism and Hospitality*. Wallingford, Oxon: CAB Publishing.

7

Travel Intermediaries – Tour Operators and Travel Agents

Learning outcomes

After reading this chapter and answering the questions, you should be able to:

- understand the functions of travel and tourism intermediaries

- be able to identify the characteristics of integrated tourism companies

- have an awareness of the significance of travel distribution channels in tourism

- outline some of the challenges facing the travel agency sector in travel retailing.

Overview

The travel product, be it a flight or hotel room, differs from manufactured goods in that it must be sold or lost; it cannot be stocked indefinitely. This feature has led to the creation of thousands of intermediaries around the world packaging two or more complementary travel elements. This chapter considers the diverse range of intermediaries in the travel and tourism industry and the challenge of technology for the travel agency sector. The issues associated with regulating the tour operator sector are discussed together with the impact of large integrated operators and the effects of consolidation and concentration in the tourism sector.

Introduction

Retailing tourism products to consumers is a key element in the production, selling and distribution of tourism services where different organizations link the supply to the source of demand. To connect supply and demand, the tourism industry has to communicate, trade and interact with the tourist and it does this through the distribution channel (i.e. how it is sold to the consumer) using intermediaries, which are agents who sell products for the industry. A distribution channel is a combination of intermediaries who seek to cooperate to sell a product, while a product may be sold through a variety of distribution channels, each of which may have different distribution channels (Figure 7.1). What the intermediaries do is transform the goods available by bundling together the raw components into a product that can be both purchased and consumed, and the pace of change in this sector can be observed by consulting industry news sites such as www.travelmole.com and www.ttglive.com.

Historically, tourism products were retailed through travel agents (intermediaries) who offered products from tour operators (who are known as principals), but, as Chapter 6 has shown, the e-tourism revolution has dramatically changed that mode of distribution. In Europe, Eurostat estimated that the tour operator and travel agency sector has 36 353 businesses involved in these activities within the 15 countries of the EU. The largest concentration of activity exists in the four main countries of Germany, with 9033 businesses with an €5925 million turnover per annum; Italy, with 6350 businesses and €6481 million turnover; France, with 2279 businesses and an €6866 million turnover and the UK with 6050 businesses and a €14 710 million turnover. The use of different distribution forms of travel products varies across the EU. Belgian, Danish, German, Greek and Austrian tourists prefer to book direct with operators, whereas in other countries travel agents are a preferred form of booking, usually for package holidays. The exception is Spain, where travel agents are also used to book domestic travel, especially for late booking in Spain and Italy.

More recent trends, such as direct selling, have changed the relationship between the tourism sector and the public and cut out the travel agent. Companies such as Portland Holidays sell direct to the customer. In recent years this relationship has changed again with the impact of information communication technologies (ICTs) such as the World Wide Web and ease of communication by email, to create a new form of distribution – a virtual distribution channel (see Insight 7.1 about Cendant). What these characteristics of different EU markets and new trends in retailing show is that the nature of tourism distribution channels has undergone profound changes in recent years via the use of ICTs but also due to industry changes. These changes to the distribution channels have not removed the need for intermediaries as they still exist. Instead the e-tourism revolution has expanded the range and scope of these for consumers and for businesses seeking to sell their products. Nevertheless, as Cooper

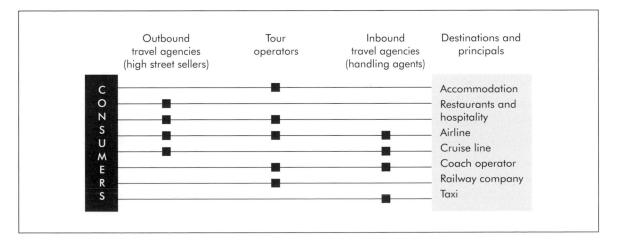

FIGURE 7.1 Tourism distribution mechanisms. Source: Modified from Buhalis and Laws (2001: 11)

et al. (2005: 422–3) reiterate, travel intermediaries, in spite of changes in ICTs, still bestow a range of advantages for:

- *producers,* in terms of bulk selling, thereby transferring risk to the tour operator and reducing promotion costs
- *consumers,* via reducing time and costs of searching for products by purchasing an inclusive tour product and by gaining the specialist knowledge and advice of the tour operator. The bulk purchasing power of tour operators may reduce consumer prices by up to 60 per cent of the price a consumer would have to pay for a non-packaged product
- **destinations**, by bringing volume business. But critics point to the growing marketing control and influence which **tour operator**s exert, as this chapter will show in terms of concentration and consolidation.

The tour operator

Defining 'the tour operator' is a far from easy process because their role, activities and form have changed dramatically from the early days when Thomas Cook first organized a package trip by rail in the 1840s (see Chapter 2). One useful approach is to identify what a tour operator does as means of establishing its characteristics and form. In simple terms, a tour operator will organize, package together (i.e. assemble different elements of the tourism experience) and offer them for sale to the public either through the medium of a brochure, leaflet or advertisement, or using ICT to display its offering. For a tour operator to offer a package, also known as an 'inclusive tour', it will normally have to have at least two elements which are offered for sale at the inclusive sale price and will involve a stay of more than 24 hours in overnight accommodation. These elements would normally include transport (aircraft seat), accommodation at a destination, return transfer from airport to accommodation, services of a tour representative, insurance and other tourist services such as car hire and excursions (Page 2003).

The nature of those packages sold by the tourism industry can normally be divided into two types: those using the traditional charter flight and those which use scheduled flights, where it is uneconomic for the tour operator to purchase charter flights. Other types of package may also exist, including multi-destination types that visit more than one country/destination and linear tours or itineraries provided by coach holidays.

The type of packages are often segmented according to:

- those focused on a mode of travel, such as ferry or coach holiday, typified in the UK by Shearings and Wallace Arnold. The package may also be based on twin-transport packages such as fly–drive, which are very popular with inbound tourists in the USA
- mode of accommodation, where hotel chains become tour operators by packaging their surplus capacity to offer weekend or short breaks in business-oriented hotels, selling rail or air transport and visits to attractions as an all-inclusive package for holiday-makers
- whether they are international or domestic packages
- length of holiday: short breaks (i.e. less than four nights away) or long holidays (of more than four nights)
- distance, where the market is divided into short-haul and long-haul: over 90 per cent of UK outbound packages are short-haul
- destination type (e.g. city breaks, beach holidays, adventure holidays) (from Page 2003).

These tours may be organized by small independent tour operators, who specialize in certain segments, or larger operators such as TUI AG, which have trans-European operations, and MyTravel Group, with global operations. In addition, there are over 300 inbound tour operators who organize the itineraries, activities and logistics of inbound visitors to countries. The British inbound tour operators are represented by their trade organization – the British Incoming Tour Operators Association (BITOA). But why do tour operators exist and why do people use them? The answer is reflected in the way they operate and the economic benefits they provide to the customer.

The Cendant Corporation – and travel distribution

The Cendant Corporation (www.cendant.com) is one of the USA's largest integrated tourism companies with a US$18192 million revenue in 2003 and pre-tax income of US$2231 million; travel revenue accounted for US$10033 million of total revenue. The corporation comprises four main activities. Real estate (property) services are one. Hospitality services are another, and Cedant is the world's largest timeshare company (e.g. RCI) and largest franchisor of hotel brands (see Chapter 10 on accommodation), and Europe's largest marketing agent for holiday rental properties. It provides vehicle services, including the Avis and Budget car rental (which it acquired in 2002) companies and provides financial services. But it is in its travel distribution services that its impact on the tourism industry is very notable, given its major investment and knowledge of ICTs. It provides a global business service in information sharing and transaction processing, which is a core element of ICTs for the tourism industry, with a leading global distribution system (see Chapter 6 for more detail) (Galileo International). This GDS distributes travel products via 43 000 travel agents, with access to 500 airlines, 30 car rental companies, 60 000 hotel properties and the leading cruise ship companies. It has developed a key role in the online distribution services, with systems for hotel operators, dynamic packaging technology for both travel agents and consumers. It has a key stake in the direct marketing to consumers via its Orbitz, cheaptickets.com and lodging.com online businesses. It also operates one of the USA's top five retail travel agency chains – Cendant Travel – and acquired similar business interests in the UK in 2003. It operates a major business travel organizer software – Travelport – to allow mid- to large-sized companies to reduce their travel costs. Cendant also announced in late 2004 that it was seeking to acquire one of the UK's leading e-tourism businesses, e-bookers, to form the basis of its European online travel distribution business.

What the example of Cendant illustrates is that the company has evolved from a multifaceted distribution chain into a multichannel distribution company. The company's move into Europe underpins the estimated scale of growth which can be achieved, since only around 10 per cent of travel bookings are made online in Europe compared to over 30 per cent in the USA. The Cendant Corporation employs over 90 000 employees and sells to consumers in over 100 countries.

The business of tour operation

Tour operators have the ability to purchase services and elements of the tourism experience from other principals or suppliers at significant discounts by buying in bulk. They fulfil a major role in the tourism sector as they allow the different tourism sectors to sell their capacity in advance – often a long time in advance as contracts are drawn up a year prior to tourists using accommodation or services. This obviates the need for smaller, specialized businesses to market and distribute their product with a wide range of potential retailers, hoping that customers will choose their product or service over and above others'. The bulk purchase agreements in large resort areas mean that, in the summer season, the complete capacity of hotels, self-catering and other forms of accommodation may be block-booked leaving the firm free to develop its own expertise in running or managing its business. Similarly, the tour operator connects together with all the ancillary services to negotiate contracts and deals which will allow a holiday to be sold and be delivered on the ground.

In operational terms, the tour operator will bulk purchase airline seats, airport transfer services from coach operators and taxis in the destination area and a whole host of local entertainment and visitor attraction opportunities to sell them to clients at the booking stage or in the destination. Tour operators traditionally have provided a guaranteed level of sales which allowed principals to fix their costs in advance and allow the operators to achieve economies of scale by giving them heavily discounted rates on their purchase. This is a business opportunity for the tourism sector, with the tour operator creating a package, product or experience by assembling the elements, and advertising and selling them using the third party agents to deliver each element on the ground. It is obvious that tourist dissatisfaction is possible under this system: service interruptions or breakdowns can occur in the delivery since so many interconnected elements are involved. Therefore, for tour operators, managing the tourist experience to ensure the holiday experience is an enjoyable and rewarding one is a key element of customer care, to which we will return later. The tour operator will often add a mark-up on the product they are selling by calculating all the input costs, their overheads, profit margin and then producing a price.

Among the risks the tour operator takes in planning a holiday include:

- estimating the likely market
- competing with long-established tour operators in a destination who have a recognizable brand
- putting major investment in human resources and infrastructure to set up a destination (Page 2003).

The business performance of tour operators is determined by the company's ability to buy its product components (i.e. aircraft seats, accommodation and transfers) at a competitive price, and resell at a price lower than a consumer could find it assembling the same product. One consequence is that tour operators standardize packages, which differ little between destinations, to keep prices low. Technology (e.g. the internet), is a challenge to this process as it may help the consumer to try and beat such prices, but tour operators have managed to remain competitive in their pricing and buying strategies.

Tour operators may keep their prices low by:

- negotiating low prices from supplier
- reducing profit margins
- cutting their cost structures (Page 2003).

Where tour operators have become integrated tourism companies and operate their own aircraft, prices for air travel can be reduced by heavy usage of an aircraft (i.e. the number of flights it can achieve each day).

To achieve cost savings, charter flights need high load factors to break even, typically 80–90 per cent, compared to 50–70 per cent for scheduled flights (depending on the cost base of the carrier). This means that any unsold seats may be unloaded on to the market at cost or less to fill the aircraft, either as seat-only sales/cheap holidays or for purchase through **consolidators** (air-brokers). Consolidators purchase surplus capacity and have the responsibility for marketing and selling such seats. For the airline/tour operator, additional passengers may yield extra revenue from onboard duty-free sales or through purchasing the company's holiday package even if a loss is made on the flight.

With charter operators, costing their price is a complex process, as 'dead legs' at the beginning and end of a season have to be incorporated. At the beginning of a season, an aircraft will fly out with tourists but return empty and vice versa at the end of the season. To extend the season, operators may provide inducements such as low-cost accommodation to attract low-season business to fill capacity. One such example is the winter flows of elderly people from Northern Europe wintering in the Mediterranean. Hotels discount their rates hoping guests will spend money in their premises and thus compensate for discounts given at a quiet time of year.

Regulating tour operating

Since the 1960s, the UK has seen a number of massive tour operator collapses, which led ABTA, the Association of British Travel Agents, to set up its bonding scheme in the 1970s. In 1975, the government introduced a compulsory contribution of 2 per cent of operator turnover by tour operators to ABTA's bonding scheme. This is to safeguard tourists from company insolvencies and being stranded overseas, as happened in the 1990s with the collapse of the International Leisure Group, which severely depleted the fund. For tour operators wishing to operate specific programmes, a licensing scheme which the Civil Aviation Authority (CAA) operates in the UK requires them to obtain an Air Travel Organizers Licence (ATOL). The ATOL data are very useful as they identify some of the dimensions of this market, as the discussion will show.

Trends in the European holiday market: Integration, consolidation and concentration

The European market is one of the most highly developed and complex areas of activity in the development of tour operators globally. It has seen a great deal of activity, particularly in investment, acquisitions and mergers. For example, in February 2005, the UK leading coach operators Shearings and Wallace Arnold merged, to create a combined passenger base of 1 million and 3400 employees; the venture capitalist 3i owned 67 per cent of the shares. This reflects issues of strategy and scale in seeking to reduce competition and develop a pan-European business. The European Travel Monitor estimated that 326 million outbound trips were taken in Europe, involving 2947 million nights away. In the European leisure travel market found that 53 per cent of Europeans had been away on a holiday, with a stronger propensity for people from the more affluent western European regions to travel than those from the southern regions (i.e. the Mediterranean).

The markets that dominate outbound travel are Germany, the UK and Scandinavia. A significant proportion of the holiday traffic is on inclusive tours to the main destinations of Spain, France and Germany, with Asia Pacific the fastest-growing area of activity. These trends and travel patterns can be explored further in the case of the UK using the ATOL data.

In Europe, large integrated tour operators dominate channels via integration:

- *vertically*, via the value chain, to include transport, business travel, tour operating and travel retailing
- *horizontally*, by amalgamations, takeovers and mergers of competing companies in the same business (e.g. TUI AG's purchase of Thomson Holidays)
- *in destination areas*, by acquiring, developing or buying equity stakes in accommodation as well as incoming tour and locally based coach operators.

Much of the growth in the European tour operator market has exhibited this pattern of concentration into fewer large integrated operators with aggressive commercial strategies of high-volume sales, purchasing or providing capacity at low cost with a resulting low profit margin. The commercial strategy seeks to grow the control of the tourism sector, with profitability based on cost control, the use of ICTs and profit based on high-volume turnover, with low profit margins per unit sold. The overall pattern of European concentration in the tour operator sector is shown in Table 7.1 which highlights five major groupings: The World of TUI, controlled by the German parent company TUI AG; Thomas Cook AG; First Choice, Airtours plc and the Rewe Group. The case of TUI AG is shown in Insight 7.2.

However, at the individual country level, the real significance of tour operators such as the World of TUI is evident in their overall control of the package holiday maker in terms of volume and extent. For this reason, attention now turns to the UK.

The UK outbound package tour market

In the UK, licensing of tour operations by the Civil Aviation Authority via its Air Travel Organizers Licensing Scheme (ATOL) provides a good insight into how far the main concerns of consumer groups and government regulatory bodies are warranted regarding the control which integrated groups have on the market. Critics have pointed to the potentially anti-competitive practices of large groups in forcing smaller operators out of the market to gain market share and control, as many Monopoly and Mergers Committee reports on the tour operator market indicated. Four main groups emerge in terms of passengers carried in the year to March 2004, dominated by TUI UK Ltd, MyTravel (despite its ongoing financial problems stemming from rapid expansion and competitive pressures), First Choice and Thomas Cook. However, a more revealing set of data exist in Table 7.3, which groups the passengers licensed to the Top Ten tour operating groups and highlights the rapid expansion of the e-tourism market, represented by the Lastminute Group and the Interactive Corporation Group. This is a major shift compared to even five years previously.

More in-depth analysis from ATOL examines the recent trends in the price of ATOL holidays but this does not cover the rapid development of flight-only purchased from low-cost airlines. However, the UK government concerns for competition in this area of holiday purchasing led to a

TABLE 7.1 Concentration in the European tour operating industry: Five major groups

Mother company and subsidiaries	Intra-European Tour-operating groups				
	The World of TUI	Thomas Cook AG	First Choice	Airtours plc (MyTravel)	Rewe Group

TOUR OPERATING ('MANUFACTURERS' – WHOLESALERS)	• TUI GERMANY
	  • TUI UK (THOMSON TG)
	  • TUI NETHERLANDS
	  • TUI AUSTRIA
	  • TUI FINLAND
	  • TUI SUISSE
	  • TUI IRELAND
	  • TUI POLAND
	• AUSTRAVEL
	• COUNTRY COTTAGES (UK & FRANCE)
	• CHEZ NOUS
	• CRYSTAL
	• BLAKES COTTAGES
	• MAGIC TRAVEL
	• SIMPLY TRAVEL
	• HORIZON
	• BUDGET TRAVEL
	• PORTLAND DIRECT
	• SKYTOURS
	• SOMETHING SPECIAL HOLIDAYS
	• SPANISH HBR
	• AIRTOURS (GER)
	• AIR CONTI
	• L'TUR
	• NOUVELLES FRONTIERES
	• TRAVEL UNIE INTERN
	• EX-ARKE
	• HOLLAND INTERN.
	  • FIRST
	  • FIRST TRAVEL MANAGEMENT
	• KRAS
	• VTB-VAB REISEN
	• JETAIR
	• FRITIDSRESOR
	  • STAR TOUR
	  • ROYAL TOURS
	  • TEMA
	  • NORDPOOL (or NRT NORDPOOL)
	• PRISMA TOURS
	• SCAN HOLIDAY
	• FINNMATKAT
	• GULET TOUROPA
	• ITV (SWITZERLAND)
	  • VOGELE
	  • IMHOLZ
	  • TRAVAK
		• JMC HOLIDAYS
		• C&N GROUP
		  • NECKERMANN REISEN
		  • NECKERMANN BELGIUM
		    • ALLAIR
		    • SUNSNACKS
		  • NECKERMANN NETHERL
		    • BROERE REISEN
		  • NECKERMANN AUSTRIA
		    • KUONI
		  • CONDOR
		• BUCHER REISEN
		• FISCHER REISEN
		• TERRAMAR
		• KREUTZER REISEN
		• THOMAS COOK HOLIDAYS
		• GRUPO VIAJES IBERIA
		• SUNWORLD
		• FLYING COLOURS
		• SUNSET
		• INSPIRATIONS
		  • CLUB 18–30
		  • NEILSON
		  • STYLE
		• ACCOLADIA
		• TIME OFF
		• AIR MARINE
		• HAVAS VOYAGES (FRANCE)
			• FIRST CHOICE HOLIDAYS
			• UNIJET
			• HAYES & JARVIS
			• RAINBOW
			• FLEXISKI
			• MEON
			• SUNSAIL
			• CROWN BLUE LINE
			• SUNQUEST
			• EXODUS
			• BARCELO TRAVEL
			• TEN TOUR
			• NAZAR
			• TAURUS
				• MYTRAVEL
				• BRIDGE TRAVEL GROUP
				• CRESTA HOLIDAYS
				• DIRECT HOLIDAYS
				• PANORAMA
				• TRADEWINDS
				• EUROSITES
				• JETSET
				• MANOS
				• LEGER
				• SUNWAY TRAVEL
				• SCANDINAVIAN LEISURE GROUP
				  • VING
				  • SAGA
				  • ALWAYS
				  • TJAEREBORG
				  • SPIES
				• FROSCH TOURISTIK INTERN (FTI)
				  • CA FERNTOURISTIK
				  • FROSCH TOURISTIK
				  • LAL SPRACHREISEN
				  • CLUB VALTUR
				  • SPORT-SCHECK REISEN
				• SUNAIR (Belgium-previous brand)
				• TRIVSELRESOR
				• MERLIN
				• VACATION EXPRESS
				• SUNTIPS
				• SUNQUEST
				• TRAVEL SERVICES INTERN
					• LTU TURISTIK
					  • MEIER'S WELTREISEN
					  • MARLBORO REISEN
					  • SMILE & FLY
					  • ITS REISEN
					  • ITS AUSTRIA
					  • ATLAS REISEN
					  • DERTOUR
					  • ADAC-REISEN
					  • JAHN
					  • TJAEREBORG
					  • MEIER'S

TRANSPORTATION (CHARTER AIRLINES)	• BRITANNIA
	  • BLUE SCANDINAVIA
	  • HAPAG LLOYD
	  • HAPAG LLOYD (CRUISE)
	  • TUI CRUISE
		• JMC AIRLINES
		• FLYING COLOURS
		• AIRWORLD
		• CALEDONIAN
		• CONDOR
			• AIR 2000	• AIRTOURS INTERN
				• FROSCH TOURISTIK INTERN
				  • FLY FTI
				• PREMIAIR
				• AIR BELGIUM
				• CARNIVAL CRUISES
				• COSTA CROCIERE
					• LTU LUFTTRANSPORT
					• UNTERNEHMEN

TABLE 7.1 continued

| Mother company and subsidiaries | Intra-European Tour-operating groups | | | | |
	The World of TUI	Thomas Cook AG	First Choice	Airtours plc (MyTravel)	Rewe Group

TRAVEL AGENICES (RETAILING AND INCOMING)	• LUNN POLY
	• HAPAG LLOYD
	• CALLERS-PEGASUS
	• SIBBALD
	• TRAVEL HOUSE ETC
	• TEAM LINCOLN
	• AUSTRAVEL
	• MCR FLIGHTS
	• PREFERRED AGENTS
	• TRAVEL UNIE INTERN
	  • (ex) ARKE REISEN
	  • HOLLAND INTERN
	  • FIRST
	  • FIRST TRAVEL
	   MANAGEMENT
	• KRAS
	• VTB-VAB REISEN
	• JETAIR
	• BELGIUM INTERN
	• TUI AUSTRIA
	• TUI SPAIN
	• SULTRAMAR
	• DR DEGENER
	• GULET TOUROPA
	• WINGE
	• PRISMA TOURS
	• SCAN HOLIDAY
		• THOMAS COOK
		• NECKERMANN REISENBURO
		  • NECKERMANN BELGIUM
		   • ALLAIR
		   • SUNSNACKS
		  • NECKERMANN NETHERL
		   • BROERE REISEN
		  • NECKERMANN AUSTRIA
		   • KUONI
		• BROERE REISENBURO
		  • BROERE NETHERL
		  • BROERE AUSTRIA
		• KARSTADT
		• QUELLE
		• PEACH
		• CARLSON WORLDCHOICE
		• ARTAC WORLDCHOICE
		• HAVAS VOYAGES (FRANCE)
		• EURO-LLOYD
		• GRUPO VIAJES IBERIA
		• LUFTHANSA CITY CENTRE
		  • LUFTHANSA CC (ITALY)
		  • LUFTHANSA CC (AUSTRIA)
			• TRAVEL CHOICE
			• LEISURE INTERN
			• TRAVEL CARE
			• BAKERS DOLPHIN
			• INTRATRAVEL
			• FERRY CHOICE
			• HOLIDAY HYPERMARKETS
			• HOLIDAY EXPRESS
			• HAVE TRAVEL
				• GOING PLACES
				• TRAVEL WORLD
				• GLOBAL TRAVEL GROUP
				• FROSCH TOURISTIK INTERN
				  • FLUBGORSE
				  • ALLKAUF
				  • FTI FERIENWELT
				  • 5 V FLUG
				• RECOMMENDED AGENTS
				• VING
				• TRAVEL SERVICES INTERN
					• DER-DEUTSCHES REISENBURO
					• ATLAS REISEN

DESTINATION	• RIU • IBEROTEL • GRECOTEL • CLUB ROBINSON • DORFHOTELS • BLUE VILLAGE	• IBEROSTAR • CLUB ALDIANA • PARADIANA		• HOTETUR • BELLEVUE	• CLUB CALIMERA

Source: Reprinted from *Tourism Management*, vol.25, Bastakis, Buhalis and Butler, 'The perception of small and medium sized tourism accommodation providers on the impacts of tour operators' power in Eastern Mediterranean', 151–71, copyright (2004), with permission from Elsevier

TABLE 7.2 TUI Airlines

Country	Company	Number of aircraft	Usage
United Kingdom	Britannia	33	Tour operations
	Thomsonfly.com	4	Low-cost airline (since summer 2004)
Sweden	Britannia Nordic	6	Tour operation
Belgium	TUI Belgium	6	Tour operation
France	Corsair	10	Tour operation
Germany	Hapag-Lloyd	34	Tour operation and low-cost airline (since 2002, HLX.com)

Airlines carried 18m passengers in 2002

Source: Adapted from TUI (2003) Annual Report and Update from TUIAG.com

INSIGHT 7.2

TUI AG – the world's largest integrated tour operator

The company evolved from the German company Preussag AG in the 1990s, when it chose to focus on services, having been an industrial conglomerate. Its entry into tourism is a significant example of corporate restructuring and repositioning to enter a growth sector – tourism. This involved divestment of former assets and investment in others, including the acquisition of Hapag-Lloyd AG in 1997 which had a global logistics, airline and travel agency chain. This was closely followed by the acquisition of TUI Deutschland, which was a brand leader for quality package holidays. The company invested in other tourism assets in tourism distribution (vertical and horizontal integration), to develop an integrated value chain. That means that, by owning companies performing key functions throughout the tourism distribution chain, it can create synergies, enter into international partnerships, form strategic alliances (see Chapter 5 for more detail) and establish quality levels across all elements of the tourism product (i.e. purchasing, transport, incoming tour handling, accommodation and ground transport). The complete integration of the product through the distribution also allows the company to provide a seamless tourism experience.

In 2000, the company continued its rapid growth in developing tourism operations, purchasing the Thomson travel group in the UK, which had a prominent brand and

market position with a quality association. Further acquisitions followed in other European countries, including Eastern Europe. By 2003, 65 per cent of the Pressaug AG group turnover was from tourism and in 2005 this rose to 85 per cent with shipping accounting for 15 per cent.

In terms of the company image, it was rebranded in 2004 to TUI AG under the aegis of the World of TUI, as illustrated in Figure 7.2 which summarizes the company's corporate profile in tourism. It is clearly the most integrated tourism operator in Europe and, as Figure 7.3 shows, it has developed a strong market presence in most European countries' outbound markets (and China). This distribution of tour operators within the TUI AG group highlights the key outbound markets of the UK, Germany, France and Scandinavia as well as the Netherlands with affluent consumers taking overseas holidays. The company's consolidation of the tour operator market is also illustrated by its investment in airlines-to-service packages and the growing low-cost market as illustrated in Table 7.2. The company-integrated operations in tourism cover retailing (travel agents, internet and other ICTs), tour operation, transportation, accommodation, business travel, incoming tourism, and cruising to provide control over the distribution channels in the destination.

The company is both visionary and strategic in its development of new markets and products, including its understanding of the fundamental changes in consumer behaviour towards the modular consumer who needs to be accommodated by innovative approaches rather than a complete, 'take it or leave it' package. For example, TUI offers seat-only sales in the UK and Belgium. The move into China with the TUI China joint venture has tapped the growing inbound, outbound and domestic Chinese tourism market (see Case Study 3.1W). The company has also developed a joint venture in Russia (TUI Mostravel) with the expansion of outbound travel among Russians to conventional Eastern European areas and new travel to the Mediterranean. Above all, innovation remains a hallmark of TUI AG as epitomized by its establishment of a travel agency of the future in a Berlin shopping mall. This uses virtual reality to allow the consumer to view the product as a sensory experience.

Image 7.1: TUI has a range of products for different markets, such as cruises or couples

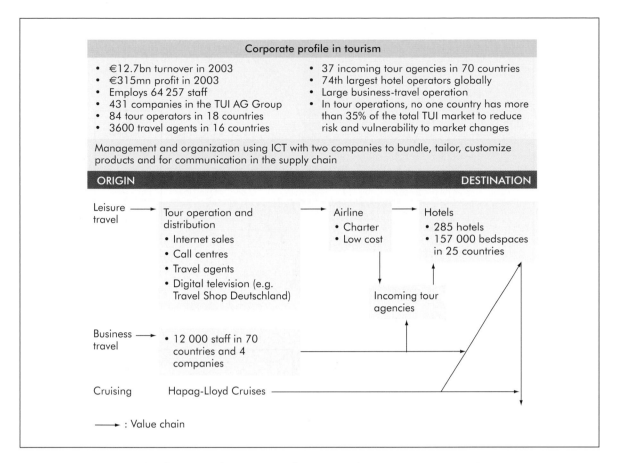

FIGURE 7.2 Example of Europe's largest vertically integrated tour operator – TUI AG. Source: Data from www.TUIAG.com

Department of Trade and Industry Foreign Package Holiday Order which stated that travel agents owned by a tour operator controlling more than 5 per cent of the package market should identify their links with suppliers in brochures and shop interiors.

Above all, the volatile nature of the package holiday market has seen the integrated companies pursue different market strategies as they:

- seek to expand market share, market dominance and position in consumers' minds

- seek to convert domestic holiday-taking to outbound travel by conveying images of low-cost holidays

- drive down the cost from suppliers and from repackaging the product, so that no-frills packages (i.e. no airport transfers, no holiday representative or in-flight meals) are provided in the market appealing to the lower end of the consumer spectrum

- drive out the smaller operators in the long-term, to further consolidate market dominance (from Page 2003).

Other strategies have been to develop new markets such as long-haul markets which now exceed 20 per cent of outbound UK business. Seat-only sales on **charter flight**s have also seen some operators expand their business, as illustrated by TUI AG. More common strategies are to seek new, cheaper destinations as over 50 per cent of UK holiday-makers are choosing packages when travelling overseas abroad at some time. One consequence has been product diversification to grow the range of possible holiday options including:

- **city break**s and additional short breaks as secondary airports open up new potential destinations such as Iceland Air's service to Reykjavik

FIGURE 7.3 The global distribution of TUI businesses, Copyright: S.J. Page

- **long-haul** and adventure travel such as ecotourism and nature holidays
- greater flexibility and tailoring of the packages to the client needs (from Page 2003).

Clearly competition will result in further consolidation among tour operators as the e-tourism revolution gains momentum. One consequence is that, in 2001, 23 ATOL-licensed companies went bankrupt and £3 million in compensation was awarded to travellers. This led Barclays Bank to launch a new bonding scheme for small operators with less than 800 passengers a year to help address the issue of insolvency. However, in the period 1985–2001, £159 million was paid to 190 000 people for 300 ATOL operators failing, which was paid from the ATOL bond it retains from tour operators. The CAA pays the shortfalls in compensation from the bond from its Air Travel Trust Fund, which in 2002 was, reportedly, £8 million in debt, highlighting the need for a re-evaluation of the role of bonds and tour operators' solvency.

To summarize, the outcome of changes in the European tour operator market is likely to be further integration and consolidation with:

- expansion via **acquisition**s
- integration of air and hotel businesses
- further widening of distribution channels

TABLE 7.3 Passengers licensed to top ten groups and companies

Group and licence holders	Passengers licensed for current year	% total	Passengers licensed for last year	% total	% change
1 TUI Group total (TUI UK Ltd; The International Academy Ltd*)	4 826 943	16	5 022 455	16	(4)
2 MyTravel Group total (MyTravel Tour Operations Ltd; Bridge Travel Service Ltd; Direct Holidays plc; Cresta Holidays Ltd; Panorama Holiday Group Ltd)	4 157 754	13	4 563 961	15	(9)
3 Thomas Cook Group total (Thomas Cook Retail Ltd; Thomas Cook Tour Operations Ltd; Thomas Cook Signature Ltd; Style Holidays Ltd)	3 173 596	10	3 295 506	11	(4)
4 First Choice Holidays Group total (First Choice Holidays & Flights Ltd; SkiBound Ltd; Exodus Travels Ltd; Schools Abroad Ltd; Meon Travel Ltd; Sunsail Ltd; Hayes and Jarvis (Travel) Ltd; Waymark Holidays Ltd; Citalia Holidays Ltd; Crown Travel Ltd; Trips Worldwide Ltd;* Adventures Worldwide Ltd*)	2 610 099	8	3 130 569	10	(17)
5 Cosmos Group total (Cosmosair plc; Cosmos Coach Tours Ltd; Avro plc; Archers Tours Ltd; The Charter Warehouse Ltd; Monarch Air Travel Ltd; Pullman Holidays (UK) Ltd; Urbanweb Ltd)	1 183 730	4	1 239 244	4	(4)
6 Gold Medal Travel Group plc	654 848	2	656 000	2	(0)
7 Trailfinders Limited	564 974	2	655 261	2	(14)
8 Lastminute Group total (Lastminute Network Ltd; The Destination Group Ltd; Globepost Ltd; Travelcoast Ltd;* Travelbargains Ltd;* Gemstone Travel Ltd;* Joint Venture Travel PLC*)	546 902	2	142 433	0	284
9 Libra Holidays Group total (Libra Holidays Ltd; Freedom Flights Ltd; Enable Holidays Ltd*; Travelseekers Worldwide Ltd)	543 955	2	581 293	2	(6)
10 Interactive Corporation Group total (Expedia.com Ltd; TV Travel Shop Holidays Ltd; Interval Travel Ltd)	536 605	2	217 440	2	147
Total passengers licensed to the top ten groups and companies	18 788 406	61	19 504 162	63	(4)
Total passengers licensed to the top four groups	14 768 392	48	16 012 491	52	(8)
Passengers licensed to all ATOL Holders	31 037 351	100	31 072 578	100	(0)

*New ATOLs in the group since last July's edition, not included in the 2003 figures for the group; numbers in brackets represent a decline.

Source: ATOL *Business Issue* 24, July 2004, © Civil Aviation Authority

- widening geographical coverage of markets and tour operators merging/entering into strategic alliances
- the impact of the euro which may allow operators to buy capacity cheaper from weaker currencies providing lower-priced holidays
- a gradual levelling of package holiday prices across the EU
- greater cost controls
- new business strategies towards products (i.e. focus on core business versus diversification)
- a greater alignment of business towards changing consumer behaviour (from Page 2003).

One consequence of these changes as the examples have shown is the growing internationalization of the tour operator. Many become TNCs (see Chapter 5) and seek further economies of scale, a wider market spread internationally and the use of multiple distribution strategies, advertising and ICTs using yield management systems (see Chapter 8 for more detail of yield management). The result in highly developed outbound markets such as the UK and Germany is that a small number of large companies now control the supply to consumers. One casualty, as already noted, was MyTravel, which sought to grow and consolidate its market position but hit financial problems, so a more international approach may not always succeed. Above all, it is important for tour operators to be cognizant of market trends, changes to consumer behaviour and the effect on their business as well as the profitability of their business operations.

The role of the 'new' consumer and future trends in tour operating

A very influential study by Poon (1993) identified the changing nature of tourists as consumers, which had implications for tourism purchasing habits. In particular Poon identified a shift from the old tourists, the less experienced travellers who purchased a homogeneous, mass-produced product that was supply driven (Chapter 4). Much of the consumption was mass resort, 'sun, sea and sand' oriented for consumers to escape the routines of daily life. In contrast, 'new' tourism is characterized by more experienced travellers who have a growing environmental concern about the impact of their holidays on the places they visit and require more individualized products rather than the mass products that are less predictable, products that are full of surprise, discovery and memorable experiences rather than simply a repetition of last year's beach holiday (Page 2003). Although 'old' and 'new' tourism coexist, 'new' tourism offers the tourism industry many growth opportunities given that tourism businesses can react to the demand for increased flexibility through greater use of ICTs. The types of factors operators need to consider are highlighted in Figure 7.4, which reveals the increasingly complex business environment which the tour operator sector now faces globally. Perhaps one of the most dominant issues to arise, however, is the growth of consumer rights, consumer action and a more discerning approach to purchasing. Yet one anomaly here is that despite consumer interest in the environment, the numbers of tourists travelling is increasing – ultimately placing more pressure on the environment.

Tour operating and consumerism

One consequence of 'new' tourism and more experienced travellers is the rise of a more demanding consumer combined with a demand for higher quality at lower cost. According to ABTA, 85 per cent of UK package holidays are ABTA bonded and in 2000 almost 5 per cent of the UKs 20 million package holiday-takers were fairly or very dissatisfied with their holidays. In 2003, ABTA received 17 000 complaints and all but 1200 were resolved quickly, with the remainder going to arbitration. However, this does not include those tourists who directly litigated via the small claims court or by other means. Complaints concerned the quality of accommodation, perceived safety standards of overseas chartered aircraft, surcharges and failure to provide what was advertised.

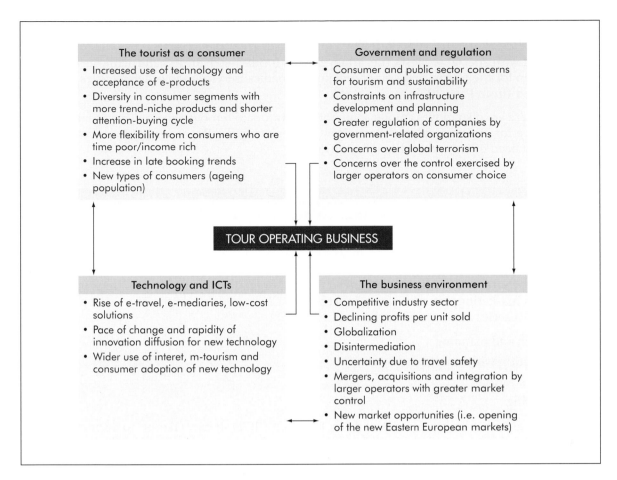

FIGURE 7.4 Factors affecting the tour operating sector

These issues remain problematic due to the gap between the consumers' perception of what they are purchasing and the reality of consumption. In the EU, the 1993 EC Directive on Package Travel required greater precision of the tour operator. As the DTI response to the directive, the following measures were implemented so that:

- all tours were licensed
- there was a greater degree of honesty in holiday brochure description
- an obligation was placed on travel agents to take responsibility for the information contained in brochures they stocked and for ensuring adequate advice to clients on:
  - health
  - passport and visa requirements
  - insurance needs

and makes the tour operator liable for losses resulting from misleading information or where suppliers do not provide the services paid for and contracted (Page 2003).

For the tour operator the DTI response highlights the need for support staff in the destination, namely the **holiday representative** ('the Rep'), so they can act as troubleshooters to remedy problems or complaints in situ. The Rep's job is very demanding as they are the public relations agent of the company, often on call 24 hours a day, 7 days a week in the peak season. They typically combine a number of roles including:

- meeting and greeting incoming and departing passengers at the airport to ensure airport transfers drop the right passengers at the correct accommodation
- handling a wide range of destination-specific inquiries, requests and provision of social events

- giving publicity to tours and services endorsed by the company for which a commission is paid to the company by the suppliers
- dealing with special requests (i.e. arrangements for disabled guests) and acting as a go-between for the tourist and hotel, local police, medical services and other agencies when required (from Page 2003).

However, there are also moves among some tour operators to remove the Rep given that they may not add value for experienced travellers. They are replacing the Reps with 24-hour contact with the company head office and quality information.

The business of tour operating: Developing the holiday brochure

The **holiday brochure** remains the most powerful marketing tool in reaching the consumer, since the intangible nature of tourism makes it imperative that the potential customer can read about what they may want to purchase (although much of this is also available electronically). To develop a brochure, a tour operator will need to plan, organize and implement a tour programme as part of its marketing and advertising process (see Chapters 15 and 16). The tour operator has to undertake a series of stages of work including:

- research and planning
- negotiation with suppliers
- administration
- marketing

all of which are now highly dependent upon the use of ICTs. It can take up to 18 months from identifying a resort and product to brochure production.

The holiday brochure has evolved from its modern-day predecessor which was introduced in 1953 by Thomas Cook (Laws 1997). This used a similar format to that of women's magazines, reflecting the important role of women as holiday decision-makers. The 1960s saw holiday brochures become glossier and packed with information and its role changing to a modern-day holiday catalogue. One possible format is shown in Figure 7.5.

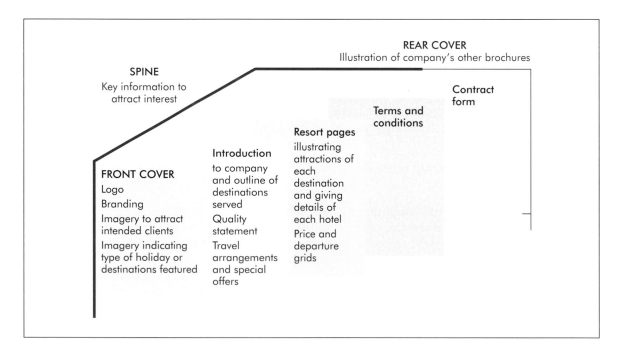

FIGURE 7.5   Structure of inclusive holiday brochures. Source: Eric Laws (1997), reproduced with the author's permission

Holiday brochures and the electronic equivalents allow **travel agent**s and e-mediaries:

- to obtain sales
- to provide information to assist purchasers' decision-making in relation to the destination, product offerings, timing (summer/winter), price, ancillary services
- to afford cost-effective distribution for the tour operator, with an attractive cover, being prominently racked in travel agents and able to generate business among agents
- to provide an effective tool to allow agents to sell holidays with detailed products/booking codes
- to allow a contract to be agreed between the tour operator and customer, providing information on procedures for changing the booking, complaints, refunds, the details of the product purchased, the client details and insurance premium paid (from Page 2003).

As Laws (1997) describes, a brochure will go through a design process to:

- identify the market audience and product
- utilize an appropriate company brand
- produce a mock-up, using a computer with illustrations and professional photographs of the hotel, destination, product offerings and services
- use a desktop publishing system which will help with brochure layout and design
- produce a proof, which is checked, and inaccuracies identified prior to printing.

Accuracy and a need to be honest and truthful in holiday brochures are now enshrined in consumer legislation in many countries. Operator groups such as ABTA's *Code of Conduct for Tour Operators* indicate that the brochure is a legal document to which complaints may refer in future claims for compensation.

Holloway (2001) identifies the following information, which must be provided in a holiday brochure for the tour operator to obtain a licence:

- 'the name of the firm responsible for the IT'
- the means of transport used, including, in the case of air transport, the name of the carrier(s), type and class of aircraft used and whether scheduled or charter aircraft are operated
- full details of destinations, itinerary and times of travel
- the duration of each tour (number of days'/nights' stay)
- full description of the location and type of accommodation provided, including any meals
- whether services of a representative are available abroad
- a clear indication of the price for each tour, including any taxes
- exact details of special arrangements, (e.g. if there is a games room in the hotel, whether this is available at all times and whether any charges are made for the use of this equipment)
- full conditions of booking, including details of cancellation conditions
- details of any insurance coverage (clients should have the right to choose their own insurance, providing this offers equivalent coverage)
- details of documentation required for travel to the destinations featured, and any health hazards or inoculations recommended.' (Source: Holloway (2001: 253–4).

Once a booking needs to be made, the tour operators will distribute the product via a wide range of channels including agents and CRSs, the internet, direct by phone and the different mechanisms discussed earlier in Figure 7.1.

One consequence of continued consolidation is that 80 per cent of inclusive tours are sold through 20 per cent of agents, with commissions paid to agents, plus an override (1–5 per cent) in addition to the basic 10 per cent for high performance.

Travel agents and retailing

Travel agents perform a role in the tourism distribution system, and in the UK they accounted for the dominant element of sales of package holidays in the late 1990s, though online retailing by tour operators and e-mediaries (see Chapter 6) has begun to challenge the travel agent's role. Yet if the consumer requires information, then the travel agent's role in tourism is to recognize and highlight that tourism is:

- *intangible*, meaning tourism is a speculative investment and an expensive purchase where the product is conveyed to the customer usually in a brochure
- *perishable*, and so can only be sold for the period it is available (it cannot be stored). This highlights the importance of last-minute bookings to sell surplus capacity
- *dynamic*, meaning that it is forever in a state of flux, especially as a product where prices can rise and fall
- *heterogeneous*, meaning it is not a standardized product which is produced and delivered in a homogeneous manner. It varies, and interactions can enhance or adversely affect it since it is dependent upon people and many unknown factors
- *inseparable*, meaning that in the consumer's mind it is purchased and consumed as an overall experience; so communicating what is being offered, its value and scope is important. Since the consumer is transported to the product, it is an unusual form of distribution, where there is a need for timely information on all of the elements as outlined in the brochure (Page 2003).

However, the rise of a new trend, **disintermediation**, has also impacted upon the traditional role of the travel agent. Disintermediation has been brought about by the rise of e-tailing and e-mediaries which have removed the dominance of the traditional high-street travel agent. Combined with changes brought about by ICTs, a number of processes in the tourism business environment are impacting upon travel agents to increase the effect of disintermediation, as Figure 7.6 shows. This is reinforced by Figure 7.4 (p. 137) which outlines changes to the environment of tour operating which are also relevant to travel agencies. Despite disintermediation, travel agents remain a key intermediary in the distribution chain, and are characterized by many features.

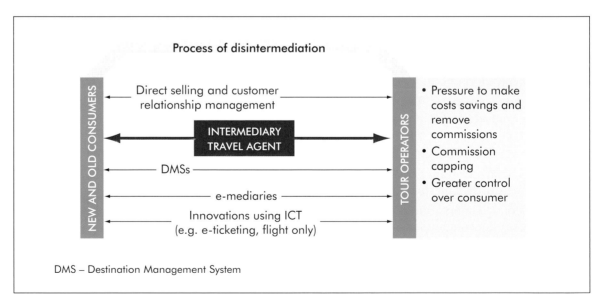

FIGURE 7.6 Disintermediation in the distribution chain

The evolution of travel agents

Travel agents in their most commercial form can be traced back to Thomas Cook and most then were independent agents, with the exception of Thomas Cook. They largely performed an agent's role in selling travel tickets for rail, sea and land-based services as well as accommodation. This was largely a brokerage role, receiving a commission on each sale. In the 1940s air-based travel emerged but agents had not reached a mass market. It was in the 1960s where the greatest changes in travel agencies occurred, with commissions, licensing and greater airline–agency relations, particularly in the sale of group travel (Laws 1997). By developing increased levels of information, service and specialized products, agents began to become more involved in the tour operation side of travel, organizing tours and selling cruises from block allocations. During the 1970s, these changes saw many travel agents expand with the growth of package travel, basing their business on volume sales. Further market change occurred in the 1980s as agencies entered into tour operating, whilst **mergers**, acquisitions and consolidation occurred. Grouping into formal alliances or consortia enabled agencies to seek greater commissions, using increased levels of technology to assist in distribution, while the high street has seen large chains emerge. In the 1980s and 1990s, travel agents bore the brunt of tour operator practices of fuel and currency surcharges which significantly impacted upon the image of the tourism sector. Similarly, in the 1990s, major challenges have included the loss of commission from airline ticket sales and other cuts in earning potential. One response for some agencies is to now charge a consultancy fee in lieu of agency fees, since commissions are the lifeblood of their revenue. One consequence is the diversification into other products such as travel insurance where the commission may counterbalance cuts in other areas of their work. Yet the internet is also allowing the cost-conscious traveller to compare insurance costs now, making this revenue more contested. Laws (1997) examined many of these changes in Table 7.4, looking at the entire post-war period and the style of travel retailing which evolved to characterize each era.

TABLE 7.4   Changes in travel retailing

Period	Trading environment	Type of travel retailing
1950s	Limited demand for holidays or other travel Reconstruction of war-damaged city centres	Full-service travel specialists located in major urban and business centres. Limited competition
1960s	Gradual increase in city centre travel retailers with the development of demand for leisure travel	Coach and other domestic holidays sold by small coach companies and through newsagents
1970s	Rapid expansion in demand for holidays	Successful retailers expand the number of outlets – proliferation of high-street retailers
1980s	Development of out-of-town shopping malls and large-scale town centres Many high streets suffer from shop closures and temporary tenants	First computerized reservations system for inclusive holidays. Larger travel agency chains grow by acquiring smaller 'miniples', consolidating ownership and putting pressure on independents. Development of specialized holiday shops, and decline of full-service travel agencies
1990s	Increasing financial pressure on travel retailers, increasing rate of acquisition and mergers	Increasingly selective racking policies Technological developments enable customers to create their own holiday packages by booking direct from home

Source: Copyright Eric Laws (1997: 122), reproduced with permission from the author

Travel agents: Roles and activities

In the UK, there are almost 6400 travel agency branches affiliated to ABTA, the Association of British Travel Agents. Table 7.5 shows the top 25 agencies by turnover which illustrates the dominance of retail multiples (i.e. chains also owned by tour operators). Like tour operating, the structure of travel agents has changed in recent years as consolidation has led to greater pressure on independent agents and less choice for the consumer, as multiples dominate the retailing of products. Interestingly, travel agents have no stock, acting on behalf of the tour operators, and so they have little financial risk and do not purchase products themselves. They receive a commission for each sale and, as agents, do not become part of the contract of sale, which is between the tour operator and the customer. Some agencies specialize, such as in airline tickets; others may aim at the larger mass-package market.

High-street agents do not specialize in business and corporate travel, although the market for specialist agents is worth over £10.5 billion a year in the UK. One very controversial area of debate in travel agents' behaviour is the process of **racking**, where the agents emphasize/display certain businesses' products (perhaps their own company's in the case of integrated businesses) to favour them as they promise higher commissions. This has concerned government bodies like the MMC who call this **directional selling** (where an agent tries to sell a product from a vertically integrated tour operator). This complex process is then developed by the travel agent through a purchase process, where matching client needs with product offerings has a key role to

TABLE 7.5	ABTA's top 25 travel agents (based on turnover)

	Number of retail outlets
Airline Network plc	0
American Express Europe Ltd	66
Brittanic Travel Ltd	22
British Airways Travel Shops Ltd	26
C W Travel Ltd	56
Co-operative Group (CWS) Ltd	379
First Choice Holiday Hypermarkets Ltd	40
First Choice Retail Ltd	203
First Choice Travel Shops Ltd	76
Flight Centre (UK) Ltd	88
Flightbookers Ltd	4
Going Places Leisure Travel Ltd	693
Hays Travel Ltd	110
Hogg Robinson (Travel) Ltd	65
Ilkeston Consumer Co-operative Society Ltd	40
Midlands Co-operative Society Ltd	107
Portman Travel Ltd	34
R E Bath Travel Service Ltd	62
RCI Europe	0
STA Travel Ltd	67
TV Travel Shop Ltd	0
The Travel Company Ltd	20
Thomas Cook Retail Ltd	637
TUI UK Ltd	900

Source: Adapted from http://www.abta.com

play. As Figure 7.7 shows, the travel agent has to establish a rapport with clients, then understand their needs, while keeping them interested and presenting various options based on product and destination knowledge. This also highlights the critical role which agency recommendation may play in shaping consumer choice of destination. Klenosky and Gitelson (1998) have produced a conceptual model to explain this which is outlined in Figure 7.8, highlighting the key role of agent knowledge in matching customer and trip variables to destination variables.

However, at a more practical level, travel agents typically deal with a diverse range of tasks including:

- making reservations
- planning itineraries (including complex round-the-world travel)
- calculating fares and charges
- producing tickets
- advising clients on destinations, resorts, airline companies and a wide range of travel products
- communicating with clients verbally and in writing
- maintaining accurate records on reservations
- ensuring racks are stocked well or supplies are kept in-house
- acting as intermediaries where customer complaints occur (from Page 2003)

and an illustration of their scale, significance and organization in Australia can be found in Insight 7.3 which examines travel retailing.

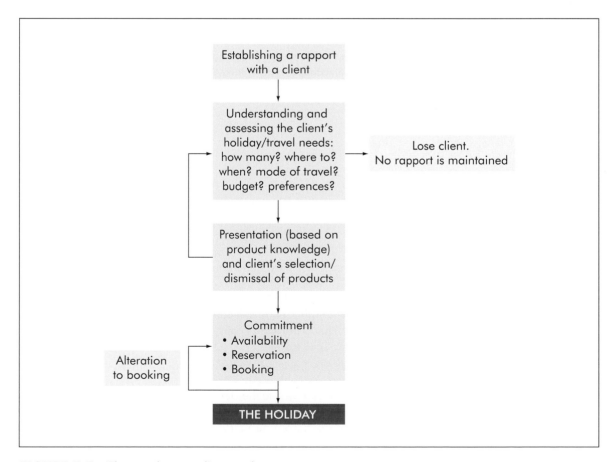

FIGURE 7.7 The travel agent–client purchase process

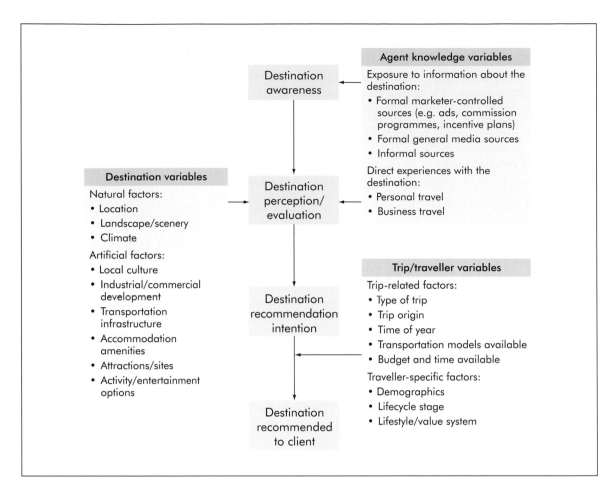

FIGURE 7.8 Conceptual model of the process and factors influencing travel agents' destination recommendations. Source: Hudson *et al.* (2001: 175), adapted from Klenosky and Gitelson (1998)

INSIGHT 7.3

Travel agencies in Australia

The Australian market, unlike those in the UK and many European countries, has witnessed a growth in the number of travel agencies operating over the last decade. Around 2800 travel agents exist in Australia and their main business is based on domestic leisure travel (60 per cent), domestic business travel (25 per cent) and international travel (15 per cent), in contrast to many of their European counterparts. The Australian travel agent sector employs a high staff:agency ratio, with 23 600 employees, due to consolidation in the market and the greater use of ICTs. As staff comprise over 75 per cent of travel agency overheads, the main area for efficiency savings is usually viewed in terms of staffing.

The market, like Europe is dominated by a number of retail multiples, with the top three agencies being:

- Flight Centre

- Flight Centre's leading rival Harvey World of Travel (incorporating mainly franchised outlets and Thomas Cook travel)

- STA Travel, with its focus on student travel.

Like Europe and the USA, online retailing has emerged as a growing element of the retail process, following the launch of travel.com.au in 1996 via the lastminute.com brand, followed by webset, zuji and wotif.com.

Business travel agents

Some travel agents also specialize in business travel (Davidson 2001). According to Davidson (2001) business travel comprises:

- individual business travel (**corporate travel**), involving business trips related to employer needs
- occasional work activities – such as conferences, conventions, events and incentive programmes.

Table 7.6 highlights the nature of each category of business travel, the key purchases, the range of intermediaries and who may supply the product. What is evident from Table 7.6 is that both private sector businesses and public sector employees (i.e. local, regional and national government bodies and charitable bodies) also engage in business travel. Not surprisingly, travel agencies

TABLE 7.6 Business travel distribution channel: Structure, players and requirements

Sector	Main buyers	Possible intermediaries	Main suppliers
Individual business travel	Companies and other organizations (governmental, professional, etc), possibly through: – inhouse travel managers – secretaries/PAs	Business/corporate travel agencies Travel management companies, possibly through: – implants – dedicated online booking services	Transport providers Accommodation and catering operators Leisure and recreation suppliers

Conferences and other meetings	Corporate sector
	Governmental sector
	Associations
	– academic
	– professional
	– trade
	– fraternal
	– religious etc, possibly through:
	  – inhouse travel managers
	  – inhouse conference organizers
	  – secretaries/PAs
		Professional conference organizers
		Venue-finding agencies
		Convention bureaux
		Destination management companies/ground handlers
		Specialist marketing consortia
			Transport providers
			Accommodation and catering operators
			Leisure and recreation suppliers
			Conference centres
			Management training centres
			Hotels meetings facilities
			Universities
			'Unusual venues'
			Audio-visual contractors
			Telecommunications companies (video/satellite conferencing facilities)
			Interpreters

Incentive travel	Corporate sector, possibly through: – inhouse travel managers – inhouse conference organizers	Incentive travel houses Business travel agencies Destination management companies/ground handlers	Transport providers Accommodation and catering operators Leisure and recreation suppliers
Exhibitions/ trade fairs	Corporate sector	Exhibition organizers	Transport providers Accommodation and catering operators Leisure and recreation suppliers Exhibition centres Stand contractors

Source: Davidson (2001: 74)

specialize in this market due to the high value of much business travel that is often sudden, unplanned and may involve premium-priced travel (i.e. business class travel). A business travel agent will manage all the client's travel arrangements and seek preferential rates, especially where volume travel occurs. Yet this sector is also very vulnerable to online travel solutions as the Cendant example in Insight 7.1 shows.

The real dilemma for many business travel agencies is that in using e-ticketing, especially for air travel, they may see disintermediation occur where direct purchasing and e-ticketing replace some of their organizing function. The largest business travel agencies in Europe are American Express, BTI Hogg Robinson and Carlson Wagonlit, as consolidation has occurred through mergers and takeovers. Where companies use these agencies, contracts can be constructed in a number of ways, but above all it seems to provide companies with greater cost controls on corporate travel and reduce costs.

The online travel revolution and the future of travel agents

The e-tourism revolution identified in Chapter 6 highlights a major problem for the travel agency sector in its current shape and form. e-mediaries, such as Microsoft's Expedia in the USA, which rose from a newcomer to one of the Top US travel agencies in four years (Buhalis 2003) have grown phenomenally due to the impact of ICTs and new forms of intermediary and distribution electronically on the conventional high-street travel agent. Expedia has purchased US business travel management firm Metropolitan Travel as it also moves into business travel. As Buhalis (2003) identified, the impact of ICTs on the travel agency sector is likely to see a reconfiguration of the existing market into three segments (see Figure 7.9). Figure 7.9 shows that the market will be characterized by:

- large global players, using ICTs, their economies of scale and scope to serve the mass market with the key brands and network of distribution channels (i.e. travel agents, online, direct selling, digital television) with the ability to also increase yields with selling surplus capacity via lastminute products
- the evolution of a new form of travel agency (real or virtual) that is more sophisticated in its use of ICTs to tailor products and profile their customers' needs, whilst adding value through specialist knowledge
- a reduction in the number of conventional high-street travel agents.

In fact Buhalis (2003) has gone as far as to suggest that the successful future travel agency will take less of a booking-office role and more of a travel management and adviser role, while adding value not accessible from online booking.

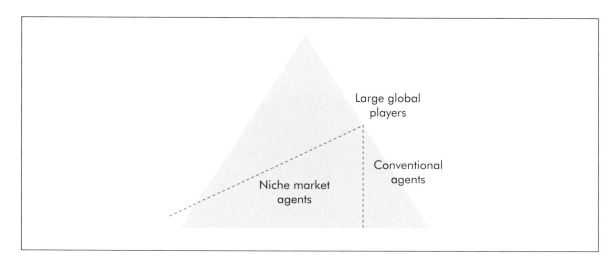

FIGURE 7.9 Future shape of the travel agency market. Source: Adapted from Buhalis (2003)

In view of the success of online travel and characterization of travel agencies as struggling to compete, there is adequate evidence of travel agents embracing new technology when its proprietary products are at a price that makes their acquisition cost effective. The notion of travel agents as technophobic is a poor representation: they have embraced technology since its inception. The main lag has been in their response to the speed of change with the internet. In fact some GDSs such as Sabre have even added European low-cost airlines to their booking systems. They have also responded to the evolution of dynamic packaging technology. In 2004, Sabre launched a MySabre internet-based agency tool to combine its product range within one site for travel agents. Plans in Europe to deregulate the GDS sector for travel agents in 2005 will provide agents with access to different systems and will most likely see use of this combined with more internet-based travel solutions. Agents able to combine face-to-face and online options are likely to retain their business, though e-ticketing is now commonplace (over 70 per cent of USA air travel tickets are now issued in this way, though it is still lower in the UK). It would seem that partnering with the low-cost airlines in providing tailored travel solutions, and moving away from the rapid growth in low-cost seat-only sales, may help agents to add value in the travel purchase process. Disintermediation will not disappear from the travel agency sector, but the introduction of dynamic packaging into this sector will allow them to compete with the online e-tourism boom. Among the future competitive pressures which travel agents will face are:

- e-tailing, especially the rise of lastminute.com and portals such as Yahoo!
- further growth in internet-only low-cost air travel sales
- continued direct selling by tour operators
- shifting consumer preferences for more value-added travel experiences.

Conclusion

In summary, it is clear that technology has had a phenomenal impact on the distribution of travel products, particularly the way in which each intermediary accesses the consumer. Technology has also made packaging products more flexible for those businesses investing in ICTs. Yet the business environment for travel distribution is changing rapidly and the consolidation of both tour operators and travel agent networks into global operations now raises issues of competition discussed in Chapter 5. Some critics point to the impact of the multiples and global players on small businesses (SMEs) (Buhalis and Laws 2001), especially the power these yield in contract negotiation, particularly in destination areas. In some smaller, more marginal tourist destinations dependent upon a number of key tour operators for their tourism market, they can have an undesirable control and power over how the country's tourism industry develops (Sastre and Benito 2001) (see also Chapter 24).

At a global scale, many of the trends identified in this chapter highlight the variability in the adoption of new technology and the effect it has had to date on travel distribution. No two countries have had similar experiences. Likewise, the importance of different stakeholders in the integrated tourism distribution chain has been highlighted as one area which the larger companies can nurture and use to add value to customers through improved quality

and greater consistency using ICTs. Companies such as TUI AG demonstrate this trend by using technology to manage supplier quality, though collaboration rather than more competitive models of doing business may make these relationships more productive where non-integrated companies provide products for tourists. Above all, supply chain issues in tourism are highly complex and less predictable, and the outcomes in terms of consumer expectations do not necessarily follow predefined outcomes. Consumers are very heterogeneous and the growing diversity of needs as tourists highlights the importance of the use of ICTs in distribution and also the role of personal involvement and contact with people. Intermediaries should always remember they are dealing with people who are the customer in the service delivery process associated with distributing tourism products. Tour operators and travel agencies are operationally driven, dealing with customers, and as distribution channels they are there first and foremost to provide information for tourists to purchase products and to enable suppliers to deliver these products effectively. Therefore ICTs in the intermediaries sector need to be harnessed to bring together buyers and sellers and create a market for a product and service as well as to help the market to function more smoothly or to expand. One element of the travel product which is integrated to travel is transport, and this is the focus of the next chapter.

Discussion questions

1 What is a tourism distribution channel?

2 Why is the European tour operator sector becoming controlled by integrated tourism companies? How is this impacting upon other operators and consumers?

3 How will travel agents evolve to compete with disintermediation?

4 How important is the e-revolution to consumer purchasing of travel products?

References

ATOL (2004) *Business Issue 24*. London: Civil Aviation Authority.

Bastakis, C., Buhalis, D. and Butler, R. (2004) 'The perception of small and medium sized accommodation providers on the impacts of the tour operators' power in Eastern Mediterranean', *Tourism Management* 25 (2): 151–70.

Buhalis, D. (2003) *eTourism: Information Technology for Strategic Tourism Management*. Harlow: Pearson Education.

Buhalis, D. and Laws, E. (eds) (2001) *Tourism Distribution Channels: Practices, Issues and Transformation*. London: Continuum.

Cooper, C., Fletcher, J., Fyall, A., Wanhill, S. and Gilbert, D. (2005) *Tourism: Principles and Practice, Third Edition*. Harlow: Pearson Education.

Davidson, R. (2001) 'Distribution channel analysis for business travel', in D. Buhalis and E. Laws (eds) (2001) *Tourism Distribution Channels: Practices, Issues and Transformations*. London: Continnum.

Holloway, J.C. (2001) *The Business of Tourism, Sixth Edition*. London: Pearson Education.

Hudson, S., Snaith, T., Miller, G. and Hudson, P. (2001) 'Travel retailing: "Switch selling" in the UK', in D. Buhalis and E. Laws (eds) *Tourism Distribution Channels: Practices, Issues and Transformations*. London: Continuum.

Klenosky, D. and Gitelson, R. (1998) 'Travel agents' destination recommendations', *Annals of Tourism Research*, 25 (3): 661–74.

Laws, E. (1997) *Managing Packaged Tourism*. London: Thomson Learning.

Page, S.J. (2003) *Tourism Management: Managing for Change*. Oxford: Butterworth-Heinemann.

Poon, A. (1993) *Tourism, Technology and Competitive Strategies*. Wallingford, Oxon: CAB International.

Sastre, F. and Benito, I. (2001) 'The role of transnational tour operators in the development of Mediterranean island tourism', in D. Ioannides, Y. Apostolopoulos and S. Sönmez (eds) *Mediterranean Island and Sustainable Tourism Development: Practices, Management and Policies*. London: Continuum.

Further reading

Buhalis, D. and Laws, E. (eds) (2001) *Tourism Distribution Channels: Practices, Issues and Transformations*. London: Continuum.

8

Transporting the Tourist

Learning outcomes

After reading this chapter and answering the questions, you should:

- be able to recognize the principal forms of tourist transport and their characteristics

- be familiar with the development of tourist transport and how it facilitates tourism development

- understand how important the experience of transport is to the mobility of tourists.

Overview

The purpose of this chapter is to introduce the concepts used to understand the relationship between transport and tourism and the characteristics of different forms of tourist transport. Transport remains the dynamic element facilitating tourist travel and it provides the opportunity for holiday making to occur. The scope of the transport sector is explored, focusing on the different travel modes used by tourists (e.g. land, air and sea-based modes).

Some of the wider development issues asssociated with globalization highlighted in Chapter 5 are explored in relation to air travel.

Introduction

Transport is a fundamental component of the tourism industry. Transport is a precondition for travel: it facilitates mobility and the movement of tourists from their place of origin (i.e. their home area) to their destination and back. Transport is frequently neglected in the analysis of tourism, often being relegated to a passive element of the tourist experience. Yet transport remains an essential service element of tourism, and in some cases it can form the focus of the tourism experience per se (e.g. cruising and scenic train journeys). Various forms of transport have been associated with the development of tourism and technological developments in transport combined with the rise in personal disposable incomes have led to the expansion of both domestic and international tourism.

Conceptualizing transport and tourism

Despite the overriding significance of transport as a mode of transit, from origin to destination, there have been few attempts to conceptualize this vital function in the tourism system. Two basic approaches have dominated the analysis of transport and tourism:

1 *Transport for tourism*: this is transport as a utilitarian or functional act which involves a mode or modes of travel in moving from origin to destination and for travel in the destination. At a global scale, Lumsdon and Page (2004: 5) point to the importance of this approach in international travel where:

- international air travel accounts for 43 per cent of international tourist trips
- road transport accounts for 42 per cent of trips
- rail travel comprises 8 per cent of trips
- sea transport accounts for 7 per cent (based on World Tourism Organization 2000).

Yet the relative importance of these different forms of transport varies by region of the world. For example, air travel is more important for international tourist travel in Latin America (see Table 8.1). In contrast, the existence of a well-developed alternative transport infrastructure in Europe means that air travel's importance is counterbalanced by the importance of road travel.

2 *Transport as tourism*; the mode of transport is integral to the overall experience of tourism such as cruising or taking a scenic railway journey. Some of the most luxurious tourist products available, such as the Orient Express and exclusive cruises, utilize the elegance, opulence and quality service attributes of the mode of travel.

What Lumsdon and Page (2004) identify is a tourist transport continuum in which transport for tourism offers a low intrinsic value in relation to the overall tourist experience (i.e. typified by using a mode of transport to simply get from origin a to destination b) through to the position where transport is developed, designed and harnessed as the containing context and the central element – as tourism (see Figure 8.1). A more in-depth study of tourism and transport linkages by Moscardo and Pearce (2004) helps to refine this continuum a stage further since it explores the tourists' motivations and interface with transport, concluding that there is a clear distinction between:

- a core motivational element related to whether people choose to travel on a particular mode of transport for tourism purposes
- a series of additional motivational elements.

This classification highlights the multiple role of transport in tourism, the influence of consumer choice and the motivating factors which contribute to the overall travel experience in terms of the continuum discussed by Lumsdon and Page (2004). This is depicted in Figure 8.2 and what the conceptual map helps us to understand is how the transport sector can create transport as tourism product by emphasizing core and additional motivating factors to aim at different markets. Figure 8.2 also helps to understand how to unlock **latent demand** (i.e. people wanting to travel if the price/service is right), as many low-cost airlines have done (i.e. via cost) or by adding improvements in the tourism value chain by raising satisfaction levels in the transport for tourism element. Above all, Moscardo and Pearce (2004) concur with the view that transport can perform multiple roles in tourism and show how successful transport operators have combined a core motivation (e.g. novelty) with an additional motivation (e.g. romance or nostalgia) to create world class products such as the Orient-Express rail journeys (http://orient-express.co.uk). With these different modes of transport in mind, attention now turns to an overview of tourist travel modes.

TABLE 8.1   Key forms of transport in Latin America

Form of transport	Importance of Latin American tourism	Examples
Air travel: short-haul/ long-haul flights	Major importance to international travel Charter flights limited, mainly scheduled flights	Most tour operators offer triangular flights between major destinations, for example, Miami, Rio, Caracas–Lima, Miami
Highways: car, hire car and coaches	Poor infrastructure in most countries, and low levels of private car ownership means limited development. Coach travel involves long hours, and lacks personal safety	There is a coach sector in each country which deals with international visitors, for example, 'Turbus' in Santiago de Chile. Most car-based tourism is for a domestic nature. Mexico is developing an independent traveller coach tourism market. Guided minibus or bus tours are popular at many destinations such as the famous charabanc tours around Cartagena in Colombia, which include a live band on board, drinks and scheduled stops for dancing
Road transfers: taxi, minibuses	Of major importance at all destinations but personal security and standardization have been a major concern of tourism authorities	In Buenos Aires a system of recognized hotel-based taxis, known as a 'Remise', has been established to offer secure transfers at a fixed price between hotels and airports
Rail: urban metro and intercity	Rail network in decay throughout Latin America with the exception of Mexico; city metro systems overcrowded	Mexico is developing its rail-based network for the US market. In most other countries the railway systems have been truncated but there are a number of tourist trains such as the train to Machu Picchu in Peru and the Train to the Clouds in Salta, Argentina
Marine: cruise and ferries	Cruise liner tourism in growth. Local ferried and river boat tourism buoyant	An increasing number of cruises call at Puerto Limon, Costa Rica. Many also call at Rio de Janeiro and Buenos Aires
Non-motorized: horse-back, cycling, walking, kayak	Very small international market	Walking as a way of getting around tourism destinations is popular but not always pleasant because of chaotic traffic systems, pollution and lack of personal security. Long-distance walking, cycling and trekking are well established and offered to niche markets as a tourism experience. Despite inherent problems of personal security it is growing; for example ecotourism groups in Costa Rica are invariably chaperoned by local guides

Source: Lumsdon and Swift (2001: 64–5)

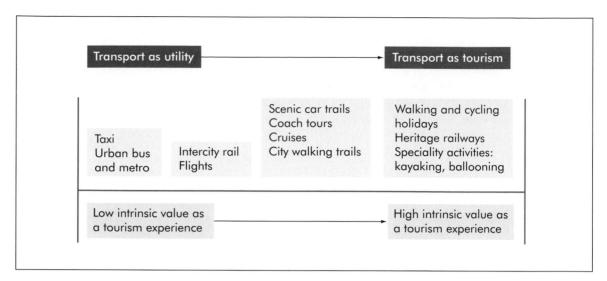

FIGURE 8.1 The tourism transport continuum. Source: Reprinted from *Tourism and Transport: Issues and Agenda for the New Millennium*, Lumsdon and Page, p.7, copyright (2004), with permission from Elsevier

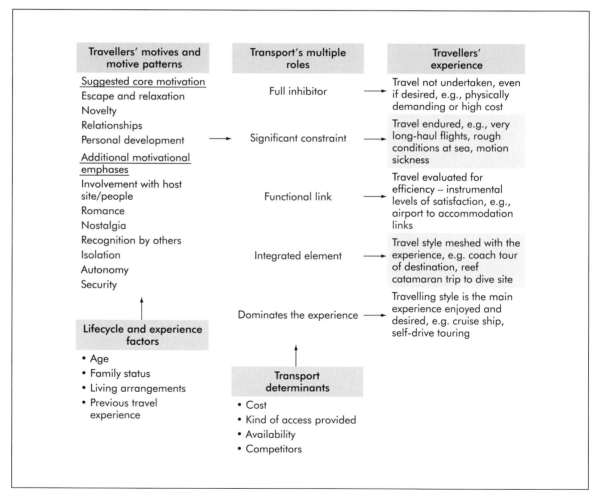

FIGURE 8.2 A conceptual map of the links between motivation, lifecycle, transport roles and the traveller's experience. Source: Reprinted from *Tourism and Transport: Issues and Agenda for the New Millennium*, Lumsdon and Page, p.32, copyright (2004), with permission from Elsevier

Tourist travel modes: A global overview

At an international scale, few studies exist to document tourists' use of different modes of transport. Even where data exist, they are specific to a certain form of transport such as air travel. At an EU level, it is possible to gauge the importance of different modes of transport for non-tourist/tourist use. Table 8.2 illustrates the trends in the use of various modes of transport 1970–2000 which indicates the dominance of two key modes: the car and air travel. In the case of the car, widening access has made it a dominant mode of travel for leisure and recreation trips, and increasingly for tourist trips in the EU. One interesting example is the August annual holiday in Paris, France, and the massive temporary migration by car to the south of France and other destinations for holidays. This causes massive congestion and highlights the problems of managing car-based tourism. The rise of air travel globally as a mode of transport for short- and long-haul travel is reflected in Table 8.2 in the context of Europe, fuelled initially by package holidays and more recently by the revolution in low-cost air travel, a phenomenon affecting many countries after being pioneered in the USA and diffused to Europe, Asia and Australasia. In contrast, the trends in rail and bus/coach travel in Europe also mirror many international trends in tourist use of these travel modes which have recorded relative declines in their use. These modes of transport do not perform the same function in moving high volumes of mass tourists that they did historically in the nineteenth and up to the mid-twentieth century. They may best be described as complementary modes of transport compared to the tourist preference for car and air-based travel. This reflects a shift from tourist use of transport in the public domain unless it is faster, more accessible and time efficient. Exceptions do exist such as the use of the **TGV** and high-speed rail services which are time competitive with air and road transport.

Land-based transport

The car

The car is still widely neglected in tourism studies because it is now such an accepted part of everyday life that in impact and use in tourism is taken for granted and overlooked. Both the early study by Wall (1971) and Patmore (1983) identify the fundamental changes in mobility in the

TABLE 8.2 Performance of EU passenger transport by mode 1970–2000 (1000 million passenger kms)

| Year | Mode of transport | | | | | |
	Passenger car	Bus and coach	Tram and metro	Railway	Air	Total
1970	1582	269	39	219	33	2142
1980	2295	348	41	248	74	3006
1990	3199	369	48	268	157	4041
1991	3257	378	48	276	166	4126
1995	3506	382	47	274	202	4410
1996	3558	391	48	282	209	4488
1997	3622	393	49	285	222	4571
1998	3702	402	50	287	241	4682
1999	3788	406	51	295	260	4801
2000	3789	413	52	303	281	4839
% change 1991–2000	+16%	+9%	+10%	+10%	+70%	+17%

Source: © European Commission, Directorate-General for Energy and Transport, EU Energy and Transport in Figures 2002

post-war period in Western industrialized society and the rise in car ownership. One of the principal changes to take place in the post-war period in both outdoor recreation and domestic tourism is the major effect of the car on patterns of travel: it has made travel more convenient and less dependent upon public transport. The car offers considerable flexibility in the way people can travel and access tourism resources and sites outside urban areas. What the car has done is transform the tourist's ability to organize and develop their own **itineraries** and activity patterns, no longer dependent upon existing transport provision. For the resource managers of sites such as National Parks, one outcome has been the need to manage the impact of the car on key sites (e.g. 'honeypots', which are high-use sites) and popular locations which tourists visit. In some cases key tourism and recreational sites where over-use is a potential threat to the local resource base (e.g. The Goyt Valley in the Peak District National Park) the use of cars has been managed through the provision of alternative forms of transport. Yet as Page (2005) shows, many National Parks in the UK are concerned about their ability to accommodate the forecast growth in car use to these sites of 267 per cent between 1992 and 2025. The essential problem posed by the car is that its use is subject to the whim of the individual and its users cannot be controlled. In urban areas, the car is also a major problem for small historic cities such as Canterbury, York, Chester and Cambridge which have provided out-of-town car parking to address the environmental impact of congestion on the town centre environment which is used by tourists.

Dickinson *et al.* (2004: 105) highlight the range of initiatives developed to try and manage the tourist's use of the car, given that in Western developed countries such as the UK, 40 per cent of mileage travelled is for leisure use. Dickinson *et al.* (2004) point to leisure travel initiatives which have sought to:

- encourage closer travel to home
- develops containment/restriction strategies such as Yosemite National Park
- generate tourist traffic to support uneconomic public transport, such as the seasonal use of rail routes to peripheral areas
- make improvements to cycling and walking opportunities such as those introduced by **SUSTRANS** in the UK.

But barriers to the adoption of these solution to managing tourist demand relate to inadequate expenditure on promoting and raising awareness of alternatives to the car, failing to make access easier to alternatives and a lack of supply-led solutions such as expanding parking provision.

In historic cities, Orbaşli and Shaw (2004) identified the need to reconfigure the road network to re-route tourist cars away from city centres to catchment areas with **park and ride** schemes. Such a scheme also requires the separation of the car from tourists on foot by provision of pedestrian-only and cycle tracks to reduce pollution, noise and conflicts. For many government agencies, the car poses a fundamental contradiction: it brings the volume of visitors many towns and cities local economies depend upon and measures to limit, deter or make city centre access inconvenient (i.e. by pricing mechanisms) or promote park and ride schemes are opposed by business groups. Consequently environmental concerns related to congestion remain dominant arguments for implementing such measures but concerns over the possible loss of business leave many local authorities in a quandry – whatever solution they adopt, opponents will be vociferous.

Coach and bus transport

In the road-based transport sector (excluding the car) a number of different forms of passenger transport serve the needs of tourists. These can be classified into:

- express scheduled coach services (domestic and international services)
- private hire services for group travel
- packaged tours on coaches
- urban and rural bus services to tourist locations
- airport taxi and shuttle services
- excursions, day trip, sightseeing tours in urban and rural areas (based on Page 2003b).

What is interesting in coach travel is that its decline in the evolution of domestic holiday-making in the post-war period has now been reversed as investment in high quality services and coach travel's redevelopment as a budget-priced option for tourist travel in the 1990s have led to a resurgence of interest.

In the EU, the bus/coach mode of travel for tourism and leisure purposes is used by around 12 per cent of the population and the countries with the greatest use were Greece, Denmark, Germany and Spain. The lowest levels of use – under 5 per cent – were in the UK, Ireland, Italy and France. At a European level, around ten million people are employed in the bus/coach sector (Page 2003b) which is much higher than the air transport sector with 3.6 million employees and railway sector with 8.4 million employees. Recent policy changes in the EU as expressed in the White Paper *European Transport Policy for 2010* (European Union 2002) outlined the potential of this sector to substitute road-based car travel for bus/coach travel. However, critics of reducing car-based travel such as Stopher (2004) indicate the practical and logistical issues of seeking to promote modal switching from car to alternative modes in the absence of government policy shifts and considering the central role of the car in the mobility of modern-day society. Furthermore, the potential of the bus can only be realized, as it has been in London, when **congestion charging** is accompanied by massive investment in buses on the road networks. This saw bus patronage rise 13 per cent 1986–2000 and a further 8 per cent in 2001–2002, although introducing one-person operated vehicles, thereby replacing icons of London such as the 1950s Routemaster (Image 8.1), may impact upon tourist use of such services. In Glasgow, First has introduced 1950s buses to nurture the interest in travelling on heritage vehicles on city tours (Image 8.2). The EU has shown that more controlled competition in bus and coach transport, as has been used in London, has been more beneficial so that the model of uncontrolled competition in the UK following the 1980 and 1985 Transport Acts is not repeated. In many mainland European countries, state monopolies still exist, though Scandinavia's limited competition model and its use in France have helped these countries to use public subsidies more effectively. The extent of public subsidies for bus travel range from 29 per cent of costs in Scotland, 32 per cent in the UK, to 60–70 per cent in Austria, Belgium, Italy and the Netherlands, dependent upon government transport policy.

These different policy approaches have led to different market structures for the management of bus and coach travel, from a public-ownership model to market-led approaches and major competition. One outcome in the UK is the development of large integrated bus-coach-rail operators such as Arriva, First, Stagecoach and National Express. Some of these operators have European and global operations: Stagecoach acquired Coach USA in July 1999 and operates services in New Zealand.

The more notable and leisure-focused services are in the express coach market. The ECMT (1999) *Regular Interurban Coach Services in Europe* report documented the growth of motorway inter-urban express services. These are epitomized in the UK by National Express. Competition for passengers with rail, following deregulation in the mid-1980s, saw passenger volumes rise, but following rail privatization the volume of passengers on such services has remained at 17.7 million passengers a year. In contrast, the UK coach holiday market (Page 2003b) generated £396 million from overseas tourists and £643 million from domestic trips. Destinations such as Canterbury in the UK receive around 900 000 coach-related visits a year estimated to generate £16 million, while leisure attractions such as Alton Towers Theme Park receive £24 million from coach day trips and Edinburgh receives £44 million from this market (Page 2003b). Whilst the traditional market for the coach holiday is the over-55-year-old group, youth travellers also make use of

Image 8.1: The iconic London 'Routemaster' was withdrawn from service in December 2005: a heritage service remains on two routes in Central London. Source: S.J. Page

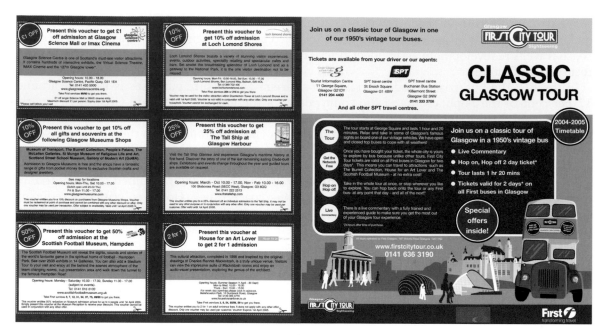

Image 8.2: Firstbus Glasgow's heritage bus service advertisement. Source: FirstBus, Glasgow

the coaches for holidays (e.g. Contiki). Outbound coach tourism from the UK is dominated by UK trips to France which accounts for over 50 per cent of the market with over 200 000 coaches crossing the English Channel via Dover/Eurotunnel each year. In the UK, the coach tourism market is dominated by a number of operators (e.g. Wallace Arnold, Shearings, Travelsphere, Titan Tours, Cosmos and Leger Travel) with Wallace Arnold the market leader, carrying over 500 000 passengers a year. Recent quality enhancements in the UK coach market (e.g. Shearings have introduced luxury vehicles with 36 seats – its Grand Tourers, costing £225 000 each, with more legroom for passengers), have further segmented the market into the low-cost, quality and luxury market.

In the EU, the express Eurolines business established in 1985 comprises 35 coach companies serving 300 cities and 500 destinations. The profile of its passengers shows that they are largely aged 16–30 years of age, most of them use the internet and over half travel alone, of whom over 55 per cent are female and 37 per cent are students. Quality enhancement to the operators' vehicles mean that the services are competitive in price with rail and air and offer an assured standard of service. The company's quality policy identifies five areas which determine the travellers' impression and satisfaction level (Figure 8.3) with communication being the most important characteristic. Eurolines indicate that around 80 per cent of consumers are satisfied with the service, although the company seeks continuous quality improvements.

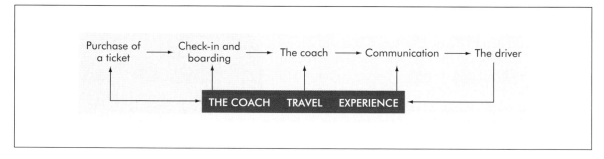

FIGURE 8.3   Model of Eurolines quality policy

Cycling

The cycle is arguably the most sustainable form of tourist transport (Lumsdon and Tolley 2004) one can use because, being non-motorized, it does not require fuel and does not always have a major impact on the built and physical environment (the exception being mountain biking where it constitutes a recreational activity). As Lumsdon and Tolley (2004) argue, after walking, cycling is the most important form of transport globally, given its significance for leisure use in developing countries such as China where it comprises 65 per cent of all trips made. In a European context, cycling is a popular form of transport in Denmark, Germany and the Netherlands (Lumsdon and Tolley 2004: 147) even though motorized transport has dominated transport policy in the inter-war and post-war period in most Westernized countries. Cycling also symbolizes many of the key principles of sustainable tourism: it has minimal environmental impacts and limited infrastructure requirements, and it is part of a wider renaissance of interest in walking and cycling in North America, Australasia and in Eastern Europe where quality of life is moving higher up the political agenda (Lumsdon and Tolley 2004: 147). This is in contrast to developing countries seeking to emulate symbols of modernization and affluence such as car ownership.

'Cycle tourism', according to SUSTRANS, is recreational visits, either overnight or visits away from home, which involves leisure cycling as a fundamental and significant part of the visit (cited in Lumsdon and Tolley 2004: 149) including:

- the recreational cyclist (e.g. the day excursionist)
- the cycle tourist (e.g. on holiday)

and may exemplify tourism as transport.

Infrastructure needs and patterns of cycle tourism Tourist cycling is now a well-established form of tourism in many countries, particularly where provision has been made through the development of cycle routeways. In the case of New Zealand, distinct patterns of cycle tourism exist (e.g. see Ritchie 1998). In the UK, developments in recreational and tourist cycling, often using redundant railway lines, are exemplified by the work of SUSTRANS (Sustainable Transport), the civil engineering charity formed in 1979, which is coordinating the National Cycle Network in Britain. This covers over 9000 miles of cycle route by 2005 (Figure 8.4). It reflects the importance of cycle routeways in the destination, which may include a network of links and loops, using a long-distance linear route or circuit trip from origin back to the origin. The national network in the UK has been planned with the intention of linking visitor attractions and the National Trust and SUSTRANS have worked on a number of joint initiatives which make journeys for cyclists more enjoyable and are largely traffic-free.

Cycling is also a popular pastime for domestic tourists and increasingly many cities are now making provision for cycle paths within the built environment which visitors can enjoy through hiring cycles. This is even evident in locations such as the Norfolk Broads in the UK where cycle routeways have been developed and managed to encourage low-impact tourism on a fragile environment. This follows good practice which is epitomized by the tourism and recreational activities that are planned and managed in the Netherlands. Here, cycling is a pastime and a sustainable form of day-to-day transport. The nature and profile of cycle users for tourism purposes is now becoming well documented as reflected in the work of Lumsdon (1997).

As Lumsdon (1997: 115) suggests, the growing importance of cycle tourism means that the market is growing and definite segments exist, including:

- *half-day/day excursionists*: occasional users who are home based and touring, typically aged 24–41 years of age and cycling 10–20 miles
- *half-day and day casual mountain bikers*: based at home and occasional users, aged 24–45 years and cycling 10–20 miles; they transport their bikes by car
- *half-day and day cycle hirers*: infrequent riders aged 18–55 years of age with a strong family element
- *the holiday tourists*: organize day rides or may be cycle tourists; they are in the upper socioeconomic groups, often transporting bikes by car
- *the holiday do-it-yourself mountain bikers*: like the previous group, but seeking harder routes

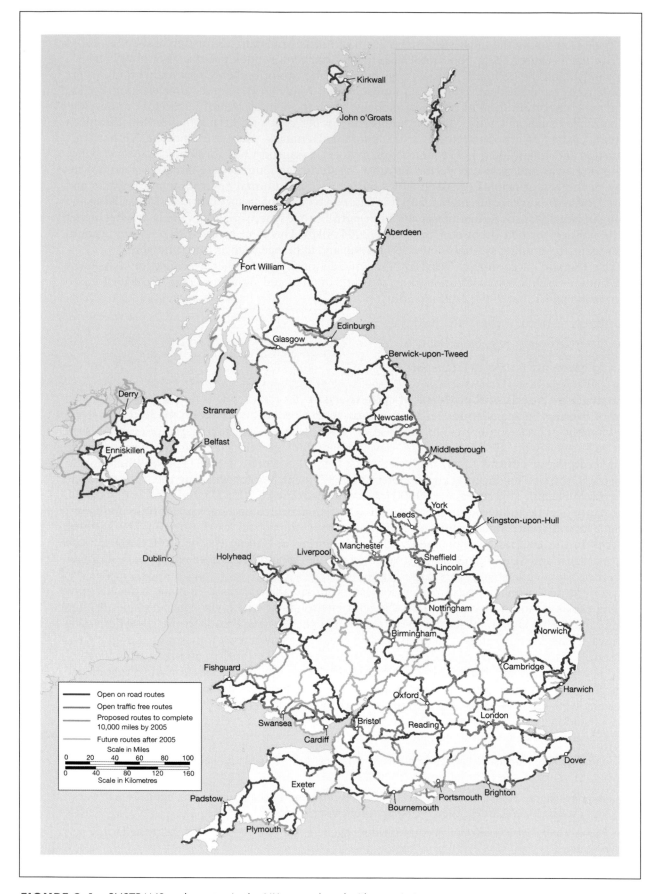

FIGURE 8.4 SUSTRANS cycle routes in the UK, reproduced with permission

- *organized, independent self-guided cycling tourists*: organize holidays and travel as a pair or group
- *organized group cyclists*: like the previous group but take guided routes
- *groups on holiday*: the cycle element is part of a multi-activitiy or cycle holiday
- *club riders*: self-arranged, long-distance riders
- *sports competitors*: undertake cycling as a sport
- *event riders*: undertake charity rides as part of a leisure experience (developed from Lumsdon 1997).

Clearly, in some contexts, cycling as an element of transport in a package or as a reason for tourism is seeing a resurgence, but one of the principal challenges for tourism planners and local authorities in destination areas is its integration into others forms of transport provision. The evidence in Loch Lomond and Trossachs National Park currently is that cycle tourists have to enter and access cycle routes by car. This is negating the principles of sustainable tourism as it adds to road-based congestion and access points by cycle are needed prior to tourists entering the park boundary. Cycle tourism provision can create a vital attraction for many destinations, but strategic planning in integrating its role and use is essential for success.

Rail travel

Train transport for tourism takes two forms: combined leisure and business, which is scheduled, and predominantly leisure-based services, 'where train travel becomes the focus of the tourist experience' (Prideaux 1999: 73). Rail transport was one of the prime movers of the leisure revolution in Victorian and Edwardian times, linked with the rise of seaside resorts since it offered an efficient mode of moving volumes of urban passengers from a city to a coastal destination. Yet for rail transport to operate effectively, a vastly expensive **capital investment** in built infrastructure is needed. Many current-day rail networks were funded by private investment in Victorian times, and have been added to and further developed by the state. Tourist use of these networks for leisure purposes has been classified by Page (2003a: 13) thus:

- the use of dedicated rail corridors which connect major gateways (airports and ports) of a country to the final destination, or as a mode of transit to the tourist accommodation in the nearby city
- the use of rapid transit systems and metros to travel within urban areas
- the use of high-speed and non-high-speed intercity rail corridors to facilitate movement as part of an itinerary or city-to-city journey, typically for business and leisure travel. These journeys may cross country borders in the EU and form part of a pan-European network
- the use of local rail services outside urban areas, often used in peak hours by commuters to journey to/from mainline/intercity rail terminals en route to other destinations
- the use of peripheral rail services which serve remote communities in the tourist season for scenic sightseeing and special interest travel.

In the case of tourist journeys by rail, the market for rail holidays has seen competition emerge with low-cost airlines although leisure day trips remain a key element of rail travel and, as discussed earlier, its use in Europe for leisure and business use on high-speed routes has seen significant growth. In Europe, rail has been subject to deregulation (Page 2003a) and it remains an expensive sector with ongoing investment requirements. Rail travel is portrayed as a more sustainable mode of travel than the car (Page 2005) and its safety record is impressive in most countries where the infrastructure is well maintained; however investment needs to occur on a rolling basis to ensure it is designed for modern-day tourist needs (i.e. time savings and convenience), examples of this being France's TGV network and dedicated city-to-airport rail routes like the British Airport Authority-funded Heathrow Express. As Page (2003a, 2005) has shown in the case of transport policy, in the years leading up to privatization, the market for leisure rail travel declined in the period 1990–5. Since privatization in 1994 (and excluding the impact of several rail crashes and the impact of foot and mouth), rail volumes have grown (Table 8.3). In contrast, rail travel in some countries (e.g. the USA) is perceived as a poorer alternative to flying but in the

TABLE 8.3 Passenger kilometres by ticket type (billions) Great Britain 1990–1 to 2003–04

	Ordinary fares	Season tickets	Total passenger kilometres	Total passenger kilometres seasonally adjusted
1990–91	22.8	10.4	33.2	33.2
1991–92	22.4	10.0	32.5	32.5
1992–93	22.3	9.4	31.7	31.7
1993–94	21.3	9.0	30.4	30.4
1994–95	20.7	8.0	28.7	28.7
1995–96	22.2	7.9	30.0	30.0
1996–97	23.4	8.7	32.1	32.1
1997–98	25.3	9.3	34.7	34.7
1998–99	26.4	9.8	36.3	36.3
1999–2000	28.0	10.4	38.5	38.5
2000–01	27.2	10.9	38.2	38.2
2001–02	28.1	11.0	39.1	39.1
2002–03	28.4	11.3	39.7	39.7
2003–04	29.1	11.8	40.9	40.9

Source: Strategic Rail Authority, reproduced with permission

Image 8.3: GNER Mallard – Coach refurbishment.
Source: Copyright, GNER

Image 8.4: GNER White Rose high-speed trains, originally built for Channel Tunnel services and now used for domestic high-speed London–Yorkshire services. Source: Copyright, GNER

UK a renaissance has occurred (see Shaw, Walton and Farrington 2003 and Page 2005). Investment in terminal facilities, innovation guides to interpret the changing landscape on Virgin Cross Country Services, state-of-the-art new trains or high quality refurbishments of rolling stock as shown by GNER (Images 8.3 and 8.4) have all created a new ambience for rail travel in the UK so the tourist or leisure traveller feels relaxed, refreshed and comfortable, and able to access the central areas of cities with ease compared to flying or via car use. Yet some of the most profound change in rail travel have occurred with the 'transport and tourism' luxury market such as the Orient Express (see Page 2005 for a case study of this innovative and successful venture). Similar examples have been developed in many countries, an example being Queensland Rail which has packaged scenery and sightseeing as key elements as discussed by Prideaux (1999). As Page (2005) observes, in Europe, further investment by the EU to create a pan-European high-speed network is a key component of its transport policy, to create a **trans-European network** (TEN) with infrastructure projects designed to provide links across country borders. This seeks to mirror the success of tourism and leisure travel achieved by other high-speed projects while improving travel efficiency, safety, mobility and European cooperation to encourage modal switching from road and air to rail.

Water-based transport

Water-borne transport is frequently overlooked in many studies of tourism since air travel dominates the world patterns of travel. However, it is certainly the case that the need to cross bodies of water, particularly where tourists use recreational vehicles (e.g. motor homes) and who then pursue land-based touring, means that crossing bodies of water presents transport operators with seasonal markets that can help offset the costs of all-year-round operation. Within the water-based transport sector, three main forms of transport can be identified: cruising, ferries and pleasure craft.

Cruising

The cruise product can take many forms; small-scale, specialist ships exist to take niche market clients to Antarctica and the Galapagos Islands and, at the other end of the spectrum, there are gigantic mass-entertainment ships which are themselves the destination. As Hoseason (2000) has shown, the use of cruise-ship capacity ratios illustrates this growth: as the ratio number drops, the luxury onboard decreases (Table 8.4). As tour operators have expanded the market for these products to a mass market (e.g. Thomson Holidays), a budget product has emerged where as new luxury ships such as the Eagle Class (Table 8.4) have a higher capacity ratio. The product, obviously, comprises both transport and accommodation – and a number of cruises out of Asia go 'nowhere' since they are provided for the gambling market. As an activity, cruising has been growing at a dramatic rate and, as Peisley (2004) acknowledges, large cruising companies dominate the market (e.g. Carnival Cruises, www.carnival.com, and Princess Cruises, www.princess.com). An associated trend is the growing size of cruise ships with the major operators now ordering 100 000-ton plus ships which bring significant economies of scale. In the USA, the Cruise Lines International Association saw the volume of passengers grow from 8.6 million in 2002 to 9.5 million in 2003, and the USA dominates world cruising market followed by the UK and Europe. These forms of luxury travel have led to a revival of cruise

Image 8.5: Cruising has now entered a new era as it provides a mass product compared to its elite role in the 1920s and 1930s

TABLE 8.4	Cruise ships' capacity ratio			
Cruise line	Ship	Tonnage	Maximum capacity	Ratio
Airtours	Sunbird	38 000	1 595	23.8
Cunard	QE II	66 450	1 800	36.9
Carnival	Imagination	70 300	2 594	27.1
Carnival	Inspiration	70 000	2 594	27.0
Carnival	Carnival Triumph	101 350	3 400	29.8
Celebrity Cruises	Galaxy	72 000	2 262	31.8
Disney Cruise Line	Disney Magic	85 000	2 400	35.4
Holland-America Line	Veendam	55 000	1 400	39.3
P&O	Oriana	69 000	1 810	38.1
Princess Cruises	Sun Princess	77 000	1 950	39.5
RCI	Eagle Class	142 000	3 838	37.0

Source: Hoseason (2000)

tourism at a global scale after the decline of the cruise liner in the post-war period when aircraft offered much lower costs of transatlantic and world travel and the luxury element lost favour. This is another example of how changes in tastes can shift demand to alternative forms of transport. Recently, cruising has been relaunched as a luxury activity (Image 8.5) which is now more accessible to greater numbers of people, but a much wider range of people from different age groups (including families) now choose this as a holiday option. In addition, the growth in new larger ships is leading cruise operators to discount their prices to fill capacity, with the new innovation of the easyCruise, another product to enter a crowded market.

Ferries

Ferries are used to cross water where it constitutes a barrier to travel. One of the busiest waterways in the world is the English Channel and a ferry service has been recorded in history between Dover and Calais since Roman times. Evidence in Medieval records also confirms the vital strategic and trade route which existed between these two ports. It remained the main crossing point between the UK and mainland Europe for many years. However, it is only since the end of the Second World War that a truly comprehensive 'product' has become available, with the size of ships increasing in order to provide more of an 'experience' for travellers and a major business activity onboard the vessels for the ferry operators. The opening of one of the largest-ever European tourist transport infrastructure projects, in the form of the Channel Tunnel, altered

---

TABLE 8.5   Ferry services in Scotland

- *Services to Orkney and Shetland* from Aberdeen and Scrabster (currently provided by P&O but transferring to NorthLink) including Aberdeen–Lerwick (Shetland), Aberdeen–Stromness (Orkney) and Scrabster–Stromness

- *Shetland inter-island ferry services* including Lerwick–Bressay, Mainland–Yell, Yell–Unst, Yell/Belmont–Fetlar, Mainland–Whalsay, Mainland–Out Skerry, South Mainland–Fair Isle, West Mainland–Foula and West Mainland–Papa Stour

- *Orkney Island services* from the mainland to Eday, Stronsay, Sanday, Flotta, Hoy, Graemsay, North Ronaldsay, Papa Westray, Westray, Rosay, Egilsay, Wyre and Shapinsay

- *Services from Shetland to the Faroe Isles and Bergen* in Norway

- *The services in the Firth of Clyde* (currently operated by Caledonian MacBrayne), including Wemyss Bay–Rothesay, Colintraive (Cowal)–Rhubodach (Bute), Largs–Cumbrae, Gourock–Dunoon, Gourock–Kilgreggan–Helensburgh and Protavadie (Cowal)–Tarbert (Kintyre)

- *Western Ferries' service* between Gourock and Dunoon

- The services to Islay, Colonsay and Gigha (currently operated by Caledonian MacBrayne), including Kennacraig (Kintyre)–Port Ellen and Port Askaig (Islay), Tayinloan (Kintryre)–Gigha and Oban–Kennacraig–Colonsay

- *The services to Mull and the Inner Hebrides* (currently operated by Caledonian MacBrayne) including Oban–Craignure (Mull), Lochaline–Fishnish (Mull), Tobermory (Mull)–Kilchoan (Ardnamuchan), Oban–Coll–Tiree, Fionnphort (Mull)–Iona and Oban–Lismore

- *Argyll and Bute Council ferry services* (Appin–Lismore and Islay–Jura)

- *The services to Skye, Raasay and the Small Isles* (currently operated by Caledonian MacBrayne) including Mallaig–Armadale (Skye), Sconser (Skye)–Raasay and Mallaig–Eigg–Muck–Rum–Canna

- *The services to the Outer Hebrides* (currently operated by Caledonian MacBrayne) including Oban/Mallaig–Castlebay (Barra)/Lochboisdale (South Uist), Uig (Skye)–Lochmaddy (North Uist), Otternish (North Uist)–Leverburgh (Harris), Uig–Tarbert (Harris) and Ullapool–Stornoway

- *Highland Council's Corran ferry* and its (directly provided) Camusnagaul–Fort William service, Mallaig–Inverie (provided under contract to Highland Council), Cromarty–Nigg (supported by Highland Council and others) and Glenelg–Kylerhea (a commercial and seasonal service across the narrows)

Source: Scottish Executive (2002: 31–2), reproduced with permission

services on this route by the end of the 1990s and provided a new form of competition with the sea-based services which were subsequently rationalized, reorganized and repositioned to compete with the new operator. What also occurred in the late 1990s was competition with another form of transport, the low-cost airlines, which has split the market three ways. In 2004 P&O Stena Line announced plans to rationalize its UK ferry operations down to around 25 vessels to counter a drop in patronage.

However, in some peripheral locations which have a highly seasonal tourist market, such as the Highlands and Islands of Scotland, the ferry services not only operate under a **public service grant** to subsidize the operation, but are a vital lifeline to a scattered series to communities as Table 8.5 shows. The volume of traffic on these services is around six million passenger journeys a year including nearly two million car crossings. The tourist market remains a key element of their business, supporting the highly seasonal tourism trade on remote and dispersed islands. In the UK, competition between the ferry operators on the North Sea and other crossings has led to their promotion of the 'cruising' qualities of sea travel to highlight the tranquillity and relaxation compared to the low-cost airline alternative, with some operators using catamaran services to offer a high-speed alternative to ferries.

Pleasure craft on inland waterways

Within countries which have an industrial heritage based on canals and inland waterways (e.g. northern European countries, the UK and Eire) a significant vacation market has developed based on pleasure boats designed to use the former canal and waterways that were previously developed to serve the transport needs of a former era. In cities such as Birmingham and Gloucester in the UK, the network of canals is so extensive that it has become the focus of urban regeneration projects. Tourist use of pleasure craft is an integral part of the strategy by British Waterways Board to relaunch the area's appeal to the tourist seeking a heritage product (Image 8.6). The extent of the canal network in the UK still offers considerable potential for expansion as a tourism and leisure resource using the historic canal boats, converted for holidays as companies such as Hoseasons have promoted.

To illustrate the scale and significance of this growing market for pleasure craft as part of a holiday experience, the example of the Norfolk Broads in the UK suggests that even seemingly sustainable modes of tourist transport such as the canal or pleasure boat are not without environmental impacts. The Norfolk Broads is a wetland region in East Anglia created through the flooding of peat diggings in the Medieval period. The region comprises a number of rivers and their tributaries which offer opportunities for recreational and tourism-related boating activities. The hire-boat industry was pioneered by John Loyne in the 1880s and popularized in 1908 by H. Blake and Company, which set up purpose-built vessels for hire aimed at the rail-based visitors. In 1995, the boat companies in the region owned 1481 motor cruises and launches hired to approximately 200 000 visitors a year but there are over 13 000 licensed boats using the Broads each year. The single most important environmental impact of the hire boat and recreation and boat industry has been the damage to the river banks caused by the wash from vessels together with a number of other impacts induced by the visitors' effect on wildlife and the potential conflict with other activities such as angling. Yet the economic impact of boating in the region is estimated to contribute £25 million to the local economy and supports over 1600 jobs, while indirect tourist spending contributes to over 5000 jobs.

Image 8.6: Since the 1990s, river tourism has become a fast-growing market in many European countries, as the appeal of cruises and trips on waterways has enjoyed a renaissance, including canal boats

Air transport

Apart from so-called 'air taxis', all civil aviation falls into one of two categories: scheduled and charter traffic. Scheduled airlines are those which operate to a clearly defined, published timetable, irrespective of whether a flight is full or not. Until the 1980s, many schedule airlines were state-owned and run for reasons of national prestige; a classic example of privatization occurred in 1987 when the British government sold British Airways. In contrast, chartered aircraft, by definition, are chartered out to a third party; this may be a seat-broker who will sell smaller blocks of seats to small tour operators or it may be a large tour operator who requires the whole aircraft for a summer or winter season's flying. In reality, the large tour operators, such as Airtours, Thomson and First Choice in the UK, possess their own airlines. The evolution of air travel is a complex area which is historically determined by international bodies such as the International Civil Aviation Organization (ICAO) and the International Air Transport Association (IATA). The regulations they established have, combined with bilateral agreements, established the framework for international air travel up until the deregulation era in the late 1970s.

One of the most complex areas is the political regulation of air travel, which dates to the 1930s and includes the 1944 Chicago Convention. Current-day aviation is regulated by international aviation law and this provides the context in which national and global carriers operate. At the national level, different countries have varying approaches to aviation competition and regulation. In the USA, anti-trust laws exist to encourage competition and reduce price fixing. This was extended under the 1978 Airline Deregulation Act. In Europe, similar legislation exists with anti-competition law in existence. In the USA, deregulation has seen the patterns of larger carriers take over many of the smaller operators and develop a **hub and spoke operation**. Here, the hub is a centralized point of operation where local flights feed passengers to the hub, to avoid operating large aircraft on local, uneconomic routes (Figure 8.5). One of the exceptions to this rule is the growth of low-cost

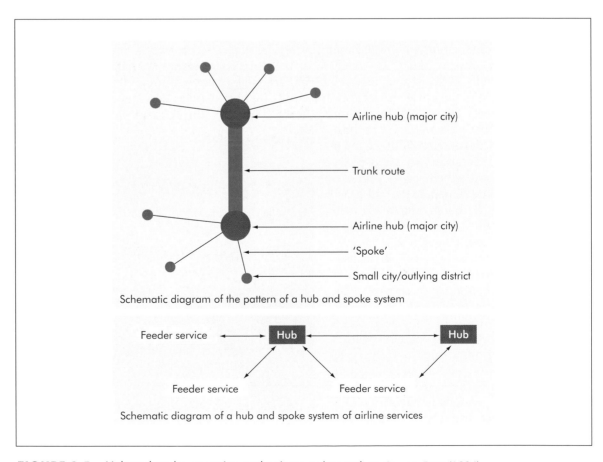

Schematic diagram of the pattern of a hub and spoke system

Schematic diagram of a hub and spoke system of airline services

FIGURE 8.5   Hub and spoke operation and point to point services. Source: Page (1994)

carriers, like Southwest Airlines in the USA, which use smaller secondary airports and offer point-to-point services, rather than a national and international network (Figure 8.5).

At an international scale, the right of airlines to fly is governed by the five freedoms of the air, outlined in Table 8.6. Airlines can gain technical and traffic rights to operate between countries,

TABLE 8.6   Freedoms of the air

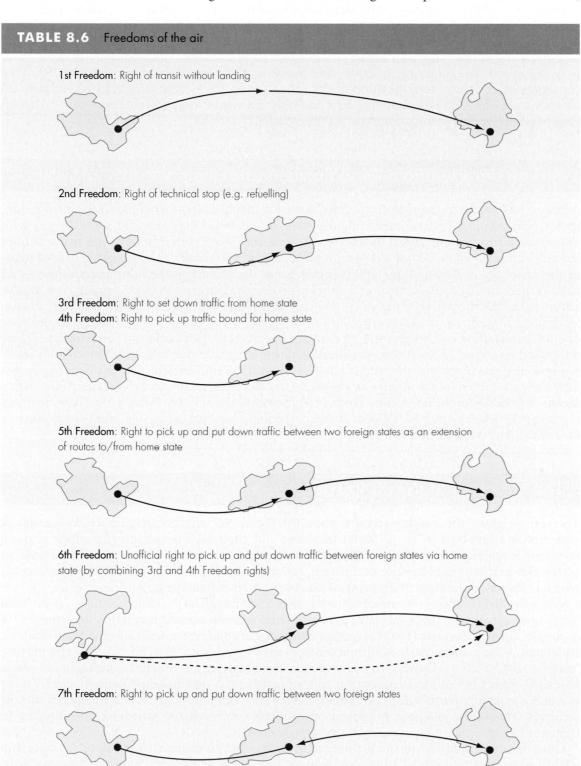

1st Freedom: Right of transit without landing

2nd Freedom: Right of technical stop (e.g. refuelling)

3rd Freedom: Right to set down traffic from home state
4th Freedom: Right to pick up traffic bound for home state

5th Freedom: Right to pick up and put down traffic between two foreign states as an extension of routes to/from home state

6th Freedom: Unofficial right to pick up and put down traffic between foreign states via home state (by combining 3rd and 4th Freedom rights)

7th Freedom: Right to pick up and put down traffic between two foreign states

Source: Redrawn from 'Figure G.1: Air transport freedom rights' which first appeared in Asia Pacific Air Transport: Challenges and Policy Reforms, ediited by Christopher Findlay, Chia Lin Sien and Karmjit Singh, p.193, with the kind permission of the publisher, Institute of Southeast Asian Studies, Singapore http://bookshop.iseas.edu.sg

based on the 1944 Chicago Convention. The rights have also been developed in subsequent years with sixth and seventh freedoms being added.

A key feature of international civil aviation in the last 20 years has been 'deregulation'. This started in the USA in 1978, when the federal government relaxed its control over route allocation and pricing leading, inevitably, to the establishment of numerous small airlines, many of which no longer exist; although it pre-dates 1978, Southwest Airlines benefited from the ability to fly on any route and has pursued a policy of issuing boarding cards instead of tickets, serving no meals and operating as many flights a day as possible (see Page 2005 for a detailed analysis of air travel in a climate of deregulation). In 2005, Southwest was serving 55 cities across the USA. One consequence of excessive competition in the airline sector was evident after 9/11 when many US airlines were already burdened with debt and only six weeks away from collapse, even though they provide the vital link for domestic and international tourism.

Airline deregulation: Globalization and alliances

Aviation has not been immune from deregulation as many governments have sought to reduce investment requirements by privatizing the state airline, which has provided some airlines with opportunities to become global businesses. In Asia and South America, however, many airlines are still state-owned and enjoy a degree of protectionism. Ironically, this has not benefited many of these airlines in Asia as Page (2005) shows, since the airlines in the other parts of the world have forged strategic alliances to enter these 'protected' markets, thereby gaining competitive advantages. The protectionism means that many of the state-owned airlines are less competitive, leading to high fares for Asian travellers (Findlay, Sieh and Singh 1997) (except where they operate low staffing cost structures), and are not operating at their optimum performance. Figure 8.6, based on Evans's (2001) conceptualization of the alliance and collaboration process for international airlines, highlights the range of motives associated with entering into such arrangements especially the potential for airlines to cooperate; for example, an alliance may offer passengers a global network without one airline having to provide all the services. This has assisted many of the larger airlines to establish a global presence through the three existing large airline alliances – Oneworld, Star Alliance and Sky Team.

The structure of the air transport sector

The complexity of the aviation sector is shown in Figure 8.7 which highlights the wide range of stakeholders involved in the aviation industry, and their significance to the wider tourism economy is apparent from Figure 8.8 which illustrates the economic impact of the air transport sector. For a vibrant airline sector to function, collaboration and a strong industry body is needed, which is shown in the Case Study 8.1W of the Association of Asia Pacific Airlines.

What the airline alliance literature shows is that a number of airline alliances have grown from 'inter-line' agreements into substantial, coordinated reservation and marketing agreements for groups of airlines. Bennett (1997) identifies two forms of alliance: tactical (informal) and strategic (informal). The tactical partnership provides marketing advantages at low risk to the parties; 'code-sharing' allows one airline to market flights from regional airports to an international one (a so-called 'hub') for onward connection to intercontinental destinations. Bennett (1997: 214) considers strategic partnerships are where longer-term commitment results in 'shared airport facilities (check-ins, lounges), improved connections (synchronized schedules), reciprocity on frequent flyer programmes...and marketing agreements'.

Ongoing consolidation in the airline industry has led to changes in alliance membership within a short space of time but one way airlines have addressed costs is through **yield management**.

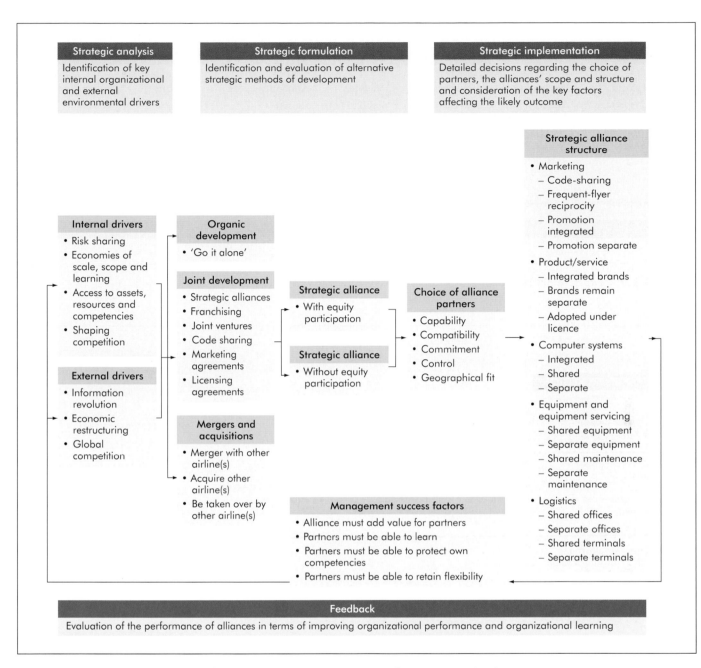

Strategic analysis	Strategic formulation	Strategic implementation
Identification of key internal organizational and external environmental drivers	Identification and evaluation of alternative strategic methods of development	Detailed decisions regarding the choice of partners, the alliances' scope and structure and consideration of the key factors affecting the likely outcome

Internal drivers
- Risk sharing
- Economies of scale, scope and learning
- Access to assets, resources and competencies
- Shaping competition

External drivers
- Information revolution
- Economic restructuring
- Global competition

Organic development
- 'Go it alone'

Joint development
- Strategic alliances
- Franchising
- Joint ventures
- Code sharing
- Marketing agreements
- Licensing agreements

Mergers and acquisitions
- Merger with other airline(s)
- Acquire other airline(s)
- Be taken over by other airline(s)

Strategic alliance
- With equity participation

Strategic alliance
- Without equity participation

Choice of alliance partners
- Capability
- Compatibility
- Commitment
- Control
- Geographical fit

Strategic alliance structure
- Marketing
  - Code-sharing
  - Frequent-flyer reciprocity
  - Promotion integrated
  - Promotion separate
- Product/service
  - Integrated brands
  - Brands remain separate
  - Adopted under licence
- Computer systems
  - Integrated
  - Shared
  - Separate
- Equipment and equipment servicing
  - Shared equipment
  - Separate equipment
  - Shared maintenance
  - Separate maintenance
- Logistics
  - Shared offices
  - Separate offices
  - Shared terminals
  - Separate terminals

Management success factors
- Alliance must add value for partners
- Partners must be able to learn
- Partners must be able to protect own competencies
- Partners must be able to retain flexibility

Feedback
Evaluation of the performance of alliances in terms of improving organizational performance and organizational learning

FIGURE 8.6 Conceptualization of the collaborative strategy process for international airlines. Source: Reprinted from *Tourism Management*, vol.22, Evans, 'Collaborative strategy: An analysis of the changing world of international airline alliances', 229–43, copyright (2001) with permission from Elsevier

Yield management and airlines

According to Kimes (2000: 3):

'yield management originated with the deregulation of the US airline industry' as the People's Express low-priced, no frills airline model of operation saw full-service operators such as American Airlines and United compete by offering a small number of similar seats on each departure. This created a diversity of passenger types and the yield (or revenue) management, a method for managing capacity profitability, has since gained widespread acceptance in the airline and hotel industries. The term 'yield' originated in the airline industry and refers to yield (or revenue) per available seat mile …Yield management is a method which can help a firm to sell the right inventory unit to the right customers, at the right time and for the right price … to maximize profit and revenue.

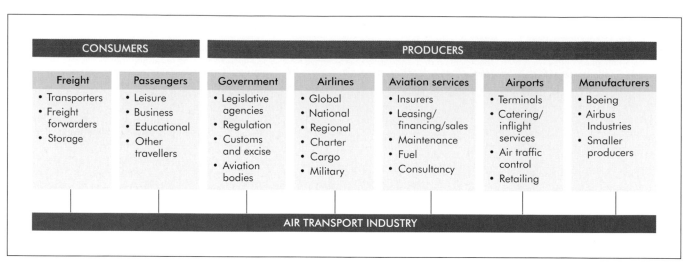

FIGURE 8.7   Structure of the aviation sector. Source: ATAG, reproduced with permission

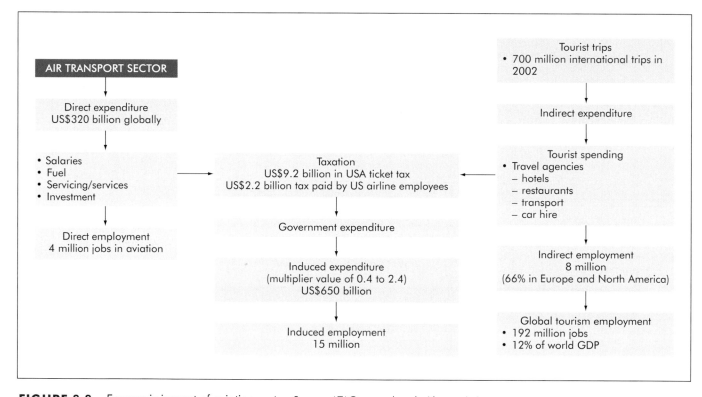

FIGURE 8.8   Economic impact of aviation sector. Source: ATAG, reproduced with permission

The concept of yield management has come to have equal validity for the hotel and cruising businesses since any capacity not sold cannot be held onto; for example, an unsold bed-night cannot be retained – it is lost revenue and better to achieve some price than none at all. Kimes (2000) identifies a number of conditions that are essential for yield management to work:

- fixed capacity
- high fixed costs
- low variable costs
- time-varied demand
- similarity of inventory units.

Added to these conditions, there are a number of required features of the business, namely:

- market segmentation capability
- historical demand and booking pattern data
- knowledge of competitor pricing
- development of an over-booking policy
- links to the corporate management information system.

Importantly, airline yield management systems enable some seats to be retained for those premium fare passengers who always book late. Page (2005) refers to research which shows 2–5 per cent revenue gains resulting from implementation of such a system.

Such systems have been successfully used by the rapidly expanding low-cost airlines in the 1990s. For example, the growth of Southwest Airlines in the USA in the 1970s has been replicated by Ryanair, easyJet and Bmibaby in the UK. This model of operation using yield management has also filtered through to Australia with Virginblue, Air Asia in Malaysia and many other competing operators in Asia such as Sky Asia and Tiger Airways (the latter two airlines developed from larger flag carriers – Thai International Airlines and Singapore Airlines) to generate new markets without diluting the full-cost and high quality service brand of the parent company. These airlines use yield management successfully to maximize revenue and passenger loadings, with low operational costs and using a distinctive business model similar to that of the highly successful Southwest Airlines (Gittell 2003). One of the key operational costs for airlines remains aviation fuel and in 2004 rising costs, according to IATA, led its 267 member airlines to report their collective losses of US$4 billion, as each 1-cent increase in aviation fuel leads to a US$500 million rise in airline costs. Yet this has not deterred the growth in low-cost travel, which remains the key driver of air travel, as the period January–August 2004 saw low-cost European carriers increase passenger volumes by 24 per cent: and they account for 25 per cent of all European air travel.

Terminal facilities and tourist travel

One of the most neglected and poorly understood areas of tourist travel is the role and significance of **terminal facilities** (Page 2005). These provide a wide range of functions from simple interchanges in the public transport setting (e.g. a coach terminal such as London's Victoria Coach Station) to the more advanced integrated transport interchanges such as Singapore Changi airport (Image 8.7) where air, rail, coach, taxi and car modes are fully integrated.

In the airline industry, terminals have traditionally been viewed as transfer points from air to other modes or air-to-air transfers. But the 1970s and 1980s have seen a revolution in airport terminal design since they offer a wide range of retailing opportunities for passengers to make the waiting and journey more pleasurable. This has also led to a growth in non-aviation revenue for airports (Graham 2000) for highly successful global airline companies such as British Airports Authority (www.baa.co.uk). Airlines have developed specialist facilities in these terminals for high-yield passengers such as first-class travellers, namely first-class lounges or VIP lounges which cater for the needs of these groups (e.g. a place to relax, work or to hold meetings).

Image 8.7: Changi Airport: A model of integrated tourist transport provision.
Source: Copyright, Civil Aviation Authority of Singapore

These facilities have to be integrated with a wide range of other functions at airports including:

- ground handling
- baggage handling
- passenger terminal operations (including check-in, passport control, customs clearance, security screening, shops, duty-free, waiting and transit areas)
- airport security
- cargo operations
- airport technical services
- air traffic control
- airport emergency services
- airport access
- car parking.

The scale and significance of such terminals in terms of the volume of traffic they handle is recorded by the global organization the Airport Council International (ACI). At a global scale, in 2003, of 3.5 billion passenger movements, 1.3 billion were in North America and 1 billion were in Europe followed by 720 million in Asia Pacific. To carry these 3.5 billion passengers, ACI airports accommodated 66.7 million total aircraft movements (including cargo flights) which include the landing and take-off of an aircraft. Table 8.7 provides a more detailed insight into the global distribution of tourist travel at the top 50 airports in 2003 by total passengers and the changes in volume on 2002. The dominance of North America, Europe and Asia Pacific is apparent, although US airports dominate the top 20 rankings given the highly developed tourism and leisure travel market and infrastructure. In the USA this accommodates a large domestic travel market as well as international travel elements. ACI statistics highlight the importance of airports in accommodating tourist travel and the need for long-term development strategies (see Page 2005 for the situation regarding UK airport policy and Page 2004 for Asia), since building a new terminal can take over a decade from inception, including the planning, development and opening phases.

Airport privatization, like airline privatization, has occurred at a global scale due to the high investment costs to governments of building new airport capacity. According to ICAO, by 2010, world airports will need US$25 billion of new investment to meet demand (Hooper 2002) and this is reflected in recent capital costs of new Asian airport developments such as KIA (US$15–20 billion) and Hong Kong's Chep Lap Kok (US$15–20 billion) (Hooper 2002).

Image 8.8: Airport ground handling of aircraft and passengers requires large expanses of land and facilities to accommodate aircraft, as shown at Singapore Changi Airport. Source: Copyright, Civil Aviation Authority of Singapore

Image 8.9: Cargo operations are a vital element of the business of air transport and they have to be accommodated alongside passenger operations. Source: Copyright, Civil Aviation Authority of Singapore

TABLE 8.7 Traffic figures for the world's top 30 airports 2003

World airport ranking by total passengers

Rank	City (Airport)	Total passengers	% change
1	Atlanta (ATL)	79 086 792	2.9
2	Chicago (ORD)	69 508 672	4.4
3	London (LHR)	63 487 136	0.2
4	Tokyo (HND)	62 876 269	2.9
5	Los Angeles (LAX)	54 982 838	(2.2)
6	Dallas/Ft. Worth Airport (DFW)	53 253 607	0.8
7	Frankfurt/Main (FRA)	48 351 664	(0.2)
8	Paris (CDG)	48 220 436	(0.3)
9	Amsterdam (AMS)	39 960 400	(1.9)
10	Denver (DEN)	37 505 138	5.2
11	Phoenix (PHX)	37 412 165	5.2
12	Las Vegas (LAS)	36 285 932	3.6
13	Madrid (MAD)	35 854 293	5.7
14	Houston (IAH)	34 154 574	0.7
15	Minneapolis/St. Paul (MSP)	33 201 860	1.8
16	Detroit (DTW)	32 664 620	0.6
17	New York (JFK)	31 732 371	6.0
18	Bangkok (BKK)	30 175 379	(6.2)
19	London (LGW)	30 007 021	1.3
20	Miami (MIA)	29 595 618	(1.5)
21	Newark (EWR)	29 431 061	0.7
22	San Francisco (SFO)	29 313 271	(6.8)
23	Orlando (MCO)	27 319 223	2.5
24	Hong Kong (HKG)	27 092 290	(20.0)
25	Seattle (SEA)	26 755 888	0.2
26	Tokyo (NRT)	26 537 406	(8.1)
27	Rome (FCO)	26 284 478	3.7
28	Sydney (SYD)	25 333 508	4.0
29	Toronto (YYZ)	24 739 312	(4.6)
30	Philadelphia (PHL)	24 671 075	(0.5)

Note: Figures in brackets represent a percentage drop

Source: ACI data, reproduced with permission

Conclusion

The tourist's use of transport begins when the tourist leaves their home and boards a form of transport. Without the transport mode, access to tourism would be very limited and restricted. It is really the post-war period that has seen the greatest revolution in transportation, making tourist destinations more accessible to a much greater population as living standards and income have increased per capita. What is also clear from this chapter is the pace of change and development in the transport sector, which provides new opportunities for tourist travel, realizing latent demand (i.e. facilitating travel where demand may not have existed because of the prohibitively high cost of travel for low income groups). The introduction of budget travel, especially the low-cost carriers, remains a major driver of tourist development that has expanded the range of destinations for the budget conscious traveller. This also leads to change in the marketplace and fierce competition between carriers to gain market share.

Among some of the current trends affecting tourist travel in different transport modes over the next decade are:

- *Air travellers' price sensitivity has increased*, as low-cost travel has challenged models of provision which have dominated many carriers, especially in markets that have only limited elements of internationalization.
- *Collaboration amongst transport providers*, especially airlines, has enabled greater cost competitiveness and an interconnected transport system at a global level and these will continue to grow in significance.

- *Quality service remains a constant pressure upon the suppliers of transport services*, especially as travellers seek more for less in terms of price. However, quality hallmarks and customer service still distinguish many well-established and successful companies that offer premium services, and there is no shortage of demand in key markets for premium services. The success of the Orient Express is a case in point.

Among key management considerations to meet increasing customer expectations in transport provisions are:

- efficient cost controls, as discussed in Chapter 5, continued savings in operational budgets and a greater use of technology to achieve these goals
- a clear understanding of strategic issues, especially the implications of transport policy changes such as the greater liberalization of air travel and process of globalization and privatization
- a need for effective and influential leadership skills to ensure operators stay ahead of the competition
- managing yields so that existing capacity and infrastructure can be used more efficiently and profitably.

A thorough understanding of the relationship between transport and tourism is a major prerequisite for any analysis of the factors which facilitate and constrain the development of tourism and any discussion of its role cannot ignore the importance of governments in shaping policy and infrastructure development to encourage inbound and outbound tourism.

Discussion questions

1 Why is transport important to the study of tourism?
2 Has the development of cruising in the late 1990s become a new product based on the concept of luxury and leisure experiences?
3 Identify the impact of low-cost airline carriers on the European airline market.
4 The interaction between transport and tourism is poorly understood. Why is this the case?

References

AAPA (2003) *Annual Report*, www.aapaillines.org.
ATAG (Air Transport Action Group) (2000) *The Economic Benefits of Air Transport*. Brussels: ATAG.
Bennett, M. (1997) 'Strategic alliances in the world airline industry', *Progress in Tourism and Hospitality Research*, 3: 213–23.

Dickinson, J., Calver, S., Watters, K. and Wilks, K. (2004) 'Journeys to heritage attractions in the UK: A case study of National Trust visitors in the South West', *Journal of Transport Geography*, 12: 103–13.
Doganis, R. (1991) *Flying Off Course: The Economics of International Airlines*. London: Routledge.

ECMT (1999) *Regular Interurban Coach Services in Europe*. Paris: ECMT.

European Union (2002) *European Transport Policy for 2010*. Brussels: EU.

Evans, N., (2001) 'Collaborative strategy: An analysis of the changing world for international airlines', *Tourism Management*, 22: 229–43.

Evans, N., Campbell, D. and Stonehouse, G. (2003) *Strategic Management for Travel and Tourism*. Oxford: Butterworth-Heinemann.

Findlay, C., Sieh, L. and Singh, K. (eds) (1997) *Asia Pacific Air Transport: Challenges and Policy Reforms*. Singapore: Institute of South East Asian Studies.

Gittell, J. (2003) *The Southwest Airlines Way*. New York: McGraw-Hill.

Graham, A. (2000) *Managing Airports*. Oxford: Butterworth-Heinemann.

Hall, C.M. and Page, S.J. (eds) (2000) *Tourism in South and South East Asia*. Oxford: Butterworth-Heinemann.

Hooper, P. (2002) 'Privatization of airports in Asia', *Journal of Air Transport Management*, 8(5): 289–300.

Hoseason, J. (2000) 'Capacity management in the cruise ship industry', in U. McMahon-Beattie, I.I. Yeoman and A. Ingold (eds) Yield Management: – *Strategies for the Service Industries, Second Edition*. London: Continuum.

Kimes, S. (2000) 'Yield management: An overview', in U. McMahon-Beattie, I.I. Yeoman and A. Ingold (eds) *Yield Management – Strategies for the Service Industries, Second Edition*. London: Continuum.

Lumsdon, L. (1997) 'Recreational cycling: Is this the way to stimulate interest in everyday urban cycling?', in R. Tolley (ed.) *The Greening of Urban Transport Planning for Walking and Cycling in Western Cities, Second Edition*. Chichester: Wiley.

Lumsdon, L. and Page, S.J. (eds) (2004) *Tourism and Transport: Issues and Agenda for the New Millennium*. Oxford: Elsevier.

Lumsdon, L. and Swift, J. (2001) *Tourism in Latin America*. London: Continuum.

Lumsdon, L. and Tolley, R. (2004) 'Non-motorised transport: A case study of cycling', in L. Lumsdon and S.J. Page (eds) *Tourism and Transport: Issues and Agenda for the New Millennium*, Oxford: Elsevier.

Moscardo, G. and Pearce, P. (2004) 'Life cycle, tourist motivation and transport: Some consequences for the tourist experience', in L. Lumsdon and S.J. Page (eds) *Tourism and Transport: Issues and Agenda for the New Millennium*. Oxford: Elsevier.

Orbaşli, A. and Shaw, S. (2004) 'Transport and visitors in historic cities', in L. Lumsdon and S.J. Page (eds) *Tourism and Transport Issues and Agenda for the New Millennium*. Oxford: Elsevier.

Page, S.J. (1994) *Transport for Tourism*. London: Routledge.

Page, S.J. (2003a) 'European bus and coach travel', *Travel and Tourism Analyst*, 1: 5–30.

Page, S.J. (2003b) 'European rail travel', *Travel and Tourism Analyst*, 5: 1–54.

Page, S.J. (2004) 'Air travel – Asia', *Travel and Tourism Analyst*, 3: 1–56.

Page, S.J. (2005) *Transport and Tourism: Global Perspectives, Second Edition*. Harlow: Prentice-Hall.

Patmore, J.A. (1983) *Recreation and Resources*. Oxford: Blackwell.

Peisley, T. (2004) 'Cruising in Europe', *Travel and Tourism Analyst*, 2: 1–39.

Prideaux, B. (1999) 'Tracks to tourism: Queensland Rail joins the tourist industry', *International Journal of Tourism Research*, 1 (2): 73–86.

Ritchie, B.W. (1998) 'Bicycle tourism in the South West of New Zealand: Planning and management issues', *Tourism Management*, 19 (6): 567–82.

Scottish Executive (2002) *Proposals for a Highlands and Islands Integrated Transport Authority: Volume 1, Main Report*. Edinburgh: Scottish Executive.

Shaw, J., Walton, W. and Farrington, J. (2003) 'Assessing the potential for a "railway renaissance" in Great Britain', *Geoforum*, 34 (2): 141–56.

Stopher, P. (2004) 'Reducing road congestion', *Transport Policy*, 11: 117–31.

Wall, G. (1971) 'Car owners and holiday activities', in P. Lavery (ed.) *Recreational Geography*. Newton Abbot: David and Charles.

WTO (2000) Data Collection and Analysis for Tourism Management; Madrid: World Tourism Organisation.

Further reading

Kimes, S. (2000) 'Yield management: An overview', in U. McMahon-Beattie, I.I. Yeoman and A. Ingold (eds) *Yield Management – Strategies for the Service Industries, Second Edition*. London: Continuum.

Page, S.J. (2005) *Transport and Tourism: Global Perspectives, Second Edition*. Harlow: Prentice Hall.

9

Visitor Attractions

Learning outcomes

After reading this chapter and answering the questions, you should:

- understand the scope and importance of visitor attractions

- be able to identify and discuss the main issues influencing the development and management of attractions

- outline future issues and themes affecting the attractions sector.

Overview

Visitor attractions are one of the key components of the tourism industry, adding to the appeal of destinations through natural and built features, as well as the hosting of special events. This chapter reviews the nature and scope of visitor attractions and explores a number of issues associated with its development, operation and management.

The different approaches used to classify visitor attractions are explored together with the various ways of conceptualising visitor attactions. The importance of management in developing successful visitor attractions is examined together with the future issues affecting the development, operation and management of visitor attractions.

Introduction

Visitor attractions form one of the basic components of the tourism industry, along with transport and accommodation, and play a crucial role in the appeal of destinations. For many tourists, the attractions on offer at a destination form the major reason for visiting. Indeed, attractions are frequently used as the basis for **destination marketing** campaigns (see Chapter 16). Attractions are a central component of leisure day visits as well as tourism trips, serving the resident community as well as those on holiday away from home. The attractions sector comprises a wide range of **built environment** and **natural environment**s, as well as cultural resources, products, **festivals and events**, which are developed and managed to provide interesting and enjoyable experiences to the visitor.

As well as providing appeal in a destination, attractions act as a focal point for visitor activity and spending, which is particularly important where tourism forms part of a wider development or area rejuvenation strategy. Therefore, a thriving attraction industry is part of an area's basic tourism infrastructure, providing opportunities for the local community, businesses and the local economy as well as visitor enjoyment. The management of attractions, however, is highly complex and beset with difficulties. Throughout this chapter, a key theme is the development, operation and management of visitor attractions as part of a prosperous tourism economy. Where examples of failed attractions are apparent, then the basic infrastructure of the tourism sector is diminished, and throughout the chapter it is apparent that those attractions that do not embrace the positive features of attraction development will either face financial problems or, more likely, fail.

The evolution of visitor attractions

While visitor attractions might be considered as a modern creation, the evolution of tourism was dependent on the existence and development of attractions. Even as far back as Roman times, travellers went to look at the Pyramids and, much later, the Grand Tour circuits were based around the major cultural attractions of Europe (see Chapter 2). As Table 9.1 indicates, some of today's major attractions existed in an embryonic form in the late nineteenth century (e.g. Blackpool Pleasure Beach, UK) and early twentieth century (e.g. De Efteling, Netherlands).

TABLE 9.1   Selection of the world's most popular theme parks

Year opened		Country	Approximate visitor numbers in 2004 (million)
1896	Blackpool Pleasure Beach	UK	6.5
1951	De Efteling	Netherlands	3.5
1955	Disneyland, Anaheim	USA	13
1964	Universal Studios, Hollywood	USA	5
1971	Magic Kingdom, Orlando	USA	15
1971	Sea World, Gold Coast	Australia	1
1977	Ocean Park	Hong Kong	3
1982	EPCOT, Orlando	USA	9
1983	Tokyo Disneyland	Japan	13
1989	Lotte World, Seoul	South Korea	8
1990	Universal Studios, Orlando	USA	7
1992	Disneyland Paris	France	10
2001	Universal Studios, Japan	Japan	7
2001	Disney Californian Adventures	USA	5.5

However, it was not really until the post-war period that visitor attractions really developed into a form that we recognize in contemporary tourism, including theme parks where the experience is highly sophisticated, using marketing and technology.

The USA is considered to be the pioneer in the development of theme parks, the first of which was Disneyland created by Walt Disney in California in 1955. The Disney vision to create a magical place which children and parents could enjoy, attracted four million visitors in its first year of opening and set the standard for the future development of the newly emerging attractions sector. Disney's second, larger resort, Walt Disney World in Florida, is now the world's most visited holiday destination. In a more global context, attractions became more prolific in number in the 1980s, with demand stimulated by tourism growth. The global distribution of major **brand**s then became a key feature (see Table 9.1), emphasizing the central theme of globalization of tourism.

The development of the attraction sector is not simply concerned with the major global theme parks. Since the 1980s, there has been a rapid growth in all types of attractions, from **country houses** to industry-related visitor centres. Thus let us turn first to the definition of the term 'visitor attraction'.

Defining attractions

As Richards (2002) argues, the study of tourism attractions is not as advanced as some other areas of tourism, and defining the scope of attractions can be problematic. With regard to basic terminology, it should be noted that visitor attractions are also known as 'tourist attractions', but because the client base of many attractions includes local residents, day visitors and tourists, the term 'visitor attraction' is a more appropriate one to use for this chapter.

The definition of attractions adopted by the NTOs in the UK, states that an attraction is:

where the main purpose is sightseeing. The attraction must be a permanent established excursion destination, a primary purpose of which is to allow access for entertainment, interest or education; rather than being primarily a retail outlet or a venue for sporting, theatrical or film performances. It must be open to the public, without prior booking, for published periods each year, and should be capable of attracting day visitors or tourists as well as local residents. In addition, the attraction must be a single business, under a single management, so that it is capable of answering the economic questions on revenue, employment ...(VisitScotland 2004: 8)

While this definition is helpful in harmonizing the collection of statistics that ascertain the volume and value of the attractions sector, it is very specific and deliberately narrow in perspective. Importantly, it excludes:

- The growing significance of shopping as a destination attraction. City centre retailing experiences increasingly form a significant draw for tourists (Timothy 2005), as well as shopping malls, clusters of specialist shops, street markets and farmers' markets. Individual shops often form an attraction in their own right, including landmark stores like Harrods through to small ventures like the House at Pooh Corner, England. Retail outlets that combine visitor services and retailing are increasingly common in tourist areas, such as the Gretna Gateway Outlet Village on the main route between Scotland and England, which attracts over one million visitors per year.

- Unique, periodic or non-permanent events and festivals (sporting, cultural and natural), which although may be one-off or infrequent, still have the capacity to create demand and associated management issues. Such events include major international events such as the Olympic Games through to the viewing of natural phenomena such as the Northern Lights.

- Images and locations viewed in films and television programmes stimulate tourist interest in destinations and have created a niche form of attraction, seen globally.

- A destination's natural, social, architectural and cultural resources act as an attraction too, including important facets of a region such as food, wine, crafts, **vernacular buildings** and indigenous people. Importantly, while such features and activities may not be deemed as part of an attractions *sector*, they are nonetheless significant in defining the *attractions* of a destination.

Therefore, a broader definition allows a wider range of attractions to be recognized. Pearce (1991: 46) presented an operational definition of a tourist attraction, which encompasses a broad spectrum of locations:

> *A tourist attraction is a named site with a specific human or natural feature which is the focus of visitor and management attention.*

As Swarbrooke (2002: 9) emphasizes, attractions must be differentiated from destinations since:

> *attractions are generally single units, individual sites or very small, easily delimited geographical areas based on a single key feature. Destinations are larger areas that include a number of individual attractions together with the support services required by tourists.*

Despite this, some attractions, such as Walt Disney World, Orlando, are of such a scale, providing substantial serviced accommodation, that they can be classed as a destination according to this definition. In terms of statistics on the visitor attraction sector internationally, there is a lack of comparable data to allow comparisons between countries. This is complicated by the different ways in which countries collect data and classify attractions.

With this debate in mind, it is clear that the scope of visitor attractions is large, and therefore it is useful to consider ways in which attractions can be categorized.

Classifications of attractions

Visitor attractions may be classified according to a number of different features (Pearce, Benckendorff and Johnstone 2000; Swarbrooke 2002; Leask 2003), for example:

Type

The **core product** offered by an attraction is one method of classification, which is commonly used by NTOs. For example, attractions can be grouped as:

- historic houses
- museums and galleries
- wildlife attractions
- castles
- gardens
- steam railways
- visitor centres
- country parks
- leisure parks.

Physical environment

Attractions can be located in the:

- natural environment, such as forests, mountains, National Parks. A further distinction can be made according to whether the natural environment is managed for visitors or left to nature
- built environment and adapted, but not originally designed for, visitor purposes, such as historic houses, workplaces, steam railways and castles
- built environment and designed for visitor purposes, such as visitor centres and leisure parks.

In addition, attractions may be located in the outdoor or indoor environment.

Ownership

Attractions are owned and managed by a range of organizations, trusts and individuals, working in the public, private and not-for-profit sectors. The shape of the attractions sector is by no means dominated by large commercial ventures. A high level of state involvement in attraction funding is evident across Europe and in other parts of the world like Canada and Singapore. In Singapore, some 48 of the 56 attractions are owned by the public sector, five are run by the voluntary sector, while only three are operated by private sector interests (see also Chapter 14, which examines the role of the public sector as an attraction operator in Scotland). Conversely, there is little public sector intervention in attractions in the USA, although many are subsidized by charitable donations and the voluntary sector. The voluntary sector includes organizations that own and manage attractions on a not-for-profit basis, and has a particularly important role in the heritage sector.

Perception

Some visitors may perceive an attraction *as* an attraction but others may not. For example, sites associated with disaster and death have become tourism attractions, known as 'dark tourism' (Lennon and Foley 2000). Whether a location such as Auchwitz should be viewed as visitor attraction poses an ethical and philosophical dilemma, and is likely to be perceived differently by different groups of people. Events such as memorial day commemorations, while not visitor attractions as such, still require a great deal of preparation by tourism organizations to cope with the participant demand for accommodation and other services (see Image 9.1 of The Old Town Jail and National Wallace Monument, Stirling, and dark tourism linkages). What undeniably 'turns a tract of land, monument, park, historic house or coastline into a heritage attraction is often the attitude of the public' (Millar 1999: 6). Allied to this aspect is the fact that public motivation to visit a site varies over time. Uzzell (1989: 14) refers to the war generation visiting battlefield sites after 1945, but as those individuals cease 'to be with us, (there is)…less to do with remembrance and more to do with a day-trip excursion, less of a memorial and more of a tourist attraction'.

Admission policy

Some attractions charge admission fees, while others are open freely to the public. Attractions operated by membership subscription organizations allow members in for no charge, an example being the National Trust for England and Wales. Other attractions operate friends' schemes, which allow subscribers free entry. Voluntary donations are requested in other attractions, such as cathedrals and churches.

Promotion campaign by Argyll, Loch Lomond, Stirling and Trossachs Tourist Board in 2004 to promote Stirling Old Town jail and the National Wallace Monument based on the appeal of 'dark tourism'. Source: Copyright, AILLST

Appeal

The market appeal of attractions can be viewed at a geographic level, where attractions might appeal: just to a local market, regionally, nationally or internationally. While the market for visitor attractions tends to be dominated by the domestic, there are strong variations according to attraction type. In Scotland, the largest proportion of visits to distilleries and castles was made by overseas tourists, whereas more domestic visitors were recorded at steam railways and country parks (VisitScotland 2004). Additionally, certain attractions may only appeal to niche markets, or particular market segments. Some attractions, like farm parks, are clearly aimed at a family market, while others, like historic houses and gardens, tend to attract larger volumes of mature visitors. Events of national significance, particularly where a range of events are held within the event itself (such as the Queen's Golden Jubilee Celebrations in London, 2002), are more likely to attract a diverse demographic and socioeconomic profile.

Size and capacity

Attractions vary in land coverage, with some housed in tiny buildings and others covering several hectares. Some are designed for a mass audience and are able to absorb large numbers of visitors compared with others. Such attractions form destinations in their own right, and may incorporate a range of resort services and facilities that enable visitors to prolong their stay, overnight or even longer. Understanding the capacity of sites is important in terms of management and marketing, as well as protection of the resource base, which may be damaged as a result of poor visitor management.

Composition

While many attractions are nodal in character, i.e. they are located at or around a specific point or feature such as a capital city, some are linear in that they follow a line or route. Good examples of linear attractions are Blackpool's Golden Mile, UK, and the Great Ocean Road, Australia, that follows Victoria's coast for over 400 km. Events may also be nodal, i.e. fixed in one venue, or may occur at a variety of locations as part of a festival: the Edinburgh Festival which, across the city, attracts 2.6 million, equivalent to the attendance at the 2002 FIFA World Cup in South Korea, is an example.

Degree of permanence

Built visitor attractions are designed with a degree of permanence. In the case of events and festivals, a short duration is expected and temporary sites, buildings or a mobile infrastructure are often used. Such events may also take part within established attractions, forming an effective method of reaching new audiences or developing an existing audience's appreciation of a site: for example, a weekend festival at a historic house. Sporadic non-permanent natural events, which are neither designed nor staged for visitors, can also attract substantial visitor interest (see Insight 9.1).

INSIGHT 9.1

Solar eclipses as a natural attraction

The magnitude of non-permanent natural attractions as generators of tourism demand is evident in the example provided by solar eclipses. Total solar eclipses are witnessed in various parts of the globe sporadically, as identified in Figure 9.1. Eclipses often attract large numbers of spectators: in Zambia where, in 2001, some 20 000 tourists were recorded, more than the country had seen before, and about US$15 million of tourist spending was generated. In the 1999 solar eclipse witnessed over Europe, 100 000 visitors to southern Belgium and 400 000 to Cornwall, southern England, were recorded. Several hundreds of tourists travelled to Antarctica in 2003 for the first recorded eclipse. Figure 9.1 illustrates the total number and path of solar eclipses in the period 1996–2020. This map identifies future eclipse paths that are likely to attract international visitors to witness the event in forthcoming years. Such forecasts also enable tourism organizations to prepare strategies that manage and maximize opportunities to welcome and accommodate visitors, while boosting the local economy.

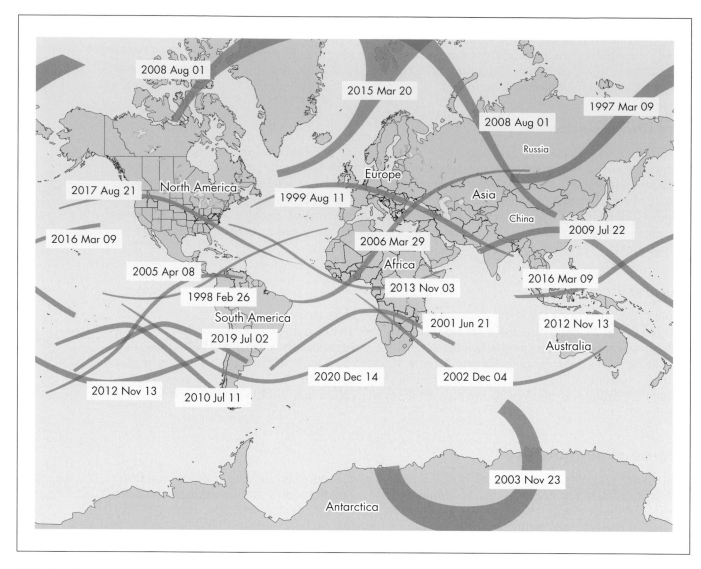

FIGURE 9.1 Total number and path of solar eclipses 1996–2020. Source: Map courtesy of Fred Espenak, NASA/Goddard Space Flight Center. For more infromation on solar and lunar eclipses, see Fred Espenak's Eclipse Home Page: sunearth.gsfc.nasa.gov/eclipse/eclipse.html

Events can be a major drawcard for tourism as this entertainer in Venice shows. Source: Venice Tourist Board

Visitor numbers

Like size and capacity, visitor attractions may also be differentiated according to the volume of visitors received over a given period of time. Some attractions regularly record visitor figures of over 500 000, while others may attract more modest numbers (Image 9.2 Venice).

Organizational complexity and risk

Extending the debate, Shone and Parry (2004: 7) suggest that a typology relating to the degree of organizational complexity and risk offers another perspective, with reference to events (see Figure 9.2).

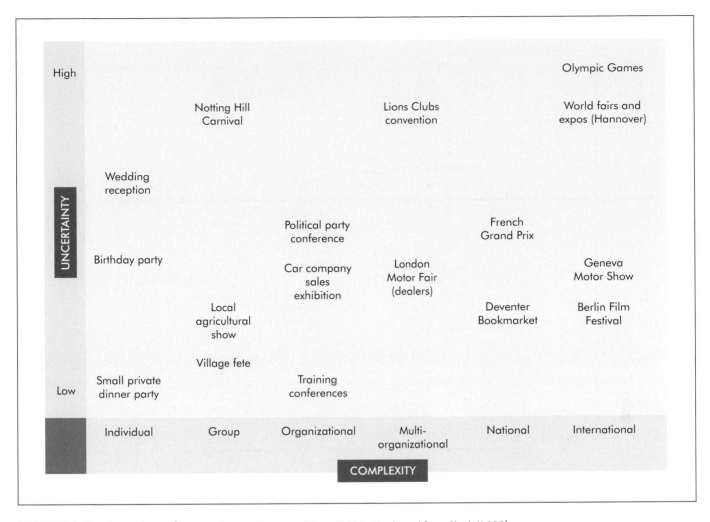

FIGURE 9.2 A typology of events. Source: Shone and Parry (2004: 5) adapted from Slack (1998)

Understanding the concept of visitor attractions

Several seminal studies were published from the 1970s enabling the development of understanding of visitor attractions. At an applied level, Gunn (1972) identified three zones in relation to the spatial or physical layout of an attraction, as illustrated in Figure 9.3:

1 the central nucleus contains the core attraction
2 the zone of closure that surrounds the nucleus contains the ancillary services associated with the attraction, such as shops, car park and tea-room
3 the inviolate belt is an area which protects the core product from the commercialized areas of the zone of closure.

At a more conceptual level, and drawing on a more **cognitive** approach to understanding visitor attractions, MacCannell (1976) identified three elements that comprise a tourism attraction:

● a tourist – a consumer with certain needs, searching for an experience
● a sight – the visitor attraction
● a marker – forms of information about the attraction, that stimulates decision-making and motivation to visit.

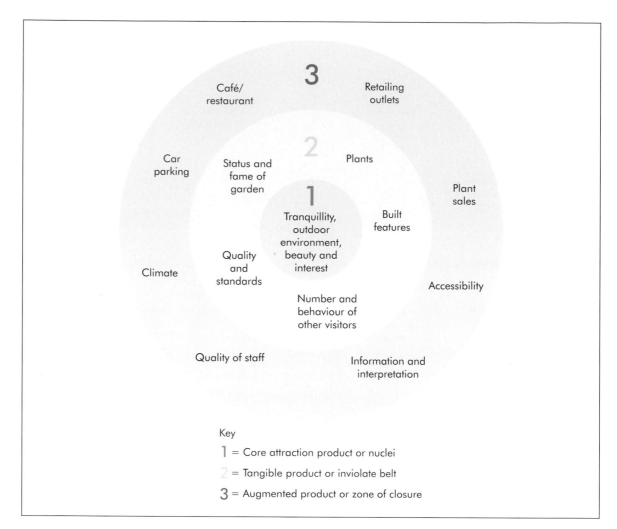

FIGURE 9.3 Spatial arrangement of a garden visitor attraction. Adapted from Gunn (1972), Kotler (1994) and Swarbrooke (2002)

This analysis is interesting, as the focus of attention may be regarded as falling simply on the 'sight', 'site' or 'nucleus'. Instead, the **attraction system** integrates the visitor and information about the attraction. Leiper's (1990) study of attractions developed the notion that attractions form part of a system, and expressed the idea in a model (Figure 9.4). Leiper suggests that tourists are not simply pulled or attracted, but *motivated* by the opportunity to experience the core product and its markers. Accordingly, when the visitor, the nucleus and the marker are linked together, the attraction system develops. By thinking about attractions as a system, it becomes more apparent how a destination 'attracts' visitors, and knowing this can assist in the development of policy and strategy (Leiper 1990).

Visits to attractions comprise a strong element of consumption, characteristic of the shift to a postmodern society in industrialized countries. In essence, the themes adopted by many attractions as their core product enable the visitor to experience a particular subject, issue or location, which has been commoditized and packaged for easy viewing or consumption. Good examples include heritage interpretation centres and workplace attractions, which tell a story based on real events made palatable (but perhaps less authentic) for the pleasure-seeking visitor (Timothy and Boyd 2003).

Lew (1987) recognized that a cognitive perspective, which places an emphasis on understanding visitor perceptions and experiences of an attraction, is crucial for those concerned with gaining an appreciation of what motivates a visit to an attraction and identifying the most enjoyable facets of a site. It is important for managers of attractions to recognize visitor experiences if they wish to capture repeat visits and stimulate recommendations, as well as provide a good core product. Understanding visitor motivations is vital in terms of marketing, product development and

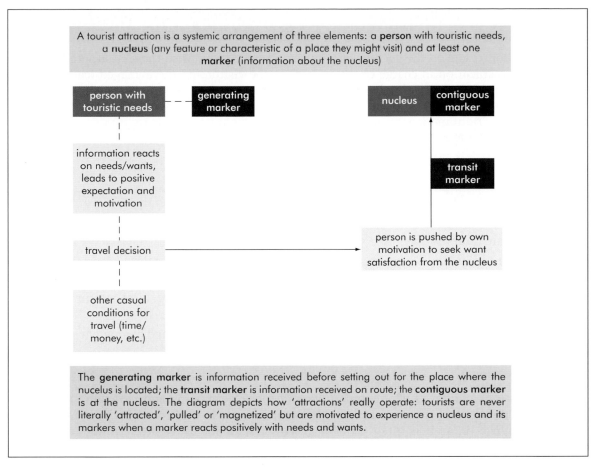

A tourist attraction is a systemic arrangement of three elements: a **person** with touristic needs, a **nucleus** (any feature or characteristic of a place they might visit) and at least one **marker** (information about the nucleus)

person with touristic needs ---- generating marker

nucleus | contiguous marker

information reacts on needs/wants, leads to positive expectation and motivation

transit marker

travel decision → person is pushed by own motivation to seek want satisfaction from the nucleus

other casual conditions for travel (time/ money, etc.)

The **generating marker** is information received before setting out for the place where the nucleus is located; the **transit marker** is information received on route; the **contiguous marker** is at the nucleus. The diagram depicts how 'attractions' really operate: tourists are never literally 'attracted', 'pulled' or 'magnetized' but are motivated to experience a nucleus and its markers when a marker reacts positively with needs and wants.

FIGURE 9.4   Leiper's model of a tourist attraction system, Copyright Leiper (1990), reproduced with permission

management of the site or event. While it might be argued that the main motivator for visiting attractions is enjoyment, specific motivators tend to vary according to attraction type and between individuals. Such an analysis is quite complex because what one individual might define as enjoyment, another might not, and individuals exhibit quite varying needs at different times. Figure 9.5 elucidates this debate, suggesting some possible reasons for attending events.

What needs to be addressed next are the factors that contribute to the success or otherwise of visitor attractions.

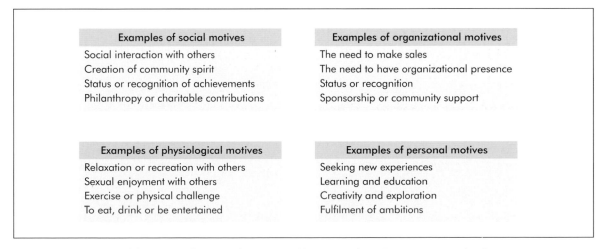

Examples of social motives	Examples of organizational motives
Social interaction with others	The need to make sales
Creation of community spirit	The need to have organizational presence
Status or recognition of achievements	Status or recognition
Philanthropy or charitable contributions	Sponsorship or community support

Examples of physiological motives	Examples of personal motives
Relaxation or recreation with others	Seeking new experiences
Sexual enjoyment with others	Learning and education
Exercise or physical challenge	Creativity and exploration
To eat, drink or be entertained	Fulfilment of ambitions

FIGURE 9.5   Possible motives for attending events (these may be primary or secondary). Source: Shone and Parry (2004: 27) adapted from McDonnell *et al.* (1999)

Influences determining the success of visitor attractions

Factors that contribute to the success of a tourist attraction comprise those associated with the operator or organization in charge of the attraction, the visitor and the managed features of the attraction (Table 9.2). Accordingly, the range of elements that constitutes a visitor attraction stretch far beyond the core focus of the attraction. In many cases, a successful attraction is one that captures the right market in the right location at the right time at the right price.

These factors include:

- professional management skills and the operator's available resources
- the type of attraction or **'product offering'**
- market demand for the product
- ease of access from major routes and centres of tourist and resident populations
- appropriate hours of opening
- provision and quality of on-site amenities, such as parking, visitor centre, signs and labels, shops, guides, refreshments, toilets, litter bins, seating and disabled provision
- proximity to and quality of near-site amenities, such as signposting, local accommodation, local services and other attractions
- quality of service, including staff appearance, attitude, behaviour and competence
- the mood, expectation, behaviour and attitude of visitors
- value for money.

The attractions market is very competitive and those developing and managing attractions increasingly understand the need to base them on innovative concepts which create a sensational experience or, as it is often termed, a 'wow' factor for the visitor. Understanding the visitor experience is a key concept for contemporary visitor attraction management, as is explored further in Chapter 25. Creating the right appeal and ambience in a fiercely uncompromising sector is crucial for visitor attractions. Neglect of an element of a visitor attraction, whether it is poor toilet cleaning or an unjustifiably high entry charge, has the potential to harm the overall experience, affecting both return visits and recommendations.

TABLE 9.2 Factors influencing the success of tourist attractions

The organization and its resources	Experience of developing and managing attractions	Financial resources	Marketing – see 'the management of the attraction'				
The product	Novel approach or new idea	Location	On-site attraction	High quality environment	Good customer service	Visitor facilities	Value for money
The market	Growth markets – targeting markets which are likely to expand						
The management of the attraction	Experienced professional managers	Adequate attention to market research	Realizing that marketing is not just about brochures and adverts	Long-term strategic view	Accepting importance of word-of-mouth	Planned marketing strategy with proper financing	Staff training

Source: Adapted from Swarbrooke (2002)

Research undertaken in Hong Kong by McKercher, Ho and du Cros (2004) revealed that five aspects influence the popularity of a cultural tourism attraction. Table 9.3 indicates that product development, visitor experience and marketing are more important in determining popularity than the historic significance of an attraction, or its meaning to local people and intrinsic worth. This research suggests that the marketing and management of an attraction are crucial and that the core product attributes alone are insufficient in determining appeal and success. Such findings only emphasize the importance of understanding the visitor experience. Visitor experiences are likely to be affected by numerous factors, some of which are inevitably not linked with the destination per se, but which hinge on the mood and personal circumstance of the visitor. Figure 9.6 illustrates the range of factors that affect the visitor's experience of an attraction.

Understanding the visitor experience is a basic facet of visitor attraction management. However, attractions are subject to a number of issues, threats and opportunities which impact on effective management. The chapter now moves on to consider a range of themes and issues involved in managing visitor attractions.

Themes and issues in the management of visitor attractions

Attractions face a number of threats from the external and internal environment that pose risks to both product quality, operational viability and the visitor experience. Consequently, it is essential for attraction managers to derive a strategy that recognizes threats and focuses on managing potential impacts in an attempt to strive for long-term viability.

TABLE 9.3 Attributes of popular cultural tourism attractions

Category	Attribute
Product	Site
	Setting
	Scale
	Access
	Purpose built or extant facility
	Complementary adaptive reuse
Experiential	Uniqueness
	Relevance to tourist
	Ease of consumption
	Focus on 'edutainment'
Marketing	Position
	Does the asset have tourism potential?
	Identification of viable market segments
	Place in attraction's hierarchy
	Product lifecycle stage and ability to rejuvenate product lifecycle
Cultural Leadership	Local vs. international social values
	Attitude to tourism
	Vision
	Ability to assess tourism potential realistically
	Ability to adopt a marketing management philosophy to the management of the asset

Source: Reprinted from *Annals of Tourism Research*, vol.31, McKercher, Ho and Du Cros, 'Attributes of popular cultural attractions in Hong Kong', 393–407, copyright (2004), with permission from Elsevier

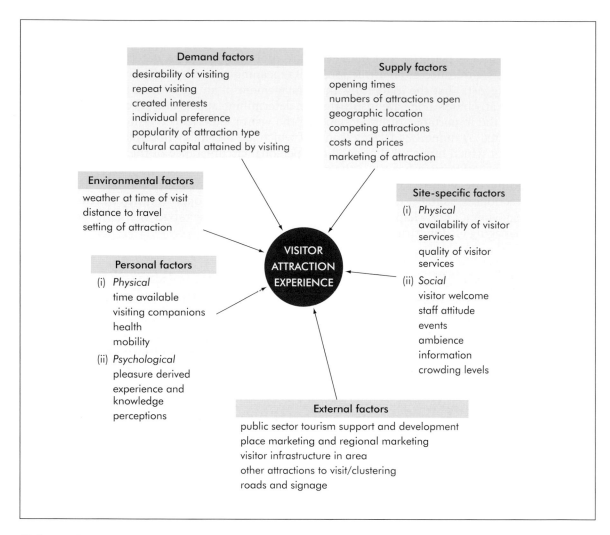

Demand factors

desirability of visiting
repeat visiting
created interests
individual preference
popularity of attraction type
cultural capital attained by visiting

Supply factors

opening times
numbers of attractions open
geographic location
competing attractions
costs and prices
marketing of attraction

Environmental factors

weather at time of visit
distance to travel
setting of attraction

Site-specific factors

(i) *Physical*
   availability of visitor
   services
   quality of visitor
   services

(ii) *Social*
   visitor welcome
   staff attitude
   events
   ambience
   information
   crowding levels

Personal factors

(i) *Physical*
   time available
   visiting companions
   health
   mobility

(ii) *Psychological*
   pleasure derived
   experience and
   knowledge
   perceptions

VISITOR ATTRACTION EXPERIENCE

External factors

public sector tourism support and development
place marketing and regional marketing
visitor infrastructure in area
other attractions to visit/clustering
roads and signage

FIGURE 9.6 Factors determining the visitor attraction experience

Management planning

Benckendorff and Pearce (2003) found in a study of Australian tourist attractions that attractions with the highest level of management planning tend to perform the best, be more profitable and have a sounder basis for the future. Accordingly, the larger the attraction, the more likely its management will engage in planning. Higher levels of planning in attractions are associated with:

- higher visitor numbers
- more gross revenue
- larger asset value
- greater total profit
- higher admission prices
- longer length of stay
- better growth
- greater confidence.

Like those in any business, the managers of an attraction must plan ahead by deciding what actions will be necessary, identifying objectives, time scales, funding and implementation of projects. Planning underpins the dynamic nature of the visitor attraction sector and is essential for the attraction's long-term survival based on renewal and innovation, which are discussed later in the chapter.

Environmental impacts

The environmental impacts caused by visitors raise a number of issues for managers of natural, built and event attractions. For example, heritage sites like Hadrian's Wall in the vicinity of the English–Scottish border receives 400 000 walking visitors following a trail alongside the wall which is a unique and fragile attraction now under threat from tourism. The construction of visitor attractions alone inevitably causes environmental impact, although some attractions positively aim to assist environmental conservation, like the Scottish Seabird Centre in North Berwick, UK (see Case Study 9.1W). Natural attractions and built attractions are prone to visitor impacts, and religious or sacred sites are vulnerable too (Shackley 2001). Garrod, Fyall and Leask (2002) identify a range of such attraction impacts, as shown in Table 9.4, and additional problems such as waste generation can be added to this.

Seasonality

In many parts of the world, seasonality is a significant issue affecting demand for tourism (see Chapter 3), and the attractions sector is particularly susceptible. In Scotland, some 68 per cent of visits to attractions were made between April and September in 2003, with 38 per cent alone made in the period July–September. Some types of attractions show a greater susceptibility to seasonality. Historic properties and monuments, steam railways, industrial/craft attractions and

TABLE 9.4 Environmental impacts relating to attractions

Overcrowding	Overcrowding of parts of a site is generally considered to be a more serious problem than overcrowding of the site as a whole. More of an issue in attractions which were not designed to accommodate visitor flow, such as castles
Wear and tear	Actions causing wear and tear are often unintentional. Erosion of footpaths, graffiti covering artefacts, control of humidity and temperature, dirty hands on glass cabinets, walls and windows, carpet wear, are examples
Litter, vandalism and stealing	Usually intentional actions. Connell (2004) found that acts of theft in garden attractions ranged from digging up plants to more professionally organized robbery of valuable statues
Transport-related	Many visitors arrive by car or coach and, consequently, there is a need to accommodate vehicles on-site by building and maintaining car parks. Road access can be a major issue. Where on-site parking is limited, vehicles may spill over into residential areas or may intrude on neighbouring private properties. Vehicular traffic also causes pollution, noise and visual impacts, as well as damage to verges and heightened road safety dangers
Behaviour	The local community and visitor interface can often be problematic (see Chapter 21). In relation to attractions, visitors may be perceived in positive or negative ways. Where an attraction encourages visitors to explore the local area in a sensitive way and spend money in local businesses, the overall effect might be positive. Attractions can provide employment for local people. Where visitors simply go to the attraction and have little benefit on the local area, a more antagonistic attitude is likely to develop. Where the actions of visitors frustrate locals, visitor management intervention is required to alleviate practical problems
Effects of visitor management on authenticity	The application of visitor management techniques, particularly in heritage properties and natural areas, while vital for protecting the resource or providing information, may be intrusive on the visitor's enjoyment. Such tools include interpretation panels, rope cordons and covers on furniture. To comply with legislation on accessibility, visitor attractions are obliged to provide the means by which less able visitors can enjoy the resource, including lifts, rails and ramps, which while necessary and to be encouraged, may detract from heritage architecture

those that charge for admission show the highest seasonal peaks and troughs in visitor numbers. Places of worship and country parks tend to suffer the least from seasonal visits, as each exhibits strong local appeal. Attractions in cities suffer less from seasonality than those located in peripheral areas. For example, in Scotland, visitor numbers to attractions in the cities of Glasgow and Edinburgh show little variation through the year, compared with the Highlands and the Western Isles, areas which are subject to much stronger patterns of seasonal visiting (VisitScotland 2004).

According to Goulding (2003), the two main operational effects of seasonality for visitor attractions include:

- staffing issues
  - recruitment costs and difficulties
  - cost of training and development
  - commitment of seasonal staff
  - loss of trained staff at the end of the season
- **capacity utilization**
  - peak season overutilization and the consequent impacts
  - **opportunity costs** of **under-utilization**
  - peaks and troughs in cash flow and revenue generation, and potential to deter capital investment due to risks of long-term payback.

Several management responses to seasonality are widely applied in visitor attractions. These include:

- accepting peak season highs by deploying more resources to generate maximum potential revenues and using the low season to develop the business or undertake maintenance and refurbishment obligations
- extending the season through product development and extension, including events and community festivals, corporate events, hiring out of the attraction and **promotion** of the attraction to local residents and educational groups. Initiatives to extend the season are often most effective when a number of attraction and visitor-related services collaborate in the promotion of out-of-season leisure opportunities. Such promotions allow potential visitors to become aware of activities and places to eat and stay at times of the year when they might not consider there to be any offerings for visitors.

Visitor numbers

Factors positively affecting visitor numbers at attractions are diverse, but the main determinants appear to be promotions and holding events, and in negative terms, global issues affecting the supply of visitors and disruptions caused by refurbishment (VisitScotland 2004). The most significant factor that affects visitor numbers both positively and negatively is one that attraction operators have little control over – the weather.

The issue of visitor demand for an attraction is relevant in management terms, depending on whether an attraction aims:

- to increase visitor numbers
- to decrease visitor numbers
- to maintain current levels of visitors
- to change the composition of an existing visitor profile.

which is underpinned by an understanding of current visitor numbers. Mechanisms for recording visitor numbers include admission tickets, car parking receipts, manual or mechanical counts. Recording visitor numbers at some sites is problematic, of course, where entry is free, where the site has multiple entry points and where the installation of mechanical counting devices (such as magic eye counters) is uneconomic.

Where there is significant visitor activity, some attractions have developed strategies to manage numbers through estimating a site's **carrying capacity**, i.e. deciding how much use can be accommodated at a given site. In reality, each attraction has a range of capacities depending on the type of visitor experience intended and the extent of resource protection required, which must be balanced against accessibility and revenue considerations. As a result, the application of carrying capacity models is a controversial issue. While physical carrying capacity is easy to determine through car park size, numbers allowed on theme park rides or number of seats in a café, more personal experiences of overcrowding known as 'perceptual carrying capacity' are difficult to define and evaluate. One method for achieving this objective is to identify primary indicators of the quality of the visitor experience, and to identify where the number of visitors at any one time exceeds both preferred and acceptable limits, and where subsequent management intervention is necessary (see Image 9.3, which shows how long tourists are prepared to wait to visit an attraction). On Alcatraz Island (within the Golden Gate National Recreation Area, San Francisco), which receives several hundred thousand visitors a year, the primary indicator was determined to be the number of other people in the prison cellhouse (the core or 'icon' attraction of Alcatraz Island) (Manning *et al.* 2002. Other indicators of quality in attractions might include the amount of time required to queue for a theme park ride, to use a toilet facility or to wait for a table in a café.

Image 9.3: Tourists queuing to visit the London Dungeon on a busy Easter weekend, which illustrates the growing interest in 'dark forms of tourism' with a sinister past. Source: S.J. Page

Attractions and destination planning

Gunn (1988) states that attractions function most effectively when they are clustered together. Many areas have adopted a strategy of **clustering** attractions and events, to provide a critical mass of activity with appeal to visitor markets. The rationale for clustering has become clear with regard to greater tourist mobility, competition between tourist areas, stronger marketing mechanisms and higher investment in development. Managers of attractions are able to work in collaboration with one another to attract visitors to an area rather than to a single attraction, with encouragement to visit all attractions, often through discount schemes and visitor passes.

The development of industry coordination mechanisms is a useful tool in boosting the profile of attractions as a key segment of the tourism product offering within a geographic area. Collaboration allows attractions to become more receptive to changes in the marketplace and assists in the formation of strong regional identities through destination marketing, rather than marketing that concentrates on specific attractions (Fyall, Leask and Garrod 2001). Investment in **flagship attractions** can act as a tool for regeneration, as seen in the example of the Guggenheim Museum, Bilbao (Law 2002) (see also Case Study 9.1W). As Law (2002) argues, the development of attractions in urban areas is not undertaken purely as a strategy to attract visitors, but also to stimulate urban renewal.

Diversification: The case of industry-based tourism

Many attractions have developed from an existing business, like farm attractions, where visitor incomes act as an essential component of a diversified agricultural business. Industry or workplace attractions have also developed through a similar process, where a company identifies an opportunity to promote its products and engender brand awareness through the visitor market. While visits to such attractions tend to be considered a phenomenon of modern tourism, Donnachie (2004) identified that tourists visited workplaces and factories as early as the eighteenth century in Britain.

Industry-based attractions fall into two categories:

1 those where visitors can watch the production process

2 those where the emphasis is on the product plus other facets, such as amusements or retailing, the product not necessarily being produced on site.

Internationally, there are many examples of companies that operate visitor centres or visitor experiences that are linked to a production process or **product** offering, as diverse as nuclear energy production and chocolate (Table 9.5). The World of Coca-Cola is one of the world's top industry-based experiences, with over 11 million visitors recorded in the 15 years following its opening in 1990. Australia offers a multitude of food and drink experiences, from its renowned range of wineries and vineyards, to a lobster factory and a ginger processing plant. In USA, there are over 1500 brewery tours on offer. In many of the coffee and tea producing countries of the world, such as Costa Rica, tourists can visit working plantations. In Alaska, even oil installations are considered tourist attractions.

Renewal and innovation

As Chapter 13 explains, innovation is a key concept in all tourism businesses. However, innovation is particularly important in the attractions industry and initiatives to extend the attraction **product lifecycle** must be built in to long-term planning. With the significant increase in competition for visitor expenditure since the 1990s across the leisure and tourism sector, a distinct visitor attraction lifecycle may be observed (Lennon 2001). Lennon (2001) argues that paid and free attractions with over 10 000 visitors a year in Scotland, tend to show the following pattern after opening:

- growth in years 1–2
- a decline in visitation in year 3
- there is a greater stability in visitor numbers to paid attractions, up to year 4
- non-paid admission attractions, on the other hand, experience a decline in years 3 and 4 then stabilization in numbers.

A decline in visitor numbers is often a reflection of a failure to innovate, refresh or expand the components of the attraction. Many attraction operators find that it is necessary to invest in major refurbishment to nurture existing customers and reinvigorate visitor interest, often using new forms of interpretation or technology. For example, a **virtual reality** trip through New York, called New York Skyride, has been developed at the Empire State Building (see www.skyride.com/index2.cfm).

TABLE 9.5   Examples of industry-based attractions

Company	Product	Location	Approximate annual visitor numbers
Tillamook	Cheese	Oregon, USA	1 000 000
Volkswagen Autostadt	Cars	Wolfsburg, Germany	1 000 000
Poole Pottery	Pottery	Poole, UK	800 000
Guinness Storehouse	Stout	Dublin, Ireland	700 000
Cadbury World	Chocolate	Birmingham, UK	535 000
Cheddar Gorge Cheese Company	Cheese	Cheddar, UK	300 000
Ben & Jerry's Visitor Centre	Ice cream	Vermont, USA	300 000
Carlsberg	Lager	Copenhagen, Denmark	150 000
The Famous Grouse Experience	Whisky	Crieff, Scotland	120 000
Cadbury World	Chocolate	Dunedin, New Zealand	100 000
British Nuclear Fuels	Nuclear energy	Sellafield, UK	100 000

Further, some attraction managers constantly introduce innovations, where diversification of the product offering and upgrading of facilities bucks the trend of the attraction lifecycle model through intervention and ongoing reinvestment. It is common to see promotional literature for attractions that boast 'New for 2006…', in an attempt to retain loyal or repeat visitors and to stimulate new visitor interest. Such strategies are commonly adopted, a good example being Cedar Point, the second oldest theme park, located in Ohio, USA. Since 1989, nine record-breaking rides have been introduced at Cedar Point, breaking the 200- and 300-foot high barriers. Cedar Point also boasted the world's tallest and fastest ride by 2003, 420 feet high and involving a speed of 120 miles per hour, with a capacity for 1500 passengers and covering eight acres of land.

Harnessing economic impacts

Attractions, and in particular events, often stimulate huge economic benefits for the areas in which they are located and it is important for tourism organizations to gauge economic impacts in order to justify spending and publicize the effects to the local community. Figure 9.7 illustrates a range of approaches used to assess the impacts of events.

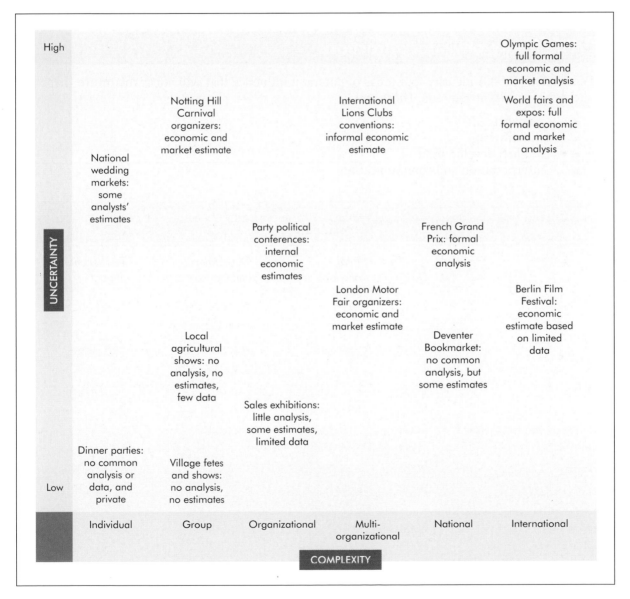

FIGURE 9.7   Some approaches to assessing the scope of the market and economic impact of events.

Source: Shone and Parry (2004: 23) adapted from Slack et al. (2001)

Local tourism economies can benefit from hosting *peripatetic* events, i.e. those that are held in different locations each year, or *rolling* events, which run on an annual basis in the same location. A good example of a rolling event is New Orleans' annual Mardi Gras, 'the greatest free show on earth', which attracts large numbers of visitors, both staying visitors and day trippers, generating significant expenditure in the city (Table 9.6). As Table 9.6 demonstrates, the range of festivals throughout the year in New Orleans creates a substantial income. While the Mardi Gras is an independent event that is not coordinated by a particular organization, it is much more common for tourism and economic development organizations to collaborate in order to attract peripatetic events and/or to provide pump-priming funds. The example of the MTV Europe Awards in Edinburgh (Insight 9.2) indicates the potential for public sector event funding to secure substantial economic returns.

Economic impacts from events are variable and often imply an opportunity cost, where public sector investment might be more effectively spent on other developments that benefit local communities. While the examples above show very positive outcomes, some events run at a loss. Therefore, running special events, and creating new visitor attractions in general, is best viewed as one option for stimulating or regenerating a local economy rather than a panacea (Shone and Parry 2004).

The future of visitor attractions

Pearce *et al.* (2000) identify four areas of potential influence that will affect the future shape and success of tourist attractions. These are:

- management
- **marketing**
- product development
- interpretation and communication.

TABLE 9.6 The economic impacts of festivals in New Orleans[1]

Event	Date	Total attendance	Out-of-town attendance	Total economic impact
Super Bowl XXXVI	2002	72 000	125 000 visitors to the city	$350 million
Bayou Classic	2002	59 745	200 000 visitors to the city	$85 million
French Quarter Festival	2004	450 000	216 000	75.5 million
New Orleans Jazz and Heritage Festival	2003	503 000	216 290	$300 million
New Orleans Wine and Food Experience	2004	13 850	6 233	N/A
Satchmo Summerfest	2004	46 000	4 171	$7.5 million
*Southern Decadence	2004	125 000	N/A	$100 million
Mardi Gras	2003	Hotel guests – 379 928	N/A	$220 532 132
Voodoo Music Festival	2004	60 000	36 000	N/A
Nokia Sugar Bowl	2004	79 342	N/A	$250.49 million

*Economic impact numbers are on $800 per person per spending average.

[1] These impacts predate the effect of Hurricane Katrina in 2005 on the area's tourism industry

Extracted from New Orleans Metropolitan Convention and Visitors Bureau 2005 at www.neworleanscvb.com/new_site/visitor/researchfestivals.cfm)

The economic impact of the MTV Europe Awards in Edinburgh, UK

The MTV Europe Music Awards, a peripatetic event, were held in Edinburgh in 2003, with finance provided the public sector (Scottish Enterprise, EventScotland and the City of Edinburgh Council) to a value of £750 000. This investment met half the cost of constructing a temporary venue capable of seating 1000 to 3000 VIPs, with a standing area for a 5000 audience; without the funding the event would not have come to Scotland. The estimated cost of hosting the event was £4.2 million. The investment in the event reaped significant returns, as the following figures (City of Edinburgh Council, Scottish Enterprise Edinburgh and Lothian and EventScotland, 2003) demonstrate:

- occupancy levels for the night of the event were 26 per cent up at 93 per cent while occupancy for the week rose by 9.4 per cent to 83 per cent compared with the same period in 2002

- hotel bookings in Edinburgh were valued at £2.2 million with 2360 more rooms being sold through the week of the event than were sold during the same week in 2002

- over 7000 bed nights were booked in the city by MTV for pop stars, their entourage and MTV staff, worth £1.5 million

- some 700 journalists stayed in the city to provide coverage of the event

- over half of the contractors providing services were from Scotland. Collectively, these companies earned £1.883 million

- some £8.9 million pounds was generated in direct spend for the local economy

- Edinburgh gained £6.4 million extra expenditure, while the surrounding area of the Lothians benefited by £300 000

- an audience of 12–14 million people in Europe watched the event on television, but many more world-wide were exposed to Edinburgh through the televising of the event, equivalent to an advertising spend of £8.6 million

- worldwide print media coverage in 2094 articles carried by 928 publications in 19 countries has an estimated value of £4.8m

- MTV's viewing audiences showed large increases over the previous year, particularly in the UK, Spain, USA and Sweden

- the event was of value in reaching younger audiences and raising the profile of Edinburgh and Scotland as a tourist destination and place to live and work, as well as showcasing Scotland's capability to stage world-class events.

New approaches to the management and training of staff, marketing and information provision focusing on the quality and experience of the core product, are a necessary part of attraction management in the twenty-first century.

Management: Revenue generation

Globally, attractions face many difficulties in the new millennium. Big-name attractions like Disney have witnessed a slump in visitor numbers and some, like Universal Studios Japan and Disneyland Paris, have experienced severe financial pressures. In the UK, several of the major attractions funded by the National Lottery have gone out of business or have failed to be as successful as predicted. Many were high-risk projects with unrealistic business plans, such as the Millennium Dome, the Earth Centre and the National Centre for Pop Music in the UK, which opened in an era of fierce competition for visitor spend.

For many attractions, creating diverse income streams is a prerequisite for achieving financial viability and success. Apart from ticket sales, attractions can generate revenue through a number of means as shown in Table 9.7. The success of such ventures is highly dependent on marketing, as well as efficient management.

TABLE 9.7   Alternative mechanisms for revenue generation in attractions

Encouraging educational visits

Providing a venue for corporate hospitality, meetings and product launches

Hosting weddings and birthday parties

Generating rental income from alternative usage of infrastructure, such as retail outlets, clubs and offices, which utilize redundant buildings or space on-site

Introducing car parking charges or leasing of the car park to a management company

Improving retail and catering initiatives that offer unique and distinctive products and experiences that reflect the ethos of the attraction

Attracting more visitors and more frequent repeat visits

Increasing length of stay by offering more activities (such as children's sleepovers at the Boston Children's Museum)

Extending opening hours to expand experiences on offer, such as night-time visiting (as in the case of Singapore Zoo)

Introducing members or friends schemes, giving privileges and discounts

Hosting high-profile events

Attracting corporate sponsorship

Marketing

Recent slumps in visitor numbers to some attractions indicate a need for attraction operators to engage in the marketing process. Marketing is central to the success of attractions. As Chapter 15 explains, marketing is not simply concerned with promotion and advertising, both of which are important to visitor attractions, but also with pricing, products and distribution channels. Most attractions produce a promotional leaflet (either as a single attraction or as a collective of attractions in a region), which can be displayed in tourist information centres or in leaflet racks maintained by distribution companies in key visitor locations. Most have websites, displaying essential information for visitors. Other means of promotion include advertising in tourist brochures, magazines, newspapers and on television, although few visitor attractions have the necessary funds for advertising. Luckily, word of mouth (WOM) recommendations remain the most powerful promotional tool for many attractions, which underlines the need for a good product that visitors will tell their friends and relations about. The most successful attractions in the world have produced professional media kits for use in public relations work, which include photographs, a brochure, maps, posters and information for different markets.

In relation to pricing, operators of attractions must be cognizant of market conditions. The market for tourism, and visitor attractions is demand elastic (see Chapter 3), so the degree of disposable income available affects an individual's propensity to visit an attraction. Many built attractions can be relatively expensive to visit, compared with the price of a holiday. If, during a family holiday, there are sufficient funds to visit only one major attraction, then individual attractions must prepare effective marketing strategies to appeal to that consumer, while offering the right product to the right person at the right time in the right place.

Image 9.4: One of the very attractions of tourism and holidays is evident in terms of the three 's's at an integrated tourist resort in Fiji: Sun, sea and sand with a tropical image of paradise.
Source: S.J. Page

Braun and Soskin (2003) note that during periods of growing or high attendance to theme parks, as in the 1980s, entry prices tend to increase, sometimes faster than inflation. Conversely, when attendance falls, increases in price may slow or prices may even decrease. Prices charged by market leaders and premium attractions, like Walt Disney World, usually act as a guide for other attractions, but such premium products often attempt to retain customer interest through heavy investment and **multi-day discounting**, which acts to limit the residual market available to competitors. Some attractions can exist in compatibility where they appeal to a different demographic, i.e. Disneyland and Universal Studios tend to charge similar entry prices, but Disney appeals more to younger families and older people, while Universal holds greater attraction for teenagers and 'twenty-somethings'. Central to this debate is the issue of product development.

Product development: Creating world class destinations

In the dynamic attraction sector, product development is a crucial aspect of economic sustainability, and is a process in which managers of attractions must constantly engage. **Innovation**s tend to be based on the development of a new concept, new technology, such as virtual reality, and through animation or enlivening the product offering through tours, **re-enactments** and personal forms of interpretation.

Following the lead set by Disney, attractions are increasingly developing into visitor destinations in their own right, with a capacity to attract international and domestic staying visitors on-site. A new era of all-inclusive, multidimensional attractions that operate all year round and offer something for everyone are developing across the world (Stevens 2003), particularly in newly emerging economies in South America, South East Asia and Eastern Europe, as well as in existing markets. Such attractions have the potential to assist in urban regeneration schemes and to put less well-known places on the tourist map. Such attractions offer retail, entertainment, relaxation, entertainment and catering facilities, some also with accommodation on-site as well. A key feature of new developments is striking architecture that creates a **'wow' factor** for visitors on arrival and becomes part of the experience.

Other product developments result from a requirement to maintain or improve standards, especially in the case of making attractions accessible and appealing to all customers. Adjustments to the layout and design of an attraction may be required to allow for easy access by wheelchair users, and adaptations to labels announcements and for those with hearing or visual impairments. Attractions that have appeal to young families must be prepared to adapt products to suit their needs: basics include a nappy-changing toilet, a child-friendly restaurant and interests for all age groups.

The key feature in creating a world-class destination is creating a product that is equal or superior to any similar product internationally, firmly centred around a clear understanding of the **visitor experience**, the principles of human resource management and a commitment to product development. Inherent in this process for operators is understanding and anticipating consumer needs and expectations, understanding the wider market and the supply of competing products, and being able to innovate.

Interpretation and communication

In relation to interpretation and communication, two broad themes are of significance:

- the role of technology (known as 'high-tech')
- the role of personal interactions (known as 'high-touch').

One of the greatest continuing developments for many attractions is the use of interactive technology to appeal to all audiences. There are several reasons why operators of attractions invest and develop technology-based elements, including:

- *Creating a unique product*, such as the example of Newseum, the world's only interactive museum of news and journalism in Arlington, Virginia, USA. Newseum offers a highly interactive product, including a newsroom and a broadcast room, where visitors find out what it is like to investigate a story and produce news programmes. It cost $50 million to develop, and 2.25 million visitors were recorded between 1997 and 2002.

- *Enhancing the visitor experience* through interpretation based on entertainment and education, where visitors are exposed to the core element of the visitor attraction product and provided with information in a fun or interactive style, different to the traditional guide book or audio-visual. Sights, sounds and smells can be replicated, a story woven into a series of exhibits and the visitor transported into a simulated environment, in which absorption of key messages may be more effective or where the thrill factor can be maximized. As an example of the last point, at the 'Borg Invasion' 3D Star Trek Experience, Las Vegas Hilton, visitors embark on a tour of a simulated research station, then to be subjected to an alien assault accompanied with physical and visual effects. The 'transporter', or theatre, has 3D main and ceiling screens, with powerful lighting and sound systems to create a formidable effect.

- *Competition*, where an attraction can boast of a unique or unusual experience, outstripping that offered by competitors. Some attractions, while not necessarily unique in nature, can create a niche through offering a particular experience that cannot be found elsewhere. Many museums have adopted technological approaches to boosting interest in their collections and artefacts. The Museum of World Religions opened in 2001 in Taipei, Taiwan. It incorporates a range of technologies including an acoustically active elevator to the main entrance, plasma screens, interactive displays, video theatres and video walls, creating a unique interplay of spirituality, religion and technology. One aim is to inspire young people to visit the museum, which has been designed with the idea that education and pleasure are compatible (see www.mwr.org.tw/en-library/en.htm).

- *Managing visitors*, where larger numbers of visitors can be formally moved through a site and its experiences by means of a technology-driven transport system, such as that found in the Yorvik Museum, York, and the New Millennium Experience at New Lanark in the UK.

- *Systems management*, where the functional activities of attraction management can be looked after by technology, including computerized ticketing, on-line booking, customer feedback and client databases.

Technological approaches in visitor attraction development are important, but so too are the personal interaction and services elements. In this respect, small and less well-resourced attractions have potential to compete with larger organizations by providing a specialized, differentiated product with an emphasis on personal service. In some attractions, a high degree of interpretation based on technology may not be required by the visitor, such as in the case of gardens, where visitors may be more content to wander freely and ask a question or two of the garden staff. More generally, helpful and friendly staff remain a crucial element in any visitor attraction, even where technology plays a big role in the attraction experience.

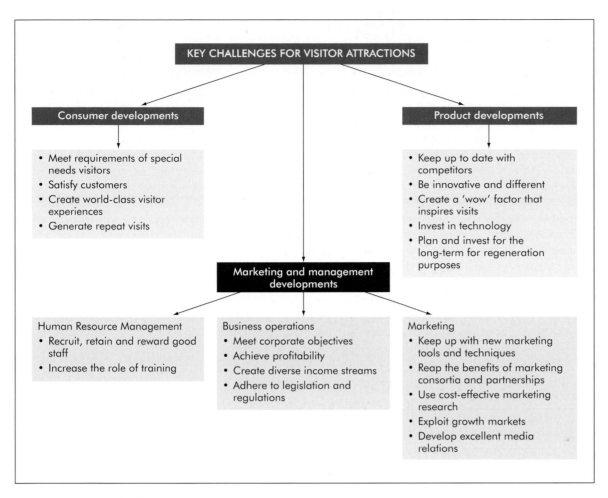

FIGURE 9.8 Key challenges for visitor attraction management. Source: Adapted and expanded from Swarbrooke (2001)

Conclusion

Attractions increased in volume and diversity through the twentieth century and continue to develop in an increasingly global marketplace, as well for local audiences, in the new millennium. Success in attraction management is never guaranteed, even with the major global brands and the future for attractions is likely to show a mix of winners and losers. Swarbrooke (2001) presents several key challenges that face managers of visitor attractions, which have been extended to incorporate more recent developments and are summarized in Figure 9.8. Most successful attractions seize new and interesting ways of stimulating visitor interest, provide multiple activities and experiences and generate multiple streams of revenue to attain financial viability.

A key tool in the future development and renewal of attractions is the augmentation of the distinctiveness of an attraction to form a 'wow' factor, or sensational experi-ence. Such developments must be based on innovation, a commitment to investment and re-investment, and a clear recogniton of market trends and visitor needs. In this respect, visitor attractions must not simply meet expectations, but exceed them. In a competitive market, contemporary attraction development centres on constant innovation and development, creating **must see places** that visitors will want to return to again. Simultaneously, attractions must be developed and managed sensitively, to sustain, reflect and care for environmental, cultural and community interests.

Attractions form just one part of the tourism and leisure industry, but display many of the key themes and issues central to other sectors. The next chapter continues the theme of supply and explores the role of accommodation and hospitality as a key part of tourism infrastructure.

Discussion questions

1 Why is the term 'visitor attraction' more appropriate to use than 'tourist attraction'?

2 Explain the approaches used to classify visitor attractions.

3 How important is the role of technology in visitor attractions?

4 What issues are likely to affect the future development of visitor attractions?

References

Benckendorff, P. and Pearce, P. (2003) 'Australian Tourist Attractions: The Links Between Organizational Characteristics and Planning', *Journal of Travel Research*, 42 (1): 24–35.

Braun, B. and Soskin, M. (2003) 'Competitive theme park strategies: Lessons from Central Florida', in A. Fyall, B. Garrod and A. Leask (eds) *Managing Visitor Attractions: New Directions*. Oxford: Butterworth-Heinemann.

City of Edinburgh Council, Scottish Enterprise Edinburgh and Lothian and EventScotland (2003) *MTV Europe Awards Edinburgh 03 Economic Impact Study*. Edinburgh: SQW and NFO.

Connell, J. (2004) '"The Purest of Human Pleasures": The characteristics and motivations of garden visitors in Great Britain', *Tourism Management*, 25 (2): 229–47.

Donnachie, I. (2004) 'Historic tourism to New Lanark and the Falls of Clyde 1795–1830. The evidence of contemporary visiting books and related sources', *Journal of Tourism and Cultural Change*, 2 (3): 145–62.

Fyall, A., Leask, A. and Garrod, B. (2001) 'Scottish visitor attractions: A collaborative future?' *International Journal of Tourism Research*, 3 (3): 211–28.

Garrod, B., Fyall, A. and Leask, A. (2002) 'Scottish visitor attractions: Managing visitor impacts', *Tourism Management*, 23: 265–79.

Goulding, P. (2003) 'Seasonality: The perennial challenge for visitor attractions', in A. Fyall, B. Garrod and A. Leask (eds) *Managing Visitor Attractions: New Directions*. Oxford: Butterworth-Heinemann.

Gunn, C.A. (1972) *Vacationscape: Designing Tourist Regions*. Austin, TX: University of Texas.

Gunn, C.A. (1988) *Tourism Planning, Second Edition*. New York: Taylor and Francis.

Kotler, P. (1994) *Marketing Management: Analysis, Planning, Implementation and Control, Eighth Edition*. Hemel Hempstead: Prentice Hall.

Law, C.M. (2002) *Urban Tourism: The Visitor Economy and the Growth of Large Cities, Second Edition*. London: Continuum.

Leask, A. (2003) 'The nature and purpose of visitor attractions', in A. Fyall, B. Garrod and A. Leask (eds) *Managing Visitor Attractions: New Directions*. Oxford: Butterworth-Heinemann.

Leiper, N. (1990) 'Tourist attraction systems', in *Tourism Systems: An Interdisciplinary Perspective*. Occasional Papers No. 2. Department of Management Systems, Massey University, Palmerston North, New Zealand.

Lennon, J. (ed.) (2001) *Tourism Statistics: International Perspectives and Current Issues*. London: Continuum.

Lennon, J. and Foley, M. (2000) *Dark Tourism: The Attraction of Death and Disaster*. London: Continuum.

Lew, A. (1987) 'A framework of tourist attraction research', *Annals of Tourism Research*, 14: 533–75.

MacCannell, D. (1976) *The Tourist: A New Theory of the Leisure Class*. London: Macmillan.

Manning, R., Wang, B., Valliere, W., Lawson, S. and Newman, P. (2002) 'Research to estimate and manage carrying capacity of a tourist attraction: A study of Alcatraz island', *Journal of Sustainable Tourism*, 10 (5): 388–404.

McDonnell, I., Bowdin, G., Allen, J. and O'Toole, W. (1999) *Festival and Special Event Management*. Brisbane: Wiley.

McKercher, B., Ho, P.S.Y. and du Cros, H. (2004) 'Attributes of popular cultural attractions in Hong Kong', *Annals of Tourism Research*, 31 (2): 393–407.

Millar, S. (1999) 'An overview of the sector', in A. Leask and I. Yeoman (eds) *Heritage Visitor Attractions: An Operations Management Perspective*. London: Cassell.

Pearce, P. (1991) 'Analysing tourist attractions', *Journal of Tourism Studies*, 2 (1): 46–55.

Pearce, P., Benckendorff, P. and Johnstone, S. (2000) 'Tourist attractions: Evolution, analysis and prospects', in B. Faulkner, G. Moscardo and E. Laws, *Tourism in the Twenty-First Century*. London: Continuum.

Richards, G. (2002) 'Tourism attraction systems: Exploring cultural behavior', *Annals of Tourism Research*, 29 (4): 1048–64.

Shackley, M. (2001) *Managing Sacred Sites*. London: Thomson.

Shone, A. and Parry, B. (2004) *Successful Event Management: A Practical Handbook, Second Edition*. London: Thomson.

Slack, N., Harrison, A., Harland, C. and Chambers, S. (2001) *Operations Management, Third Edition*. London: Pitman.

Stevens, T. (2003) 'The future of visitor attractions', in A. Fyall, B. Garrod and A. Leask (eds) *Managing Visitor Attractions: New Directions*. Oxford: Butterworth-Heinemann.

Swarbrooke, J. (2001) 'Visitor attraction management in a competitive market', *Insights*, A41–52, London: English Tourism Council.

Swarbrooke, J. (2002) *The Development and Management of Visitor Attractions, Second Edition*. Oxford: Butterworth-Heinemann.

Timothy, D. (2005) *Shopping Tourism, Retailing and Leisure*. Clevedon: Channel View Publications.

Timothy, D. and Boyd, S. (2003) *Heritage Tourism*. Harlow: Prentice Hall.

Uzzell, D.L. (1989) 'The hot interpretation of war and conflict', in D.L. Uzzell (ed.) *Heritage Interpretation: Volume 1 The Natural and Built Environment*. London: Belhaven.

VisitScotland (2004) *The 2003 Visitor Attraction Monitor*. Glasgow: Moffat Centre, Glasgow Caledonian University.

Further reading

Swarbrooke, J. (2002) *The Development and Management of Visitor Attractions, Second Edition*. Oxford: Butterworth-Heinemann.

10

Tourism Accommodation and Hospitality Services

Learning outcomes

After reading this chapter and answering the questions, you should:

- understand the scope and nature of the hospitality industry

- be aware of the diverse range of accommodation for tourism

- be familiar with the operational issues affecting the accommodation sector

- be able to identify the different types of accommodation and hospitality services used by tourists.

Overview

The purpose of this chapter is to provide the reader with an appreciation of the various types of accommodation and hospitality services and some of the issues which impact upon the sector. The growing diversity of the accommodation sector mirrors trends in the wider tourism sector, as it focuses on attracting customers and profitability as well as quality issues. The sector is often a trend-setter and innovator in its pursuit of ways to stay ahead of the competition as well as its anticipation of changing tourist behaviour and the pursuit of niche products.

Introduction

The concept of **hospitality** underpins much of what the tourist experiences as a traveller, namely the consumption of food, drink and accommodation away from the home environment. As Lashley (2000) observed, it is this context where such activities create a range of relationships, some of which occur in commercial, social and private settings. As Lashley (2000) explains, hospitality may occur in three domains:

- *The private domain* – guests experience the provision of food, drink and accommodation in domestic settings. This involves hosting and hospitality by the **host**. This personal relationship sometimes has a reciprocal nature (i.e. if you host a friend there is often an expectation that they will host you at some point in the future), where the **guest** may be the host on a future occasion (i.e. involving family and friends) and may also characterize some of the relationships experienced by guests in bed-and-breakfast establishments.

- *The social domain* – historically many societies valued the social setting in which hospitality occurs, particularly the trait to act with generosity as a host to visitors. This traditionally involved being charitable to strangers, especially travellers in pre-industrial societies, and bestowed status on the host.

- *The commercial domain* – now characterizes many industrial societies where the experience of hospitality is a purely commercial relationship and not based on charitableness or social reciprocity in the main. A commoditized relationship now exists where the guest pays the host for the services/products consumed via a bill. However, being treated as a valued customer does not infer that a business is offering personal hospitality. Indeed, the cost controls used by large hospitality businesses in terms of portion control, well-defined limits to the scope and extent of the hospitality experience to be delivered are certainly very distant from the notions of hospitality in the private domain. Nevertheless, hospitality is a relationship between host and guest and the different contexts in which tourists consume such hospitality is the focus of this chapter.

The hospitality industry

Historical studies of the hospitality sector indicate that 'commercial hospitality has its roots in supplying to travellers through the market, the basic human needs of food, drink, shelter and rest' (Walton 2000: 57). From the early ale houses of Medieval times, to inns and the emerging public houses, such establishments met travellers' needs. Yet it was the Victorian era that saw the rise of the hotel, restaurant and large scale caterer in the form of public dining rooms in London from the 1820s. As Littlejohn (2003) indicated, the concept of a hotel developed in mid-seventeenth century Paris. In 1780 it crossed to London with the founding of Nero's hotel, aimed at an affluent clientele. In the mid-Victorian period, the provision of railway hotels catering for middle-class travellers created a major development boost to the urban expansion of hotels. Littlejohn (2003) argues that a hotel is a culturally bound phenomenon, given that cultural rules and customs affect hospitality provision and certain behaviour and social codes prevail (i.e. certain codes of conduct are encouraged/discouraged). National codes of regulation also affect hospitality establishments impacting upon what they provide and the roles they fulfil in tourism. This can complicate attempts to define the scope and nature of hospitality services in tourism.

Defining the scope of the hospitality industry

According to Jones (2002), various criteria and measures have been used to define the scope of the hospitality sector. He points to the use of the UK's Standard Industrial Classification (SIC) developed initially in 1948 to statistically track the development of industry. Revised in 1968 and 1980, the SIC (Table 10.1) divides hospitality into its constituent parts of establishments providing meals and light refreshments, drink and accommodation. Much of the hospitality industry is classified under the Division 6, services, Class 66 – hotels and catering, which is then subdivided into six groups.

An indication of the scale and scope of the hospitality industry in the UK is apparent from the Hospitality Training Foundation (HTF) Labour Market Intelligence studies (see www.IHF.org) indicated that in the UK there were 27 700 hotels, 122 300 restaurants, 110 500 public houses, clubs and bars and 25 500 contract catering companies. These employed 1.6 million main jobs in hospitality and a further 111 000 second jobs. These statistics show that hospitality is both a significant employer and whilst accommodation is not the largest sector, it does assume a critical role in the hospitality experience of visitors.

TABLE 10.1   The Standard Industrial Classification of the hospitality industry

Division 6 Class Group		Services Activity	
66	Hotels and catering		
	661		Restaurants, snack bars, cafés and other eating places
		6611	Eating places supplying food for consumption on the premises
			a. Licensed places b. Unlicensed places
		6612	Take-away food shops
	662	6620	Public houses and bars
	663	6630	Night clubs and licensed clubs
	664	6640	Canteens and messes
			a. Catering contractors
			b. Other canteens and messes
	665	6650	Hotel trade
			a. Licensed premises
			b. Unlicensed premises
	667	6670	Other tourist or short-stay accommodation
			a. Camping and caravan sites
			b. Holiday camps
			c. Other tourist or short-stay accommodation not elsewhere specified
Division 9		Other services	
		9310	Catering services ancillary to higher education institutions
		9320	Catering services ancillary to schools
		9330	Catering services ancillary to educational and vocational training not elsewhere specified
		9510	Convalescent and rest homes with medical care
		9611	Social and residential homes

Source: Jones (2002)

Accommodation

According to Medlik and Ingram (2000: 4):

> *hotels play an important role in most countries in providing facilities for the transaction of business, for meetings and conferences, for recreation and entertainment … In many areas hotels are important attractions for visitors who bring to them spending power and who tend to spend at a higher rate than when they do when they are at home.*

What Medlik and Ingram's (2000) key study of the hotel sector shows is that for many forms of tourism (excluding visiting friends or visiting relatives), the tourist requires some form of accommodation for an overnight stay or longer. And part of that accommodation consumption often involves discretionary spending which is at a higher rate than their normal leisure spending or household expenditure. Accommodation provides the base from which tourists can engage in the process of staying at a destination. The accommodation sector is among the capital-intensive infrastructure which tourists utilize and is very labour-intensive in servicing visitors' needs. But it has the advantage in that by hosting guests it also has the potential to generate additional revenue from **food and beverage** services. In that sense accommodation in the tourism and wider hospitality sector has the potential to realize spending from visitors at different rates, particularly as the diversification of the accommodation sector into a wide variety of niche markets and products based on price has offered a new range of opportunities for the tourist in recent years (e.g. the growth of budget accommodation). The accomodation sector is one of the most visible and tangible elements in the tourist's trip and experience, since the premises hosts the visit. Therefore, the underlying premise in accommodation provision, aside from operating profitably, should be to provide a conducive environment where the visitor feels comfortable and welcomed. This involves considerable investment in the accommodation infrastructure. The accommodation sector is perhaps, one of the most capital-intensive areas of the tourism industry given the real-estate value of accommodation venues.

The accommodation product, according to Medlik and Ingram (2002), comprises:

- the *location* of the establishment (i.e. where it is based in terms of a city or rural area and its relative accessibility to tourists and customers)
- its *facilities* (i.e. its bedrooms, bars, restaurants, meeting rooms and sports and recreation facilities)
- its *service* (i.e. what level of service the provider offers will depend upon its grading and facilities and market niche)
- its *image* (i.e. how it is portrayed to customers and the way it is marketed)
- its *price* which is function of the location, facilities, service and image.

In addition, the price will also depend upon the customers being sought since accommodation units appeal to a range of users. Tourist accommodation has been developed, over time, to a position where virtually all tastes are catered for; from holiday villages that encourage guests to spend their time on-site to basic bunk-house barns that cater for a single-night stay at very low cost. Another variation is the concept of time share, which provides an investment for one or two weeks per year in a property with the option of exchanging weeks for locations elsewhere.

Image 10.1: Brands such as Crowne Plaza are significant features in the post-modern tourism environment

Forms of accommodation have been developed to meet the purposes of individual and group travellers. En route accommodation has evolved with changes in mode of transport such that the railway terminus hotel of the nineteenth and twentieth centuries is today represented by the airport hotel where accommodation at major gateways now comprise a significant sector of the accommodation stock in many countries. Motels represent the logical extension of the coaching inn although some companies have restored these older properties to high-standard contemporary business use and in the USA and Australasia they represent a major sector of accommodation supply. The boom in China's 878 million domestic tourists travelling each year has created a demand for motels as the rapid growth in car ownership and road building has fuelled a demand for travel. An illustration of the growth of accommodation in one location – the Gold Coast – is shown in Insight 10.1.

In some countries, the state is or has been directly involved in the operation of accommodation. The former Eastern European countries are an example. Here, the state identified the supply in relation to the demand, although state involvement has been waning globally due to costs of operation and high capital requirements for upgrading schemes and an absence of management skills. As state involvement has waned, private sector involvement, especially through global interests, has grown.

INSIGHT 10.1

The development of Surfers Paradise, Gold Coast, Queensland, Australia

In Australia, the Gold Coast is the country's main tourist destination (after Sydney). Located in the south east corner of Queensland (Figure 10.1), the region is 70 km south of the state capital, Brisbane. Tourism accommodation has developed since the early 1900s (Warnken, Russell and Faulkner 2003) from the initial use as recreational destination with tents, boarding houses and small hotels, at Coolangatta. As Table 10.2 shows, five phases can be discerned in the growth of accommodation, as the initial development at Coolangatta reached its peak along the coastal strip along Surfers Paradise, Broadbeach, Barleigh and Carrumbin. As Figure 10.2 shows, the growth of tourism accommodation along the Gold Coast was promoted by the extension of rail services from Brisbane and the entrepreneurial activities of early guest houses and accommodation.

In the 1950s and 1960s, Warnken et al. (2003) observed that demand for more sophisticated leisure and entertainment options saw Coolangatta decline and Surfers Paradise grow. This was at a time when all the coastal plots had been divided into 500–900m² sections and developed into holiday homes. High-rise development did not occur until the 1960s, although three-storey hotels emerged (Table 10.2).

The infilling of land for tourism use and upgrading of Coolangatta airport in the 1960s widened access to the region from domestic and overseas markets, although the area still only had a population of 38 000. The growth of high-rise buildings in the 1960s and 1970s was followed by the areas further development as a tourism node. This was followed by a growing intensity of accommodation development to serve tourists and new infrastructure provision. In the 1980s and 1990s, high-rise accommodation resulted with some low-value, low-density residential properties redeveloped to create the tourist destination – the Gold Coast, focused on Surfers Paradise.

As Warnken et al. (2003) show, condominium development (self-catering apartments and properties) and different development booms created a distinctive accommodation landscape and southern Surfers Paradise, enjoyed a massive building boom in the early 1980s (Figure 10.2). These condominiums can operate with much lower overheads than hotels, especially in the number of employees needed to service them. Yet as such properties may be driven by property development opposed to tourism demand, occupancy levels rarely exceed 70 per cent. Where such infrastructures age and deteriorate and do not have ongoing reinvestment (in contrast to luxury hotels), the only option may be lower prices. A downward spiral of decay may begin as the properties do not get maintained as profits drop. On the Gold Coast, Warnken et al. (2003) point to the threat that condominium development may pose to the long-term sustainability of tourism, if investors in such developments leave when financial returns are no longer attractive, further intensifying the spiral of decline. In the Surfers Paradise case, the clustering of buildings of a similar age has the potential for long-term environmental deterioration and a negative aesthetic impact when they age, so that an entire district will have a visual and image problem 20–25 years after development. This highlights the wider importance of individual accommodation providers to the image of a destination and the consequences of market forces, oversupply and link between a condominium's visual attractiveness and ongoing demand for its use.

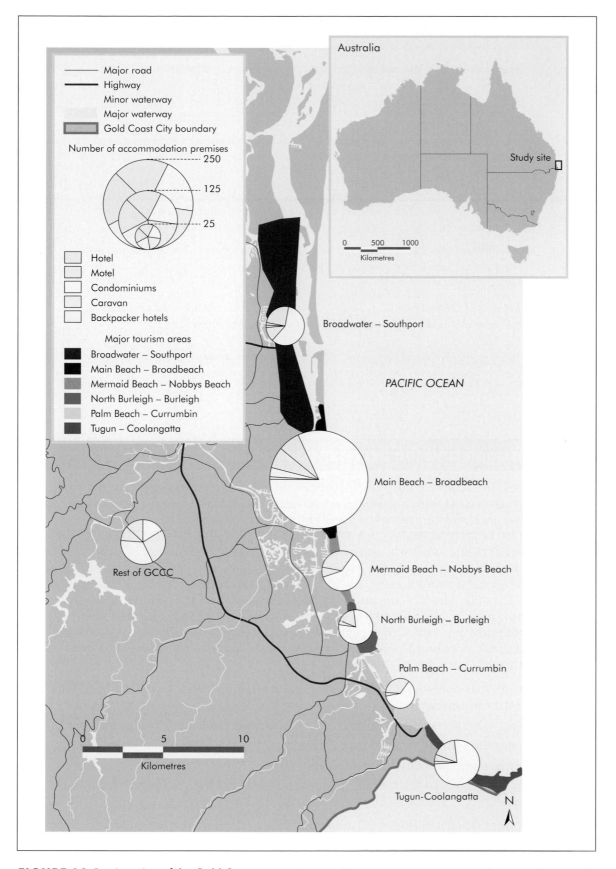

FIGURE 10.1 Location of the Gold Coast. Source: Reprinted from *Tourism Management*, vol.24, Warnken, Russell and Faulkner, 'Condominium developments in maturing destinations: Potentials and problems of long-term sustainability', 155–68, copyright (2003), with permission from Elsevier

TABLE 10.2 Succession of accommodation facilities on the Gold Coast

Stage	Type of tourist accommodation	Location, distribution
One (pre-WWII)	Early days: tents, boarding houses and small hotels	Mostly around headlands, along protected beaches
Two (post-WWII)	Low-key development: summer holiday houses, small motels (one storey), two- or three-storey hotels	Development spreading north from headlands
Three (1950s–1960s)	Intermediate phase: multi-storey holiday apartment complexes, two-storey motels, multi-storey hotels	Development filling in area between headlands and main coastal road running parallel to the beaches
Four (1960s–1970s)	First high-rise buildings: 6–10-storey brick and concrete condominium complexes, 10–20-storey hotels	Establishment of major tourism node: Surfers Paradise
Five (1980s–1990s)	Built-up: >20-storey high-rise condominium resorts, >20-storey hotels	Consolidation of destination's tourist centre, Surfers Paradise

Source: Reprinted from *Tourism Management*, vol.24, Warnken, Russell and Faulkner, 'Condominium developments in maturing destinations: Potentials and problems of long-term sustainability', 155–68, copyright (2003), with permission from Elsevier

Globalization and the accommodation sector

As we discussed in Chapter 1, the term 'globalization' refers to the process of internationalization which is now associated with a growing worldwide trend towards products and tastes among consumers that are now being recognized and fulfilled by international companies. Some critics of globalization in the accommodation sector argue that this is leading to the **McDonaldization** of the tourism product line, where the experience of a hotel stay in one country is identical to that in another country. In other words, the experience of products and services is becoming homogenized by the global operators, especially in the accommodation sector where the consumer can be assured of a standard level of service and provision regardless of the country they visit. Yet this standardization may in fact be running contrary to the wider changes in consumer tastes for different experiences but still with a guaranteed quality threshold. Within the accommodation sector, any company pursuing a global strategy can operate in countries, where their head office is not located, through a number of strategies:

- **franchising** its operation to other businesses in other countries (see Chapter 13 for a discussion of franchising)
- **licensing** other companies or premises to operate using its brand, logo or trademark
- making non-investment management agreements
- acquiring overseas properties and interests
- engaging in mergers to horizontally integrate business interests to operate in a number of countries.

In the field of international business, these approaches are called 'market entry choices': a company decides to enter a foreign market and chooses the best mode of entry into that market; other approaches may involve forming strategic alliances, as discussed in Chapter 5 and 8, and joining consortia which can support those companies that choose franchising options. In some cases, companies will choose to become sole owners of a hotel but, whatever entry mode is chosen, strategic planning will be important to set out the business case and logic for a particular entry mode.

FIGURE 10.2 Accommodation on the Gold Coast. Source: Reprinted from *Tourism Management*, vol.24, Warnken, Russell and Faulkner, 'Condominium developments in maturing destinations: Potentials and problems of long-term sustainability', 155–68, copyright (2003), with permission from Elsevier

Image 10.2: Hotels are a major form of the hospitality sector – especially the global chains such as Crowne Plaza

As Page (2003) indicates, these changes have led to nearly 30 per cent of all of the world's accommodation stock being chain controlled (Image 10.2): being part of international businesses operating globally. For many countries, chain hotels mean that profits are expatriated back to the country in which the hotel chain is based. In addition, many of the chains have highly developed distribution channels, being affiliated to major global distribution systems that distribute the product electronically to travel agents. By 2050, the Horwarth and Horwarth Worldwide Hotel Industry report predicted that up to 60 per cent of hotels will be affiliated to global chains, continuing the consolidation trend to integrated tourism companies across the tourism sector discussed in Chapter 7.

Hotel chains

The WTO estimate that there are over 17 million rooms in hotels, a growth of nearly three million on 1997. The importance of the USA in the evolution of hotel chains can be dated to the period after 1952, when Kemmons Wilson established Holiday Inn to produce a standardized product across a chain of properties (Image 10.3). This standardization created a focus on a guarantee of quality but also enabled operators to set and control prices and operational costs. Over 50 years since this evolution of the chain concept, 67 per cent of US accommodation is branded (see Chapter 16 for more discussion of branding), largely franchised compared to just over 25 per cent in Europe. Marvel (2004a) indicates that the USA has over 6.1 million hotel rooms although Europe dominates, with 6.3 million; there are 4.1 million in Asia. The global differences are between the more historic and ageing stock in Europe and the relatively newer properties in the USA and Asia. The impact of chain development in Europe varies by country, with Marvel (2004a) pointing to the highest proportions (exceeding 30 per cent of capacity) in France, the UK and the Netherlands, with Germany and Spain with over 20 per cent of capacity controlled by chains. In some countries, such as France, the chains have focused on the lower-grade properties (up to two-star) for chain development. In the UK the major growth in chain ownership has been in the establishment of budget brands. For example, Marvel (2004a) points to the trebling of budget capacity in the UK 1996–2002 with around 57 000 rooms in this sector, accounting for a third of branded capacity. The major players in the UK are:

- Travel Inn, Travelodge, Premier Lodge, Express by Holiday Inn; many of these are controlled by diversified pub and restaurant groups (e.g. Whitbread) highlighting the wider importance of integration in the tourism and hospitality sector
- new entrants, including the Cendant Corporation (see Chapter 7) with its Days Inn brand.

Image 10.3: Two important global brands for the hotel sector are the Holiday Inn and Intercontinental logo

Much of the growth and development has been geographically concentrated in centres of tourism and leisure demand (e.g. city centres) together with arterial transit routes, such as the M25 motorway corridor around London, and at motorway junctions, replicating the pattern of growth along arterial routes in the US motel sector in the 1950s and 1960s. In 2005, Travelodge announced plans to double its room capacity in the UK by 2011, adding a further 15 000 rooms. In some cities, such as Paris, Marvel (2004a) points to 60 per cent of hotels being controlled by brands. In a European context, the most important chains are Accor (with its Ibis, Mercure and Novotel brands), Intercontinental, Best Western, Societé du Louvre and Hilton International (Marvel 2004a). Yet the expansion of development of hotels as part of a corporate strategy also depends upon the professional and high quality management of individual properties and, for this reason, attention now focuses on hotel management.

Hotel management

According to Jones and Lockwood (2002: 1) a hotel 'is an operation that provides accommodation and ancillary services to people away from home' and the elements of what a hotel provides can be classified into 'tangible components', such as rooms, and more 'intangible' elements, such as room ambience which are assessed by visitors as part of their experience of staying at a property. This molecular model of hotel management highlights the central element for hotel management – the human element (i.e. the staff) and the way they interact with guests to create a favourable impression where the intangible and tangible elements come together. However, at a more generic level, hotel management needs to ensure that each accommodation unit can function profitably. It also needs to ensure high levels of customer satisfaction and a quality experience by generating income and profit from customer demand while managing the supply elements (i.e. asset protection and development, employees, service standards and quality and productivity levels). The assets include the buildings, rooms and infrastructure which the customer experiences, and the scope of the areas to manage are shown in Table 10.3. This illustrates the wide range of skills which a hotel manager must possess in seeking to integrate all elements of the hotel to ensure they run smoothly and work towards a common set of goals. As demand and supply for hotels varies, hotels will also need to utilize technology to manage different situations which may arise, including where supply exceeds demand or where demand exceeds supply, so as to maximize the business and revenue opportunities.

Yet these operational issues also have to be balanced against developments in the area of distribution channels (i.e. e-solutions such as lastminute.com to sell surplus capacity), and in making pricing decisions and capacity decisions on how much to sell and at what price to generate sales and profit. For example, in 2004, the world's largest hotel company, Marriot International Inc., agreed to sell rooms in over 2000 of its worldwide stock of hotels via Expedia.com and Hotels.com as one additional distribution channel for its products. One part of this strategy is to attempt to improve room **occupancy** and sales, and to this end such companies employ sophisticated yield management systems, as discussed in Chapter 8.

In operational terms, the outcome of hotel management and the selection of different distribution channels for selling hotel rooms has been analysed by KPMG's (2004) *Global Hotel Distribution Survey*. This showed that some parts of the world still had a high level of bookings direct to the hotel in the absence of online travel sites (e.g. Eastern Europe) whereas other markets use online booking more frequently. KPMG noted that the cheapest room rates in the USA which could be gained from online intermediaries while corporate travel agents gained the best rates for business

TABLE 10.3 Functional areas for hotel management

Front-of-house

- Reception
- Reservations
- Conference facilities/telephone-fax-internet services

Food and beverage

- Restaurant
- Bars
- Room service
- Banqueting facilities

Back-of-house

- Food production
- Cleaning
- Laundry

Leisure facilities

travellers. The most important distribution channels in 2004 in order of importance were online agents, corporate agents, hotel websites, central reservations (call centre) and direct calls to the hotel. This highlights and reiterates the overwhelming importance of technology, the World Wide Web and e-travel. For e-bookers using websites, KPMG (2004) confirmed many of the findings of other studies of online travel, that the ability to navigate around sites, their content (i.e. information it contained) together with its functionality (i.e. how well it worked) and customer relationship management were key factors. Whilst KPMG (2004) identified the need for hotels to review their distribution strategies, the USA and Canada were seen as the most advanced in the use and management of technology to achieve effective distribution of capacity.

Operational performance of hotels

Different studies on the performance of the worldwide hotel industry exist, mainly undertaken by large global consulting firms with the resources to track and monitor it. One of the most detailed is Deloitte's (2004) *HotelBenchmark Survey* (www.hotelbenchmark.com) which surveys 6000 hotels worldwide (excluding the USA). The study has many key features, but for the purpose of analysing hotel performance, three useful indicators are:

- *occupancy rates* (i.e. how many people stayed in the hotel as a percentage of the number of available rooms, where complete occupancy would be 100 per cent)
- *average room rate (ARR)*, which is the average price charged for a room, taking into account the highest and lowest rates which are then averaged
- *revenue per available room* (Rev Par), being the amount of revenue from each guest which is received after costs of supplying the room have been deducted, as a form of profit.

Table 10.4, from Deloitte's survey, examines the operational performance of hotels in the main capital cities around the world which highlights:

- the relatively high occupancy rates in Asia Pacific and Europe
- high room rates in Europe, particularly in Paris, London and Madrid, which are rivalled in Asia by Tokyo
- the high Rev Par rates for Tokyo, Amsterdam, London, Madrid, Paris and Rome.

In Asia Pacific, studies such as Horwath's *Asia Pacific Hotel Industry Survey of Operations* highlighted the contribution which cost controls in food and beverage operations made to increased Rev Par in luxury hotels while yields in resorts dropped and serviced apartments saw a growth in operating profit in 2004. To understand why there are noticeable differences in the various sectors of the accommodation industry, it is useful to examine the characteristics of the accommodation sector.

Characteristics of the accommodation sector

All types of accommodation are confronted with some common characteristics – *seasonality*, which affects those properties where one market, such as 'summer sun', dominates. In these situations, marketing efforts attempt to fill rooms at off-peak times through short breaks or other incentives (see Chapter 21 for more discussion of seasonality and urban tourism). Many accommodation providers work with their regional tourist board to develop local products such as festivals in the spring and autumn to spread the demand across seasons which may be quieter.

Related to seasonality is the issue of *occupancy level*, as discussed above. For large hotels occupancy levels have been assisted with the development of yield management systems which seek to achieve a better fit with the market so that occupancy is spread across the week and month and year to avoid too many peaks and troughs in their business. **Location** can be of paramount importance in the siting of accommodation units. Ashworth (1989) proposed a model of urban hotel location based on one simple principle: distance decay – the prestigious properties located in the central locations with the greatest accessibility to the market and adjacent to convention centres and other large venues.

Chapter 10 Tourism Accommodation and Hospitality Services

TABLE 10.4   The *HotelBenchmark* Survey by Deloitte – summary report

The *HotelBenchmark Survey* by Deloitte is the leading survey of its kind, containing data from over **6000** hotels across all areas of the world outside of North America. The results below reflect a sample of the **320** markets on which we report on a monthly basis, providing depth of coverage and sample sizes which are unsurpassed in the majority of regions. To learn more, visit our website at **www.HotelBenchmark.com** or contact us at **HotelBenchmark@deloitte.co.uk**

1/2003 to 12/2003	Occupancy		Average room rate		RevPAR	
	2003 %	Change	2003 US$	Change	2003 US$	Change
Asia Pacific (HotelBenchmark sample represents approximately 1000 hotels across the region)						
Auckland	71.8	0.3%	79	28.0%	57	28.4%
Beijing	55.2	−26.2%	77	2.8%	43	−24.2%
Hong Kong	62.5	−20.5%	113	−2.5%	71	−22.4%
Singapore	61.1	−13.3%	79	−7.1%	48	−19.4%
Sydney	74.7	4.5%	112	30.6%	83	36.4%
Tokyo	78.2	−3.1%	178	7.9%	139	4.5%
Caribbean & Latin America (HotelBenchmark sample represents approx 120 hotels across region)						
Buenos Aires	55.0	36.1%	74	−1.4%	41	34.2%
Mexico City	65.8	1.3%	120	−2.3%	79	−1.0%
Quito	62.1	8.6%	73	0.4%	46	9.0%
Sau Paulo	49.5	8.3%	76	−14.2%	38	−7.1%
Santiago	55.8	8.3%	90	−7.2%	50	0.4%
Europe (HotelBenchmark sample represents approximately 3500 hotels across the region)						
Amsterdam	73.8	−5.5%	147	10.5%	109	4.4%
Berlin	64.1	1.7%	98	9.2%	63	11.1%
Brussels	64.2	−1.0%	108	18.0%	69	16.8%
London	73.7	−1.4%	156	5.6%	115	4.1%
Madrid	66.5	−2.7%	161	14.5%	107	11.4%
Paris	65.9	−8.3%	202	14.5%	133	5.0%
Rome	65.4	−2.4%	197	16.3%	129	13.6%
Vienna	71.5	6.5%	102	23.3%	73	31.4%
Middle East (HotelBenchmark sample represents approximately 500 hotels across the region						
Cairo	64.2	−0.1%	62	−3.9%	40	−3.9%
Dubai	77.6	0.2%	128	9.4%	99	9.6%
Jerusalem	34.6	22.2%	81	8.4%	28	32.5%
Riyadh	55.7	−9.5%	114	0.2%	64	−9.3%

Source: © Deloitte (2004), reproduced with permission

There is a tendency for hotels to locate in urban areas and to seek out the most accessible locations, as railway hotels did in the nineteenth century, next to the source of demand. In some situations, conversion of former office blocks and redundant warehouses (the Palace Hotel in Manchester is located in a listed insurance building) are used as prestigious locations for up-market hotels. At the same time, gateways such as airports remain high value locations. Intersections on major routeways (e.g. motorways) are also assuming a significant role for mid-range hotels in the absence of available in-town sites. In rural environments, location is often related to the scenic and aesthetic qualities of the landscape so that visitors can enjoy the rustic image and landscape attraction and, in coastal locations, sea views assume a premium price in the location of accommodation.

Grading systems according to Cooper *et al.* (2005) incorporate classifications and grading of accommodation, and the former relates to the assignment of hotels to a category in relation to its facilities and services. In contrast, grading emphasizes the internal quality elements of the property. The result is that classification and grading schemes are used to establish a standardized approach to service and product range and to communicate with consumers on what is provided at each property. It also enables accommodation providers to market, segment and compete on the basis of its distinctive features while setting minimum standards for consumers. In 1999, the UK finally harmonized the tourist board 'crown' scheme with the 'stars' awarded by the two motoring organizations, the RAC and the AA. The result: stars for hotels and diamonds for other serviced accommodation. England does not operate a statutory registration scheme for tourist accommodation; at a major conference organized by the English Tourism Council (now subsumed into VisitBritain) in 1999, some of the arguments given for the introduction of one were: "the unacceptable level of customer dissatisfaction ... no formal channel for complaints ... no mechanism for taking action against persistent offenders... [the] enforcement of fire regulations, building controls, environmental health is poorly resourced' and a similar debate is ongoing in Scotland over compulsory registration. Opponents of statutory grading schemes argue that further regulations stifle enterprise and that there is no firm evidence that in countries where it has been implemented standards have been raised. Furthermore, the tourist experience includes visits to theatres, restaurants and shops but these are not subject to grading; despite the latter point, there is little doubt that, for many tourists, their accommodation acts as a 'base' whilst on holiday and although they may tolerate low standards in some shops the same cannot be applied to where they sleep.

Classifying the accommodation sector

The accommodation sector is a diverse and complex phenomenon which is in a state of constant change and evolution. As a result, it is impossible to come up with a definitive classification that will embrace all forms of accommodation at any one point in time because of the pace of change in this sector, although Figure 10.3 attempts to develop a typology based on the form of journey/visit being undertaken and the purpose of the trip which highlights the complexity of classifying the sector. However, for the purpose of simplifying the nature of the accommodation sector, the first major distinction one can make is between the serviced and non-serviced sectors. The serviced sector is accommodation with services and facilities provided which can be included in the charge for the product. In the non-serviced sector, the product is accommodation only.

Serviced accommodation

Hotels

As mentioned already, the hotel is among the most visible and easily identifiable subsectors within the accommodation business (which is referred to as the 'lodging sector' in the USA), employing large numbers of staff. Whilst globally the sector is dominated by small family-owned businesses, the competition with chains and reinvestment costs have forced many out of this sector. Many of the surviving hotels in the small family sector have identified distinct niches. The ownership of hotels is a complex area, typically grouped under three forms (based on the discussion earlier of entry mode):

- those hotels owned and operated by hotel companies under their own name
- those which are franchised, which may use a brand (in the USA the Hospitality Franchise Systems company operates many franchises on behalf of brands but owns few properties; it is reputed to be the largest global hotel company although it does not have an identifiable physical presence)
- management of the hotel on behalf of an owner – such as Hilton and Marriott.

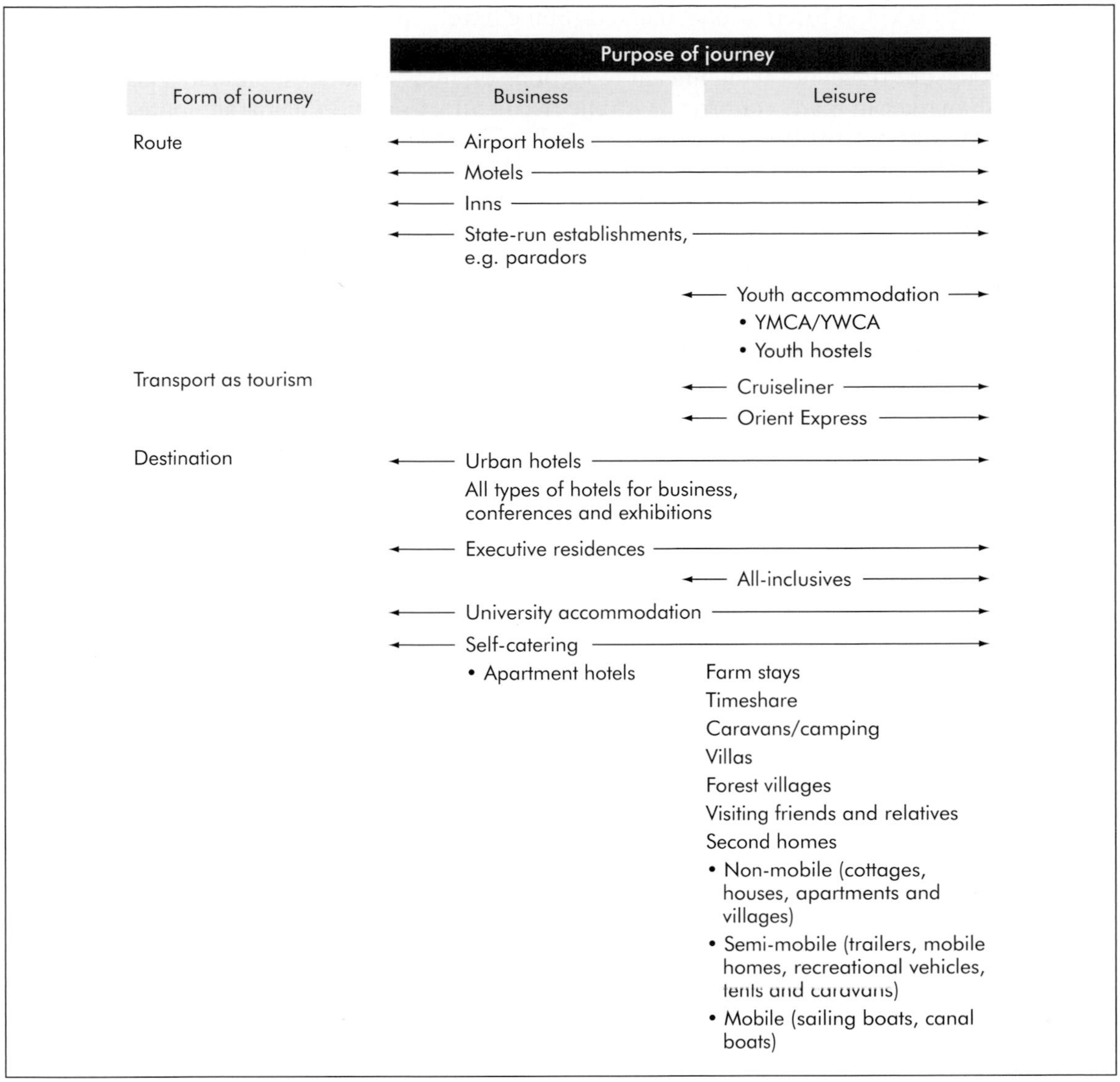

FIGURE 10.3 Accommodation types. Source: Adapted from Hall and Page (1999); Hall and Müller (2004)

What has characterized hotels in the last 20 years is the low rates of return on investment, with many city centre hotels purchased more for their long-term asset value than for profitability, as occupancy levels have posed problems in achieving profit thresholds. However, the last decade has seen a greater pressure on hotel chains to meet profit thresholds given their investors' demands for greater returns.

Recent developments in the hotel sector include the growth of health resorts (which is one of the fastest-growing sectors of the business in Europe, particularly the luxury end of the market with tariffs of £1000 a night) and the introduction of long-stay five star hotels such as Marriott Executive Residences, including their recently opened property in Budapest, and TownePlace Suites which has properties in different American states.

According to Jones (2002), the different sources of demand for accommodation include:

- government officials
- business travellers
- leisure travellers
- tour groups
- conference participants
- other users

from both domestic and international markets. Some hotels specialize in certain markets, such as city centre business and conference hotels with premium prices which use weekend capacity for short-break leisure travellers at significant reductions on mid-week rates. Similarly, airport hotels are a growth market in many countries with the rise in air travel and the market for accommodating flight crews and transiting passengers as well as inbound and outbound travellers. Periods which sometimes prove problematic for airport hotels are weekends and holiday periods such as Easter and Christmas and some have diversified by catering for weddings.

The rise of the hotel chains, the development of newer, more innovative forms of hotel accommodation and the decline of the traditional seaside resorts in many western European locations have seen a shift towards urban and rural properties and a focus on areas of potential and growth at a global scale that are apparent in Table 10.5. In many respects, the small family-owned hotel is in decline and is being superseded by the globalization of the high-yield locations in cities and resorts. The small family-run sector is left with the less profitable and lifestyle properties with much smaller profit margins. One notable exception is the growth of smaller prestigious boutique hotels. This is evident in the evolution of new luxury health resorts and hotels which are moving the hotel sector into new market segments. Traditional family-run businesses relying upon domestic tourists are facing increased competition in many countries from the larger hotels and the appeal of cheap package holidays and new products (e.g. cruises and motoring holidays).

One example of a response to the development of chain hotels has been the formation of independent groupings and a number of consortia have developed in recent decades in order to compete with the power of the hotel chains; independent hotels group together to obtain the benefits of national and international marketing and bulk-purchasing discounts. A range of other developments, including the rise of the resort offering a more diverse range of accommodation and services is shown in Insight 10.2 with the rise of the mega resort hotel in Las Vegas. The Insight indicates that the accommodation sector cannot easily be separated from the tourism sector since it is key element of the tourism economy and is linked to the image and concept of the destination although in some cases it can create an enclave where the tourist stays within the resort and has little interaction with the area they are staying in.

TABLE 10.5   A selection of development themes in the global accommodation sector

- In Beijing, power shortages due to massive urban growth have led the government to consider rationing power and hotels may have to cut their consumption by 20 per cent

- Large hotel chains dependent upon lucrative but volatile business and conference meetings and convention business have sought to diversify into the leisure market, as the example of www.LeisureSuitTraveler.com shows

- In 2006, the Poseidon Undersea Resort will open in the Bahamas with 44 rooms at a cost of US$40 million. Room rates will be up to US$1500 a night, and half of the rooms will be underwater with acrylic walls to see out. This is following the example of the Jules Undersea Lodge in Key Largo, Florida

- Boutique hotels with chic interiors and designs are set to open with room rates of up to US$700 a night after the Marriot brand, Ritz-Carlton, entered into an agreement to build hotels with a Rome jewellery and perfume house. Armani and Ferragamo are also seeking to develop this area, since designer brands add class and prestige to the locations and will attract the fashion-conscious traveller

- In the UK, the entrepreneur S. Woodroffe plans to replicate his success from setting and selling his Yo! Sushi café concept by developing Yotel, a budget hotel concept. Yotel is based on the idea of the pods used in space-saving hotels in Tokyo and aims to use redundant space in cities (e.g. basements) to develop these cabin-like entities of 10 m² based on the British Airways First Class cabins with upmarket furnishing. Yotel will charge around £75 a night. Initial properties are planned for airports in London

The mega resort hotel and Las Vegas

Las Vegas is an interesting example of a destination built in the desert environment of Nevada, USA, and with a tourism sector based on entertainment and gambling. It was only in 1997 that the destination exceeded the 100 000-room point but, because of the scale of building, there were over 125 000 hotel rooms in 2000 and the number continues to increase. Table 10.6 illustrates the size of some Las Vegas hotels.

Relating to the origin of their names, The Venetian 'includes a Grand Canal with gondolas, a 315-foot campanile, Doges Palace, Bridge of Sighs and St Mark's Square' whereas Hilton's Paris features 'a 50 storey half-scale Eiffel Tower'. The Las Vegas Convention and Visitors Authority projects that for every 1000 new rooms opened, an extra 275 000 visitors a year are needed. Given the scale of development, active marketing needs to be complemented by new direct flights, since many visitors arrive by air.

In 2004, MGM announced plans to create a multi-billion dollar Project CityCentre in Las Vegas on a 66-acre site in the heart of the Las Vegas strip. The first phase of the development would be an 18 million square foot development with a 4000-room hotel and casino with three 400-room boutique hotels operated by other Las Vegas hotel operators. This would also contain 550 000 square foot of retail space and 1650 condominiums. The first phase of this ambitious project is to be opened in 2010. This would extend MGM Mirage's national presence from the 11 casino resorts it currently operates in in the USA and the three additional casino resorts it has invested in the USA as well as interests in the UK. To view further statistics, the reader is recommended to the website at www.lasvegas24hours.com.

TABLE 10.6   A selection of Las Vegas' 'mega-hotels' and casinos

	Number of rooms
MGM Grand Hotel & Casino	5034
Excalibur Hotel Casino	4008
Mandalay Bay	4000+
Circus Circus Hotel & Casino	3770
Las Vegas Hilton	3174
The Venetian	3036
Paris Hilton	2916
Bally's	2814
Aladdin	2567
Imperial Palace	2700
Sahara Hotel	2000
Tropicana	1874
Golden Nugget	1800

The resort and accommodation

The term 'resort' is here taken to mean the provision of accommodation and substantial other services at one location. Poon (1998: 62) defines all-inclusive resorts as those 'which include virtually everything in the prepaid price – from airport transfers, baggage handling, government taxes, rooms, all meals, snacks, drinks and cigarettes to the use of all facilities, equipment and certified instructors ... the result is that the use of cash is eliminated'.

The all-inclusive concept originates from holiday camps and villages such as Butlin's in Britain and the French-based Club Méditerranée (Club Med). Club Med, which developed in the 1950s, now dominates the league table of all-inclusive chains, as Table 10.7 illustrates, and is the market leader in France (Marvel 2003) for French holidays, with 25 000 rooms and two million customers in 2004. Its global operations cover France, Mediterranean Europe, Asia, the Caribbean, Africa, the South Pacific and the USA.

Budget accommodation

At the low-cost end of the serviced market are forms of **budget accommodation**. Some forms have developed as a result of transport improvements and the innovation by entrepreneurs and these include motels, budget hotels (e.g. the easy.com brand) and some guest-houses. Branding assists the process of marketing as it informs the customer that a Travelodge at one end of the country is likely to offer the same facilities 300 miles away; there are over 190 of these lodges in the UK all offering en suite rooms with satellite television and easy check-in/out. What is apparent in the budget hotel sector is its rapid response to consumer demand since the 1980s, as the demand for low-cost accommodation shifted from bed-and-breakfasts and small family-owned hotels to new low-cost, high-quality room-only priced units. This has also meant greater competition at the one- or two-star accommodation level and a rise in business travel which can account for up to 50 per cent of budget hotel business in the UK. This has been because budget hotels offer many of the facilities of higher-grade hotels (en suite facilities, direct dial telephones, televisions) and are often on sites easily accessed by car.

The Days Inn's concept of 'budget-luxury' is another example of market segmentation. As a result of travelling in New England, Cecil B. Day, the founder of Days Inns, realized that there was a gap in accommodation for the typical American family travelling on a limited budget. Day opened his first motel, which combined budget and luxury features, in Tybee Island, Georgia, in April 1970 on the premise of providing quality lodging at a fair and reasonable price. Since then, Days Inn has grown into one of the largest franchised lodging systems in the world, opening its 1900th hotel in November 1999. There are now Days Inns in Canada, China, Colombia, the Czech Republic, Hungary, India, Mexico, Philippines, South Africa, the United Kingdom and Uruguay in addition to the USA and the chain is now owned, as discussed in Chapter 7, by Cendant Corporation. At a lower cost, the Youth Men's Christian Association (YMCA), Youth Women's Christian Association (YWCA) and YHA (www.yha.org.uk) are notable. The market has also grown as entrepreneurs have set up backpackers' establishments to cater for the global growth in dormitory-style accommodation for backpackers in youth and mature markets. The rise of more luxurious backpacker establishments akin to budget hotels also highlights one of the trends in this growing market. Yet one of the most established forms of budget accommodation is the YHA.

The YHA is more than simply an accommodation provider, it is virtually an environmental movement in its own right and has expressed opinions on afforestation in the Lake District and industrial development in the countryside with its aim 'to promote love, care and understanding of the countryside in principle and in practice'. The association is represented on 20 official or

TABLE 10.7 *Major all-inclusive chains*

Resort	*Headquarters*
Club Med	France
Allegro Resorts	Dominican Republic
Robinson Clubs	Germany
Club Valtur	Italy
Super Clubs	Jamaica
Club Aldiana	Germany
Clubs International	USA
Sandals	Jamaica

Source: Developed from Poon (1998); Marvel (2003); industry websites

voluntary bodies connected with the environment and has developed its own seven-point Environmental Charter for youth hostels globally. This is a notable development in the accommodation sector, as the environmental impacts of their stay have assumed a greater role in consumers' awareness.

Environmental concerns

The environmental issues in the accommodation sector are complex. These are issues of concern to consumers (i.e. water use, energy use, recycling, waste disposal, the impact of the hotel when it is located in a fragile location) and accommodation establishments who have used their environmental friendliness to achieve a competitive edge. The International Hotels Environment Initiative (IHF) (www.ihei.org), created in 1992, aims for continuous improvements in the hotel industry worldwide. It uses benchmarking to examine how different forms of accommodation consume resources in comparison with similar properties worldwide and it advises on what type of programmes can be used to reduce consumption (i.e. in energy and fresh water consumption, waste minimization and purchasing). Among its influential publications are its *Environmental Pack for Hotels: A User Friendly Guide for all Hotel Staff* and its widely acclaimed *Environmental Management for Hotels: An Industry Guide to Best Practice Manual*.

The non-serviced accommodation sector

In contrast to the serviced sector the growth of **self-catering** accommodation has been a major change for the post-war accommodation industry in many countries and much of this growth has been at the expense of the traditional guest-house and small family-run hotel sector. Some self-catering complexes have provided recreational and entertainment facilities such as Center Parcs (www.centerparcs.co.uk), a company that has sites in Germany, Belgium, France and the Netherlands, from where it first developed. When it took over the Oasis holiday village, it acquired 750 villas at the Penrith location on the edge of the English Lake District. The all-inclusive nature of this complex means that there is no reason to leave the site (the Oasis Penrith location covers 400 acres) and, given that the villas are let on a self-catering basis, the clientele are encouraged to buy from the on-site supermarket if they do not patronize the restaurants. What is notable about Center Parcs is that occupancy rates are around 90 per cent and repeat visits are running at 60 per cent, which is a significant achievement for this innovative form of accommodation. In the early years of operation, the Rural Development Commission in the UK concluded that Center Parcs Sherwood Forest and Elveden Forest villages had an economic impact of £4 million on the local economy, with visitors also spending £2 million locally. Through the multiplier effect (see Chapter 17 for an explanation of how this works) Center Parcs' impact on the local area of each village is £14 million based on initial estimates. This highlights the impact which the accommodation sector can have on the local economy.

Apartments form a central component of the accommodation provided in self-catering units and in the Mediterranean, the USA and Australasia. This market has been a popular addition to both coastal and urban locations. This sector also includes developments such as gîtes (French holiday cottages) and second homes (see Case Study 10.1W). In some cases self-catering accommodation is also being packaged in the mass markets by specialist operators while new innovations (e.g. house swaps) have also added additional capacity for holiday accommodation to compete with the serviced sector following the 1980s boom in global timeshare.

Timeshare and holiday rental intermediaries

According to Marvel (2004b), holiday rental intermediaries (HRIs) link owners and clients of holiday properties together, with around 4000 companies in the USA and 600 000 properties. In Europe, there are over one million properties accounting for 38 million holidays, dominated by France, Spain and the UK. In Europe, the main player is Cendant, and in the USA, Resort Quest.

These companies are beginning to compete with hotels as condominiums and **timeshares** continue to become more fashionable especially for families with young children. The rise of the low-cost airlines has made this accommodation-only option more accessible to holiday-makers. The market is experiencing growth as niche operators enter, such as internet-based companies (e.g. Vacation Rentals by Owner and hotelrentals.com). Further forms of accommodation which are notable are university campus accommodation (see Connell 2000), camping and caravan sites while specialist operators such as Eurocamp have developed sited tents and caravans for the budget-conscious family and small groups of travellers.

Caravanning and camping

In Europe one of the leading caravanning organizations, the Caravan Club, points to 315 000 touring caravans in use. The volume of members has seen a growth from 50 000 in 1966 to 100 000 in 1972 with the greatest rise occurring 1972–1990 when membership exceeded 250 000. The organization offers over five million pitch nights each year on 200 sites and via a further 2700 certified sites in private ownership on farms and rural sites. It accounts for 17 per cent of UK holiday spending and is worth £2 billion a year in the UK, employing 90 000 people as a result of the UK's 18 million bed nights spent in caravans. The average caravanner spend a relatively low at £25 a night, but this generates £210 million for the local economies in which caravans are pitched. However, there is an ongoing debate on the aesthetic impact of mobile and static caravans on the rural and coastal environment, given that many campsites were constructed prior to planning legislation becoming formalized in many countries, and remains a contentious issue in many national parks where they are often viewed as a blight on the landscape.

One of the least-known and understood sectors which is not strictly non-serviced is the visiting relatives (VFR) category. In some cities such as Auckland in New Zealand, up to 50 per cent of the inbound UK visiting relatives market stay in the home of a relative or acquaintance and while it makes a major contribution to the local tourism economy it is poorly understood in relation to domestic tourism. Similarly, the growth of global family networks in an age of increasing travel among certain ethnic groups such as the Chinese may also create a market for visiting relatives who do not use serviced accommodation or non-serviced accommodation but stay with a network of family and friends in different countries. Yet, at some point during a visit, tourists will make use of non-accommodation hospitality services.

Non-accommodation hospitality services

The hospitality services which are often associated with the accommodation sector are not always provided by this sector. In many locations, these services are also provided outside accommodation establishments and comprise restaurants, fast-food outlets, cafeterias and public houses, bars, clubs and canteens. This sector has undergone massive change in the UK reflected in employment change in hotel and catering. One of the greatest changes has occurred in the fast-food sector which has grown nationally in the UK while other sectors have expanded through the use of part-time employment. The dominance of transnational corporations such as McDonald's, KFC and Burger King have resulted in the market being dominated by a limited number of brands. For the tourist, this has meant that the fast-food sector has competed directly with other forms of food retailing in city and small town locations and is a good illustration of the theme of globalization.

In a European context, the European Hotels, Restaurant and Café Association (HOTREC, www.hotrec.org) noted that there are over one million businesses in the EU restaurant and café sector employing five million people. This illustrates the small-scale nature of many of these hospitality establishments, with fewer than ten employees and typically four employees per establishment. The sector generated around €92 billion in 2001, equivalent to 4 per cent of the service sector (HOTREC 2004). 'Restaurant' is a wide-ranging term used to incorporate establishments serving food from the full-service gastronomie through to fast-food establishments. Changing trends in the way and how people eat in their leisure time has meant that lifestyle changes have impacted upon the sector. In the UK, Mintel (2004) observed that whilst there is an increased frequency of eating out, it has become a function of greater disposable income and more a way of life than a treat, following trends in North America and other countries. In fact, Mintel (2004) found that half the population eat at public houses; the boom in fast-food consumption has been challenged by concerns over healthy eating, leading many fast food chains to launch healthy options.

However, the restaurant sector is a highly volatile sector as it relies on a mix of tourism and leisure trade (Image 10.4), with high rates of business failure and ownership change. Among key drivers of change in this sector of leisure consumption are service, quality and branding. In the coffee consumption expansion in many cities across the world, chains such as Starbucks and Costas increased competition and coffee as a takeaway and casual drink has become a key consumption experience for visitors and non-visitors alike, leading to comments that we now live in a cappuccino society where the café is a central element of socializing and enjoying hospitality. Whilst the eating-out expansion in many countries has seen massive growth, in part, fuelled by tourism and leisure spending, the competition and involvement of chains have also impacted upon this sector. Competition remains intense as the restaurant sector takes a major part of the tourist spend. One measure of the importance of the dynamic nature of this sector is the growth of one chain in the UK: J.D. Wetherspoons (see Insight 10.3).

INSIGHT 10.3

J.D. Wetherspoons: The growth of a hospitality chain

J.D. Wetherspoons is a large hospitality chain created in 1979 by entrepreneur Tim Martin (www.jdwetherspoon.co.uk). He strove to offer good value for money and cask-conditioned beers. The concept was extended to offer all-day food, non-smoking areas and a clean, convivial atmosphere. The company's pubs were initially located in north London followed by other areas of London and the Home Counties (south east England). After stock market floatation in 1992, the company began a national plan of pub acquisitions, beginning in the Midlands (Birmingham) followed by other major cities: Liverpool, Bristol and Manchester. The company adopted a strategy of acquiring sites or pubs in key locations and competing locally on its strengths. In 2004, the company had over 640 premises (including lodges) selling its products, which is a massive growth for any company. In 2004, its turnover was £787 million with a profit of £77 million; 40 per cent of sales are from food and soft drinks.

The pattern of growth in the period 2001–2004 is shown in Figure 10.4 and it shows the company's entry into the UK's main conurbations up to 2001 and a gradual consolidation and further expansion into other regions such as Scotland after that date. Figure 10.4 also highlights the scale of growth in a three-year period by region, illustrating the principal areas of development and how the company has developed a wider scale of operations, becoming a national brand.

Among some of the critical factors that distinguishes Wetherspoon's from the competition are:

- good quality food and drink provision

- being ahead of the competition with its use of non-smoking areas, in view of impending changes to UK smoking law
- the use of well-trained and friendly staff
- individually designed pubs to create a unique experience as opposed to a McDonaldized homogeneous experience
- high standards of repair and maintenance
- low operating margins (around 9–10 per cent) to keep prices low
- including food sales and service as a key growth sector for leisure spending
- holding beer festivals to promote traditional ales from British, Irish and micro breweries to exceed the capacity sold by the Annual Campaign for Real Ale (CAMRA) Great British Beer Festival
- using a non-music policy to deter a binge-drinking environment and introducing family areas for early evening dining
- working in an environment of deregulation of the pub trade in the 1980s when the major breweries were required to divest a large number of their tied pubs to improve competition
- operating annual performance-related bonus schemes for all staff, based on profitability and operating standards. It also operates a share scheme to motivate staff, especially those who interface with the public
- operating an environmental policy via its corporate social responsibility group.

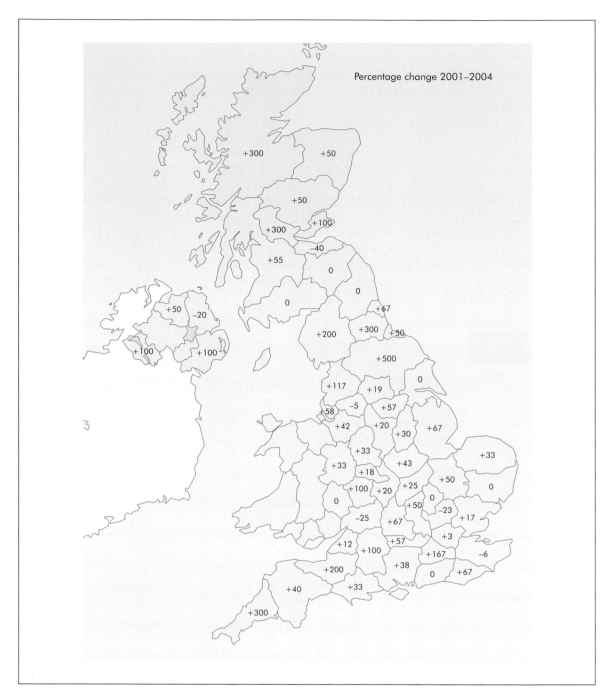

Percentage change 2001–2004

FIGURE 10.4 Geographical expansion of J.D. Wetherspoon pubs in 2001–2004. Copyright S.J. Page

Image 10.4:
The restaurant
sector provides key
service and form of
hospitality to tourists

Insight 10.3 shows one of the major difficulties with quantifying the impact of both the accommodation and more complex and diverse hospitality sector in terms of the users. In certain destinations, for example the tourist-historic city, those establishments offering food and possibly other entertainment tend to cluster. This is demonstrated most clearly in many Dutch cities where entertainment facilities (e.g. sex shops and brothels) are located in a distinct area with other food and hospitality services developing nearby given the nature of the attraction and visitor appeal of these icons of the built environment. Yet hospitality and the consumption of food and drink may also have wider uses in tourism, since regional specialization, marketing and promotion may lead to themed forms of tourism based on these experiences, which can be integrated with local accommodation providers to develop new forms of tourism.

Contemporary issues in hospitality management

Managing accommodation and hospitality premises poses many complex issues for those in a managerial role. In western Europe, the impact of government and transnational bodies like the EU has generated a wide range of legislation with which managers need to be conversant. As Table 10.8 illustrates, in the accommodation sector the legislation covers a wide range of concerns, many of which are related to providing a safe experience and environment for guests and employees. However, for many smaller businesses this has led to criticisms of unnecessary red tape which increases compliance costs; an example of such a piece of legislation is the 2002 Disability Act to make public places such as hotels accessible to the less able. In extreme cases, some businesses will cease operating when compliance costs cannot be financed or will push the business into a loss.

Attracting and retaining staff also remains a problem area for the hospitality sector, as Chapter 11 will show later. Rates of high staff turnover in many European countries has led some hotel managers to recruit economic migrants from the former Eastern Europe to fill gaps in the hospitality workforce.

To address these labour shortages in recruiting skilled workers, resulting from poor wage rates compared to other industries, employers have de-skilled some vital areas of hospitality work. A response to this is the use of **contract caterers** (Haywood and Wilson 2003), who provide systems solutions with pre-packed chilled prepared food which does not need skilled

---

TABLE 10.8   Principal legislation issues for accommodation providers

- Planning permission and building regulations
- Fire safety (including fire certificates)
- Signage
- Business rates for the premises
- Utility supplies (water, gas and electricity)
- Health and safety
  - for guests, the public and employees
  - insurance cover
  - workplace-based safety
  - food safety (hygiene, handling and labelling)
  - liquor licensing
- The business of tourists/visitors as consumers
  - pricing and charging
  - accepting guests (i.e. disabled access)
  - cancellations
  - recording guests
- Other areas of regulation as an employer
  - national minimum wage
  - paternity and maternity leave
  - employee rights
  - taxation

Source: Adapted from VisitBritain (2004)

Image 10.5: Raffles Hotel, Singapore. The former colonial landmark is an exclusive tourism location

food preparation. Among the successful companies operating in this sector are The Compass Group plc, now one of the world's largest food service companies, with revenue in excess of £11.7 billion; the group also owns brands such as Burger King and many catering franchises. Many hotels now rely upon just-in-time delivery from contract caterers, such as Brake Brothers in the UK. Globally, this market is estimated to be worth in excess of US$290 billion.

Management skills have also assumed a growing importance now larger hotel chains seek increased profits for shareholders (Image 10.5). As Riley (2003) observes, in the hotel sector, two sources of uncertainty characterize hospitality: demand and the consumer's subjective evaluation of products and services. The increasing role of technology has meant that hospitality managers are needing to use e-solutions for securing customers, in-house management (especially yield management) and procuring supplies via supply chains to achieve economies of scale.

Mergers and acquisitions and **corporate strategy** in hospitality and changing operational conditions have led many international firms to choose a strategy of either concentration or of obtaining scale economies by offering a uniform product with preferred management approaches including strategic alliances, franchising, management contracts, joint ventures and acquisitions, as discussed in Chapter 5. This has meant change is the only constant in the sector. The need also to understand the lifecycle of a product, the effect of competitors and technology has become critical for managers. Innovative marketing by new entrants may remove the existing competitive advantage of a product, particularly where consumer sales and promotion expenditure are targeted at encouraging brand switching. Operating in a global marketplace, expanded by the impact of technology and the bypassing of existing intermediaries, has seen e-mediaries and dedicated accommodation sites gain ground. As a result, accommodation businesses will need to harness new marketing techniques such as **relationship marketing** (see Chapter 15) and to embrace new approaches such as one-to-one marketing, using ICTs to individualize the interaction (i.e. via email). They will also need to make a greater effort to retain customers, since it is cheaper to retain an existing customer than to recruit a new one. Hotels in particular are facing a growing pressure to deliver customer value, to meet expectations and to have quality as an all-embracing feature throughout all levels of their organization.

Conclusion

Within the accommodation and hospitality services sector, the global brand has emerged as one of the most significant developments and is an ongoing trend. The process of globalization is evident from the hotel sector to restaurants and even cafés, as a reassurance of quality. The consequence for the built environment and the tourist experience, as critics would argue, is the growing McDonaldization of the accommodation and hospitality services sector. Yet one trend running contrary to this is the development in local and regional cuisine and hospitality as reflected in the wine and food festivals and theming of tourism products to emphasize local and regional distinctiveness.

The market for accommodation is very diverse with a product and price range being developed for an increasingly sophisticated tourist market. This is evident in the rise of the internet as a search tool for consumers to identify a wider range of products to consider in booking accommodation and travel services. Added to this is the rise of the environmental lobby, reflected in consumer demands for a greater attention to environmental sensitivity (see Stabler and Goodall 1997). Hotels are now achieving cost savings as a result, by seizing the environmental advantages of less laundering, savings in water consumption and reduction in the use of consumables. Thus, the accommodation sector cannot be separated from trends in the wider tourism sector and in some cases this sector is leading the way forward in environmental management, where such initiatives are developed and implemented. The accommodation sector is also a key element of the tourist's experience of a destination and is often sold as part of a product; therefore quality standards and tourists' satisfaction levels with their holiday experiences are intrinsically linked to the accommodation sector. The consumer is consuming an experience where tourism, hospitality and accommodation are integrated. Yet the constant theme in this sector is the quality of the staff who interface with visitors and for this reason the next chapter examines human resource issues in tourism.

Discussion questions

1 What image does the hotel sector have within the tourism and hospitality industries?

2 Discuss the problem of staff turnover in the hospitality industry.

3 How has the development of self-catering accommodation villages such as Centre Parcs impacted upon the serviced sector in European coastal resorts?

4 The rise of budget accommodation in the serviced sector is now driven by the demand for quality at a lower cost. How far does this result from wider developments in the tourism industry?

References

Ashworth, G.J. (1989) 'Urban tourism: An imbalance in attention', in C.P. Cooper (ed.) *Progress in Tourism, Recreation and Hospitality Management Volume 1.* London: Belhaven.

Connell, J.J. (2000) 'The role of tourism in the socially responsible university', *Current Issues in Tourism*, 3 (1): 1–19.

Cooper, C., Fletcher, J., Fyall, A., Gilbert, D. and Wanhill, S. (2005) *Tourism: Principles and Practice, Third Edition.* Harlow: Pearson Education.

Deloitte (2004) Hotel Benchmark Survey: Summary Report, http://www.hotelbenchmark.com, accessed 8.1.2005.

Hall, C.M. and Müller, D. (2004) 'Introduction: Second homes, curse or blessing? Revisited' in C.M. Hall and D. Müller (eds) *Tourism, Mobility and Second Homes.* Clevedon: Channel View.

Hall, C.M. and Page, S.J. (1999) *The Geography of Tourism and Recreation: Environment, Place and Space, Second Edition.* London: Routledge.

Hall, C.M. and Sharples, L. (2003) 'The consumption of experiences or the experience of consumption? An introduction to the tourism of taste', in C.M. Hall, L. Sharples, R. Mitchell, N. Macionis and B. Cambourne, *Food Tourism Around the World.* Oxford: Butterworth-Heinemann.

Haywood, K. and Wilson, G. (2003) 'Contract food service', in B. Brotherton (ed.) *The International Hospitality Industry: Structure, Characteristics and Issues.* Oxford: Butterworth-Heinemann.

HOTREC (2004) What is on the EU menu for restaurants? An overview of European issues affecting restaurants, http://www.hotrec.org, accessed 10.1.2005.

Jones, P. (ed.) (2002) *Introduction to Hospitality Operations: An Indispensable Guide to the Industry, Second Edition.* London: Continuum.

Jones, P. and Lockwood, A. (eds) (2002) *The Management of Hotel Operations: An Innovative Approach to the Study of Hotel Management.* London: Continuum.

KPMG (2004) *Global Hotel Distribution Survey.* London: KPMG.

Lashley, C. (2000) 'Towards a theoretical understanding', in C. Lashley and A. Morrison (eds) *In Search of Hospitality: Theoretical Perspectives and Debates.* Oxford: Butterworth-Heinemann.

Littlejohn, D. (2003) 'Hotels', in B. Brotherton (ed.) *The International Hospitality Industry: Structure, Characteristics and Issues.* Oxford: Butterworth-Heinemann.

Marvel, M. (2003) 'All-inclusives – the major players', *Travel and Tourism Analyst*, June.

Marvel, M. (2004a) 'European hotel chain expansion', *Travel and Tourism Analyst*, May.

Marvel, M. (2004b) 'Holiday rental intermediaries', *Travel and Tourism Analyst*, September.

Medlik, R. and Ingram, S. (2000) *The Business of Hotels, Fourth Edition.* Oxford: Butterworth-Heinemann.

Mintel (2004) *Eating out habits.* London: Mintel.

Page, S.J. (2003) *Tourism Management: Managing for Change.* Oxford: Butterworth-Heinemann.

Poon, A. (1998) 'All-inclusive resorts', *Travel and Tourism Analyst*, 6: 62–77.

Riley, M. (2003) 'Operational dilemmas', in B. Brotherton (ed.) *The International Hospitality Industry: Structure, Characteristics and Issues.* Oxford: Butterworth-Heinemann.

Stabler, M.J. and Goodall, B. (1997) 'Environmental awareness, action and performance in the Guernsey hospitality sector', *Tourism Management*, 18 (1): 19–33.

VisitBritain (2004) *The Pink Booklet: A Practical Guide to Legislation for Accommodation Providers.* London: VisitBritain.

Walton, J. (2000) 'The hospitality trades: A social history', in C. Lashley and A. Morrison (eds) *In Search of Hospitality: Theoretical Perspectives and Debates.* Oxford: Butterworth-Heinemann.

Warnken, J., Russell, R. and Faulkner, B. (2003) 'Condominium developments in maturing destinations: potentials and problems of long-term sustainability', *Tourism Management*, 24 (2): 155–68.

Further reading

Medlik, R. and Ingram, S. (2002) *The Business of Hotels, Fourth Edition.* Oxford: Butterworth-Heinemann.

Managing Tourist Operations and Communicating with the Visitor

In Parts I and II, the factors impacting upon and shaping both the demand and supply of tourism were outlined and we saw the scope of issues associated with both the tourist and the sectors which comprise the tourism industry. The major challenge for the tourism sector is the maximization of demand to meet its supply. This management challenge is one which concerns tourism managers globally and dominates both strategic long-term goals and day-to-day tourism operations where the tourism sector seeks to fill demand and meet the customer's needs through a range of mechanisms. This section of the book focuses on the wider context of tourism operations, by examining the tools and issues which the tourism industry has to deal with on a day-to-day basis as well as those which assume strategic importance. This is reflected in the first major issue which most tourism enterprises see as critical to maintaining a competitive business – having appropriate staff for the tasks in hand.

As will have become apparent from the different chapters in the book, tourism is a people business and so having the right kind of people doing the right kinds of jobs to delight the tourist must be central to the management of successful tourism enterprises. This is discussed in Chapter 11 in relation to global issues of human resource management which affect the tourism industry. The nature of human resource management and the particular challenges it poses for the future development of tourism are reviewed, emphasizing the new ways of thinking about human resource issues, the challenge of technology, more flexible working and the insatiable demand for labour in many developed countries. As people are a major cost in most tourism enterprises, it is appropriate to focus on the range of financial issues associated with setting up, developing and managing a tourism enterprise. This is a specialized area of tourism activity vital to the development of tourism businesses and operational performance and cannot be separated from the wider operational issues associated with managing a tourism business. Surprisingly, finance is largely neglected in many studies of tourism despite its key role in understanding how businesses operate and the financial management to retain profitable and able to develop. Therefore, Chapter 12 introduces some of the broad concepts and principles which tourism managers need to understand; it also examines how different tourism businesses secure funding and the various techniques used to review a businesses financial performance. This is very much linked to the next chapter (Chapter 13) which examines the vital area of tourism and entrepreneurship and the characteristics and activities of key individuals who have had a major impact on a specific sector of the tourism industry. The chapter highlights the influence of key individuals who are responsible, along with companies they own and operate, for the provision of tourism services and experiences.

In both chapters, it is also important to recognize that a key management tool used by successful businesses is ICTs, especially in the e-tourism revolution discussed in Chapter 6. Therefore, this tool which has been used to manage tourism supply issues, as well as in managing business operations, in interfacing with customers and in business to business relationships should not be seen in isolation from Chapters 11, 12 and 13 because some of the influential entrepreneurs in the low-cost airline revolution have utilized ICTs as their key strategy to compete in and develop their markets. But one of the major actors in facilitating and promoting (as well as constraining tourism) is the public sector, which is discussed in Chapter 14. Here the emphasis is on the role which the public sector plays at all geographical scales from the international level right down to the role of the local authority in helping to manage tourism as well as promoting, facilitating and pump-priming tourism in some cases. This role is often overlooked in a business context, but the public sector plays a complementary role to the private sector especially where the two work in partnership to grow the benefits of tourism for countries and localities. In many cases, they are also charged with a role in marketing tourism.

For this reason, Chapter 15 introduces many of the key marketing concepts used by businesses to develop a customer-focused organization, through a marketing orientation. This is vital for both the private and public sector for the long-term sustainability of tourism as an economic activity and much of the chapter highlights how marketing concepts are operationalized by businesses and organizations to develop valued relationships between the tourism industry and its potential and actual customers. One context in which this occurs in a highly visible manner is the destination. Therefore, Chapter 16 discusses the concept of destination marketing and its role in promoting places for tourism. Critical issues and concepts such as the marketing mix, communicating with the tourist and the role of advertising in tourism are discussed. Many of the key concepts developed in Chapter 15 are then applied in a destination context to show how organizations seek to market and advertise destinations to influence people to visit, using powerful tools such as branding as part of their advertising and promotional campaigns.

11

Human Resource Management in Tourism

Learning outcomes

After reading this chapter and answering the questions, you should be able to:

- understand the people dimension in tourism as a fundamental element in the success of tourism enterprises

- assess the scope of the human resource manager's job in tourism

- consider how agencies are involved in human resource management issues in tourism

- examine how future changes in work patterns will affect human resource issues in tourism

- assess the role of human resource issues in small tourism businesses

- understand how empowerment impacts upon the success of human resource issues in tourism organizations.

Overview

Human resource management issues are vital in the successful operation, development and long-term sustainability of tourism organizations. These issues are global in nature, although they may also have local ramifications, but the indisputable feature of tourism is its reliance on people as the vital ingredient in making an experience a success or failure. Even where experiences may be affected by negative events, empowered staff with initiative and a grasp of how to make a difference can often rescue a negative tourism experience. At the same time, many countries are reporting problems in recruiting and retaining staff and many new initiatives and developments are occurring globally to try and address some of these issues.

Introduction

Tourism is a people industry: tourists are people, customers and clients, and their activities are subject to the normal vagaries of human behaviour (i.e. decision-making about what to buy and consume) which are both predictable and unpredictable depending on the situation and context. The tourism experience or product is entirely dependent upon people for its delivery – or, more simply put, it is dependent upon the human factor in a service sector such as tourism, which is characterized by high levels of human involvement in the development and delivery of services or vacation experiences. Watson, D'Annunzio-Green and Maxwell (2004: 1) acknowledge that delivering hospitality and tourism products and services across international frontiers to discerning customers in highly competitive and dynamic market conditions presents a range of organizational challenges. **Human resource management** (HRM) presents a valuable tool for meeting many of these challenges and adding value in organizations (Baum 1993) and it frequently involves contact with people from different backgrounds, locations and cultures. Therefore, tourism can be conceptualized as a client purchasing 'the skills, service and commitment of a range of human contributors to the experience that they are about to embark upon' (Baum 1993: 4) and, as Baum and Kokkranikel (2005: 86) argue, 'The human resource dimension is one of the most important elements of any industry sector, none more so than for the tourism experience to be successful, managers within the tourism industry need to ensure that the tourism product or experience is "mediated" to the customer' which by its very nature means a wide range of human resource issues emerge.

As Baum and Kokkranikel (2005) indicate, the distinctive features of tourism as a human contact industry, based on service delivery, means than a number of issues impact upon HRM in tourism settings. Figure 11.1 summarizes some of these issues, which highlight the **perishability** of tourism products and services (i.e. they cannot be stored), their intangibility and the importance of employees in making the visitor's experience memorable and enjoyable is critical. Figure 11.1 highlights that, as a service delivered in specific places (i.e. destinations or in settings like a restaurant), tourism has a people-intensive nature. As a result, human resource managers need to be aware, at the very least, of a number of key issues as shown in Table 11.1. Yet Baum and

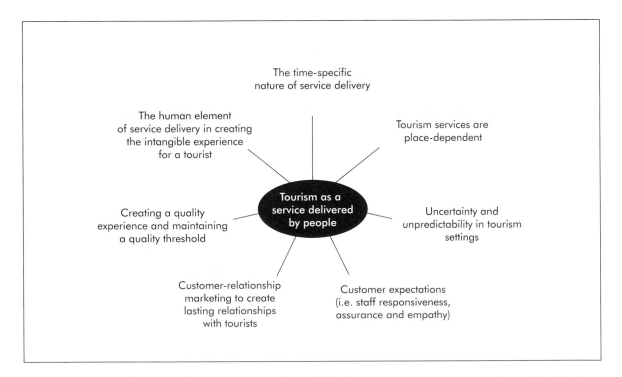

FIGURE 11.1   The nature of tourism as a service and the human resource component. Source: Developed from Baum and Kokkranikel (2005)

TABLE 11.1 The scope of human resource management issues for a tourism industry manager

1. A critical awareness of the scope and nature of the labour market
2. The design of jobs
3. Recruitment, selection, appointment and retention of staff
4. Induction, equal opportunities, training and development
5. Evaluation of staff performance
6. Salaries and incentives
7. Employment termination, grievance and dispute procedures
8. Industrial relations and employment law
9. Motivation of staff

Source: Adapted from Baum (1993)

Kokkranikel (2005) argue that HRM in tourism is characterized by 'adhocism', since managers and industry leaders have often had ambivalent attitudes to investing in the human capital (i.e. the people) who are the lifeblood of the tourism sector. One consequence of the long history of underinvestment in the human capital in the tourism sector is the development of global concern over how future labour requirements will be met if the growth of the sector is to be maintained. Labour shortages will constrain the growth ambitions of many governments that see tourism growth as one way of expanding and diversifying their economies: this hinges upon recruiting and training the right staff for the jobs available. This poses many challenges for individual businesses at the destination level and globally, where transnational operators concerned with their growth strategies will require labour to meet expansion plans. For the individual firm, these issues can be best summarized in Table 11.1 which outlines the scope of the activities a manager might have to consider.

Since tourism is a global business, with many enterprises operating transnationally or as multinational enterprises across several continents, certain sectors of the industry (e.g. the hotel sector) also have to adopt an international or global approach to HRM. Within the published studies of HRM in tourism, there are a common range of themes that consistently emerge which help to identify a number of elements that need to be considered when attempting to define the nature and scope of HRM in tourism. Baum (1993: 9–10) cites the following 'universal themes' which consistently feature in the analysis of HRM in tourism and these remain in force almost a decade later:

- demographic issues related to the shrinking pool of potential employees and labour shortages, which surface when the economy is performing well and other career options offer higher rates of pay
- the tourism industry's image as an employer: it is seen as a low payer, providing routine and mundane work roles
- cultural and traditional perceptions of the tourism industry
- rewards and compensation for working in the sector
- education and training and the need to constantly upgrade skills in a growing technical age
- skill shortages at the senior and technical levels, especially in developed countries (Baum 2002)
- linking human resource concerns with service and product quality
- poor manpower planning, especially a lack of innovation and **empowerment** of staff (see Insight 11.1) and the reluctance to introduce boundary-spanning roles for staff breaking down traditional functional job roles to meet customer needs
- a remedial rather than a proactive approach to human resource issues

and these are summarized in Figure 11.2.

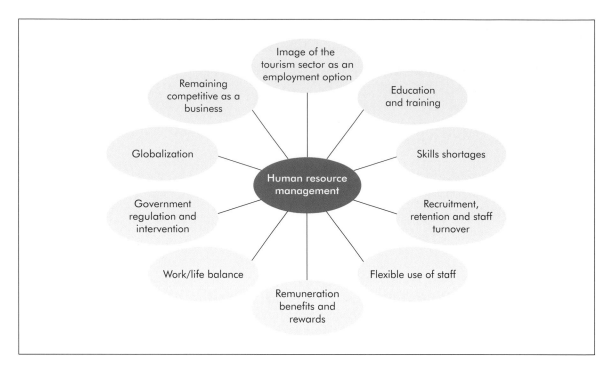

FIGURE 11.2 Contemporary themes in human resource management in tourism. Source: Adapted from Baum (1993)

Aside from the scope of HRM issues identified in Table 11.1, it is evident that the tourism sector also has a number of unique problems which need to be considered when attempting to define the scope of HRM in tourism.

So what do we mean by the term 'human resource management'?

In simple terms, HRM can be termed as a form of employment management which is focused on the managerial need for human resources to be provided and deployed. In line with the functions of management, the concern within HRM is the planning, monitoring and control of the human resource as a management activity. More complex analyses of HRM identify the need for the individual human resource system within any organization to realize the strategic objectives of the organization (i.e. the delivery of excellent **customer service** to tourism consumers). One can also distinguish between 'hard' and 'soft' HRM approaches. 'Hard' approaches are essentially financially driven and concerned with controlling the salary cost; they are extremely directive and this type of approach is therefore described as utilitarian and managerialist. In contrast, 'soft' approaches to HRM are centred on the principle of the development of the employees and are much more humanist, with employees as assets rather than liabilities. In practice most organizations adopt a pragmatic approach to HRM depending on a wide range of factors including the economic and operating environment, the size of the organization, the extent to which the labour market is supplied with adequate staff and the corporate culture. What should be evident from this brief discussion of HRM is that it is far more than simple personnel management and in its most highly effective state it should adopt a holistic approach to employment management. In a 'people' business such as tourism, this approach assumes a significant role because of the need to derive quality from the employees and their interaction and exchanges with customers so that it becomes critical that the people with the right skills are in the right jobs. Since tourism is a global business which operates at a wide range of scales, this chapter will examine HRM issues in tourism at the international and the individual levels of tourism enterprise to illustrate the issues which students need to be aware of when examining the tourism sector. (For a more specific discussion of the detailed nature of HRM functions readers are directed to the further reading section at the end of this chapter.)

Agencies and HRM issues in tourism: International perspectives

Among the existing studies of HRM in tourism, there is a reasonable consistent view on the human problems which face the tourism industry, and at the international scale there are a wide range of approaches and responses to the problems. They assume a key role for governments in countries seeking to expand their tourism economy. For example, in Croatia international tourism generated a ratio of 1:13.3 jobs that equates to around 300 000 jobs in total. One important scheme which has helped Croatia to capitalize upon its HR potential is the EU's *Travel and Tourism Capital Investment Programme* which aims to help provide a trained and responsive workforce, given Croatia's growing high dependence upon this growth sector compared to some of its neighbours (e.g. the Czech Republic has 12.4 per cent of employment based on tourism, Bulgaria 12.1 per cent, Hungary 10.3 per cent and Romania 5 per cent). With tourism employment set to grow 3.8 per cent per annum, training and HRM will prove to be key issues. Not surprisingly, in many of the **tourism master plan**s developed for countries, human resource issues assume a significant position. There are also a range of bodies which have an active involvement in HRM issues in tourism such as the World Travel and Tourism Council (WTTC), as discussed in Insight 11.1.

INSIGHT 11.1

The role of the World Travel and Tourism Council – Human Resources Taskforce and the future role of HRM

The WTTC is a global business leader's forum for travel and tourism from all sectors of the industry. It has representatives and offices throughout the world and it sponsors a WTTC human resource centre which has produced a publication entitled *Global Good Practices in Travel and Tourism Human Resource Development* with the publication sponsored by American Express. It provides case studies of good education and training across the tourism sector with a view to disseminating real-world experiences to a worldwide audience of human resource professionals. Pizam (1999) reports the results of a study funded by the WTTC and American Express on tourism and human resource issues in Latin America. In 2001, WTTC also undertook an in-depth study of the main human resource challenges facing the global tourism sector, given forecasts of 4.5 per cent growth per annum and the need to supply well-trained staff. This resulted in the WTTC Task Force report (WTTC 2001). The six areas the Task Force focused on were:

- the future role of HR and **e-HR**
- the attraction and retention of staff
- education and training
- **leadership** and management development
- gender and racial prejudice
- raising the awareness of tourism as a generator of employment.

The Task Force indicated that HR functions in the future will be very different, especially as HR moves from a localized to a global function, with locally led teams in different locations. Above all, employers need to be flexible so that employees can have a decent work–life balance. With the growth of technology, it will be possible to deliver HR services electronically, via e-HR computer systems. What is clear is that organizations in tourism of the future will move away from the traditional, highly structured, hierarchical form (see Chapter 5) to more flexible forms that might resemble a spider's web containing smaller clusters of teams distributed across the organization.

This, according to management theorists such as Drucker, Peters and Handy, is to accommodate continuous innovation (see Chapter 13), to cut implementation times and to head off competition. A more goal-oriented form of organization (see Insight 11.2 on empowerment and Southwest Airlines) with ICTs will need to be used to communicate and manage these teams, collaborating to achieve a common goal. As a result, a hierarchy will be replaced by a looser corporate umbrella, with more empowered teams working in a flexible manner. Self-managed and empowered teams will be a key element of this new organizational structure.

One consequence for tourism organizations may be a greater use of part-time staff and contractors and consultants rather than full-time employees, with a greater use of online recruitment. Part of this culture change will also be creating organizations people want to work in and in e-HR, which can help in facilitating a greater interaction between staff and the organization so people feel they can participate in the management of the organization. Using web-based training and e-learning offers employees more flexible training options.

In terms of the recruitment and **retention of staff**, the Task Force noted some of the high costs and reasons for staff turnover, which results in lost knowledge, were due to:

- inadequate opportunities for promotion
- dissatisfaction with company management
- dissatisfaction with pay
- lack of flexibility and lack of empowerment to take responsibility
- poor career paths
- bad working environments
- conflict with manager/staff
- unhappy with employee benefits.

To address such issues, the Task Force pointed to good practice across the tourism sector by companies to address such issues by:

- improving internal communications about the organization and strategy
- improving remuneration and benefits

- taking a greater focus on retention strategies
- focusing on new recruitment audiences such as retirees, returners and the disabled
- providing employment flexibility
- recruiting based on competencies to do the work (i.e. Southwest Airlines) and improved recruitment literature.

Even so, the major challenge for tourism employers will be:

- recruiting employees with industry experience
- retaining good staff
- introducing performance-based rewards
- providing a better image of the sector.

In terms of education and training, the value of human capital and the importance of integrating new HR practices will be dependent upon organizational **leadership** to recognize and implement these issues. The adhocism reported by Baum (2002) was critical of progress in this area. However, changes are gradually filtering into larger organizations (as opposed to the SME sectors) as they recruit effective leaders, and Figure 11.3 highlights some of the essential leadership qualities which the Task Force identified.

The tourism sector also has to address gender and racial prejudices to reduce dissatisfaction and turnover and to comply with the legislation in different countries. This involves recruiting a diverse workforce.

FIGURE 11.3   Characteristics of effective leadership

In some countries, the public sector is actively involved in the provision of organizations and assistance for the tourism sector to assist in human resource development, through policies, planning and the implementation of initiatives. A good example of this is the establishment of CERT in Ireland nearly 40 years ago as a national initiative funded by the state government. However, where the state is involved, it may often be the case that a range of bodies have overlapping responsibilities. The organizations which are typically involved are state education provision, private training and educational providers, national employment or manpower agencies, and associated bodies such as trade unions and the national, regional and local tourism agencies. Coordinating and liaising with such a host of bodies can be complex and time consuming. Furthermore, changes in political philosophy, such as in the UK after 1979, have seen state assistance progressively cut back and the emphasis being placed on the private sector. Where national tourism organizations (NTOs) are involved in training, their function can range from direct control of the training system at one extreme through to a limited policy role.

Image 11.1: Human resource issues and training are vital in face to face encounters such as check-in at airports where tourists rate the efficiency and friendliness of the encounter. Source: Civil Aviation Authority of Singapore

The World Tourism Organization (WTO) collates information from time to time and publishes it in reports, but even those data are partial. More progressive countries such as Singapore, with its Singapore 21 Strategy, have a key concern for human resource issues in tourism and this reflects the vast investment and significance of tourism to their national economies (Image 11.1). At a pan-European level, the EU (2001) report *Working Together for the Future of European Tourism* identified a number of priorities for concerted EU action in the field of tourism including:

- the need to upgrade skills in the tourism workforce, which is characterized by low skill levels, with potential barriers to improvement being high levels of staff turnover
- the need for holistic solutions to training, including creating partnerships between training institutes, the tourism sector and other stakeholders through the concept of learning areas. The report advocated the use of structural funds to support innovative solutions
- the need to monitor the tourism labour environment better, with a focus on the staff in this sector
- the development of a handbook for learning areas in tourism to turn learning to innovation
- an improvement in the quality of tourism products in the EU, which will require a better trained and skilled workforce.

In the UK, the Department of Culture, Media and Sport's (2004) *Tomorrow's Tourism Today* identified the importance of skills and education to provide a workforce to deliver a quality product. It also indicated the need for high quality training strategies from hands on skills to management to improve the workforce. It cited the launch in 2004 of yet another agency with an input to HR issues in tourism, the sector Skills Council on Hospitality, Leisure, Travel and Tourism – People First, which needs to engage with other stakeholders to develop a cooperative approach to:

- identify skills shortages affecting the industry and regional variations
- develop proposals building on best practice to improve training, **recruitment** and skills
- to ensure government initiatives in skills and training are available to the tourism industry.

To implement Tomorrow's Tourism, public sector agency support from regional development agencies, the Local Government Association and business group, the Tourism Alliance will need to be actively involved. At the same time, one of many organizations already involved in

Image 11.2: Airline service and customer interaction are still rated highly even on low cost airlines such as easyJet, where low cost fares still have to be accompanied by professional and consistent levels of service. Source: easyJet

training is Springboard. This is an agency created to provide more holistic solutions to improving the image of tourism as a work option (www.springboard.org.uk). It offers a specialist careers service and promotes tourism education in schools and colleges as well as seeking to help those with disabilities, the unemployed and adult returners who have had family career breaks to re-enter the workforce. In addition, national tourist boards such as VisitBritain run various training schemes for tourism businesses including Welcome Host, to improve customer care skills and skills training to develop customer–employee relationships. Yet not all state agencies adopt a singularly supportive view of tourism development based on investing in this sector. However, political changes such as the recent expansion of the EU to include a further ten countries has been widely welcomed by western Europe's hotel sector. This has provided opportunities for east to west urban migration to fill employment vacancies, given the wage rate differential between east and western Europe. Many hotel chains in the UK quickly responded to this political change by recruiting eastern European chefs and staff although other hotels pursue a 'grow your own' policy via investing in the training and retention of their staff, as other companies also do (Image 11.2).

The scope and extent of many human resource issues in countries seeking to develop their tourism industry are evident in Table 11.2 where the range of problems which the state and private sector need to address through a more coordinated approach to HRM in tourism are apparent. However, focusing on the role of the state and public sector as the agents responsible for HRM issues overlooks the fact that individual businesses need to take an active role and for that reason the discussion now turns to this issue.

TABLE 11.2 Human resource management problems in the Latin American tourism industry

1. A lack of effective managerial training

2. Educational institutions have inappropriate provision for the needs of the tourism industry

3. Lack of coordination between the educational sector and the tourism industry

4. Limited number of tourism instructors

5. Inadequate investment in training by the private sector

6. Insufficient and inadequately designed in-house training programmes

7. Limited exposure to foreign language training

8. A lack of travel agency training programmes

9. Service delivery and customer relations given inadequate attention together with inadequate levels of education among employees

10. Too few internship opportunities for tourism students

11. Poor regulation of training institutions

12. Inadequate government fiscal incentives to facilitate industry training

13. Limited public sector support for tourism

14. Low wages and salary levels for employees in the tourism industry

15. Negative attitudes towards service occupations

Source: Adapted from Pizam (1999)

Tourism and HRM issues: The response and role of the individual business

For the individual business, there is a need to recognize the macroeconomic processes which are at work within the business environment. For example, one of the greatest challenges for the future development of tourism employment is the change to the nature of work as discussed in Case Study 11.1W.

For the medium and large tourism enterprises, human resource issues and the factors affecting their performance are usually linked to the staff and workforce (Image 11.3) and therefore recognizing the role of recruitment and ongoing development of the staff resource to achieve strategic goals become essential. A re-investment in the human resource, through ongoing training and development of the employees' skills and abilities to create and add value to the organization, is an inherent quality which successful tourism enterprises are recognized for throughout the world. The scale of the human resource function will often reflect the size of the organization and specific functions (e.g. training and development) may be allocated to specific individuals whereas, in smaller organizations, the commitment to core functions (recruitment and retention) may be all that is possible due to work pressures and constraints on staff time. However, one also has to recognize that in some countries, the larger tourism organizations (e.g. airlines and hotel chains) may be major employers but the backbone of the tourism industry is the small business sector with its own range of issues.

Human resource management issues in small tourism businesses

According to Morrison (1996: 400):

a small tourism business is financed by one individual or small group and is directly managed by its owner(s), in a personalized manner and not through the medium of a formalized management structure…it is perceived as small, in terms of physical facilities, production/service capacity, market share and the number of employees.

The definition of a small tourism business according to employee size varies with each research study. For example, a Deloitte Touche Tomatsu (1994) study of small tourism businesses adopted a cut-off of fewer than ten employees. In contrast, Thomas *et al.*'s (1997) study in the UK acknowledged that in the EU a small business could range up to 50 employees, with micro enterprises employing fewer than ten employees. Morrison (1996: 401) has argued that 'traditionally the tourism industry has been dominated by the small business and this still remains true in the 1990s. Currently in Ireland…firms with less than 15 employees account for around 79 per cent of all Irish tourism businesses'. In New Zealand, it is nearer to 90 per cent. In this sector of the tourism industry, the literature on small businesses indicates that four types of firm can be discerned which has a bearing on HRM. Table 11.3 highlights the typology. This is also reflected in the different management differences between small and large firms as highlighted in Table 11.4. The short-term time horizon of small businesses and owner-managed structure relies more on personal skills, especially leadership qualities and experience. The implications for HRM in small tourism firms are as follows:

* small businesses normally have constraints on their resource base and therefore are unable to fund developments in HRM to the same degree as large firms

Image 11.3: Hospitality staff should be efficient and customer-focused when serving the varying needs of large numbers of tourists

- HRM is widely acknowledged as a major component in small businesses becoming more competitive and productive as well as in organizational success
- HRM is often of marginal interest for family-owners where a family business exists
- the most important area for small businesses to improve their performance is in the recruitment and selection of personnel
- small firms tend to use marginally qualified staff in the tourism sector, especially in the rural environment
- management training is normally limited among owner-managers, with time constraints and a perception of no need for training limiting the development of human resource processes
- many managers in small businesses do not apply strict principles of HRM, being unable to delegate, and fail to define lines of authority and responsibility for employees.

TABLE 11.3 Organizational structures and entrepreneurial characteristics

Category	Entrepreneurial characteristics
Self-employed	Use of family labour, little market stability, low levels of capital investment, tendency towards weakly developed management skills
Small employer	Use of family and non-family labour; less economically marginalized but shares other characteristics of self-employed group
Owner-controllers	Use of non-family labour, higher levels of capital investment, often formal system of management control but no separation of ownership and control
Owner-directors	Separation of ownership and management functions, highest levels of capital investment

Source: Adapted from Goffee and Scase (1983)

TABLE 11.4 Management differences between small and large firms

Small firms	Large firms
Short-term planning horizon	Long-term planning horizon
Reacts to the environment	Develops environmental strategy
Limited knowledge of the environment	Environment assessment
Personalized company objectives	Corporate strategy
Communication informal	Formal and structured communication
Informal communication systems	Formalized control systems
Loose and informal task structure	Job descriptions
Wide range of management skills	High specialist/technical skills demanded
Income directly at risk in decision-making	Income derived from a wider performance base
Personal motivations directly affect performance	Broader-based company performance

Source: Adapted from Carter (1996)

As Morrison and Teixeira (2004: 245) argue 'human resource management appears consistently as an aspect that significantly challenges small firms'. In some cases, some SMEs opt for an approach to management where family members report fewer HRM problems than paid employees (Morrison and Teixeira 2004). Habberson and Williams (1999) report this as:

- creating a more unique, family-oriented workplace with more customer care
- having more flexible work practices
- experiencing family members as more productive than non-family employees
- communicating effectively through a common family language
- unusual motivation, improved trust and improved loyalties generated by family relationships
- low transaction costs
- informal and efficient decision-making (cited in Morrison and Teixeira 2004: 25).

To illustrate the problems of HRM issues in small tourism businesses, Case Study 11.2W of New Zealand outlines the recent expansion of its tourism industry and successful development. Therefore, what Case Study 11.2W shows is that while small tourism businesses may be the backbone of the tourism sector in many countries, the extent to which HRM practices are developed and implemented in this sector are limited according to surveys undertaken in this area. Probably the greatest challenge for this sector is to communicate the benefits of investing human resources where a company decides to invest in its major asset – its staff (Image 11.4).

Managing HRM issues in the tourism sector in the new millennium

The major challenges for the tourism industry in the new millennium are associated with developing a high quality staff who do really make a difference in what is undoubtedly a people business. Yet within many of the international research studies of HRM in tourism, there are concerns that there is and will continue to be a severe shortage of trained and able staff. One of the greatest challenges which faces any employee in the tourism sector is the ability to respond and adapt to change, especially at a managerial level. In a high-technology sector where knowledge and managerial skills are vital, managing staff and the recruitment and retention of high calibre staff are also vital. The 1980s and early 1990s can best be described as years of unsophisticated and reactive human resource policies in the tourism sector, and in the new millennium a new economic climate in which tourism operates combined with the growth of the knowledge economy means that change and competition will continue to intensify. Those businesses which are not adopting progressive human resource policies in line with other sectors of the service sector will be left behind and find it difficult to compete when much of the work is people and skills based. More sophisticated human resource policies need to be developed and implemented in the following areas for the tourism sector to be responsive to add value to its staff and change the sectors' image as an employer:

- **induction** of staff
- **appraisal** and staff performance evaluation
- effective staff communication
- reward of initiative and excellence
- empowerment of staff
- **industry–education collaboration**.

Image 11.4: Singapore offers a benchmark of good practice in hotel management within Asia, particularly in the four and five-star hotels located in the waterfront district

As Jones and Lockwood (2002) argue, one of the real solutions in the hotel sector in accommodating staff and demand, is the introduction of flexible working. They point to four types of flexibility:

- *functional flexibility,* being the ability of employees to handle different tasks and to move between jobs
- *numerical flexibility,* being able to adjust the numbers of workers and hours worked
- *pay flexibility,* which may reward scarce skills or individual performance
- *distancing strategies,* such as contracting out operations to shift the burden or risk elsewhere

and different methods of work flexibility are illustrated in Table 11.5. These may help with:

- workforce development
- improving employee job satisfaction, particularly work–life balance
- attracting and retaining staff
- reducing risks in some areas, especially the problem of stress for those staff working in face-to-face delivery of services and those involved in long hours of work.

But these issues are part of the growing recognition in some tourism and hospitality organizations of the need for greater flexibility in the way staff are able to perform their tasks and of the rise of empowerment, which is examined in Insight 11.2.

One other area of activity among tourism businesses has been the investment in service quality training for employees to deliver high quality tourism experiences in the service encounter between tourist and staff. Baum and Kokkranikel (2005) summarize the importance of this and the criteria used by Grönroos (1988) which hinges upon the staff–customer interaction around a

---

TABLE 11.5 Methods of work flexibility

Functional

- Multi-skilling
- Horizontal job enlargement
- Vertical job enlargement – up
- Vertical job enlargement – down
- Job rotation
- Career development
- Task group approaches
- Total retaining

Numerical

- Part time
- Temporary
- Job sharing
- Overtime
- Sabbaticals etc.
- Flexible daily hours
- Flexible weekly hours
- Compressed working work
- Annual hours contracts
- Committed hours schemes
- Shift-work systems
- Short-term contracts

Distancing

- Agency staff
- Subcontracting
- Home working
- Computer terminal systems
- Government-subsidized trainees

Pay

- Incentive schemes
- Rare skills payments
- Multi-skill payments
- Pay/performance links

Source: Jones and Lockwood (2002:61)

Empowerment, HRM and the Southwest Airlines model

One of the growing areas of interest in HRM and services in recent years is empowerment (Lashley 2004), which sets out to enable employees to feel more in control and able to use their power in dealing with work issues, especially human interactions with customers. It gives them the discretion to make decisions and is designed to give employees a positive emotional state in the workplace. In service delivery situations it should help employees to feel a commitment to the customer. As Table 11.6 shows, Lashley (2004) points to relational elements of empowerment, which means the power relationships that exist between an employer and manager. Table 11.6 outlines some of the contexts and approaches which organizations can use to embrace a greater empowerment of employees. Yet empowerment also has a motivational element, meaning that the employee needs to be able to perceive their ability to be empowered and to use the power effectively in everyday situations. A feeling of empowerment has to be followed by the power to take decisions which make a difference. Both the relational and motivational elements of empowerment need to be recognized if an organization wishes to empower employees. Figure 11.4, based on Lashley (2004: 205–206), outlines five stages to empowerment in a practical tourism and hospitality operational context to combine the relation and motivational elements of empowerment.

Figure 11.4 provides an illustration of how teams in organizations can be led so that the emotional state of empowerment is engendered to engage employees progressively through a number of stages. Organizations such as McDonald's have used empowerment models for employment, as many of its managers have previously trained as part of the operational 'crew' with the new recruits trained in all aspects of operation so as to provide a foundation for leading a team or progressing to a managerial role.

One high-profile example of a tourism-related business which has used empowerment as part of its HRM practices is Southwest Airlines, the original low-cost airline in the USA (Gittell 2003). As Gittell (2003) explains, the company transformed itself from a regional carrier to a national carrier by:

- building an organization able to build and sustain relationships, with shared goals, knowledge and mutual respect
- having an intense focus on quality
- using a non-unionized workforce in a highly unionized industry
- having influential leadership and a clear strategy
- creating a unique **corporate culture**

- having a quick **turnaround of aircraft**
- having high levels of coordination.

As the airline is built upon the efforts of its staff, the airline has a highly empowered culture of inclusivity for its staff and well-organized teams where all staff work together. A high ratio of supervisor to team members (1:12 or 1:10) is the highest in the US airline sector, but it empowers managers and supervisors also to perform the work of other staff. So they work as 'player-coaches' to use a US football team analogy, undertaking the work of **frontline** staff: a policy that is conducive to building shared goals, relationships and problem-solving. It also helps to eliminate staff not suited to working at Southwest. As a result, Southwest's HRM focus is on employing people with teamwork abilities. Internal promotions also create internal job mobility so staff acquire knowledge across the organization, helping to break down barriers between departments. The organization also has a well-established conflict resolution process for staff, when conflicts are not addressed immediately, to improve working relationships.

HRM strategy at Southwest encourages staff to be themselves, so employees identify with the company, and seeks to maintain the **family–life balance** by having flexibility in scheduling of staff. One innovation is in 'shift trading', allowing staff to negotiate their work–life balance to fit the workplace. The airline does not endorse negative controls through functional accountability (i.e. finger pointing when things go wrong), seeking instead to learn from mistakes so as not to undermine the corporate culture. It does this by looking at the overall results and performance of the organization rather than narrow functions, department by department, and their outputs. By having flexible job boundaries, staff can help each other so they can cross functional boundaries and managers can work alongside frontline employees. As a result Southwest is characterized by:

- investing in frontline leadership
- empowering staff via job flexibility and team working
- training staff for competencies such as an ability to build relationships
- using conflict to build rather than destroy relationships
- being a caring employer
- investing in people, their careers and thereby their organizational commitment via flexible working practices.

Underpinning much of the culture at Southwest is its empowering of staff at all levels to work towards shared goals, which involves caring about relationships inside the organization, with its customers and with its suppliers.

number of the customer's perceived tangible and intangible elements of the service encounter, including:

- professionalism and skill in the service encounter
- staff attitudes and behaviour
- customers being able to access staff and feeling they are flexible and able to respond to their needs
- reliability and trustworthiness of staff
- recovery of a situation when things go wrong
- ensuring the brand image of a product has a reputation and credibility.

Since quality is seen as critical to being competitive in tourism, and most of the tangible and intangible criteria of perceived good service are largely human-resource related, this illustrates the critical nature of employing staff with the skills or ability to be trained to add value to these service encounters.

TABLE 11.6 Analysing the rational aspects of empowerment

Degree of involvement	Directive – tell, tell and sell
	Consultative – tell and test, seek
	Participative – joint problem solving, delegation
	Direct – all employees
Form of involvement	Indirect – representatives of employees
	Financial – shares, profits, bonuses
	Tasks – how tasks are done
Level of involvement	Department – who does what; tactical issues
	Corporation – business strategy and goals
	Service delivery – meeting customer needs, complaints
Range of issues involved	Employment issues – pay and conditions of employment
	General organization conduct – general purpose and aims
	Making the decision stick
Power	Who makes the final decision – recommending or deciding?

Source: Lashley (2004: 202)

Level 1 Waits to be told

Typically the team member has never performed the task before. They wait to be told and shown how to complete the task.

The team leader is demonstrating, explaining, training and giving feedback to the employee and will be present throughout the time the task is being done.

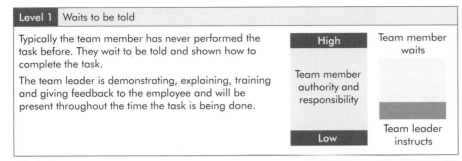

High

Team member authority and responsibility

Low

Team member waits

Team leader instructs

Level 2 Asks what to do

The team member is aware that a task needs doing or that there is a way of getting round a problem, but does not know how to do it. They ask what needs to be done and are shown the task.

The team leader is involved in demonstrating, explaining, training and giving feedback, though this would be reduced because the employee has at least a basic grasp of the issue to be undertaken.

High

Team member authority and responsibility

Low

Team member asks

Team leader explains

Level 3 Recommends what to do

The team member is familiar with the job or task and is confident enough to make recommendations for correction or improvement. They are still not skilled, experienced or knowledgeable enough to take action themselves.

The team leader should now be receiving and deciding on the suggestion, getting the team member working on the task and giving feedback on their efforts, and will need to spend less time on direct supervision on their work.

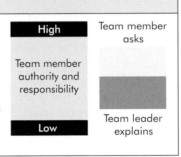

High

Team member authority and responsibility

Low

Team member asks

Team leader explains

Level 4 Takes action, reports immediately

The team member is confident and familiar with task, but will not have completed it without supervision in the past. They now need to do the task, but check back that they have done it correctly.

The team leader is confirming correct action, or preventing an action that might cause damage to the unit or a loss of confidence in the team member. Minimal supervision of the person undertaking the task.

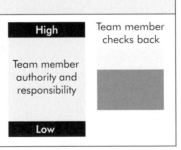

High

Team member authority and responsibility

Low

Team member checks back

Level 5 Takes action reports routinely

The team member is skilled, knowledgeable and confident enough to get on with the task and do whatever is needed. They will not need to inform you of their actions immediately, though will routinely report to you.

The team leader needs to provide feedback on a regular basis so that team member is informed about their progress and their motivation levels are maintained. There is virtually no direct supervision of the team member, though you will be indirectly monitoring progress.

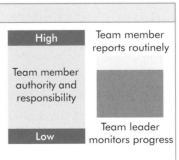

High

Team member authority and responsibility

Low

Team member reports routinely

Team leader monitors progress

FIGURE 11.4   Five stages in individual empowerment. Source: Lashley (2004)

Conclusion

Worldwide many universities embraced tourism and hospitality education in the 1990s to improve provision in the area, although critics might argue that the rush to capitalize on this new growth area has led to poor provision among some providers who have seen the growth in student numbers and revenue as more important than the qualities they engender and career direction of its graduates. Instead of investing educational resources in a few centres of excellence with well-funded programmes and industry linkages to ensure careers for its graduates, the resource base is spread thinly with providers competing intensely for student numbers. More important, tourism education and training globally needs to take stock of what human resource requirements are needed in each area; a theme highlighted by WTTC and other governmental bodies as well as by Wanhill's (1992) analysis of human resource planning and an understanding of the **productivity** and wastage rates (i.e. staff leaving the industry). Looking at the Australian tourism sector Hall (2003) outlined its tourism productivity rates and its relatively low outputs compared to some other sectors of the economy as well as its lower operating profit margins of 15.2 per cent compared to 22 for other industries. Herein lies the problem for the sector: it needs to improve labour productivity so it can raise profit margins and thereby invest further in the human capital. Of course tourism is not alone in having low profit levels, since this characterizes many areas of service provision. Adding value to the tourism experience is one obvious way of being able to levy higher profits. Understanding these concepts is critical to education and training as well as investing in life-long learning and upskilling, once graduates have entered a career in this dynamic sector of economic activity. Without addressing these issues, the tourism sector and interface with education providers will not be bridged to improve HRM for the industry.

What is interesting is the continued existence of ongoing problems in HRM and tourism, which have altered little in the last decade. If anything, changes in the demand for tourism labour have intensified the pressure on employers. As the WTTC Task Force report observed, the demand for workers will continue to increase as the numbers employed are forecast to grow from 198 million globally in 2002 to 249 million in 2012. At the same time, an ageing population in developed countries will reduce the pool of employees. The telling recommendation of the Task Force is that companies must place learning and education for their workforce centre-stage in their business strategy. This is because, increasingly, the performance of a business in tourism will be based on the quality of its human talent. At the frontline of delivery, quality of service will continue to be a surrogate of corporate performance, especially given the need to impress first time visitors and also to nurture repeat customers (Petrik 2004). The importance of word of mouth recommendation to build a loyal customer base will grow in significance, and delivering consistent quality will be a challenge. New ways of working within organizations will need to be found to address the high turnover of first-time employees who leave disenchanted with an industry, associated with glamour in some sectors, but also involving long hours of work and poor training opportunities. There are many examples of good practice now being developed across the tourism and hospitality industries to overcome these negative images by developing career paths for employees so that tourism careers rather than jobs become the norm. Only by raising global awareness of tourism's critical role in the economy, and through more innovative and attractive labour market policies, will tourism address future HRM issues.

Discussion questions

1 What is the purpose of human resource management?

2 What problems do tourism businesses face in relation to human resource issues?

3 How do the human resource problems facing small and large tourism businesses differ?

4 What types of role does a human resource manager play in a large tourism organization?

References

Baum, T. (1993) *Human Resource Issues in International Tourism.* Oxford: Butterworth-Heinemann.

Baum, T. (2002) 'Skills and training for the hospitality sector: A review of issues', *Journal of Vocational Education and Training,* 54 (3): 343–63.

Baum, T. and Kokkranikel, J. (2005) 'Human resource management in tourism', in L. Pender and R. Sharpley (eds) *The Management of Tourism.* London: Sage.

Carter, S. (1996) 'Small business marketing', in M. Warner (ed.) *International Encyclopedia of Business and Management.* London: International Thomson Business Publishing.

Deloitte Touche Tomatsu (1994) *Small Business Survey 1994: New Zealand Tourism Industry.* Christchurch: Deloitte Touche Tomatsu Tourism and Leisure Consulting Group.

Department of Culture, Media and Sport (2004) *Tomorrow's Tourism Today.* London: DCMS.

Eichaikul, R. and Baum, T. (1998) 'The case for government involvement in human resource development: A study of the Thai hotel industry', *Tourism Management* 19 (4): 359–70.

EU (2001) *Working Together for the Future European Tourism.* Brussels: EU.

Gittell, J. (2003) *The Southwest Airlines Way.* New York: McGraw Hill.

Goffee, R. and Scase, R. (1983) 'Class, entrepreneurship and the service sector: Towards a conceptual clarification', *Service Industries Journal,* 3: 146–60.

Grönroos, C. (1988) 'Service quality: The six criteria of good perceived service quality', *Review of Business,* 9 (3): 10–13.

Habberson, T. and Williams, M. (1999) *A Resource Based Framework for Assessing the Strategic Advantage of Family Firms.* Working Paper Series, No 101. The Wharton School, University of Pennsylvania.

Hall, C.M. (2003) *Introduction to Tourism in Australia: Dimensions and Issues, Fourth Edition.* Frenchs Forest, NSW: Hospitality Press.

Jones, P. and Lockwood, A. (2002) *The Management of Hotel Operations: An Innovative Approach to the Study of Hotel Management.* London: Continuum.

Lashley, C. (2004) 'A feeling for empowerment?', in N. D'Annunzio-Green, G. Maxwell and S. Watson (eds) *Human Resource Management: International Perspectives in Hospitality and Tourism.* London: Thomson.

Morrison, A. (1996) 'Marketing the small tourism business', in A. Seaton and M. Bennett (eds) *Marketing Tourism Products: Concepts, Issues and Cases.* London: International Thomson Business Publishing.

Morrison, A. and Teixeira, R. (2004) 'Small firm performance in the context of agent and structure: A cross cultural comparison in the tourist accommodation sector', in R. Thomas (ed.) *Small Firms in Tourism: International Perspectives.* Oxford: Elsevier.

Petrik, J. (2004) 'Are loyal visitors desired visitors?', *Tourism Management,* 25 (4): 463–71.

Pizam, A. (1999) 'The state of travel and tourism human resources in Latin America', *Tourism Management,* 20 (5): 575–86.

Thomas, R., Friel, M., Jameson, S. and Parsons, D. (1997) *The National Survey of Small Tourism and Hospitality Firms Annual Report 1996–1997.* Leeds: Leeds Metropolitan University.

Wanhill, S. (1992) 'Tourism manpower planning: The case of Nepal', in P. Johnston and B. Thomas (eds) *Perspectives on Tourism Policy.* London: Mansell.

Watson, S., D'Annunzio-Green, N. and Maxwell, G. (2004) 'Human resource management issues in international hospitality and tourism; Identifying the priorities', in N. D'Annunzio-Green, G. Maxwell and S. Watson (eds) *Human Resource Management: International Perspectives in Hospitality and Tourism.* London: Thomson.

WTTC (2001) *Human Resources Task Force: HR Opportunities and Challenges.* London: WTTC.

Further reading

D'Annunzio-Green, N., Maxwell, G. and Watson, S. (eds) (2004) *Human Resources Management: International Perspectives in Hospitality and Tourism.* London: Thomson.

Financing Tourism Operations – John Pinfold and Stephen J. Page

Learning outcomes

After reading this chapter and answering the questions, you should be able to:

- understand how financial decisions are made in terms of funding tourism businesses

- identify sources of funding for tourism businesses and the obstacles they face

- comprehend some of the features of published company accounts.

Overview

The purpose of this chapter is to provide the reader with an appreciation of the world of finance as it applies to the tourism industry. It does not attempt to provide a detailed knowledge of financial management; it merely introduces the reader to the basic principles and provides examples of financing issues in tourism together with an analysis of company accounts and how to read them focusing on the experience of easyJet.

Introduction

The development and management of the tourism industry is dependent upon the accessibility to capital and sources of finance so that new businesses can be developed and existing businesses can expand and develop their markets for tourism products and services. Many tourism businesses are based within the private sector and they normally source finance for investment purposes from banks, finance houses and other lending institutions. However, there are also a number of other public sector agencies which assist the tourism sector with pump-priming funds and product development as will be discussed in Chapter 14. The issue of finance and investment is largely neglected in existing studies of tourism, especially in many textbooks. Much of the published literature is based on finance and accounting texts which are not specifically rooted in tourism and hospitality research. This chapter seeks to adopt a tourism focus in which the various elements of financing tourism operations and their financial performance are examined.

The problem of financing tourism businesses

Generating the idea for a business venture is not the most decisive factor in the creation of a new business. Finding the funding is the crucial hurdle which only the minority of prospective new ventures can overcome. Funding requirements vary greatly, ranging from the part-time venture easily funded by family, to the multi-million-dollar development requiring a syndicate of investors. Expansion brings the need for more capital, and often the growth prospects of the business mean that additional outside funding is required if it is ever to reach its potential. For a venture to be a viable business it must be able to provide its working proprietors, if any, with an income at market rates for the hours they work, as well as providing an adequate return on invested funds commensurate with the risk involved. To attract funding not only must a business have the ability to provide an adequate return, but its management must also be able to instil confidence in potential investors.

The location and nature of the business can affect its ability to attract finance. Urban businesses and those located in resort areas tend to have a greater attraction for investors given the defined tourism market and greater access to a volume of potential customers (residents and visitors). In contrast, rural tourism businesses tend to have characteristics which make them risky propositions when viewed from the financiers' perspective. They are often remotely located, which means they are distant from business services, such as accountants and consultants, that can assist the business if it gets into difficulty. A **receivership** or **mortgage** sale to recover a **defaulting loan** will then be difficult and expensive. The **assets** of a tourism business may be specialized in nature and have little resale value if the venture is not successful, and hence may be of limited value as security for a loan. Many tourist businesses are seasonal in nature, which makes them difficult to sustain through the off-peak periods, and also makes financing more difficult.

Financiers are often sceptical that entrepreneurs have the management and financial skills necessary to manage a business, especially when they have no track record in successfully operating such ventures. Given the dominance worldwide of small tourism businesses as the **modus operandi** in tourism (Thomas 2004), the small size of the business proposition will provide an additional incentive not to invest. Taylor, Simpson and Howie (1998) rightly point to the importance of finance in tourism operations in both the establishment of a venture as well as the subsequent resourcing and growth of a business (if it succeeds). Generally the **financier** will want to be able to visit and monitor the business's progress on a regular basis. Where the size of investment is small, the estimated costs of administering and monitoring the business are often greater than the financier's margin on the loan. Nevertheless, finance is certainly readily available to small businesses, but it will be concentrated on activities where the risks are known and business assets have recognized market values.

Banks will prefer to invest in small business sectors that they know well, for example farming and businesses which service the farming industry, because they have a long history of financing these sectors and know the risks and rewards available. If a farmer fails to operate profitably the bank knows it will normally be possible to hold a mortgagee sale of the property and other assets to recover the money owed. On the other hand, the tourism enterprises will generally involve an innovative but unproven idea. The financier may decline to invest simply because the risks are not quantifiable (i.e. the financier cannot determine the likelihood of success or the value of the business assets in the event of the business failing).

Sources of funding

The difficulty experienced by small tourism businesses in raising debt finance is well known (Taylor *et al.* 1998). When the reasons for small businesses' lack of access to financial markets were investigated in Australia, Campbell (1981) found that it could not be attributed to any lack of efficiency in the allocation of financial resources but was directly related to the higher cost and risk of lending to small enterprises. Keasey and Watson (1994) arrived at the same conclusions when studying the situation in the UK. A Deloitte Touche Tohmatsu (1994) study of 400 small tourism businesses in New Zealand demonstrated the consequences of banks' reluctance to lend to small business. Some 44 per cent of the businesses in the study relied totally on their own funding, and only 22 per cent sourced 50 per cent or more of their funds from banks. This means the majority of small tourism ventures typically need to find the major source of their funding outside the banking industry. Nevertheless, seeking bank funding will be the logical first step for the tourist venture needing to fund its operations.

In situations where **entrepreneur**s cannot fund the operation from their own resources or obtain bank finances it will normally be necessary to invite other shareholders to participate in the business. Small tourism firms, especially start-up ventures, normally first draw on the 'four fs' for financing. These are:

- founders
- family
- friends
- the foolhardy.

Often the last three of these are only called upon because banks loans are unavailable. While the '**venture capital**' industry may be regarded as a logical source of finance in these situations, the reality is that the vast majority of ventures will not meet typical venture capitalists' requirements, and in fact the venture capital industry is not the major source of private capital. Florida (1994) reported that while US venture capitalists financed 10 per cent of new high-technology business start-ups they invested in less than 1 per cent of business start-ups as a whole. Fried and Hirsrich (1988) asserted that fewer than 2 per cent of venture capital proposals are ever funded. Clearly, venture capital, given the limited role it plays in financing other sectors of business, cannot be considered a likely source of capital for the tourist industry as a whole.

While the majority of capital in all new ventures comes from entrepreneurs, their friends and relatives, the major outside source is what are known as **angels**. 'Angels' are difficult to identify accurately in spite of the known importance of their role. They are wealthy individuals and companies with capital to invest in new ventures. In the tourist industry they are likely to be individuals with experience in the industry or companies who already operate in the sector. They can often add expertise and create synergistic benefits such as the ability to tap into an existing customer base. It is not necessarily easy to locate angels or to convince them of the merits of an investment; however, they are the most likely outside source of capital, particularly for the expansion of proven concepts constrained by undercapitalization.

Mason and Harrison (1994) found that the majority of angels in the UK located the companies in which they invested through sources other than the generally recognized ones such as accountants, lawyers, banks and consultants. He found that 16.3 per cent were located through friends, 24.7 per cent through business associates and 15.1 per cent through personal searches for investment opportunities. Few angels made investments as a result of referrals from accountants and other professional sources. The Deloitte Touche Tohmatsu (1994) study, which found that only 6 per cent of the sample of small New Zealand tourist businesses had outside investors providing half or more of their funding requirements, reflects the relatively small role outside investors currently play in financing the sector, and this is probably true in other countries.

While **debt** from banks and other finance houses will be a key source of finance for those that can meet the lender's requirements, there is another source of debt type finance that should not be overlooked. Leasing is the second most important source of external debt after bank loans. With a lease, the leasing company owns the asset and the business gains the use of the asset in exchange for periodic payments, but the lease is fixed for a certain period of time usually and commits the organization to expenditure on the lease. Some sectors of the tourism industry are largely financed using leases, for example the airline industry, due to the high capital cost of fixed assets. Other transport operators are also big users of lease finance as it is relatively easy to finance the entire purchase price of a vehicle by leasing it rather that purchasing it. The leasing companies have specialist expertise in the industries in which they operate and are able to readily place the assets they finance with other operators should the lessee fail to make the required payments. The accommodation sector is also a large user of leased property. Hotel chains, while they may own buildings, will also manage buildings leased from property investors. In this way those with the expertise in running accommodation-based ventures can profit from their expertise without the need to finance the buildings themselves. This operates to the advantage of both parties. Those wishing to invest in tourist accommodation can do so without the need to possess expertise in hotel management. In addition, by leasing to a hotel chain, they can obtain the leverage of leading international branding and marketing networks. Hotel operators can profit from their brands and management expertise without needing the capital to pay for buildings.

Investment evaluation

Financial risk can be regarded in two ways: either the risk of the business failing and the investment being lost or as a measure of the variability of the possible return on the investment. Providers of debt have a fixed rate of return and hence the probability of losing all or part of their investment is the focus of their analysis. They will generally look only at propositions where the probability of such a loss is small, and this inevitably means that assets must be pledged as security for the loan. It must be remembered, however, that financiers will not lend money simply because they can recover the loan by realizing securities. They look upon this as a last resort and must be satisfied of the viability of the venture as well as of the worth of the security offered.

Risk capital investors, that is, anyone who puts up money which is unsecured, are in a different position. Here the loss of the investment is a real possibility even in well-established businesses. Taking this risk can be justified only if the investor can share in the profits. In addition to the risk of losing the investment, it is necessary for them to look at the variability of the returns which might be achieved. The more uncertain or variable the future income stream is likely to be the greater is the risk. The greater the risk, the higher the return the rational investor will require.

Estimating **investment risk** is an extremely difficult task, particularly where new ventures are concerned. The risk will always be high due to the high **failure rate**s of start-up businesses. Birch (1987) and Altman (1993) put the number of US firms failing within five years at 50 per cent. Ganguly (1985) produced a figure of 52 per cent for similar UK firms. Pinfold (2000) studied failure rates in New Zealand and found that 57.5 per cent of new ventures failed within five years, and that 50.5 per cent of similar projects started up by existing firms also failed.

Based on the reports cited above, a figure of 50 per cent can be used as a rule of thumb for estimating the probability that a start-up business will fail. The likely failure rate of individual businesses varies from this figure, and the previously mentioned characteristics of many rural tourist ventures put them at the higher end of the risk spectrum. Thus, in determining the returns required it is realistic to assume a 50 per cent or higher chance that the total amount of risk capital invested will be lost. The returns that can be achieved from the business if it is a success must be high enough to compensate for the risk. Given the high risks faced by entrepreneurs, the rewards must also be high.

One method of calculating the required return, which is probably the most useful, is to use a risk-adjusted rate of return when calculating the **discounted cash flow** of the investment. Exactly what rate of return is required for a particular level of risk is a vexing question and comes down largely to a matter of opinion. As a guide, a UK study by Mason and Harrison (1994) found that informal investors or angels required a minimum annual rate of return of 45 per cent for businesses in their pre-start-up phase, 32 per cent for start-ups and 21 per cent for established firms. Schilit (1993) put the minimum rate of return required by US venture capital firms at 38 per cent per annum, and Fried and Hirsrich (1994) gave a range of 30–70 per cent.

Net present value method to evaluate an investment

The evaluation of an investment to see if it meets the required rate of return is made using a discounted cashflow technique. The method most accepted as being correct is the **net present value method** (or NPV), although the use of internal rates of return (IRR), a very similar method, is probably more widespread in practice. The principle behind the NPV method is that investors will only invest £1 today if they expect to get £1 plus their required rate back in one year's time. The cash flow from the investment each year is therefore discounted back on an annual basis by the required rate of return to find out its value at the present time. When all the present values of the future cash flows are added together the total must be equal to or greater than the cash to be invested, otherwise less than the required rate of return will have been achieved. When calculating this return, only cash flows to the investor (i.e. dividends) are used, not accounting profits. In addition, any salary paid to owners of the business for their work in the business is excluded.

To illustrate the returns required, assume someone invests £10 000 in a start-up business today and requires a return of 38 per cent. As we are dealing with a **start-up business**, assume that all the profits will need to be ploughed back into the business and in five years' time the business will be sold to realize this return. At what price will the investment need to be sold to get this required rate of return? The calculation is:

$$£10\,000 \times (1.38)^s = £50\,000$$

It must be remembered that this is a start-up business and there is a 50 per cent chance that it will fail and the entire investment be lost. Assume there are only two possible outcomes: a 50 per cent chance of failure and a 50 per cent chance the business will be profitable enough to sell at a price high enough to achieve the required rate of return. As we expect to get nothing back 50 per cent of the time we must get a higher return when the business succeeds if on average we are to receive £50 000. Therefore:

$$expected\ return = (return\ if\ business\ fails \times 0.5) + (return\ if\ business\ succeeds \times 0.5)$$

$$£50\,000 = (£0 \times 0.5) + (return\ if\ business\ succeeds \times 0.5)\ £50\,000 = (£0 \times 0.5) + (£100\,000 \times 0.5)$$

This means that the investment, if successful, must sell for at least £100 000 in five years' time to achieve the required rate of return. What level of profit will the business need to be generating in five years' time to achieve this price? A reasonable estimate of the price a small business will fetch is four times its after-tax earnings. For the £10 000 investment the after-tax earnings would need to be:

$$£100\,000 \div 4 = £25\,000.$$

In other words, the business will need to be generating around £2.50 per annum of after-tax profit in five years' time for each £1 of risk capital invested today. This is a very daunting task but illustrates the type of investment performance required by so-called 'rational investors' before they will risk their money. Entrepreneurs are by nature optimistic and will base decisions on their estimates of the risks and returns available, which may be very different from the more jaundiced eye of the professional financier.

In larger firms, especially those with **shareholders**, they usually expect to receive a percentage of the annual profits and this is taken in the form of a **dividend**; at the same time, they believe the value of their shares will improve. From the company perspective, raising finance through the issue of more shares is attractive since it is relatively low risk, i.e. if the company does not make a profit, they will not issue a dividend whereas a bank loan must be serviced regardless of profits. Retained profits are another source for financing new developments. An alternative is for a company to raise finance by selling bonds; these are loans with a fixed rate of interest which are repaid over a specified period of time. In November 1998, the large vertically integrated tour operator Airtours launched a £250 million **convertible bond** issue through finance company Merrill Lynch; interest was to be paid at between 5.25 and 5.75 per cent until January 2004 when the bonds converted into ordinary shares at a 20–25 per cent premium over Airtours' share price on the date the bond was issued.

To remain competitive, businesses need to invest either in the replacement of **fixed assets**, the addition of more assets or a combination of both. In making these decisions, companies will assess such capital investment programmes using methods such as payback period, net present value (NPV) and **internal rate of return** (IRR). Discounted cash flow methods such as NPV and IRR are almost universally accepted as the methods that lead to the correct investment decision, however the **payback** method is still widely used as it is easy to calculate and understand. Brounen, de Jong and Koedijk (2004) surveyed European firms and found that national averages for the use of the payback method as the favourite decision-making tool varied between 50.9 and 69.2 per cent.

Payback shows how quickly an investment will have covered its cost through the cash flow it generates. An example of a payback calculation is contained in Table 12.1. In this example, a white-water rafting company intends to expand its business. It has found two types of raft that suit its needs. It can buy Xtreme Inflatables that are cheaper and hold one more passenger, or Ultra Catacraft which are more flexible, safer and less prone to damage; hence they have lower maintenance costs and a longer average life. We can see that the after-tax cash flows generated by the Xtreme Inflatables are equal to the amount invested by the end of year 2. It takes 2.2 years for the cash flows from the Ultra Catarafts to payback the original investment. Using the payback method we would decide to invest in the Xtreme Inflatables as they have a shorter payback period.

One major drawback with this method is that it does not include cash flow beyond the payback period despite the asset having a residual value. Messenger and Shaw (1993: 212) state that a project may be chosen in preference to another just because it has a quick payback time while another with a slower time may in fact have a longer life with greater cash flows. An additional problem with the payback method is that it does not take risk into account. Risky investments require higher returns, and the payback method does not consider the required rate of return.

Go and Pine (1995), however, believe net present value (NPV) and internal rate of return (IRR) to be the most commonly used measures of investment in the tourism industry. Messenger and Shaw (1993: 217) consider the main advantage of NPV is 'that it considers the time value of money, so that the value of money received in the future can be compared with present sums'. NPV makes the assumption that money received now has a higher value than money received next month or next year, i.e. the sooner it is received, the sooner it can be invested in alternative projects. In Table 12.2 the white-water rafting investment is analysed using the NPV method. We assume that a project of this risk requires an after-tax return of 20 per cent. We can see that the Xtreme Inflatables have future cash flows that exceed the required return by £52 362 when valued in today's pounds or, in other words, have an NPV of £52 362. However, the Ultra Catarafts have an NPV of £87 289 and are therefore a better investment. If we had calculated the actual return on investment, which is the discount rate that will give a NPV of zero, we would discover the Xtreme Inflatables produce an IRR of 32.8 per cent and the Ultra Catarafts 35.7 per cent. Obviously we would chose the investment that gives us the highest return.

TABLE 12.1 Investment decision using payback method

	Xtreme Inflatables	Ultra Catarafts
Capital expenditure	£210 000	£225 000
Cash flow – Year 1	£100 000	£85 000
Cash flow – Year 2	£110 000	£115 000
Cash flow – Year 3	£110 000	£115 000
Cash flow – Year 4	£60 000	£95 000
Cash flow – Year 5	£25 000	£85 000
Cash flow – Year 6	£0	£45 000
Payback period	2.0 years	2.2 years
Preferred investment	✓	

TABLE 12.2 Investment decision using NPV method

	Now	Year 1	Year 2	Year 3	Year 4	Year 5	Year 6
Cost of Xtreme Inflatables	−£210 000						
After tax cash flow from the investment		£100 000	£110 000	£110 000	£60 000	£25 000	£0
Required return at 20% per annum		1.2	$(1.2)^2$	$(1.3)^3$	$(1.2)^4$	$(1.2)^5$	$(1.2)^6$ ·
Present value of annual cash flows		£83 333	£76 389	£63 657	£28 935	£10 047	£0
Total present value of future cash flows	£262 362						
Net present value	£52 362						
	Now	Year 1	Year 2	Year 3	Year 4	Year 5	Year 6
Cost of Ultra Catarafts	−£225 000						
After tax cash flow from the investment		£85 000	£115 000	£115 000	£95 000	£85 000	£45 000
Required return at 20% per annum		1.2	$(1.2)^2$	$(1.3)^3$	$(1.2)^4$	$(1.2)^5$	$(1.2)^6$
Present value of annual cash flows		£70 833	£79 861	£66 551	£45 814	£34 160	£15 070
Total present value of future cash flows	£312 289						
Net present value	£87 289						

The business plan

A business seeking finance, especially a start-up, will almost inevitably be asked to provide a **business plan** as this is the first thing that financiers and investors look at when deciding whether or not they will provide finance. The business plan must not only show the expected returns, it must also produce evidence of how these returns will be achieved. This means that a comprehensive plan for all aspects of the business must be presented. The website www.scotexchange.net, funded by Scottish Enterprise and hosted by the national tourism organization VisitScotland, has a site entitled 'Business development' aimed at entrepreneurs seeking to start their own business.

The site examines:

- how do I get started?
- marketing
- knowing your market
- networking
- staff-related issues
- risks in setting up a business
- business types

with related links to Scottish Enterprise advice through its network of 22 local enterprise companies and its Small Business Gateway site (www.sbgateway.com). Above all, these sites highlight much of the conventional wisdom on small business start-ups in tourism and hospitality, and the importance of developing a good business plan. As Page (2003) illustrates, a wide range of issues have to be considered aside from the financing of the business including the market for the product or venture. Where a large investment over and above the resources of a small business are involved, a more substantial feasibility study may also be commissioned or undertaken, as Page (2003) shows in the case of a visitor attraction that attempts to model the business it will generate and how the initial investment will yield a profit over the payback period of the initial investment.

The effect of financial availability on the shape of the industry

The difficulties of meeting the debt financiers' **lending criteria**, coupled with the difficulties of generating sufficient return to attract outside equity investors, inevitably shapes the type of investments which are made in tourism. The idyllic country lodge may be very aesthetically appealing to a small-scale entrepreneur, but once it consistently fails to operate at a profit its market price may well be a small fraction of its construction cost, if it can be sold at all. A bank may well decide that if a mortgage over the property is the only security available, then the maximum size of loan that can be offered is only a small percentage of the construction cost. For the equity investor the potential profit will probably be insufficient to cover the risk, given the high capital cost coupled with the fixed revenue that can be generated. Both the bank and the equity investor will find that investing in a similar venture in an urban location provides a similar return for substantially less risk, given the concentration of tourist visitors compared to the tendency for a dispersed geographical pattern in rural areas.

The type of ventures able to overcome the financing hurdle will be those which have the best **risk to reward ratio**. These are ones where the capital investment required is small in relation to the size of the potential market, and probably small in absolute terms. Investing in outdoor recreation activities such as river rafting and wilderness trekking, for example, can be contrasted with capital-intensive and fixed facilities like accommodation. In ventures where accommodation is built it will normally be in places where customer demand is already established, because the risks are lower. Development will therefore tend to form clusters, with each enterprise building on the success of those which have gone before. In a rural context, the use of home-stays will be an attractive method of accommodating tourists because it does not need significant additional capital, though it needs to be remembered that this type of accommodation does not follow the established pattern of geographical clustering, especially where the prevailing patterns of rural activity are space-extensive.

Assets purchased will tend to be ones that can be readily sold or moved to another area if a venture is not successful, such as vehicles, boats and equipment. The investments will tend to be ones which can be started on a small scale and grown once they are successful, for example an adventure tour operator starting with one or two vehicles and building to a large fleet as business grows. Additional capital for expansion will prove difficult to obtain; hence, the involvement of larger chains will often be necessary to develop more successful concepts. Those looking to start rural tourism ventures should be mindful of these characteristics. Large-scale outside funding is unlikely to be available in most cases, and business activities which can start on a small scale using personal funding have a better chance of progressing beyond the planning stage.

An additional source of funding for tourism businesses may the government, as in some countries there are government schemes that assist new businesses to set up. In the UK a multitude of agencies exist to fund new ventures (see Thomas 2004 for more detail) and in the 1970s tourist boards funded some tourism ventures to help upgrade infrastructure. However, critics have argued that the tourism sector should not be subsidized unduly as it may distort the market and support unprofitable ventures with a public sector funding culture. Yet in Scotland agencies such as Scottish Enterprise play an active role in the generation of new business development as Chapter 14 will show. In the case of countries seeking to expand the range of tourism businesses able to serve tourists' needs and to provide much needed employment, government assistance may be a central part of the expansion strategy as is the case in South Africa. As Insight 12.1 shows, to promote indigenous and foreign investment in tourism, various schemes are available to help reduce the risk of investing in tourism, as well as the provision of advice and information in the process of business development.

INSIGHT 12.1

Funding opportunities for tourism businesses in South Africa

Tourism has emerged as a major element of the economy of the new South Africa following the ending of apartheid and it is the leading country for tourism on the African continent. To help facilitate the development of tourism businesses in South Africa, government agencies have put in place different funding programmes as the sector seeks to grow the numbers employed from the 820 000 people currently indirectly and directly employed in tourism. As Nuntsu, Tassiopoulos and Haydan (2004) show, much of the focus is on the potential of entrepreneurs and micro-scale businesses to accommodate the expected doubling of inbound tourism every four years.

Although Nuntsu *et al.*'s (2004) and Rogerson's (2004) studies of South Africa's bed-and-breakfast sector identified a number of barriers to growth including lack of access in finance, the Department of Environmental Affairs and Tourism's Funding Programmes for Tourism Businesses (www.environment.pw.gov.za) do outline the following schemes which resulted from collaboration between the Tourism Business Council of South Africa (established in 1996) and the Department of Environmental Affairs and Tourism. The main programmes include:

- The small and medium enterprise development programme, which is a cash grant incentive scheme for new or expansion projects to help reduce investment costs and to attract overseas investment.

- The Industrial Development Corporation, with its Tourism Business Unit providing finance as a loan for capital-intensive projects such as accommodation facilities, buildings, furniture and fittings, renovations and expansion with loans of 5–15 years in duration and other finance options.

- The Development Bank of Southern Africa, with finance and expertise through support for investment in attractions, accommodation, transport, enabling infrastructure (e.g. basic services and telecommunications) and training.

- Khula Enterprise Finance, which is a credit guarantee scheme for investors without the financial resources to start up a business. The Khuala Guarantee acts as up to 80 per cent of the collateral.

- The National Empowerment Fund, established in 1998 to empower disadvantaged people by financing and investment in projects.

- Business Partners Ltd, which is an unlisted public company established in 1981 to help with business planning, advice and support including a mentoring programme.

- Community Public Private Partnerships Programme, launched in 1999 to link resource-rich rural communities and private sector investors to unlock the economic potential of the country, promoting the sustainable use of resources in the country's poorest areas to address poverty. Tourism is now a focus of the programme including archaeological and anthropological remains and their use in tourism.

- National Lottery Distribution Trust Fund, established in 1997 to distribute the proceeds of a National Lottery, with a focus on the arts, heritage (natural and cultural) and the environment in much the same vein as the UK's National Lottery. The scheme funds projects of national significance, especially in rural areas.

- Eastern Cape Development Corporation, to help fund the rapidly growing tourism sector in the country's cape.

- Ganteng Tourism Authority Tourism Development Fund, which funds tourism infrastructure to help increase tourism growth and community participation in tourism, as well as focusing on key tourism gateways, routeways, nodes and clusters (i.e. areas where tourism activities come together to create a critical mass, and so a tourism cluster develops). The scheme also supports tourism training, capacity building (i.e. investing in the human resource potential of employees) as well as seeking to improve the overall visitor experience.

- Northern Cape Department of Economic Affairs and Tourism, to help reduce poverty and to engage the unemployed and underemployed in the formation of micro-enterprise formation through a credit guarantee scheme and innovation fund.

- Western Cape Department of Economic Development and Tourism, which aims to help develop infrastructure so that marginalized rural communities benefit from tourism. It seeks to help in the creation of new entrepreneurs, and with training support. A wide range of areas can benefit, for example the craft sector which can be helped to link to tourism opportunities.

- Kwa Zula Natal, with its ITHALA Development Finance Corporation to facilitate tourism investment in the province (i.e. in the Kingdom of Zula) via new or existing tourism projects. It offers finance for buildings as a lead organization and is willing to enter into equity schemes via joint ventures if an entrepreneur lacks the funding. The project has the opportunity to buy out ITHALA's involvement in the venture at a later stage. It also helps finance buildings and equipment, providing loan capital for up to five years and it runs a Black Empowerment Fund to encourage involvement in the tourism sector. ITHALA also offers consultancy services, from feasibility analysis through to post-establishment services including maintenance management.

Source: Adapted from Department of Environmental Affairs and Tourism's Funding Programmes for Tourism Businesses (www.environment.pw.gov.za), accessed 15.1.2005.

References

Nuntsu, N., Tassiopoulos, D. and Haydan, N. (2004) 'The bed and breakfast market of Buffalo city (BC), South Africa: Present status, constraints and success', *Tourism Management*, 25 (4): 512–22.

Rogerson, C. (2004) 'Tourism, small firm development and empowerment in post-apartheid South Africa', in R. Thomas (ed.) *Small Firms in Tourism: International Perspectives*. Oxford: Elsevier.

After the business is financed, the next major hurdle is making a success of the venture. This is dependent upon the management of the business and the marketing of its products and services. For this reason, it is useful to examine the principles of financial management that are crucial to the success of the business.

Financial management in tourism

The financial skills required to manage a tourism operation are essentially the same as those required for managing any other business, and it is well beyond the scope of this chapter to cover the subject comprehensively. It is worthwhile, however, to draw attention to some of the key issues. While it must seem obvious that managers must monitor the ongoing financial position of the business, in practice many businesses find out how profitable they have been only some time after year end when their accountant prepares the annual tax accounts. Haswell and Holmes (1989) pointed out the significance of a lack of accounting records and showed half of all failed businesses have deficient accounting records or none at all. Williams (1987) investigated 5646 failed Australian firms and found that inadequate, inaccurate or non-existent books and records were one of the reasons for failure in 55.3 per cent of the businesses. The need for adequate financial records is clearly not in dispute, but many small-business owners have little perception of what is required. Many specialist texts exist in tourism (e.g. Owen 1994) that document the importance of keeping financial records and how to assess profitability, **liquidity** and efficiency in the business, in the initial set up and development stage of a business. Wilcox (1976) studied various financial models which were being developed to predict company failures and found that in all cases the key determinant of failure was the ratio of cash flow to total assets. While the value of such models in predicting failure is arguable, they clearly demonstrate the importance of cash flow in business survival. The old cliché that businesses do not fail because they run at a loss but, rather, because they run out of money is very true, and the event which spells the end for many companies is the day they do not have enough money to pay the wages.

Cash-flow management is a key activity in financial management. It can be divided into short- and long-term cash management. The short-term cash management involves listing out, on a day-to-day basis, the cash which the business expects to receive from all sources and the cash it will pay out (e.g. to its suppliers, staff, for rent rates and taxes). From this information the company can calculate its projected bank balance and hence ensure that adequate funds are available. Typically the daily cash flow is projected out for a two-month period and is revised once a month, or more often where there are changes in projected cash flows. The longer-term cash flows form part of a company's budgeting process, whereby at least once a year the business should project its balance sheet, profit and loss, and cash flow for the next year, and preferably for two years or longer. Longer-term projections are advisable where the business is young or expanding rapidly. The business's actual financial position should be compared on a monthly basis with these budget projections.

While budgets are notoriously unreliable indicators of actual performance, the process of generating budgets and monitoring performance against them is in itself very important, as through it management is able to understand the business and monitor its progress. In this way problems are detected early and can be dealt with before they become crises. Ask a bank manager for a temporary increase in a loan facility because you cannot pay this week's wages and the answer is likely to be a receiver walking through the door. Tell the same bank manager that you expect to need an additional short-term loan in three months' time and the chances of success are greatly enhanced.

The type of financial skill required to carry out this process may be beyond the expertise of many managers, and the accounting profession obviously provides this input for many businesses. However, the business's own managers should do as much as possible of the financial management, for only they can follow developments on a day-by-day basis. In a hospitality context, Beal (2003) points to the importance of managing costs in operating a business, especially labour, which is one of the major items of expenditure. Also, the cost of a heavy input of professional services may reduce the profitability of the business and be self-defeating. However, once the business is up and running, it is important for tourism ventures to be able to access financial information to make management decisions such as costing a product or service or understanding the break-even point and the relationship of sales to profitability (Messenger and Shaw 1993). One of the most important areas is in preparing and understanding financial information in company accounts.

Understanding company accounts and financial information

As Page (1994) notes, an annual report is used by companies to provide a review of the year's activities and it contains company accounts which are prepared within accounting guidelines in force in the country where the head office is based. Beal (2003) points to a growing trend towards greater transparency in **financial reporting** in lodging operations and investment performance, (with the exception of Asia). Bird and Rutherford (1989) argue that company accounts contain messages which use specialist jargon to deal with a complex situation. Once the specialist jargon is decoded by the reader, company accounts provide an insight into the financial performance of businesses. There are two key elements within company accounts:

- a **balance sheet**
- a profit and loss account.

On one side (figuratively speaking) of the balance sheet, the items owned by the company are listed; in other words, its assets. On the other side of the balance sheet the way in which these assets are financed is listed. Part of this will be financed by the owners, in other words the shareholders' funds, and part will be financed by the company's financiers such as its bank. Both the shareholders and the financiers require a return for investing in the company. In addition to this, part of the business is financed at no cost to the business. This finance is provided by creditors who have supplied goods or services to the company but have yet to be paid, by staff who have holiday pay owing to them, and by other such accruals. The assets, by definition, are exactly balanced by the creditors and plus the shareholders' funds. By convention assets and liabilities are divided into current and fixed categories. Current assets and liabilities are items will be converted into cash, discharged, or used up within 12 months' time.

The **profit and loss account** reveals the company's turnover and level of profit for the year. It provides a detailed picture of the changes in the retained earnings part of the owners' equity during the year. The profit and loss account is more correctly called the 'statement of financial performance', as it is the measure of how the company performed during the year.

It should be recognized that a balance sheet and profit and loss provide a snapshot of an organization's activities at one point in time. Therefore, analysts tend to consider company accounts over a three- to five-year period to give a more realistic assessment of an organization's business performance. There is a great deal of debate among accountants over the reliability of such documents, due to the degree of creative accounting which characterizes them, especially the unaudited accounts of private companies. Even with publicly listed companies it requires considerable expertise to fully analyse accounts as key disclosures may only be revealed in the notes to the accounts. Investors often carry out a due diligence process before investing in a company so they can obtain the information behind the accounts and interpret it for themselves.

As an example of a set of accounts, the 2003 consolidated profit and loss account for easyJet is provided in Table 12.3 and the balance sheet in Table 12.4. From these we can establish easyJet's level of profitability in 2003 and compare it with its performance in 2002. From the balance sheet we can see the assets that easyJet uses to produce its revenue and how those assets are financed, and look at the movements in assets and liabililties over the year. From Table 12.3 we can see that during 2003 the turnover increased from £552 million to £932 million and that the gross profit increased from £139 million to £157 million. However, after taking distribution, marketing and administration costs into account the operating profit showed a decline from £69.5 million to £48.5 million. This resulted in the retained profit (net profit after tax) declining from £49 million to £32.4 million. This retained profit is the money available to distribute to shareholders as dividends or to reinvest in the business.

TABLE 12.3   easyJet consolidated profit and loss account for the year ended 30 September 2003

	2003 £000	2002 £000
Turnover	931 845	551 844
Cost of sales	(774 989)	(413 209)
Gross profit	156 856	138 635
Distribution and marketing expenses	(60 985)	(40 634)
Administrative expenses	(47 422)	(28 429)
Group operating profit	48 449	69 572
Loss from interest in associated undertaking: committed contribution to Deutsche BA	(1 329)	(1 359)
Total operating profit: group and share of associate	47 120	68 213
Amounts written off investments	(7 777)	(7 159)
Interest receivable and similar income	13 729	15 751
Interest payable	(1 549)	(5 228)
Profit on ordinary activities before taxation	51 523	71 577
Tax on profit on ordinary activities	(19 121)	(22 568)
Retained profit for the financial year	32 402	49 009
	Pence	*Pence*
Earnings per share		
Basic	8.24	14.61
Diluted	8.04	13.89
Basic, before goodwill amortization	12.72	15.53
Diluted, before goodwill amortization	12.40	14.78
Basic, before goodwill amortisation, committed contribution to Deutsche BA, amounts written off investments, costs of integrating the businesses of easyJet and Go Fly and accelerated depreciation of certain owned aircraft	18.01	18.95
Diluted, before goodwill amortization, committed contribution to Deutsche BA, amounts written off investments, costs of integrating the businesses of easyJet and Go Fly and accelerated depreciation of certain owned aircraft	17.56	18.02

All activities relate to continuing operations in the current and previous year

Source: easyJet (2003: 50)

TABLE 12.4 easyJet consolidated balance sheet as at 30 September 2003

	2003 £000	2002 £000
Fixed assets		
Intangible assets	329 836	–349 685
Tangible assets	320 772	185 098
Investments	–	6 624
Total fixed assets	650 608	541 407
Current assets		
Debtors	141 564	96 005
Cash at bank and in hand	335 405	427 894
Total current assets	476 969	523 899
Creditors: amounts falling due within one year	(260 925)	(260 614)
Net current assets	216 044	263 285
Total assets less current liabilities	866 652	804 692
Creditors: amounts falling due after more than one year	(65 322)	(48 600)
Provisions for liabilities and charges	(42 869)	(28 388)
Net assets	758 461	727 704
Capital and reserves		
Called-up share capital	98 485	97 919
Share premium account	539 632	533 263
Profit and loss account	120 344	96 522
Shareholders' funds – equity	758 461	727 704

Source: easyJet (2003: 51)

When we look at easyJet's balance sheet we can see that it has fixed assets of £651 million and current assets of £477 million, which gives it total assets of £1128 million. Of these assets £320 million are intangible (**goodwill**). Shareholders fund 70 per cent of the assets with shareholders' funds of £758 million. As the company has cash in hand or in the bank of £335 million and only has a small amount of debt, the balance sheet looks very safe. However, caution tells us we should read the notes to the accounts to see if there are parts of the picture that are not immediately obvious. From these notes we find that the company leases aircraft which are accounted for as operating leases; in other words, the rental is charged directly to the profit and loss account but the aircraft are not included in the balance sheet. Note 20 of the accounts (easyJet 2003: 71) tells us the annual lease commitments for aircraft are £82.4 million. It also tells us that easyJet has agreed to purchase 119 Airbus A319 aircraft for approximately £3.2 billion, as well as assorted Boeing aircraft. This may lead you to ponder what the balance sheet would look like if all the leased aircraft were owned by the company and the purchase of the new aircraft complete. It is probable that the purchase commitment for these aircraft will be financed by operating leases and will never appear on the balance sheet, but it points to the need for a more detailed analysis of the turnover easyJet will need in the future to fill these aircraft and the associated risks.

Multinational enterprises and globalization

With increasing globalization of tourism enterprises (see Chapter 5), many have become multinational corporations (MNCs) (Image 12.1). In some tourist destinations, especially developing countries, the power and size of transnational corporations has an enormous impact because their investment remains seductive. Initially, development may bring jobs and increased prosperity but long-term stability is not guaranteed. Destination choice changes with consumer fashion and the country may experience relatively little benefit once leakages are accounted for. Financing such companies assumes a greater international dimension where their activities are able to attract not only government inducements and sweeteners in the case of large resort developments in less developed countries, but are attractive to large finance companies which may be assured of significant financial returns. Tribe (1995: 234) refers to the French government providing a comprehensive infrastructure package including new roads and rail connections (and) a loan at preferential interest rates in order to enable Disney to locate their attraction in the country. Apart from the estimate that the development would lead to 18 000 construction and 12 000 operational jobs, the attraction was predicted to earn US$700 million in foreign currency each year. A substantial portion of the risk associated with the venture was taken by European equity investors who subscribed for shares in the Euro Disneyland IPO. These investors lost substantial sums when the company failed to meet projections. The Walt Disney Company itself had structured the transaction in such a way that it was largely insulated from the risks of the project. The project does, however, show how large multinational enterprises can be powerful agents in the tourism development process, especially from the financial perspective, and how governmental involvement can allow ventures to proceed by taking financial risk in order to secure other economic benefits.

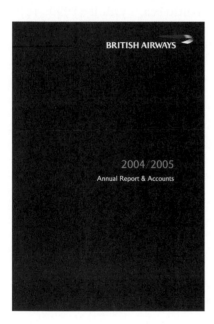

Key Results

			2004-05	2003-04
Group results				
Turnover	m	up 3.3%	7,813	7,560
Operating profit	m	up 33.3%	540	405
Profit before tax	m	up 80.4%	415	230
Attributable profit for the year	m	up 93.1%	251	130
Net assets	m	up 12.0%	2,684	2,397
Basic earnings per share	p	up 93.4%	23.4	12.1
Key financial statistics				
Airline operations yield	p/RPK	down 4.4%	6.02	6.30
Operating margin	%	up 1.5 points	6.9	5.4
Net debt/total capital ratio	%	down 11.4 points	42.7	54.1
Group operating statistics				
Passengers carried	'000	down 1.1%	35,717	36,103
Revenue passenger kilometres	m	up 4.7%	107,892	103,092
Revenue tonne kilometres	m	up 6.5%	15,731	14,771
Available tonne kilometres	m	up 3.2%	22,565	21,859
Passenger load factor	%	up 1.8 points	74.8	73.0

Contents

Image 12.1: Extracts from the
British Airways Annual Report 2004

Multinational corporations are often able to structure their operations in ways that minimize tax, or defer it for long periods of time. The opportunities for creating tax advantages available to multinational firms are much greater than those for domestic firms. The details of the ways in which investments are structured and operated in order to take advance of tax breaks are complex and well beyond the scope of this text; they also vary from country to country according to the tax legislation of the countries involved. Tax minimization can involve such things as having holding companies registered in tax havens, using transfer pricing to shift profits from high tax jurisdictions to ones with lower tax rates, and delaying the repatriation of dividends to delay tax liability. Countries generally attempt to protect their tax bases so they block taxation loopholes on an ongoing basis while the tax lawyers try to keep one step ahead. However, not all tax breaks exploited by multinationals are disapproved of by tax authorities as the taxation system is often used as a way of providing incentives for attracting offshore investment. Tax planning by multinationals can allow them to invest in projects that would otherwise be unattractive, and can influence where tourist investment occurs.

Supranational investment

A number of institutions exist at supranational level, i.e. beyond the boundaries of one nation, and some have a significant effect on the international tourism industry. One example will be reviewed here: the World Bank. Businesses in areas of Europe that have been designated for EU assistance can apply for grant aid from the EU, although it is usually on a matched funding basis, i.e. the applicant will be supported pound for pound, or euro for euro. The impact of EU funding is not well researched and neither is there a commonly agreed method to measure it according to Bull (1999: 149). Research on the island of Bornholm, in the Baltic sea, by Bull (1999: 157) showed that for many of the small businesses, the EU support was crucial because it opened the channels to commercial capital at a time when access to loans was extremely difficult. The approval of support from the EU was conceived of as a credibility stamp for the project, which made it easier to obtain additional capital from other sources.

The World Bank Group

In 1944, representatives from a number of nations met at Bretton Woods in New Hampshire to discuss the reconstruction that would be necessary after the war; the World Bank and the International Monetary Fund (IMF) were the result of this summit. The World Bank Group comprises the International Bank for Reconstruction and Development (IBRD), the International Finance Corporation (IFC), the International Development Agency (IDA), the International Centre for Settlement of Investment Disputes (ICSID) and the Multilateral Investment Guarantee Agency (MIGA).

The not-for-profit sector

The not-for-profit or voluntary sector, as it is frequently termed, has different objectives to the commercial world. This does not mean that operational practices are inefficient; in fact, the reverse can be true. In Britain, the largest organization in this sector to affect tourism is the National Trust, a registered charity, which was established in 1895 and is now the custodian of many assets. The trust has to balance the needs of visitors with the requirements of conservation for future generations and relies on a variety of financial sources including membership subscriptions, donations, government grants and bequests in wills.

Conclusion

The ability to raise finance is clearly very important in tourism development; entrepreneurs with a proven track record will find access to capital much more straightforward than individuals with just a business idea. All too often in the analysis of tourism growth and development, the hidden role of finance is neglected, since major infrastructure projects such as large attractions and accommodation units require substantial investment and funding to make the projects reach fruition. One of the difficulties which certain parts of the tourism sector face is the payback period over which finance and investment are expected to make a return. Where the private sector has been unable to finance large projects, there is growing evidence in many countries that the public sector will assist private sector projects such as tourist attractions which can be seen to have a wider community benefit beyond usage by tourists, thus justifying public sector assistance. This also reflects the integral role which tourism can play in certain communities where financing tourism projects creates local employment.

This chapter has also indicated that financing arrangements can frequently be a matter of putting together a combination of bank loans, public sector support and, perhaps, venture capital funds. In making investment decisions, bankers and investors will focus on the risks they bear and the returns they expect and meeting their expectations is essential to secure finance for a project. It is important to note that other factors, such as the composition of the senior management team, will also be considered by investors. This provides an important backdrop to those individuals and groups of individuals who establish new ventures, entrepreneurs, who are the focus of the next chapter.

Discussion questions

1 Why would you use the net present value method in financial decision-making in tourism?

2 How important are company accounts for potential investors? What pitfalls are associated with them?

3 What problems do new ventures face when seeking finance?

4 How important is the location of a new venture for its ability to raise capital and funding?

References

Altman, E.E. (1993) *Corporate Financial Distress and Bankruptcy, Second Edition*. New York: Wiley.

Beal, P. (2003) 'Financial management', in B. Brotherton (ed.) *The International Hospitality Industry: Structure, Characteristics and Issues*. Oxford: Butterworth-Heinemann.

Birch, D.L. (1987) *Job Creation in America*. New York: Free Press.

Bird, P. and Rutherford, B. (1989) *Understanding Company Accounts*. London: Pitman.

Brounen, D., de Jong, A. and Koedijk, K. (2004) *Corporate Finance in Europe Confronting Theory with Practice*. Working paper. Rotterdam: Erasmus University.

Bull, B. (1999) 'Encouraging tourism development through the EU structural funds: A case study of the implementation of EU programmes on Bornholm', *International Journal of Tourism Research*, 1 (3): 149–65.

Campbell, J.K. (1981) *Report of the Committee of Inquiry into the Australian Financial System*. Canberra: AGPS.

Deloitte Touche Tomatsu (1994) *Small Business Survey 1994: New Zealand Tourism Industry*. Christchurch: Deloitte Touche Tomatsu.

easyJet (2003) *Annual Report*. Luton: easyJet.

Florida, R. (1994) 'What start-ups don't need is money', *INC*, April: 27.

Fried, V.H. and Hirsrich, R.D. (1988) 'Venture capital research: Past, present and future', *Entrepreneurship: Theory and Practice*, 13: 15–28.

Fried, V.H. and Hirsrich, R.D. (1994) 'Towards a model of venture capital investment decision making', *Financial Management*, 23 (3): 28–37.

Ganguly, P. (1985) *UK Small Business Statistics and International Comparisons*. London: Harper & Rowe.

Go, F. and Pine, R. (1995) *Globalization Strategy in the Hotel Industry*. London: Routledge.

Haswell, S. and Holmes, S. (1989) 'Estimating the small business failure rate: A reappraisal', *Journal of Small Business Management*, 27(3): 68–74.

Keasey, K. and Watson, R. (1994) 'The bank financing of small firms in the UK: Issues and evidence', *Small Business Economics*, 6 (5): 349–62.

Mason, C. and Harrison, R. (1994) 'Informal venture capital in the UK', in A. Hughes and D.J. Storey (eds) *Finance and the Small Firm*. London: Routledge.

Messenger, S. and Shaw, H. (1993) *Financial Management for the Hospitality, Tourism and Leisure Industries*. Basingstoke: Macmillan.

Nuntsu, N., Tassiopoulos, D. and Haydan, N. (2004) 'The bed and breakfast market of Buffalo City (BC), South Africa: Present status, constraints and success', *Tourism Management*, 25 (4): 515–22.

Owen, G. (1994) *Accounting for Hospitality and Tourism*. London: Pitman.

Page, S.J. (1994) *Transport for Tourism*. London: Routledge.

Page, S.J. (2003) *Tourism Management: Managing for Change*. Oxford: Butterworth-Heinemann.

Pinfold, J.F. (2000) 'Examining new venture failure rates: A New Zealand study', *Small Enterprise Research*, 8 (1): 56–72.

Schilit, W.K. (1993) 'The performance of venture capital funds, stocks and bonds', *International Review of Strategic Management*, 4: 304.

Taylor, S., Simpson, J. and Howie, H. (1998) 'Financing small businesses', in R. Thomas (ed.) *The Management of Small Tourism and Hospitality Firms*. London: Cassell.

Thomas, R. (ed.) (2004) *Small Firms in Tourism: International Perspectives*. Oxford: Elsevier.

Tribe, J. (1995) *The Economics of Leisure and Tourism Environments, Markets and Impacts*. Oxford: Butterworth-Heinemann.

Wilcox, J.W. (1976) 'The gamblers ruin approach to business risk', *Sloan Management Review*, 18 (1): 33–46.

Williams, A.J. (1987) 'A longitudinal analysis of the characteristics and performance of small business in Australia', *Australian Small Business and Entrepreneurship Research: Proceedings of the Third National Conference*. Newcastle, NSW: University of Newcastle, Institute of Industrial Economics.

Further reading

An interesting case study on funding a new fleet of aircraft can be found in:

Branson, R. (1998) *Losing my Virginity The Autobiography*. London: Virgin Publishing.

and for an in-depth discussion of accounting principles in tourism and hospitality see:

Moncarz, E. and Portocarrero, N. (2003) *Accounting for the Hospitality Industry*. London: Pearson Education.

Tourism and Entrepreneurship

Learning outcomes

After reading this chapter and answering the questions you should be able to:

- understand the range of characteristics common to entrepreneurs

- outline how entrepreneurship is linked to tourism

- analyse the factors affecting entrepreneurs

- identify the features of innovation and its significance to tourism

- comprehend the wide variety of successful tourism entrepreneurs.

Overview

Tourism throughout history has been dependent upon entrepreneurs identifying business opportunities and in turning their ideas into businesses. This process of development has largely driven the process of new firm development in tourism and governments support this type of activity on the premise that these types of ventures create wealth and employment, while the small firm of today may be the large company of tomorrow if it succeeds. Much of the success in the business field is dependent upon individual entrepreneurs and their vision, business acumen and ability to see opportunities.

Introduction

Entrepreneurship is a major force in economic development, since it is responsible for generating growth and acts as a vehicle for innovation and change in the economy (Lordkipanidze, Brezet and Backman 2005). Tourism is one of the sectors of the service economy that is in a constant state of change and flux, and innovation and change are vital if businesses are to grow and provide the diversity of products to accommodate changing patterns of tourism consumption. Our knowledge and understanding of entrepreneurship in tourism have progressed substantially since the comments of Shaw and Williams (1990: 67) that there is 'relatively little appreciation of the specific operating characteristics of tourism firms, and especially of tourism entrepreneurship'. Indeed as Shaw (2004: 122) notes, 'during the last 20 years there has been a growing recognition of the importance of entrepreneurship within the tourism industry', especially as small tourism businesses become more fully understood alongside the large research literature on tourism as an element of international business. There are many important examples within the history of tourism, such as Thomas Cook, Richard Branson and V. Raitz, in innovating to generate significant tourism businesses and many of their successes have evolved into global brands and products we are all familiar with (i.e. Thomas Cook, Virgin and package holidays). Such success can be found in many countries and underpins the economic vitality of the tourism sector.

This chapter examines the nature of tourism entrepreneurship, especially the importance of innovation and small business development. This is assuming a growing international significance, as Chapter 5 explained, with changes in the nature of how businesses are organized in an increasingly globalized world. To keep ahead of the competition, innovation and change are vital and, whilst many tourism enterprises are small-scale in nature, there has been a significant paradigm shift in how firms are organized. As Table 13.1 shows, globalization is now making business networks increasingly important, with opportunities emerging for small firms able to use new technology to develop into flexible entities. Table 13.1 builds upon many of the points made by the WTTC (2001) Task Force report discussed in Chapter 11 on the changing nature of the organization and the need for flexible working (Peper, Doorne-Huiskes and den Dulk 2005) and the need for change and innovation on how tourism is delivered by organizations. For entrepreneurs and innovators within organizations an ability to harness technology to nurture business-to-business relationships in the tourism supply chain and business-to-consumer relationships in terms of demand will lead to a redefining of how organizations interact with each other, with customers and how they are operated as organizations. As a result, the need for 'enterprise' and 'enterprising people' has never been greater in tourism.

TABLE 13.1 A paradigm shift in the organization of the firm

Element	Old organization	New organization
Structure	Vertical hierarchy	Network and horizontal relationships
Size	Large, many layers	Downsized, de-layered, smaller
Basis of action	Control	Empowerment
Operating environment	Static	Dynamic, changing
Decision-making	Centralized	Decentralized, disaggregated and autonomous
Work organization	Departmentalization	Multifunctional teamwork, project work
Production	On-site, owned by firm	Dispersed, outsourced
Communication	Formal	Informal, flexible
Personnel focus	Managers	Professionals, technical competency
Compensation basis	Position in hierarchy	Accomplishment, value of skills and value added
Values	Masculine	Feminine
Learning and competency of employees	Narrow and specific	Broad and continuous, flexible specialization

Source: Lennon (2001: 116) adapted and extended from Tapscott and Caston (1993)

Understanding the nature of entrepreneurship

According to Drucker (1985) there is no explanation 'as to why entrepreneurship emerged as it did in the late nineteenth century and as it seems to be doing again today … The changes are likely to lie in changes in values, perception, and attitude, changes in demographics, in institutions … perhaps changes in education as well' (Drucker 1985: 12). Besides the lack of explanation for entrepreneurship, there is little in the way of economic theory for the entrepreneur. Casson (1982: 9) considers that the subject has become the domain of 'sociologists, psychologists and political scientists'; in his view, this is because of the assumption that we all have 'free access' to the information needed for decision-making which, therefore, becomes 'the mechanical application of mathematical rules for optimization … trivializes decision-making, and makes it impossible to analyse the role of entrepreneurs in taking decisions of a particular kind' implying that it is a complex area to understand. Medlik (1996: 94) argues that an entrepreneur is 'a person who undertakes an enterprise, makes decisions on and controls its conduct, and bears the risk'. Youell (1996: 79), similarly, emphasizes that it is 'an individual who is prepared to take a risk and accept a challenge or undertake a venture that has no guarantee of success'. The challenge and risk elements are evident when many tourism businesses are reviewed. Significantly, the process of entrepreneurship is 'more holistic and dynamic' (Morrison 1998: 1) than any one perspective can explain: nonetheless, the focal point is the individual. More recent research in management science has identified the need to understand the individual characteristics and the stories of individual entrepreneurs so as to appreciate the diversity of experiences and successes (Hjorth and Steyaert 2004).

Shaw (2004) points to the fact that entrepreneurs have traditionally been perceived as innovators based on the economic development perspective by Schumpeter (1934) (a subject which is extensively reviewed by Reisman (2004) in relation to his contribution to entrepreneurship research). This perspective highlights the entrepreneur as a business pioneer driven by profit motives. Yet Shaw (2004) is critical of such perspectives, since few small-scale entrepreneurs actually pioneer: they tend to be 'reproducers', taking ideas from elsewhere and making them work in their context. This has led Shaw (2004) to identify different entrepreneurial types in tourism, such as classical entrepreneurs interested in being their own independent boss, managerial types and the artisan entrepreneur. There is a tendency to classify small-scale tourism entrepreneurs into:

- *lifestyle entrepreneurs,* who often have low managerial skills and expertise and focus on niche products with limited capital (Shaw and Williams 2004a) which Morrison, Rimmington and Williams (1999) observed as comprising the majority of small businesses in the UK where non-economic motives are important in tourism entrepreneurship

- *business-oriented entrepreneurs,* who are motivated by profit.

Whatever categorization one adopts, what is clear is that the entry into entrepreneurship is in itself a life-changing experience for most people and is often related to a desire to exercise some control over their working lives as well as to seek to seize the economic potential of perceived opportunities (Shane 2004). Not surprisingly, the majority of studies of tourism entrepreneurship have been focused on small businesses although examples of individual successes in the low-cost airline market exist in relation to popular biographies of influential entrepreneurs and the companies they have set up (Image 13.1). Yet what are some of the reasons for people seeking to become tourism entrepreneurs?

Image 13.1: easyJet founder Stelios is now a well-known entrepreneurial figure in the tourism and leisure sector with its low cost brands such as easyJet. Source: easyJet

Characteristics of entrepreneurs

A common belief is that entrepreneurs are born rather than made and, indeed, some personalities appear to have an innate ability: Casson (1982: 6) argued that 'many of the qualities with which the heroic stereotype is imbued are simply a reflection of contemporary cultural attitudes ... the stereotype is useful as an articulation of the view that there is a correlation between various personal characteristics and entrepreneurial activity'. There can be no doubt that entrepreneurship comprises a number of elements. McMullan and Long (1990) consider these to be a combination of **creativity** and/or innovation, uncertainty and/or risk taking, and managerial and/or business capabilities. Taking personal characteristics a stage further, Stalinbrass (1980), Brown (1987) and Shaw and Williams (1994: 133) recognize that entrepreneurs at the owner-manager level may well have '*non-economic motives* for entering the business'. In Getz and Petersen's (2005) study of profit-oriented entrepreneurship among family business-owners in tourism and hospitality, lifestyle and autonomy were key attributes. Interestingly, they found that owners of restaurants and forms of accommodation are more motivated by profit and growth than owners of arts and crafts and Bed and Breakfasts (B&Bs), who are more motivated by lifestyle and autonomy. Lifestyle motives comprise a need for independence, the need to achieve (Hisrich and Peters 1992), job satisfaction – or self-actualization, and 'environmental factors' (Shaw and Williams 1990: 77).

Not surprisingly perhaps, there are also differences in motivation between males and females as discussed in Fielden and Davidson (2005). The 'overwhelming majority' of women in Goffee and Scase's (1985: 62) survey who had started their own businesses were 'university graduates who had been employed in a variety of middle-management positions ... [whose] career prospects were limited because of the existence of various gender-related prejudices'. Of particular interest is the observation that many of these female entrepreneurs 'organize their businesses on the basis of trust ... employees are committed to the employer's goals' and will accept lower wages because of greater individual autonomy and job satisfaction; the 'pay-off' for the entrepreneur is that a 'high trust organizational culture, then, has important economic advantages' (Goffee and Scase 1985: 68). One of the most widely cited classifications of entrepreneurs remains Goffee and Scase (1985) as shown in Table 13.2. This outlines their model of organizational structures and entrepreneurial characteristics, where the self-employed and small firms tend to dominate the accommodation sector. This raises the issue of what constitutes a small firm. Definitions vary, as discussed by Page, Forer and Lawton (1999) where up to 70 exist, a feature reiterated by Thomas (2004). The term 'small or medium enterprise' (SME) tends to complicate things, since the EU definition of 'medium enterprise' is of 100–499 employees while 'small' is 10–99 employees. The only agreement is on the micro enterprise, employing fewer than ten people (Thomas 2004) with the majority located in this category in the tourism and hospitality sector in many countries.

TABLE 13.2 Organizational structures and entrepreneurial characteristics

Category	Entrepreneurial characteristics
Self-employed	Use of family labour, little market stability, low levels of capital investment, tendency towards weakly developed management skills
Small employer	Use of family and non-family labour; less economically marginalized but shares other characteristics of self-employed group
Owner-controllers	Use of non-family labour, higher levels of capital investment, often formal system of management control but no separation of ownership and control
Owner-directors	Separation of ownership and management functions, highest levels of capital investment

Source: Adapted from Goffee and Scase (1985); Shaw and Williams (1994)

According to Brown and Scase (1994: 158), the appeal of entrepreneurship for graduates lies in 'possibilities for obtaining a greater degree of personal independence whereby their life chances will not be controlled by the arbitrary and discretionary judgements of others'. Drucker (1985) considers that longer years in education played a part in the emergence of the entrepreneurial economy in the United States. Ultimately, 'personal qualities which are rewarded through entrepreneurship are imagination and foresight, and skill in organizing and delegating work' (Casson 1982: 347). In seeking to understand what shapes the process of becoming and/or being an entrepreneur, a range of issues exist which can be broadly classified as the political/economic environment, the social/cultural environment and innovation and creativity.

The political/economic environment

Not surprisingly, larger tourism economies 'have a wider range of entrepreneurial opportunities' (Shaw and Williams 1994: 121) and political changes such as deregulation and privatization (Mudambi 2003) which have provided opportunities in the tourism sector for entrepreneurs to succeed. The advent of the 1979 Conservative government in Britain led to sweeping changes to many national policies: 'rolling back the frontiers of the state' created opportunities for both established and budding entrepreneurs. In the United States the deregulation of civil aviation in 1978 immediately spawned a range of low-cost carriers; the deregulation of the coach transport business came in 1982 and led to the creation of many small-scale businesses with only Greyhound surviving out of the two large operators. In recent years, Greek-born entrepreneur Stelios Haji-Ioannou has developed the direct-sell, low-cost carrier easyJet which was discussed in Chapter 5. Again this reinforces the importance of opportunities in the wider context of why entrepreneurs set up new ventures. Recent research on the concept of **effectuation**, which argues that the future is unpredictable but can be controlled has been cited as one factor associated in such activity (Sarasvathy 2005). Effectuation research also argues that rather than simply focusing on the traits of entrepreneurs, one should also look more closely at their expertise as a key element in setting up new ventures and success.

British deregulation of the passenger coach business, created by the 1980 Transport Act, allowed brother and sister Brian Souter and Ann Gloag, with their company Stagecoach, to develop national bus routes (www.stagecoach.co.uk). They also bid for railway interests with the privatization of British Rail and the acquisition of various interests in rail franchises and a recent success is the megabus.com brand for low-cost coach travel. Music and aviation entrepreneur Richard Branson expanded his travel interests by acquiring the 'cross-country' and West Coast Inter-City franchises, thereby creating Virgin Rail – having already benefited from the 'liberalization' of flights within the European Union and Virgin Blue in Australia (Branson 1998).

The sociocultural environment

Drucker (1985: 1) observed in the United States, 'a profound shift from a "managerial" to an "entrepreneurial" economy'. This has been further enhanced by social innovation, just as the commercial bank and civil service resulted from the Industrial Revolution: 'the present age of entrepreneurship will be [as] important for its social innovations – and especially for innovations in politics, government, education, and economics – as for any new technology or material product' (Drucker 1989: 247). Entrepreneurship is an integral part of North American culture and is, indeed, 'taught in school from kindergarten through to the twelfth grade, it has been integrated into college and university curricula, and is … promoted through … government Small Business Development Centers in every state' (Welsch 1998: 59). Entrepreneurs on that continent have the status of 'modern hero'.

However, in societies which show a marked respect for 'seniority' and authority the environment is unlikely to be conducive to the creation of large numbers of entrepreneurs. Dondo and Ngumo (1998: 18) consider the education, especially in primary schools, received by Kenyans is not only very conformist but that 'natural curiosity is suppressed'. When this factor is coupled with respect for 'rank', they believe the cultural environment is a poor base for entrepreneurship; a feature also examined by Echtner (1995). Shaw (2004) also noted the **cultural brokerage** role tourism entrepreneurs play within host communities, acting as a bridge between the world of the tourist and the local community, which is most vivid in developing countries (Dahles 1999). Getz and Carlsen (2000) found in Australian family-run businesses that social motives were very dominant, particularly in their prioritization of family life as opposed to business. Here the household has a major role to play in production. In Ghana, Gartner (2004) observed the importance of extended family being employed in these settings. Yet for businesses to remain viable, the process of innovation is crucial to success.

Innovation and creativity

According to Hjagler (2002: 465) 'innovation' has been used to describe the behaviour of tourism enterprises, destinations and the tourism sector and innovation can occur in a variety of contexts. 'Innovation' is a comparatively recent term to be examined in entrepreneurship (Schumpeter 1952) and Storey (2004) provides an excellent overview of contributions to this area. Hisrich and Peters (1992: 8) observe that innovation 'is one of the most difficult tasks for the entrepreneur. It takes not only the ability to create and conceptualize but also the ability to understand all the forces at work in the environment' and yet it is now one of the most all-embracing terms used in the tourism sector.

Schumpeter's seminal work in this area identified five types of innovation:

- introduction of a new good – or an improvement in the quality of an existing good
- introduction of a new method of production
- opening of a new market
- conquest of a new source of supply of raw-materials or half-manufactured good
- creation of a new type of industrial organization.

Some of these types can be observed by reviewing Branson's Virgin Atlantic airline: quality has been raised across the board through competition, true sleeper-beds have been introduced, new markets were opened to Tokyo (1991), Hong Kong (1994), Washington DC and Johannesburg (1996) and St. Lucia (1999). This was made possible by the introduction of the Airbus A340-300 with its new configurations and greater operational economies available for medium- to long-haul operations. The company's plans to develop new products and services onboard their future aircraft, the A380 (see Chapter 29 for more detail of the A380) will see the continued innovation by Virgin.

Hjagler (2002) outlined five types of innovation:

- *product innovations for new services* (e.g. airline loyalty programmes)
- *process innovations* to improve the performance of operations, such as ICTs
- *management innovations* (e.g. staff empowerment, as discussed in Chapter 11)
- *logistics innovations*, such as vertical links between restaurants and food producers
- *institutional innovations*, where new regulations such as government legislation provide new opportunities such as the deregulation of the aviation sector

while Wan, Ong and Lee (2005) simplify this typology into:

- technical/administrative innovation (e.g. booking via the internet)
- product and process innovation
- radical and incremental innovation.

Hjagler (2002) points to the Abernathy and Clark model (Figure 13.1) which explains whether innovation makes business linkages redundant (the horizontal axis) or leads to retrenchment. The vertical axis points to the knowledge and competencies used to produce things, leading to four types of innovation:

- *regular innovation*, such as ongoing investment in upgrading a hotel
- *niche innovations*, where new suppliers may enter the tourism supply chain or the creation of a marketing alliance
- *architectural innovations*, creating new infrastructure or capacity to develop a new product such as an event-led destination, remodelling the concept of tourism in that locality
- *revolutionary innovations*, such as the use of e-services to reach customers.

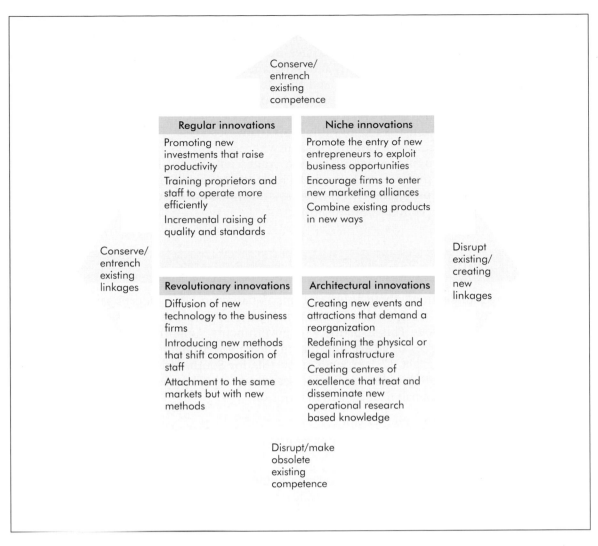

FIGURE 13.1 The Abernathy and Clarke model. Source: Reprinted from *Tourism Management*, vol.5, Hjagler, 'Repairing innovation defectiveness in tourism', 464–74, copyright (2002), with permission from Elsevier

For innovation to occur, the innovator has to acquire the knowledge and then be able to use it. As Chapter 11 argued, the EU (2001) saw obstacles to innovation diffusion might be removed by better dissemination of existing knowledge by a guide book. This model has been widely used by Scottish Enterprise companies in Scotland, with examples of best practice (see www.scotexchange.net) and the innovation exchange to disseminate knowledge and information. The major problem facing the tourism sector is its dominance by small firms, especially the micro enterprise (Wanhill 2000). This was one reason for the EU's financial support for the industry to help facilitate entrepreneurial activity and job creation. Not surprising, many of the cases of best practice in innovation tend to be large enterprises, such as the Disney Corporation discussed by Page (2003). It is widely emulated and studied in the tourism sector for its customer care programme, attention to detail, high level of repeat business (50–70 per cent) and desire to exceed customer expectations based on three propositions:

- *a quality staff experience,* since each individual staff member impacts on the customer experience
- *a quality customer experience,* based on being customer driven and seeking to exceed customers' needs and expectations rather than simply meeting them
- *a quality set of business practices,* where knowledge, marketing, innovation and other elements are blended to ensure commercial success.

Disney empowers its staff to put things right when they go wrong, with its 'How can I help?' philosophy and focus on what it describes as **service debugging**. It is also widely admired for its innovation in being able to manage massive numbers of visitors in its theme parks with visitor management tools such as an Early Bird Programme, Fast Passes and Tip Boards to advise on waiting times. However, competition and the global diffusion of innovations mean that a market leader will be quickly replicated, unless the product is patented and licensed. Yet even when an innovative idea has been created, it needs to be developed and commercialized in the tourism sector if it is to be marketed and this faces many obstacles. To exploit the idea, one of the most significant obstacles is funding it, and where a business is set up to progress the concept, it may go through a series of growth stages which will have many barriers and constraints. One way to understand these is to look at how small firms grow; thus one will understand better what problems entrepreneurs and innovators face and therefore how to develop the business idea, concept or innovation.

How do small tourism firms grow?

Much of what we understand about tourism firms is based on large enterprises but, as many researchers acknowledge, the growth of small firms today in a number of cases may create the large company of tomorrow. This explains why governments support this activity. Table 13.3 outlines some of the sources of advice and funding from governments for entrepreneurship in different countries and Insight 12.1 expands upon this for South Africa. The role of economic geography (e.g. Hjagler 1999) and small firms researchers (e.g. Thomas 2004) have traditionally examined the dynamics of small firm growth in terms of:

- births (creation of new enterprises)
- deaths (business failures, where firms enter into receivership, go bankrupt or cease operation for personal reasons).

Morrison *et al.* (1999) interestingly observed the following stages of growth which small firms pass through after establishment (failure typically occurs in the first couple years of operation):

- existence
- survival
- success
- take-off
- resource maturity.

The experiences of the business in each stage will be dependent upon the management style and skills, style of organization and problems faced by the company. As was discussed in Chapter 12, finance and working capital are key problems in the set-up and existence stage and it is here that

TABLE 13.3 Sources of advice and assistance for entrepreneurs in selected countries

Ireland	www.intertradeireland.com
Scotland	www.scottish-enterprise.com
England	www.sbs.gov.uk
Canada	bsa.cbsc.org
Malta	www.maltaenterprise.com
Fiji	www.fiji.gov.fj
Japan	www.chusho.meti.go.jp
USA	www.business.gov/
Thailand	www.dip.go.th

the management skills and abilities of the entrepreneur are crucial. Even in the survival stage, Shaw (2004) pointed to the weakness of formal management systems and the result is that many tourism lifestyle businesses remain in the survival stage, staving off failure.

Where businesses enter the success stage, they may opt for a steady-state, stable option to meet lifestyle choices, or go for growth. Yet the main constraint to growth which many studies identify (e.g. Page *et al.* 1999), is a lack of finance. Other key features which will impact upon the business in the growth stage include:

- cash flow (see Chapter 12)
- staff and technology
- marketing and business planning
- management skills (i.e. personal skills and qualities and formal management skills).

These all affect the performance of small tourism ventures, and have also been observed among the critical factors for ecotourism businesses in Australia (McKercher 1998). Yet entrepreneurship does not just exist in the private sector, as the case of **intrapreneurship** will show.

Public sector entrepreneurship: Intrapreneurship in tourism

As Morrison *et al.* (1999) discuss, in existing private and public sector organizations, the process of intrapreneurship may occur. This is when an individual or group of people may envision something and make it happen. These types of entrepreneur are often branded as 'product' or 'business' champions, epitomized by First Scotrail's new rail franchise in Scotland (www.firstscotrail.com) and its customer service 'champion' to bring continuous improvements. Such a change master requires important personal qualities to overcome those resistant to innovation and change – the 'laggards'. To overcome such barriers to innovation, innovators will need to progress the following strategies to win over staff, highlighting the benefits to employees and the importance of change:

- education and communications
- participation and involvement in a change management strategy when re-engineering business processes
- facilitation and support
- negotiation to secure agreement
- manipulation and cooperation
- explicit and implicit coercion to remove barriers.

For example, Maria Glot, Eddie Fenn and Ian Page performed this role at **Bradford** City Council in the early 1980s by putting an industrial city on the tourist map in what was described as a difficult area (Buckley and Witt 1985). What is interesting in this case is the role which the public sector and key drivers of change (the intrapreneurs) did in the 1980s. Davidson and Maitland (1997: 177) note that in the public sector, in Britain, there was 'an element of hegemonic change … in the face of evidence that the Thatcher values of enterprise and initiative were actually taken up by local government staff. In many cases, there was a change in attitude from regulation to entrepreneurship' making it possible to use tourism as process for urban regeneration, with the public sector taking a lead role (see Chapter 14 for more detail on the public sector).

The demise of traditional manufacturing in the early 1980s prompted Bradford City Council to set aside funds for the development of tourism to the area; textiles and engineering had dominated up until the 1970s but, by the 1980s, the city's image was one of bleak de-industrialization. Themed packages, such as 'The Flavours of Asia' and ones based on the Brontë Sisters, were developed: 2000 were sold in 1981/82 rising to 25 000 over the following two years (as Table 13.4, based on the review of Bradford by Hope and Klemm 2001, shows). This confirms that there can be entrepreneurship in a public service institution although it is likely to be 'far more difficult to innovate than even the most bureaucratic company' (Drucker 1985: 163). Davidson

TABLE 13.4 Bradford: Changes in the city and its tourism summarized

	The mid-1980s	The late 1990s
Hotel rooms	897	1677
Hotel occupancy	65% (1985)	39% (1997/8 estimated)
Bednights	85 000	370 570
Population	280 700	484 500
Ethnic minorities	N/A	94 260
Employment in tourism, leisure and cultural industries	N/A	12 977
Unemployment	N/A	8% city-wide 14% in Bradford's objective 2 area (under EU regional development funding)
Targeted market segments	Tourists on short breaks based on the following themes: The Brontës Industrial heritage Bradford mill shops television and film themes, (*Wuthering Heights*, *Emmerdale Farm*, *Last of the Summer Wine*) National Museum of Film Photography and Television.	Business and conference visitors on weekdays, short-break leisure tourists at weekends New themes: 'Flavours of Asia' Bradford festival New Imax theatre Salts Mill and David Hockney Gallery Cathedral 2000 Project
Role of city council funding	Lead role in developing and marketing tourism	Tourism partnership between public and private sectors
Funding	Local council, central government and tourist board grants	European grants Private sector funding from hotels and retailers Millennium Commission grants

Source: Reprinted from *Tourism Management*, vol.22, Hope and Klemm 'Tourism in difficult areas revisited: The case of Bradford', 629–635, copyright (2001), reprinted with permission from Elsevier

and Maitland (1997: 176) argue that 'a new approach to planning is emerging which seeks to combine private-sector requirements with a greater sense of public purpose: entrepreneurial planning' although the research by Hope and Klemm (2001) also pointed to changes in public sector involvement and emphasis in the 1990s. One of the key features of developing a destination such as Bradford is the role which innovation played across the entire city (Acs 2003) and the need for collaboration and joint working so that organizations can realize the wider tourism objectives for the city. For this reason, it is useful to examine the strategies which SMEs can develop in relation to innovation in tourism.

Strategies for SME innovation in tourism: Collaboration

In the pursuit of innovation, many SMEs are widely acknowledged as at a comparative disadvantage compared to large businesses due to their isolation, lack of resources and inadequate networking (Pyka and Küpper 2002). Here one of the most powerful tools which has been recognized is the process of collaboration. As tourism is a fragmented and diverse industry, with many linkages across sectors, joining up some of these links may prove beneficial to SMEs (Image 13.2). The formation of partnerships to develop collaborations can have win–win outcomes for SMEs and destinations and these have been widely encouraged by public sector agencies in the creation of business networks. The culture of business-to-business networks and public–private partnerships can help with information sharing and in influencing policy-making to lobby agencies for support; they are also well known in sustainable tourism projects for bringing stakeholders together (Selin 1999). This may help with developing new products where inter-organizational collaboration may lead to a supply chain being formed. The application of the idea in rural tourism is also well developed.

Hallenga-Brink and Brezet (2005) identified potential innovation strategies which might result in micro-tourism enterprises where a brainstorming method (i.e. getting the stakeholders together at a meeting to explore to the range of potential innovations perceived by business owners). Possible innovations include:

- *at the company level*, introducing a level of socially responsible entrepreneurship by an ecovolunteer programme and business collaboration to create new products such as a laundry service for hotels
- *for local infrastructure development*, clustering tourist activity to reduce seasonal pressure
- *at the product level*, developing quiet beaches where low-impact activities could be developed
- *aimed at the guest*, green marketing on menus.

What collaboration may also achieve is a greater competitive advantage (Lerner and Haber 2001), by allowing SMEs to concentrate on their core competencies, pooling their resources, creating economies of scale, reducing costs and creating a model which competitors cannot easily imitate (Evans, Campbell and Stonehouse 2003). As a result, to foster innovation, collaboration may by horizontal, cooperating with similar businesses undertaking similar activities, as well as vertical, with businesses undertaking different activities. With the use of ICTs, some of these organizations may be virtual.

Collaboration is preferable to competition in the SME sector which, in its most highly developed form, can lead to value chains, creating interdependencies which provide the competitive advantage. Much of the thinking in this area results from the influential work of Michael Porter (1985) on how to gain competitive advantage. Some of the forms which these collaborations may take include, as Shaw and Williams (2004a) show:

- informal inter-firm relationships
- supply strategies, such as those used by tour operators
- long-term strategic alliances
- mergers and acquisitions

although the latter two categories are much more common in larger tourism firms.

However, much of the success of entrepreneurship is dependent upon the individual entrepreneur. While tourism remains characterized by relatively easy access in forming a business, personal traits still play a powerful role (Dewhurst and Horobin 1998) and the following section examines the characteristics of some influential entrepreneurs in the tourism sector.

Image 13.2: In tourist destinations, the growth and development of small businesses, like this café in Venice, is supported through servicing tourist needs

Travel and tourism entrepreneurs

Brian Souter and Ann Gloag, representing rail and coach operation, and Richard Branson, with an airline and rail businesses, have already been mentioned. When it comes to tour operating, there are few barriers to entry into the business: the single greatest in Britain is probably the Civil Aviation Authority's ATOL (Air Travel Organizer's Licence) financial requirement. This is one reason why tourism is so attractive to entrepreneurs: thus, in the SME sector, entry barriers and capital needs may be low (unless a major technological investment is envisaged). In the United States, Sheldon (1995: 405) cites the growth from 588 tour operating firms in 1978 to 1001 by 1985 although only 34 per cent of those operating in 1978 were still in business seven years later; she notes that 'the situation is similar in European countries and seems to be characteristic of the industry'. Instability is largely a result of the easy entry and exit from this sector of tourism. When reviewing tour operations, Yale's (1995: 24) comments are particularly apposite: 'starting a new tour operating company can be seen as a creative business requiring imagination and strong nerves, so it has tended to attract entrepreneurial characters with strong personalities, most of them men'. The British tour operating industry is strewn with well-known names and their former brands: Harry Goodman and Intasun, Freddy Laker – whose Skytrain Holidays evolved out of the airline – and Vic Fatah, founder of SunMed and managing director of Inspirations, to name but three. However, a large number of contemporary entrepreneurs are simply emulating names from the past such as Vladimir Raitz who, many would argue, first established the mass market for package holidays by air charter in 1950. (See Bray and Raitz 2001 for a detailed analysis of Raitz's entrepreneurial activies.) A more recent example in the UK is the development of Palm Air based in Bournemouth which received a highly complimentary review from the consumer magazine *Holiday Which* and retains its small characteristics as an entrepreneurial business (see www.bathtravel.co.uk). To illustrate some of the key characteristics of entrepreneurs, attention now turns to vignettes of a range of travel and tourism entrepreneurs in Insight 13.1, and Web Case studies 13.1 and 13.2: some have a national profile and others a local one but all display a wide range of entrepreneurial characteristics and have impacted upon the tourism sector.

INSIGHT 13.1

Stelios Haji-Ioannou and the easyGroup

Born in Athens in 1967, Stelios obtained an economics degree from the London School of Economics in 1987 and a Master's in shipping trade and finance from the City University the following year. Joining his father's Troodos shipping company, Stelios became the founding chairman of the Cyprus Marine Environment Protection Association in 1992; this group of Cyprus-based business people pursue a common interest in sustainable development.

Stelios' first venture, Stelmar Tankers, was formed in 1992, involving his older brother and younger sister as shareholders. Three years later, easyJet was launched as a low-cost carrier flying out of Luton. In 1998, a holding company called easyGroup was formed in order to build on recognition of the 'easy' brand. The first of these new ventures was easyEverything – more than cyber-cafés, these internet access outlets contain between 400 and 600 terminals offering cheap 'surfing'; the first began trading in June 1999 and more are planned across Europe. In spring 2000, easyRentaCar was launched, taking on the might of the established companies Avis, Hertz, National and Europcar, with the unique idea of only one model of car and very low hire cost.

Stelios says that what motivates him is 'succeeding in using new technology, particularly the internet, to bring down the price of goods and services to consumers' and he enjoys the challenge of developing an idea from inception to implementation and then moving on to a new project, such as the easyhotel.com, while leaving the former business in competent management to run unimpeded. Website address: www.easy.com

Conclusion

What emerges from the discussion of entrepreneurs and entrepreneurship is an understanding that successful entrepreneurs are likely to possess a number of personal characteristics although no two will be alike; one individual may exhibit a high degree of innovation but wish to limit the amount of risk exposure, another will perceive the 'self-actualization' process as more important. A good track record in a previous business is undoubtedly of great help and provides a network of contacts to draw upon. These skills are vital in the early stage of business formation to survive and then to make informed decisions on how to grow the business. As SMEs dominate the tourism sector worldwide, the issues they face in the twenty-first century in the foundation by entrepreneurs is a valuable area of study, and researchers have begun to try and recognize what characteristics contribute to success. An example is the BBC series in 2005 *The Apprentice* (Sugar 2005) which tested many of the characteristics needed to be successful in business. Besides these individual features, the wider economic and political environment is extremely important; in a highly regulated environment, there is little incentive for personal enterprise. What is widely acknowledged is that certain sectors such as the restaurant and catering sector have high failure rates while other SMEs in tourism may hover around financial viability due to lifestyle reasons and cost subsidization from the use of family labour. Yet identifying the scale and extent of business failure in the tourism sector is notoriously difficult due to the sector's wide-ranging nature and data limitations in many countries. Even so, business failure does not deter serial entrepreneurs, especially as the experience of the dot.com boom illustrates: many of those who failed started up again later. Whilst crises like foot and mouth and 9/11 tipped many small businesses into liquidation, other companies got stronger by weathering such events. In developing countries, Gartner (2004) for example, notes the links between entrepreneurs and working in the informal economy where regulations or a lack of capital prohibit a formal business structure. Finally, the sociocultural environment must be considered to have a major effect. Media portrayal of entrepreneurs in the United States frequently show success as something to be admired whereas respect tends to be more grudging in western Europe.

Understanding entrepreneurship in tourism, particularly the process of innovation, is critical to fostering a competitive tourism sector. As agencies such as Scottish Enterprise show (www.scottish-enterprise.com), fostering innovation via its Tourism Innovation Development Awards, supporting an online innovation exchange and providing online case studies of successful innovation are all part of the wider support structure entrepreneurs and businesses require if they are to aim to do things better. Tourism innovation will continue to be one of the key buzz words which remains associated with supporting entrepreneurial and intrapreneurial activity to raise the standards, invest in new products and to drive tourism forward in all areas of the industry.

Discussion questions

1 Why is the study of entrepreneurship important in tourism?

2 What makes a successful tourism entrepreneur?

3 Identify the pre-conditions in the wider economy conducive to tourism entrepreneurship.

4 Why does the tourism sector have low entry barriers to starting a new business, and is this detrimental to the long-term viability of the sector?

References

Acs, Z. (2003) *Innovation and the Growth of Cities*. Cheltenham: Edward Elgar.

Branson, R. (1998) *Losing my Virginity – the Autobiography*. London: Virgin Publishing.

Bray, R. and Raitz, V. (2001) *Flight to the Sun: The Story of the Holiday Revolution*. London: Continuum.

Brown, B. (1987) 'Recent tourism in S.E. Dorset', in G. Shaw and A. Williams (eds) *Tourism and Development: Overviews and Case Studies of the UK and the SW Region*. Working Paper No. 4. Exeter: Department of Geography, University of Exeter.

Brown, P. and Scase, R. (1994) *Higher Education and Corporate Realities – Class, Culture and the Decline of Graduate Careers*. London: UCL Press.

Buckley, P. and Witt, S. (1985) 'Tourism in difficult areas: Case studies of Bradford, Bristol, Glasgow and Hamm', *Tourism Management*, 6 (3): 205–13.

Casson, M.C. (1982) *The Entrepreneur: An Economic Theory*. Oxford: Martin Robertson.

Dahles, H. (1999) 'Tourism small entrepreneurs in developing countries: A theoretical perspective', in H. Dahles and K. Braw (eds) *Tourism and Small Entrepreneurs, Development, National Policy and Entrepreneurial Culture: Indonesian Cases*. New York: Cognizant.

Davidson, R. and Maitland, R. (1997) *Tourism Destinations*. London: Hodder and Stoughton.

Dewhurst, P. and Horobin, H. (1998) 'Small business owners', in R. Thomas (ed.) *The Management of Small Tourism and Hospitality Firms*. London: Cassell.

Dondo, A. and Ngumo, M. (1998) 'Africa: Kenya', in A. Morrison, M. Rimmington and C. Williams, *Entrepreneurship in the Hospitality Tourism and Leisure Industries*. Oxford: Butterworth-Heinemann.

Drucker, P.F. (1985) *Innovation and Entrepreneurship*. London: Heinemann.

Drucker, P.F. (1989) *The New Realities*. London: Heinemann.

Echtner, C.M. (1995) 'Entrepreneurial training in developing countries', *Annals of Tourism Research*, 22 (1): 119–134.

EU (2001) *Working Together for the Future of European Tourism*. Brussels: EU.

Evans, N., Campbell, D. and Stonehouse, G. (2003) *Strategic Management for Travel and Tourism*. Oxford: Butterworth-Heinemann.

Fielden, L. and Davidson, M. (eds) (2005) *International Handbook of Women and Small Business Entrepreneurship*. Cheltenham: Edward Elgar.

Gartner, W. (2004) 'Factors affecting small firms in tourism: A Ghanaian perspective', in R. Thomas (ed.) *Small Firms in Tourism International Perspectives*. Oxford: Elsevier.

Getz, D. and Carlsen, J. (2000) 'Characteristics and goals of family and owner-operated businesses in rural tourism and hospitality sectors', *Tourism Management*, 21 (6): 547–60.

Getz, D. and Petersen, T. (2005) 'Growth and profit oriented entrepreneurship among family business owners in the tourism and hospitality industry', *Hospitality Management*, 24 (2): 219–42.

Goffee, R. and Scase, R. (1985) *Women in Charge: The Experiences of Female Entrepreneurs*. London: Allen and Unwin.

Hallenga-Brink, S. and Brezet, J. (2005) 'The sustainable innovation design diamond for micro-sized enterprises in tourism', *Journal of Cleaner Production*, 13: 141–9.

Hisrich, R.D. and Peters, M.P. (1992) *Entrepreneurship – Starting, Developing and Managing a New Enterprise, Second Edition*. Homewood, Irwin: IL.

Hjagler, A. (1999) 'The ecology of organizations in Danish tourism: A regional labour perspective', *Tourism Geographies*, 1(2): 164–82.

Hjagler, A. (2002) 'Repairing innovation defectiveness in tourism', *Tourism Management*, 23 (4): 464–74.

Hjorth, D. and Steyaert, C. (eds) (2004) *Narrative and Discursive Approaches to Entrepreneurship*. Cheltenham: Edward Elgar.

Hope, C. and Klemm, M. (2001)'Tourism in difficult areas revisited: The case of Bradford', *Tourism Management*, 22 (6): 629–35.

Lashley, C. and Morrison, A. (eds) (2000) *Franchising Hospitality Services*. Oxford: Butterworth-Heinemann.

Lennon, J. (ed.) (2001) *Tourism Statistics: International Perspectives and Current Issues*. London: Continuum.

Lerner, M. and Haber, S. (2001) 'Performance factors of small tourism ventures: The interface of tourism, entrepreneurship and the environment', *Journal of Business Venturing*, 16 (1): 77–100.

Lordkipanidze, M., Brezet, H. and Backman, M. (2005) 'The entrepreneurial factor in sustainable tourism development', *Journal of Cleaner Production*, 13: 787–98.

McKercher, B. (1998) *The Business of Nature Tourism*. Melbourne: Hospitality Press.

McMullan, W. and Long, W.A. (1990) *Developing New Ventures: The Entrepreneurial Option*. London: Harcourt Brace Jovanovitch.

Medlik, S. (1996) *Dictionary of Travel, Tourism and Hospitality, Second Edition*. Oxford: Butterworth-Heinemann.

Morrison, A. (ed.) (1998) *Entrepreneurship – An International Perspective*. Oxford: Butterworth-Heinemann.

Morrison, A., Rimmington, M. and Williams, C. (1999) *Entrepreneurship in the Hospitality Tourism and Leisure Industries*. Oxford: Butterworth-Heinemann.

Mudambi, R. (ed.) (2003) *Privatisation and Globalisation: The Changing Role of the State in Business*. Cheltenham: Edward Elgar.

Page, S.J. (2003) *Tourism Management: Managing for Change*. Oxford: Butterworth-Heinemann.

Page, S.J., Forer, P. and Lawton, G.R. (1999) 'Small business development and tourism: *Terra incognita?*' *Tourism Management*, 20, 435–59.

Peper, B., Doorne-Huiskes, A. and den Dulk, L. (eds) (2005) *Flexible Working and Organisational Change: The Integration of Work and Personal Life*. Cheltenham: Edward Elgar.

Porter, M. (1985) *Competitive Advantage: Creating and Sustaining Superior Performance*. New York: The Free Press.

Pyka, A. and Küpper, G. (eds) (2002) *Innovation Networks: Theory and Practice*. Cheltenham: Edward Elgar.

Reisman, D. (2004) *Schumpeter's Market: Enterprise and Evolution*. Cheltenham: Edward Elgar.

Sarasvathy, S. (2005) *Effectuation: Elements of Entrepreneurial Expertise*. Cheltenham: Edward Elgar.

Schumpeter, J. (1934) *The Theory of Economic Development*. Cambridge MA: Harvard University Press.

Schumpeter, J. (1952) *Can Capitalism Survive?* New York: Harper & Row.

Selin, S. (1999) 'Developing a typology of sustainable tourism partnerships', *Journal of Sustainable Tourism*, 7 (3/4): 260–73.

Shane, S. (2004) *A General Theory of Entrepreneurship: The Individual-Opportunity Nexus*. Cheltenham: Edward Elgar.

Shaw, G. (2004) 'Entrepreneurial cultures and small business enterprises in tourism', in A. Lew, C.M. Hall and A. Williams (eds) *A Companion of Tourism*. Oxford: Blackwell.

Shaw, G. and Williams, A.M. (1990) 'Tourism, economic development and the role of entrepreneurial activity', in C.P. Cooper (ed.) *Progress in Tourism, Recreation and Hospitality Management, Volume 2*. London: Belhaven

Shaw, G. and Williams, A.M. (1994) *Critical Issues in Tourism: A Geographical Perspective*. Oxford: Blackwell.

Shaw, G. and Williams, A. (2004a) 'From lifestyle consumption to lifestyle production: Changing patterns of tourism consumption', R. Thomas (ed.) *Small Firms in Tourism: International Perspectives*. Oxford: Elsevier.

Shaw, G. and Williams, A. (2004b) *Tourism and Tourism Spaces*. London: Sage.

Sheldon, P.J. (1995) 'Tour operators', in S.F. Witt and L. Moutinho (eds) *Tourism Marketing and Management Handbook*. Hemel Hempstead: Prentice Hall.

Smit, T. (1997) *The Lost Gardens of Heligan*. London: Victor Gollancz in association with Channel 4 Books.

Stalinbrass, C. (1980) 'Seaside resorts and the hotel accommodation industry', *Progress in Planning*, 13(2): 103–74.

Storey, D. (ed.) (2004) *The Management of Innovation*. Cheltenham: Edward Elgar.

Sugar, A. (2005) *The Apprentice*. London: BBC Books.

Tapscott, D. and Caston, A. (1993) *Paradigm Shift: The New Promise of Information Technology*. New York: McGraw Hill.

Thomas, R. (2004) *Small Firms in Tourism: International Perspectives*. Oxford, Elsevier.

Wan, D., Ong, C. and Lee, F. (2005) 'Determinants of firm innovation in Singapore', *Technovation*, 25(3): 261–8.

Wanhill, S. (2000) 'Small and medium tourism enterprises', *Annals of Tourism Research*, 27 (1): 132–47.

Welsch, H. (1998) 'America: North', in A. Morrison, (ed) *Entrepreneurship – An International Perspective*. Oxford: Butterworth-Heinemann.

WTTC (2001) *HR Opportunities and Challenges, A Report by the WTTC Human Resources Task Force*, Accessed 12.1.2005.

Yale, P. (1995) *The Business of Tour Operations*. Harlow: Longman.

Youell, R. (1996) *The Complete A–Z Leisure, Travel and Tourism Handbook*. London: Hodder and Stoughton.

Further reading

Thomas, R. (2004) *Small Firms in Tourism: International Perspectives*. Oxford: Elsevier.

The Role of the Public Sector in Tourism

Learning outcomes

After reading the chapter, and answering the questions the reader should be able to understand:

- the rationale for public sector intervention in tourism

- the function and role of the public sector in tourism activity

- the development and implementation of tourism policies in the public domain

- the role and responsibilities of national tourism organizations and other public sector agencies in the tourism sector.

Overview

This chapter discusses the role of the government and other agencies in the facilitation and development of tourism. The structure and activities of national tourism organizations and their regional partners are explored along with their coordination and liaison roles. The main focus of the chapter is on the reasons for public sector involvement in tourism, the activities of the sector and the mechanisms through which public sector objectives in tourism are achieved. International examples of public sector involvement and intervention in tourism are also discussed to highlight the impact and effect of policies and interventions on the tourism sector.

Introduction

The private sector, largely typified by profit-driven motives and entrepreneurial activity operating in a free market economy, forms a significant driver in tourism (see Chapter 12). However, as Pearce (1989) states:

> Provision of services and facilities characteristically involves a wide range of agents of development. Some of these will be involved indirectly and primarily with meeting the needs of tourists, a role that has fallen predominantly to the private sector in most countries. Other agents will facilitate, control or limit development...through the provision of basic infrastructure, planning or regulation. Such activities have commonly been the responsibility of the public sector with the government at various levels being charged with looking after the public's interest and providing goods and services whose cost cannot be attributed directly to groups or individuals. (Pearce 1989: 32)

This quotation from Pearce summarizes the basic issues that this chapter will examine:

- Why is the public sector involved in tourism?
- How do different organizations in the public sector manage tourism?

The development of tourism in specific countries is a function of the individual **government**'s predisposition towards this type of economic activity. In the case of outbound tourism, governments may curb the desire for mobility and travel by limiting the opportunities for travel through currency restrictions, as South Korea did in the 1980s, while still encouraging inbound travel. Similarly, in the USSR under the former Communist rule, the opportunities for domestic tourism were controlled by a limited supply of holiday infrastructure. However, such examples are not usual because most governments seek to maximize the domestic population's opportunities for mobility and travel by the provision of various modes of transport to facilitate the efficient movement of goods and people at a national level. To achieve the objective of encouraging tourism, policies must be formulated to guide the organization, management and development of tourism, which is where the public sector has an important role to play.

The government is a major influence in society and in tourism, and Elliot (1997) argues that the success of entrepreneurs like Thomas Cook would not have been possible without a stable and supportive government. The public sector plays a very significant role in facilitating, controlling and/or providing the context for tourism development.

Defining the public sector

The public sector is a somewhat nebulous grouping of organizations which comprises a range of government and government-based organizations. Their unifying focus is to deliver government policy and they have power to make decisions on aspects of strategic importance. Public sector bodies with an interest in tourism are linked together in a complex set of working relationships, designed to achieve objectives for wider good. To do this, the public sector uses taxation revenue to develop and implement policies and initiatives that benefit the community that it serves. Organizations that comprise the public sector are not commercially oriented institutions, although increasingly they operate with commercially driven objectives to ensure internal and external efficiency in utilizing limited resources.

The public sector operates at a number of different geographic levels in tourism, including:

- *Supra-national organizations,* working in the international or regional arena and involving a number of countries working in cooperation, the organization having greater power than individual countries on issues that transcend national interests. These organizations are likely to influence tourism planning and policy (e.g. United Nations, EU, ASEAN, APEC)
- *International organizations,* working on particular issues on an international policy area often in an advisory capacity (e.g. World Tourism Organization, UNESCO)
- *National governments,* working at the level of the state or country and often operated by a democratically elected group that represent the wider populace, supported by an employed

civil service. However, other styles of governance include dictatorships and non-democratic systems. National governments usually oversee tourism development through a **ministry** which may have tourism among a portfolio of other interests or which may be specifically focused on tourism. The level of national government involvement in tourism differs significantly between countries

- *Government-funded agencies*, often working within a particular policy or geographic area, these bodies are charged with implementing national or local government policy but with the freedom to manage their own affairs. These bodies are termed **QUANGO**s (quasi-autonomous non-governmental organizations) in the UK, and in many Western countries there has been a proliferation of such organizations since the 1980s (van Thiel 2004). Many national tourism organizations (NTOs) fall into this category

- *Local authorities*, working at the local level of a county or administrative area, and, in a democratic system, elected by the local community and supported by an employed staff. Local councils often play an important part in tourism development and promotion at the local level as Insight 14.1 shows.

Public sector interest in tourism stretches across all of these organizational and geographic dimensions. However, tourism development usually requires support and guidance from national government through policy. As Gunn and Var (2002: 114) state, governments 'have the choice of doing nothing or doing something constructive about public tourism policy'. Policy issues will be explored later in the chapter, but now the discussion moves on to consider why public sector interest in tourism exists.

INSIGHT 14.1

The role of local authorities in tourism in Scotland

There are 32 local authorities (known also as councils) across Scotland, and the role that they play in tourism is of crucial importance to ensuring that visitors have a satisfying and rewarding experience in the area. The main areas of involvement for local authorities includes:

- providing and maintaining infrastructure to support tourism

- ensuring that attractions are accessible

- providing useful information on local attractions and events

- achieving a high standard in the maintenance of the physical environment

- paying attention to safety, for example through street lighting, policing and inspection of premises

- assisting in the development of new and enhanced tourism products.

From this, it is clear that Scottish local authorities play a multifarious role in tourism facilitation and development. However, they also comprise a major stakeholder in tourism, providing direct and proactive contribution to the tourism product, as well as performing a support role. Tourism functions of local authorities are now explored below under two main headings.

Tourism support role

Within their area of jurisdiction, local authorities:

- are responsible for roads, planning, signposting, environmental health, public safety, licensing, trading standards and public transport coordination, all of which have a role to play in the potential success of an area's tourism product

- own, fund and manage public amenities, including museums and galleries, country parks, leisure facilities and public parks to serve the local community, but which facilities are also attractive to visitors

- employ a tourism officer or person whose portfolio includes tourism development

- provide information about their area and operate a website.

Such functions are fairly typical among local authorities on an international level. However, where Scotland differs from many regions is in the more direct role that the local authority plays in tourism, as illustrated below.

Tourism operations role

Funding
Scottish local authorities fund tourism through various means, for example:

1 They supply the main source of funding for the area tourist boards (ATBs), providing one-third of ATBs' revenue income overall. For some tourist boards, local authority funding is as high as 60 per cent of revenue.

2 Local authorities are a major promoter of tourism-related initiatives that are eligible for European Union (EU) funding, and during the period 1994–9, expenditure by Scottish councils on tourism-related projects funded by EU schemes was estimated at £71.8 million, mainly focused on the range, quality and marketing of the tourism product. Such a level of funding reflects the importance of tourism as part of an holistic approach to improving social and economic development.

Visitor attraction ownership

Contrary to the ethos that many governments have adopted with regard to tourism operations, in Scotland, many local authorities own visitor attractions, and thus directly interact with and profit from visitors. Local authorities own 47 per cent of the 1999 attractions not charging an admission fee, and 6 per cent of all 318 paid attractions. Of these attractions, local authorities are charged with running 21.5 per cent of the total. In 2001, sites owned by local authorities attracted around 15 million visitors and accounted for over 45 per cent of all visits to attractions in Scotland. One of the major areas of activity for local authorities is the museums and galleries sector, as shown in Table 14.1. Another particularly important feature of the tourism asset in Scotland is the provision of genealogical services for those seeking their ancestral roots, a service provided by the local authority library services.

In addition, the range of assets owned by local authorities which tourists use are diverse, from harbours and fisheries to arts venues, car parks, golf courses and even a racecourse, as well as the more traditional conference centres, parks and sporting facilities. Local authorities also fund and coordinate festivals and events, such as Highland Games and Hogmanay celebrations.

Tourism development and marketing

Local authorities are also major funders of direct services and partnership arrangements to support tourism development and marketing. Examples include:

- design and implementation of promotional campaigns
- film location support
- coordination, promotion and sponsorship of events
- town twinning
- interpretation of sites, such as town trails and country park guided walks
- tourism brochures and 'what's on' guides for the local area
- town centre management and enhancement schemes
- advice and support to tourism businesses through Small Business Gateway and Scottish Enterprise.

Local authorities are charged with applying commercial values in the operation and delivery of services, and adhere to a strict policy of 'best value'. This means that much of the work of Scottish local authorities in tourism is achieved through collaborative working with other public sector organizations and, where appropriate, the private sector, to achieve maximum efficiency.

A new system of public sector tourism support in Scotland has been introduced in the form of a new Integrated Scottish Tourism Network that replaces ATBs with 14 hubs integrated with the NTO, VisitScotland. In terms of the previous system of local authority funding for ATBs, grants have been replaced by partnership agreements where each local authority negotiates with VisitScotland for the tourism services they require. This will enable authorities to specify exactly what they receive for their money (www.scotexchange.net 'FAQs on the Tourism Review').

Source: Adapted from SLAED (2002); COSLA (2002); Economic Development and Planning Executive Group and VisitScotland (2004) www.scotexchange.net/tourism organisations.

TABLE 14.1 Visitor attractions owned by local authorities (LAs) in Scotland

Type of attraction	No. of sites owned by Scottish LAs	% of all sites in category owned by Scottish LAs	% of visitors to all sites in category owned by Scottish LAs
Museums/galleries	65	42	55
Heritage visitor centres	16	24	12
Country parks	12	80	97
Gardens	4	13	29
Historic houses	4	10	21
Historic sites	4	14	36
Safari/zoos	2	25	9

Source: Adapted from VisitScotland (2001) Visitor Attraction Monitor

The rationale for public sector involvement in tourism

Lickorish and Jenkins (1997) argued that tourism is too important for governments to leave to market forces alone due to the array of positive and negative impacts that tourism can create (see Chapters 17–20) that require some form of intervention. Such mitigating activity transcends the scope of the private sector. The scope and extent of national government involvement in tourism varies between countries and regions, depending on political ideology (i.e. a system of belief about an issue that structures our thoughts), level of national economic development and the importance of the industry. Ooi (2002) compares the different approaches taken by the governments of Singapore and Denmark as shown in Table 14.2, where Singapore retains strong state control in promoting a profit-driven culture, while in Denmark the state maintains a clear separation between private and public sectors and only offers the infrastructure necessary to stimulate business. Often, there is a direct and positive relationship between the importance of the industry and the amount of government involvement, so where tourism is a very significant part of a country's economy, or where tourism impacts are prominent, it is likely that government involvement will be high (Kerr 2003). For example, tourism has grown rapidly since the late 1980s in Ireland as a result of government policy to develop and maintain the growth and success of the sector within the nation's economy (Deegan and Dineen 1997), and government involvement remains strong. In Paris, on the other hand, tourism was never highlighted as a key policy area but subsumed in a wider urban strategy. Since the 1990s, tourism in the city has been addressed more directly by the public sector due to the negative impacts of traffic congestion and parking, rather than a direct approach to develop tourism (Pearce 1998).

Normally, the public sector does not have an involvement in tourism to directly profit from interaction with tourists, although conversely, in some regions, the public sector is a major stakeholder in tourism. Indeed, the work of the public sector in fulfilling its primary responsibility to

TABLE 14.2 Different approaches of the Danish and Singaporean tourism authorities		
	Copenhagen: Wonderful Copenhagen (WoCo) and Danish Tourist Board (DTB)	*Singapore: Singapore Tourist Board (STB)*
Cooperation with industry	Build cooperation with other business agencies	Cooperates with other state agencies in their social engineering programmes
	WoCo coordinates five tourism-related business networks	Cooperates with and offers policy support and financial resources to tourism businesses, such as retailers, attraction operators, and travel agencies
	DTB licenses tourist information centres around Denmark	License attraction operators, travel agencies, and guides in Singapore
Role of tourism authorities	Provide infrastructure for tourism businesses	Provides infrastructure for tourism businesses Initiates, manages, and provides financial and institutional support for tourism activities Engages in state social engineering programmes
Public–private separation	Maintains separation between public and private sectors	Merges private sector interest with public social interests
Business and culture relations	Advocates that business influences on culture should be balanced by letting these two spheres of activities decide for themselves	Advocates that business and culture complement each other

Source: Reprinted from *Annals of Tourism Research*, vol.29, Ooi, 'Contrasting tourism strategies: Tourism in Denmark and Singapore', 689–706, copyright (2002), reprinted with permission from Elsevier

its tax-paying citizens creates spin-offs from which tourists benefit, such as providing and maintaining infrastructure. The public sector also subsidizes and manages facilities and services for local people, from museums to swimming pools, and official events to national attractions, such as New Year celebrations, which are equally attractive to visitors and assist in developing tourism products and economic benefits for local communities.

The traditional rationale for public sector activity in tourism is to generate economic benefits, although in the new millennium a much wider rationale exists. The dominant policy of economic growth through tourism has been superseded in many destinations around the world by a broader base of objectives, including:

- community welfare
- **visitor satisfaction**
- **environmental and cultural protection**
- economic benefits.

Finding the balance to make these often conflicting goals work is fraught with difficulties, as Chapter 20 on sustainable tourism will further explore. Accordingly, government involvement in tourism crosses the spectrum of economic, environmental, social and political interests. The reasons outlined in Table 14.3 characterize public sector interest in tourism. So, having established the basic reasons as to why the public sector has an interest in tourism activity, the mechanisms through which involvement becomes manifest and the multiple roles that the sector plays are now explored.

The role of the public sector in tourism

A number of public sector tourism roles can be identified, which will vary in importance according to place. Drawing from the work of the International Union of Official Travel Organisations (IUOTO) in identifying the role of the state, Hall (2000) argues that the government now plays eight roles in tourism as follows:

Coordination

Duplication of resources between government-based tourism bodies and private bodies can be better avoided through greater coordination and information sharing, based on a common strategy which is founded on cooperation between agencies. However, as van Westering and Niel (2003) highlight, public sector organizations at different levels sometimes experience difficulties in working together towards collective goals and communications may be impaired due to differing political loyalties.

Planning

The wide remit of **planning** including the application and enforcement of development control strategies as well as tourism development strategies, allows the state to identify which areas and sectors are appropriate to develop for specified uses, in consultation with stakeholders (Chapter 25 provides a more detailed discussion on tourism planning processes). More recent functions which the public sector has assumed in view of the increasingly volatile nature of international tourism is the preparation of crisis management plans in anticipation of impending events, including scenario planning exercises associated with global issues such as the potential flu pandemic which was a subject of intense debate in 2005.

Legislation and regulation

Legislation and regulations not directly aimed at the tourism sector impinge upon its growth and development, ranging from immigration and visa regulations to employment policy. These and other statutory responsibilities are not an active form of intervention in tourism in most cases, but form the regulatory framework to which tourism activity must adhere. In some

TABLE 14.3   Public sector interest in tourism: Influential factors

Economic factors

- To improve the balance of payments in a country by generating hard currency through tourism
- To aid regional or local economic development and economic restructuring
- To help diversify the economy and encourage commercial developments
- To increase income levels in a country, region or specific locality
- To increase state revenues from taxation of tourism activity
- To generate new employment opportunities

Political factors

- To achieve political goals in relation to promoting a country's political acceptability as a place to visit, for example in Spain in the 1960s, the government promoted tourism to stimulate political acceptance of the Franco regime as well as foreign exchange
- To promote the development process through tourism, especially in less developed countries
- To ensure that development is consistent with political ideology, e.g. in Cuba, where there was an embargo on American visitors

Social and cultural factors

- To ensure the well-being of the individual, by legislating for paid holiday time and supporting 'social tourism', exemplified by the Soviet Union's network of holiday centres for workers
- To act as a catalyst of social change, for example facilitating closer interaction between host cultures and those from other countries
- To promote cultural awareness, appreciation and development through tourism

Environmental factors

- To address market failure, where unrestricted operation of the private sector results in, for example, degradation of the environment, exploitation of labour or erosion of culture
- To coordinate and undertake environmental enhancement works and visitor management schemes to manage the effects of tourism, as well as improving areas to attract visitors
- To raise awareness and support for environmental initiatives and regeneration schemes, such as visitor payback schemes

instances, regulations for tourism businesses have been proven to be unnecessarily bureaucratic as the UK government recognized in the 'Tomorrow's Tourism' policy (Department of Culture, Media and Sport 2004). Conversely, in other parts of the world, increased regulation of tourism has been argued for with respect to environmental and human rights issues.

Entrepreneurship

Governments and public sector bodies often own and operate tourism ventures or may own or manage land resources. This type of entrepreneurial activity appears to be declining particularly in countries where less public sector intervention is sought where there is an increase in **public–private partnerships** (see Chapters 12 and 13); in the latter case a direct financial return is sought by the public sector rather than development being undertaken for the public good. It is exemplified in urban and rural as well as seaside regeneration schemes where the life-cycle model has reached stagnation.

Stimulation

Mill and Morrison (1985) argue that stimulation may occur in three ways:

1 The public sector stimulates tourism supply through financial incentives such as providing tax relief to overseas investors in tourist developments to encourage foreign investment and generate employment. This may be necessary in destinations where there is insufficient experience or capital to finance tourism projects.

2 Sponsoring research to assist the development of the sector through knowledge and understanding of markets and product innovation. A good example of this is provided by the partnership work of VisitScotland, Scottish Enterprise and Tourism Knowledge Scotland (TKS), a consortium of Tourism Researchers in Scottish Universities, where dissemination of academic research is facilitated through an online database accessible to industry (see www.scotexchange.net/knowyourmarket).

3 Stimulation of demand through marketing and **promotion**, which is a significant area of work for the public sector (see below) and is explored more fully in Chapter 16 on destination marketing.

Marketing and promotion

One of the primary roles of the public sector in tourism is marketing and promotion aimed at increasing consumer interest in a destination (see Chapters 15 and 16). Such activity is undertaken at different geographic levels but is normally coordinated through an NTO, which reflects national tourism policies. The curiosity in this is that the public sector promotion rarely has much control over the products that are being marketed which are largely owned, managed and operated within the private sector. But NTOs have embraced the concept of destination branding globally, as well as unique selling propositions (USPs), the unique features of a locality and area which gives it a distinct competitive advantage (Morgan and Pritchard 2002), which are explored further in Chapter 16. Such marketing activities are outside the scope of private sector alone, although the private sector is an integral part of the marketing process.

Providing social tourism

Historically, many governments actively participated in or issued policy statements on social tourism: providing holiday opportunities to marginalized groups such as those on low incomes or for the general population within a state-supported framework, as seen in the former USSR (Worthington 2003). There has been a substantial decline in social tourism in recent years reflecting a reduced governmental intervention on the individual as opposed to the public interest. An exception is the Kyrgyzstan Republic, which is actively developing mechanisms for social tourism. Social tourism activity now occurs more in the not-for-profit sector (e.g. the Family Holidays Association in the UK) and is more common in Scandinavia and Europe. Examples can be found on the International Bureau of Social Tourism website (www.bits-int.org).

Protector of the public interest

The government's role is to serve as an intermediary between competing interests and act as a balance between those seeking short-term gain and those with long-term interests. The public sector's responsibility is to act in the collective interest to prevent such abuses and resolve conflict (Jeffries 2001). This is not the case in non-democratic countries with a centralized approach to development, in instances where the democratic process is brought into question or simply when dubious decisions are made within democratic processes. Indeed, governments can sometimes act against community interests in the cause of generating economic benefits from tourism, as in the case of the build-up to Visit Myanmar Year in 2000, where the military government of Myanmar forced communities to move in order to build new tourist accommodation (see Chapter 24).

Pearce (1989) contests that the public sector does not have clearly defined responsibilities in relation to tourism and because there are often a large number of different bodies with a tourism interest, a resultant lack of coordination, duplication of effort or in some cases, neglect occurs. For example, in 2003 the UK national government launched its UK Airport Policy plan to expand many UK airports and many of the schemes compromised local and regional government schemes for their localities, illustrating a less than harmonious approach to tourism-related development. Such a diverse set of functions and roles normally require a *policy* to guide public sector activity. Although by no means a panacea, a defined policy and integrated system for implementation can help to achieve strategic objectives more effectively.

Tourism policy

The term 'policy' is frequently used to denote the direction and objectives an organization wishes to pursue over a set period of time. Policy tends to focus at the macro level, while planning (see Chapter 25) normally focuses more at the micro level and implementation of policy (Hall 2000). According to Turner (1997), the policy process is a function of three interrelated issues:

- the intentions of political and other key actors
- the way in which decisions and non-decisions are made
- the implications of these decisions.

The policy-making process is a continuous process and Figure 14.1 outlines a simplified model of the policy process which is applicable to the way tourism issues are considered by government bodies. Hall and Jenkins (1995) argue that state policy is a consequence of the political environment, values and ideologies, the distribution of power, institutional frameworks and the decision-making process within a country. Tourism policy reflects the strategic direction that a government deems appropriate to follow although, in a democratic context, the process of policy formulation is also open to industry stakeholders, communities, development agencies and those with an interest in tourism development. Hall (2000) argues that it is more effective for countries to follow a tourism policy than a wider economic development strategy that incorporates tourism.

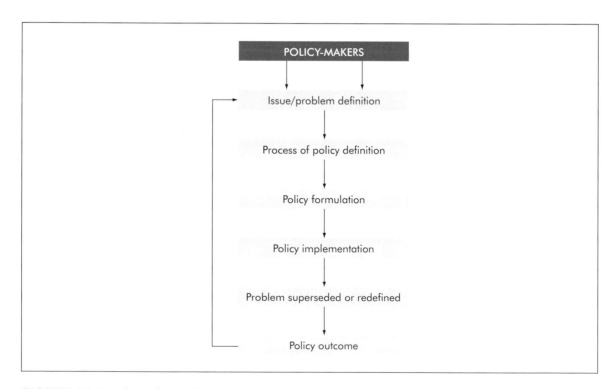

FIGURE 14.1 The policy-making process

Some countries have followed tourism policies for many years, while others have more recently developed a framework for tourism as they have emerged as international players, e.g. the Baltic States. In the case of India, which issued its first tourism policy in 1982, the key elements of the redesigned 2002 National Tourism Policy aim to position tourism as a major engine of economic growth and to harness the potential of India as a destination. The policy acknowledges the critical role of government acting as a proactive facilitator and catalyst, working in partnership with other bodies. In the UK, national government policy focuses on promoting a favourable economic climate for enterprise and investment and therefore assisting the industry to develop. Part of this strategy, for example, focuses on reducing or simplifying burdensome regulations for businesses. However, the national approach also acknowledges a

Image 14.1: Tourism policy in India has utilized many of its heritage resources, such as the Taj Mahal

need for integrated or 'joined-up' thinking in tourism as an industry that is impacted on by a number of government areas, such as transport, planning, operational regulations and licensing, employment regulations and strategic funding.

While there are certainly some generic features of tourism policy, particularly in terms of economic impacts, some governments are particularly focused on other aspects of development and the role that tourism can play in fostering growth in specific parts of the economy. One example is Nigeria, where the main thrust of government policy on tourism introduced in 1990, aside from the more universal objectives of generating foreign exchange and employment, is to encourage rural development by promoting tourism-based rural enterprises and accelerating rural urban integration and exchange.

One other interesting example of tourism policy and changing political ideology is the case of China. China first opened its doors to the West and tourism in 1978, as discussed by Zhang, King and Ap (1999) and after during the 1980s and 1990s it went through considerable change to accommodate growth, development, investment and change to attract international visitors. The following features summarize the principal policy changes which occurred:

- China to all intents and purposes was a developing country in terms of tourism in 1978, with a limited private sector able to develop tourism
- the government played a major role as an operator of tourism infrastructure and plant up to 1978
- post-1978, the role of the state expanded to become one of regulator, stimulator of investment, promoter of tourism opportunities, coordinator of tourism activities among government departments and promotor of the establishment of education and training initiatives
- as a planner, with a National Tourism Plan, the state set the direction of tourism policy and development with a shift from politics to economics in the philosophy underpinning tourism development
- in a developing country such as China, tourism may need to be pump-primed and a lead taken by the state to promote development
- the state needed to foster overseas investment where internal resources are limited. The investment climate is essential to gain internationally recognized and quality development
- in the policy arena, the power base, key actors (e.g. Deng Xiao-Ping), institutional arrangements and interest groups provide a powerful influence on tourism policy-making and policy measures can gradually change the direction and nature of tourism development.

This example shows that tourism policy-making is a key element shaping public sector involvement and, for this reason, it is pertinent to now focus on the public policy framework in which tourism is developed and managed.

The public policy framework for tourism

At a global scale, there are a number of agencies who have an influential impact upon tourism. The most significant of these is the World Tourism Organization (WTO), a specialist agency of the United Nations Development Programme established to maximize the benefits of tourism while minimizing the negative impacts. The WTO was originally set up as the International Congress of Official Tourist Traffic Associations in 1925, becoming the WTO in 1975. The WTO encourages government involvement in tourism in partnership with other stakeholders, including the private sector, local authorities and non-government organizations (NGOs). It promotes international cooperation, serves as a forum for tourism issues globally and provides more practical assistance for its members, such as tourism planning, market intelligence, statistical information (as outlined in Chapter 3), education and training. The WTO also plays an advisory role in relation to, for example, technological development in tourism, harmonization of policies and practices in terms of trade, quality and safety, achieving sustainable development through tourism and funding sources. The WTO is based in Madrid and has a very useful website (www.world-tourism.org) which provides regular newsletters and press releases as well as a statistics database (for subscribers) and a list of the reports it produces. At an international level, a number of associated organizations also undertake activities which impact upon tourism, including transport industry bodies such as the International Air Transport Association (IATA), the International Civil Aviation Organization (ICAO) and interest groups such as the Air Transport Action Group (ATAG). The Organization for Economic Co-operation and Development (OECD) also has an involvement in tourism, producing publications for its member countries. These bodies have a coordinating and influencing role on governments and, at a regional level, bodies such as the Pacific Asia Tourism Associaton (PATA) exercise considerable influence over tourism organization and policy. The European Union (EU) is a good example of a transnational body which provides a policy framework for tourism and this seeks to coordinate and liaise with the diverse stakeholders interest groups and organizations to consider.

According to Cooper *et al.* (2005) the EU's role in tourism is one of simplifying, harmonizing and reducing restrictions on trade, which in this case is travel. The main thrust of the EU's tourism activities are directed towards improving the quality of tourism services, encouraging the development of inbound tourism from outside the EU as well as improving the business environment for tourism enterprises and ensuring a sustainable environment for tourism. Given the diversity of tourism products and experiences within member states, the EU effectively leaves tourism policy to the member states. However, the EU's main action occurs in relation to the gathering of tourism statistics, improvements to transport infrastructure that impacts upon tourism and the easing of frontier formalities and image promotion with the European Travel Commission (a non-profit-making body with 21 member countries). The impact of EU grants on tourism has been extensively researched and a number of good studies exist (e.g. Pearce 1992 and Bull 1999). Beyond the standard arguments for unification, the reason for the EU's intervention in tourism, as Hall (2000) and Cooper *et al.* (2005) argue, can be summarized as follows:

- the transnational character and operation of some tourism business calls for a European-wide policy framework
- concerns about environmental, social and cultural dimensions of tourism development, necessitating the drive towards safeguarding natural and cultural resources and sustainable and balanced tourism growth
- development of **regional policy**, particularly in disadvantaged areas, where public sector financial support is required to kick-start and sustain businesses as well as providing or improving essential infrastructure
- improving the quality and competitiveness of the tourism product, through funding programmes, dissemination of **best practice**, market information and training
- retaining cultural identity and the promotion of the concept of 'Europe'.

Information on EU tourism activity can be found on the website europa.eu.int. While organizations working in the international arena play an important role in tourism, it is national governments and agencies that exercise the greatest level of influence over tourism activities within a country.

National tourism organizations

One of the most useful sources to consult on tourism organizations is Pearce (1992) which examines a wide range of country examples of tourism organizations, especially NTOS. There are wide variations in the administrative frameworks developed within countries to manage and promote tourism. Figure 14.2 illustrates the statutory framework for the administration of tourism in the UK. The NTO is usually a state-funded or hybrid organization which is state-private sector funded

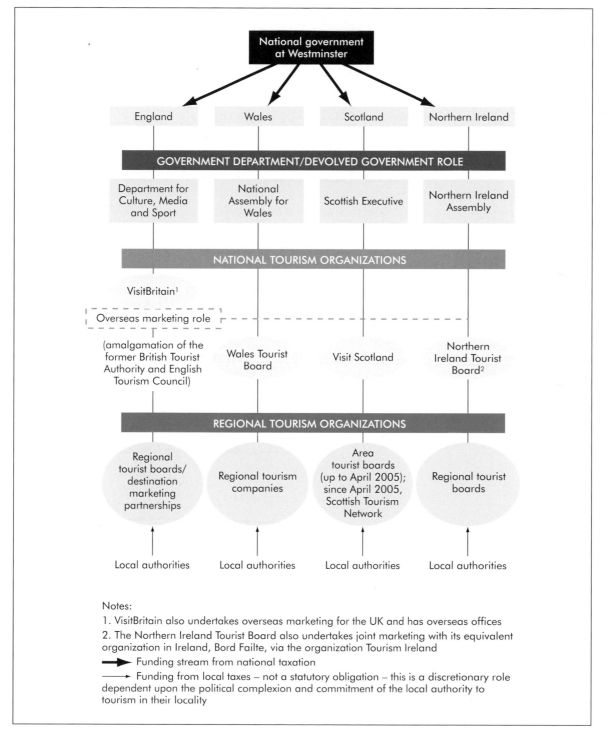

FIGURE 14.2   The statutory framework for the administration of tourism in the UK

and often located within a ministry of tourism (see Figure 14.3 for the structure of an NTO in Greece). The NTO may be inside or outside the ministry of tourism, depending on whether the state wants a government or semi-government agency to direct tourism. It normally has a board of directors, a constitution enacted by law and a degree of independence from the political system. The funding of the NTO is usually agreed by the ministry by a purchasing or direct funding agreement, typically annually. In some countries, the NTO is termed a 'convention and visitor bureau', where revenue is raised from a range of sources (such as the private sector and sometimes through tourist taxes). Many NTOs operate overseas offices from where overseas marketing can be more effectively organized, for example VisitBritain has 31 overseas offices,

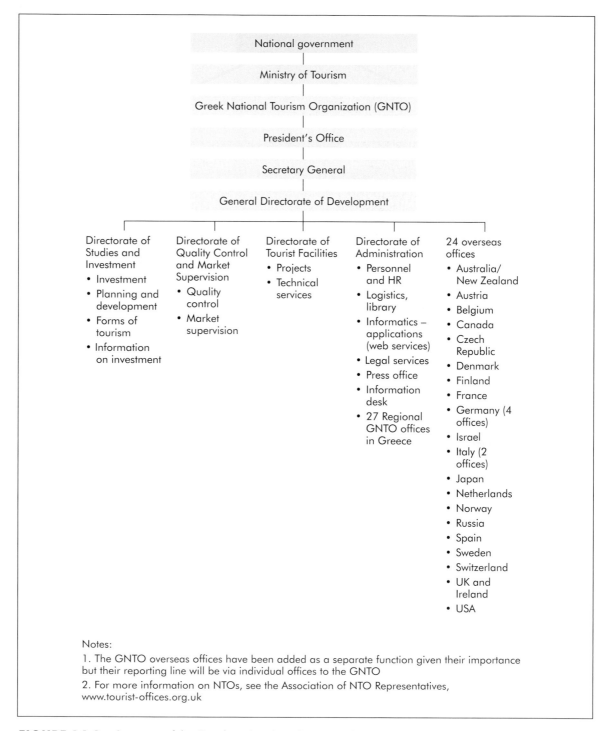

FIGURE 14.3 Structure of the Greek national tourism organization

including newly emerging markets like South Korea and Russia. Overseas NTO offices work with the local media and travel trade to stimulate interest in visiting their particular country.

Not all nations have government-funded NTO. Despite being one of the country's largest industries, the United States Congress voted to suspend funding of its tourism office (US Travel and Tourism Administration) in 1996. Without a nationally funded and coordinated tourism marketing agency, the Travel Industry Association of America (TIA), a non-profit industry association, stepped in. The TIA created the universal brand for the US tourism product 'SeeAmerica' (see Chapter 16) in partnership with more than 2000 leading travel industry organizations to promote the United States as the world's premier tourism destination. However, while there is no federal body in charge of tourism in the USA, there are a large number of state tourism offices and a small number of regional organizations consisting of states, such as Discover New England. In addition, there are many destination marketing organizations that work on a much smaller scale such as counties, resorts and towns. Government funding is made available to support tourism development objectives, for example the US$10m approved by Congress in November 2004 to build on efforts to promote the USA as an international travel destination after a dramatic decline post-9/11 (also see Chapter 26).

The 1990s have seen many changes to NTOs, particularly to their funding, as states have sought to encourage the private sector to contribute more to the running of NTOs with some countries using tourist taxes as a means of funding the NTO. The structure of the Singapore Tourism Board (STB), which can be consulted at www.stb.com.sg, shows that the STB is one of the larger NTOs in an international context. It is funded by the state and was established in 1964 to promote Singapore as a tourist destination. In 1996, the STB launched its 'Tourism 21: Vision of a Tourism Capital' (see Insight 14.2) which was a public–private sector initiative for developing tourism in Singapore in the new millennium so Singapore would become a regional tourism capital in South East Asia.

Clearly, the NTO performs a wide range of roles but its main functions can largely be categorized into:

- development (including **research** and tourism plans)
- information provision
- pricing
- controlling access to key tourist sites
- marketing.

It is the latter function – marketing – to which attention now turns.

INSIGHT 14.2

The Singapore Tourism Board's vision for tourism and Tourism 21

The STB's vision of Singapore as a tourism capital embodies an exciting and memorable destination; a regional hub for travellers and tourism investors; and a centre of excellence in tourism business expertise, ideas and networks. It is a vision of a vibrant and progressive city-state, yet filled with Asian warmth and hospitality; a place where East and West meet, and the old and new coexist in harmony; a gateway for travellers and business professionals to make their voyage in to the region and beyond.

Source: Modified from STB (www.stb.com.sg/corporate/index/htm)

In terms of Tourism 21, the STB will be realized through six strategic thrusts:

- redefining tourism
- reformulating the product
- developing tourism as an industry
- configuring new tourism space
- partnering for success
- championing tourism.

This is designed as a new blueprint for Singapore's tourism industry in the new millennium.

Marketing tourism and the NTO

Marketing is usually the primary function of an NTO. Oppermann and Chon (1997) highlight a key factor associated with the growth of tourism in less developed countries (LDCs) which is the aggressive marketing by NTOs. However, NTO finances are quite variable and, as Morgan and Pritchard (2000) point out, the budgets of some of the US state travel offices exceed that of some countries' national tourism budgets. Pike (2004) identified the top ten budgets of NTOs as shown in Table 14.4. The grant-in-aid provided by the Department for Media, Culture and Sport to promote Britain overseas for 2004/05 was £35.5m. As Morgan and Pritchard (2000) and Pike (2004) comment, such figures pale into insignificance when compared with the budgets of other global brands competing for consumers' discretionary spend.

The marketing activity of an NTO includes a number of tasks, from preparing a marketing plan and subsequent advertising campaigns to organizing familiarization tours for the press or travel industry, creating newsletters and attending trade and consumer exhibitions. The NTO is increasingly charged with creating a **brand image** of a destination, which is discussed in Chapter 16.

The process of identifying a destination's key tourism resources is a key component of marketing planning, as discussed in the next chapter, which shows that tourism assets can be a competitive advantage. For example, the Canadian Tourism Commission created a vision and a **mission statement** for tourism using an audit process shown in Table 14.5. This illustrates the initial assessment of Canada's market position and natural tourism assets. From this, a vision and mission was developed, and the mission was:

Canada's tourism industry will deliver world-class cultural and leisure experiences year round, while preserving and sharing Canada's clean, safe, natural environments. The industry will be guided by the values of respect, integrity and empathy. (Smith 2003: 130)

In terms of developing this mission, Smith identified a number of challenges: 'For example, while the vision was seen as laudable for the nation as a whole, not every business or destination has a realistic opportunity to develop into a world-class, four-season operation' (Smith 2003: 130).

Other agencies involved in tourism in the public sector

Below the NTO in most countries there is often a complex web of organizations which complement the work of the NTO at the regional and local level. While their activities are often a scaled-down version of the NTO's work at a regional level, they often implement national policy and pursue integrated activities with the NTO providing guidance in a top-down approach. Pearce (1992) examines the activities of the regional tourism organizations (RTOs) in different countries and discusses their varied roles.

Other organizations also exist with a wide remit for enhancing economic development in a locality, such as Enterprise Companies, often have a tourism interest in this respect, with an agenda to boost or diversify the economy (see Insight 14.3 at the end of the chapter). In addition, public sector bodies also encompass agencies like National Park Authorities, who have a substantial interest in tourism planning and visitor management at park level.

One of the growing areas of activity in the 1980s and 1990s in the public sector has been an increase in interest and response at the local level, often at the city or area level, where tourism has become a major issue to manage. Page and Thorn (1997, 2002) examine the situation in New Zealand where the Resource Management Act and its principles of sustainable planning combined with a market-led approach to tourism policy and planning placed the emphasis on the public sector in the regions and localities to plan and manage tourism growth. An interesting insight is provided by Page and Hall (1999) who point to the 1997 Inquiry by the Parliamentary Commissioner for the Environment on the management of the environmental effects associated with the tourism sector, which highlighted the potential for negative environmental and sociocultural impacts from tourism development, particularly with respected to Maori. The Inquiry concluded that the environmental qualities underpinning tourism are at risk

TABLE 14.4 The world's top ten National Tourism Organization budgets in 1997

Country	Budget (US$ millions)
Spain	147
Mexico	103
Thailand	94
Brazil	92
Australia	88
Singapore	87
Puerto Rico	79
China/Hong Kong	68
South Korea	63
France	58

Source: Reprinted from *Destination Marketing Organisations*, Pike, copyright (2004), reprinted with permission from Elsevier

TABLE 14.5 Initial assessment of Canadian market position

Image	Core competencies	General product base	International advantages
Moose, mountains and Mounties	Natural beauty, protected in parks	Wide-open spaces	Cities (e.g., Québec City, Montréal, Toronto, Calgary, Vancouver)
Space	Clean, safe, sophisticated cities	Cities	Resorts, including skiing and golf
Scenery	Easy accessibility	Extensive inventory of protected spaces	Touring corridors (e.g., Windsor–Québec City, North-of-Superior, BC Coast, Rockies, Atlantic Canada)
Spiritual	Proximity of cities/outdoors	Culture (including Aboriginal, immigrant, bilingual)	Sportfishing (both fresh and salt)
Safe	Culture	Skiing (long/narrow runs and bowls, heli-skiing, reliable snow)	Ecotourism
Oasis of calm	Safety	Four seasons	
Socially conscious	Hospitable population	Festivals and events	
Civility	Little pollution		
Clean	Not densely developed		
Unspoiled	Price		
Multi-cultural	Canadian Arctic Variety of coastal areas Wine regions Strong packaging potential Strong regional products		

Source: Reprinted from *Tourism Management*, vol.24, Smith, 'A vision for the Canadian tourism industry', 123–33, copyright (2003), with permission from Elsevier

in some areas and noted that visitor pressure on some 'icon' attractions (e.g. Waitomo Caves and Milford Sound) could not be sustained in the medium term without attention being given to reducing adverse visitor effects. In the light of the new NZTB (New Zealand Tourism Board) tourism marketing campaign for New Zealand it is also notable that the Inquiry concluded that the marketing activities of NZTB may have outstripped the capacity of the tourism sector to manage the environmental consequences of tourism growth.

This is interesting as it shows another government agency questioning the market-driven approach of the NZTB. Page and Thorn (1997, 2002) illustrate that the role of local and regional councils in New Zealand highlighted that many localities were unprepared for the impact of tourism. As a consequence, there is a greater role for the public sector, as Dredge and Moore (1992: 20) mooted where

> increased tourism growth will result in greater challenges for the integration of tourism and town planning. These challenges will be brought about by the need for the development of attractions, transport, support services and infrastructure to cater for increased visitor numbers, and the implications this will have for land use planning...Planners have a responsibility to meet challenges offered by the growth in tourism and to understand how their activities affect tourism.

The outcome of this statement is reflected in many destinations around the world, where local government becomes responsible for implementing visitor management measures to manage tourism more effectively. For example, some 600 coaches (often old, noisy and polluting) a day used to visit Salzburg in the 1990s, and passengers often spent less than two hours in the city. The city council prohibited coaches from entering the centre unless passengers were staying overnight. However, businesses complained of a decline in patronage as a result of fewer coach visitors (Orbaşli and Shaw 2004). Another good example is the historic city of York in the UK, which attracts about four million visitors per year, creating about £291 million in visitor spend and supporting over 9000 jobs (10 per cent of the population) in 2003. The council's view until recently was to control and contain tourism, and the city was not actively promoted as a destination (Meethan 1997). Traffic management has been a key theme, as about two-thirds of visitors arrive by car. Measures to address this include park and ride, pedestrianization, a ban on coaches entering the city centre and signposting to aid visitor flow around the centre. However, a policy change to boost economic growth has seen York City Council establishing the public–private partnership 'First Stop York' in 1995, with the main aims of maximizing economic and employment benefits from tourism and emphasizing quality, as well as managing negative environmental and social impacts and stimulating resident support for tourism (see Snaith and Haley 1999). Some of the key achievements have included:

- generating 14.8 per cent more longer stays in the city
- increasing visitor expenditure by 22.4 per cent
- increasing the number of jobs opportunities for local people
- launching popular events
- new destination signs on the A1 trunk road
- a substantial improvement in the standing of tourism in the city (York Tourism Bureau 2003).

Local authorities play an important role in shaping the role and impact of tourism in local areas, often in tandem with other public and private sector organizations. However, Hope and Klemm (2001) argue that support for tourism from local government cannot be relied on for two reasons. First, local authorities do not have a statutory responsibility to promote tourism and, second, it is difficult to obtain data that prove that tourism contributes to the local economy. In addition, as Ashworth and Tunbridge (2000: 66) argue, and as shown in the example of York, tourism can sometimes be viewed 'as a problem to be contained, not an opportunity to be welcomed' in cities such as Venice (see Chapter 21).

Public sector intervention in tourism

While some governments view the market economy as an adequate arena for tourism to operate within, others actively pursue interventionist policies to produce desired outcomes. Governments that are more likely to use interventionist policies are those whose countries are dependent on tourism as an economic agent or where tourism is creating significant problems (Kerr 2003). Some examples of intervention include:

1. Incentives to developers

The government has the capacity to alter regulations in order to provide an appealing climate for developers, particularly foreign investors able to bring in capital to start projects and developments that will bring economic benefits to a country or region in the longer term. The Indian government views tourism as a major growth area and generator of economic benefits and the new tourism policy aims to assist the development of physical infrastructure. Incentives to developers that have been approved include:

- concession rates on customs duty of 25 per cent for goods that are required for the initial setting up or substantial expansion of hotels
- fifty per cent of profits derived by hotels, travel agents and tour operators in foreign exchange are exempt from income tax. The remaining profits are also exempt if reinvested in a tourism-related project
- approved hotels are entitled to import essential goods relating to the hotel and tourism industry up to the value of 25 per cent of the foreign exchange earned by them in the preceding licensing year. This limit for approved travel agents/tour operators is 10 per cent
- hotels in locations other than the four major metro cities (Bombay, Delhi, Calcutta and Madras) are entitled to a 30 per cent deduction from profit, for a ten-year period, and hotels in designated tourist areas or heritage areas (adapted from www.tourismofindia.com 2002).

2. Tourist taxes

Governments often levy taxes on the tourism sector, the most common in the form of taxes on airport departure and hotel occupancy, for the sole purpose of raising revenue. More recently, taxes have been levied on tourists for environmental reasons. The best cited example is that of the Balearic Islands, where the pressure of mass tourism has led to significant environmental problems. The government of the Balearic Islands established an ecotax in 2002 which was levied on individuals staying in tourist accommodation per night. The revenue generated is drawn into a fund to address environmental initiatives on the islands (Palmer and Riera 2003). However, in 2003 the Minister for Tourism claimed that the ecotax had had a negative effect on tourism to the islands and resulted in a competitive disadvantage with other island destinations.

Byron Bay in Australia, which receives in excess of 1.7 million tourists per year, is a town that has witnessed huge tourism growth. As a result of an influx of tourists and second home owners, the **local authority** has a funding crisis, unable, for instance, to place adequate resources into improving sewerage capacities and placing pressure on other services, such as hospitals and public transport. One of the main reasons why this situation has arisen is that the revenue gained from the small permanent population through rates is insufficient to cover the costs associated with the tourist population. Suggestions to improve the flow of funding have included imposing a fee on day visitors and tourists by designating Byron Bay as a National Park. Recommendations being considered more widely in Australia include imposing a surcharge on airline tickets, provision of a fee from state government to the local authority based on numbers of tourists, placing a 50 per cent surcharge on the rates payable on second home owners and charging a toll on certain highways. In Brisbane, a local government consortium suggested placing a levy of $200 on international tourists to cover tourism infrastructure costs. Such measures represent mechanisms by which local authorities can shift the burden of expenditure from their own budgets (and local residents) to visitors, but are often contentious, as many believe that increases in holiday costs may motivate tourists to find alternative destinations.

INSIGHT 14.3

The role of Scottish Enterprise in the development of tourism, Paul McCafferty, Scottish Enterprise Forth Valley

Scottish Enterprise (SE) was formed in 1990 by the New Towns and Enterprise Scotland Act 1990, which brought together the Scottish Development Agency and the Training Agency.

SE is Scotland's main economic development agency, funded by the Scottish Executive, and the mission of the organization is to help the people and businesses of Scotland succeed. In doing so, the aim is to build a world-class economy. As well as companies and individuals, SE also works with universities, colleges, local authorities and other public sector bodies to achieve these goals.

The organization's headquarters are located at Atlantic Quay in Glasgow. It also has 12 local offices (local enterprise companies) across the country. SE covers the southern half of Scotland, from the Grampians right down to the Borders. Similar services are provided by Highlands and Islands Enterprise within the Highlands of Scotland.

The budget of SE in 2003/04 was approximately £445 million to support the commitment by the Scottish Executive to develop Scotland's economy.

The development of tourism is one of many areas in which SE commits resources. The organization's role in the development of the tourism industry is driven by the Scottish Executive's economic development strategy, 'A Smart, Successful, Scotland.' This identifies three key priorities – growing businesses, developing skills and learning and strengthening global connections.

A key focus of SE's work with tourism businesses is to stimulate innovation and creativity in Scottish tourism businesses, which encourages the development of new or refreshed products and services to attract or retain visitors. Investment in the quality and skills of staff is another area of priority as this has a fundamental impact on business performance. The final priority for activity by SE in tourism development is in supporting Scotland to be internationally competitive in tourism, through investment in the right tourism infrastructure to enable visitors to access and enjoy what Scotland has to offer and to provide an environment in which tourism businesses can successfully compete with other destinations.

Much of the tourism development activity delivered by the agency is done in partnership, both with the private sector and with other public agencies involved in tourism delivery.

These include VisitScotland and its local network of offices, as well as local authorities, the National Park Authorities and Forestry Commission Scotland, amongst others.

Examples of project delivery

Innovation

SE is involved in a range of projects and activities to help companies to develop new and improved ways of working.

These include the development and delivery of a Tourism Innovation Toolkit which contains practical techniques for use by companies to assist in identifying potential new products and services. To support the implementation of the best ideas, SE operates a Tourism Innovation Development Awards scheme, which can provide up to £15 000 matched funding to those projects and ideas which demonstrate genuine innovation.

Recognizing the importance of knowledge transfer in the innovation process, SE has worked with VisitScotland to establish Tourism Knowledge Scotland, which is a network of tourism experts from within Scottish universities who have established a range of mechanisms to highlight research relevant to industry.

Product development

SE has undertaken substantial research into product development in a number of destinations, and has discovered that the most popular tourist destinations have focused their product development around their unique areas of competitive advantage.

Some examples of product development activity in which SE has been involved includes, Scotlandwhisky, which is an industry-led initiative which aims to highlight Scotland as a quality tourism destination through the global recognition of whisky. The project has developed a network of 40 whisky embassies, where staff have been trained and where visitors can be assured of a positive whisky experience. Ancestral Tourism is another product development project in which SE has played a part. SE is a member of the project steering group, which has prepared a plan to enhance the customer experience by improving access to information, encouraging businesses to work together to develop new products and working with VisitScotland to ensure a cohesive approach to marketing.

Skills

A variety of courses and events have been developed by SE to ensure that staff are equipped with the knowledge and experience required by businesses.

The programme is the most comprehensive in the UK, and includes the highly successful Gleneagles Masterclasses series which attract world-class inspirational and motivational speakers. A number of Executive Development Learning Journeys have been delivered to a range of locations, including the Disney Learning Institute in Florida, Cape Cod and Schindlerhof Hotel and Creative Conference Centre in Nuremburg in Germany.

Destination development

A number of initiatives have been developed which are designed to improve the quality of the visitor experience at some of Scotland's key tourism destinations. The approach is to work closely with industry and public sector partners. Destinations where this approach has been applied include St Andrews, where the St Andrews World Class project has been developed, and the Loch Lomond and Trossachs National Park, where Destination Loch Lomond is emerging as an integrated programme of activity to maximize the quality of the destination.

Local context

Scottish Enterprise Forth Valley is one of the 12 local enterprise companies that form the SE network. Covering the local authority areas of Stirling, Falkirk and Clackmannanshire, tourism is one of the key sectors which the enterprise company supports as a priority. The area also boasts part of Scotland's first National Park, in the Loch Lomond and Trossachs area; Scotland's newest designated city, in Stirling; and one of the most successful recent additions to Scotland's visitor attraction portfolio, in the Falkirk Wheel (Image 14.2).

The performance of the area in terms of economic impact generated by tourism within the Forth Valley area can be illustrated using STEAM data, which is a trend model which estimates tourism volumes and values to a region (see Table 14.6).

SE Forth Valley has prioritized its tourism investment within the city of Stirling area, and in the Loch Lomond and Trossachs National Park, which covers much of rural Stirling.

Within the city, a range of projects have been developed in partnership with Stirling Council as part of the strategy 'Making Stirling Work'. The projects developed include a programme for investment in the city centre public realm, to improve the quality of the city centre for visitors, tourists and locals alike, as well as encouraging private sector investment. A new strategy for orientation and interpretation has also been prepared for implementation in future years. An events strategy for the Stirling area has also been developed, which will aim to both generate economic benefit to the region, as well as assisting in raising the profile of Stirling as a tourism destination.

The commitment which SE Forth Valley has made to the Loch Lomond and Trossachs National Park, forms part of SE's destination development activity.

The priorities for investing in projects within the park have been developed around a number of key themes as shown in Table 14.7.

Investment by Scottish Enterprise Forth Valley in the Loch Lomond and Trossachs National Park around these themes in the period of 2002–2008 is likely to be in the region of £3 million.

Further information

Further information on Scottish Enterprise activity in developing tourism can be found at:
www.scottish-enterprise.com
www.scotexchange.net
or contact tourisminformation@scotent.co.uk

Image 14.2: Scottish Enterprise and other public sector agencies supported the development of this flagship attraction – the Falkirk Wheel

TABLE 14.6   Tourism revenue for the Forth Valley area 2002–2003

Revenue by district	2003 £m	2002 £m	% change
Clackmannanshire	16.41	15.06	9
Falkirk	65.84	60.68	9
City of Stirling	236.03	230.66	2
Rural Stirling	115.40	108.78	6
Total	**433.69**	**415.18**	**4**

Source: STEAM data 2002 and 2003, provided by Global Tourism Solutions 2003

TABLE 14.7   Scottish Enterprise priorities for investment in Loch Lomond and Trossachs National Park based on key themes to develop tourism potential

Key theme	Rationale
Early Action Works	First-time visitors to the new park will arrive with heightened expectations based on the international concept of National Parks. The experience will therefore require meeting these expectations from the start to ensure a successful long-term outcome
Gateway Projects	Gateways are important for two key reasons. First, as the initial point of contact with the park they will create first impressions. Second, the Gateways will act as the main service centres for the park through providing a range of services
Improving the tourism product	If Scotland is to be globally competitive in tourism, it must have a globally competitive product. It is recognized that despite a number of natural advantages, much of the build environment of the park is not yet internationally competitive
Developing the infrastructure base	Infrastructure is what holds the park together. It will get people to the park and take them around it. It will act as the support to all the other activities and will require meeting the aspirations of the wide range of tourists and visitors
Growing tourism businesses	The key stakeholders in the project will be the businesses who operate from and provide services to the visitors and tourists. It is generally recognized that many of Scotland's tourism businesses fail to aspire to the level required if the park is to be internationally successful

Conclusion

This chapter has examined the role of the public sector in the management and organization of tourism, emphasizing the role of different agencies and bodies in this process. The formulation and implementation of tourism policies is not a static unchanging process. Tourism is highly politicized as, in practice, tourism policies are often vehicles of national political ambitions by countries seeking to harness the economic and political benefits of a buoyant tourism industry. One of the key objectives of the NTO is to assist in the development of supply and promote the growth and management of demand to meet supply. Through the **policy** dimension, the NTO and government departments may use a range of instruments and other government measures such as land use planning and control measures, building regulations, measures to regulate and direct the market as well as investment incentives. The state can also play a major role in non-tourism areas such as the provision of transport infrastructure and this area is not always planned with tourism interests in mind, though in countries with an increasingly private sector demand-driven focus, the needs of the tourism sector are more carefully programmed into new developments such as airports and new infrastructure projects. There is also growing evidence of the NTOs seeking private sector finance through partnerships with industry to develop areas of their work for the tourism industry. Without a strong public sector role in tourism, the wider public good of the tourism sector and society is not easily reconciled with the needs of the private sector for profit and development. The public sector acts as an anchor and counterbalance to the private sector, although it needs to work in harmony with the private sector rather than in opposition to it for a viable and successful industry. One area of cooperation is marketing, as Chapter 15 will now examine.

Discussion questions

1 What is the significance of declining government funding for the tourism sector, and should the private sector play a greater role in funding this activity?

2 Do governments need tourism ministers? If so, why and what functions should they undertake?

3 Review the roles which national, regional and local tourism organizations might play in tourism. Do they have overlapping roles, and if so, how would you address this problem?

4 What are tourist taxes? What role can they play in funding the tourism sector?

References

Ashworth, G. and Tunbridge, J. (2000) *The Tourist-Historic City. Retrospect and Prospect of Managing the Historic City*. Oxford: Elsevier.

Bull, B. (1999) 'Encouraging tourism development through the EU structural funds: A case study of the implementation of EU programmes on Bornholm', *International Journal of Tourism Research*, 1: 149–65.

Cooper, C., Fletcher, J., Fyall, A., Gilbert, D. and Wanhill, S. (2005) *Tourism: Principles and Practices, Third Edition*. Harlow: Prentice Hall.

COSLA (2002) *Review of the Area Tourist Boards*. COSLA, Edinburgh.

Deegan, J. and Dineen, D.A. (1997) *Tourism Policy and Performance – the Irish experience*. London: International Thomson Business Press.

Department of Culture, Media and Sport (2004) *Tomorrow's Tourism Today*. London: DCMS.

Downes, J. (1999) 'European Union progress on a common tourism sector policy', *Travel and Tourism Analyst*, 1: 74–87.

Dredge, D. and Moore, S. (1992) 'A methodology for the integration of tourism in town planning', *Journal of Tourism Studies*, 3 (1): 8–21.

Economic Development and Planning Executive Group and VisitScotland (2004) *FAQs on the Tourism Review*. http://www.scotexchange.net; accessed 1 March 2005.

Elliot, J. (1997) *Tourism: Politics and Public Sector Management*. London: Routledge.

Gunn, C. and Var, T. (2002) *Tourism Planning: Basics, Concepts, Cases*. London: Routledge.

Hall, C.M. (2000) *Tourism Planning: Policies, Processes and Relationships*. Harlow: Prentice Hall.

Hall, C.M. and Jenkins, J. (1995) *Tourism and Public Policy*, Fourth *Edition*. London: Routledge.

Hope, C. and Klemm, M. (2001) 'Tourism in difficult areas revisited: The case of Bradford', *Tourism Management,* 22 (6): 629–35.

Jeffries, D. (2001) *Governments and Tourism.* Oxford: Butterworth-Heinemann.

Kerr, W. (2003) *Tourism Public Policy, and the Strategic Mangement of Failure.* Oxford: Elsevier.

Lickorish, L.J. and Jenkins, C.L. (1997) *An Introduction to Tourism.* Oxford: Butterworth-Heinemann.

Meethan, K. (1997) 'York: Managing the tourist city', *Cities,* (14) 6: 333–42.

Mill, R.C. and Morrison, A.M. (1985) *The Tourism System: An Introductory Text.* Englewood Cliffs, NJ: Prentice Hall International.

Morgan, N. and Pritchard, A. (2000) *Advertising in Tourism and Leisure.* Oxford: Butterworth-Heinemann.

Morgan, N. and Pritchard, A. (2002) 'Contextualising destination branding', in N. Morgan, A. Pritchard and R. Pride (eds) *Destination Branding: Creating the Unique Destination Proposition.* Oxford: Butterworth-Heinemann.

Ooi, C. (2002) 'Contrasting strategies: Tourism in Denmark and Singapore', *Annals of Tourism Research,* 29 (3): 689–706.

Oppermann, M. and Chon, K. (1997) *Tourism in Developing Countries.* London: International Thomson Business Press.

Orbaşli, A. and Shaw, S. (2004) 'Transport and visitors in historic cities', in L. Lumsdon, and S.J. Page (eds) *Tourism and Transport: Issues and Agendas for the New Millennium.* Oxford: Elsevier.

Page, S.J. and Hall, C.M. (1999) 'New Zealand', *International Tourism Report,* 4: 47–76.

Page, S.J. and Thorn, K. (1997) 'Towards sustainable tourism planning in New Zealand: Public sector planning responses', *Journal of Sustainable Tourism,* 5 (1): 59–77.

Page, S.J. and Thorn, K. (2002) 'Towards sustainable tourism development and planning in New Zealand: the public sector response revisited', *Journal of Sustainable Tourism,* 10 (3): 222–38.

Palmer, T. and Riera, A. (2003) 'Tourism and environmental taxes. With special reference to the "Balearic Ecotax", *Tourism Management,* 24 (6): 665–74.

Pearce, D.G. (1989) *Tourist Development.* London: Harlow.

Pearce, D.G. (1992) *Tourist Organizations.* Longman: Harlow.

Pearce, D.G. (1998) 'Tourism development in Paris: Public intervention', *Annals of Tourism Research,* 25 (2): 457–76.

Pike, S. (2004) *Destination Marketing Organizations.* Oxford: Elsevier.

SLAED (Scottish Local Authority Economic Development Group) (2002) *The Role of Scottish Councils in Tourism.* Edinburgh: SLAED.

Smith, S.L.J. (2003) 'A vision for the Canadian tourism industry', *Tourism Management,* 24 (1): 123–33.

Snaith, T. and Haley, A. (1999) 'Residents' opinions of tourism development in the historic city of York, England', *Tourism Management,* 20 (5): 595–603.

Turner, J. (1997) 'The policy process', in B. Axford, G. Browning, R. Huggins, B. Rosamond and J. Turner (eds) *Politics: An Introduction* London: Routledge.

van Thiel, S. (2004) 'Trends in the public sector: Why governments prefer quasi-autonomous organisations', *Journal of Theoretical Politics,* 16 (2): 175–201.

van Westering, J. and Niel, E. (2003) 'The organization of wine tourism in France: The involvement of the French public sector', *Journal of Travel and Tourism Marketing,* 14 (3/4): 35–47.

VisitScotland (2001) *Visitor Attraction Monitor.* Edinburgh: VisitScotland.

Worthington, B. (2003) 'Change in an Estonian resort: Contrasting development contexts', *Annals of Tourism Research,* 30 (2): 369–85.

Zhang, H., King, C. and Ap, J. (1999) 'An analysis of tourism policy in modern China', *Tourism Management,* 20 (4): 471–86.

Further reading

Hall, C.M. (2000) *Tourism Planning: Policies, Processes and Relationships.* Harlow: Prentice Hall.

Marketing Tourism

Learning outcomes

After reading this chapter and answering the questions, you should be able to:

- understand some of the main terms associated with marketing and the concept of value

- recognize the consequences of marketing in the tourism industry, and be aware of its distinguishing features as a service activity

- realize the importance of understanding the customers' needs, the marketing mix and market segmentation

- explain the role and nature of marketing plans, describing some of the main analytical techniques used.

Overview

Marketing is central to tourism to enable organizations to create value through their transactions with consumers. Core marketing concepts and issues are fairly universal and constant, but tourism marketing reflects some of the special characteristics of this industry. This chapter introduces a range of concepts and issues related to tourism marketing emphasizing the role of value in the marketing process, the importance of understanding the marketing mix, understanding customers needs and the role of marketing planning and various techniques used to analyse the marketing environment.

Introduction

In the evolution of tourism, the practice of marketing has a long tradition, evident from the early work of Thomas Cook in using promotional material for tourism (see Chapter 2). Yet the formal identification of the concept of marketing emerged in the 1950s (Kotler *et al.* 2004), and reviews of the evolution of marketing in tourism (e.g. Cooper *et al.* 2005) highlight a number of different stages including:

- *a production era*, based on the notion that if products were priced cheaply, they would sell regardless of consumer preferences. This was deemed an inward, product-oriented focus with little concern for consumers
- *a sales era*, where selling was the prime focus regardless of the market's willingness to accept the product
- *a marketing era*, replacing the preceding approaches: businesses now produced products they could sell which were tailored to consumer needs to satisfy the purchaser, effectively making the organization more outward looking.

This shows that marketing has become more sophisticated as a process and tool used by businesses to nurture customers and to add value to their experience of tourism, as well as to seek to develop their loyalty through innovative reward schemes (e.g. frequent flyer programmes). Yet marketing is not a substitute for good business performance and vice versa. The cost of marketing (especially advertising) makes this an expensive activity for many SMEs which often fail to penetrate the tourism market through limited marketing. Equally, some large flagship projects developed with tourism in mind, have also failed in the attraction sector due to inadequately conceived marketing plans and activity as Chapter 9 highlighted. In contrast, sectors like the airline and tour operator sector make sophisticated use of marketing to reach growing consumer markets in tourism where they achieve economies of scale in their marketing efforts. Indeed, the low-cost airline sector exemplifies the role of marketing-oriented tourism organizations as chapters 5 and 8 have shown.

The concept of marketing

As approaches to marketing have evolved, the consumer has also evolved in sophistication. The tourism sector has responded to meet their needs, as markets and sub-markets have developed, reflected in the use of segmentation techniques. A number of useful texts exist on tourism marketing (e.g. Middleton and Clarke 2001; Holloway 2004; Fyall and Garrod 2005) and there is a general acceptance of the definition provided by the UK Chartered Institute of Marketing that marketing is 'the management process responsible for identifying, anticipating and satisfying customer requirements profitably'.

This definition can be expanded to incorporate the growing sophistication of the consumer and the need to deliver value. As Kotler *et al.* (2004: 6) argue, marketing is:

A social and managerial process by which individuals and groups obtain what they need and want through creating and exchanging products and value with others.

Whilst Chapters 3 and 4 have highlighted the importance of human needs, wants and demand, the key feature here to stress is how marketing is based on a *value* proposition, which are the benefits which organizations put forward to satisfy consumers' needs (see Insight 15.1) as the *marketing offer* (i.e. the combination of products, services, experiences) to satisfy needs and wants. Consumers make decisions based on the **perceived value** of an overall product's capacity to satisfy their needs/wants and the marketing process is based on the concept of an *exchange* occurring between an organization and consumer (often a commercial transaction but not in every case). For this exchange to take place, two parties need to agree on the basis for the exchange, which will usually be a *transaction*, where two parties or more trade value, usually in response to some **marketing offer** made by the organization (see Kotler *et al.* 2004 for more detail).

The concept of perceived value in tourism marketing

There is a growing interest among marketers in the concept of value for tourists, given its potential to provide businesses with a competitive advantage if it is understood and built into the marketing offer. Sánchez *et al.* (2006) recognized the dynamic nature of this seemingly subjective concept which is perceived by tourists in several ways:

- before a purchase
- at the moment of purchase
- at the point of use
- post-use.

Different elements of what tourists value may receive attention or focus at the various stages of purchase or use. For example, price may be a dominant issue at the point of purchase whereas at the point of consumption other elements may be more significant than price.

Perceived value is a key element in the concept of relationship marketing and the nurturing of consumers. Perceived value is a complex concept which may best be understood as a multifaceted phenomenon based upon elements such as:

- notions of quality
- emotional responses
- monetary price
- behavioural price
- reputation.

Tourism experiences based on the notion of fun, pleasure and emotional responses are assuming a growing importance in seeking to understand tourist behaviour. One of the underpinning methods of explaining perceived value in consumer behaviour is the Cognition–Affect–Behaviour approach (Chapter 16) which argues that:

- *cognition* is associated with how consumers process information in consumption experiences, and how they develop meanings and beliefs about what they buy
- *affect* is associated with emotional elements (e.g. anxiety, hate and pleasure) which help to understand the types of feelings consumers develop
- *behaviour* relates to the purchasing and consumption element, where the enjoyment of a purchase or experience manifests itself.

This approach to consumer behaviour is a more complex one than more simplistic notions that all human behaviour in a consumption context is rational, which certainly would not help in studying hedonistic activities like tourism. To try and measure perceived value in tourism, different dimensions have been examined: *perceived quality* through social value, *emotional elements* (perceived quality of the product) and the *functional value* (price and value for money). Sánchez *et al.* (2006) noted that in the case of a tourism package, the consumer has a holistic notion of its perceived value which is more complex than simplistic notions of quality and price, since affective elements have a key role to play. This is reflected in the social value attached to tourism purchases. For example, a family may place a great deal of value on being able to spend their leisure time together, and so a family tourism product will need to emphasize some of the affective elements that can be perceived as adding value to the marketing offer.

As a result, the marketing implications of perceived value in tourism are clear. Tourism businesses need to focus on the intangible elements of tourism products, communicating these to consumers.

In tourism, the adding of value to the transaction has become a core concept in marketing, especially in the development of *relationship marketing* to build long-term relationships between customers and suppliers, with consistent quality and value-laden transactions that are mutually beneficial. The tangible outcome of value in tourism is often framed in terms of perceived notions of product and service quality, which we will return to in Chapter 25 on the tourist experience. For the tourism company, this means that they need to develop both marketing know-how and expertise to understand how to interpret customer needs. This may involve the training of staff to add value or, in extreme cases, **re-engineering** an organization to be more customer-focused, as British Airways did in the 1980s. Thus, marketing in tourism needs to be a philosophy adopted towards one's business operations that transcends simple notions of selling to the consumer: all the core elements of marketing (i.e. research, product, value creation, promotion and sales) need to be integrated around a core focus on the consumer. Therefore, tourism marketing requires organizations to understand both the short-term needs to recruit customers and long-term goals to retain and nurture them, in a cost-effective and efficient manner.

Tourism marketing

In most organizations, marketing is a key component where consumer products are sold, and Lumsdon (1997: 27) outlined some of the characteristics which marketing orientated tourism businesses might exhibit (Table 15.1). This orientation may be informed by one or more of the different philosophies that have developed in marketing, as shown in more detail in Table 15.2. In practice, different organizations define and apply their marketing activities in a way that is most

---

TABLE 15.1 Marketing orientation

An organization would exhibit some or all of the following characteristics:

- A clearly defined approach to existing, potential and long-term markets

- Policies and actions which reflect concern for consumer wants in relation to societal and environmental requirements

- Implementation which involves internal marketing (own staff), consumer orientation and consideration of stakeholders including host communities

- Market environmental scanning which includes short- and long-term scenarios

- Marketing planning process which is part of the culture of the organization and includes genuine reappraisal of internal resources

- A structure and culture which leads to long-term vision

Source: Lumsdon (1997: 27)

TABLE 15.2 The marketing concept: Different approaches

The product concept

An approach that assumes that customers are mainly interested in the quality, performance or features of the product. Thus marketing activities focus on product development and improvement.

The production concept

An approach which believes that customers are generally price sensitive. Here the aim will be to make products efficiently and distribute them widely enough to raise volume and drive down costs.

The selling concept

Assumes that customers need to be persuaded to buy enough of the firm's products. Here a greater emphasis will be placed on advertising and promotion.

The marketing concept

Has, as its basis, the importance of understanding customer needs and the aim to fulfil them more effectively than the competition.

The societal concept

Here a concern for society is expressed, rather than simply satisfying customers and generating profits. Marketing approaches aim to encompass the interests of society as well as the customers concerned.

Source: Adapted from Peattie (1992)

relevant to their product or service. Organizations, having examined their own marketing needs, should also:

- *develop a marketing information system* to undertake market research on customers, competitors and internal effectiveness to operate in particular markets
- *develop* **marketing planning**, to analyse the marketing environment and strategy to operate in certain markets and segments
- *plan tactical campaigns*
- *develop marketing operations*, including coordinating the internal marketing functions and communications internally and externally (i.e. public relations functions) as well as a monitoring and control function to manage the marketing function (after Lumsdon (1997).

This will also require an organization to be able to understand the external marketing environment (Table 15.3) at both the firm level and macro level, to understand how tourism operates and

TABLE 15.3 The external marketing environment

Factor	Examples
1. Political environment	• Government interest in free trade and exchange of visitors • Government and intergovernmental involvement in rules and regulations (international airline routes) • Environmental awareness and legislation • Growth of interest (lobbying on behalf of commercial sectors) and pressure group influence
2. Economic environment	• Affluence of 'North' and debt-laden 'South' • Growth in economies, such as Asia • Differential rates of personal discretionary income available for tourist expenditure • Changing consumer patterns of expenditure, leisure and tourism are now more important • Privatization and lesser role of government in tourism provision
3. Social/cultural environment	• Changing patterns of cultural values • Fragmentation of societies into subcultural groupings • Changing patterns of lifecycle and lifestyles such as more single households • Environmental and social consciousness • Growth of 'skilled customers' i.e. more knowledgeable
4. Technological environment	• Accelerating pace of technological change • Accessibility and rapid diffusion of technology in Western countries • Technological enhancements in the home, including 'virtual reality' holidays in near future • Positive regulation of technical change
5. Ecological environment	• Increasing consumer and governmental awareness of ecological issues especially pollution and depletion of resources • Continued questioning of short-termism by increasingly articulate groups • Consumer choice based on environmentally friendly tourism offerings
6. Demographics	• Population growth in developing countries • Slowdown in birth rate in Western economies • Ageism in Western economies • Geographical shifts of population • Migration to cities in developing countries and the opposite in advanced economies • Change in family structures and fragmentation of lifecycles

Source: Lumsdon (1997: 15)

how different factors may affect its business. As the tourism industry is regarded as a 'service' industry, there are several attributes that distinguish the marketing needs of tourism from those of marketing a specific product. These characteristics are reflected in Table 15.4 and include intangibility, perishability, heterogeneity and inseperability. These can be expanded to also include a number of other considerations as shown in Table 15.5.

As Tables 15.4 and 15.5 suggest, the tourism product can be more accurately thought of as a combination of several different services. While some of the basic principles of marketing apply to all products, there are clearly some special considerations to make in investigating the tourism industry. Lumsdon (1997) has shown that there is a conceptual continuum between goods and services where either tangible or intangible elements are dominant, and Figure 15.1 shows that, in most cases, tourism is an intangible offering. Therefore, in a business context, organizations providing tourism service need to have:

- a customer orientation
- a focus on the firm's external environment
- accurate marketing research information, particularly in relation to customers and competitors
- products that meet tourists' needs
- a strategy of differentiation, i.e. that the tourism firm's products are different in some way from the competition
- the ability to manipulate various marketing opportunities in such a way to create customer satisfaction.

TABLE 15.4 The underlying principles of services marketing

Principle	Explanation	Implications
Intangibility	Unlike products, services are mainly intangible by nature. It is impossible for the consumer to touch, smell, feel or hear the service offering in the same way as they can test a product	Tourism marketers tend to 'tangiblize' the tourism offering in brochures and videos – visual displays of the real thing
Perishability	It is not possible to store services. An unoccupied seat on a train or bed in a guest house is lost forever unlike a product which can be stockpiled until demand rises once more	The management task emphasizes managing demand and capacity to a degree of fine tuning. For example, airlines offer standby fares to those willing to fill unexpected empty seats at short notice
Heterogeneity	It is difficult for service marketers to standardize service provision given the close contact between staff and consumers. Performance varies regardless of processes designed to minimize this factor	Tourism marketers design processes to minimize differences in service encounters and provision between different outlets or between different shifts at a hotel, for example. Provision of uniforms and of similar physical surroundings illustrates evidence of standardization
Inseparability	The service provision and consumption occur at the same time and both provider and consumer interact in the process of delivery. This obviously is why standardization of service is so difficult as consumer involvement is high	Marketers attempt to devise systems which ease interaction and invest in campaigns to educate staff and consumers as to how to get the best from the interaction. Training in hotels emphasizes how staff can manage the interaction
Lack of ownership	The consumer does not take title of goods as in product marketing. They bring back memories and feelings from a holiday	The marketer emphasizes pictorial reference and souvenirs to reinforce image of holiday experience

Source: Lumsdon (1997: 29)

TABLE 15.5   Additional features of tourism that highlight the need for services marketing

Inelasticity of supply

Tourism products are inelastic in that often they cannot be easily adapted. If demand suddenly falls, this is unlikely to have a significant effect on the price. Tourism products are dependent on existing structures (hotels, transport and facilities) at destinations.

Elasticity of demand

While it is more difficult to quickly adapt tourism products, demand is very elastic. Sudden events, such as fuel price rises, terrorist acts and exchange rate changes can quickly influence demand. Moreover, certain destinations can quickly become less fashionable.

Complementarity

When a holiday is purchased, often it is not just a single service, but several sub-products that complement each other. Failure in one if these areas (e.g. airport delays) can seriously affect the overall experience.

High fixed costs

The cost of developing tourism products, such as a holiday, involves high fixed costs (hotels, aircraft and trains). Such investment is not a guarantee of future profits.

Labour intensity

Tourism is a labour intensive industry and the tourist's experience is greatly influenced by the skill of the staff they come into contact with.

Source: Adapted from Baker (1993); Cannon (1992); Vellas and Becherel (1999)

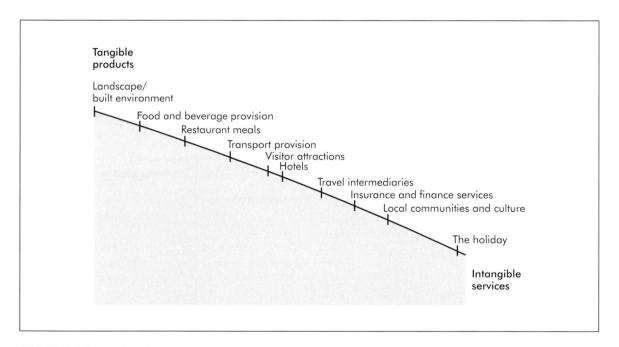

FIGURE 15.1   Good–services continuum in tourism. Source: Lumsdon (1997: 27)

It is against this background that marketing managers in tourism need to operate, since the marketing function is at the heart of an organization's strategy. Here, the most crucial question the marketing manager must ask is: 'Why should my customers buy my products, rather than those of my competitors?' (Holloway and Robinson 1995: 23). The remainder of this chapter will introduce some of the relevant concepts and issues associated with addressing this question.

The marketing planning process and the marketing mix

Within the services marketing literature, there is a considerable debate over the precise nature of tourism as a consumer activity and its marketing needs. At a generic level, there is a debate over the nature of tourism consumption compared to the conventional consumption of goods through the pre-consumption, consumption and post-consumption stages as shown in Figure 15.2. This suggests that businesses have to plan their marketing activities to fit to these different stages. As Jones and Lockwood (2002) point out, in the marketing process within tourism and hospitality firms, the marketing planning process usually occurs in Stage 1, but has a lesser role in services marketing as much of the 'production' or 'delivery' occurs in Stage 2, which is contact or people dependent. They also point to the element of remixing which often occurs in services in Stage 2, meaning the re-adjustment of pricing levels by monitoring consumer activity, typically through ICTs. Thus, Stage 2 is critical in tourism marketing and this highlights the importance of different marketing tactics and strategies which focus on the marketing mix.

The marketing mix

Marketers need to have a thorough understanding of the tourism products they offer and long-term success requires an understanding of how potential tourists respond to a number of variables when deciding whether to respond to the marketing offer and purchase a product or service.

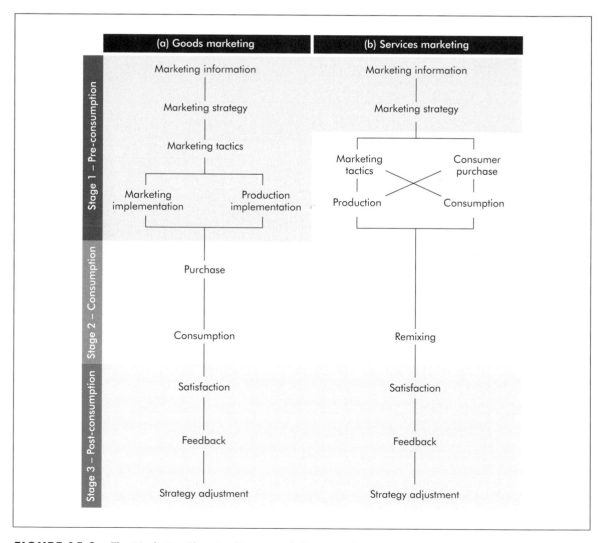

FIGURE 15.2   The Marketing Planning Process and Consumption stages. Source: Jones and Lockwood (2002: 69)

It is the mix of these variables that will help to determine the extent to which an organization satisfies the needs of the market. These variables are referred to as the 'Marketing mix' and are outlined in the Booms and Bitner model in Table 15.6. These are often simplified to the four **P**s of product, **price**, **place** and promotion as discussed in Case Study 15.1W.

It is the contribution of these variables, which constitutes the total product and provides the basic opportunity for satisfying customer needs. The interaction of factors shaping the marketing mix is illustrated in Figure 15.3 and different types of marketing decisions/marketing mixes will need to be made for different types of tourists since 'different markets require different marketing mixes at different times in their life cycle' (Vellas and Becherel 1999: 98). But there is some debate as to whether the four Ps are comprehensive enough to reflect the nature of marketing decisions in the tourism industry, with Vellas and Becherel (1999) referring to an additional three Ps being necessary in the case of service providers. These are:

People In the tourism industry, people, i.e. staff, are important particularly in terms of their skills of customer care, how friendly they are and their appearance.

Physical evidence Within accommodation, for example, considerations of the furnishings, décor, environment, ambience, layout, cleanliness and noise level are all important.

Process Here aspects such as how efficiently procedures work, for example, service time, waiting time, customer forms and documents all need to be evaluated.

TABLE 15.6 Booms' and Bitner's marketing mix for services

Product:
- range
- quality
- level
- brand name
- warranty
- after-sales service

Place:
- location
- channels of distribution
- coverage
- accessibility

Price:
- level
- discounts
- terms
- differentiation

Promotion:
- advertising
- selling
- sales promotion
- public relations
- publicity
- merchandising

People:
- personnel:
  - training
  - commitment
  - appearance
  - incentives
  - social skills
- attitudes
- other customers

Physical evidence:
- environment:
  - colour
  - layout
  - furnishing
- facilitating goods
- tangible clues

Process:
- policies
- procedures
- mechanisms
- employee discretion
- customer involvement
- flow of activities
- customer direction

Source: Jones and Lockwood (2002: 70)

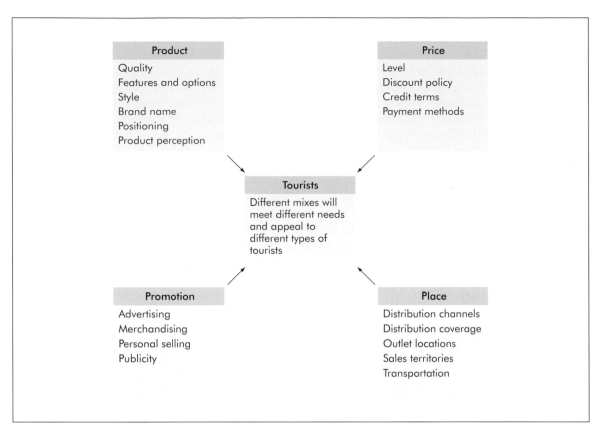

FIGURE 15.3   The marketing mix. Source: Developed from Cannon (1992); Holloway and Robinson (1995)

However, marketing mix decisions need to aim at the right target market and be consistent with the marketing concept of the particular tourism organization. Case Study 15.2W reveals how the marketing mix needs to understand cultural issues in a growing market, Chinese outbound tourism (which is also examined in Case Study 3.1W). Knowing the customer and meeting their expectations is the only way to succeed, as the next section emphasizes.

Knowing the customer

Marketers in the tourism industry need to understand the buying behaviour of the customers within their target markets. Some of the questions tourism marketers need to answer in respect of tourist buying behaviour include:

- Who are the customers/tourists?
- What types of tourism products do they buy?
- With whom do they travel (alone, couple, family)?
- Which suppliers do they use?
- What are the needs they aim to satisfy?
- Where/how do they buy their tourism products?
- When do they buy them (last minute, in advance)?
- How long do they go on holiday for?
- How often do they travel?
- How much are they prepared to pay?
- How do they decide which tourism products to buy?

- What influences their travel decisions?
- How do previous holidays affect future plans?

The answers to these questions will clearly help the marketer to decide how best to market their products as well as natural advantages (Image 15.1). For most tourism businesses it is unlikely that their range of products will appeal equally to all types of potential tourist. Rather, the products are aimed primarily at particular types of tourist (e.g. young adults who are singles, travelling with friends, without children). Such groups represent the 'target market' and Vellas and Becherel (1999: 59) refer to three options for targeting markets:

Undifferentiated marketing

This is where a tourism business tries to sell as much as possible and their products have to the broadest appeal. This would be a characteristic of mass-market tour operators.

Differentiated marketing

Here the company aims at particular target markets, and designs separate products and marketing programmes for each market. The costs to the firm of this are larger, but total sales may be greater.

Concentrated marketing

In this approach the business concentrates on a specific target market. Rather than aim at all tourists, it chooses a specific market and aims to capture a large share of this particular market. Dacko (2004) examined the price-sensitive online last minute market including the three largest providers (Travelocity.com, Expedia.com and Orbitz.com) and the strategies used to target this type of consumer. These forms of purchasing reflect the global growth of internet use which now exceeds over 600 million users worldwide. Tourism organizations may choose different virtual marketing solutions, including:

- *a virtual face*, to achieve a low-cost approach to market products and services via the web
- *a co-alliance* (a shared partnership) joining part of a consortium with a more sophisticated website
- *a star alliance*, comprising a number of core companies surrounded by others who draw on the expertise of the core
- *a value alliance*, based on a supply-chain model, using ICTs not previously available and facilitating the packaging of services and products in one place and able to respond quickly to the market
- *a market alliance*, with non-competing products and as a portal for the group
- *a virtual broker*, where third-party suppliers provide a virtual structure for different services
- *a virtual space*, which is entirely based on virtual contact with the customer, with an online marketing channel for distribution (Source: Burn and Barnett 1999; Lee *et al.* 2004)

Image 15.1: One of Iceland's strengths is its natural features, like geysers (see Table 15.8)

in seeking to target the online consumer. This highlights that a strategy to approach a target market is necessary, but tourists buy their holidays in different ways. Some people buy a holiday after careful study of travel brochures and guides, online press reviews, discussions with their friends and colleagues and a careful comparison of competing products. Others, who purchase the same holiday, may do so on impulse, after happening to see it advertised. For the purchase of most products, there is a buying process, as discussed in Chapter 4 and is simplified for the purchase of a holiday as outlined in Figure 15.4 and which will be returned to in Chapter 16 in relation to the impact of advertising on this process.

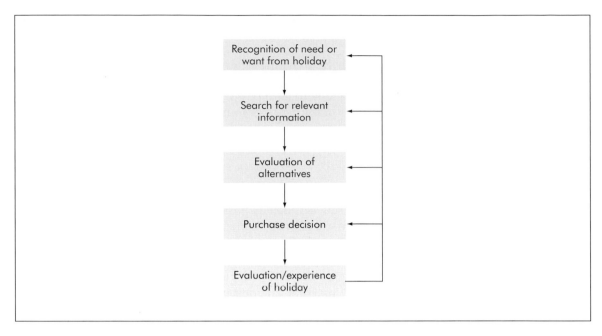

FIGURE 15.4 The buying process

At each stage in the buying process there are implications for the tourism marketer. Of particular importance is how potential tourists search for relevant information on which to base their decisions. This is of special relevance in the tourism industry where attracting new visitors to a destination or new customers to a tourism service is always necessary. Here, marketers need to communicate their products to new customers, but to do this they need to know where the potential customer searches for that information and, as Chapter 6 highlighted, the internet is increasingly being used to fulfil this role as 'lookers' search the millions of sites available. This has meant many tourism organizations have had to develop a web presence to be more outwardly facing in this new environment for marketing products and services. Increasingly, organizations in the tourism sector are having to be more cognizant of the wider external environment discussed earlier as well as the diverse range of information sources now influencing tourist holiday-buying behaviour as shown in Table 15.7.

TABLE 15.7   Sources of information used by tourists to decide on travel

The following sources of travel decision-making are commonly used:

- Experience of previous visit
- Friends and family
- Travel guide books
- Newspaper advertisements
- Newspaper articles
- The internet
- Destination websites
- Television advertising
- Travel programmes on television
- Magazine advertising
- Travel fairs
- Radio

The buying behaviour for a holiday is a complex process, and marketing communications have to be targeted at specific markets and types of consumers as Chapter 16 will show. One technique developed and widely used in marketing, as discussed in Chapter 4, is market segmentation to identify target markets. For example, the Argentinian National Tourism Organization is segmenting the inbound market into specific target markets comprising:

- active tourism (i.e. adventure activities)
- world heritage
- ecotourism
- thermal tourism
- rural tourism
- youth tourism.

As Vellas and Becherel (1999: 60) state, market segmentation can improve the 'competitive position and better serve the needs of customers'. Achieving advantage over the competition introduces a new dimension in marketing, which is discussed next.

Competition

Identifying a market and presenting a distinctive service to a market segment are only the first stages of effectively developing a market. Having developed the tourism product, the business must hold onto it (Image 15.2). As Chapter 5 discussed, competition for markets and consumers is intense in tourism and this illustrates the need for a well-developed strategy towards marketing and the marketplace. One of the most widely cited studies of the degree of competitive intensity a company will face is Porter's (1980) competitive strategy. As Figure 15.5 shows, Porter pointed to five key forces (degree of rivalry, new entrants, buyers, suppliers, substitutes) which impact upon a tourism setting and Lumsdon (1997) discusses this in the context of visitor attractions. This illustrates the importance of marketers undertaking competitor analysis using the tools and techniques which are discussed later in this chapter (e.g. SWOT analysis) and the need for ongoing monitoring of the marketplace. This helps to explain why market intelligence reports from organizations such as Mintel (www.mintel.com) can command premium prices as they track the market and identify trends, future scenarios and the level of competition in the marketplace. Such research is critical for organizations who wish to develop or retain competitive advantages, seeking to cement the three-way relationship between the company, its products and consumers. Kotler (1988) argues that businesses need to know the following about their competitors:

- who they are
- what are their strategies
- what are their objectives
- what their strengths and weaknesses are
- how they react.

Image 15.2: Icons, such as Denmark's familiar mermaid statue, provide a memorable element when seeking to promote a country or destination

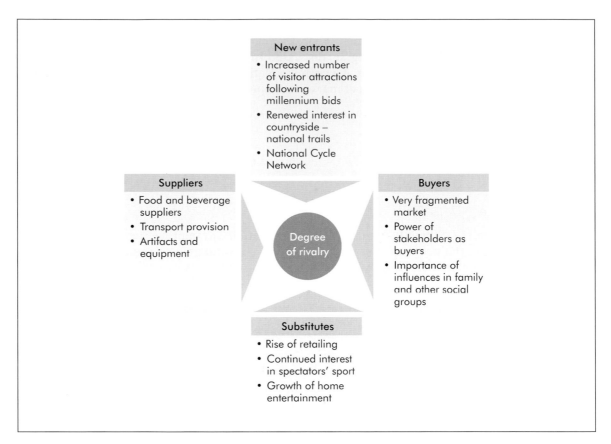

FIGURE 15.5 Porter's five forces: Degree of competitive intensity. Source: Lumsdon (1997: 89)

Planning for the future: Marketing planning and analysis

Most commercial organizations in the tourism industry aim to survive, make a profit and, in many cases, grow. To do this requires that the firm have a strategic marketing plan in place which is flexible and a regular feature of managerial activity. According to Lumsdon (1997: 79) 'Marketing planning is the process by which an organization attempts to analyse its existing resources and marketing environment in order to predict the direction it should take in the future'. This is necessary to plan for the future. One needs to be forward thinking and innovative while thinking about the markets one serves/will serve, thereby ensuring that the organization is outward facing. Whilst different researchers adopt various approaches to outline the nature of the marketing planning process it is likely to have many of the features outlined in Figure 15.6. Planning like this will apply to larger tourism organizations, since Chapter 13 highlighted the lack of planning by many tourism SMEs. Yet marketing planning may be one of many planning processes for tourism organizations (e.g. financial planning, HRM planning and other lower-profile activities such as environmental planning to reduce waste).

As part of the marketing planning process, a number of questions to consider are:

- What is the core business and what are the firm's overall objectives?
- What is the current position in the marketplace?
- What are the firm's marketing objectives?
- What is the nature of the environment in which the firm operates and how will this change in the future?
- What strategies are there to achieve marketing objectives?
- What tactics are there to achieve the strategies?
- Is there a sufficient budget for this activity?

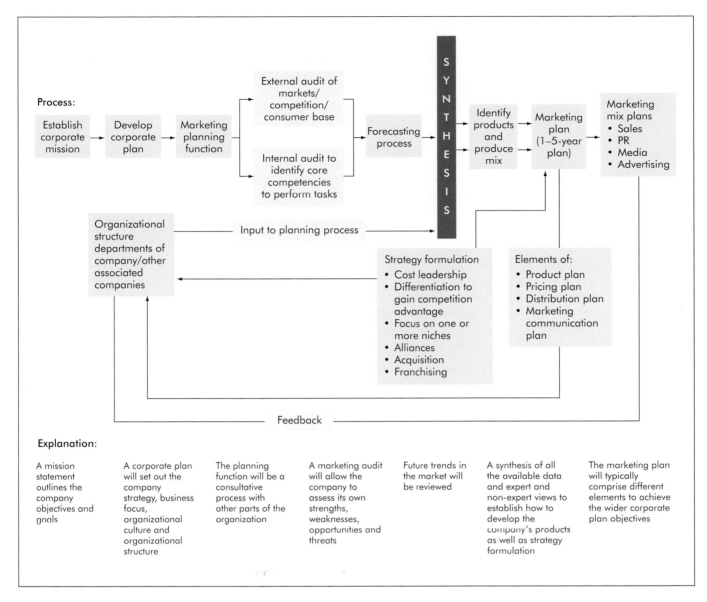

FIGURE 15.6 The marketing planning process in tourism. Source: Adapted from Atkinson and Wilson (1996); Lumsdon (1997)

As Figure 15.6 illustrates, these questions will be dealt with in a systematic manner to address wider management concerns over corporate strategy and the type of tourism business they aspire to be. One of the first steps in the marketing planning process is the marketing audit, to identify the company's strengths, weaknesses and ability to react to opportunities and threats. This wider analysis of the marketing environment may involve a **PEST** or **SWOT** analysis, since to overlook these issues may mean that competition or events erode a company's competitive advantage.

PEST analysis

PEST analysis is an acronym for 'political, economic, sociocultural and technological', and refers to the external environment within which the firm operates. To inform future plans, this method provides a framework to help investigate the various factors that will affect the firm. While some of these are beyond the control of the individual business, an awareness of them is important.

- *Political*: What is the political environment of the destination area? Are there visa restrictions? Is there political stability or government elections? What is the government's attitude to tourism?

- *Economic*: What are the economic positions of both generating and destination areas? What effect will exchange rates, inflation, credit charges and labour costs have on the business?
- *Sociocultural*: What are the attitudes of the host community to tourism? What are the attitudes of tourists in the target market? What effect will new fashions and preferences have? What is the role of the family?
- *Technology*: What effects will new electronic forms of promotion, distribution and ticketing have?

PEST analysis is particularly important in the tourism industry due to the rapidity of change and this highlights the importance of the marketing planning process in Figure 15.6. While PEST provides an awareness of the external environment, SWOT analysis is one of the main tools in developing business strategies.

SWOT analysis

SWOT is an acronym for 'strengths, weaknesses, opportunities and threats'. This technique provides a framework that enables an organization to assess their position within a market in relation to the competition. Information gathered in a marketing audit can assess the company's internal strengths and weaknesses and the external opportunities and threats that it faces. SWOT analysis is not limited to marketing; it can be applied to the whole company, to destinations or tourism products. Some of the common factors that could be considered are:

- *Strengths and weaknesses – internal*: Products, people, the organization, financial position.
- *Opportunities and threats – external*: Competition, nature of the market, new technology, economic position, legal framework, political situation.

These are illustrated by the SWOT analysis for Iceland (Table 15.8) which also outlines the context of tourism against which a SWOT analysis should be considered.

Approaches to marketing planning

Marketing plans are central to company strategy and, in tourism, short-term activities such as festivals or events may equally need professional marketing to make them a success and to attract the target market. As Figure 15.7 shows, the marketing plan for an event will follow a similar

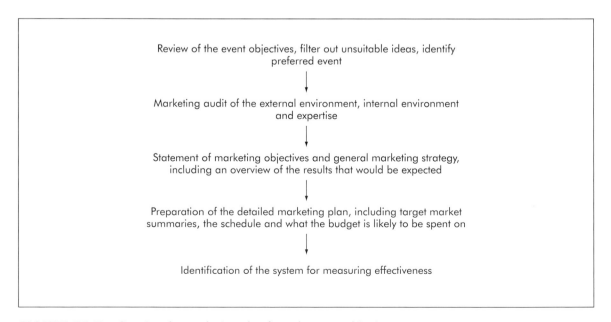

FIGURE 15.7   Creating the marketing plan from the event objectives. Source: Shone and Parry (2004)

TABLE 15.8 SWOT analysis of Iceland

Tourism in Iceland in 2004

In 2004, tourism constituted 13 per cent of income in Iceland's economy, generated 5400 jobs and accounted for 4.5 per cent of GNP. Arrivals have been growing at 9 per cent per annum and, in 2002, international arrivals were 277 300 with the largest groups from Nordic countries (73 900), the USA and Canada (47 700), the UK (42 600) and Germany (33 000) with a further 30 100 cruise ship arrivals annually. Bed spaces are 12 600 in 248 hotels and guesthouses, with 31 per cent located in the capital. A large proportion of visitors are from professional groups, motivated by nature, culture/history and cost. Around 80–90 per cent of visitors are on holiday, the majority independently organized with an average stay of ten nights in summer and five nights in winter.

Strengths:
- Distinctive and exotic environment (geysers, volcanic mountains, lava deserts, glaciers, midnight sun, abundant bird life)
- Established cultural and historic heritage (saga sites, Viking culture)
- Good access via Keflavik airport and reasonable accommodation stocks, particularly in the capital, Reykjavik
- Well-established profile with committed specialist tour operators

Weaknesses:
- Seen as remote and largely outside the average tourist's 'consideration set' as a destination
- An expensive destination
- Extreme seasonality of climate and travel conditions mainly dictate summer visitation, especially into the interior
- Poor family destination due to lack of things for children to enjoy
- Poor travel infrastructure (no trains, poor roads, especially in interior)
- Poor historic built environment since little architecture survives from pre-1900

Opportunities:
- Excellent development possibilities for specialist interest markets including green tourism, natural history enthusiasts, sporting enthusiasts (fishing, river rafting, climbing)
- Opportunity for short city-break development with capital Reykjavik as a trendy centre for upmarket done-everything tourists looking for something different
- Opportunity to develop Reykjavik as conference centre (Gorbachev and President Reagan held Reykjavik summit in the 1980s)

Threats:
- Other Scandinavian destinations
- Cost factor put Iceland at a major competitive disadvantage to other resorts
- Continuing difficulty of finding funds to market/promote awareness/destination image (Iceland had a tourist base of less than 200 000 in the 1990s, so expensive promotional budgets are impossible. See also www.icetourist.is

Source: Modified from Seaton and Bennett (1996: 119); Iceland Tourist Board, www.icetourist.is

process to that discussed earlier, albeit in a very time compressed period due to the staging of the event. The precise nature of an event marketing plan is shown in Figure 15.8 which highlights the strategic and operational issues which an event will have to deal with. An event, like any other tourism product or service will seek to target potential visitors (i.e. buyers) as well as sponsors and the budget available to implement the marketing plan will often reflect the scale and significance of the event. Edgell, Ruf and Agarwal (1999) suggest a six-stage framework to help marketers analyse the marketplace and develop a strategic marketing plan. While such plans will obviously differ, in accordance with the particular tourism product, these stages represent a useful structure based on Edgell *et al.* (1999).

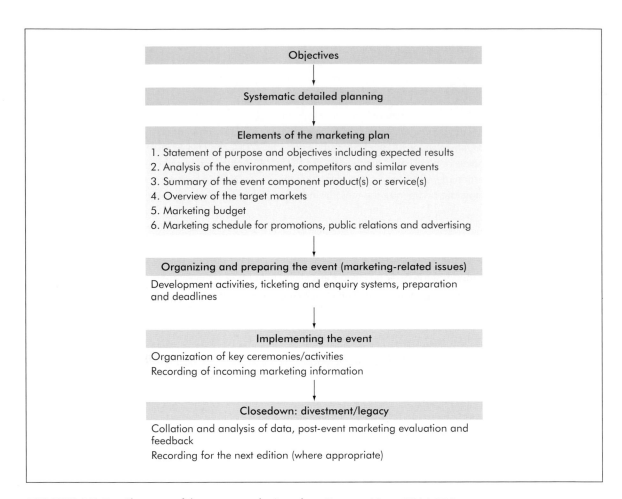

FIGURE 15.8 Elements of the event marketing plan. Shone and Parry (2004:154)

Needs analysis

Here the first step is to articulate the general objectives of the organization. This might include increasing the number of customers, the services they purchase and their repeat custom.

Research and analysis

Detailed analysis in all respects is an important second stage. Such methods may include SWOT and other types of examination of the marketing function within the organization. Externally PEST analysis is useful, as are other forms of competitor analysis. Customer research is also important, to include market segmentation and target market identification as shown in Case Study 15.3W on recording of visitor information at the Geneva Motor Show.

Creative infusion

Edgell *et al.* (1999) suggest that after reviewing the results of the research, a stage of creativity, of finding ideas to distinguish the organization's marketing plan from its competitors, should be undertaken.

Strategic positioning

This will involve reviewing the organization's position in terms of its current and future customer needs, **competitive advantage** and competitor's position, together with a creative component has helped to shape the strategic position.

Marketing plan development

Each market segment should have a separate marketing plan to capture new and repeat custom. Such plans have **SMART** goals ('specific, measurable, achievable, relevant and time-bound'). The accomplishment of goals is achieved through an identification of critical success factors (tasks that are vital to overall success). A definition of the marketing mix is also important to include aspects of pricing and promotion strategies.

Training, implementation, evaluation and adjustment

Training all who might be involved with the tourism product or service (including other organizations) is essential to remain competitive, aware of consumer needs and to maintain a viable business. Following this, once implemented, continual evaluation and adjustment of plans are needed so that particular marketing campaigns can be examined in terms of their success.

Conclusion

Harris and Katz (1996: 26) state that tourism marketing 'is not an easy task... it is more than just advertising; it requires a co-ordinated, phased plan involving dozens of specialised tasks' and in tourism people are a central component. Of crucial importance to the tourism marketer is being able to plan for the future using carefully designed, flexible marketing plans. As changes in tourism, involving technology and lifestyle preferences constantly evolve, marketers who are able to adapt their strategies and marketing methods accordingly are more likely to achieve success.

There is a growing debate within marketing as a subject, that the speed of technological change and direct access to customers via electronic means has redefined the nature of marketing as a business activity. Businesses are experiencing the ongoing fragmentation of markets as disintermediation occurs, more demanding consumers seek perceived value and competition in some sectors is intense, notably in the package holiday market. As Lumsdon (1997: 81) argued, the tourism organization in the twenty-first century which is market driven will need to be concerned with:

- customer attraction and retention
- segmentation by benefits (real and perceived)
- having a precise understanding of consumer values, choice and attitudes with marketing aligned to the consumer
- investment in ICTs to understand and track consumers
- innovating and being perceived as a flexible organization
- a proactive approach to consumers
- being able to understand and outflank one's competitors
- principles of societal and sustainable tourism principles and how to implement them (e.g. corporate social responsibility and environmental policies and plans, as discussed in Chapters 19 and 20).

Therefore, the successful tourism organization of the twenty-first century will not only need to be managed successfully, but also be able to understand the role of innovative and creative marketing to nurture consumers.

Discussion questions

1 Identify a business in the tourism industry. From the information you have how would you describe its marketing mix?

2 Analyse the marketing implications of launching a new product such as low-cost hotel rooms.

3 Evaluate the importance of online marketing for the tourism industry and its range of uses to create value and facilitate the marketing exchange process.

4 Discuss the contention that the battle for customers in tomorrow's tourism industry will be fought not over price but over hearts and minds.

References

Atkinson, J. and Wilson, I. (1996) *Strategic Marketing: Cases, Concepts and Challenges*. London: HarperCollins.

Baker, M.J. (ed.) (1993) *Chartered Institute of Marketing: The Marketing Book, Second Edition*. Oxford: Butterworth-Heinemann.

Booms, B. and Bitner, M. (1982) 'Marketing services by managing the environment', *Cornell HRA Quarterly*, May, 35–9.

Brassington, F. and Petit, S. (2003) *Principles of Marketing, Third Edition*. Harlow: Prentice Hall.

Burn, J. and Barnett, M. (1999) 'Communicating for advantage in the virtual organization', *IEEE Transactions on Professional Communication*, 42 (4): 215–22.

Cannon, T. (1992) *Basic Marketing, Third Edition*. London: Cassell.

Chartered Institute of Marketing (1984) in L. Lumsdon (1997) *Tourism Marketing*. London: International Thomson Business Press.

Cooper, C., Fletcher, J., Fyall, A., Gilbert, D. and Wanhill, S. (2005) *Tourism: Principles and Practice, Third Edition*. Harlow: Prentice Hall.

Dacko, S. (2004) 'Marketing strategies for last-minute travel and tourism: Profitability and revenue management implications', *Journal of Travel and Tourism Marketing*, 16 (4): 7–20.

Edgell, D.L., Ruf, K.M. and Agarwal, A. (1999) 'Strategic marketing planning for the tourism industry', *Journal of Travel and Tourism Marketing*, 8 (3): 111–20.

Fayos-Sola, E. (1996) 'Tourism policy: A midsummer nights dream', *Tourism Management*, 17 (6): 405–12.

Fyall, A. and Garrod, B. (2005) *Tourism Marketing: A Collaborative Approach*. Clevedon: Channel View.

Harris, G. and Katz, K. (1996) *Promoting International Tourism*. Los Angeles: The American Group.

Holloway, J.C. (2004) *Marketing for Tourism, Fourth Edition*. Harlow: Pearson.

Holloway, J.C. and Robinson, C. (1995) *Marketing for Tourism*. Harlow: Longman.

Jones, P. and Lockwood, A. (2002) *The Management of Hotel Operations*. London: Continuum.

Kotler, P. (1988) *Marketing Management: Analysis, Planning, Implementation and Control, Sixth Edition*. Englewood Cliffs, NJ: Prentice Hall.

Kotler, P., Wong, A., Saunders, J. and Armstrong, G. (2004) *Principles of Marketing: Fourth European Edition*. Harlow: Prentice Hall.

Lee, J., Sung, H., DeFranco, A. and Arnold, R. (2004) 'Developing, operating and maintaining a travel agency website: Attending to e-consumers and internet marketing issues', *Journal of Travel and Tourism Marketing*, 17 (2/3): 205–23.

Lumsdon, L. (1997) *Tourism Marketing*. London: Thomson Learning.

Middleton, V.T.C. and Clarke, J. (2001) *Marketing in Travel and Tourism, Third Edition*. Oxford: Butterworth-Heinemann.

Peattie, K. (1992) *Green Marketing*. Harlow: Longman.

Porter, M. (1980) *Competitive Strategy: Techniques for Analysing Industries and Competitors*. New York: Collier and Macmillan, Free Press.

Sánchez, J., Callarisa, L., Rodriguez, M. and Moliner, A. (2006) 'Perceived value of the purchase of a tourism product', *Tourism Management* 27.

Seaton, A. and Bennett, M. (1996) *Marketing Tourism Products*. London, Thomson Learning.

Shone, A. and Parry, B. (2004) *Successful Event Management, Second Edition*. London: Thomson Learning.

Vellas, F. and Becherel, L. (eds) (1999) *The International Marketing of Travel and Tourism: A Strategic Approach*. London: Macmillan.

Further reading

The best book in marketing remains:

Kotler, P., Wong, V., Saunders, J. and Armstrong, G. (2004) *Principles of Marketing, Fourth European Edition*. Harlow: Prentice Hall.

With a new text on tourism marketing by:

Fyall, A. and Garrod, B. (2005) *Tourism Marketing: A Collaborative Approach*. Clevedon: Channel View.

A recent review of the state of tourism research in marketing is a good overview:

Oh, H., Kim, B. and Shin, J. (2004) 'Hospitality and tourism marketing: Recent developments in research and future directions', *International Journal of Hospitality Management*, 23: 425–47.

16

Marketing Tourism Destinatations

Learning outcomes

After reading this chapter and answering the questions, you should be able to:

- understand the concept and elements of a destination

- recognize the role of destination marketing and destination marketing organizations.

- identify aspects of marketing planning, imagery and advertising for reaching target consumers

- understand the need for branding in destination marketing.

Overview

The application of marketing and advertising principles in tourism is largely undertaken by the private sector, seeking to communicate and sell their products and services to tourists. Yet since tourism services and products are an amalgam of different elements of tourism supply by businesses, an organizing framework is needed to integrate these components of supply into a means by which tourists can easily understand the products different places can offer. One mechanism to do this, is to develop the concept of a destination, around which the marketing, advertising and development of tourism products and services is undertaken. This often requires an organization such as an NTO or destination management organization to lead this process, around which the unique selling proposition of the destination is developed to give it a competitive advantage.

Introduction

Destinations are often seen by the tourist as the outwardly facing element of a tourism service or product, being a place where their consumption occurs. At a global scale, the growth of international and domestic tourism has seen the exponential expansion of places seeking to develop their tourism potential. Even very unlikely and unattractive places have developed a tourism economy, based on the principles of creating a destination and a demand for the products and services they offer. This chapter examines the concept of a destination and how it has been used in a marketing context, and it develops many of the ideas covered in Chapter 15 on the role of the public sector, as well as the marketing and advertising concepts covered in Chapter 14. In this respect, it provides a synthesis of how destinations harness marketing principles and implement them. One of the central themes of this chapter is also to show how tourists perceive destinations, and how they develop destination images. In a strategic management context, this chapter also highlights the link which marketing and management have in seeking to ensure the long-term sustainability and prosperity of destinations, the need to delight the visitor and engender notions of satisfaction from their experiences and to ensure that the area does not decline (Buhalis 2000). One of the very early tourism marketing texts by Wahab *et al.* (1976: 24) outlined the scope of tourism destination marketing:

> *The management process through which the National Tourist organizations and/or tourist enterprises identify their selected tourist, actual and potential, communicate with them to ascertain and influence their wishes, needs, motivations, likes and dislikes, on local, regional, national and international levels and to formulate and adapt their tourist products accordingly in view of achieving optimal tourist satisfaction thereby fulfilling their objectives.*

In operational terms, destination marketing has a crucial role in ensuring that the destination lifecycle does not enter into a stage of saturation or decline, in communicating with the target markets at each stage of develop (i.e. to raise visitors' awareness at the initial stage of development, to inform in the growth stage, to persuade visitors to come in a mature and saturation stage and to retain visitors and introduce new markets in the declining stages) (Buhalis 2000). As Chapter 15 and the resort lifecycle suggest, marketing is also vital since other destinations develop in competition, thus destinations have to formulate strategies to differentiate themselves. As Porter's model in Chapter 15 shows, destinations need to compete but are constrained by one critical constraint, the resource base and its sustainability, since once the resource base is destroyed it cannot be replaced. Nevertheless, destination marketing has to make critical decisions on strategic issues related to product, promotion, price and distribution strategies for tourism, since the resort lifecycle means that the destination is constantly evolving and changing, making strategic marketing a necessity. In extreme cases, destinations overrun by visitors may also have to use marketing to de-market their locality through dissuading visitors from coming at peak times in conjunction with **visitor management** tools.

One interesting attempt to set the destination in a competitive framework was made by Gilbert (1990), who argued that destinations could be classified along a continuum. At the initial stages of development, a destination achieves a status at which its unique attributes are not substitutable, so consumer loyalty and willingness to pay to visit are high. Through time, as the destination develops and competing destinations come on stream, decisions to visit it are based more on price competitiveness and high-spending visitors are not attracted. The destination then assumes a commodity status, though in reality Buhalis (2000) suggests that most destinations are located at some point between these status and commodity positions. In some cases, destinations have sought to develop niche markets as a process of continuous innovation, in order to diversify their market base and remain competitive, retaining their unique appeal. However, in locations that have followed cost-leadership strategies, mass tourism has caused irrevocable damage to the resource base. Whatever approach to destination marketing an area develops, the starting point must be a fundamental understanding of the elements, which coalesce to form the destination.

The destination concept

Tourist destinations are a mix of tourism products, experiences and other intangible items promoted to consumers. This is not a new concept, since resorts and many areas which developed large tourism industries in the eighteenth and nineteenth century used guide books, posters and brochures to promote travel to their area. At a general level, this concept of a destination can be developed to represent geographically defined entities such as groups of countries, countries, regions in a country (i.e. The Rockies in North America), a city (e.g. London), a rural area (e.g. The Swan Valley, a wine tourism region in Western Australia), a resort or a wide range of experiences created by tourism marketers. Increasingly, the notion of a destination is something perceived by consumers, although most conventional definitions emphasize the geographical element of a specific place. From a tourist's perspective, a destination may usually be classified into one of the following: conventional resorts; environmental destinations; business tourism centres; places one stops en route to another place; a short-break destination and day-trip destinations. In essence, destinations are places which tourists visit and stay at. Whatever way one approaches the concept of a destination (i.e. from an industry-supply perspective or from the consumer's viewpoint), there are a range of six components which comprise a destination as Figure 16.1 shows.

The destination is often refered to as an amalgam of the six As:

- available packages
- accessibility
- attractions
- amenities
- activities
- ancillary services

and in the most developed destinations, a public/public-private or private sector organization may be responsible for the coordination, planning and promotion of the destination.

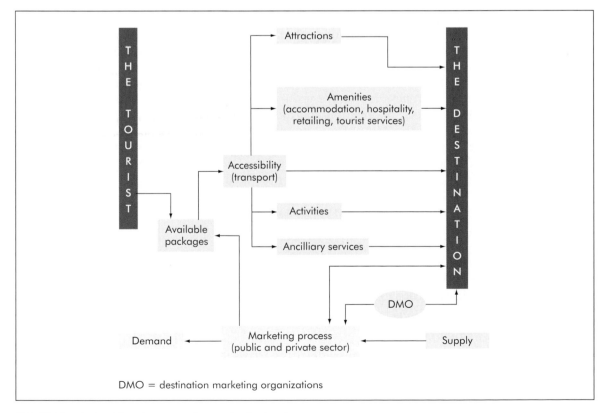

FIGURE 16.1   The elements of a tourist destination

One of the principal tasks of **destination marketing organization**s (DMOs) is to increase visitation levels in a marketing context. However, DMOs also have a management function including the coordination of planning, economic development, the role of stakeholders including the host community, private sector tourism interests, public sector (including local and national government), tourists and other bodies such as pressure groups. These different stakeholders are an important focus for planning, since they may have different political agendas which makes seeking to derive a consensus destination marketing a complex task and illustrates the importance of collaboration.

Formulating the destination marketing mix: The role of the DMO

A central feature of any destination **marketing strategy** will be the formulation of a destination product. In some cases, a destination may find that competitive forces have caused it to begin to decline. This may be due to a wide range of reasons such as lacklustre performance or complacency by the DMO or NTO or both, since NTOs will market countries as destinations, while DMOs will develop their own distinctive approach at the local destination level to develop a unique selling point and highlight key factors to appeal to visitors. As Middleton and Clarke (2001) suggest, most DMOs do not have the ability to control tourist travel to destinations: they can only influence it because, as Chapters 3 and 4 have shown, a wide range of factors impact upon demand. DMOs are only part of the total marketing spend for a destination, since the private sector also uses brochures, websites and other campaigns to promote the products available for sale in the destination as Figure 16.1 shows. In the best case scenario, only a small proportion of these suppliers will have formal links with an NTO or DMO, although experiments in online DMOs such as VisitScotland.com have started to change this situation.

One starting point for DMOs is the marketing strategy, which will identify the marketing mix needed to promote the area after a marketing plan has been created. At a generic level, destination marketers need to constantly evaluate the strategic fit of the destination product with changing consumer tastes. The case of VisitScotland (Insight 16.2) also sets out a blueprint for the tourism industry to develop destination products in each area of Scotland's product portfolio, to maximize the impact of product campaigns. This emphasizes the need for a DMO to provide leadership and a focus for industry coordination and planning of marketing efforts to gain synergies, consistent marketing messages to consumers and partnerships to facilitate joint **marketing campaigns**.

In formulating the destination product, the DMO will always have an intentional focus, meaning that it will be directly seeking to influence visitors to come in the short-term as well as aiming to raise general awareness for future visits. One of the core functions of any DMO in communicating to stakeholders its direction and focus will be its strategy document; in Insight 16.1 the strategy document for a DMO at the state level in Australia – Tourism New South Wales – is outlined. This not only gives its strategies for 2003–2006, it is also an example of a domestic marketing strategy for showcasing the destination and the DMO's support for the tourism industry in terms of advertising, public relations and direct marketing.

Middleton and Clarke (2001) point to the wider role which NTOs can play in support of DMOs such as TNSW in the source markets and in support of the tourism industry:

- providing market intelligence and research data
- running web-based advertising
- organizing trade shows
- hosting familiarization trips for foreign travel agents, travel writers and tour operators
- providing online travel trade manuals as reference guides
- participating in joint marketing
- running a DMS (see Chapter 6) to provide direct access to consumers and bookings
- running destination quality schemes to raise standards and engender a wider concern for tourist well-being (see Chapter 26 for more detail).

INSIGHT 16.1

Tourism New South Wales marketing strategy

In 2005, the readers of the North American newspaper *USA Today* voted Australia as the most desirable tourist destination to visit. This underpins the phenomenal success of Australia's growth as a visitor destination in the 1990s. On of the country's major gateways is Sydney, New South Wales, and this provides many opportunities for the state's tourism organization – Tourism New South Wales (TNSW). TNSW has developed a strategy which is consumer driven. In 2003/2004 TNSW saw its main challenge was to:

- target and increase visitor nights, mainly from inter-state markets (i.e. other states in Australia)
- to target long-stay holidays currently being lost to Queensland
- to continue to attract international markets.

For 2003–2006, TNSW outlined ten key strategies:

- to lead the New South Wales tourism industry
- to align marketing efforts with corporate objectives (i.e. to increase visitor nights, to target new and emerging markets, off-peak and mid-week travel and to aid the geographical dispersion of visitors in New South Wales whilst also increasing yields)
- to build strong tourism brands to differentiate TNSW from its competitors
- to take a fresh look at the way we view markets
- to integrate marketing activity across TNSW, its regions and in the use of the promotional tools it uses, including the web
- to develop new strategic product offers such as holidays for mature people
- to showcase TSNW via its brands, products and showcasing experiences to bridge the brand–product link
- to adopt a new approach to regional tourism partnerships

- to develop a new approach to international marketing, working in close cooperation with the Australian Tourist Commission.

As part of the marketing efforts of TNSW, three methods of communicating to the consumer focus on:

- the brand, with the 2003/2004 'Freedom' and 'Feel Free' campaign;
- showcasing the top six experiences which distinguish TNSW from its competitors:
  - Sydney
  - nature
  - Discovery/Drive (a touring experience)
  - food and wine
  - beaches
  - sports and events product, which comprises the holiday experiences.

Table 16.1 provides one example of how TNSW set about showcasing the region to provide potential visitors with the reason to visit, with the retail products already in place for consumers to purchase. Table 16.1 also shows how the different elements of the marketing strategy, using the concept of showcasing the region, were put into action by TSNW 2003/2004 to lead the promotion in line with its marketing strategy and goals. This should also be read together with TNSW's *Towards 2020 – New South Wales Tourism Masterplan* (Tourism New South Wales 2003a), which sets out state tourism policies/planning issues, measures to improve the effectiveness and efficiency of the tourism industry and measures designed to enhance the destination and visitor experience. The plan also incorporates the measures designed to adopt a state-wide destination positioning and promotion strategy based upon capital city tourism, regional tourism events, business tourism and aboriginal tourism.

There's no place in the world like Sydney

Image 16.1: Tourism New South Wales branding of Sydney – 'There's no place like Sydney', Source: Copyright, Tourism New South Wales

TABLE 16.1 Domestic partnership marketing activity: Showcase-led experiences/destinations (one-year plan 2003/2004)

DOMESTIC PARTNERSHIP MARKETING ACTIVITY SHOWCASE – Lead Experiences/Destinations	2003 July	Aug	Sept	Oct	Nov	Dec	Jan	2004 Feb	Mar	April	May	June
CONSUMER MARKETING SUPPORT												
ADVERTISING												
John Farnham 'Freedom' TVC (VIC/QLD/SD)	A		A	A					A	A		
Brand Sydney					A Sydney summer campaign						A Sydney winter campaign	
Showcasing	BC	BC	BC	E	E	E	C	C	B	B	D	D
Experience and product offer print	BC	BC	BC	E	E	E	C	C	B	B	D	D
PUBLIC RELATIONS												
Publicity/editorial	ABCF	ABCDF	BCDEF	BCEF	AF	ACF	ACF	ABCDEF	BDEF	BDF	ACF	ACF
Promotions		B			D		A		B		D	A
Media familiarizations*						ALL YEAR						
DIRECT MARKETING												
e-marketing						ALL YEAR						
Database marketing		B						C			C	
Consumer shows										Sydney & Melbourne Caravan, Camping & 4WD Holiday Super Show	Melbourne Caravan, Camping, 4WD & Holiday Super Show	Brisbane Caravan, Camping, 4WD & Holiday Super Show Collateral
COLLATERAL												
Regional holiday planners*						ALL YEAR						
TRADE MARKETING												
Summer in the City						A	A					
Sydney on Sale	A											

Legend

A Sydney B Nature C Discovery D Food and wine E Beaches F Sports events ALL YEAR – will occur throughout the year across the spectrum themes
VIC Victoria QLD Queensland SD Sydney

Source: Tourism New South Wales (2003b)

What these potential roles and support functions of the DMO highlight is the need to undertake the following generic tasks in a marketing (and destination management) context:

- understanding consumer markets
- ensuring accessibility to the market (e.g. the Scottish Executive provided a £6 million fund to help fund the establishment of new flights to Scotland to make it more accessible as a destination)
- understanding and communicating the core offering
- recognizing, analysing and addressing the competitive forces affecting the destination
- identifying the tourism development needs of the destination to nurture visitors and to improve their experiences as Insight 16.1 illustrates

- coordinating and leading destination marketing activities
- reformulating the marketing mix
- monitoring **sustainability** to ensure that activities do not destroy the long-term marketability and resource base in the destination
- identifying new ideas, trends and how to be an outwardly facing organization able in order to understand the global marketplace and adopt a creative approach to destination marketing.

DMOs also have a key role in understanding the pricing of the destination product, even though this is largely in the control of the private sector businesses. In the case of the large European tour operators who have been accused of driving down the prices paid to local operators, their size and power illustrates that small local businesses must address reduced profit margins by new strategies (i.e. overpricing local services and products). DMOs have a central role to play in working with intermediaries (including e-mediaries) such as those involved in staging meetings, incentives, conferences and exhibitions (MICE) who may bring lucrative business travellers.

As Chapter 15 has shown, DMOs may have a communication role in promoting the destination by organizing a coordinated campaign. This may include *above-the-line promotional activity*, such as advertising, to develop the destination brand; this is discussed later. *Below-the-line promotion*, such as attending trade fairs and distributing brochures while meeting with intermediaries, is also undertaken. But how do tourists select a destination to visit, given the highly competitive marketing which many places are now undertaking?

Selecting a tourist destination

According to Seddighi and Theocharous (2002) understanding how tourists select the destinations they visit is central to destination marketers so they can decide upon which marketing strategies to use to influence consumer behaviour. At a simplistic level, any traveller is faced with a range of motives. In the case of business travel, this is often not a choice-related form of travel and is dictated by employment needs, although conference and incentive travel may be influenced by choice. It is the leisure holiday which has attracted the greatest amount of research, where the initial choice of destination facing the tourist is either a domestic or overseas destination(s), the decision being partly based upon the purchasing power of the consumer. The attitudes and perception of the prospective tourist towards alternative destinations leads to different preferences, as a multi-stage process. As Chapter 4 discussed, a wide range of demographic, gender, income and level of education impact upon holiday-taking. Seddighi and Theocharous (2002) also develop the importance of destination-specific factors including:

- whether the visitor has been to the destination before
- the cost of living at the destination
- the price of the tourist package
- facilities at the destination
- the cost of transportation and time taken in travelling
- the quality of the promotion and advertising
- the quality of services
- any political instability at the destination.

This highlights the importance of destination marketing, as Buckley and Papadopolous (1986: 86) argued, where

Greater attention must be paid to the characteristics of visitors when trying to develop a marketing strategy ... a clear market segment must be identified and an investigation made of the buying decision factors, which predominate in that segment ... It is, however, important to recognise that the tourist product is a composite product and that there is more than one type of client.

This also indicates the importance of buyer behaviour as a key element in destination choice. As Middleton and Clarke (2001) indicate, models of consumer behaviour have traditionally emphasized price as the key determinant of a purchase. But growing consumer sophistication has seen branding and other non-rational considerations and attitudes influence buyer behaviour. In a simplified form, this process can be summarized as follows:

- destinations promote competitive products to consumers direct, and via the travel trade/intermediaries
- advertising, promotion and the interplay of personal recommendation, family, friends, consumer trends, taste and the internet combine to shape buyer characteristics
- these buyer characteristics are filtered by the **learning behaviour** of consumers, which has been influenced by marketing/recommendation. For example, Ashworth and Goodall (1988) observed that if a tourist is dissatisfied they will not recommend the destination to others; a reminder of the importance of visitor satisfaction and word of mouth. It is also shaped by the perceptions of consumers of brands and images of the destination, and their experience of travel (i.e. prior travel to destinations)
- these characteristics combine in the buyer decision-making process where learning, perceptions and experience lead to the motivation to buy
- at the motivation stage, the characteristics of the consumer (i.e. demographic, economic and social profile) combine with their psychographic characteristics as well as their attitudes to create: needs, wants and goals. In tourism purchases, Morgan (1996) suggests the family often acts as a single decision-making unit and Zalaton (1998) noted male–female differences in purchases
- the consumer then chooses between different goods or services to purchase a product or brand to fulfil their motivation.

Within buyer behaviour research, which derives from the sub-area of marketing called 'consumer behaviour', the DMO may apply marketing segmentation techniques as described in Chapter 4. Yet one of the most influential factors in the consumer's choice of destination is the **destination image** which is not necessarily grounded in experience or facts but is a key motivator in travel and tourism. Images and the expectations of travel experiences are closely linked in prospective customers' minds and the ultimate objective of destination marketing is to: 'Sustain, alter or develop images in order to influence prospective buyers' expectations' (Middleton and Clarke 2001: 127). Again, this reiterates the importance of marketing research in seeking to understand the intrinsic attractiveness of a destination's image to a visitor, as well as how the perceived image can be used to position the destination to derive a competitive advantage.

The tourist destination image

Within the literature on tourism marketing, the study of destination imagery is one of the major areas of academic endeavour. For this reason, this section will examine the factors which impact upon destination image including how to approach the study of image formation. According to Gallarza, Saura and Garciá (2002: 58), the initial development of destination image research can be dated to Hunt (1975). Most academic studies have focused on:

- the conceptualization and dimensions of TDI
- the destination image formation process
- the assessment and measurement of destination image
- the influence of distance on destination image
- destination image change over time
- the active and passive role of residents in the image of destinations
- destination image management (i.e. positioning and promotion).

This proliferation of studies has made the definition of TDI a complex task, with no consensus of the term and its scope, although it is broadly concerned with the way individuals and groups develop mental constructions about destinations, focusing on different attributes which are shaped by their beliefs, values, ideas, perceptions and impressions. As Beerli and Martin (2004a) suggest, the image of the destination might be classified into nine items as shown in Table 16.2, based on the attributes of the destination which are vast and very difficult to reduce to a series of simple constructs. A study

TABLE 16.2   Dimensions and attributes determining the perceived tourist destination image

Natural resources	General infrastructure	Tourist infrastructure

Weather
  Temperature
  Rainfall
  Humidity
  Hours of sunshine
Beaches
  Quality of seawater
  Sandy or rocky beaches
  Length of beaches
  Overcrowding of beaches
Richness of the scenery
  Protected nature reserves
  Lakes, mountains, deserts etc.
Variety and uniqueness of flora and
  fauna
	Development and quality of roads,
	  airports and ports
	Private and public transport facilities
	Development of health services
	Development of telecommunications
	Development of commercial
	  infrastructures
	Extent of building development
		Hotel and self-catering accommodation
		  Number of beds
		  Categories
		  Quality
		Restaurants
		  Number
		  Categories
		  Quality
		Bars, discoteques and clubs
		Ease of access to destination
		Excursions at the destination
		Tourist centres
		Network of tourist information

Tourist leisure and recreation	**Culture, history and art**	**Political and economic factors**

Theme parks
Entertainment and sports activities
  Golf, fishing, hunting, skiing, scuba
  etc.
  Water parks
  Zoos
  Trekking
  Adventure activities
  Casinos
  Nightlife
  Shopping
	Museums, historical buildings,
	  monuments etc
	Festival, concerts etc
	Handicraft
	Gastronomy
	Folklore
	Religion
	Customs and ways of life
		Political stability
		Political tendencies
		Economic development
		Safety
		  Crime rate
		  Terrorist attacks
		Prices

Natural environment	**Social environment**	**Atmosphere of the place**
Beauty of the scenery Beauty of the cities and towns Cleanliness Overcrowding Air and noise pollution Traffic congestion	Hospitality and friendliness of the local residents Underprivileged and poverty Quality of life Language barriers	Luxurious place Fashionable place Place with fame and reputation Place oriented toward families Exotic place Mystic place Relaxing place Stressful place Happy, enjoyable place Pleasant place Boring place Attractive or interesting place

Source: Reprinted from *Tourism Management*, vol.25, Beerli and Martin, 'Tourists' characteristics and the perceived image of tourist destinations: A quantitative analysis – a case study of Lanzarote, Spain', 623–36, copyright (2004), with permission from Elsevier

by Echtner and Ritchie (1991) has added some clarity to the wide range of definitions which exist by pointing to the existence of three axes that support the image of a destination:

- a psychological/functional dimension
- the common/unique dimension
- holistic/attribute axes.

As Beerli and Martin (2004a) suggest, a number of attributes have been studied in TDI studies which can be classified according to the functional–psychological axis. These studies can help in understanding what Gunn (1988) described as the personal factors affecting the tourist formation of a destination image:

- the accumulation of images of the destination
- modifying the initial image after gathering more information, creating an induced image
- deciding to visit the destination
- visiting the destination
- sharing the destination
- returning home
- modifying the image based on experience to create an organic and induced image. This organic image, based upon non-commercial sources of data, is influenced by the media and friends. In contrast, the induced image is the result of commercial data and information such as destination or industry advertising.

One consequence of these studies of TDI is that whatever measures are developed to understand imagery, one needs a framework within which to understand image formation.

A model of destination image formulation

Baloglu and McCleary (1999) provided a framework to analyse TDI, which is conditioned by two key elements:

- stimulus factors (external stimuli, physical objects, personal experience)
- personal factors (social and psychological characteristics of the consumer).

As a result, three determinants of TDI were identified by Baloglu and McCleary (1999):

- tourism motivations
- sociodemographic factors
- information sources.

These determinants help shape the TDI as an attitudinal construct, that comprises a consumer's mental understanding of knowledge, feelings and global impression of a destination. As we discussed in Chapter 15, the image has a perceptual/cognitive as well as an affective element which generate responses to create an overall image of the destination as shown in Figure 16.2.

The construction of images of destination is clearly an area which can be studied using quantitative research methods to measure the elements of a TDI and the visitors' preferences. Yet there is also a growing interest in more qualitative studies which seek to examine the images portrayed in brochures by marketers to promote destinations. In the case of less developed world tourism destinations, Echtner and Prasad (2003) examined the visual elements in the brochures. They found images of lands which were unchanged, where unrestrained behaviour could occur and where 'uncivilized' people existed. They also highlighted the myths created in destination images by tour operators to represent the less developed world to appeal to particular market segments. Such destination imagery is demeaning to the host population and that this may attract visitors with false expectations and a form of tourism that is not compatible with the destination.

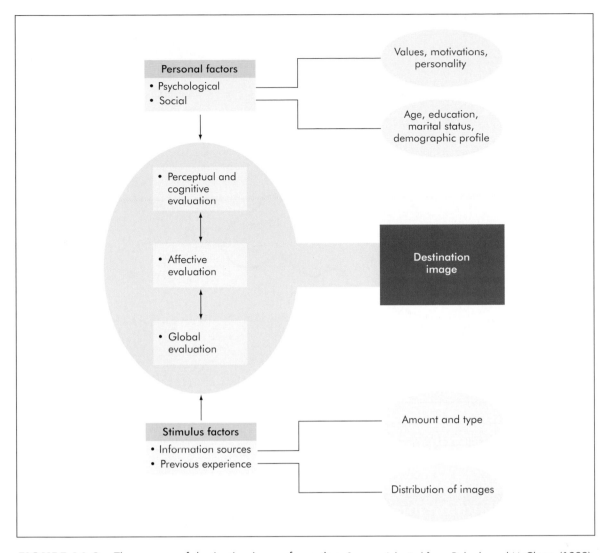

FIGURE 16.2   The process of destination image formation. Source: Adapted from Baloglu and McCleary (1999)

Kim and Richardson (2003) point to a similar effect that may be generated by motion pictures on destination images. Such images enter the domain of popular culture and the impact on place images can be very influential. In fact Gartner (1993) highlighted the interrelationship of cognitive and affective elements of destination images which have a strong impact on the decision to visit. One example of this effect occurred in Scotland following the launch of a childrens's programme, *Balamory*, set on a fictitious island of the same name, which was, in real life, the Isle of Mull, in the town of Tobermory (Figure 16.3) with its painted houses. This led to a tourism boom, following the rise of toddler tourism (Connell 2005). The local area tourist board, AILLST, promoted the area using Tobermory on the front cover of their 2004 holiday brochure, adding to the tourist boom (Image 16.2). As Connell (2005) has shown, such place imagery can have an immediate impact on a destination, particularly when the images generated by popular culture (e.g. the BBC) are not matched in reality, and small-scale destinations find themselves besieged in the peak tourist season.

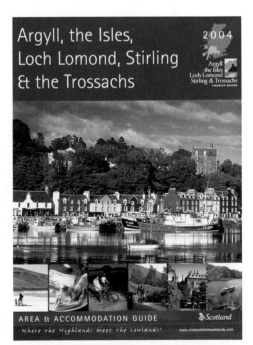

Image 16.2: Argyll, the Islands, Loch Lomond, Stirling and the Trossachs Tourist Board Holiday Brochure, 2004 with image of Tobermory, reproduced courtesy of AILLST

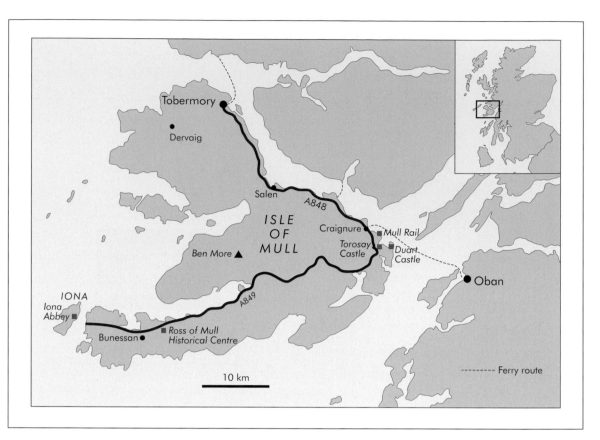

FIGURE 16.3 Location of 'Balamory'. Source: Copyright J. Connell

Using destination imagery to gain competitive advantage

With growing global competition for tourists, destination marketers are constantly seeking new ways to overcome the problem of **destination substitutability**. The global expansion of destination advertising is highly competitive as the use of print media and the World Wide Web along with the travel sections of European Sunday newspapers show. Competitiveness is a byword for destinations in the twenty-first century. One method developed is **destination positioning** (DP). As Pike and Ryan (2004) observe, DP is based on three propositions:

- in modern society, people are bombarded with information on a daily basis
- the mind has developed a defence mechanism against this process of information overload
- the only way to reach the consumer is through simplified and focused messages.

The core element of DP is image, which is the simplified messages and information associated with destination. These messages try and influence buyer behaviour, given the intangible nature of tourism and its experiences. DP requires a DMO to create a lasting favourable image or perception among prospective consumers. In technical terms, the destination marketer will need to understand the cognitive, affective and choice element in the decision or intent to visit a destination (the 'conative image'). To operationalize this, marketers will need to identify the important attributes which visitors perceive in the destination, and its attractiveness to the **target market**. This needs to be understood in relation to how the competition performs. Through complex statistical analysis (e.g. factor analysis and importance–performance analysis), it is possible to group destinations in a matrix. This allows marketers to identify one or two key features to differentiate the destination image from that of the competition, whilst providing a mechanism to communicate that image to consumers. A typical affective response matrix for competing destinations in the adventure tourism destination market is shown in Figure 16.4.

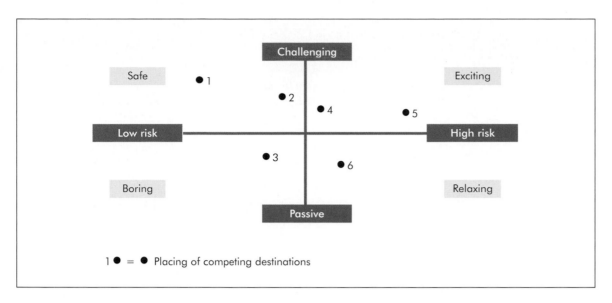

FIGURE 16.4   Affective response matrix for competing adventure tourism destinations

For example, Destination 1 is perceived as a relatively low-risk but challenging place to undertake adventure tourism whereas Destination 3 is perceived as a relatively passive and boring location and should reconsider the suitability of its image for the market it is trying to attract. Figure 16.4 shows that this type of competitor analysis is helpful in that each destination can see how suited it is to specific promotional messages which are aligned to consumer perception. A study by van der Ark and Richards (2007) examined the attractiveness of European capital cities in terms of culture to assess their relative positions as destinations, with their attractiveness dominated by London, Paris and Rome whose culture enhanced their rankings.

Communicating the destination image: The role of advertising

Marketing concepts in tourism allow us to understand some of the tools and techniques used to communicate with consumers, yet to the consumer these may seem abstract and very distant from the real world. This is because the tourist only sees the outwardly facing elements of marketing by businesses and destinations, and the most visible elements of this is advertising. According to Middleton and Clarke (2001: 237), advertising and public relations

> are primary means of manipulating demand and influencing buyer behaviour. Simply stated, they enable businesses to reach people in their homes or other places away from the places of production and delivery, and to communicate to them messages intended to influence their purchasing behaviour.

This suggests that buyer behaviour is a very complex process. Advertising is one of the most widely used marketing communication tool in tourism, mainly because the product or service is intangible. It is often based on real or perceived images of tourism and destination. What is notable in tourism is the massive scale of advertising spend. According to Middleton and Clarke (2001), advertising spend on display advertising for tourism in the UK in the late 1990s was £425 million. The tourism sector is a high spender on tourism advertising to get its messages across as any review of post-Christmas television advertising by European tour operators will show. This is designed to influence consumers in the traditional December–January period when they are looking to book summer holidays.

More recent data for the USA were compiled by Wöber and Fesenmaier (2004) who noted that US state tourism offices spent US$178.2 million on domestic and US$49.7 million on international advertising which was over 30 per cent of the total US$685.1 million of combined budgets of these tourism offices. A selection of these expenditures can be found in Table 16.3 which illustrates the significance placed on tourism in states with a highly developed tourism

TABLE 16.3   Selected US state tourism budgets 2000 – 2001

	(US$)		
	Domestic advertising budget	*International advertising budget*	*Other sources of advertising revenue*
Illinois	8 534 000	5 400 000	47 125 000
California	4 650 000	830 000	9 120 000
Florida	10 175 221	4 119 857	45 499 632
Mississippi	3 496 200	400 000	9 557 370
New York	7 462 400	316 000	12 160 700
Nevada	1 631 332	524 937	9 101 127
Texas	16 921 000	2 186 590	19 065 160
Washington	996 000	250 000	2 579 020

Source: Adapted from Wöber and Fesenmaier (2004)

industry. But it is expensive to undertake advertising and hard to assess its impact. Yet for the highly developed and competitive tourism marketplace, it is not the only tool used to inform, persuade and attempt to induce consumer activity in the fast-moving consumer goods sector, where products such as holidays have a limited shelf life. Advertising in a marketing context is part of the promotional mix identified in marketing plans and strategies, but it has to be viewed as part of a more integrated communication strategy for businesses and NTOs to speak with one voice to their existing or potential customers.

Advertising and tourism: An integral relationship?

The consumer buying process in tourism often involves the consumer seeing imagery of places, products and services, rather than being able to physically experience them before buying. Consequently, advertising is important in developing the buyer attitudes, behaviour and the perceived image of a prospective purchase. The holiday brochure, combined with powerful television images, is a major mechanism used by tour operators to seek to influence consumers that they will derive personal value and benefits from their holiday product. At the same time, such intentional advertising is often supported by destination marketing in terms of posters, billboards, brochures and media advertising to reinforce and encourage an interest in a certain destination. One illustration of one facet of a media campaign and the cost for industry partners can be seen in the SeeAmerica.org media promotion in the UK market in 2005.

SeeAmerica.Org media planning for promotion in the UK market in 2005

In 2004, over four million UK residents visited the USA. Despite the growth in arrivals of 8 per cent 2002–2003 and 11 per cent 2003–2004, the Tourism Industry Association of America (TIA) launched the See America campaign (as discussed in Chapter 14). In 2005, See America launched a campaign to offset the negative imagery associated with the Iraq war and to target the growing UK market. This was part of a US$4 million advertising campaign led by See America. As part of the advertising programme for 2005, See America provided US tourism operators with the opportunity to advertise in the following UK consumer publications as travel supplements:

- January 2005, *Sunday Times*, national edition (1.4 million circulation and 3.25 million readership)
- March 2005, *Sunday Times*, regional editions, and the *Mail on Saturday* (one million circulation and two million readership)
- September 2005, *Sunday Times*, regional editions, and the *Mail on Sunday*.

A direct mail to UK ABTA members in February, April and September was also planned to 16 000 members, reaching 96 000 tourism trade readers.

What is interesting from an advertising perspective, is the cost to See American members. A programme with advertising, editorial coverage, supplements in consumer publications, an online sweepstake, opportunity to join a database of interested readers and the ABTA mail out was priced thus:

For three-time participation in the programme (and one time in brackets)
½ page display advert US$130 000 ($55 000)
¼ page display advert US$73 000 ($32 500)
⅛ page display advert US$41 000 ($17 050) (Adapted from www.seeamerica.org See America 2005 UK Campaign, February 2005)

which highlights the high cost of advertising in the media. Yet such advertising is only part of communicating the destination image, which needs to be understood in the wider context of advertising.

The process of communicating the destination image

In its simplest form, advertising in tourism is a process and much of the discussion which follows is as relevant to destination marketing as it is for tourism businesses. In an operational context Middleton and Clarke (2001: 241) point to the six stages of advertising:

- advertising objectives (i.e. what is one seeking to achieve?)
- target audience identification
- creative planning (the pictures, images and symbols to use to convey the advertising message)
- media planning (i.e. what forms of advertising to use)
- media costs
- measuring the results and effectiveness of advertising; this typically falls into response measurement (i.e. in relation to a brochure request advertisement) and more in-depth market research studies of the communication effect. This will often be a costly market research exercise to test measures of awareness, interest, attitudes and recall of advertising.

The outcome of the advertising, as a communication process for destinations (and individual businesses) is shown in Figure 16.5. This combines much of the conventional research from consumer behaviour which suggests that advertising will be targeted at consumers, but only around 12 per cent of the target is reached, since messages are filtered out by the consumer subconsciously. Once the message reaches the final proportion of consumers, a variety of different models of consumer behaviour suggest that potential visitors go through a series of steps before deciding to visit a destination. One model, shown in Figure 16.5, is the AIDA (attention–interest–desire–action) approach which dates to Strong (1925). Alternative models include the Awareness to Reinforcement Process as described by Morgan and Pritchard (2000) as well as that discussed by McWilliams and Crompton (1997).

To convert consumers to buyers, advertisers need to be aware of the following issues:

- *advertising objectives*: the identification of what a DMO or business wishes to achieve in its target markets, namely awareness, interest and activity resulting in a visit or purchase
- *target audience identification*, by examining their media habits

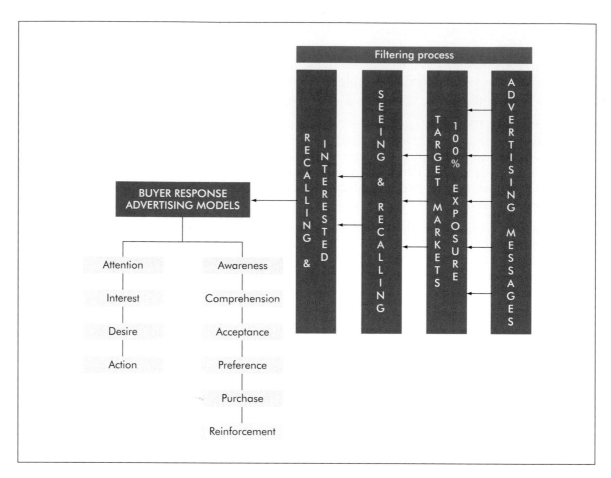

FIGURE 16.5 The advertising communication process in destination marketing. Source: Developed from Middleton and Clarke (2001); Morgan and Pritchard (2000); McWilliams and Crompton (1997)

- *creative planning*, where pictures, symbols and words are used to convey the message simply, as discussed under destination positioning above. An example is British Airways and the World's Favourite Airline image. The tourism sector, like many other industries, uses the creative talents of private sector advertising agencies to develop a creative set of concepts, which are tested on consumers using focus groups before launching the campaign

- *media planning*, identifying and programming which advertisements will be shown. This involves identifying which audiences to target, the cost of reaching them, the scope for creative activity depending on the media used, the space sought and receptiveness of the audience

- *media costs*, where advertising costs are identified as cost per thousand reached.

To reach the target market, various rules of advertising have been developed since the 1950s which include:

- have a unique selling proposition (USP).
- a memorable slogan is needed.
- a logo is needed in any advertisement.
- humour is not necessary.
- the product needs to be visible in the advertisement (Adapted from Morgan and Pritchard 2000).

However as Morgan and Pritchard (2000) demonstrate, these rules have been developed during the last decade to reflect the importance of creativity in gaining consumer attention. Thus the USP may be replaced with emotional selling propositions and irrational appeals, while humour is valid, as are slogans and logos. As Santos (2004) found in the case of Portugal, the opinions of travel writers can also be extremely influential in the promotion and advertising of tourism products and destinations. In some cases, this can also lead to misrepresentations of destinations. Historically, such writers have been important opinion leaders and influencers of tourist visitation, creating images that have even been incorporated into the advertising of destinations. These intangible elements of a destination image have led many DMOs to use more sophisticated tools to develop this emotional link between the consumer and the destination, through branding.

Destination branding

Branding is about helping destinations to harness their USP to promote their attractive features (e.g. history, culture, landscape, the people and destination attributes) by building a brand. Branding is designed, as Morgan and Pritchard (2002) argue, to connect the consumer with the destination in the present or future. As Morgan and Pritchard (2000: 216) suggest, 'modern branding is not just about developing appealing communication strategies, it is also about defining and delivering leading edge product or service quality to match or exceed customer expectations'. It requires a vision for the brand to be established so that consumers will buy into it; this can be expressed as the brand's core values. These values should be credible, plausible, drivable and deliverable. These values are consistently reinforced through the product, the service and in all marketing communciations in all media to maintain a brand presence (Image 16.3). Modern-day brands have an emotional appeal, evoking trust, quality and reliability.

Building a brand is a long process but destination advertising is crucial where a brand has been developed to position the destination firmly in the target markets. Insight 16.2 illustrates this process in the case of Scotland which has recently re-imaged and repositioned itself as a destination. Among the benefits of branding are:

- it allows consumers to identify with the produce or place. These are constantly evolving propositions: New York's Convention Bureau and Visitors' Bureau coined the 'Big Apple' in the 1970s, and the State of New York also developed the 'I Love New York' slogan at the same time. In 2005, the city of New York filed an application to trademark a new slogan – The World's Second Home

- it helps to create an image of the product or service and raises visibility. In a more sophisticated use of branding, it may help a destination to target different markets, where multiple brands are developed. For example, in 2006, the resort company Sandals used branding to differentiate its resorts into Signature and Classic brands according to service levels. The Signature brand became the elite product with five-star restaurants and butler service

- it helps to reinforce imagery among customers and intermediaries selling tourism experiences and may add prestige to the destination

- a corporate logo, symbol or trademark may help to distinguish the destination from competitors.

There's no place in the world like Sydney

Nowhere else can you travel minutes from the city to one of over forty beautiful, secluded harbourside beaches. Soak up the views, letting the world's most stunning harbour be your canvas for summer, sun and life. To plan your Sydney summer escape, go to seesydney.com.au or call NSW Holidays on 1300 666 787.

Image 16.3: Promotional campaign for Sydney focusing on 'There's no place in the world like Sydney' and its harbourside beaches, 2005 campaign. Source: Copyright, Tourism New South Wales

INSIGHT 16.2

Re-imaging a destination – the case of Scotland

Scotland has an international and domestic image as a destination but, by 2000, visitor numbers were declining and tourism industry critics were pointing to the ineffective marketing and promotion by the national tourism organization, the Scottish Tourist Board (STB). After a government review and reassessment of Scotland's tourism organizations and product, the Minister for Tourism launched a Tourism Framework for Action in 2002 as shown in Figure 16.6. This, combined with the newly re-formed VisitScotland (VS), to replace STB and relaunch Scotland's tourism products, highlighted the need for different stakeholders to work together based on three priorities:

- market position
- consumer focus
- enhanced status.

This is currently under review with ambitions to increase tourism revenue by 50 per cent by 2015, to promote Scotland across its product areas and to develop new markets as well as enhancing e-business capability.

Based on extensive research in 2001/2002, VS examined the reasons why visitors came to Scotland, the country's values as a brand with the importance of icons such as whisky, tartan, golf, a rich imagery and powerful associations. VS set out to create a brand wheel to symbolize a new brand for Scottish Tourism (Figure 16.7) which was based on three essential words:

- *enduring*: buildings, history and culture
- *dramatic*: reflected in the scenery, changing weather and light
- *human*: the people were perceived as innovative, having integrity and pride.

This helped VS to formulate four core values: integrity, pride, proficiency (knowing our customers and able to use best practice) and innovation. These are embodied in the VS brand wheel where the brand values were translated into the rational and emotional elements to help describe the complex formulation of a proposition which could be communicated to the visitor, via the *Live It* campaign, in television, cinema, press and poster promotions which engaged the five senses to portray the life-enhancing qualities one would experience by visiting Scotland (i.e. The See It, Touch it, Hear it, Taste it and Smell Campaign, which can be seen as a video clip on www.scotexchange.net/promote your business).

This was underpinned by more specialist campaigns focused on Scotland's product portfolio –

- *Active Scotland*, with walking, cycling and extreme sports
- *Freedom of Scotland*, touring and wildlife viewing
- *business tourism*, conferences, meetings, incentive travel and exhibitions
- *cities*, with their attractions, shopping, nightlife and restaurants
- *culture and heritage*, with festivals, heritage, the arts, genealogy, museums/galleries.

As a result, the brand wheel helps to focus tourism marketing efforts on strengths and care products, while the re-imaging exercise has helped to build a more defined market position, a clearer consumer focus and enhanced status for tourism in Scotland as a key element of the economy. Part of this process is also the improvement of quality and continuous innovation.

Source: Adapted from www.scotexchange.net/know your market; personal communication with VisitScotland and Scottish Executive.

As Insight 16.2 shows, a destination brand has been built by focusing on the emotional attachment which visitors have with Scotland, so that it is exciting, conveys powerful ideas, resonates with the consumer and is reinforced by the advertising campaign: 'Live it – Scotland'. Another highly successful advertising campaign in the 1980s was 'Glasgow – miles better', while New Zealand's '100% Pure' and Torbay in Devon's English Riviera campaign in the 1990s were successful too. But how can destinations evaluate the efficiency of their marketing efforts? One approach now being considered is **destination benchmarking**.

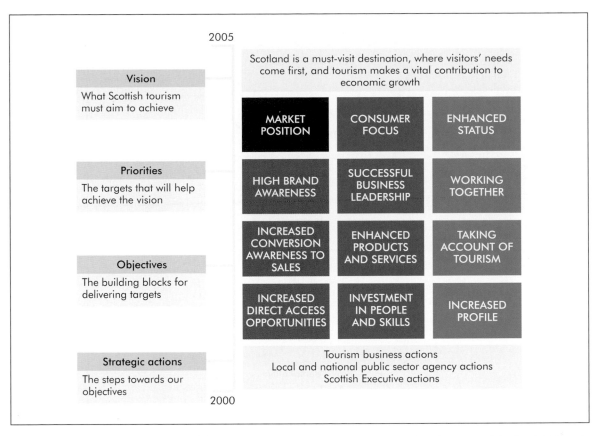

FIGURE 16.6   Tourism Framework for Action. Source: Scottish Executive, reproduced courtesy of the Scottish Executive

Destination benchmarking

Benchmarking is a technique which has gained increased popularity in the tourism industry since the 1990s. It looks at the performance of similar businesses or sectors to gauge how one is performing relative to competitors. It has seen applications in measuring destination competitiveness, particularly in relation to productivity and the effectiveness of advertising and marketing in relation to measurable outcomes (e.g. visitor arrivals, bed nights and receipts) as well as for more subjective measures. Wöber and Fesenmaier (2004) used Data Envelopment Analysis (DEA) to assess the efficiency of destination marketing in the USA. By examining the 48 state tourism offices (excluding Alaska and Hawaii), they examined three advertising elements:

- total state tourism office domestic advertising budgets
- total state tourism office international advertising budgets
- other budget services.

This highlighted that 15 states were extremely efficient while 33 faced challenges in justifying the advertising budgets given the visitor expenditure and employment generated. This highlights the value of DEA in benchmarking performance based on observed operations. It may also be useful when reviewing promotional campaigns, advertising and the long-term value of branding. In the case of branding, benchmarking may help to point to the brand lifecycle to see if it is achieving the desired effects. As Morgan and Pritchard (2002) argue, brands (like the destination lifecycle) pass through stages of growth when the brand is fashionable through to being famous, then familiar and then fatigued, when they need to be refreshed, relaunched or redeveloped. The key point here is that a destination's brand values will need to be reviewed, and benchmarking may be a technique to evaluate performance in a competitive context.

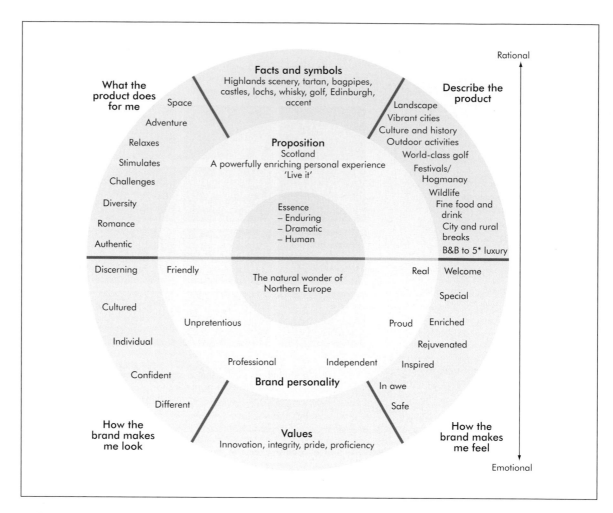

FIGURE 16.7 The VisitScotland brand essence wheel. Source: VisitScotland, reproduced courtesy of VisitScotland

Conclusion: The future of destination marketing

With the rapid changes in consumer behaviour brought about by technology and changing tastes and trends, destination marketing will need to harness market research to understand how such changes impact upon a destination. DMOs have many challenges to face and innovation will be a critical component, when harnessed with creative solutions to attract the future visitor. Among key concerns, according to Buhalis (2000), are:

- public-private sector partnerships to gain cooperation to pool resources and collaborate on marketing initiatives
- creating a comprehensive marketing strategy and mix to support the competitiveness of the destination
- taking advantage of the new ICTs, particularly the use of DMS to coordinate the products and services offered locally, so as to promote globally
- understanding the value of different markets, especially the yields of higher-spending tourists which can be more lucrative than mass markets
- pinpointing target markets and ensuring that the marketing strategy for the destination does not alienate residents through unsustainable development.

This highlights the importance of marketing destinations which can affect the success or failure of a destination. Understanding how tourists select a destination is clearly important, as are the more specific aspects of destination image, promotion and segmentation within the marketing planning process as discussed in Chapter 15. There is a constant process of change in tourism destinations as they pass through various stages of the destination lifecycle and, within any region or country, destinations will be at various stages of development. Destinations compete with each other for both domestic and international visitors to ensure their viability, and the growth of greater cooperative marketing efforts among destinations adjacent to each other can assist in a wider regional marketing of regions with a cluster of destinations and attractions. These types of collaborative efforts are beginning to affect the way destinations within defined regions are now beginning to see the benefits of collaboration rather than wasteful competitive marketing. Destination marketing in the future will be increasingly more dependent upon achieving a competitive advantage, and this will be done through more sophisticated research, creative marketing and the use of ICTs. The global marketplace is now a reality for many destinations, but more responsible, sustainable and product-driven marketing will be the key to successful destination development. Yet one of the ongoing issues for all destinations will be the stage of development they have reached in the destination lifecycle, and the impacts which tourism development generates. This is now the focus of Part IV of the book to understand the effects of tourist demand, the supply by the industry and effect upon localities and destinations.

The destination policy formulation process needs to consider the various stakeholders and external influences that will impinge upon future marketing strategies. Given the wide variety of people involved, disagreements are inevitable. Laws (1995: 39) notes that parties can be 'poles apart', with some arguing for 'further development, others opposing it, perhaps even arguing for a reduction of current levels of tourism activity'.

Discussion questions

1 Identify and describe the main components of a selected destination.

2 What activities do DMOs undertake in order to market a destination?

3 How do tourists choose which destination to visit?

4 How significant is the advertising process to destinations? What types of advertising can you identify for a destination you are familiar with?

References

Ashworth, G. and Goodall, B. (eds) (1988) *Marketing in the Tourism Industry: The Promotion of Destination Regions*. Beckenham: Croom Helm.

Baloglu, S. and McCleary, K. (1999) 'A model of destination image formation', *Annals of Tourism Research*, 26 (4): 868–97.

Beerli, A. and Martin, J. (2004a) 'Factors influencing destination image', *Annals of Tourism Research*, 31 (3): 657–81.

Beerli, A. and Martin, J. (2004b) 'Tourists' characteristics and the perceived image of tourist destinations: A quantitative analysis – a case study of Lanzarote, Spain', *Tourism Management*, 25 (5): 623–36

Buckley, P. and Papadopolous, S. (1986) 'Marketing Greek tourism – the planning process', *Tourism Management*, 7 (2): 82–100.

Buhalis, D. (2000) 'Marketing the competitive destination of the future', *Tourism Management*, 21 (1): 97–116.

Connell, J. (2005) 'Toddler, tourism and Tobermory: Destination marketing issues and television-induced tourism', *Tourism Management*, 26 (5): 763–76.

Echtner, C. and Ritchie, J.B. (1991) 'The meaning and measurement of destination image', *Journal of Tourism Studies*, 2 (2): 2–12.

Echtner, C. and Ritchie, J.B.R. (1993) 'The measurement of destination image: An empirical assessment', *Journal of Travel Research*, 31 (4): 3–13.

Echtner, C. and Prasad, P. (2003) 'The context of third world marketing', *Annals of Tourism Research*, 30 (3): 660–82.

Gallarza, M., Saura, I. and Garciá, H. (2002) 'Destination image: Towards a conceptual framework', *Annals of Tourism Research*, 29 (1): 56–78.

Gartner, W. (1993) 'Image formation process', in M. Uysal and D. Fesenmaier (eds) *Communication and Channel Systems in Tourism Marketing*. New York: Haworth Press.

Gilbert, D. (1990) 'Strategic marketing planning for national tourism', *The Tourist Review*, 1 (1): 18–27.

Gunn, C. (1988) *Vacationscape: Designing Tourist Regions, Second Edition*. New York: Van Nostrand Reinhold.

Hunt, J. (1975) 'Image as a factor in tourism development', *Journal of Travel Research*, 13 (3): 1–17.

Jenkins, O.H. (1999) 'Understanding and measuring tourist destination images', *International Journal of Tourism Research*, 1 (2): 1–15.

Kim, H. and Richardson, S. (2003) 'Motion picture impacts on destination images', *Annals of Tourism Research*, 30 (1): 216–37.

Laws, E. (1995) *Tourist Destination Management*. London: Routledge.

McWilliams and Crompton, J. (1997) 'An expanded framework for measuring the effectivness of destination advertising', *Tourism Management*, 18 (3): 127–37.

Middleton, V. and Clarke, J. (2001) *Marketing in Travel and Tourism, Third Edition*. Oxford: Butterworth-Heinemann.

Morgan, M. (1996) *Marketing for Leisure and Tourism*. Hemel Hempstead: Prentice Hall.

Morgan, N. and Pritchard, A. (2000) *Advertising in Tourism and Leisure*. Oxford: Butterworth-Heinemann.

Morgan, N. and Pritchard, A. (eds) (2002) *Destination Branding: Creating the Unique Destination Proposition*. Oxford: Butterworth-Heinemann.

Pike, S. and Ryan, C. (2004) 'Destination positioning analysis through a comparison of cognitive, affective and conative perceptions', *Journal of Travel Research*, 42, May, 333–42.

Santos, C. (2004) 'Framing Portugal: Representational dynamics', *Annals of Tourism Research*, 31 (1): 122–38.

Seddighi, H. and Theocharous, A. (2002) 'A model of tourism destination choice: A theoretical and empirical analysis', *Tourism Management*, 23 (4): 475–87.

Strong, E. (1925) 'Theories of selling', *The Journal of Applied Psychology*, 9: 75–86.

Tourism New South Wales (2003a) *Towards 2020 – New South Wales Tourism Marketplan*. Sydney: Tourism New South Wales.

Tourism New South Wales (2003b) *Three year Marketing Strategy 2003/06*. Sydney: Tourism New South Wales, tnsw.gov.av, accessed 18.2.2005.

Van der Ark, L. and Richards, G. (2007) 'Attractiveness of cultural activities in European cities: A latent class approach', *Tourism Management*, 28, in press.

Wahab, S., Crampon, L. and Rothfield, L. (1976) *Tourism Marketing*. London: Tourism International Press.

Wöber, K. and Fesenmaier, D. (2004) 'Multi-critical approach to destination benchmarking: A case study of state tourism advertising programmes in the United States', *Journal of Travel and Tourism Marketing*, 16 (2/3): 1–18.

Zalaton, A. (1998) 'Wives involvement in the tourism decision process', *Annals of Tourism Research*, 25 (4): 890–903.

Further reading

Pike, S. (2004) *Destination Marketing Organizations*. Oxford: Elsevier.

IV

The Impact of Tourism

In this section of the book, the impacts associated with tourist activities and effects are considered as a way of understanding some of the costs and benefits of tourism. Impacts are a major element of tourist activity and their scope, effect and duration on the host society are complex. They vary in terms of their intensity and effect according to the specific location and nature of the impacts, and as Part V of the book will also show the impacts are highly variable depending on the type of environment in which tourism develops and operates. In Chapter 17, the most frequently cited impact used by governments and private sector enterprises to justify tourism activity – economic impacts – are reviewed. The chapter not only examines the nature of economics as a framework for understanding economic impacts but also critically examines both the costs and benefits of tourism as an activity that can generate employment and foreign currency while contributing to the balance of payments at a national level. Some of the more sophisticated tools now being used to measure and monitor these impacts (e.g. Tourism Satellite Accounts) are also introduced.

This is followed by Chapter 18 which discusses some of the social and cultural impacts that are inevitably associated with tourism development. The chapter evaluates the problems of gauging the extent to which tourism-induced changes to societies and their cultural values are a direct result of tourist activity. The chapter considers many of the concepts and frameworks developed by anthropologists and sociologists to evaluate the effect of tourism on host societies.

Chapter 19 focuses on tourism's impact on the built and natural environment. The environment is viewed as finite resource which is also directly affected by tourism development and examples of impacts and measures to ameliorate these impacts are discussed. The tourism impacts associated with the environment have also generated a wide range of opinions and views on how to accommodate tourism and the environment, given their symbiotic relationship. Therefore, Chapter 20 considers the challenge of sustainability, which reviews the evolution of the debate on the extent to which tourism can be a sustainable development option. This is controversial and has become one of the most widely researched areas of tourism since the 1990s.

341

17

Economic Impacts

Learning outcomes

After reading this chapter, and answering the questions, you should be able to:

- explain what is meant by the terms 'economics', 'supply' and 'demand'

- define the positive and negative economic impacts of tourism

- outline methods for measuring tourism's economic impacts.

Overview

Among the most significant reasons used by government and private sector tourism businesses for developing tourism is the associated economic gain. Tourism can assist in generating foreign exchange, and improve the economy and employment prospects of countries, regions and cities. While the economic advantages of tourism are certainly clear, many negative aspects are apparent and to understand the nature of the economic impacts of tourism, it is important to have an understanding of economic concepts and how they relate to tourism. In addition, the tools used to measure the impact of tourism are introduced to an insight into the ways economists have developed new ways of depicting how tourism interacts with the national economy.

Introduction

The economic aspects of tourism have been widely studied and has been extensively published in academic journals such as *Tourism Management* and *Tourism Economics*. However, much of the early research on tourism impacts tended to be rather uncritical and focused on the positive economic gains rather than any negative aspects relating to the environment and society. The justification for tourism development generally focuses on the potential for positive economic impacts and tourism has flourished across the world because of its perceived benefit: it is heralded as the world's largest industry. The global economic importance of tourism is illustrated by the World Travel and Tourism Council (WTTC).

Tourism generates:

- 11 per cent of gross domestic product
- 207 million jobs
- 8 per cent of total employment
- 5.5 million new jobs per year which will continue up to until 2010 (WTTC 2004)

although there are concerns about the validity of such measures due to the problems of validating such estimates of global tourism activity.

According to Mathieson and Wall (1982), the magnitude of the economic impacts of tourism is influenced by five factors:

- the type of tourism facility and attraction for tourists
- the volume and level of tourist spending
- the level of economic development in the region
- the extent to which tourist spending is maintained and recirculated in the region
- the extent of seasonality in the region.

These factors determine whether economic impacts are positive or negative.

Tourism gives rise to different benefits and costs and the nature and scope of economic impacts tend to depend on geography and socioeconomic structures. There are distinctions between developed and less developed countries and core and peripheral areas within a country. For this reason, establishing the economic impact of tourism for specific countries is a difficult exercise. To derive a greater understanding of tourism and the economic impacts it generates, attention now turns to the nature of economics to explain the concepts which are used to study the economic effects of tourism.

What is economics?

Like many social science subjects, there is little agreement on how to define the area of study that is economics. However, according to Craven (1990: 3) 'economics is concerned with the economy or economic system… [and]… the problem of allocating resources is a central theme of economics, because most resources are scarce'. Therefore Craven (1990: 4) argues that economics is the study of methods of allocating scarce resources and distributing the product of those resources, and the study of the consequences of these methods of allocation and distribution.

What is meant by scarcity and resources? The term 'scarcity' is used to illustrate the fact that most resources in society are finite and decisions have to be made on the best way to use and sustain these resources. Economists define resources in terms of:

- natural resources (e.g. the land)
- labour (e.g. human resources and entrepreneurship)
- capital (e.g. artificial aids to assist in producing goods)

and collectively these resources constitute the factors of production which are used to produce commodities. These commodities can be divided into:

- goods (e.g. tangible products, such as an aircraft or a hotel room)
- services (e.g. intangible items, such as services of a tour guide)

and the total output of all commodities in a country over a period of time, normally a year, is known as the *national product*. The creation of products and services is termed *production* and the use of these goods and services is called *consumption*. Since, in any society, the production of goods and services can only satisfy a small fraction of consumers' needs, choices have to be made on the allocation of resources to determine which goods and services to produce (Lipsey 1989). The way in which goods and services are divided among people has been examined by economists in terms of the distribution of income and the degree of equality and efficiency in their distribution. Many of these issues are dealt with under the heading of *microeconomics*, which Craven defines as:

> the study of individual decisions and the interactions of these decisions... [including] ... consumers' decisions on what to buy, firms' decisions on what to produce and the interactions of these decisions, which determine whether people can buy what they would like, whether firms can sell all that they produce and the profits firms make by providing and selling (Craven 1990: 4).

Therefore, microeconomics is concerned with certain issues, namely:

- the firm
- the consumer
- production and selling
- the demand for goods
- the supply of goods.

Economists also examine a broader range of economic issues in terms of *macroeconomics* which is concerned with:

> the entire economy and interactions within it, including the population, income, total unemployment, the average rate of price increases (the inflation rate), the extent of companies' capacities to produce goods and the total amount of money in use in the country (Craven 1990: 5).

Therefore, macroeconomics is mainly concerned with:

- how the national economy operates
- employment and unemployment
- inflation
- national production and consumption
- the money supply in a country.

Within micro- and macroeconomics, tourism economists examine different aspects of the tourism system, based on the analysis of the concepts of demand and supply.

Demand

Within economics, the concern with the allocation of resources to satisfy individuals' desire to travel means that transport economists examine the demand for different modes of travel and the competition between such modes in relation to price, speed, convenience and reliability. Economists attempt to understand what affects people's tourism behaviour and the significance of tourism in a destination.

Tourism economists have examined the demand for travel and tourist products, recognizing the significance of demand as a driving force in the economy. This stimulates entrepreneurial activity to produce the goods and services to satisfy the demand (Bull 1995). More specifically, tourism economists examine the **effective demand** for goods or services: the aggregate or overall demand over a period of time. Since income has an important effect on tourism demand, economists measure the impact using a term known as the **elasticity of demand**. As Bull (1995) has shown, it is measured using a ratio calculated thus:

$$Elasticity\ of\ demand\ =\ \frac{percentage\ change\ in\ tourism\ demand}{percentage\ change\ in\ disposable\ income}$$

in relation to two equal time periods. The significance of this concept is that the demand for goods to fulfil basic needs (e.g. food, water and shelter) is relatively unchanging or *inelastic* while the demand for luxury items, such as holiday and pleasure travel, is variable or *elastic*, being subject to fluctuations in demand due to factors such as income or price. Thus, 'elasticity' is used to express the extent to which tourists are sensitive to changes in price and service. For example, primary demand is usually more elastic than derived demand. The different elements which comprise the tourism product (e.g. transport, accommodation and attractions) are complementary and it is difficult to separate out one individual item as exerting a dominant effect on price since each is interrelated in terms of what is purchased and consumed.

To assess the impact of price on the demand for tourism, economists examine the **price elasticity** of demand, where an inverse relationship exists between demand and price (Bull 1995). For example, it is generally accepted that the greater the price, the less demand there will be for a tourism product due to the limited amount of the population's disposable income which is available to purchase the product. It is calculated thus:

$$Price\ elasticity\ =\ \frac{percentage\ change\ in\ quantity\ of\ tourism\ product\ demanded}{percentage\ change\ in\ tourism\ product\ price}$$

The concept of **cross-elasticity** needs to be considered as destinations tend to be considered substitutes when they are in a similar area or offer a similar product. Waggle and Fish (1999) examined Hong Kong, China and Taiwan to see if the tourism markets are complementary or competitive. Their research indicated that Hong Kong and China are competitive destinations whereas a different outcome was noted in the case of Hong Kong and Taiwan. This has ramifications for marketing policies and the effects of currency fluctuations, unrest and other external factors.

Other contributory factors which influence the demand for tourism include the impact of tourist taxation and the amount of holiday entitlement available to potential tourists as well as the effects of weather, climate and cultural preferences for holiday-making which are expressed in terms of seasonality. These factors also need to be viewed in the context of the economics of each specific part of the tourism product and the aggregate impact upon tourism demand leads economists to look ahead and forecast the likely growth which will occur in the future (i.e. tourism forecasting, see Chapter 27). The WTTC (2004) provides a snapshot of those countries which are forecast to see above average growth in international tourism demand for the period 2004–13, illustrated in Table 17.1. This shows the importance of developing countries in achieving forecast growth in demand.

TABLE 17.1	Growth in demand for tourism 2004–13
Top ten countries	*% annualized real growth*
1 Angola	9.5
2 Mexico	9.5
3 Turkey	9.2
4 China	8.9
5 India	8.8
6 Botswana	8.5
7 Laos	8.4
8 Malaysia	8.2
9 Hong Kong	8.1
10 Vanuatu	7.8

Source: WTTC (2004)

Supply

Economists are also interested in the *supply* of a commodity (e.g. hotel rooms) which is often seen as a function of its price and the price of alternative goods. Price is often influenced by the cost of the factors of production.

Bull (1995) suggests that the principle questions in which economists are interested from the supply side are:

- what to produce
- how to produce it
- when and where to produce it.

Supply may be viewed from two perspectives. First, increasing demand requires an increase in facilities and infrastructure to cope with added pressure – this centres on the concept of extending capacity. Second, tourism may be stimulated by the provision of more facilities – this is creation and/or anticipation of demand. Borooah (1999) suggests that, for hotels, it is those who are already constrained by capacity who are responsible for most room increases. Borooah undertook an **econometric** analysis (mathematical analysis) of the supply of hotel rooms in Queensland, Australia, and found that the sector is strongly responsive to increase in earnings per occupied room but less influenced by increases in room occupancy rate or by changes in the interest rate. For commercial operators, the main objective in supply terms is to maximize profitability from the available capacity, as discussed in Chapter 10.

The economic characteristics of the tourism industry

There are numerous debates within the tourism literature on the extent to which tourism is a business, an industry, a service or just a phenomenon. The WTTC outline the extent to which the terms of tourism industry and tourism economy can be defined, where the 'travel and tourism industry' describes the direct effect of travel demand and relates to services such as accommodation, catering, entertainment, transport and attractions. WTTC portray this as the tip of the iceberg. In contrast, the 'travel and tourism economy' refers to the wider effects of flow-through of travel demand across the economy. This includes the 'travel and tourism industry' but also those businesses which support it, such as printers, publishers, wholesalers, utilities, administration, computing and security.

One of the main justifications for tourism development is the potential for economic benefits. Tourism is often encouraged to draw in much-needed foreign exchange, generate employment and improve economic and social prospects in a destination area. There are a number of characteristics of tourism which distinguish it from other industries, goods and services. These are as follows:

- *Tourism is an invisible export industry* – there is no tangible product and consumers tend to make a purchase without seeing the product first-hand.
- *Tourists require supporting goods and services* – the expansion of existing infrastructure and services may be required or new ones created.
- *Tourism is a fragmented product* – it consists of a number of elements, such as transport and accommodation as well as landscape and cultural resources.
- *Tourism is a highly price- and income-elastic product.*
- *Tourism is a perishable product* – if a hotel room is not booked one night, then that income is lost.
- *Tourism is subject to unpredictable external influences*, such as currency, politics, tourist motivation and taste, and these features are discussed in more detail in Chapter 27 (source: Mathieson and Wall 1982; Holloway and Robinson 1995).

Murphy (1985) states that the only constant in tourism is change. It is an industry dependent on a complexity of external factors. At a general level, the demand for tourism is governed by three economic cycles:

Short-term economic cycles

This type of **economic cycle** defines periods of dramatic change. Short-term cycles tend to be highly visible and predictable. Good examples of these include seasonality, such as summer peaks and winter troughs and the period in between, shoulder seasons. The problems with short-term cycles such as seasonality are pressure on the resource (congestion, overcrowding, staff stress) and issues of economic efficiency (too much summer trade, insufficient off-peak trade). For some tourism services, it might be necessary to maximize revenue during the summer season to ensure all-year-round survival (Murphy 1985). A commitment to a quality industry, including maintaining acceptable staff levels year-round and a thriving industry is a challenge, requiring knowledge of the market and the tools which may assist in reducing fluctuating demand. In some instances, reduced demand out of season is desirable for environmental reasons or as part of a business strategy.

Medium-term economic cycles

Medium-term cycles relate to changes over a period of several years. These changes tend to reflect consumer attitudes and the demand for specific tourism products. Consumer preferences tend to be fickle. Natural events, such as floods, hurricanes and earthquakes, can also affect tourism in the medium term (also see Chapter 26 on the 2004 tsunami). Yet there are no set rules on the recovery of tourist destinations after unpredictable events. Other economic aspects, such as currency devaluation and the strength of currencies, have significant effects on tourist numbers. The crisis in the economy of South East Asia in the late 1990s led to a rise in incoming tourism as visitors saw the opportunity of a cheap holiday and a weak currency.

Long-term economic cycles

Over a longer period of time, tourism products go through an evolutionary process. The tourism area lifecycle (Butler 1980) model examines the growth of a destination and its ultimate decline or regeneration. Much of the work by economists seeking to model such cycles is derived from the ideas of Kondratiev, based in turn on the economic ideas of Schumpter in 1939, where four phases in long economic cycles could be discerned: boom, recession, depression, recovery. In the Kondratiev model, these waves last around 40–50 years (Berry, Kim and Kim 1993) but they are becoming much shorter in the global economy.

Economic benefits

The balance of payments

The balance of payments account for a country is a record of transactions during a period of time between residents of that country and the rest of the world. This includes all imports and exports. Improving the balance of payments is probably the most significant justification used by governments to promote tourism. The contribution of tourism to the overall balance of payments of a nation is calculated by working out the difference between the amount spent by overseas visitors in that country and the amount spent overseas by residents of the country. This figure will either be a net surplus or deficit on the tourism account of a national economy. Tourists are viewed as 'invisible exports' which have an impact on national economies. Some of the highest negative travel accounts in the world are displayed by Germany and Japan as residents spend more on tourism trips than all the incoming visitors do. The United States of America had the most positive account.

The industrial structure of developing countries, within the national economy is comparatively weakly developed with less scope for exporting manufactured goods. Reliance is on low-cost primary product and imported high-cost products, particularly in the case of luxury hotel developments that often use imported rather than indigenous resources. Tourism development can improve the balance of payments by bringing in foreign spending to the local economy.

Income

As tourism stimulates economic activity in a destination, it assists in improving the overall economic status of a country. The measurement of economic production and nation wealth is **gross domestic product** (GDP). Tourism can lead to increases in GDP. Table 17.2 outlines the GDP for Asian countries and indicates how GDP has recovered since the Asian economic crisis and SARS crisis. For example, in the Caribbean and Pacific Islands, over 40 per cent of GDP for many small islands is derived from tourism, which rises to 88 per cent in the case of the Maldives. At the micro level, this can also mean such islands need to be aware of the value of tourism. Orams (1999) examined the economic value of whale watching to the economy of the South Pacific island of Vava'u in Tonga and highlights the significance of one major tourist activity for the local economy (see Table 17.3). From this, Orams notes that whales are worth about $750 000 in revenue to the community of Vava'u each year.

Mules (1998) examined the economic contribution of tourists by identifying three components: numbers of tourists, length of stay, and average expenditure and how tourism expenditure changes over time. The results have implications for government policy aimed at achieving higher GDP through tourism. The study showed that, for Australian tourism, real expenditure over time from 1985 to 1995 was dependent on growth in tourist volume, in particular the narrow market segment of the mass Asian market.

TABLE 17.2 Economic Indicators for selected Asian countries 1997–2002

Region/country	Population in 2002 (million)	Real GDP growth						% change 1998–2002
		1997	1998	1999	2000	2001	2002	
North East Asia								
China	1284.3	8.8	7.8	7.1	8.0	7.3	8.0	7.7
Hong Kong SAR	6.8	5.1	−5.0	3.4	10.2	0.5	2.3	2.1
Japan	127.1	1.8	−1.1	0.1	2.8	0.4	0.2	0.4
South Korea	47.6	5.0	−6.7	10.9	9.3	3.1	6.3	4.4
Taiwan	22.4	6.7	4.6	5.4	5.9	−2.2	3.6	3.4
South East Asia								
Brunei	0.4	3.6	−4.0	2.6	2.8	3.0	3.2	1.5
Indonesia	214.2	4.9	−13.3	0.8	4.9	3.4	3.7	−0.3
Malaysia	24.5	7.3	−7.4	6.1	8.3	0.4	4.1	2.2
The Philippines	83	5.2	−0.6	3.4	4.4	3.0	4.4	3.2
Singapore	4.2	8.5	−0.9	6.4	9.4	−2.4	2.2	2.9
Thailand	63.5	−1.3	−10.5	4.4	4.6	1.9	5.2	1.0
Vietnam	80.3	8.2	5.8	4.8	6.8	6.8	7.0	6.2
APEC	—	3.9	2.0	3.6	4.0	0.7	2.4	2.5
World	—	3.5	2.3	3.0	4.0	1.2	1.9	2.5
World[1]	—	4.2	2.8	3.6	4.7	2.3	3.0	3.2

Note

1. Using the previous year's GDP, valued at purchasing power parity exchange rates as weights.

Source: Developed from *2003 APEC Economic Outlook*. Reproduced with permission from APEC Secretariat. Data from *2003 APEC Economic Outlook*, ISSN 0218–9763 APEC#203-EC-01.1. For full publication, please visit www.apec.org

TABLE 17.3 The economic value of whale watching in Vava'u, the kingdom of Tonga

	Direct expenditure of visitors on whale watching[1]	Other expenditure of whale tourists[2]	Whale watch operators' expenditure in Vava'u[3]	Whale watch business employees' expenditure in Vava'u[4]	TOTAL
Estimated totals for all permitted whale watch operators	$78 000–$116 000	$570 000	$47 000	$44 000	$739 000–$777 000

Source: © Mark Orams (1999) reproduced with permission.

1 Direct expenditure includes items such as boat fares, food, camera film and souvenirs. Given as a range
2 Other expenditure includes accommodation, transport, other food and souvenirs, other attractions
3 Whale watch operators' expenditure includes wages, fuel, boat maintenance, supplies and administrative costs
4 Estimate of the proportion of wage bill spent in the local community

Employment

There are three types of employment which may be generated by tourism:

- **direct employment** – jobs created as a result of visitor expenditure and directly supporting tourism activity, e.g. hotels
- **indirect employment** – jobs created within the tourism supply sector but not as a direct result of tourism activity
- **induced employment** – jobs created as a result of tourism expenditure as local residents spend money earned from tourism.

Several factors influence tourism-related employment patterns. The type of tourist activity has an effect on employment as some forms of tourism are more labour intensive than others. Farm tourism, particularly farm accommodation, does not necessarily create new employment, whereas resort development will create a variety of new jobs. Employment opportunities for host communities may also be questioned as the benefits of tourism employment may not always be widely felt by local people. Employment of local people will be based on the local skill base. In most cases, there will be few managerial posts in local tourism development but many jobs requiring minimal skill – with low pay and little reward. Managerial grade jobs may be advertised across a wide geographic area to attract well-qualified and experienced candidates and, in less developed countries and small island states, expatriate workers are often imported on higher salaries. Employment benefits may often be disguised as tourism jobs to attract people from other sectors or people not normally part of the economic workforce. This includes those who take second jobs, holiday work or those who generate extra revenue from an existing business (such as farm tourism). One attempt to quantify the future growth employment 2004–13 in terms of jobs created by expected global tourism growth is shown in Table 17.4. This underlines the economic significance of tourism in developing and developed countries.

Economic benefits to the tourism environment may be directly induced from tourism spending. While it is accepted that spending to a greater or lesser extent assists in local economic development, more refined ways of ensuring a flow of money to specific development projects requires a more innovative approach. One of the ways this is currently being evaluated is the **visitor payback** concept which is outlined in Case Study 17.1W – visitor payback schemes.

As tourism continues to grow, many destinations do not have budgets and resources to cope with environmental damage and the costs associated with tourist development. In many places, there are no entrance fees and public sector finance is often unable to meet the demands for conservation and restoration work, particularly in game reserves and National Parks in Africa.

TABLE 17.4	WTTC forecasts of travel and tourism employment 2004–2013	
Top ten countries	No. of jobs to be created in tourism	
1 China	11 493	
2 Indonesia	4 192	
3 Mexico	3 914	
4 India	3 845	
5 CIS*	2 221	
6 Brazil	1 854	
7 United States	1 559	
8 Bangladesh	1 104	
9 Spain	971	
10 Pakistan	968	

* Former Soviet Union

Source: WTTC (2004)

Tourist taxes on businesses often do not directly benefit those managing tourism. Bearing this in mind, visitor payback schemes (see the Tourism Company 1998) give an opportunity of generating revenue which can be used to fund projects in the local area in a targeted way.

Economic costs

Inflation

Tourism development often creates **inflation**ary effects on local economies, relating to land, property and goods. The increased demand for land increases the price. While this is beneficial to those selling land, there is a negative side-effect on the local population, particularly those who are not involved in tourism. Local people are then forced into competition for land and housing with tourism development interests. The consequences for local residents in places such as Polperro in Cornwall is social exclusion from their own community even though they provide local labour.

Opportunity costs

Opportunity costs relate to the time, effort and money of developing tourism at the expense of other activities or areas of investment. If a government invests in tourism, then the money spent is unavailable for other uses. This may be detrimental to the well-being of local communities. Tourism investment can, of course, benefit local people through improved infrastructure, services and employment potential. This necessitates a cost-benefit approach to the analysis of tourism impacts, which is often expressed in terms of the leverage of additional investment or tourist spending, where a public sector investment occurs.

Dependency

Heavy reliance on a single industry in any region or country is a risky strategy in the long-term. **Economic dependency** on tourism is a much criticized policy, particularly for less developed countries and peripheral regions in the developed world. Some less developed countries rely on tourists from a small number of generating countries, which is the case for many small islands. Changes in their markets are not controllable and decreases in demand for tourism will have huge effects on the receiving country. The Concentration Index is used to identify the level of dependency on one or more generating countries and is calculated as follows:

$$\frac{Tourist\ arrivals\ from\ primary\ markets}{All\ tourist\ arrivals} \times 100$$

It is more favourable for a destination to attract a broad base of tourists so that, if there is a downturn in one particular market, then the consequences are not so damaging.

Seasonality

Seasonality is one of the major disadvantages in tourism and can cause negative economic effects on a destination. Although the high season may bring the opportunity to generate significant revenue from tourism, the economic gain must be sufficient to allow an income which will support individuals and the economy throughout the year. A high incidence of seasonality generally means that employees have jobs for only part of the year. It also means that the investment made in the tourism business is idle for part of the year. So, profits have to be made in a shorter time period than in most industries and spread across the year may not seem as lucrative as imagined. Some hotels, attractions and other tourism-related enterprises close down entirely in the off-peak season. Others, depending on location and climate, attempt market diversification, promotion and incentives to retain more even business or may stage events (Image 17.1).

Leakage

In many cases, foreign exchange generated by tourism activity may not benefit the economy of the destination. Foreign investors in the shape of multinational corporations (MNCs) which control accommodation, travel and tour organization receive substantial proportions of tourist spending. **Leakage** may occur through:

- repatriation of profits generated from foreign capital investment
- vertical integration
- not sourcing services and goods locally
- payment for holidays made in the generating country
- ownership of transport (e.g. the national airline).

Bull (1995) notes that large, well-developed destinations demonstrate the lowest leakage rates as they contain supply industries which can compete with foreign imports and therefore retain more money within the local or regional economy. In less developed countries, there is a higher propensity to import due to a lack of supporting industries (see Chapter 24). In this case, the **tourism multiplier** effect cannot develop to its full potential as most of the tourist revenue filters out of the destination. In the coastal area in Belize, for example, around 90 per cent of tourist development is in foreign hands. Martin De Holan and Phillips (1997) state that leakage as high as 75 per cent occurs in Cuba for four reasons:

- lack of industries producing goods and services to support tourism
- inadequate distribution systems
- the enormity of firms' inefficiencies in the local economy
- presence of international hotels.

Oppermann and Chon (1997) found leakage rates of 27–38 per cent in Singapore and Fletcher and Snee (1989) found 53 cents of every dollar leaked out of the Pacific island of Palau. Figure 17.1 shows this process of leakage, which can occur at each stage of tourist spending; it

Image 17.1: Events such as the Glastonbury music festival in the UK can have a significant economic impact on the local area also shows how the infusion of spending into the local community is passed on, via tourist employees, to the community or destination.

Income and employment

While promoters of tourism promise jobs and improved income to host communities, in many cases there is a negative aspect to this. Better paid, managerial posts may not be available to local people. The income generated by tourism activity may not benefit the poorest in a society. First, it may leak out of the destination to a foreign investor and, second, it may only filter to those who have direct interest in a tourism business or those who exist within a certain type of economy. Oppermann and Chon (1997) question whether tourism is a useful tool in securing regional economic development in developing countries. Martin de Holan and Phillips (1997) also question Cuba's strategy of low-cost high-volume tourism, which is explored in Case Study 17.2W.

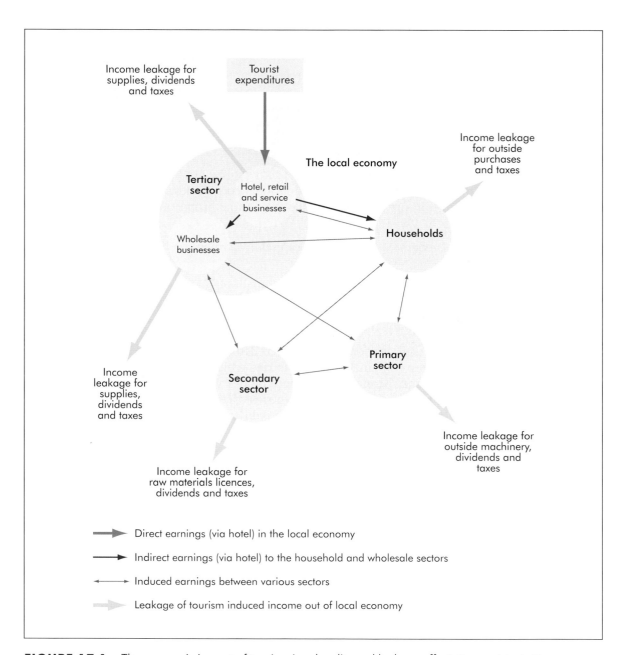

FIGURE 17.1 The economic impact of tourism in a locality and leakage effect. Source: Adapted from Kreutzwiser (1973), Murphy (1985) and Page (1995)

Measuring the economic impacts of tourism

There has been considerable debate has arisen over methodological problems in the economic analysis of tourism. These debates focus on three areas:

- economic multipliers and cost-benefit analyses
- evaluation of opportunity costs
- the role of tourism in economic development.

There are significant problems in trying to obtain accurate measures of the economic impacts of tourism but several measures can be used to give an overview of the effect of tourism. Multipliers are used extensively to examine the effect of revenue generation from tourism.

The tourism multiplier

A multiplier is a statistical expression of how much income or employment (depending on whether one is referring to income or employment multipliers) is generated by a certain amount of tourist spending. The multiplier concept is based on the premise that tourist expenditure will inject additional cash flow into the regional economy and increase regional income. The size of the multiplier is based on the proportion of additional income spent within the region. The income is received by other businesses who also spend within the region and so on. The income multiplier is the ratio of income to the tourist spending that generated it. There are three types of spending:

- *direct spending* – this is the money spent by tourists on the services they need on holiday, such as accommodation, food, shops, attractions (Image 17.2)
- *indirect or generated spending* – this represents the expenditure of tourism businesses on goods and services
- *induced or additional spending* – this is expenditure by the resident community of income earned directly or indirectly from direct spending (tourist expenditure).

The multiplier does not show how income generation through tourism affects each sector of the local economy. To do this, another method is utilized called the **input-output model** (IO). This shows the flow of current transactions through a given economy for a given time period. Various types of businesses are grouped together into industrial sectors and arranged in a matrix. The total value of all sales made by each sector is calculated. This is a slightly more satisfactory method. Studies that demonstrate the IO model in operation include Leones, Colby and Crandall's (1998) study of ecotourists in Arizona and La Lopa, Chen and Nelson (1998) use of multiplier and IO methods to assess the economic impact of the 1996 Oldsmobile Classic (golfing tournament) on the Greater Lansing area of Michigan, USA. The total spending by those who attended the event was $1 811 055. The IO analysis showed a 76 per cent capture rate ('capture rate' indicates the amount of spending retained in the local economy), giving a total of $1 376 401.46. The multiplier generated a figure of 2.39, indicating a significant economic effect. This means that for every $1 spent by a visitor to the tournament, the total economic impact was $2.39, which illustrates the significance of event-led strategies to promote tourism, as discussed by Connell and Page (2005), particularly where annual events are staged such as Edinburgh's New Year Hogmanay celebrations and Festival.

Image 17.2: Tourist shopping helps to boost the local economy

Alternative measures

Despite the development of different techniques to examine the economic aspects of tourism, Dwyer, Forsyth and Spurr (2004: 307) argue that 'The fundamental problem with Input-Output analysis is that it is incomplete: it ignores key aspects of the economy'. This fails to adequately model the economy and 'in nearly all cases, the changes in economic activity which they come up with, whether relating to output, income or value added, are much greater than the net increase in activity in the economy overall...The old models give results which are hazardous to use for policy purposes' (Dwyer *et al.* 2004: 308).

One of the newer techniques used to rectify these imperfections in estimating the economic impact of tourism, is the **computable general equilibrium model** (CGE). Whilst the CGE incorporates an IO framework, it also models a wider range of elements, ranging from basic to more complex forms, and may be static (i.e. for one point in time) or dynamic. But CGEs are often expensive to undertake, despite the availability of computer models.

One of the most widely adapted elements of CGEs is their development of static snapshots in the form of *Tourism Satellite Accounts* (TSAs) (WTO 1999). TSAs set out to measure the economic contribution of tourism in a fairly descriptive, yet detailed manner and WTTC (2004) estimated the TSA for global tourism in Table 17.5. An example of a TSA can be seen in Insight 17.1.

Other techniques used to evaluate economic values include 'contingent valuation' (Lindberg and Johnson 1997) and the use of a 'social accounting matrix' (SAM) (see Wagner 1997). Walpole and Goodwin (2000) provide an alternative method of researching the economic impact of tourism, stating that macroeconomic techniques (such as IO analysis) are inappropriate for use at local levels due to lack of existing data. Walpole and Goodwin's study of the effects of ecotourism in the Komodo National Park of Indonesia set out to examine employment, distribution effects and tourism-induced change rather than regional economic impact. Techniques used included estimations from survey-based data and use of secondary data sources, referred to as 'local economic inquiry' (Walpole and Goodwin 2000: 565). This may be the only feasible approach to assessment if there is a lack of data for the area.

Tourism and economic development

The economic effects of tourism do not occur in isolation from the area and regions in which tourism develops. In destination areas and different regions of countries where tourism has been developed, the effect of tourism translates into economic development. That development occurs in time and space and follows distinct economic cycles; it may need public sector intervention to pump-prime it, via incentives such as tax benefits.

Since tourism is a powerful tool in stimulating economic development, it has been widely used by governments to diversify a country's economic base, to stimulate a new economic sector and/or, as part of the regeneration of urban, rural and coastal areas, to underpin property redevelopment and to create new attractions and activities for tourists. In some cases, governments have developed purpose-built tourist resorts, such as Languedoc–Roussillon in southern France, to achieve regional economic development benefits via tourism. This highlights the significance of tourism and economic policies, with long-term growth in this productive activity. More commonplace, is the intervention at the local level by the public sector as part of an urban regeneration scheme (see Chapter 21) to assist in the redevelopment of an urban environment. This intervention is often justified, as Chapter 14 has shown, to break the cycle of decline or to rectify a failure in the local economy. Through such an intervention, public investment is often seen as a positive step to stimulate and leverage additional public and private sector investment focused around a dedicated tourism project or mixed tourism and other uses development. In theory, this is supposed to kick start economic development, as exemplified by the spectacular redevelopment of Cardiff's waterfront and Tiger Bay area.

TABLE 17.5 WTTC TSA estimates and forecasts 2004 and 2004–2013

World	2004 US % Bn	2004 % of total	% growth*
Personal travel & tourism (T&T)	2 294.6	10.1	3.7
Business travel	524.8	—	3.7
Government expenditure	236.5	3.9	3.0
Capital investment	730.9	9.6	4.3
Visitor exports	605.1	6.0	7.1
Other exports	535.2	5.3	7.2
Travel & tourism demand	4 926.8	—	4.6
T&T industry GDP	1 374.8	3.7	3.6
T&T economy GDP	3 787.2	10.3	3.9
T&T industry employment	69 737.8	2.7	2.2
T&T economy employment	200 967.0	7.7	2.4

*2004–2013 annualized real growth adjusted for inflation (%); 000 jobs

Source: WTTC (2004)

INSIGHT 17.1

The tourism satellite account in New Zealand

In June 1999, the Department of Statistics in New Zealand released its findings from developing a pilot TSA using 1995 data and this has been updated for 1999–2003 (www.trcnz.govt.nz). The TSA, developed in line with OECD and WTO guidelines, provides a wide range of economic data related to tourism by identifying the impact of tourism from the national accounts and other data sources. The findings enable one to identify a number of features including:

- the direct impact of tourism on GDP

- tourism expenditure as a percentage of GDP

- direct employment as a percentage of total employment

- international travel expenditure as a percentage of total travel expenditure

- domestic personal travel expenditure as a percentage of total travel expenditure

- domestic business and government travel expenditure as a percentage of total travel expenditure

- the value of taxes (i.e. Good Services Tax, GST) paid by tourists.

Other features such as the indirect tourism value added can also be quantified and this is modelled for 2003 in Figure 17.2 which summarizes the principal findings from the TSA. For the year ended March 1995, total tourism expenditure in New Zealand totalled NZ$9.1 billion and this had grown to NZ$16.5 billion in 2003, which highlights the substantial contribution the sector made in the 1990s to the national economy. This has been underpinned by the impact of the America's Cup in 2003/04 and film tourism associated with The Lord of the Rings. Figure 17.2 also examines the direct value that tourism adds to GDP, which measures the direct value added by the sellers of products to tourists. Not only does this permit cross-industry comparisons that highlight the contribution other industries make to GDP, it also illustrates the significance of the diverse range of service sector activities which contribute to tourism. As a result of the TSA, tourism employment in New Zealand is estimated to comprise 104 000 full-time equivalent employees (FTEs) directly employed in tourism activities. The majority of the those employed in tourism work for 16 000 tourism-related small businesses complemented by major employers such as the airlines and the airports. For further detail on the TSA, consult www.trcnz.govt.nz and the WTO (1999) report.

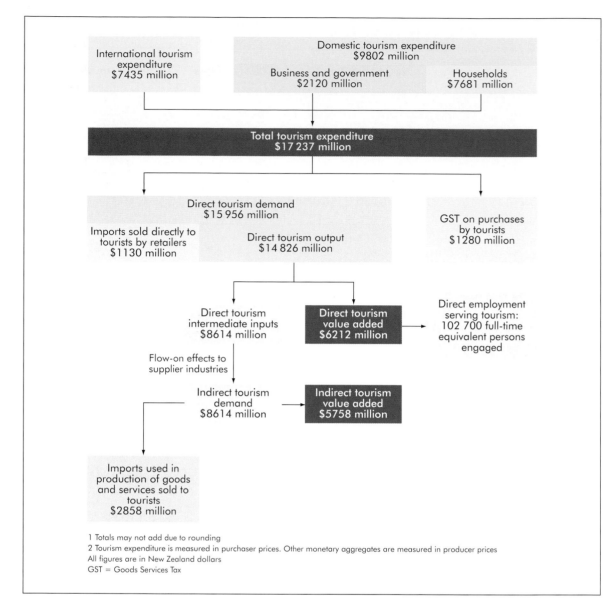

FIGURE 17.2 Flows of tourism expenditure through the New Zealand economy, year ended March 2004,
Source: http://www.trenz.govt.nz

Conclusion

Tourism is a major global industry that provides huge opportunity for economic growth, foreign exchange earnings, employment and income generation. It has been seen that tourism results in a range of economic impacts, both positive and negative, depending on the location and socioeconomic foundation of a destination. Future challenges for the industry include:

- reducing leakage of tourism revenue from destination economy
- ensuring wider and more equal distribution of economic benefits
- developing strategies to ensure appropriate return on investment
- balancing the needs of commercial operators with socioeconomic stability in destination areas.

For any government seeking to develop tourism, greater attention to these aspects will assist the tourism industry in striving towards a more sustainable future. All too often, a critical awareness of the true economic costs of tourism to host communities and regions are obscured or glossed over in attempts to develop employment in declining regions or cities as well as in the less developed world. Yet for tourism to reach its full potential, developing a tourism product and visitor industry based on the ability of the local economy and environment to support tourism-related growth needs careful planning and management. The economic aspects of tourism cannot be seen in isolation from the wider economic growth and development of countries, regions and places since they need to be carefully integrated into the existing social and cultural structures. In this respect, development planning in less developed countries needs to adopt a broader evaluation of tourism so that the expected benefits are balanced with the costs and impacts to the area being developed.

Discussion questions

1 Explain the effect of leakage on a tourism destination.
2 What is the tourism multiplier and how does it work?
3 Discuss the positive and negative economic impacts of tourism.
4 Explain the meanings of 'macroeconomics' and 'microeconomics'. Discuss how these concepts relate to the tourism industry.

References

Berry, B., Kim, H. and Kim, H. (1993) 'Are long waves driven by techno-economic transformations? Evidence for the US and the UK', *Technological Forecasting and Social Change*, 44: 111–35.

Borooah, V.K. (1999) 'The supply of hotel rooms in Queensland, Australia', *Annals of Tourism Research*, 26 (4): 985–1003.

Bull, A. (1995) *The Economics of Travel and Tourism, Second Edition*. Melbourne: Longman.

Butler, R. (1980) 'The concept of the tourist area life cycle of evolution: Implications for management of resources', *Canadian Geographer*, 14 (5): 5–12.

Connell, J. and Page, S.J. (2005) 'Evaluating the economic and spatial effects of an event: The case of the World Medical and Health Games', *Tourism Geographies*, 7 (1): 63–85.

Cooper, C., Fletcher, J., Gilbert, D., Shepherd, R. and Wanhill, S. (1998) *Tourism: Principles and Practice, Second Edition*. Harlow: Longman.

Craven, J. (1990) *Introduction to Economics, Second Edition*. Oxford: Blackwell.

Dwyer, L., Forsyth, P. and Spurr, R. (2004) 'Evaluating tourism's economic effects: new and old approaches', *Tourism Management*, 25 (3): 307–17.

Fletcher, J. and Snee, H. (1989) 'Tourism in the South Pacific Islands', in C. Cooper (ed.) *Progress in Tourism, Recreation and Hospitality Management, Volume One*. London: Belhaven.

Henthorne, T. and Miller, M. (2003) 'Cuban tourism in the Caribbean context: A regional impact assessment', *Journal of Travel Research*, 42 (1): 84–93.

Holloway, J.C. and Robinson, C. (1995) *Marketing for Tourism*. Harlow: Longman.

Jayawardena, C. (2003) 'Revolution to revolution: Why is tourism booming in Cuba?', *International Journal of Contemporary Hospitality Management*, 15 (1): 52–8.

Kreutzwiser, R. (1973) 'A methodology for estimating tourist spending in Ontario counties', unpublished MA thesis, University of Waterloo, Ontario.

Leones, J., Colby, B. and Crandall, K. (1998) 'Tracking expenditures of the elusive nature tourists of Southeastern Arizona', *Journal of Travel Research*, 36: 56–64.

Lindberg, K. and Johnson, R.L. (1997) 'The economic values of tourism's social impacts', *Annals of Tourism Research*, 24 (1): 90–116.

Lipsey, R.G. (1989) *An Introduction to Positive Economics, Seventh Edition*. London: Weidenfeld & Nicolson.

La Lopa, J.M., Chen, K. and Nelson, K. (1998) 'Economic impact of the 1996 Oldsmobile Classic Golf Tournament in the Greater Lansing Area', *Journal of Vacation Marketing*, 4 (2): 175–85.

Martin de Holan, P. and Phillips, N. (1997) 'Sun, sand, and hard currency. Tourism in Cuba', *Annals of Tourism Research*, 24 (4): 777–95.

Mathieson, A. and Wall, G. (1982) *Tourism. Economic, Social and Physical Impacts*. Harlow: Longman.

Mules, T. (1998) 'Decomposition of Australian tourist expenditure', *Tourism Management*, 19 (3): 267–71.

Murphy, P. (1985) *Tourism. A Community Approach*. London: Routledge.

Oppermann, M. and Chon, K. (1997) *Tourism in Developing Countries*. London: International Thomson Business Press.

Orams, M. (1999) *The Economic Benefits of Whale Watching in Vava'u, the Kingdom of Tonga*. Auckland, New Zealand: Centre for Tourism Research, Massey University at Albany.

Page, S.J. (1995) *Urban Tourism*. London: Routledge.

The Tourism Company (1998) *Visitor Payback. Encouraging Tourists to Give Money Voluntarily to Conserve the Places they Visit*. Ledbury: The Tourism Company.

Waggle, D. and Fish, M. (1999) 'International tourism cross-elasticity', *Annals of Tourism Research*, 26 (1): 191–4.

Wagner, J. (1997) 'Estimating the economic impacts of tourism', *Annals of Tourism Research*, 24 (3): 592–608.

Walpole, M.J. and Goodwin, H.J. (2000) 'Local economic impacts of dragon tourism in Indonesia', *Annals of Tourism Research*, 27 (3): 559–76.

WTO (World Tourism Organization) (1999) *Tourism Satellite Account: The Conceptual Framework*: Madrid: World Tourism Organization.

WTTC (World Travel and Tourism Council) (2004) *Summary Statistics*, www.wttc.org, accessed 1 February 2005.

Further reading

Vanhove, N. (2004) *Economics of Tourist Destinations*. Oxford: Butterworth-Heinemann.

18

Social and Cultural Impacts

Learning outcomes

After reading this chapter, and answering the questions, you should be able to:

- define the social and cultural impacts of tourism

- explain the factors which affect the extent of social and cultural impacts

- understand a range of current issues illustrating social and cultural impacts.

Overview

For many nations, tourism is seen as an easy way of generating income, particularly foreign exchange (see Chapter 17). In some cases, little capital expenditure is required by the host society as external investment is available. The economic spin-offs are viewed as the most important aspect of tourism development. As the economic impacts of tourism are more readily measurable, other types of impact tend to remain more hidden; in particular, the social and cultural effects. However, insidious social and cultural change may incur more significant costs than economic benefits in the long-term. This chapter explores the nature of the impacts of tourism from this perspective.

Introduction

The history of tourism indicates that tourism is a social event. **Resort development** and sightseeing came about partly through fashions and social responses to the natural and built environments. Tourism is a global phenomenon which is essentially taste driven, with regions coming in and out of fashion and often the topic of social conversation. This is often embodied in the concept of which places are 'in vogue' and 'must see' destinations. This is reflected in the example of Ireland in the late 1990s: the country benefited from a global Celtic revival based on Irish culture and heritage which had a profound effect on promoting the country as a tourist destination (Cronin and O'Connor 2003). In this respect, tourism is about people and how people as tourists interact with other locations and peoples, engaging in experiences that may influence their own or the host community attitudes, expectations, opinions and lifestyles. This domain of study within tourism studies is normally identified with **anthropology** (Nash 2005) and, to a lesser degree, **sociology** (Cohen 2004). This interest is reflected in a number of seminal studies in tourism and its social and cultural impact embodied in MacCannell's (1976) *The Tourist*, Smith's (1977) *Hosts and Guests* and De Kadt's (1979) *Tourism: Passport to Development*. Each of these studies confirm what Murphy (1985: 117) argued that tourism is a 'sociocultural event for the traveller and the host' (it is sometimes difficult to separate social and cultural elements and so the term 'sociocultural' tends to be used frequently in tourism literature).

The nature of sociocultural impacts

Sociocultural impacts relate to changes in societal value systems, individual behaviour, social relationships, lifestyles, modes of expression and community structures. The focus of sociocultural impacts tends to be the host community, i.e. the people who reside in tourist destinations, rather than the tourist-generating region. Mathieson and Wall (1982) state that sociocultural impacts are 'about the effects on the people of host communities, of their direct and indirect associations with tourists'. Lea (1988) outlines the dimensions of **tourist–host encounters** and provides a useful starting point from which to define social and cultural aspects. This is illustrated in Figure 18.1

Elements of culture

According to Mathieson and Wall (1982: 158), culture is the 'conditioning elements of behaviour and the products of that behaviour', consisting of 12 elements:

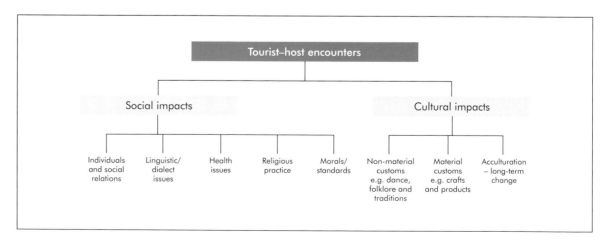

FIGURE 18.1   The dimensions of tourist–host encounters. Source: Modified from Shaw and Williams (1994: 87)

- handicrafts
- language
- traditions
- gastronomy
- art and music
- history

- local work
- architecture
- religion
- educational system
- dress
- leisure activities.

Sharpley (1994) states that from a social and cultural perspective, the rapid expansion of tourism is important in two respects:

1 The development of tourism as a vehicle for economic modernization and diversification almost invariably leads to changes and developments in the structure of society. These may be positive and negative. In the positive sense, there may be society-wide improvements in income, employment opportunities, education, local infrastructure and services. On the negative side, there may be a threat posed to traditional social values, the creation of factions of society who may take advantages of others and adaptation or weakening of cultural values.

2 All tourists, to a lesser or greater extent, inevitably take on holiday their own beliefs, values and behavioural modes: what may be termed **cultural baggage**. Cohen (1972) states that people tend to travel in an **environmental bubble** (see Murphy 1985: 6). Therefore, the scope for mixing of cultures is great.

This gives rise to two ideas about the sociocultural effect of tourism. First, that the interaction between host and guest could dilute or destroy traditional cultures. This reflects the literature that considers tourism primarily as a threat to culture and peoples. Second, that the interaction between host and guest could create new opportunities for peace and greater understanding. This alternative perspective acknowledges the benefits that tourism can have in allowing exchange of cultures in promoting greater awareness on both sides (Image 18.1). There is evidence to prove both of these aspects exist and a consensus is by no means easy to generate.

While it is possible to generalize about sociocultural impacts, it is more problematic to define the extent to which they have occurred. The study of impacts on society and culture is complicated by the nature of more general social and cultural change. The forces of change are many and varied, tourism being just one factor. Other aspects which must be acknowledged include the role of advertising and media, the effect of multinational corporations, the aspirations of government, education and immigrants. Given the complexity of influencing factors, it is hard to extrapolate tourism as a single example of potential sociocultural impact. It might be argued that if cultures are continually changing, what is wrong with change as a result of tourism? Leaving this debate to one side, the main assumption about sociocultural impacts is that if the tourist generating country has a 'stronger' economy and culture than the receiving country, then the sociocultural impact is likely to be higher than if the other way around. The greater the difference, the greater the impact. Thus, for example, the sociocultural effect of British holiday-makers to France is less than it would be on a developing country such as Vietnam.

Image 18.1: The cultural dimension in tourism has seen many indigenous people, such as the Maori in New Zealand, provide interpretation of a rich cultural past embodied in visits to community meeting houses (Marae). Source: S.J. Page

Factors influencing sociocultural impacts

Having explored the general context, it is now apposite to consider the range of factors which influence the nature and extent of sociocultural impacts. Sharpley (1994) outlines four factors which shape the effects.

- *Types and numbers of tourists*: The traditional view is that low numbers of tourists, particularly independent travellers, result in a low impact, therefore a high tourist volume results in a high impact. In other words, those who integrate with local services and people have less impact than those who rely on externally provided mass tourism facilities. Yet the independent traveller may have more effect on an isolated community that has not been exposed to outside influence than a large, established resort might. Therefore, it might be argued that mass tourism in self-contained resorts e.g. **Club Mediterranée** may have less impact. This is a much debated point (see e.g. Wheeller 1993).

- *Importance of the tourism industry*: The primary purpose of tourism as an industry is economic growth and/or diversification of the local economy. The impacts of tourism are likely to be less in a mixed economy than on an economy reliant on tourism.

- *Size and development of the tourism industry*: A large number of tourists in a small community will tend to have a large impact. Larger communities may remain less affected. In relation to the tourism lifecycle model, there are more likely to be impacts in the developmental stage as facilities grow and changes take place. Many areas in the UK now want smaller numbers of higher-spending tourists to visit and some countries are following this particular mode of development, e.g the Seychelles. Established resorts are likely to experience less change than newly emerging destinations.

- *Pace of tourism development*: Some destinations have witnessed rapid growth which has been relatively uncontrolled. Social impacts are likely to be higher in these areas. Local communities need to adapt gradually to the needs and benefits of change and tourists.

Other related aspects which need to be considered include the nature of the host–guest encounter, the nature of the destination, and cultural similarities. Williams (1998) comments that cultural similarity or dissimilarity is one of the major factors in shaping sociocultural impacts. Impacts tend to be greater where the host and guest relationship is both culturally and geographically distant. This is represented in Figure 18.2.

Thus, where the tourist and the host are culturally similar, as in the case of western Europeans or Americans and Canadians, then the sociocultural impacts will be limited. Williams (1998) notes that even for the rapidly expanding markets of South East Asia, over 75 per cent of international visitors originate from within the region (ie. these are intra-regional travellers). In a part of

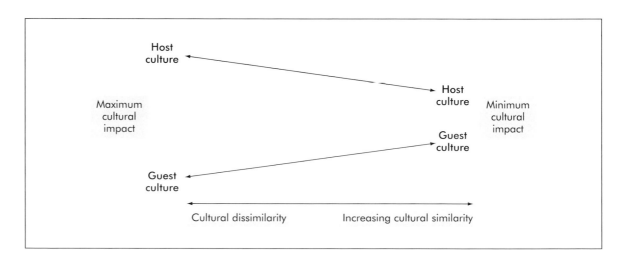

FIGURE 18.2   Host and guest relationship. Source: Modified from Williams (1998)

the world where impacts might be expected to be significant, a large proportion of visitors will share a sufficiently similiar sociocultural background for fewer impacts to occur than might be anticipated.

The nature of the **host–guest relationship** and community attitudes to tourism generally depend on:

- type of contact between host and guest
- importance of the tourism industry to the community
- community tolerance threshold (de Kadt 1979).

Contact between host and guest may arise in three scenarios:

- tourist purchase of goods and services from local people (shops, hotels)
- tourist and local resident use of same facilities (beaches, shops, bars)
- purposeful meeting to exchange ideas and information.

The demonstration effect

De Kadt (1979) defines the **demonstration effect** as 'changes in attitudes, values or behaviour which can result from merely observing tourists'. This may be advantageous or disadvantageous to the host community. It is said that observing other peoples may encourage hosts, particularly in developing countries, to adapt or work for things they lack; in other words, it may assist development. More commonly it is detrimental, causing discontent and resentment (Mathieson and Wall 1982) because the degree of wealth and freedom of behaviour displayed by the tourist imposes an impossible goal. Local people may turn to illegal means to obtain the level of wealth they desire, thus crime rates may increase as a result of tourism in a destination. The demonstration effect has the greatest influence on young people and may create generation gaps and class differences between those who desire change and those who wish to retain traditional ways of life. The young and especially the educated tend to migrate. Norberg-Hodge (1992) observes the effect of a sudden influx of Western tourists in Ladakh, Nepal, on young men and states that feelings of inferiority have resulted. 'They rush after the symbols of modernity: sunglasses, Walkmans, and blue jeans several sizes too small – not because they find those jeans more attractive or comfortable, but because they are symbols of modern life' (Norberg-Hodge 1992: 98). An increase in aggression was also noted. The young people want the material side of modern life but cannot see so readily the negative aspects of it – such as stress, unemployment, environmental degradation, disenfranchisement. This type of change may be a disruptive force to traditional kinship over time.

Acculturation

Many impacts of tourism appear relatively quickly while others tend to manifest themselves more gradually. Cultural change falls into this last category and, over time, more long-term cultural change may result from tourism. External influences and the evolution of society results in change, regardless of the existence of tourism. Enhanced networks of communication, technology and the emergence of the global market are all part of this process. However, the role of tourism needs to be understood to ensure that culture is not unnecessarily damaged. The infiltration of Western culture into less developed countries is viewed as problematic as different views, attitudes, behaviour patterns, aspirations and expenditure patterns may not be easily adapted from one culture to another. In addition, unique and interesting ways of life may be pushed aside for Western ideals which are not necessarily appropriate for the future of global society. Sharpley (1994) notes the example of tourism in Nepal, now becoming a mainstream tourist destination where there is a visible Westernization of Kathmandu is occurring as a result of tourism. This type of change is sometimes referred to as **coca-colonization**. Ritzer (1996) has considered this in terms of the effects of globalization in the fast-food industry as 'McDonaldization' – the wider implications of this are worthy of consideration as this relates to acculturation through tourism.

International tourism is thought to influence sociocultural change through the process of acculturation. The theory of acculturation rests on the notion that contact between cultures results in sharing and adoption of one another's values and attitudes. A major concern is that when a culturally weak society comes into contact with a culturally strong one, the process will be more one way; that is, the values and attitudes of the strong nation are transferred to the weak nation. Thus, acculturation is more pronounced in less developed countries, particularly those which have had less contact with Western society in the past. Tourism induced acculturation may be difficult to disentangle from wider cultural change.

Two arguments dominate the literature on the cultural impacts of tourism.

1   Tourism results in the transformation of cultural events into commercialized products or spectacles which are devoid of all meaning. Culture may be trivialized by tourism in an attempt to make it a product for tourists to consume. The process of cultural commodification is much criticized by authors such as Urry (1990).

2   Tourism results in the preservation and revitalization of traditional cultural practices by providing financial support and engendering community pride. This is seen as positively contributing to the goals of sustainable tourism.

Furze, De Lacy and Birckhead (1996) state that the development of consciousness assists in defending indigenous societies against the might of multinational companies, developers and governments and cite the example of Australian aboriginal communities. Pedregal (cited in Bossevain 1996) talks about the idea of self-consciousness in the south Spanish coastal community of Zahara de los Atunes in response to tourist arrivals. The summer season is said to drive the locals crazy and they feel hostile towards the presence of tourists or 'others'. The end result is that local people close themselves off from tourists and continue their own cultural pastimes but away from the eyes of tourists. Host communities may be subject to what is termed 'zooification' if tourists are curious about local people and their way of life. This refers to tribal people being turned into sights to be viewed by the tourist. This is particularly marked for tribal people. Tribal people may put on special events for visitors such as demonstrations of dancing or traditional customs. The danger is that these events may lose their cultural significance if performed at inappropriate times and reasons. The Padaung women of Thailand have become victims of this.

From the tourist perspective this raises questions of authenticity and objectification of culture from the host perspective. For example, in the transition of eastern Europe from Communism to independence (Worthington 2003), tourism has boomed in many places, now realizing their tourism potential and their low costs of production relative to western Europe. Hughes and Allen (2005) examined the perception of image formers in national tourist boards responsible for promoting cultural tourism in eastern Europe. They found that respondents felt that the promotion of tourism did not displace, distort or devalue local culture. Indeed, respondents pointed to the seemingly genuine folk performances in Bulgaria and Poland as evidence of tourism's positive impact. In contrast, Mathieson and Wall (1982) outline the developed world interest in the material culture of Aboriginals (see also Simons 2000). The ancient sand paintings of desert tribes have been adapted to the use of acrylics and canvas for the export market. This cheapens and degrades the traditional artwork because the aesthetic qualities are deemed to be more important than true meanings and function. Cohen (1972) constructed a framework to illustrate tourist settings in relation to authenticity (see Figure 18.3).

The sociocultural effects of tourism

Language

As a social vehicle of communication, language is a key indicator of acculturation. Tourism can lead to language change in three ways:

- economic changes through the hiring of immigrant or expatriate labour. Seasonal workers and second home owners may exacerbate this. In some areas, there may be a diminishing trend of local dialects due to migration patterns, e.g. on the Isle of Skye, Scotland

Nature of scene	Real	Staged
Real	Authentic e.g. visit to a living, working town. The function of the settlement is unchanged by the tourist presence and the host community continues to go about their daily business. Visitors integrate into the scene	Denial of authenticity (staging suspicion) e.g. costumed hosts in Thai villages, where traditional apparel is worn regardless of tourist presence. Visitors may think locals are dressing up especially
Staged	Staged authenticity (covert tourist space) e.g. tribal dancing for visitors, where the tourists believe that they are witnessing a culturally important event but the host community have set it up deliberately as entertainment	Contrived (overt tourist space) e.g. tourist village, heritage centre. The visitor is fully aware that the attraction is not authentic and visits knowingly

FIGURE 18.3   Tourist perception of a scene. Source: Adapted from Cohen (1972)

- demonstration effect, where the local community aspires to achieving the status of the visitor
- direct social contact and the need to converse to make commercial transactions. Sometimes, the host is obliged to learn the main incoming tourist language in order to deal with their requirements and to ease the transition to a foreign destination.

Religion

In some tourist regions, religion has become a commodity. Religious buildings and events are spectacles to view. Many religious sites attract large numbers of visitors, who may or may not possess the beliefs of that particular religion. Some of the most well-visited sites have religious connections, such as cathedrals, abbeys and spiritual centres, such as Mecca, Bethlehem and Lourdes. Increasing conflict exists between local worshippers, devout visitors and sightseers. Traditional ceremonies, rites and practices are not always recognized by the tourist, who may view such events in a frivolous and direspectful way. It has been known for tourists to be spectators at burials and weddings. In Bhutan, tourists are not permitted to visit certain monasteries, in a bid to prevent tourism from disrupting religious life. In many countries, particularly Islamic ones, tourist clothing can cause offence. For example, in the Gambia, with its predominantly Muslim population, female tourists who wear tight clothes, shorts or a short skirt and men wearing short-sleeved shirts are viewed as indecent. In the Maldives, where the population is Islamic, no topless bathing is allowed. In Zanzibar, Islamic beliefs are offended by improper tourist clothing and behaviour. These are just a few examples. Philp and Mercer (1999) discuss the extent to which Buddhism has become commodified in contemporary Burma in an attempt by the military junta to legitimate its authority. The promotion of tourism has relied on strong images of Buddhist traditions and cultural heritage. There has been concern about authenticity issues as well as substantive effects on indigenous peoples in the creation of a strategic tourist product and adverse impacts have also been associated with the impact of tourists on health of residents and through crime, as the case of prostitution's growth alongside tourism in South East Asia suggests (Oppermann 1999) (see Chapter 26 for more detail on these issues).

Host perceptions of impacts

There is substantial literature on the host perception of tourism impacts (e.g. Hernandez and Cohen 1996; Korca 1996; Faulkner and Tideswell 1997). Variables which contribute to host perception of tourism can be categorized as:

- extrinsic
- intrinsic.

Extrinsic factors are those factors that affect the community at a broader level, such as the pace of tourism development, type of tourism, cultural differences between host and guest and the **tourist–host ratio**. *Intrinsic factors* relate more specifically to the people, such as their demographic structure, employment in the tourism industry and proximity of residence to tourism areas. In fact many studies of the social impacts of tourism have been undertaken in less developed countries. While this research is important, there must be caution in applying research findings from one culture to another. Page and Lawton (1996) found that in the case of a host community in Devonport, Auckland, New Zealand, residents would be prepared to accept a growth in tourist numbers if the growth was appropriately managed, despite initial concerns by local politicians that tourism growth should be halted. This illustrates the importance of developing locally based research to understand these highly contentious issues.

Frameworks for measuring sociocultural impacts

Ways of assessing the extent of social impacts have emerged over the last 30 years in an attempt to provide some evidence of the effects of tourism on host communities. Doxey's **Irridex** (irritation index) (Figure 18.4) was developed following research in Barbados, the West Indies and Ontario in 1975 and remains one of the most widely cited frameworks for thinking about host responses to tourism. The model supposes that impacts of tourism on the host community may be translated to degrees of resident irritation. It is based on four stages of response which increase through time in sequence as the destination lifecycle unfolds and resident attitudes change. The initial stage – euphoria – arises at the outset of tourism and describes the scenario where a small number of travellers arrive in a location. There is little tourist infrastructure so visitors use local accommodation and services. Hence, there is a high degree of informal contact between host and guest and high economic benefits as local people benefit directly from tourism activity (Image 18.2). Tourists are welcomed and the host population feels euphoric. As time progresses and tourism development begins, the host population may start to take tourism for granted (apathy). This may reflect an increasingly formal type of contact between host and guest as more services are developed, foreign investors begin to take control of the industry and local people begin to get used to servile roles. The annoyance stage generally reflects the stage when a destination reaches the saturation point, where tourism has become a dominant force in the environment and adaptations are necessary to cope with the numbers of tourists. The final stage of the *Irridex* – antagonism – is an extreme point where the host population blames tourism for all the negative aspects of life in the area.

Image 18.2: Local crafts for sale so tourists can create economic benefits for local people, but is this 'commoditization of culture'?

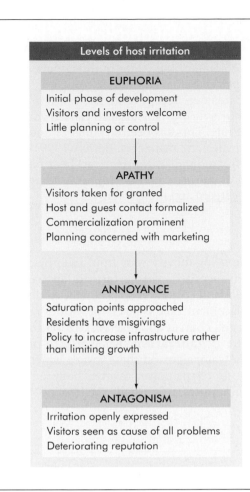

FIGURE 18.4   Doxey's Irridex. Source: Modified from Doxey (1975)

Teo's study of the sociocultural impacts in Singapore (1994), illustrates the negative effects of lack of contact between the host and guest. The average length of stay, three days, implies minimal contact and no opportunity to engage. Tourists tend to remain in enclaves or 'ghettoes'. Teo's attempt to measure the host response to tourism using Doxey's *Irridex* showed that:

- 75 per cent welcomed tourists for economic purposes
- 75 per cent thought that locals received poorer levels of service than tourists
- 99 per cent thought that tourists were overcharged
- 78 per cent rarely communicated with tourists – if they did, it was to give directions.

The results of a survey of residents indicated that the appropriate measure using the *Irridex* was apathy. Ap and Crompton (1998) have developed a tourism impact scale which has yielded valid and reliable data on resident perceptions of impacts and is more reliable than the widely cited study by Doxey and other research which has imitated the same conceptual framework. This is because Ap and Crompton (1993) recognize that host communities are not homogenous. Many published studies still using unidirectional and redundant models such as Doxey have still not grasped the major progress made in the analysis of social and cultural impacts in tourism research. Krippendorf (1987) defines four categories of local person: those who are in continuous and direct contact with tourist; those who own tourism businesses but have little contact with tourists; those who are in direct and frequent contact with tourists but only gain part of their income from tourism; and those who have little or no contact with tourists. People in each category are likely to have a different view of tourism and its impacts.

Wider issues relating to social and cultural impacts of tourism

It is also important to recognize some of the wider ramifications of tourism development where economic objectives have been placed before community concerns (Gursoy and Rutherford 2004). One of the most significant debates over recent years has centred on the **displacement** of local communities to make way for tourism. Tourism has also caused governments to act in ways which contravene the rights of local people. This has been a primary issue for indigenous peoples as they enter into tourism as both spectacles and managers. Berno (1999) suggests that where the expectations of tourists and residents are similar, tourism can be a beneficial exchange process, but where the two do not meet, local culture can be compromised and indigenous people may find tourism contributes to low self-esteem and is exploitative.

Displacement

Various instances of local people being moved away from their place of residence to make way for tourism development have been recorded. This is termed 'spatial displacement', and Ryan and Aicken (2005) also identify social and cultural displacement, as discussed in the various sections above. In the case of spatial displacement, land is taken for various reasons, such as the construction of hotels, tourist infrastructure, golf courses and reserves. **Tourism Concern** (www.tourismcon-cern.org) the **non-government organization** that works to protect communities affected by tourism has run many successful campaigns on these issues which can be seen on their website. Displacement illustrates the nature of the power relation between the forces of tourism development, government and local communities. It is usually the local people who lose out (Insight 18.1).

INSIGHT 18.1

Examples of displacement

- In Guatemala, 300 families were evicted in June 1996 from land they claimed belonged to the state. Police burned down their homes to create the land needed for a Spanish businessman's plan for a tourist complex.

- The Masai tribe in Kenya have been subject to the vagaries of government wishes since the end of the Second World War and moved away from certain areas of land for conservation reasons. It was thought that pastoral agriculture was to blame for the degradation of the environment. Tribes were moved to other areas and reserves created for tourism. Wildlife numbers have not increased as a result.

- One of the most famous cases of displacement occurred in Burma in the mid-1990s. The year 1996 was declared 'Visit Myanmar Year' by the military government. Communities were forced to relocate their homes and clear up shabby buildings to make way for hotels. Worse than this was the claim that over two million people were forced into labour camps to build the necessary tourism infrastructure (roads, railways, hotels and other facilities) for Burma to become a favoured destination.

- In October 1992 and for some time after, the radical Islamic group El-Gamaat el Islamiya campaigned against tourism in Egypt, stating that mass tourism offends Islam. Thirty Western tourists were injured and five died after shootings and bombings. The main issue centred around tourist's lack of respect for the values of the host community – for example, Islamic women dress in a style which covers their bodies from head to toe and alcohol is not consumed. The actions cut tourism industry revenue by one third.

- At Kuah, Malaysia in 1989, 29 shop owners living close to a jetty were forced to move and their shops and homes were demolished. This was because the Tourism Development Committee considered the building to be an eyesore. As part of a later Tourist Development Beautification Project, a new tourist shop and restaurant were constructed on the site.

- About 300 native Hawaiians were evicted from Makua Beach, Honolulu, by the Hawaiian government in 1996 to release the land for development into a beach park.

The Universal Declaration of Human Rights (1948) which states the basic standards that must underpin contemporary global society is clearly contravened by some examples of tourism development, examples of which are illustrated in Table 18.1.

TABLE 18.1 Contravention of human rights associated with tourism development

Human right	Examples of where contravened by tourism
The right to freedom of movement	Local people are restricted from using some tourist beaches in the Caribbean, e.g. Grenada In Kenya, tribal families are not permitted to graze cattle in the Keilado Ghana sanctuary any longer
The right to land, water and natural resources	In Goa, local people suffer from water shortages while tourists in luxury hotels have fresh, piped supplies
The right to health and well-being	In Thailand, the health of residents living next to golf courses has been affected by toxins in water supplies from chemical grass treatments
The right to respect and dignity	In Hawaii, much of the hotel development has taken place on sacred and culturally significant sites In St Lucia, an all-inclusive resort development was built on the sacred site of the first inhabitants of the island
The right of the child to protection	Sex tourism in Sri Lanka has resulted in many children working as prostitutes

Source: Based on a speech by Cecil Rajendra, Malaysia, Tourism Concern (1992); Pattullo (1996)

Tourism and local communities – planning and management issues

Much work has been undertaken to identify ways in which the impact of tourism on local communities might be lessened. In conjunction with this, attempts to involve the local community in the tourism development and management process should be noted. If one of the objectives of tourism development is to benefit the host population, some consideration must be given to the host perspective on impacts and local community carrying capacity values (see Chapter 19) should be part of tourism planning. This is important in all host communities but is a more sensitive issue in relation to tourism which affects tribal and **indigenous peoples**.

Indigenous tourism

According to Butler and Hinch (1996), indigenous tourism relates to a form of tourism that is directed by indigenous peoples or where indigenous culture is the tourist attraction. Figure 18.5 illustrates the theoretical nature of tourism as it relates to indigenous culture. Ryan and Aicken (2005) point to the value of indigenous culture in allowing tourism destinations to promote the distinctive cultural features, which may contribute to a cultural revival if the local culture is managed appropriately. Yet where it does not occur in a sensitive manner, it may illustrate the link between the notions of culture and control.

Altman and Finlayson (1993) outline some of the previous research on Aboriginal tourism which has tended to find that Aboriginal people are reluctant to participate directly in tourism activity because they feel that involvement with non-Aborigines is intrusive and negative. Sociocultural considerations are put before economic ones as Aborigines do not feel it important to participate in the formal labour market. Aboriginal people tend to be directly involved in the manufacture and sale of artefacts and so based in the cultural tourism sphere. However, there are many examples of successful ventures where there is a high degree of Aboriginal control, appropriate scale of enterprise, accommodation of social and cultural factors and an element of consumer and industry education, also noted by Dyer, Aberdeen and Schuler (2003).

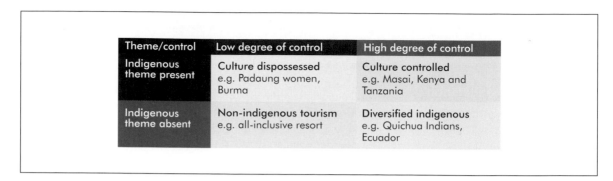

Theme/control	Low degree of control	High degree of control
Indigenous theme present	Culture dispossessed e.g. Padaung women, Burma	Culture controlled e.g. Masai, Kenya and Tanzania
Indigenous theme absent	Non-indigenous tourism e.g. all-inclusive resort	Diversified indigenous e.g. Quichua Indians, Ecuador

FIGURE 18.5   Indigenous culture, control and tourism. Source: Adapted from Butler and Hinch (1996)

Involving the community in tourism planning

Involving local communities in managing tourism is one of the precepts of sustainable tourism development and, as Ap and Crompton (1998: 120) state, 'for tourism to thrive in an area it needs support from the area's residents'. The rationale for involving the host community in tourism decision-making includes allowing those who will be involved with or affected by tourism to have their say in how it should be developed. Another reason is that local people often have knowledge of their home environment which can assist in planning tourism development. The overall aim of community involvement is to reduce the conflict between tourism and the host community (Swarbrooke 1999). Methods of community involvement are varied but may include consultation with the host community about tourism plans and proposals or allowing some input to policies. Yet as Teye, Sönmez and Sirakaya (2002) found in a review of projects funded by aid donors in Ghana, local people were effectively excluded from involvement which failed to meet their expectations and created resentment among those working in the tourism sector.

The host community with the assistance of a supporting organization may promote **codes of conduct** for incoming tourists as Tourism Concern do on their website. In some instances, local people have been the progenitors of tourism projects. The Quicha Indians in Ecuador are a good example. While some social and cultural change is inevitable, it seems more appropriate for local communities to control the rate of change through tourism. The fast pace of change in North Sulawesi has meant that it has been difficult for the host community to contribute and adapt to the development of tourism. Tour operators have taken control of the industry and policies have not been imposed to ensure appropriate forms of development which benefit local people (see Ross and Wall 1999).

A crucial component of the community-based tourism concept is empowerment of local people in the development process, a percursor in encouraging participation. Central to this process, is ensuring that access to information is sufficient and that systems of governance actively promote meaningful interaction between the public sector, developers and local people, resulting in a collaborative approach to decision-making (see Murphy and Murphy 2004). Techniques used by the public sector that seek to advocate community approaches to tourism development often extend beyond consultation. Common tools include establishing marketing partnerships with groups of tourism providers, facilitating links between stakeholders and assisting with skills development through training. Examples of community-controlled projects, where a group of residents take charge of developing, promoting and operating a particular tourism product that produces economic and social benefits for that community, are increasingly common in both developed and less developed countries. However, the outcome and effectiveness of community approaches shows substantive variation, according to cultural and business environments, strength and direction of governance, levels of existing tourism infrastructure development and degree of community interest.

Conclusion

Tourism results in a range of social and cultural impacts of varying magnitude. Several factors influence the extent of social and cultural impacts. It must be acknowledged that while tourism may have economic benefits which are generally easy to assess, it is likely that there will be some impact on the host community in both the short and long-term. Discussion of social and cultural impacts often emphasizes the negative aspects but it must be remembered that there are positive angles too. It is difficult to make accurate assessments of the extent to which tourism causes social and cultural change because it is just one force of change which operates.

This type of change is not really tangible and occurs gradually. Despite this, it is certainly clear that those who control tourism activity must take some responsibility for the cost to host communities. It is also apparent that in some cases tourism has been developed at the expense of the host community, where economic gain has been placed as a higher priority than the well-being and integrity of the local people. There are signs that more innovative ways of managing host–guest conflict are emerging but there is still a great deal of concern about the long-term implications of an ever-growing global tourism industry.

Discussion questions

1 Discuss whether tourism results in communication or corruption of culture.

2 Explain why local community involvement in tourism development and management can reduce sociocultural impacts.

3 Discuss the factors which seem to influence the extent of sociocultural impacts in relation to tourism.

4 Why do the sociocultural impacts of tourism appear to be more pronounced in developing countries?

References

Altman, J. and Finlayson, J. (1993) 'Aborigines, tourism and sustainable development', Journal of Tourism Studies, 4 (1): 38–50.

Ap, J. and Crompton, J.L. (1993) 'Residents' strategies for responding to tourism impacts', Journal of Travel Research, 22 (1): 47–9.

Ap, J. and Crompton, J.L. (1998) 'Developing and testing a tourism impact scale', Journal of Travel Research, 37: 120–30.

Berno, T. (1999) 'When a guest is a guest: Cook Islanders view tourism', Annals of Tourism Research, 26 (3): 656–75.

Bossevain, J. (ed.) (1996) Coping with Tourists. European Reactions to Mass Tourism. Oxford: Berghahn.

Butler, R. and Hinch, T. (eds) (1996) Tourism and Indigenous People. London: Routledge.

Cohen, E. (1972) 'Rethinking the sociology of tourism', Annals of Tourism Research, 6 (1): 18–35.

Cohen, E. (2004) Contemporary Tourism. Oxford: Elsevier.

Cronin, M. and O'Connor, B. (eds) (2003) Irish Tourism: Image, Culture and Identity. Clevedon: Channel View.

De Kadt, E. (1979) Tourism – Passport to Development. New York: Oxford University Press.

Doxey, G.V. (1975) 'A causation theory of visitor-resident irritants, methodology and research inferences', Conference Proceedings: Sixth Annual Conference of Travel Research Association, San Diego, 195–8.

Dyer, P., Aberdeen, L. and Schuler, S. (2003) 'Tourism impacts on an Australian indigenous community: A Djabugay case study', Tourism Management, 24 (1): 83–95.

Faulkner, B. and Tideswell, C. (1997) 'A framework for monitoring community impacts of tourism', Journal of Sustainable Tourism, 5 (1): 3–28.

Furze, B., De Lacy, T. and Birckhead, J. (1996) Culture, Conservation, and Biodiversity: the Social Dimension of Linking Local Level Development and Conservation Through Protected Areas. Chichester: John Wiley.

Gursoy, D. and Rutherford, D. (2004) 'Host attitudes towards tourism: An improved structural model', Annals of Tourism Research, 31 (3): 495–516.

Hernandez, S. and Cohen, J. (1996) 'Residents' attitudes towards an instant resort enclave', Annals of Tourism Research, 23 (4): 755–79.

Hughes, H. and Allen, D. (2005) 'Cultural tourism in Eastern Europe: The views of induced image formation agents', Tourism Management, 26 (2): 173–84.

Korca, P. (1996) 'Resident attitudes towards tourism impacts', *Annals of Tourism Research,* 23 (3): 695–7.

Krippendorf, J. (1987) *The Holidaymakers.* Oxford: Butterworth-Heinemann.

Lea, J. (1988) *Tourism and Development in the Third World.* London: Routledge.

MacCannell, D. (1976) *The Tourist: A New Theory of Leisure Class.* London: Macmillan.

Mathieson, G. and Wall, A. (1982) *Tourism: Economic, Social and Environmental Impacts.* Harlow: Longman.

Mowforth, M. and Munt, I. (1998) *Tourism and Sustainability. New Tourism in the Third World.* London: Routledge.

Murphy, P. (1985) *Tourism: A Community Approach.* London: Routledge.

Nash, D. (2005) *Beginnings of an Anthropology of Tourism.* Oxford: Elsevier.

Norberg-Hodge, H. (1992) *Ancient Futures. Learning from Ladakh.* London: Rider.

Oppermann, M. (1999) 'Sex tourism', *Annals of Tourism Research,* 26 (2): 251–66.

Page, S.J. and Lawton, G. (1996) 'The impact of urban tourism on destination communities: implications for community-based tourism in Auckland', in J. Jenkins, G. Kearsley and C.M. Hall (eds) *Tourism Planning and Policy in Australia and New Zealand.* Melbourne: Irwin.

Pattullo, P. (1996) *Last Resorts. The Cost of Tourism in the Caribbean.* London: Cassell.

Philp, J. and Mercer, D. (1999) 'Commodification of Buddhism in contemporary Burma', *Annals of Tourism Research,* 26 (1): 21–54.

Ritzer, G. (1996) *The McDonaldization of Society.* Thousand Oaks, NJ: Pine Forge Press.

Ross, S. and Wall, G. (1999) 'Ecotourism: Towards congruence between theory and practice', *Tourism Management,* 20 (1): 123–32.

Ryan, C. and Aicken, M. (eds) (2005) *Indigenous Tourism.* Oxford: Elsevier.

Sharpley, R. (1994) *Tourists, Tourism and Society.* Huntingdon: Elm.

Shaw, G. and Williams, A. (1994) *Critical Issues in Tourism.* Blackwell: Oxford.

Simons, M.S. (2000) 'Aboriginal heritage art and moral rights', *Annals of Tourism Research,* 27 (2): 412–31.

Smith, V. (ed.) (1977) *Hosts and Guests: An Anthropology of Tourism.* Philadelphia: University of Pennsylvania Press.

Swarbrooke, J. (1999) *Sustainable Tourism Management.* Wallingford, Oxon: CAB International.

Teo, P. (1994) 'Assessing sociocultural impacts: The case of Singapore', *Tourism Management,* 15 (2): 126–36.

Teye, V., Sönmez, S. and Sirakaya, E. (2002) 'Resident attitudes towards tourism development', *Annals of Tourism Research,* 29 (3): 666–86.

Urry, J. (1990) *The Tourist Gaze.* London: Sage.

Wheeller, B. (1993) 'Sustaining the ego', *Journal of Sustainable Tourism,* 1 (2): 121–9.

Williams, S. (1998) *Tourism Geographies.* London: Routledge.

Worthington, B. (2003) 'Change in an Estonian resort: Contrasting development contexts', *Annals of Tourism Research,* 30 (2): 369–85.

References

Two recent books which provide a good introduction to this subject are:

Nash, D. (2005) *Beginnings of an Anthropology of Tourism.* Oxford: Elsevier.

Ryan, C. and Aicken, M. (eds) (2005) *Indigenous Tourism.* Oxford: Elsevier.

19

Environmental Impacts

Learning outcomes

After reading this chapter and answering the questions, you should be able to:

- understand the importance of the environment as a tourism resource

- recognize the positive and negative impacts of tourism on the natural environment

- identify a range of examples of environmental impacts.

Overview

One of the phrases most frequently used by tour operators and tourism marketers to describe a destination is 'unspoilt'. For many tourists, the desire to escape to a seemingly untouched environment is strong and tourism generally takes place in the world's most attractive environments. Since the onset of mass travel, concern has developed about the desirability of tourism. In many locations, tourism development has taken place with little regard for the natural environment. While it is recognized that tourism is an important contributor to the economy, there is a growing body of knowledge that recognizes the importance of managing and protecting the environment. This chapter outlines the major environmental impacts of tourism and future challenges for tourism such as climate change.

Introduction

Tourism development in many places has led to a deterioration in environmental quality. The growth of tourism has prompted debate about environmental consequences and the desirability of further development. In the 1960s, the effects of mass tourism and increasing awareness of the human impact on the environment led to a general realization that nature is not an inexhaustible resource, and this was embodied in the seminal study by Young (1973) *Tourism: Blessing or Blight?* This was a notable turning point in the analysis of tourism's impact on the natural and built environment, questioning the validity of uncontrolled growth. More recent studies in this vein are Krippendorf's (1987) *The Holidaymakers* and Wood and House's (1991) *The Good Tourist*. These studies are symptomatic of the fact that not only have total international tourist numbers risen rapidly at a global scale but also the regional distribution has changed away from a European focus to a more widespread pattern, covering less developed countries and new, exotic and extreme locations. There has also been a switch to more environmentally sensitive forms of tourism such as **ecotourism** and **wildlife-based tourism**, which still brings with it major environmental concerns. For some destinations, the environmental effects of tourism have led to direct threats to the industry, as the success in attracting tourists leads to negative impacts on the attractiveness of the **environment**.

Attributing environmental damage to tourism is difficult for a number of reasons, as outlined by Mathieson and Wall (1982). The main problem is that of disentangling the effects of tourism from the effects of human existence. Coupled with the complex and fragmented nature of tourism provision, the problem is further compounded. Nevertheless, Edington and Edington (1986: 2) point out that 'a proper understanding of biological, or more specifically, ecological factors can significantly reduce the scale of environmental damage associated with recreational and tourist development'.

As Gössling (2002: 284) observed, globally tourism contributes to:

- changes in land use, as tourism is a major consumer of land (e.g. airport development)
- energy use, as tourism may be a major consumer of **fossil fuels**
- extinction of wild species
- the geographical spread of disease, such as SARS and avian flu (see www.who.int)
- changes to the perception of the environment, which becomes a resource to be consumed as part of an experience.

The relationship between tourism and the environment is complex but may be viewed from three perspectives. This demonstrates the holistic approach to the term 'environment', which includes the natural and sociocultural interface. The three perspectives are:

- tourist–environment interactions
- tourist–host interactions
- host–environment interactions.

When these relationships break down, problems inevitably ensue. While the term 'environment' may be used to denote an all-encompassing view of both the natural and social worlds, for the purposes of this chapter, concentration is focused on the natural or physical environment, defined by Mieczkowski (1995: 8) as the 'combination of non-living, i.e. abiotic, physical components, with biological resources, or the biosphere, including flora and fauna'. Tourism and the environment are closely linked – without an attractive environment, tourism cannot succeed and, in some cases, without tourism, environmental conservation is at risk. In other words, a **symbiotic relationship** exists between tourism and the environment: each is dependent upon the other for maintaining a balance so that if the environment deteriorates it will directly impact upon tourism. Mathieson and Wall (1982: 97) argue that 'In the absence of an attractive environment, there would be little tourism. Ranging from the basic attractions of sun, sea and sand to the undoubted appeal of historic sites and structures, the environment is the foundation of the tourist industry.' Farrell and Runyan (1991: 26) also suggest that 'natural resources, the ecosystem, regional ecology … contribute to all tourist locations', emphasizing the need to recognize environmental impacts.

The nature and scope of the environmental impacts of tourism

To facilitate the study of environmental impacts of tourism, it is advisable to break 'tourism' into its component parts. While there is some overlap between these categories, this provides a satisfactory basis for analysis. Broadly, tourism comprises:

1 Travel
2 Tourism destination development
3 Tourism associated activities.

Travel

Much concern has been expressed about increasing levels of transport on roads and in the air in industrialized nations, and the consequent wider effects on the environment and human health (Page 2005). Awareness of **pollution** emanating from various transport modes as well as direct effects on landscape and amenity values have escalated as transport infrastructure is further developed. The study of transport is one aspect of tourism which highlights the conflict between the environment and the industry. On the one hand, enabling travel is an essential criterion for tourism; roads, cars, aircraft and airports are all needed to permit the easy passage of tourists from home to destination and back again. Conversely, the negative effects are the pollution of the natural environment and damage to the quality of landscapes. Balance is required between these two aspects but this is not readily achievable. Gössling *et al.* (2005) examined the eco-efficiency of tourism by examining its energy efficiency in relation to economic performance. Tourist travel is responsible for around 50 per cent of all global travel and is a major consumer of fossil fuel. In locations such as the Seychelles, tourism was seven times less eco-efficient than tourism in France which consumed only 10 per cent of the global average for tourism. Gössling *et al.* concluded that at current estimates tourism is not sustainable as an economic activity. This is compounded when one considers the following figures for air travel in the UK discussed by Page (2005):

- during 1970–2002, air travel rose from 32 million to 189 million passengers, a five-fold increase
- by 2020, there will be 350–460 million passengers
- half the UK population now flies once a year, 70 per cent of which flights are destined overseas (though this finding is debatable, since it depends upon how one calculates participation rates)
- the economy increasingly depends upon air travel (for exports, tourism and inward investment) and supports 200 000 direct jobs and 600 000 jobs indirectly), contributing £13 billion to UK GDP (Source: Page (2005); Department for Transport (2003)

This is a useful insight into why air travel is such a contentious issue, not least because of its environmental impacts.

Air travel

Worldwide, over one billion people (one fifth of the world's population) now travel by air. The damage caused to the environment starts before the aircraft even takes off. Airports require substantial tracts of land in order to operate safely and efficiently. Scale of destruction linked with building an airport is significant – for example, Frankfurt's third runway resulted in the felling of half-a-million trees. Aircraft account for 13 per cent of total transport fuel consumption. Jet kerosine is currently the only significant fuel used. Like all fuels, on combustion kerosine produces:

- carbon dioxide (CO_2)
- water (H_2O)
- carbon monoxide (CO)

- hydrocarbons (HCs)
- nitrogen oxide (No$_x$)
- sulphur dioxide (SO$_2$).

Emission standards for unburned hydrocarbons, CO$_2$ and No$_x$ are laid down for new aircraft by the International Civil Aviation Organization but these only apply to take-off and landing. The key factor in the environmental effect of air travel is altitude. Although aircraft are responsible for only a small amount of hazardous pollutants, emissions have a greater impact because of the highly sensitive regions where they are emitted – particularly in the upper atmosphere. Nitrogen oxides (1–1.5 million tonnes per year) in the lower atmosphere (35–39 000 feet) lead to ozone formation at ground level and urban smog, and contribute to global warming, which is discussed later. As the Royal Commission on the Environment (2002) noted, these concerns are related to:

- **climate change**, including **greenhouse gases**
- the reduction of ozone in the **stratosphere**, contributing to increased surface ultra-violet (UV) radiation
- regional pollution downwind from airports and local pollution in terms of noise, decreased air quality and additional ground transportation pollution from airport expansion.

An in-depth discussion of aviation impacts can be found in Insight 19.1.

INSIGHT 19.1

British Airways Environmental Report

BA as a global airline had a turnover of £7.5 billion in 2003/2004. The recent group statistics are shown in Table 19.1 and the company operated a fleet of 291 aircraft in 2003/2004 to 157 destinations in 76 countries, with 49 per cent of its revenue derived from Europe. Air travel impacts on the environment are discussed in their widely used *Environmental and Social Report* under the following headings.

Noise

BA (2003) show that they have made considerable progress towards noise reduction targets with a 5.8 per cent reduction 2002–2003 (which rises to 8 per cent if Concorde is excluded) and it has 78 per cent of its fleet already meeting the new ICAO Chapter 4 noise standards, up from 60 per cent in 1998–9. The global distribution of noise pollution by BA aircraft at airports it uses is shown in Table 19.2 which illustrates the pattern of operations, dominated by its London bases. To further help reduce noise pollution on arrival at airports, the airline has a code of practice – the Continuous Descent Approach, which seeks to reduce noise and improve fuel efficiency when it is safe to use this approach.

Emissions, fuel efficiency and energy

The growing concern over global warming and 'greenhouse gases' (e.g. CFCs, CO$_2$, NO$_x$ and methane) arising from aviation (Table 19.3) are significant as BA estimated that

civil aviation accounts for 400–500 million tonnes of carbon dioxide from 20 000 million tonnes of fossil fuels. This recognizes that almost 50 per cent of global warming may be a consequence of man's activities, with civil aviation's contribution accounting for 3 per cent of the total effect of global warming. BA also indicated that NO$_x$ emissions remain the main airport-related pollution issue for airlines. BA also reports that 97.6 per cent of its fleet conform to the new ICAO certification levels for NO$_x$ emissions, and that by making modifications to almost half of its Boeing 747-400 fleet it has been able to reduce NO$_x$ emissions in-flight. It also points to the combined effect of CO$_2$, NO$_x$, particles and water vapour which combine to produce **radiative forcing**, that is a process resulting from airline pollution which contributes towards global warming. They indicate that global aviation contributes about 3.5 per cent to this process.

Congestion

Congestion is viewed by BA as one of the most pressing problems it faces. For Heathrow, Gatwick and Manchester the cost of additional fuel burnt due to congestion was £3.6 million. BA points to the additional fuel burnt by aircraft being held in locations above the airports they want to land at (known as *stacking*). Additional fuel was also burnt due to aeroplanes carrying excess fuel in case of delays occurring at Heathrow, Gatwick and Manchester.

TABLE 19.1 Key group statistics – BA 2002–2004

Measure	2001/02	2002/03	2003/04	Change (%)
Turnover (£m)	8 340	7 688	7 560	−1.7
Average manpower equivalent (MPE)	60 468	53 440	49 072	−8.2
Passengers (000)	40 004	38 019	36 103	−5.0
Cargo (000 tonnes)	755	764	796	+4.0
Overall load factor (%)	64.0	66.6	67.6	+1.5
Available tonne kilometres (ATKs) (m)	22 848	21 328	21 859	+2.4
Revenue tonne kilometres (RTKs) (m)	14 632	14 213	14 771	+3.8
Revenue passenger kilometres (RPKs) (m)	106 270	100 112	103 092	+2.9

Notes: Group statistics do not include those of associated undertakings (Qantas Airways, Comair and Iberia) and franchises (British Mediterranean Airways, GB Airways, Maersk Air, Loganair, Sun Air (Scandinavia), Regional Air and Zambian Air Services). British Regional Airlines was acquired by British Airways in May 2001 so is included in statistics 2001/02.

Source: © BA (2004: 2), reproduced courtesy of British Airways

TABLE 19.2 Noise impact of British Airways operations by airport

Airport	Percentage of British Airways global noise	Approximate number of annual aircraft movements*
Heathrow	35.1	184 700
Gatwick	9.9	74 100
New York – JFK	2.8	5 900
Manchester	2.5	21 300
Paris – CDG	1.7	14 800
Edinburgh	2.0	17 300
Glasgow	1.8	14 600
Singapore	1.5	2 900
Aberdeen	1.0	7 200
Amsterdam	1.0	9 700

* An aircraft movement = take-off or landing

Source: © BA (2004:14), reproduced courtesy of British Airways

Tourism destination development

Tourism destinations comprise a wide diversity of environments, from purpose-built resorts to remote natural areas. In general it is possible to identify broad categories of impact that may affect all destinations to a greater or lesser extent as outlined by Wood and House (1991): inappropriate development, loss of habitat, extinction of species, pollution, and loss of spirit. According to the

TABLE 19.3   Airline emissions[1]

Emission	Environmental effects	Approximate emissions (millions of tonnes)	
		Commercial aviation	Worldwide (fossil fuels)
Oxides of nitrogen	Acid rain. Ozone formation at cruise altitudes and smog and ozone at low levels	1.6	69[2]
Hydrocarbons	Ozone and smog formation at low levels	0.4	57[2]
Carbon monoxide	Toxic	0.9	193[2]
Carbon dioxide	Stable – contributes to greenhouse effect by absorption and reflection of infrared radiation	500–600	20,000[2]
Sulphur dioxide	Acid rain	1.1	110[2]
Water vapour	Greenhouse effect by absorption and reflection of infrared radiation	200–300	7,900[3]
Smoke	Nuisance – effects depend on composition	negligible	N/A

[1] Other emissions, mainly from paints and cleaning solvents, are associated with aircraft maintenance and also from ground transport supporting the airline's operation.

[2] OECD Secretariat estimates (for 1980), from OECD Environmental Data 1989.

[3] Derived from BP *Statistical Review of Energy* 1991.

Aviation figures from AEA estimates apart from NO_x (Egli, Chimia 44, 369–371, 1990).

Source: British Airways (1992: 8). Reproduced courtesy of British Airways. For a more up to date assessment of the situation readers may also like to consult the Intergovernmental Panel on Climate Change (IPCC) report produced in 1999 which updates this general assessment, entitled *Aviation and Global Atmosphere*, which provides the most recent data.

European Environment Agency (1998), tourism creates significant contributions to the following environmental problems:

- waste
- reducing levels of **biodiversity**
- pollution of inland waters
- pollution of marine and coastal zones.

In a European context, the environments which tend to be most directly affected by tourism are coastal and alpine areas. Table 19.4 illustrates a range of environmental impacts in relation to specific habitats. A habitat is defined as 'the place in which a species of animal or plant lives, providing a particular set of environmental conditions' (Cordrey undated).

There are two types of environmental impacts which occur in destination development:

- those affecting the integrity and composition of the natural environment
- those affecting the tourist experience of the environment.

In essence, these two categories overlap but need to be viewed from different perspectives. For example, the effects of **trampling** on vegetation induce direct environmental change whereas overcrowding affects tourist enjoyment but has a different overall impact on the natural environment. It is also interesting to consider the question of responsibility for tourism impacts. Kavallinis and Pizam (1994) found in a study of the perception of tourism impacts on the Greek island of Mykonos that tourists were more critical of impacts than the host community. Tourists considered residents and entrepreneurs to have greater responsibility for producing negative environmental impacts. Residents believed that they were to blame for much of the environmental impact. It is not always appropriate to say that 'tourists' damage the environment – there is in reality a complexity of interactions, decision-making, economic imperatives and responsibilities which affect the outcome. Nevertheless, WWF (2002) have developed an **ecological footprint**

TABLE 19.4 Summary of environmental impacts in specific habitats

Habitats influenced	Effect of tourism development
Marine waters	Pollution from sewage outfall Dumping of waste in the sea Oil pollution from tourist boats Litter and threat to marine creatures
Coastal habitats	Habitat loss and fragmentation Deterioration in ecological diversity Destabilization of sand dunes Erosion of coastal landscape
Inland waters	Sewage pollution Eutrophication Oil pollution from boats and barges Disturbance of bird communities by watercraft
Upland heaths, mires and tundra	Erosion Habitat loss and fragmentation Disturbance to nesting birds
Agricultural land	Loss of area for production Conflict between adjacent agricultural uses and tourism
Semi-natural grasslands	Loss of open landscape Habitat loss
Heathlands, scrub, rocky area	Habitat loss and fragmentation
Forests	Habitat loss and fragmentation Disturbance from recreational activities

Source: Adapted from European Environment Agency (1998)

to help tourists to understand how different types of holidays affect the environment in terms of the consumption of resources and impacts.

The following sections outline the major environmental impacts of tourism in destinations.

1. Inappropriate development

Tourism development whether it takes place on the micro or macro scale may be classed as inappropriate where it fails to be sensitive to the natural environment. Large tracts of the Mediterranean coastal strip are now covered by urban sprawl to cater for the mass tourism market. Theroux (1996: 34) describes the Spanish coast as 'utterly blighted' and continues 'I felt intensely that the Spanish coast, especially here on the Costa del Sol, had undergone a powerful colonisation, of a modern kind...It had robbed the shore of its natural features, displaced headlands and gullies and harbours with futile badly-made structures' (1996: 35). This type of development occurs as a result of short-term planning in environmental terms. Resort developments, while contained on specific sites, are normally built on green-field sites in undeveloped areas, often with no planning control. A chain reaction of tourism-related development often follows. The Waikiki area of Honolulu has also been subject to high-density tourism development with skyscraper hotels obscuring views of the coast. Newly developing resorts in less developed countries are also displaying signs of unplanned development, such as Pattaya, in Thailand, which is considered to be overdeveloped.

In some cases, inappropriate development has been removed: the poorly built hotels of Calvia, Mallorca, were demolished in the late 1990s to make way for environmental enhancements. In England, the National Trust has been active in turning the tide of inappropriate developments. At Kynance Cove, Cornwall, the Trust demolished unsightly cafés and shop buildings which had contributed to site erosion as visitors would follow a particular route past them. The Trust re-routed the paths, restoring the damaged ground surface and controlling the movement of visitors to reduce the physical impact of visitors to the site. However, this has been seen to cause conflict with the local community in some cases, for some local businesses are dependent on visitors who stay on such sites.

2. Loss of natural habitat and effects on wildlife

Development of facilities and subsequent tourist use may result in rapid or more gradual effects on habitats. In Nepal, deforestation resulting in the felling of thousands of trees for building tourist lodges and provision of hot water, heating and cooking fuelwood has resulted in a dramatic depletion of the country's forest cover: one trekker consumes five to ten times more wood than a Nepali in a day and a single lodge may consume one hectare of virgin forest per year for running facilities. Trampling, for example, through walking or horse-riding, causes disturbance to vegetation and soil. Reduced ground vegetation cover or loss of tree seedlings through trampling causes soil to become exposed and therefore vulnerable to both erosion and compaction. Trail widening and muddiness may result.

There is much research on the effects of tourism on wildlife and nature conservation (Page and Dowling 2002). As a result of habitat effects and as a direct result of tourism activity, wildlife can be disturbed. There is a debate about whether tourism and nature conservation can co-exist in mutual benefit and it is possible to identify a number of examples of instances where tourism has incurred costs and benefits. One example is the Golden Toad, known only to exist in the Monteverde Cloud Rain Forest in Costa Rica, which is on the verge of extinction. This orange-coloured toad, depicted on postcards and on entrance signs to one of the most popular lodges in the area, has declined in numbers at the same time as ecotourism has evolved in the area. It is possible that an alien organism brought in by ecotourists may have caused a plague (Honey 1999).

Another species more directly affected by tourism activity is the Loggerhead Turtle. Prunier, Sweeney and Geen (1993) provide evidence for this having studied the turtles on the Greek island of Zakynthos, one of the most important nesting areas in the Mediterranean. Nesting takes place in the peak tourist season between June and August and of the hatchlings, only one or two in every thousand will reach adulthood. Concern was expressed in 1979 about this 'endangered species'. The development of tourism threatens the turtle in six ways:

1 *Loss of beach nesting areas* – developers and tourists encroach on the habitat, and tree planting to provide shade for tourists may cause a barrier to successful nesting

2 *Nestings females and young turtles disoriented by artifical illumination* – the turtle is phototactic and moves towards a light source. The usual movement is towards the reflection of the sun on the sea but lights from beachfront developments attract the turtles inland where they dehydrate or become road casualties

3 *Noise* – turtles are confused by loud noises

4 *Traffic* – on the beach, traffic causes sand compaction, creates an imbalance of gases absorbed by the eggs and may activate hatchlings at the wrong time

5 *Pollution* – litter and boat oil may be consumed and cause choking and death

6 *Activities in water* – turtles become entangled in fishing lines, drown in nets and are injured in collision with watercraft.

The Galapagos Islands, 600 miles of the coast of Ecuador, are considered to be one of the foremost locations for wildlife tourism. Organized ecotourism started in the late 1960s with visitor numbers of about 6 000. In 1996, these visitor numbers were up to 62 000. The environment of the Galapagos is the main attraction – sea lions, marine iguanas, giant tortoises, penguins and an array of unusual reptiles, birds, plants, insects and fish. Strict rules on tourist activity apply. Visitors must follow guides, stay on paths, not take food, not drop litter and wash off before going to another island. Despite this, red- and blue-footed boobies have been observed to change their nesting locations and

display behaviour in relation to tourist use of trails. Iguanas wait for tourists to feed them bananas.

Wildlife viewing is increasing in popularity and forms one of the major activities associated with ecotourism (Image 19.1). The impacts of this are trampling of vegetation by foot and vehicular traffic and disruption of wildlife behaviour. In the Amboseli National Park, Kenya, cheetahs have learned to avoid tourists and delay their activities according to tourist presence. Feeding and harassment of wildlife causes unnatural behaviour changes which may result in spatial and temporal displacement leading to lower quality food sources, inferior cover and increased competition. Longer-term changes may lead to the alteration of the structure and size of the population and local extinction. Whale watching has become one of the boom sectors in ecotourism but even this has impacts on wildlife. Insight 19.2 explores this in more detail.

Image 19.1: Ecotourism trips, such as this in Africa, often cause disturbances to wildlife

3. Pollution

Water quality and sewage treatment are often neglected following tourism development, sometimes due to lack of planning controls, sometimes due to lack of finance to back schemes. In the Mediterranean, horror stories of raw sewage being pumped straight out to sea have been prolific. This results in a number of different impacts. Increased nutrients in the water robs the water of oxygen causing eutrophication in lakes and subsequent death to aquatic life. Plagues of jellyfish feed on the increased nutrients and float ashore, causing problems for sea-bathing tourists. Water-borne diseases such as diarrhoea and typhoid can also occur. There has been a move

---

INSIGHT 19.2

Whale and dolphin-watching: A global growth sector

According to Hoyt (2001), in 1995 5.4 million tourists engaged in this activity and by 2001 the figure was 9 million. They spent US$ 500 million in 1995 and US1 billion industry by 2001. The activity of whale and dolphin watching has seen significant growth over the last ten years and is enjoyed in a variety of international locations, from the poles to the equator. It now occurs in 87 countries and in 492 communities. Whale watching has been growing by 12 per cent a year in visitor numbers and, since 1994, 22 new countries have joined the market for this activity. In 1994, only the USA had one million visitors whale watching a year but by 1998 this had extended to Canada and the Canary Islands, with Australia and South Africa recording 500 000 visits a year. Some localities have seen remarkable growth such as Taiwan growing from zero to 30 000 visits 1994–8. While there are no international regulations, many countries have introduced strict regulations to protect the creatures, such as limiting the noise and speed of boats, the number of boats, the distance allowed from creatures and swimming. Some are calling a halt to activities. In New

Zealand and the Azores, concern has been expressed about the amount of human contact between the creatures and swimmers, which is thought to cause stress among whales. At Kaikoura, South Island, New Zealand, there is a moratorium on the setting up of new tourist business related to whale watching and existing businesses have agreed to a voluntary code of practice to allow the whales sufficient rest time. The Whale and Dolphin Conservation Society (www.wdcs.org) is currently campaigning for an international ban on swimming with all marine creatures. Boats also cause problems by following the creatures too closely. Contact with the creatures can lead to changes in behaviour, such as more leaping, and disturbance to habits, such as the need to rest during the day and hunt at night. More research is required to prove that human contact does cause whales stress problems but, until then, the precautionary principle should be adhered to. Whale watching has been proven to be beneficial to conservation when its economic potential exceeds that of hunting, as discussed in Chapter 17 in the case of Tonga.

towards limitation of problems and preventative measures have been installed in many locations. Tighter regulations, new technology, improved waste-water management systems and innovations such as ultra-violet treatment systems are important environmental measures for resorts.

According to the Marine Conservation Society (MCS) (www.mcsuk.org), plastic debris is the greatest hazard to marine creatures. Sea creatures can become entangled in items such as plastic loops used to hold drinks cans together or can swallow plastic bags. More than 90 per cent of gannet nests on the Welsh island of Grassholm contain plastic litter.

4. Loss of spirit

Much less of a tangible effect but still crucial is the impact of tourism on the ambience of a location (Image 19.2). A loss of atmosphere might be individually perceived but it may also have wider implications for tourism. The spirit of a place might be the main attraction and once that spirit is diminished, then tourists may no longer desire to visit. That is over and beyond the ramifications for the integrity of the environment and the host community. Changes in character may be incremental so the loss of spirit may occur gradually or may take place more rapidly, in the instance of resort development.

5. Overcrowding and traffic congestion

When the volume of tourists exceeds the capacity of an environment, then overcrowding occurs. Geographical and temporal considerations are required when assessing overcrowding because in general it affects certain parts of a site and/or certain times of the day or year. Overcrowding is a problem for two reasons:

- it poses an increased risk of environmental damage through erosion
- it restricts visitor appreciation of the destination.

Traffic, particularly the private car, attracts much attention as an area of research. In the UK, concern is directed at both rural and urban tourism. While tourist traffic is not generally the major cause of congestion, at certain times of the year and in particular regions and destinations, it adds significantly to the pressures of general road use. A large proportion of rural tourists visit the countryside by car and the biggest increase in car use is predicted for rural areas. For towns and cities, growing congestion from commuter and tourist traffic is leading to restrictions being imposed on use of roads at certain times. Road traffic can damage the built environment through pollution and vibration as well as negatively affecting tranquility and atmosphere. Car parks are required to contain traffic volume at destinations but in some locations inappropriate parking causes damage to verges and vegetation, for example off-road parking on moorlands. The increasing popularity of off-road driving damages vegetation, causes erosion and adds to localized pollution. At the extreme end of the spectrum, in some of the National Parks of the UK and the USA road closures have been necessary to stem the untenable flow of traffic (e.g. Yellowstone and the Peak District) and air quality problems have been perceived to be a significant effect of tourism – mainly from exhaust fumes from tourist vehicles in these environments (Wang and Miko 1997). Koenen, Chon and Christianson (1995) calculated that about 19 per cent of carbon monoxide air pollution in Las Vegas is caused by tourism. Congestion often results in new journey patterns where people travel to different places to avoid queues and/or where they know they are able to park. This spreads the problem to a wider area.

Image 19.2: The environment acts as a major influence on tourism demand but overcrowding can lead to a loss of appeal

6. Wear and tear

Physical damage to the environment is often more marked in the countryside but is also an issue for urban areas. Sensitive locations, such as peat moorlands and sand dunes, are prone to serious damage by a range of users, such as horse-riders, mountain bikers, walkers and off-road vehicles.

Riverbanks are subject to the wash from pleasure boats, a problem suffered in the Norfolk Broads, UK, where the problem is exacerbated by the weakening of reeds by fertilizer run-off. Other problems of wear and tear include litter. On Dartmoor, UK, up to 250 trailer loads of litter are collected every year from one small area. In Rome, coins thrown by tourists into the Trevi Fountain are chipping the marble. The English Tourist Board and Employment Department Group (1991) report that Westminster Abbey's three million annual visitors cause damage to the physical fabric of the interior. The thirteenth-century Cosmati pavement in front of the high altar is literally being worn away. Pieces of statuary are stolen and the increased exposure to humidity, light and dust from the volume of visitors is a threat to artwork, materials and ornamentation. The famous caves at Lascaux in the Dordogne, southern France, containing 17 000-year-old Quaternary cave paintings, illustrate where action was needed to eliminate the effect of tourism on the integrity of the resource base. Perspiration and breath from the large numbers of tourists to the caves altered the microclimate, leading to an increase in carbon dioxide, temperature and humidity. In addition, artificial lights used to illuminate the interior gave favourable conditions for the growth of mosses, algae and bacteria. This began to have a damaging effect on the quality of the paintings. The caves were closed to visitors in 1963 and are now only open to scholars by arrangement. They must go through a disinfectant chamber before entry, must not speak once inside and are allowed a maximum of 20 minutes in the caves. A replica, named 'Lascaux Two' was constructed in 1983 to enable 2000 tourists per day to experience something of the paintings.

7. Activities

In relation to the impact of tourism activities, it is worth drawing out examples to indicate to what extent popular holiday activities can affect the natural environment.

Skiing/alpine tourism Mountain ecosystems are generally quite fragile but many are prone to intensive use, through skiing, trekking and other mountain/snow sports. Skiing is seen by many as a damaging activity because it requires associated developments, such as lodges, resorts, roads and ski-slopes and causes severe erosion and deforestation (Hudson 1999). A great deal of damage is caused in the initial construction and development stages. In some resorts, lack of snowfall and tourist demand for the snow experience means that snow cannons have been employed. These require large amounts of waters to produce sufficient snow to form a satisfactory slope for skiing and, according to May (1995), lead to a shorter growing season, reduced river currents affecting fish populations and destruction of forest cover causing soil erosion.

Ecotourism While the premise of ecotourism is to assist in conservation and the well-being of local communities, it is often the case that ecotourism-based activities lead to deterioration in environmental quality. Swarbrooke (1999: 320), for example, argues that 'today's ecotourism package can easily become tomorrow's mass market tourism product'. Early ecotourism destinations such as Kenya, the Galapagos Islands and Thailand have already suffered extensive negative impacts as a result of increased numbers of ecotourists. Cater (1993) cites the example of Belize, where development has involved the clearance of mangrove swampland, drainage and infilling using topsoil literally shaved off the wetland savannah a few miles inland. Thus, two distinctive ecosystems have been destroyed. Well-documented cases of lack of planning, improper management and negative impacts indicate that a desire for short-term benefits has in some cases resulted in inappropriate forms of development (Wight 1993) as well as the wider distribution of tourism across the globe to sensitive environments like Antarctica.

Positive environmental impacts of tourism

The damaging aspects of tourism are significant and receive deserved attention. However, it is essential to recognize that positive impacts may be gained from tourism activity. Doswell (1997) notes that tourism can focus attention on significant environmental issues and stimulate initiatives to conserve and enhance the environment. The main areas to examine are three-fold.

Conservation of redundant and/or historic buildings for alternative uses

Tourism can provide the impetus for converting disused buildings into foci for tourism activity. Many buildings retain their character yet can be carefully modernized to form new visitor attractions. Examples are old woollen mills and industrial premises, which may be given an alternative role through tourism use. Tourism may provide the financial means to restore and/or maintain historic buildings in an appropriate way. This may also provide the basis for future development in tourism with planning approvals likely to be more easily obtained for building conversion or brown-field sites rather than new, green-field locations. If existing buildings can be used in creative yet sensitive ways, tourism can prove to be a beneficial force of redevelopment. Use of derelict land for development of urban parks or country parks is widespread in industrialized nations. Despoiled land, such as the old open-cast coal mines of Northumberland, have been restored to both agricultural land and recreational areas and polluted brown-field sites in cities have been redeveloped for tourism uses, as the London Dome project showcased. This is a vital part of all Olympic City bids (see Chapter 21) to leave an enviromental legacy.

Enhancement of local environments

If tourism is viewed as an important source of income (Image 19.3), it is likely that local government will seek to retain and increase visitor numbers by improving the general amenity value of the local environment. This is relevant to a range of environments, including rural, coastal and urban areas. For many historic cities, improvements may consist of landscaping which reflects the heritage character of the townscape and simultaneously assists the visitor experience. However, it might be said that such enhancements detract from the original form. The **Center Parcs** development in Sherwood Forest, UK, resulted in the planting of 500 000 trees, the seeding of native grasses and wild flower species, heathland re-creation and management and an overall increase in ecological diversity. While developments of these type tend to be criticized for their scale and siting in natural areas, in most cases, the environmental management which accompanies development improves the environment, which might have been subject to previous intensive use, such as forestry plantation. Heathland fauna, such as the Nightjar and Grass Wave Moth, are reappearing. Creation of waterways has attracted 12 species of dragonfly and damselfly (sufficient number to meet English Nature's criteria for selection as a Site of Special Scientific Interest). The first recorded sighting in Nottinghamshire of an Emperor Dragonfly has been recorded at Sherwood Forest.

Protection of wildlife

It has been seen in various locations worldwide that tourism discourages poaching because it places economic value on wildlife and protection of natural resources. In many less developed countries, tourism acts as a force of conservation as it offers an alternative economic use. National Parks, such as Amoseli in Kenya and Etosha in Namibia, are viewed as tools of conservation and economic development. Tourist spending generates local employment, demand for local goods and crafts and helps to justify protection of natural resources. Doswell (1997) comments that tourism draws attention to issues relating to biodiversity, endangered species and the human impact on the environment. However, Sindiga and Kanunah (1999) state that in some of the Kenyan National Parks tourist carrying capacities have been exceeded and animals are harassed by tourist vehicles, which disrupt their usual habits and behaviour. Appropriate environmental policy and management is required to ensure protection of the environment and a satisfactory visitor experience. But one of the main environmental problems affecting tourism as a global issue is **global warming** and climate change.

Image 19.3: The splendour of the natural environment creates a magnet for tourist visits, such as in the awe-inspiring landscapes of the US National Parks

Tourism, global warming and climate change

One of the most serious global environmental issues facing the tourism industry is the issue of climate change (Becken 2004; Hall and Higham 2005) (see Image 19.4). According to the current forecasts for tourism activity, by 2050 tourism is expected to see its contribution to greenhouse gas emissions rise from its current 3 per cent to 7 per cent. One consequence of global warming is the negative effects it may have on tourism and the environments it occurs in. The first international tourism and climate change conference hosted by the World Tourism Organization (WTO) in 2003 in Djerba (WTO 2003) endorsed the need for action to reduce tourism's global impacts by endorsing the **Kyoto Protocol** on reducing emissions (The **Djerba Declaration**) which highlights the expected impacts of climate change on different environments. One of the most widely discussed is the rising sea levels and the effect on small islands, combined with extreme climatic events such as a decrease in rainfall in some areas and increases elsewhere. These are significant since climate and temperature are important determinants of destination selection. These will thus be to a greater analysis of **tourism comfort indices** (i.e. mean temperature, maximum temperature, humidity, precipitation, sunshine hours and wind) in choosing destinations (Lise and Tol 2002). Some of the expected effects may be:

- there will be a decline in European sun, sea and sand holidays in the Mediterranean due to the increased temperatures (Lohmann 2001)
- rising temperatures in central European culture cities in peak season will lead to a decline in visitors
- specific ecosystems such as coral reefs will be affected as they have shown great sensitivity to minor changes in temperature; an increase of 1–2°C causes coral bleaching
- rising temperatures on the USA seaboards will trigger a move inland for holidays in the peak season, leading to people taking coastal holidays in the spring and autumn as Florida and California lose their popularity
- in the Caribbean, erosion may make their products less attractive
- in Alpine areas, shorter skiing seasons may arise
- in France, temperatures may rise by 2°C by 2050, with 15 per cent less rainfall in summer and 20 per cent more in winter. There may be a drop in winter snow for ski fields while in coastal areas, erosion and rising sea levels will impact upon the environment
- water shortages in the tourism sector may be exacerbated as Kent *et al.* (2002) discuss in the case of Mallorca.

A number of global organizations are currently working in the field of global warming (see Table 19.5) as experts begin to understand how climate change may lead to reverses in the shape of seasonality with a growing demand for coolness in summer, leading to increased energy consumption for air conditioning, along with a greater number of extreme weather events which could disrupt tourism, such as flooding, sand storms, droughts and summer fires. Above all this highlights the need for stakeholders (e.g. governments, the tourism sector, tourists and other bodies as well as scientists) to develop solutions to this global problem. However, one of the biggest stumbling blocks remains the largest fossil fuel consumer – the USA – refusing to sign up to the Kyoto Protocol, given their concerns related to limits it may impose on economic activity. In addition, the rapid industrialization of developing countries such as China pose major problems for progress towards reducing energy consumption as they are expanding their demand for fuel and energy at an exponential rate.

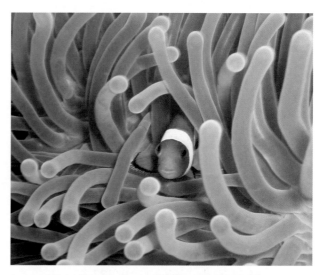

Image 19.4: Coral reefs on the Great Barrier reef are under significant threat from climate change

TABLE 19.5 Selected organizations working on climate change
• World Tourism Organisation, www.world-tourism.org • Caribbean Planning for Adaptation to Global Climate Change, www.cpacc.org • Climate Research Unit, University of East Anglia, www.cru.uea.ac.uk • Friends of the Earth, www.foe.co.uk • The Carbon Trust, www.thecarbontrust.co.uk • United Nations Framework Convention on Climate Change, www.unfcc.int • World Wildlife Fund, www.wwf.org.uk • Aviation Environment Forum, www.airportwatch.org

Conclusion

Many environmental impacts resulting from tourism have been acknowledged. In some cases, programmes of work have been established to reduce these effects and a pledge towards developing more responsible forms of tourism has been made. In other instances, effects are less well-known and/or accepted by those who seek to gain maximum economic benefits, regardless of the environmental costs. It is likely that the future will involve closer examination of environmental impacts as the case of climate change has shown – the environmental impacts of tourism have come centre stage. Research is at a relatively early stage of development and there is still much work to be undertaken to establish clear knowledge of cause, effect, systems and interactions, but tourism's polluting role and massive fossil fuel consumption is now being recognized through techniques such as eco-efficiency and ecological footprinting. Wider uptake of auditing procedures and improvements in corporate environmental management through legislation and consumer demand will invoke a higher degree of environmental consciousness in tourism-based enterprises. These aspects are more fully discussed in Chapter 20.

Discussion questions

1 Why might it be argued that the ultimate success of tourism relies on an understanding of the environmental impacts?

2 Argue the case that tourism and the environment are mutually beneficial.

3 How would you prioritize which impacts are more serious: those which directly affect the physical environment or those which directly affect tourist enjoyment?

4 To what extent is the tourist responsible for environmental impacts of tourism?

References

BA (2003) 2002/2003 Social and Environmental Report. Harmondsworth: British Airways.

BA (2004) Environmental and Social Report 2003/2004. Harmondsworth: British Airways, www.ba.com.

Becken, S. (2004) 'How tourists and tourism experts perceive climate change and carbon offsetting schemes', Journal of Sustainable Tourism, 12 (4): 332–45.

Cater, E. (1993) 'Ecotourism in the Third World: Problems for sustainable tourism development', Tourism Management, 14 (2) 85–90.

Cordrey, L. (ed.) The Biodiversity of the South West. An Audit of the South West Biological Resource, RSPB and County Wildlife Trusts and South West Regional Planning Conference.

Department for Transport (2003) *Airport Policy*. White Paper. London: HMSO.

Doswell, R. (1997) Tourism: *How Effective Management Makes a Difference*. Oxford: Butterworth-Heinemann.

Edington, J.M. and Edington, M.A. (1986) *Ecology, Recreation and Tourism*. Cambridge: Cambridge University Press.

English Tourist Board and Employment Department Group (1991) *Tourism and the Environment. Maintaining the Balance*. London: English Tourist Board and Employment Department Group.

European Environment Agency (1998) *Europe's Environment: The Second Assessment*. Luxembourg: OOPEC.

Farrell, B.H. and Runyan, D. (1991) 'Ecology and tourism', *Annals of Tourism Research*, 18 (1): 26–40.

Gössling, S. (2002) 'Global environmental consequences of tourism', *Global Environmental Change*, 12 (4): 283–302.

Gössling, S., Peeters, P., Ceron, J., Dubois, Patterson, T. and Richardson, R. (2005) 'The eco-efficiency of tourism', *Ecological Economics* 54 (4): 417–34.

Hall, C.M. and Higham, J. (eds) (2005) *Tourism, Recreation and Climate Change*. Clevedon: Channel View.

Honey, M. (1999) *Ecotourism and Sustainable Development. Who Owns Paradise?* Washington, DC: Island Press.

Hoyt, E. (2001) Whale watching 2001: Worldwide Numbers, Expenditure and expanding socioeconomic benefits. Crowborough: Whale and Dolphin Conservation Society. www.wdcs.org

Hudson, S. (1999) *Snow Business: A Study of the International Ski Industry*, London: Continuum.

Kavallinis, I. and Pizam, A. (1994) 'The environmental impacts of tourism – whose responsibility is it anyway? The case study of Mykonos', *Journal of Travel Research*, 23 (2): 26–32.

Kent, M., Newnham, R. and Essex, S. (2002) 'Tourism and sustainable water supply in Mallorca: A geographical analysis, *Applied Geography*, 22 (4): 351–74.

Koenen, J.P., Chon, K-S. and Christianson, D.J. (1995) 'Effects of tourism growth on air quality: The case of Las Vegas', *Journal of Sustainable Tourism*, 3 (3): 135–42.

Krippendorf. J. (1987) *The Holidaymakers*. Oxford: Butterworth-Heinemann.

Lise, W. and Tol, R. (2002) 'Impact of climate on tourism', *Climatic Change*, 55 (4): 429–49.

Lohmann, M. (2001) 'Coastal resorts and climate change', in A. Lockwood and R. Medlik (eds) *Tourism and Hospitality in the Twenty First Century*. Oxford: Butterworth-Heinemann.

Mathieson, A. and Wall, G. (1982) *Tourism. Economic, Physical and Social Impacts*. Harlow: Longman.

May, V. (1995) 'Environmental implications of the 1992 Winter Olympic Games', *Tourism Management*, 16 (4): 269–75

Mieczkowski, Z. (1995) *Environmental Issues of Tourism and Recreation*. Lanham: University Press of America.

Page, S.J. (2005) *Transport and Tourism: Global Perspectives, Second Edition*. Harlow: Prentice Hall.

Page, S.J and Dowling, R. (2002) *Ecotourism*. Harlow: Prentice Hall.

Prunier, E., Sweeney, A. and Geen, A. (1993) 'Tourism and the environment: The case of Zakynthos', *Tourism Management*, 14 (2): 137–41.

Royal Commission on Environmental Pollution (2002) *The Environmental Effects of Civil Aircraft in Flight*. London: HMSO.

Sindiga, I. and Kanuhah, M. (1999) 'Unplanned tourism development in sub-Saharan Africa with special reference to Kenya', Journal of Tourism Studies, 10 (1): 25–39.

Swarbrooke, J. (1999) *Sustainable Tourism Management*. Wallingford, Oxon: CABI.

Theroux, P. (1996) *The Pillars of Hercules*. London: Penguin.

Wang, C-Y. and Miko, P.S. (1997) 'Environmental impacts of tourism on U.S. National Parks', *Journal of Travel Research*, 35 (4): 31–6.

Wight, P. (1993) 'Sustainable ecotourism: Balancing economic, environmental and social goals within an ethical framework', *Journal of Tourism Studies*, 4 (2): 54–66.

Wood, S. and House, K. (1991) *The Good Tourist*. London: Mandarin.

WTO (2003) *The Djerba Declaration on Tourism and Climate Change*. Madrid: World Tourism Organization.

WWF (2002) 'Ecological footprint', www.wwf.org.uk/researcher/issues/footprint/index.asp.

Young, G. (1973) *Tourism: Blessing or Blight?* Harmondsworth: Penguin.

Further reading

United Nations Environment Programme: Impacts of Tourism, http://www.uneptie.org

20

The Challenge of Sustainability

Learning outcomes

After reading this chapter and answering the questions, you should be able to:

- understand the principles of sustainable development and the link with tourism

- define the meaning of sustainable tourism

- outline the principles and a range of sustainable practice in global tourism

- state the difficulties of achieving sustainable tourism.

Overview

One of the most important aspects of tourism management in the twenty-first century is in devising ways of improving environmental performance. Tourism managers and decision-makers need to be fully conversant in the need to minimize impacts on host communities and the natural environment while at the same time ensuring the existence of a viable tourism industry and maximum local benefits. This chapter explores the underlying principles of the argument for sustainable tourism and outlines how some tourism organizations are introducing new practices to improve environmental performance.

Introduction

As the impacts of tourism become apparent, concern about the quality of the environment and the future of the tourism industry begin to emerge. Increasingly wide recognition of the negative environmental effects of tourism development and activity (see Chapter 19) has led to a focus on alternative forms of tourism and improved environmental practice. The principle which underlies this focus is sustainable development; translated to tourism it is known as **sustainable tourism**. A large amount of literature exists on the topic of sustainable tourism, in the academic arena (e.g. Swarbrooke 1999; Mowforth and Munt 2003, plus a journal dedicated to the topic – the *Journal of Sustainable Tourism*) and Page (2005) has argued that this has been one of the most researched areas of tourism since the 1990s. Consumer-oriented interest in such issues has been framed in terms of the green consumer, and the media have also focused on sustainability with television travel shows (the British Airways *Tourism for Tomorrow Awards* are televised on the ITV travel programme *Wish You Were Here* in the UK). According to Prosser (1994: 19), sustainable tourism 'seeks to sustain the quantity, quality and productivity of both human and natural resource systems over time, while respecting and accommodating the dynamics of such systems'. This is based on the idea of optimizing returns while protecting the resource base. Prior to exploring the concept and practice of sustainable tourism, it is necessary to gain some understanding of the context in which the concept of sustainability developed. This is best accomplished by considering the evolution of development in environmental thinking.

The rise of environmental concern

It is a commonly held view that the 'green' movement is a recent invention. However, the roots of concern about the human impact on the environment can be traced back to ancient civilizations (Hardy, Beeton and Pearson 2002). Ancient Greek literature reveals the philosophy of the earth being viewed as a living goddess. In Roman times, written evidence exists of concerns about land degradation and soil erosion through intensive use and even the effect on human health from using lead cooking vessels. Through the sixteenth and seventeenth centuries, the dominant view of the environment in Europe was centred around humans' mastery of nature – that people could conquer the environment and use its resources for human progress. This tends to be viewed as the imperial or **anthropocentric** perspective on the environment and it has dominated human thinking to the present day. Conversely, the scientific study of nature around the late 1700s onwards gave rise to the notion of the interrelationships of the natural world and a valuing of flora and fauna – the Arcadian or **ecocentric** perspective. This is illustrated in Figure 20.1.

Many commentators began to realize the negative implications of growth (in industry and population) and challenged the notion of this dominant world view. One of the early critics was Thomas **Malthus**, who stated that human population growth was increasing at a rate which would outstrip food production. The rapid social and economic changes of the nineteenth century brought about a need for resource management and preservation, best exemplified by the emergence of wilderness preservation societies and early proponents of the National Parks movement in North America. **Ecology** as an academic discipline became recognized from 1850 and gave rise to a new era in environmental thinking which built on the foundations of the Arcadians.

Ecocentrism	Anthropocentrism
Natural environment is the core concern. Quality of the environment more important than human progress	Humans are a dominant force. Mastery of the natural environment for maximum human gain

FIGURE 20.1   A simplified illustration of environmental thinking

The early part of the twentieth century demonstrated a preponderance of groups dedicated to preserving and conserving habitats, species, built heritage and access to open areas. However, the environment became high profile in a social and political sense in the 1960s. Policies for economic growth post-1945 worked on the premise that the more goods the industrial system produced, the more satisfied consumers would be (the greatest happiness for the greatest number of people or 'maximum utility'). The age of consumerism and the industrial processes that gave rise to it did not recognize any environmental responsibilities and production continued while environmental pollution began to increase. Tourism, while not an industrial process, may be seen to be part of this production process, as it requires resources and produces pollution in a number of different forms. From the 1960s, the conventions of economic growth began to be questioned and this, along with several high-profile environmental catastrophes (such as the *Torrey Canyon* oil disaster in 1967), sparked off the beginning of the contemporary environmental movement. Many environmental groups, such as Friends of the Earth, also originate from this period.

The development of the sustainability concept

Early proponents of a new approach to the economy and the environment came in the form of authors (from economists such as J.K. Galbraith to biologists such as Rachel Carson) and pressure groups (concerned with micro and macro issues). Concern focused on both environmental and societal issues. Discussion at international government levels were also apparent. The 1962 United Nations conference promoted the idea of a balance between social and economic development and from then on instigated several long-term subgroups to examine areas of concern (e.g. the Research Institute for Social Development, Environment Programme). Representatives from the governments and non-government organizations of 119 countries met in 1972 at Stockholm (United Nations Conference on the Human Environment) in an attempt to consider environmental problems. The conclusion reached by the conference was that development and the environment could exist together in mutual benefit but no indication was given as to how this might be achieved.

The International Union for the Conservation of Nature and Natural Resources (IUCN) published the World Conservation Strategy which promoted sustainable development in 1980. In 1984, the United Nations General Assembly appointed a commission headed by the Norwegian Prime Minister Gro Harlem Brundtland. The commission, entitled the **World Commission on Environment and Development**, was charged with exploring environmental and development philosophies and putting forward proposals for change and action. The resulting publication *Our Common Future* set out critical objectives for the future of economic growth and the environment and stated that some painful decisions would have to be made by governments. 'Sustainable development' was defined in the document as development that meets the needs of the present without compromising the needs of those of future generations. Indeed, Robinson (2004) suggests that sustainability goes to the heart of the interconnected debates on environmental, social and economic issues: it adopts adopt a long-term perspective which is particularly suited to communities where conflicting views among stakeholders of the concept of sustainability, need to be accommodated as a political process.

Defining sustainability and sustainable tourism

The most widely accepted definition of sustainable development is that cited in *Our Common Future*:

> *Development that meets the needs of the present without compromising the needs of future generations.*
> (World Commission on Environment and Development 1987: 8)

While this provides a relatively neat summary, the meaning and application of the concept is more problematic. Sustainable development allows for economic development but within the parameters of resource conservation. Sustainability as a concept may be viewed from opposites: at one extreme is economic sustainability where what is being sustained is the economy at whatever cost; diametrically opposed to this is ecological sustainability, where the natural environment takes priority over any economic development. In addition to defining sustainability, there is a need to consider degrees of sustainability. Turner, Pearce and Bateman (1994) produced a spectrum of sustainable development, defining positions ranging from 'very weak' sustainability to 'very strong' sustainability, as illustrated in Figure 20.2.

The deep ecologist Arne Naess pointed out the distinction between **shallow ecology** and **deep ecology** (Devall and Sessions 1985). This has become widely accepted and is even reflected in the tourism literature in reference to tourism by Acott, La Trobe and Howard (1998), who outline the characteristics of deep and shallow forms of ecotourism and emphasize the relationship between tourism and wider debates about sustainability and the environment. In other words, sustainability and sustainable tourism do not represent an absolute standard.

The challenge of sustainability in tourism

Recognition of the damaging effects of tourism has led to a focus on encouraging 'alternative tourism'. Alternative tourism raises the question 'alternative to what?' Most commentators agree that it refers to an alternative to mass tourism. If viewed in this way, then sustainable tourism becomes a niche market. In reality, this is what seems to have occurred. A variety of niche markets with an alternative theme have emerged and terms such as 'ecotourism', 'green tourism', 'sustainable tourism', 'nature tourism', 'soft tourism' and 'adventure tourism' to name but a few have become part of international and domestic tourism markets. Growth in these areas has been particularly marked since the beginning of the 1990s.

To some extent, this pattern of product growth is contrary to the ideals of sustainable development. The reason for this is that the diversity of tourism products and environments has increased (as alternative tourism favours less exploited areas, environmentally sensitive or rural areas and culturally different regions which are prone to negative impacts if improperly managed) while mass tourism destinations continue to exist within the traditional management framework. The conclusion to this argument is that sustainable tourism should be viewed more as an ethos than a product or niche market. The ideals of sustainability need to infiltrate the entire tourism system if environments and people are to be protected from the negative forces of change.

There are signs that this is beginning to happen. Attention to environmental management (a more practical and achievable perspective of tackling the problems from a business perspective) is becoming more widespread. Large companies, such as tour operators, hotel chains and airlines, are starting to demonstrate an awareness of the consequences of tourism development and activity as noted in the **Tour Operators Initiative** (www.toinitiative.org). There is some criticism that this type of reaction is merely 'lip-service' but it is at least a step in the right direction. In addition, it is impossible to imagine any kind of tourism activity being developed and then operating without in some way, reducing the quantity and/or quality of natural resources somewhere. Some of these aspects will be discussed in this chapter.

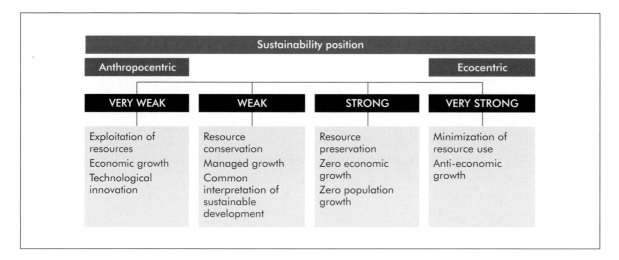

FIGURE 20.2 Degrees of sustainability. Source: Adapted from Turner, Pearce and Bateman (1994)

What is sustainable tourism?

The word 'green' connotes many ideas and contradictions. What is 'green' to one individual or society may not be to another. Deep green environmentalists argue that truly environmentally aware individuals would spurn holidays altogether. Krippendorf (1987) states that if people can be persuaded to stay at home, they may be encouraged to improve their own environment rather than escape from it and damage another elsewhere. Krippendorf argues for greater 'humanism' in life, of which tourism is just one small component. The idea of humanism seeks to reverse trends of consumerism and encourage greater satisfaction in non-consumptive forms of activity. However, what has happened in reality is that people expect more and more. Instead of finding satisfaction in a two-week full-board holiday in Torquay, the travel market has encouraged more sophisticated travellers who wish to see more unusual environments. So, the reality is very complex. If home and work are more satisfying, does this remove the need to escape? Probably not. Tourism has become part of modern life and the way forward is to not try to stop tourism but to explore alternative ways of developing and operating the tourism sector. A response to the recognition of the impacts of tourism has led to the development of an alternative approach generally known as 'sustainable tourism' and Table 20.1 illustrates some of the growing range of international reports, actions and declarations on sustainable tourism since the 1980s. As Page (2005) observes, this has generated a large volume of literature in tourism, although much of it reworks the same basic ideas (see Liu 2003 for a review).

Initially, sustainable tourism was considered to be most relevant in the countryside, where the relationship between the visitor and the natural environment is most obvious (see Chapter 22).

TABLE 20.1   The evolution of international tourism action on sustainable tourism since 1980

- WTO (1980) Manilla Declaration on World Tourism
- WTO (1985) Tourism Bill of Rights and Tourist Code
- Tourism Concern and World Wildlife Fund for Nature (1992) Beyond the Green Horizon: Principles for Sustainable Tourism
- WTO/UNEP/UNESCO/EU (1995) Charter for Sustainable Tourism, Lanzarote
- Federation of Nature and National Parks of Europe (1997) European Charter for Sustainable Tourism
- WTO (1997) Malé Declaration on Sustainable Tourism Development
- Calvià Declaration on Tourism and Sustainable Development in the Mediterranean (1997)
- EU/UNEP/IUCN and Industry Bodies (1997) Berlin Declaration
- UNEP/WTO (1998) Programme of Action for Sustainable Tourism in Small Island Developing States
- WTTC/WTO/Earth Council (1995, 1996, 1998) Agenda 21 for the Travel and Tourism Industry, Rio Earth Summit
- Commission on Sustainable Development (1999) Working Programme for Sustainable Tourism
- WTO (1999) Global Code of Ethics for Tourism
- WTO (1999) Sustainable Tourism and Cultural Heritage
- UNEP (2000) Principles for the Implementation of Sustainable Tourism
- WTO (2001) Sustainable Development of Tourism
- Tour Operators Initiative for Sustainable Tourism Development (2000)
- WTO (2002) Hainan Declaration – Sustainable Tourism in the Islands of the Asia-Pacific Regions
- WTTC (2002) Industry as a Partner for Sustainable Development: Tourism, Johannesburg Earth Summit
- WTO (2004) Indicators of Sustainable Development for Tourism Destinations: A Guidebook (including guidelines for local authorities, ecotourism, protected areas, SMEs and the built environment)
- WTO (2005) Muscat Declaration on Built Environment for Sustainable Tourism
- WTO (2005) Tourism Congestion Management at Natural and Cultural Sites

This led to a concentration on what was generally termed 'green tourism' – the 'green' emphasizing use and conservation of natural resources. In UK, the first major event where **green tourism** was at the fore was the 1990 'Shades of Green – Working Towards Green Tourism in the Countryside' conference held in Leeds. Sponsored by the Countryside Commission, English Tourist Board and Rural Development Commission, the objective was to encourage good practice in rural tourism – good practice defined as tourism that respects the environment and community. In this respect, 'green tourism' is nothing new. Walking, cycling, staying in small-scale accommodation, eating local food, using public transport, observing wildlife – these activities, encouraged by marketers of green tourism, are acutely traditional. What is new is the marketing, promotion and packaging behind it. Since the 1990s, the 'green' term has generally fallen away and a more overarching term – 'sustainable tourism' – has become more prominent.

Defining sustainable tourism

Sustainable tourism is a nebulous concept and to some extent has become moulded to fit the needs of conservationists, governments, communities and developers. Thus, there is no universally accepted definition, but in 2004 the WTO (www.world-tourism.org/sustainable) did attempt to address this vast range of definitions by establishing that sustainability principles apply to environmental, economic and sociocultural aspects of tourism, so that a suitable balance needs to be achieved between these interconnected elements to guarantee the long-term sustainability of tourism. The WTO outlined that sustainable tourism should:

- *make optimal use of environmental resources* (while maintaining the essential ecological processes while helping to conserve the natural heritage and biodiversity)
- *respect the sociocultural authenticity of host communities* (helping to conserve the cultural heritage and traditional values as well as seeking to engender intercultural understanding and tolerance)
- *ensure viable, long-term economic operations, providing socioeconomic benefits to all stakeholders*

which requires involvement of all stakeholders as well as ongoing monitoring of the impacts of tourism. This allows for preventive or corrective measures to be taken when needed, as well as seeking to maintain high levels of tourist satisfaction and their awareness of sustainability issues. What this confirms is that the main remit of sustainable tourism is to strike a balance between the *host* (local community), the *guest* (visitors) and the *environment*. This three-way relationship is at the core of sustainable tourism principles and requires careful consideration to maximize positive benefits and minimize negative effects. It is clear that sustainable tourism does not imply a 'no-growth' policy, but it does recognize that limits to growth exist and that environments must be managed in a long-term way. Clarke (1997) suggests four ways in which sustainability in tourism can be viewed:

- *as polar opposites* – sustainable and mass tourism are at opposite ends of the spectrum
- *as a continuum* – where shades of sustainability and mass tourism are recognized
- *as movement* – where positive action can make mass tourism more sustainable
- *as convergence* – where all tourism strives to be sustainable.

Swarbrooke (1999: 13) provides a useful definition of sustainable tourism: 'tourism which is economically viable but does not destroy the resources on which the future of tourism will depend, notably the physical environment and the social fabric of the host community', observing the need to achieve a balance in the tourists' use of tourist resources and environments they visit and consume.

In both academic and **practitioner** circles, there has been an emphasis on sustainable tourism as a major focus of attention – illustrated by the amount of published work and the plethora of applied initiatives globally. There is much debate as to the meaning of sustainable tourism but two strands seem to summarize the main contention:

1 Development centred
2 Ecologically centred.

Development-centred ideas consider sustainable tourism as a way of sustaining the tourism industry, while *ecologically centred ideas* concentrate on placing priority on the environment and biodiversity over economic gain. These terms are mutually exclusive so the debate is polarized. If these lines are pursued then no consensus can be achieved. Therefore, one of the challenges of sustainability is to move towards a clear, workable definition with which all stakeholders are reasonably satisfied. Further to this, the concept of sustainable tourism appears to be composed of two elements. The first is *acting in an environmentally conscious way*. This relates to integration of environmental practices into everyday processes and operations, such as: using products which cause less harm to the environment, such as biodegradable washing powders, ozone-friendly cleaning sprays; conserving energy; minimizing waste through purchasing package-free goods or composting and recycling; using locally produced organic produce; reducing the need to travel. These are practical kinds of activities that individuals and businesses can participate in. The second way is *sustainable tourism as an underpinning philosophy*. Sustainable tourism constitutes a way of thinking about the environment where tourism takes place, respecting the landscape, wildlife, people, existing infrastructure and cultural heritage of a tourism destination. The latter is a more holistic, philosophical perspective that underlies the first element and Table 20.2 outlines a rationale for developing sustainable tourism which may be a useful framework for considering the principles used when sustainable tourism is put into practice.

Sustainable tourism in practice

The evidence for the existence of sustainable tourism lies in case studies and examples of good practice which exist globally. It is clear that sustainable tourism can be interpreted in a variety of ways, from small-scale community ventures to environmental/technical management in hotels. Interestingly, it has been the large corporations with multinational interests that have responded most quickly to pressure rather than smaller, locally based tourism ventures, as they have greater financial resources. Many of these early initiatives are well documented, including:

- 1990 – Consort Hotels adopted message 'Conservation in Comfort' which was translated to a number of selected hotels. An example of how this translated to practice is an example of a package – the 'Go Green Weekend' which included talks by local naturalists, nature walks, a nature interpretation room and fresh wholefood produce on the menu. The general aim was to fill surplus capacity in the off-season and create a new niche market

TABLE 20.2 The rationale for sustainable tourism

Tourism which is sustainable should:

- Stimulate awareness of tourism impacts
- Be well-planned, with a strategy identifying limits of acceptable change/carrying capacities
- Generate direct and indirect local employment
- Support viability of local enterprises
- Provide income which is retained in the local area as much as possible
- Support diversification in local and regional economies
- Encourage local community involvement
- Support existing infrastructure and provides justification for retention and improvement of local services
- Respect the integrity of the local environment, culture, people, infrastructure and character of an area
- Promote local pride
- Assist in conservation works in the natural and built environment
- Be carefully monitored and strategies for minimizing negative impacts should be in place

- 1991 – Inter-Continental Hotels Group put together an environmental reference manual giving guidelines and instructions to staff on environmental management. The aim of this manual was to increase staff awareness of environmental concerns and encourage a more proactive approach

- 1992 – The International Hotels Environment Initiative produced a revised manual *Environmental Management for Hotels: The Industry Guide to Best Practice*. This included a voluntary code of conduct and useful reference material on how to upgrade procedures and systems, such as waste management, energy consumption, noise, congestion, purchasing and training. A second edition was published in 1996 (see IHEI 1996)

- Canadian Pacific Hotels launched *The Green Partnership Guide* which identifies environmental improvements and how they might lead to reduced operating costs (also see the magazine *The Greenhotelier* on www.greenhotelier.com).

There have been a significant number of what might be termed 'area' projects based on sustainable tourism development. Some have achieved success, others less so. These can generally be classed as follows:

- *Regional rural projects.* These cover a large area of mainly rural regions, such as the Alto Minho region of Portugal, and tend to focus on regional economic development with a tourism focus. Usually run in partnership between public sector bodies.

- *District-wide projects.* Usually run by a single authority (often in partnership) and covering a specific, generally politically defined area, such as Project Explore in south east Cornwall and National Park Authority projects such as Kruger National Park, South Africa (see Middleton and Hawkins 1998).

- *Local community initiatives.* Originated and run by local people, these take a 'bottom-up' rather than a 'top-down' approach. Good examples of these are beginning to emerge in the international arena: Rathlin Island off the coast of Northern Ireland; the Big Apple in Herefordshire, UK; Capirona in Ecuador where a community of Quichua Indian families have developed ecotourism as a means of economic development.

- *Urban/single-site visitor management.* Includes town centre management, schemes set up to restore part of a historic city incorporating tourism objectives, environmental management in seaside resorts (e.g. Malaga city). This also includes management of particular locations, such as a honeypot site or visitor attraction, e.g. Niagara Falls, Ayers Rock and Pompeii. Single-site sustainable tourism incorporates visitor attractions based on the sustainability theme, such as The Eden Project in the UK.

INSIGHT 20.1

The Ecological Footprint as an indicator of sustainable tourism

There is a growing literature in environmental research that argues a need to develop indicators capable of accounting for the tourist's impacts on the environment. One technique now being developed and debated in tourism is the Ecological Footprint (EF), as mentioned in Chapter 19. Ecological Footprinting is a tool by which an estimate of resource consumption and waste generated by economic activity, such as tourism, can be generated in a given area. The technique examines the consumption of energy, foodstuffs, raw materials, water, transport impacts, waste generated and loss of land from development. While criticisms exist over the methods of analysis used to calculate the EF, it is now being used by public sector agencies to highlight issues of sustainability. Gössling (2002) used this technique to illustrate the EF for tourism in The Seychelles per tourist, using the common

unit of measurement 'gha' (global hectares), which is the way demand of an activity on natural resources results in its consumption. In The Seychelles, values of 1.9 gha per year for the EF were 90% the result of air travel. For a typical two-week holiday in The Mediterranean, the WWF study noted in Chapter 19 observed that a gha of 0.37 resulted in Majorca and 0.93 in Cyprus. In each case, air travel was the contributor to over 50% of the EF. The value of the EF technique is that it allows you to compare the overall ecological impact of tourism products on global biological resources.

Further Reading

Hunter, C. (2002) 'Sustainable tourism and the tourist ecological footprint', Environment, Development and Sustainability, 4 (1): 7–20.

Tools for sustainability

One of the great drawbacks of sustainability is the difficulty in finding ways to put it into practice. To ease this, processes and practices have been developed and Tribe *et al.* (2000: 99–100) identify a range of environmental instruments which can be used: laws and regulations; special designation of sites and resources; taxes, subsidies and grants; tradeable rights and permits; community programmes; ecolabelling; environmental management systems set up by companies; and award schemes to disseminate good practice . The concept of 'best practice' environmental management is now widely accepted as a means of achieving total quality management in all industries and is of direct relevance to tourism. Evaluation processes have existed since the 1970s in the manufacturing industries and have developed from business organization theory and global management perspectives. However, as Tribe *et al.* (2000) acknowledge, some of the self-regulating schemes may not set high enough standards and a number are now reviewed.

Corporate environmental management

From the late 1980s, environmental management procedures have become part of the tourism industry, initially assisted by the Rio Summit in 1992 and subsequent Earth Summits (e.g. www.earthsummit2002.org). A survey of tour operators and environmental awareness in 1991 found that most businesses had not seriously addressed environmental issues and that the recession meant that they were not even on the agenda. Most tended to follow the strategy of 'see it now before it's gone'. Several studies in the 1990s attempted to track the behaviour of tour operators as research and awareness of tourism impacts became more widespread in the consumer market (Holden and Kealy 1996; Carey, Gountas and Gilbert 1997). The launch of the Tour Operator Initiative in 2000 (www.toinitiative.org), developed with the support of WTO/UNEP/UNESCO, focused on cooperation with destinations and sustainability reporting, including performance indicators in sustainable tourism. Some of the largest tour operators have joined the scheme (e.g. Thomas Cook, TUI, First Choice) and there were 23 members in 2005. In the UK, the British Standards Institute have developed a standard procedure and kitemarking system for **corporate environmental management**. This is known as BS 7750 (known internationally as ISO 14000/140001. The procedure entails an annual independent assessment of company environmental practice.

Environmental impact assessment

An **environmental impact assessment** (EIA) is a project assessment of the adverse and beneficial impacts of a specific development used in the planning control system. The assessment covers the period from initial planning to post-development. It is an in-depth, coordinated assessment of the environmental ramifications of development, which covers not only impacts but quality of environmental management systems (Middleton and Hawkins 1998). This information assists decision-makers in evaluating the consequences of a development and thus deciding whether an application should be approved or made conditional on implementing environmental management procedures. For tourism purposes, developments such as marinas, ski resorts, holiday villages (such as Center Parcs) and other large-scale resort developments would require EIA. As Ding and Pigram (1995) note, if the process is effective and meets the correct objectives, then it is a very useful technique. However, there are three main issues upon which one can criticize the effectiveness of EIA.

- Global implementation is patchy. While most developed nations have adopted legislation on EIAs, many less developed countries have not done so. The USA was at the forefront of EIA in the 1970s, while the European Union adopted legislation in 1985. In Australia as in many other countries, proposed tourism developments are subject to EIA before planning approval is given.

- While it is a mandatory requirement for large-scale development, smaller developments are not generally subject to the same process. Therefore, environmental damage is still likely to occur over the long-term through the operation of smaller enterprises.

- EIA is only applicable to new developments, not existing operations which cause environmental damage.

In addition, there are secondary issues to consider. The developer is generally assigned to collect data on the proposals so the accuracy may be questioned. EIA is also individual project-based rather than taking into account wider strategic issues as those who would develop a Strategic EIA have argued. Thus, EIA fails to recognize effects on an interactive and cumulative level, not integrating environmental, social and economic factors very effectively. For example, the issue of overdevelopment in the area may not be acknowledged. There are also concerns about the lack of a feedback loop for ensuring effective monitoring, as Ramjeawon and Beedassy (2004) found in the case of Mauritius. Their discussion of coastal development and tourism activity found no baseline studies of the ecological and environment existed and economic impacts were generally treated favourably.

Environmental auditing

One of the most innovative projects emanating from attempts to look at the environmental performance of existing tourism businesses is the idea of **environmental auditing**. Auditing is different to EIA because it evaluates existing business practice rather than potential problems. Ding and Pigram (1995) state this is a relatively new idea and not yet well developed in Australia. In the UK, the Green Audit Kit has been developed as an auditing tool. The kit comprises a loose-leaf binder containing six sections on aspects of environmental management. These are energy, transport, purchasing, waste, health and local environment. It is designed as a 'do-it-yourself' environmental audit manual. The kit was first trialled as part of the South Devon Green Tourism Initiative which ran 1992–4 and later adopted by the Countryside Agency for wide use across England, as will be discussed in Chapter 22. Many subsequent environmental initiatives have followed this model. This type of environmental evaluation is voluntary. The deficiencies in EIA procedure can be resolved to some extent by applying the two processes together; that is, EIA prior to development, then auditing following development. Auditing can provide the feedback required to assess impact prediction. One new technique gaining prominence – Ecological Footprinting – can be seen in Insight 20.1.

Environmental policies and statements

Many companies have developed statements about their environmental performance, **environmental policies** and practices (Image 20.1). These range in length from a sentence or two (e.g. most tour operators), a page in a brochure to a full booklet (e.g. Center Parcs) and even an annual report (e.g. British Airways). In many cases, very little of substance is conveyed but some organizations provide detailed information about how environmental and community work is contributed to or how impacts are assessed and monitored. The essential aspect is to ensure that policies are put into action otherwise they are useless, as is shown in Insight 20.2.

However, a more innovative approach to draw these issues together can be found with the formation in Scotland in 1994 of the Tourism and Environment Forum (www.greentourism.org). As a partnership of public and private sector organizations, it has helped organizations put many of these sustainability tools into practice and some of its recent achievements include:

- establishment of 'Wild Scotland', an association for Scottish wildlife and nature tourism operators
- the development of a Green Tourism Business Scheme for accommodation and visitor attractions, which is an environmental accreditation scheme with over 500 members in the UK (www.green-business.co.uk), pursuing a sustainable philosophy towards tourism.

Image 20.1: There should be certain areas of the world, such as the Antarctic with its fragile ecosystem that are off-limits to tourism: Do you agree?

INSIGHT 20.2

British Airways Environmental Affairs Department

British Airways, based at Heathrow airport, UK, is the world's largest international passenger airline. The company recognizes the significance of environmental issues and takes an active role in attempting to minimize impacts and create opportunities for conservation and communities. The Environmental Affairs Branch of British Airways advises, supports, monitors and measures environmental performance.

Environmental policy

The corporate goal of British Airways is to be a 'good neighbour, concerned for the community and the environment'. Policy objectives include:

● to develop awareness and understanding of the interactions between the airline's operations and the environment

● to maintain a healthy working environment for all employees

● to consider and respect the environment and to seek to protect the environment in the course of its activities.

British Airways has produced an environmental strategy as a way of achieving these broad objectives. Policy is then translated into practice which is measured through target setting.

Environmental impacts and environmental management

Tackling environmental issues is achieved through a dedicated section within British Airways – the Environmental Affairs Branch. An annual environment and social report is produced, which charts current practice and progress and sets targets for improved environmental performance. Through reviews and consultation, five environmental issues have been highlighted as significant in the operation of British Airways, discussed in Chapter 19.

However, probably the most influential catalyst for change in this area was the formulation of Agenda 21, which brought sustainable tourism issues more into the mainstream in a public policy and planning context.

Agenda 21

Despite the commendable attempts by the United Nations to raise awareness and stimulate action on social and environmental issues worldwide, there was very little evidence of action. A process of change began after the 1992 United Nations Earth Summit in Rio de Janeiro where commitments to action were made by governments across the globe. One of the key outcomes of this conference was **Agenda 21** – an international action plan or 'blueprint' for sustainable development. Signed by 182 heads of state, Agenda 21 commits national governments to considering the environment and development across a number of different activities and is now being implemented in countries across the world. About two thirds of the Agenda 21 action plan requires implementation at local levels and local authorities and communities are working together to achieve this objective.

Agenda 21 affects most areas of global activity, including tourism. Tourism has been recognized in some local action plans, for example Devon County Council in the UK and Calvià in Majorca (see Chapter 23) – both of which are important regions for tourism activity. In addition, defined elements of tourism activity, such as transport, food, accommodation, waste management and entrepreneurship, are an integral part of local Agenda 21 plans. Various methods of assessing the potential and actual impact of tourism have been generated, mostly to assist in planning procedures and in improving environmental performance. The idea of Agenda 21 has been adapted more specifically to the tourism industry by the WTTC, the WTO and the Earth Council (this last is the body established to translate Agenda 21 principles into practice). Agenda 21 for the Travel and Tourism Industry by the WTTC in 1996 recommended actions for tourism specific organizations in the public and private sector to adopt sustainable principles. Grant (1996) provides a useful overview of this. More recently, sustainability issues have assumed a more centre-stage place in global environmental policies, since the Johannesburg Summit in 2002 saw tourism included as three chapters in the reports on sustainable development, pushing tourism explicitly into the public arena.

Visitor management

At the core of sustainable tourism lies good practice in **visitor management**, as the WTO reports on sustainable tourism suggest (Table 20.1), particularly the 2005 report on tourism congestion management. Visitor management is an approach which aims to protect the environment while providing for visitor enjoyment. There are different methods for different types of location which work on both macro (i.e. a nation, region or area) and a micro (settlement, site) level. Strategic decisions about visitor management must be made in relation to **carrying capacity**. Visitor management covers a broad spectrum of strategies and tools but generally, there are three main areas – as demonstrated in Figure 20.3.

Visitor management may also be divided into two forms (Grant 1994):

1 *Hard measures* – aligned with physical and financial restrictions on access. Examples are road closures, parking fees, entrance charges, fencing, zoning, and restrictions on vehicle size.

2 *Soft measures* – associated with encouraging desired behaviour rather than restricting undesirable activities. Examples are marketing and promotional material, signs, interpretation, information provision and guided walks.

The two forms are not mutually exclusive. The hard measures are somewhat easier to apply with immediate results but may not solve the problem alone. A combination of hard and soft initiatives is considered appropriate in most cases.

Spatial distribution as a visitor management strategy aims to spread economic benefits of visitor activity geographically, extend recreational opportunities and experiences and reduce pressure on stressed environments. This may be achieved through a number of tools:

- information packs, outlining attractions and accommodation in the wider area
- marketing areas that are less well known areas
- ticketing strategies (e.g. joint ticketing, discounts, high charges)
- visitor assistants
- interpretation (e.g. trails, information, routeing, tours)
- transport links.

In addition to protecting environmental resources, sometimes it is necessary to prevent conflict between recreational users of an area. Zoning is a method of managing conflicting activities by spatial separation; it is commonly found on reservoirs and lakes where sailing, water-skiing, angling and conservation purposes might be at odds. The Peak District National Park is zoned into five recreational areas, indicating levels of intensity of use, from wild areas through to areas of highest-intensity recreational use. Lundy Island, England's only marine nature reserve, is managed partly through a system of zoning designed to meet the needs of marine conservation and recreation.

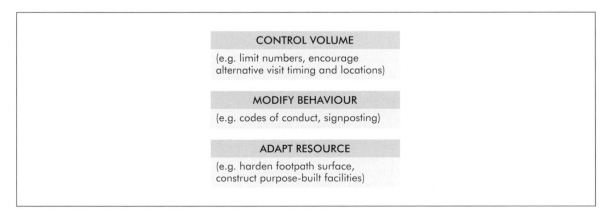

FIGURE 20.3 Summary of visitor management strategies. Source: Modified from Employment Department Group and English Tourist Board (1991)

Temporal distribution aspects address how visits might be spread throughout the year rather than just at peak times. Tools of temporal distribution are:

- timed ticketing
- promotion of out-of-season packages
- special events
- all-year facilities.

In addition, 'de-marketing' is an active policy of not marketing a location is another option for areas where visitor capacity has been reached or attempts are being made to limit promotion of a more fragile environment.

Ways of altering visitor behaviour are also an important part of visitor management. One method employed quite extensively is use of codes of conduct. The aim of a code of conduct is to change tourists' behaviour and attitude. Mowforth and Mason (1995) provide a useful overview of codes of conduct. Friends of Conservation have produced guidelines aimed at tourists to assist in maintaining a balance between enjoyment and conservation. Entitled the *Traveller's Code*, it covers issues of accommodation, culture, dress, food and drink, out and about, shopping, transport, adventure and booking.

Carrying capacity and the limits of acceptable change

Much of the discussion about managing environmental and tourist resources considers the concept of carrying capacity. There are four main types of carrying capacity, illustrated in Figure 20.4.

The notion of carrying capacity, while quite acceptable in theory, is criticized for its inherent difficulty in application. Swarbrooke (1999) provides a critique of the carrying capacity idea:

- some types of capacity are subjective
- measuring techniques are crude, not taking into account
  1 type of destination and nature of environment/community
  2 type of tourism and tourists

PHYSICAL
A measure of the number of tourists that may be accommodated on a site

PERCEPTUAL
A measure of the number of people that may be accommodated on a site before the visitor experience is damaged

ECONOMIC
A measure of the number of people that may be welcomed to a location before the economy of the area is adversely affected

ECOLOGICAL
A measure of the number of people that may be accommodated on a site before damage occurs to the environment

FIGURE 20.4 Types of carrying capacity

- carrying capacity does not address the complexity of the issue of acceptable/unacceptable situations. It is too simplistic to say that a few extra people make a difference
- measurements of carrying capacity do not take account of the costs of reducing capacity, such as jobs and income.

A more recent approach to this subject is the **limits of acceptable change** (LAC) which incorporate a more holistic approach. Limits are set according to how much environmental change is permissible.

The importance of drawing up appropriate policies to manage tourism is illustrated by Ritchie (1998, 1999) who reports the findings of work conducted in the Banff-Bow Valley, Canada. This is one of the most comprehensive studies of its type carried out in Canada. The results demonstrate the importance of involving the local community, a need to identify appropriate activities for an environment, the requirement for extensive and accurate environmental information and an understanding of visitor services and behaviour. Lane (1994) concurs with this and cites the difference between conventional and sustainable tourism planning.

Difficulties in achieving sustainable tourism: Challenges for the future

One of the main problems with achieving sustainable tourism is the lack of consensus as to what it actually means in practice. While this might seem to be an academic argument, it has practical ramifications of a critical nature. Without a precise understanding of what the term means, no progress can be made towards achieving it. Hoodwinking must be avoided at all cost as Wheeller (1991: 94) states: 'Examples of positive management of the tourist influx are the exception, not the rule'. This raises the question: 'Is sustainable tourism for the elite only?' The development of new tourism has attracted new tourists. Many existing and new tourism destinations wish to attract a small number of high-spending tourists. Mass tourism is associated with low-spending, high-volume tourism. This highlights one of the essential problems in sustainable tourism. If this alternative approach to tourism is to work in protecting the environment, it cannot work in isolation. It should aim to cover every aspect of tourism, from the Costa del Sol to the rainforest of Belize. As tourism growth proceeds, the answer to lessening the impacts is obviously not in attracting low-spending high-volume tourism. This is the dilemma for policy-makers in destinations. Insight 20.3 demonstrates how a mass tourism resort is tackling the idea of sustainability.

INSIGHT 20.3

Alcúdia's plan of highest quality

Alcúdia is a small peninsula on the north-eastern coast of Mallorca (see Figure 23.4) and is one of the most visited parts of the island. It offers natural beauty, varied scenery, history and a range of tourist facilities. Mass tourism has developed over the last 20 years.

- Pol-lèntia is an outstanding archaeological site, with evidence of Roman settlement. The site has been interpreted for visitors and a self-guided trail leaflet is available.
- S'albufera de Mallorca is the largest and most important wetland area in the Balearics and its first protected area (declared a national park in 1988). The site is

characterized by its ecological richness, including plants, fish, invertebrates, fungi, mammals and, most significantly, birds.

- Cycling is promoted through a booklet freely available to tourists, describing ten cycling routes which give opportunities to explore off the beaten track.
- Alcúdia is promoted as an 'ecotouristic community' through a leaflet outlining the major plant and animal species to be found and the location of nature reserves.
- Representatives attend the World Travel Market in London to promote the area's attraction and the ideals of sustainable tourism.

There are dangers in promoting sustainable tourism because it might lead to the results witnessed through mass tourism development. Green policies tend to focus on spreading the tourist benefits, which include the temporal (widening the tourist season by encouraging off-peak visiting) and spatial (promoting a wider area for tourism). For Alcúdia, the potential for tourist interest in the fragile natural and historical sites necessitates a strategic approach to the planning, management and monitoring of the environment.

Monitoring the effects of tourism and of sustainable tourism projects needs further consideration and the English Tourism Council (ETC 2001) established a series of national sustainable tourism indicators. Due to institutional reorganization, the implementation has not occurred since the responsibility for this task has been passed to another body and no further information is available on this in 2005. This is a disappointing and missed opportunity for sustainable tourism, in seeking to move Agenda 21 from rhetoric to local action. Without monitoring, it is impossible to say whether tourism is becoming more sustainable or not. The ETC (2001) report also set out a series of criteria by which to monitor and evaluate progress, expanding upon other studies of sustainable tourism planning (Dymond 1997; Page and Thorn 2002). This is becoming an accepted part of sustainable development on an international scale. Achieving sustainable tourism is difficult for four reasons, according to Muller (1994):

- too many theories and experts – too few resources and little time to act
- there is a continuing boom in tourism demand
- while there is a growing awareness of the environment, the predominance of a hedonistic philosophy means a trend towards indulgence of pleasures on holiday rather than responsibility
- a change of paradigm is needed to move towards socially and environmentally compatible lifestyles – a long and difficult process.

Sisman (1994: 60) suggests that 'environmentalism should be much more integrated into society as a whole, not an adjunct to it'. The implications of this is that sustainable tourism should be a philosophy that infiltrates the whole of the tourism industry rather than being a niche market or minority view. To be successful, Sisman advocates 'a working partnership that blends good environmental practice and profitable business for mutual long-term advantages' (Sisman 1994: 59). A plethora of environmental guidelines and charters have been prepared by environmental groups for the tourism industry to implement. Sisman believes these have failed because such groups lack an understanding of business. No doubt environmental groups would counter this with the view that business does not understand the environment! This is at the core of the problem of achieving sustainability. Redclift (1987: 36) cites the importance of integrating the sustainable development concept into international structures, otherwise there is a danger that it will become 'yet another discarded development concept'. However, ending on a positive note, the recent launch by the Travel Foundation in the UK (a charity which promotes sustainable tourism among travellers) of its *Insider Guide: Make a difference when you travel* is a good practice guide to promote wider understanding of our impact and how to minimize it (www.travelfoundation.org.uk).

Conclusion

Despite confusion over meanings of sustainable tourism, it is clear that protection of the resources which tourism depends on is central to sustainable development (Page and Thorn 2002) but implementation involves a very complex process in different localities. It is vital to recognize this complexity and not to be fooled into thinking that sustainable tourism can be achieved by devising a policy statement or undertaking one aspect of environmental management. In reality, sustainable tourism is somewhat of an oxymoron – while appropriate management is achievable at the site level, it cannot be achieved overall because of the need for travel. The best that the tourism industry as a whole can do is move towards better environmental practice. May (1991) provides six steps which can be taken to move closer to the goal of sustainability:

- better understanding of the value of environments
- more complete information about environments, local values and susceptibility to outside influences
- greater attention to the regional effects of development

- use of environmental economics in relation to assessing development
- improved measurements of environmental factors for use in environmental accounting
- developments should be designed with long-term environmental quality in mind.

These issues provide a continuing challenge for the development and management of tourism in the twenty-first century, since Carvalho (2001: 70) argued that we need to do more in our conceptualization of sustainable development if we are to give it more meaning in the case of tourism, rather than retaining 'the notion as something that can be achieved in the current system with just a little tweaking and slight greening of the current development model'. We need a new philosophy that reconceptualizes the tourism development model, since as Page (2003) has shown, tourism has the potential to self-destruct in localities and environments once the development process gets out of control.

Discussion questions

1 Why is ecotourism not necessarily a form of sustainable tourism?
2 To what extent are multinational corporations in tourism displaying green credentials?
3 Explain the meaning of sustainability in a tourism context and suggest why this might conflict with other perceptions of sustainability.
4 Why is sustainable tourism so difficult to achieve?

References

Acott, T. La Trobe, H. and Howard, S. (1998) 'An evaluation of deep ecotourism and shallow ecotourism', *Journal of Sustainable Tourism*, 6 (3): 238–53.

Carey, S., Gountas, Y. and Gilbert, D. (1997) 'Tour operators and destination sustainability', *Tourism Management*, 18 (7): 425–31.

Carvalho, G. (2001) 'Sustainable development: Is it achievable within the existing international political economy context?' *Sustainable Development*, 9: 61–73.

Clarke, J. (1997) 'A framework of approaches to sustainable tourism', *Journal of Sustainable Tourism*, 5: 224–33.

Devall, B. and Sessions, G. (1985) *Deep Ecology. Living as if Nature Mattered.* Utah: Gibbs Smith.

Ding, P. and Pigram, J. (1995) 'Environmental audits: An emerging concept in sustainable development', *Journal of Tourism Studies*, 6 (2): 2–10.

Dymond, S. (1997) 'Indicators of sustainable tourism in New Zealand: A local government perspective', *Journal of Sustainable Tourism*, 15 (4): 279–93.

Employment Department Group and English Tourist Board (1991) *Tourism and the Environment. Maintaining the Balance.* London: English Tourist Board.

ETC (English Tourism Council) (2001) *The Sustainable Growth of Tourism to Britain.* London: English Tourist Board.

Grant, M. (1994) 'Visitor management', *Insights*, A41–6, London: English Tourist Board.

Grant, M. (1996) 'Tourism, sustainability and agenda 21', *Insights*, A85–90, London: English Tourist Board.

Hardy, A., Beeton, R. and Pearson, L. (2002) 'Sustainable tourism: An overview of the concept and its position in relation to conceptualisation of tourism', *Journal of Sustainable Tourism*, 10 (6): 475–96.

Holden, A. and Kealy, H. (1996) 'A profile of UK outbound "environmentally friendly" tour operators', *Tourism Management*, 17 (1): 60–4.

IHEI (International Hotels Environment Initiative) (1996) *Environmental Management for Hotels: The Industry Guide to Best Practice, Second Edtion.* Oxford: Butterworth-Heinemann.

Krippendorf, J. (1987) *The Holidaymakers.* Oxford: Butterworth-Heinemann.

Lane, B. (1994) 'Sustainable rural tourism strategies: A tool for development and conservation', *Journal of Sustainable Tourism*, 2 (1 and 2): 102–111.

Liu, Z. (2003) 'Sustainable tourism development: A critique', *Journal of Sustainable Tourism*, 11 (6): 459–75.

May, V. (1991) 'Tourism, environment and development. Values, sustainability and stewardship', *Tourism Management*, 12 (2): 112–18.

Middleton, V.T.C. and Hawkins, R. (1998) *Sustainable Tourism. A Marketing Approach.* Oxford: Butterworth-Heinemann.

Mowforth, M. and Mason, P. (1995) *Codes of Conduct in Tourism.* Occasional Papers in Geography, No. 1. Plymouth: Department of Geographical Sciences, University of Plymouth.

Mowforth, M. and Munt, I. (2003) *Tourism and Sustainability. New Tourism in the Third World, Second Edition.* London: Routledge.

Muller, H. (1994) 'The thorny path to sustainable tourism development', *Journal of Sustainable Tourism*, 2 (3): 131–6.

Page, S.J. (2003) *Tourism Management: Managing for Change.* Oxford: Butterworth-Heinemann.

Page, S.J. (2005) 'Tourism planning and management', in C. Ryan, S.J. Page and M. Aicken (eds) *Taking Tourism to the Limits: Issues, Concepts and Managerial Perspectives.* Oxford: Elsevier.

Page, S.J. and Thorn, K. (2002) 'Towards sustainable tourism development and planning in New Zealand: The public sector response revisited', *Journal of Sustainable Tourism*, 10 (3): 222–38.

Prosser, R. (1994) 'Societal change and growth in international tourism', in E. Cater and G. Lowman (eds) (1994) *Ecotourism: A Sustainable Option?* Chichester: John Wiley and Sons.

Ramjeawon, T. and Beedsay, R. (2004) 'Evaluation of the EIA system on the island of Mauritius and development of an environmental monitoring plan framework', *Environmental Impact Analysis*, 24: 537–49.

Redclift, M. (1987) *Sustainable Development. Exploring the Contradictions.* London: Routledge.

Ritchie, J.R.B. (1998) 'Managing the human presence in ecologically sensitive tourism destinations: Insights from the Banff-Bow Valley study', *Journal of Sustainable Tourism*, 6 (4): 293–313.

Ritchie, J.R.B. (1999) 'Policy formulation at the tourism/environment interface: Insights and recommendations from the Banff-Bow Valley study', *Journal of Travel Research*, 38: 100–10.

Robinson, J. (2004) 'Squaring the circle? Some thoughts on the idea of sustainable development', *Ecological Economics*, 48: 369–84.

Sisman, D. (1994) 'Tourism: Environmental relevance', in E. Cater and G. Lowman (eds) *Ecotourism: A Sustainable Option?* Chichester: John Wiley and Sons.

Swarbrooke, J. (1999) *Sustainable Tourism Management.* Wallingford, Oxon: CAB International.

Tribe, J., Font, X., Griffiths, N., Vickery, R. and Yale, K. (2000) *Environmental Management for Rural Tourism and Recreation.* London: Cassell.

Turner, R.K., Pearce, D. and Bateman, I. (1994) *Environmental Economics: An Elementary Introduction.* New York: Harvester Wheatsheaf.

Wheeller, B. (1991) 'Tourism's troubled times. Responsible tourism is not the answer', *Tourism Management*, 12 (2): 91–6.

World Commission on Environment and Development (1987) *Our Common Future.* Oxford: Oxford University Press.

Further reading

Mowforth, M. and Munt, I. (2003) *Tourism and Sustainability. New Tourism in the Third World, Second Edition.* London: Routledge.

Trends and Themes in the use of Tourist Resources

Having reviewed the impact of tourism in Part IV, attention now turns to a number of different forms of tourism which have impacts on the environment. This section reviews the main tourism environments which attract tourist activity and discusses the nature of tourism in each context as well as the principal issues associated with each particular form of tourism. With the development and growth of tourist destinations, a consistent theme in recent research over the last 20 years is the concept of **tourist resource**s which are consumed at specific points in time by tourists in different environments. In the following four chapters, the issue of tourist resources in specific environments is examined in a variety of different contexts ranging from the urban through to rural, coastal and resort environments to the less developed world. To understand the synergies and themes which unify these chapters it is interesting to begin by highlighting a number of fundamental concepts which have evolved in both the tourism and recreational literature in the last 25 years and have influenced the way we look at, analyse and understand tourist resource environments.

Concepts and themes in the analysis of tourist resources

In some respects, the overlap between recreation and tourism is evident when one begins to try and explain how concepts have been devised to understand how tourists use certain resources (see Hall and Page 1999 for a discussion of the recreation-tourism continuum). In 1960, Clawson, Held and Stoddart (1960) examined ways of classifying outdoor recreation and resources based on the principle of distance and zones of influence in terms of whether the resource base had a national, regional, sub-regional, intermediate or local zone of influence. This research is shown in Table 21.1, which helped explain the 'pull' of the resource, and they identified a simple model of use where three zones existed:

- A 0–16km zone, many resource needs for recreation can be met in terms of golf, urban parks and the urban fringe.
- A 16–32km zone, the range of activities is greater, though particular types of resource tend to dominate activity patterns (e.g. horse-riding, hiking and field sports).

- A 32km or greater, sports and physical pursuits with specific resource requirements (e.g. orienteering, canoeing, skiing and rock-climbing) exist.

What Clawson et al. (1960) highlight is that while the majority of recreational activities are undertaken near to home, it is the more distant resources within countries and outside of countries (i.e. overseas) that are the focus of the tourist. With increased mobility, resources have become much more accessible to those tourists able to afford the cost of travel although, in terms of domestic tourism, Clawson et al.'s (1960) classification to a large degree is still a good analysis of the difference between recreational and tourist resource users.

For tourists, the principle inherent in this research was that visitors would use different resources depending upon their accessibility, appeal and attraction base. This has led to research which describes the features and attractions of specific resource environments. For example, inventories of the attractions and accommodation in resorts are frequently undertaken by tourist agencies and the differences are noted in relation to the status and quality of destinations to identify the strengths, weaknesses, opportunities and threats (SWOT analysis). Much of the research on the tourist and recreationalist use of resources has been undertaken by geographers (Hall and Page 2005) and they use specific concepts and approaches to model and classify the users of specific resources.

In Chapter 21, the significance of urban tourism is discussed as a context for many forms of tourist visit and the problems of accurately analysing this form of tourism are discussed. The impact of urban tourism on city environments and the interactions it has with the city economy are reviewed together with the nature of tourist activities in city environments. Chapter 22 in direct contrast, examines rural tourism. The problems of defining what comprises rural tourism is a major task of the chapter and the impacts and effects of this form of tourism are considered. This is followed in Chapter 23 with a review of the stereotypical tourism environment – the coastal environment and resort tourism. Chapter 23 discusses both the evolution of the coast as a context for tourism activity and its predisposition as a location for resort development, with its concentration of services and facilities to service tourist needs. Last, Chapter 24 reviews the impact of tourism activity in the less developed world which has become a popular destination in recent years for tourist trips due to the exotic appeal and relatively low costs now offered to Western tourists through package travel. In each chapter, the nature of the form of tourism is discussed and, where possible, examples illustrating the impacts of tourism activity highlighted in the previous section of the book are outlined to show how the impacts occur in specific tourism environments.

References

Clawson, M., Held, R. and Stoddart, C. (1960) Land for the Future. Baltimore: John Hopkins Press.

Hall, C.M. and Page, S.J. (1999) The Geography of Tourism and Recreation: Environment, Place and Space. London: Routledge.

Hall, C.M. and Page, S.J. (2005) The Geography of Tourism and Recreation: Environment, Place and Space, Third Edition. London: Routledge.

Chapter 21 Urban Tourism

TABLE 21.1 A general classification of outdoor recreational uses and resources: Implications for tourism resource use

| Item | Type of recreation area | | |
	User-oriented	Resource-based	Intermediate
General location	Close to users; on whatever resources are available	Where outstanding resources can be found; may be distant from most users	Must not be too remote from users; on best resources available within distance limitation
Major types of activity	Games such as golf and tennis; swimming; picnicking; walks; horse-riding; zoos; play by children	Major sightseeing, scientific, historical interest; hiking, mountain climbing, camping, fishing and hunting	Camping, picnicking, hiking, swimming, hunting and fishing
When major use occurs	After hours (school or work)	Vacations (i.e. tourism)	Day outings and weekends (possibly some domestic tourism)
Typical size of areas	One to a hundred or at most to a few hundred acres	Usually some thousands of acres, perhaps many thousands	A hundred to several thousand acres
Common types of agency responsibility	City, county or other local government; private	National parks and national forests primarily; state parks in some cases; private especially for seashore and major lakes	Federal reservoirs; state parks; private

Source: Adapted from Clawson, Held and Stoddart (1960: 136)

21

Urban Tourism

Learning outcomes

After reading this chapter and answering the questions, you should be able to:

- appreciate the significance of cities as tourism destinations

- consider the ways in which urban areas fulfill a wide range of tourist needs

- identify why tourism has been used as a tool for urban regeneration

- develop an understanding of the complexity of towns and cities in the analysis of tourist resources.

Overview

Cities have long been the centre of tourist activity, from the early times of civilization through to their very highly developed state in the global economy of the twenty-first century, where world cities not only perform important roles as centres of business and trade but also as tourist destinations for leisure and business travellers and day trippers. Cities hold a particular fascination for tourists, from the vast, highly developed world cities right down to the small historic towns, where heritage, history and an intimate scale enable the visitor to feel embodied in a past landscape which has been adapted for modern day use. Urban tourism is arguably one of the most highly developed forms of tourism at a global scale, since most of the major tourist gateways are urban in nature, and yet it is still a poorly understood aspect in the wider tourism system.

Introduction

Urbanization is a major force contributing to the development of towns and cities, where people live, work and shop. Towns and cities function as places where the population concentrates in a defined area, and economic activities locate in the same area or nearby, to provide the opportunity for the production and consumption of goods and services in capitalist societies. Consequently, towns and cities provide the context for a diverse range of social, cultural and economic activities which the population engage in and where tourism, leisure and entertainment form major service activities. These environments also function as meeting places, major tourist gateways, accommodation and transportation hubs, and as central places to service the needs of visitors. Most tourist trips will contain some experience of an urban area; for example, when an urban dweller departs from a major gateway in a city, arrives at a gateway in another city-region and stays in accommodation in an urban area. Within cities, however, the line between tourism and recreation blurs to the extent that at times one is indistinguishable from the other, with tourists and recreationalists using the same facilities, resources and environments although some notable differences exist. Therefore, many tourists and recreationalists will intermingle in many urban contexts. Most tourists will experience urban tourism in some form during their holiday, visit to friends and relatives, business trip or visit for another reason.

Urban tourism: A relevant area for study?

Ashworth's (1989) landmark study of **urban tourism** acknowledges that 'a double neglect has occurred. Those interested in the study of tourism have tended to neglect the urban context in which much of it is set, while those interested in urban studies ... have been equally neglectful of the importance of the tourist function in cities' (Ashworth 1989: 33). While more recent studies have examined urban tourism research in a spatial context (e.g. Pearce 1998, 2001), it still remains a comparatively unresearched area despite the growing interest in the relationship between urban regeneration (also referred to as rejuvenation by some commentators) and tourism. The problem is also reiterated in a number of subsequent studies as one explanation of the neglect of urban tourism. Despite this problem, which is more a function of perceived than real difficulties in understanding urban tourism phenomena, a range of studies now provide evidence of a growing body of literature on the topic as reviewed in Page and Hall (2002). Yet much of the research which is published on urban tourism research remains quite descriptive, mainly case-study driven.

Interestingly Ashworth (1992) argued that urban tourism has not emerged as a distinct research focus: research is focused on tourism in cities. This strange paradox can be explained by the failure by planners, commercial interests and residents to recognize tourism as one of the main economic rationales for cities. Tourism is often seen as an adjunct or necessary evil to generate additional revenue, while the main economic activities of the locality are not perceived as tourism related, unless tourism is a central component of urban regeneration strategies. Such negative views of urban tourism have meant that the public and private sector have used the temporary, seasonal and ephemeral nature of tourism to neglect serious research on this theme. Consequently, a vicious circle exists: the absence of public and private sector research makes access to research data difficult and the large-scale funding necessary to break the vicious circle, and underwrite primary data collection using social survey techniques, is rarely available. However, with the pressure posed by tourists in many European tourist cities (e.g., Canterbury, London, York, Venice and Florence), this perception is changing now that the public and private sector are belatedly acknowledging the necessity of visitor management (see Chapter 20 and 25 for a discussion of this issue) as a mechanism to enhance, manage and improve the tourists' experience of towns and places to visit. Insight 21.1 examines the scope of many of these issues in relation to one of the world's most fascinating **historic cities** – Venice.

INSIGHT 21.1

Tourism in a small historic city – Venice

Venice is world famous as the only amphibious city. It developed towards the end of the Roman Empire and has a long history associated with a seafaring race, the Venetians, who created this small historic city, full of cultural antiquities including its world-famous fifteenth-century Renaissance art. It also has a long tradition of tourism, epitomized by the rich and leisured classes who visited in the eighteenth and nineteenth centuries. What makes Venice unusual and popular with visitors is its location on a series of islands in a lagoon (Figure 21.1), serving as the capital of the Veneto region of Italy. Despite economic growth in the region since the 1960s, the historic city of Venice experienced continued population loss during this period, dropping from 175 000 people in 1951 to now under 78 000. At the same time, many of the city's historic buildings are under constant threat from the sea (Image 21.2) although this is not new and debates in the Victorian period saw poets such as Ruskin debating the modernizing influence of industrialization on the romantic aspects of the city. Among the main environmental threats facing Venice are a sinking ground level, a rising sea level, periodic flooding of the lagoon in which it is located and atmospheric pollution which impacts upon the foundations of its buildings and the very building fabric. But one of the most visible and persistent issues is the effect of tourism.

Image 21.2: St Mark's Basin aerial view illustrates the dominance of the sea in Venice's location. Source: Venice Tourist Board

As one of the city's prominent residents whose popular BBC Television series – Venice, outlined:

Building gondolas, rowing them, blowing glass and fashioning masks were once essential livelihoods in the economy of a great city: now they merely capitalize on the tourist industry although the very layout of the city [Figure 21.1], its canal structure and intimate urban landscape make it one of the most memorable cultural tourism experiences in Europe (Mosta 2004: 204).

The scale of tourism is apparent from Mosta's observation that:

A reputed 15 million visitors flock to the city every year…and the cultural distinctiveness of Venice are threatened by the intense pressures of mass tourism. Cruise ships bring tourists right into the heart of Venice. There is much concern that this is damaging the fragile infrastructure of the city (Mosta 2004: 206).

Image 21.1: The Doge's Palace is a fine example of Venice's heritage. Source: Venice Tourist Board

These visitor numbers are swelled by a large day-visitor market from other parts of Italy, especially the Adriatic beach resorts and Alpine areas and the concentration at key points such as St Mark's Square (Image 21.3). Montanari and Muscara (1995) recognized that Venice was saturated at key times in the year (e.g. Easter) and that the police have had to close the Ponte del Liberta temporarily since the optimum flow of 21 000 tourists a day has been exceeded (e.g. 60 000 at Easter and 100 000 in the summer). The diversity of people attracted to the city is evident from Montanari and Muscara's (1995) nine-fold classification of tourists:

Image 21.3: St Mark's Square, a focal point for tourist activity and sightseeing in Venice, Source: Venice Tourist Board

- first-time visitors on an organized tour
- the rich tourist
- the lover of Venice
- the backpacker camper
- the worldly-wise tourist
- the return tourist
- the resident artist
- the beach tourist
- the visitor with a purpose.

Whilst excursionists comprise over 85 per cent of all visitors to the city, additional pressures have arisen by making the destination more accessible through the advent of low-cost airlines. Since the opening up of eastern Europe, the city has also seen an influx of eastern Europeans, with city officials reporting 60 000 Czechs arriving in 1200 coaches in one day. In Venice, van der Borg, Costa and Gotti (1996: 314) calculated the visitor:resident (host) ratio of 89.4:1 which may explain why residents may feel besieged by the tourists. The large volume of visitors who descend on Venice each year not only exceeds the desirable limits of tourism for the city but also poses a range of social and economic problems for planners. As van der Borg (1992: 52) observes

the negative external effects connected with the overloading of the carrying capacity are rapidly increasing, frustrating the centre's economy and society … excursionism [day tripping] is becoming increasingly important, while residential tourism is losing relevance for the local tourism market … [and] … the local benefits are diminishing. Tourism is becoming increasingly ineffective for Venice.

A number of positive measures have been enacted to address the saturation of the historic city by day visitors including denying access to the city by unauthorized tour coaches via the main coach terminal. Glasson et al. (1995: 116) summarize the problem of seeking to manage visitors and their environmental impact in Venice:

every city must be kept as accessible as possible for some specific categories of users, such as inhabitants, visitors to offices and firms located in the city, and commuters studying or working in the city. At the same time, the art city needs to be kept as inaccessible as possible to some other user categories (the excursionist/day-trippers in particular).

The city has a well-developed heritage of traditional festivals and events (see below) and these attract more cultural tourists. The city's heritage includes a number of more sustainable transport solutions to cater for the tourist market including the gondola (Image 21.6).

This Insight is significant in that it highlights the prevailing problems affecting many historic cities around the world which are not peculiar to Venice. Whilst pollution is a grave problem for Venice, the greatest threat are day trippers who contribute little to the economy. Yet, as the example of Venice shows, it takes a determined political will to address the pressures posed by tourism since vested interests do not want to see the economy decline if visitors are not attracted. The launch of the Venice Card in 2004 is to control tourism, giving visitors priority via pre-booking, and to manage

Images 21.4 and 21.5: Venice has many festivals and events, some of which have a long history, including the Carnival where masks were first worn in 1268, which are a cultural artefact of Venice's rich and varied history.
Source: Venice Tourist Board

visitor numbers. It will need one million subscribers a year to work, so visitor numbers can be limited to 25 000 a day when on some days 200 000 arrive (Van der Borg 2004).

Probably the greatest dilemma is in reaching a sustainable solution – a balance which is poignantly voiced by Mosta (2004: 211): 'The future of Venice is uncertain. I hope that its remarkable history will be preserved along with its monuments, and that a balance can be found between opening up this city of wonders for modern visitors and restoring the integrity and vitality of the Venetian population' in view of the declining resident population base and prevailing concerns that the city will eventually become a peopleless museum or devoid of Venetians as second home owners buy apartments. In such a case it would lose much of its appeal as a living and working city.

Image 21.6: The gondola is a sustainable form of transport for tourists and a major attraction in its own right as the tourists travel along the canals and go under the Bridge of Sighs and Bridge of Paglia. Source: Venice Tourist Board

Understanding the nature and concept of urban tourism: Theoretical debates

Shaw and Williams (1994) argue that urban areas offer geographical concentration of facilities and attractions that are conveniently located to meet both visitor and resident needs alike. But the diversity and variety among urban tourist destinations has led researchers to examine the extent to which they display unique and similar features. Shaw and Williams (1994) identify three perspectives:

- the diversity of urban areas means that their size, function, location and history contributes to their uniqueness
- towns and cities are multi-functional areas, meaning that they simultaneously provide various functions for different groups of users
- the tourist functions of towns and cities are rarely produced or consumed solely by tourists, given the variety of user groups in urban areas.

Ashworth (1992) conceptualizes urban tourism by identifying three approaches towards its analysis, where researchers have focused on:

- *the supply of tourism facilities in urban areas*, involving inventories (e.g. the spatial distribution of accommodation, entertainment complexes and tourist-related services), where urban ecological models, developed by urban geographers have been used (see Page 1995). In addition, the facility approach has been used to identify the tourism product offered by destinations
- *the demand generated by urban tourists*, to examine how many people visit urban areas, why they choose to visit and their patterns of behaviour, perception and expectations in relation to their visit
- *urban tourism policy*, where the public sector (e.g. planners) and private sector agencies have undertaken or commissioned research to investigate specific issues of interest to their own interests for urban tourism.

Theoretical studies of urban tourism by Mullins (1991) and Roche (1992) are focused on the many former towns and cities with a declining industrial base that are now looking towards

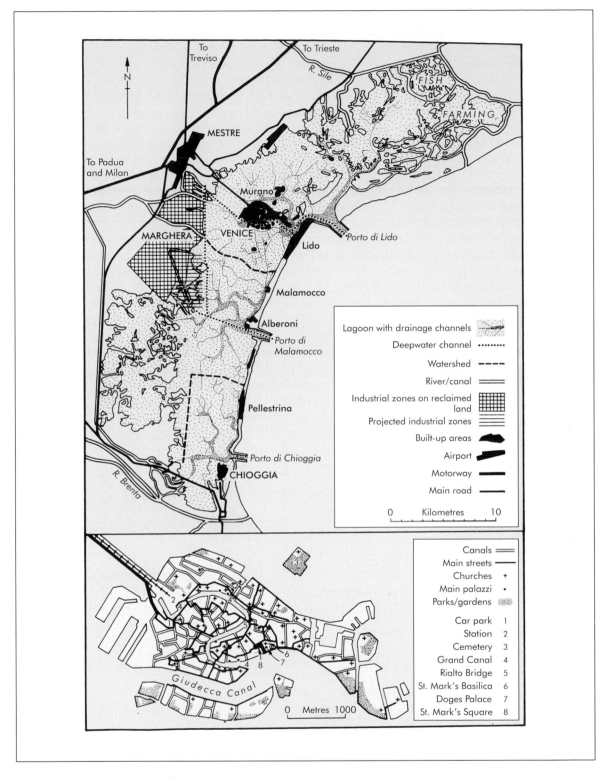

FIGURE 21.1   Location of Venice. Source: King (1987), reproduced with kind permission R. King

service sector activities such as tourism that have the potential to generate new employment opportunities through regeneration, as discussed later. These studies examine urban tourism in **post-industrial** society and question the types of process now shaping the operation and development of tourism in post-industrial cities, and the implications for public sector tourism policy.

Mullins' initial research has been followed by studies which argue that a 'new urban tourism' exists in a post-industrial society, based on the consumption of places. Indeed, sociologists such as Meethan (1996) suggest urban areas now see this consumption as a complex process of transforming the landscape into one of pleasure and fun. A variety of activities exist such as promenading, eating, drinking, watching events and appreciating the heritage and culture of the place. Hannigan's (1998) **Fantasy City** depicts many of these features in the North American city, while other studies have pointed to the globalization of such trends in the post-modern city. Critics such as Ritzer (1996) suggest that this process of globalization has led to the McDonaldization of production and consumption in such cities, meaning that in these environments one now has a similar experience regardless of location due to the process of globalization. Whatever theoretical perspective one adopts, urban places in the developed world (and former Communist eastern bloc) are in the process of transformation based on the consumption of tourism. Global capital has realized the benefits of investing in regeneration schemes to transform redundant areas for profit. What is also apparent is that the urban landscape of the twenty-first century is littered with symbols of globalization, such as the multinational hotel chains and hospitality brands such as KFC and Starbucks, as well as a wide range of locally produced elements that retain a degree of distinctiveness for the destination. However, the competition for global investment and visitors has led to complex forms of place-marketing to promote each locality, its identity, brands and a variety of markets. In some cases, highly developed urban tourism resorts have evolved (e.g. Las Vegas, Australia's Gold Coast) as part of what Mullins and others have described as 'tourism urbanization'. Many of these places, solely developed through tourism, operate 24 hours a day and have a defined theme (e.g. gambling and entertainment in Las Vegas).

What the tourism urbanization studies highlight is the role of the state, especially local government in seeking to develop service industries based on tourism consumption. For example, many local authorities in western Europe are pump-priming tourism development as a means of stimulating the urban economy, particularly where leisure and culture-based spending can be harnessed to create new employment. Consequently, one can identify the following types of urban tourist destination:

- capital cities
- metropolitan centres, walled historic cities and small fortress cities
- large historic cities
- inner city areas
- revitalized waterfront areas
- industrial cities
- seaside resorts and winter sport resorts
- purpose-built integrated tourist resorts
- tourist-entertainment complexes
- specialized tourist service centres
- cultural/art cities
- sport cities (Page and Hall 2002).

The market for urban tourism

Identifying the scale, volume and different markets for urban tourism remains a perennial problem for researchers. Urban tourism is a major economic activity in many of Europe's capital cities but identifying the tourism markets in each area is problematic. The principal international data sources on urban tourism are the published statistics of the WTO and the Organization for Economic Co-operation and Development. Such data sources commonly use the domestic and international tourist use of accommodation as one measure of the scale of tourism activity. In the context of urban tourism, researchers must have an understanding of the geographical distribution of tourist accommodation in each country to identify the scale and distribution of tourist visits. In countries where the majority of accommodation is urban based, such statistics may provide preliminary source of data for research. Whilst this may be relevant for certain categories of tourist (e.g. business travellers and holiday-makers), those visitors staying with friends and relatives within an urban environment would not be included in the statistics. Even where statistics can be used, they only provide a preliminary assessment of scale and volume and more detailed sources are needed to assess specific markets for urban tourism. Figure 21.2 describes a method of classifying urban tourists based on individual motives for visiting urban destinations, although Jansen-Verbeke (1986) points to the methodological problem of distinguishing between the different users of the tourist city. For example, Burtenshaw *et al.* (1991) discuss the concept of functional areas within the city, where different visitors seek certain attributes for their city visit (e.g. the historic city, the culture city, the night life city, the shopping city and the tourist city, to which Page and Hall (2002) have added the sport city as shown in Figure 21.3) where no one group has a monopoly over its use. Residents of the city and its hinterland, visitors and workers all use the resources within the tourist city, but some user groups identify with certain areas more than others. Thus, the tourist city is a multifunctional area which complicates attempts to identify a definitive classification of users and the areas/facilities they visit.

A study by Romero, Ortuño and Suriñach (2002) identified the main groups of urban visitors in terms of:

- business users
- fairs and congress attendees
- visiting friends and relatives
- vacation travellers
- short-break visitors

although these markets do exhibit different degrees of seasonality.

Ashworth and Tunbridge (1990) prefer to approach the market for urban tourism from the perspective of the consumers' motives, focusing on the purchasing intent of users, their attitudes,

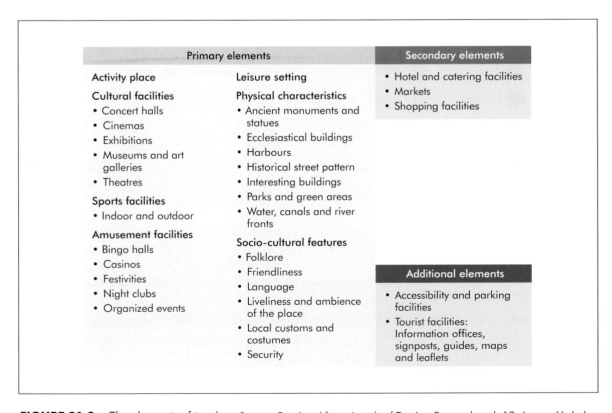

FIGURE 21.2   The elements of tourism. Source: Reprinted from Annals of Tourism Research, vol. 13, Jansen-Verbeke, 'Inner-city tourism', 79–100, copyright (1986), with permission from Elsevier

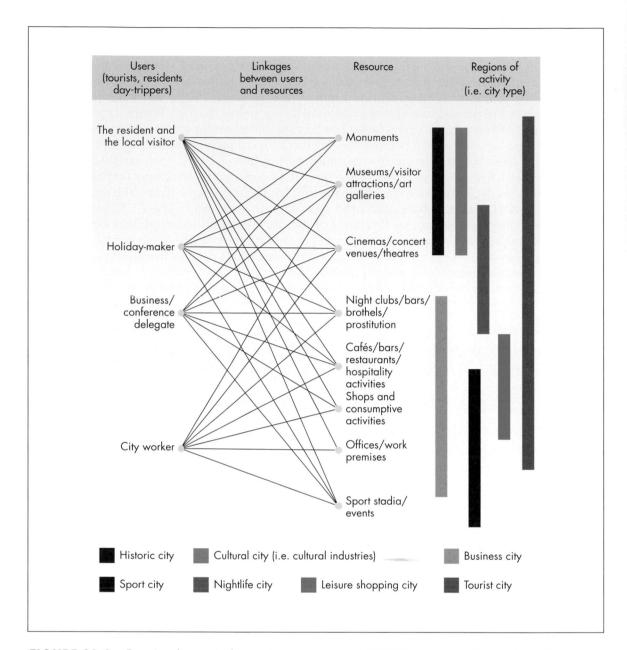

FIGURE 21.3 Functional areas in the city. Source: Page and Hall (2002), reproduced with permission from Pearson Education

opinions and interests for specific urban tourism products. The most important distinction they make is between use/non-use of tourism resources, leading them to identify intentional users (who are motivated by the character of the city) and incidental users (who view the character of the city as irrelevant to their use). This two-fold typology is then used by Ashworth and Tunbridge (1990) to identify four specific types of users:

- intentional users from outside the city-region (e.g., holiday-makers and heritage tourists)
- intentional users from inside the city-region (e.g., those using recreational and entertainment facilities – recreating residents)
- incidental users from outside the city-region (e.g., business and conference/exhibition tourists and those on family visits – non-recreating visitors)
- incidental users from inside the city-region (e.g., residents going about their daily activities – non-recreating residents).

Such an approach recognizes the significance of attitudes and the use made of the city and services rather than the geographical origin of the visitor as the starting point for analysis. This is a more sophisticated approach to understanding the tourist demand for urban areas. But it does raise a practical problem – that tourists tend to cite one main motive for visiting a city, but in any destination there are likely to be a wider range of motives beyond one principal reason to visit. It is likely that there will a variety of user groups. This multi-use nature of urban visitors advanced by Ashworth and Tunbridge (1990, 2000) was also developed in a geographical context by Getz (1993) in terms of the tourism business district where the attractions of the city, the central business functions and services provided in the city were consumed by three user groups: residents, workers and visitors. This makes it difficult to precisely identify the contribution of the tourist in supporting these services and resources. Yet it is evident that the economic value of such groups can be harnessed when seeking to regenerate areas to create a tourism sector.

Tourism and urban regeneration

In the post-modern city, one of the defining features of tourism is the way in which city authorities and planners have formed partnerships with investors, developers and other stakeholders to realize the development potential of tourism. One of the principal features of this approach to urban areas is the realization that, by forming partnerships, as discussed by Maitland (2002), across public–private sector interest groups, wider benefits can be achieved by turning areas to destinations in their own right such as the European Year of Culture scheme. For example, the urban redevelopment of London Docklands since the 1980s has seen the area marketed as a destination within London's vibrant tourism economy. By adding transport infrastructure (i.e. the Dockland Light Railway and Jubilee Line) and an accommodation base along with attractions, areas deemed to be deprived have seen tourism grow. The link between tourism and regeneration and some of the potential benefits of potential development projects can be seen in Case Study 21.1W which examines the potential impact of hosting the Olympic Games in New York.

The urban tourist experience: Behavioural issues

Any assessment of urban tourist activities, patterns and perceptions of urban locations will be influenced by the supply of services, attractions and facilities in each location. In an urban context, we need to try and understand how the urban visitor consumes the services and resources produced for their visit and experience. One useful framework developed in the Netherlands by Jansen-Verbeke (1986) to accommodate the analysis of what the tourist consumes and what is produced for their visit is that of the '**leisure product**' (Figure 21.2). As Figure 21.2 shows, the facilities in an urban environment can be divided into the 'primary elements', 'secondary elements' and 'additional elements'. To distinguish between user groups, Jansen-Verbeke (1986) identified the first and second reasons of 'tourists' and 'recreationalists' for visiting three Dutch towns (Deneter, Kampen and Zwolle). Jansen-Verbeke found that the inner city environment provided a leisure function for various visitors regardless of the prime motivation for visiting. As Jansen-Verbeke (1986: 88–9) suggests: 'On an average day, the proportion of visitors coming from beyond the city-region [tourists] is about one-third of all visitors. A distinction that needs to be made between week days, market days and Sundays'. Among the different user groups, tourists tended to stay longer, with a strong correlation with 'taking a day out' sightseeing and visiting a museum' as the main motivation to visit. Nevertheless, leisure shopping was also a major 'pull factor' for recreationalists and tourists, though it is of greater significance for the recreationalists. Using a scaling technique, Jansen-Verbeke (1986) asked visitors to evaluate how important different elements of the leisure product were to their visit. The results indicate that there is not a great degree of difference between tourists' and recreationalists' rating of elements and characteristics of the city's leisure product. While recreationalists attach more importance to shopping facilities than events and museums, the historical characteristics of the environment and decorative elements combine with other elements such as markets, restaurants, markets and the compact nature of the inner city to attract visitors. Thus, 'the conceptual approach to the system of inner-city tourism is inspired by common features of the inner-city environment, tourists' behaviour and appreciation and promotion activities' (Jansen-Verbeke 1986: 97). Such findings illustrate the value of relating empirical results to a conceptual framework for the analysis of urban tourism and the necessity of replicating similar studies in other urban environments to test the validity of the framework and interpretation of urban tourists' **visitor behaviour**.

Such studies also have a vital role in tourism marketing, when the elements of urban tourism are disaggregated and examined. For example, if one accepts the notion that urban destinations are competing for visitors, then these 'elements' of tourism can help to understand how consumers generate an image of the urban destination and choose to visit/not visit. The image is also influential in the intention to revisit, if the initial visit was able to meet the visitor's expectations.

Tourist perception and cognition of the urban environment

How individual tourists interact and acquire information about the urban environment remains a relatively poorly researched area in tourism studies, particularly in relation to towns and cities. This area of research is traditionally seen as the forte of social psychologists with an interest in tourism, though much of the research by social psychologists has focused on motivation (e.g. Guy and Curtis 1986, on the development of perceptual maps). Reviews of the social psychology of tourism indicate that there has been a paucity of studies of tourists' behaviour and their adaptation to new environments they visit. This is somewhat surprising since 'tourists are people who temporarily visit areas less familiar to them than their home area' (Walmesley and Jenkins 1992: 269). Therefore, one needs to consider a number of fundamental questions related to:

- How will the tourists know the areas they visit?
- How do they find their way around unfamiliar environments?
- How do they find their way in unfamiliar environments?
- What type of **mental maps** and images do they develop?

These issues are important in a tourism planning context since the facilities which tourists use and the opportunities they seek will be conditioned by their environmental awareness. This may also affect the commercial operation of attractions and facilities, since a lack of awareness of the urban environment and the attractions within it may mean tourists fail to visit them. Understanding how tourists interact with the environment to create an image of the real world has been the focus of a research in social psychology and behavioural geography (see Walmesley and Lewis 1993: 95–126). Geographers have developed a growing interest in the geographic space perception of all types of individuals (Downs 1970), without explicitly considering tourists in most instances. Behavioural geographers emphasize the need to examine how people store spatial information and 'their choice of different activities and locations within the environment' (Walmesley and Lewis 1993: 95). The process through which individuals perceive the urban environment is shown in Figure 21.4. Whilst this is a simplification, Haynes (1980) notes that no two individuals will have an identical image of the urban environment because the information they receive is subject to mental processing. This is

FIGURE 21.4   How individuals perceive the tourism environment

conditioned by the information signals received through one's senses (e.g. sight, hearing, smell, taste and touch) and this part of the process is known as 'perception'. As our senses may only comprehend a small proportion of the total information received, the human brain sorts the information and relates it to the knowledge, values and attitudes of the individual through the process of **cognition** (Page 1995: 222). The final outcome of the perception and cognition process is the formation of a mental image of a place. These images are an individual's own view of reality, but they are important to the individual and group when making decisions about their experience of a destination, whether to visit again, and their feelings in relation to the tourist experience of place.

As Walmesley and Lewis (1993: 96) suggest:

> the distinction between perception and cognition is, however, a heuristic device (i.e. something which helps one to learn) rather than a fundamental dichotomy because in many senses, the latter subsumes the former and both are mediated by experience, beliefs, values, attitudes, and personality such that, in interacting with their environment, humans only see what they want to see.

Consequently, individual tourists knowledge of the environment is created in their mind as they interact with the unfamiliar environment (or familiar environment on a return visit) they are visiting.

According to Powell (1978: 17–18) an image of the environment comprises ten key features which include:

1 a spatial component accounting for an individual's location in the world
2 a personal component relating to the individual to other people and organizations
3 a temporal component concerned with the flow of time
4 a relational component concerned with the individual's picture of the universe as a system of regularities
5 conscious, subconscious, and unconscious elements
6 a blend of certainty and uncertainty
7 a mixture of reality and unreality
8 a public and private component expressing the degree to which an image is shared
9 a value component that orders parts of the image according to whether they are good or bad
10 an affectional component whereby the image is imbued with feeling.

Among geographers, the spatial component to **behavioural research** has attracted most interest, and they derive much of their inspiration from the pioneering research by Lynch (1960). Lynch asked respondents in North American cities to sketch maps of their individual cities and, by simplifying their sketches, derived images of the city. Lynch developed a specific technique to measure people's urban images in which respondents drew a map of the centre of the city from memory, marking on it the streets, parks, buildings, districts and features they considered important. 'Lynch found many common elements in these mental maps that appeared to be of fundamental importance to the way people collect information about the city' (Burgess and Hollis 1977: 155) and recent studies of transport have refined this area of research in relation to **cognitive map**s (Golledge and Garling 2004) and mental maps (Weston and Handy 2004). Lynch (1960) found five elements in the resulting maps after simplifying the maps. These were:

1 *paths* which are the channels along which individuals move
2 *edges* which are barriers (e.g. rivers) or lines separating one region from another
3 *districts* which are medium-to-large sections of the city with an identifiable character
4 *nodes* which are the strategic points in a city which the individual can enter and which serve as foci for travel
5 *landmarks* which are points of reference used in navigation and way finding, as shown in Figure 21.5 for Armidale, New South Wales, Australia.

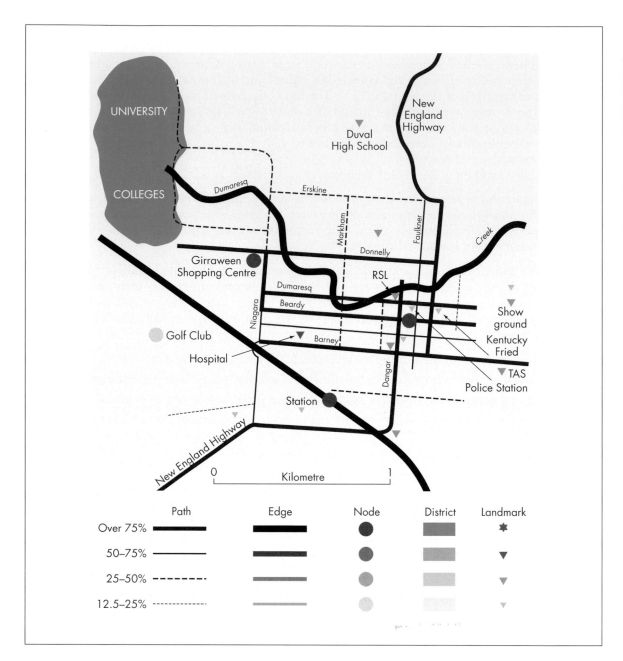

FIGURE 21.5 Lynchean landscape of the city. Source: Walmesley and Lewis (1993), reproduced with permission from Pearson Education

Pearce (1981) reviewed pioneering studies of cognitive maps of tourists, noting that visitors were quick to develop cognitive maps, often by the second day of the visit. The interesting feature of the study is that there is evidence of an environmental learning process at work. Walmesley and Jenkins' (1992: 272) critique of Pearce's findings note that:

- the number of landmarks, paths and districts increased over time
- the number of landmarks identified increased over a period of 2–6 days, while recognition of the number of districts increased from 2 to 3
- the resulting sketch maps were complex with no one element dominating them.

The significance of such research for the tourist and visitor to the urban environment is that the information they collect during a visit will shape their image of the place, influencing their feelings and impressions of it. Furthermore, this imageability of a place is closely related to the:

legibility by which is meant the extent to which parts of the city can be recognized and interpreted by an individual as belonging to a coherent pattern. Thus a legible city would be one where the paths, edges, districts, nodes and landmarks are both clearly identifiable and clearly positioned relative to each other. (Walmesley and Lewis 1993: 98)

But among the most important issues for city managers, tourism businesses and planners, is how the visitor enjoyed their stay, particularly the level of satisfaction they derived. This is becoming a key element in the competitiveness of urban destinations, and this issue can assume an even greater complexity given the development of multi-destination urban trips within and between countries. This allows the visitor to compare and contrast their experience of urban tourism. In the USA, over 31 per cent of the six million inbound trips by European, Asian and Latin American travellers fall into the category of urban tourism (Hwang, Gretzel and Fesenmaier 2002). Whilst such trips provide opportunities for the tourism industry to market products to such visitors, it may highlight why some cities feature prominently as self-standing destinations (e.g. Orlando) while other destinations such as San Diego are always part of a multi-city trip.

Conclusion

Tourism's development in urban areas is not a new phenomenon. But its recognition as a significant activity to study in its own right is only belatedly gaining the recognition it deserves within tourism studies. The reasons why tourists visit urban environments, to consume a bundle of tourism products, continue to be overlooked by the private sector which often neglects the fundamental issue – cities are multifunctional places. Despite the growing interest in urban tourism research, the failure of many large and small cities which promote tourism to understand the reasons why people visit, the links between the various motivations and the deeper reasons why people are attracted to cities all remain fertile areas for theoretically informed and methodologically sound research. The consequences for cities of not understanding urban tourism are significant, given the large-scale public sector investment in regeneration schemes and in building large facilities for events (e.g. conference centres and Olympic sporting venues) which can sometimes require major public subsidies when the markets do not materialize. Furthermore, not understanding urban tourism simply leads to missed business opportunities where common sense issues, such as providing transport to link together the components of attraction system to help visitors navigate and travel around the city, leads to lost spending and unviable attractions. Some cities have addressed this issue well, most notably Melbourne in Australia with its free tourist tram. Many other cities are beginning to recognize the importance of monitoring visitor perceptions and satisfaction and the activity patterns and behaviour of tourists. For the public and private sector planners and managers with an interest, involvement or stake in urban tourism, the main concern continues to be the potential for harnessing the all-year-round appeal of urban tourism activity, despite

the fact that such visitors are often only short stay. Ensuring that such stays are part of a high quality experience, where visitor expectations are realistically met through well-researched, targeted and innovative products, continues to stimulate interest among tour operators and other stakeholders in urban tourism provision.

These concerns should force cities seeking to develop an urban tourism economy to reconsider the feasibility of pursuing a strategy to revitalize the city-region through tourism-led regeneration. All too often both the private and public sectors have moved headlong into economic regeneration strategies for urban areas, seeking a tourism component as a likely back-up for property and commercial redevelopment. The implication is that tourism issues are not given the serious treatment they deserve. Where the visitors' needs and spatial behaviour are poorly understood and neglected in the decision-making process, the planning, development and eventual outcome of the urban tourism environment are affected. Therefore, tourist behaviour, the tourism system and its constituent components need to be evaluated in the context of future growth in urban tourism to understand the visitor as a central component in the visitor experience. Managing the different elements of this experience in a realistic manner is requiring more attention among those towns and cities competing aggressively for visitors, using the quality experience approach as a new-found marketing tool. Future research needs to focus on the behaviour, attitudes and needs of existing and prospective urban tourists to reduce the gap between their expectations and the service delivered. But ensuring that the tourism system within cities can deliver the service and experience marketed through promotional literature in a sensitive and meaningful way is now one of the major challenges for urban tourism managers.

Discussion questions

1 Why is urban tourism important as an economic activity for cities?

2 Why do tourists seek urban tourism experiences?

3 How can tourism be used to aid economic regeneration in cities?

4 To what extent do cities provide a diverse tourism product which can cater for all types of tourists needs?

References

Ashworth, G. (1989) 'Urban tourism: An imbalance in attention', in C.P. Cooper (ed.) *Progress in Tourism, Recreation and Hospitality Management, Vol. 1*. London: Belhaven.

Ashworth, G.J. (1992) 'Is there an urban tourism?' *Tourism Recreation Research*, 17 (2): 3–8.

Ashworth, G.J. and Tunbridge, J.E. (1990) *The Tourist – Historic City*. London: Belhaven.

Ashworth, G.J. and Tunbridge, J.E. (2000) *The Tourist – Historic City: Retrospect and Prospect of Managing the Heritage City*. Oxford: Pergamon.

Burgess, J. and Hollis, G. (1977) 'Personal London' Geographical Magazine, December

Burtenshaw, D., Bateman, M. and Ashworth, G.J. (1991) *The City in West Europe, Second Edition*. Chichester: Wiley.

Clawson, M., Held, R. and Stoddart, C. (1960) *Land for the Future*. Baltimore, MD: Johns Hopkins Press.

Downs, R. (1970) 'Geographic space perception: Past approaches and future prospects', *Progress in Geography*, 2: 65–108.

Getz, D. (1993) 'Planning for tourism business districts', *Annals of Tourism Research*, 20: 583–600.

Glasson, J., Godfrey, K. and Goodey, B. with Absalom, H. and Van der Borg, J. (1995) *Towards Visitor Impact Management: Visitor Impacts, Carrying Capacity and Management Responses in Europe's Historic Towns and Cities*. Aldershot: Ashgate.

Golledge, R. and Garling, T. (2004) 'Cognitive maps and urban travel', in D. Hensher, K. Button, K. Haynes and P. Stopher (eds) *Handbook of Transport Geography and Spatial Systems 5*. Oxford: Elsevier.

Guy, B.S. and Curtis, W.W. (1986) 'Consumer learning or retail environment: A tourism and travel approach', in W. Benoy Joseph (ed.), *Tourism Services Marketing: Advances in Theory and Practice*. American Academy of Marketing Conference, Cleveland University.

Hannigan, J. (1998) *Fantasy City*. London: Routledge.

Haynes, R. (1980) *Geographical Images and Mental Maps*. London: Macmillan.

Hwang, Y., Gretzel, V. and Fesenmaier, D. (2002) 'Multi-city pleasure trip patterns: An analysis of international travellers to the US', in K. Wober (ed.) *City Tourism 2002*. Vienna: Springer Verlag.

Jansen-Verbeke, M. (1986) 'Inner-city tourism: Resources, tourists and promoters', *Annals of Tourism Research*, 13 (1): 79–100.

Law, C. (2002) *Urban Tourism: The Visitor Economy and the Growth of Large Cities, Second Edition*. London: Continuum.

Lynch, K. (1960), *The Image of the City*. Cambridge, MA: MIT Press.

Maitland, R. (2002) 'Partnership and collaboration in destination management: The case of Cambridge, UK', in K. Wober (ed.) *City Tourism 2002*. Vienna: Springer Verlag.

Meethan, K. (1996) 'Consumed in the civilised city', *Annals of Tourism Research*, 32 (2): 322–40.

Montanari, A. and Muscara, C. (1995) 'Evaluating tourist flows in historic cities: The case of Venice', *Tijdschrift Voor Economische en Sociale Geografice*, 86 (1): 86–7.

Mosta, F. (2004) *Venice: The Dramatic History of the World's Most Beautiful City*. London: BBC Books.

Mullins, P. (1991) 'Tourism urbanization', *International Journal of Urban and Regional Research*, 15: 326–43.

Page, S.J. (1995) *Urban Tourism*. London: Routledge.

Page, S.J. and Hall, C.M. (2002) *Managing Urban Tourism*. Harlow: Prentice Hall.

Pearce, D. (1998) 'Tourist districts in Paris: Structure and functions', *Tourism Management*, 19 (1): 49–65.

Pearce, D. (2001) 'An integrative framework for urban tourism', *Annals of Tourism Research*, 28 (4): 926–46.

Pearce, P.L. (1981) 'Route maps: A study of travellers' perceptions of a section of countryside', *Journal of Environmental Psychology*, 1: 141–55.

Powell, J.M. (1978) *Mirrors of the New World: Images and Image-makers in the Settlement Process*. Canberra: Australian National University Press.

Ritzer, D. (1996) *The McDonaldisation of Society, Revised Edition*. Thousand Oaks, CA: Pine Forge.

Roche, M. (1992) 'Mega-events and micro-modernisation: On the sociology of the new urban tourism', *British Journal of Sociology*, 43 (4): 563–600.

Romero, M., Ortuño, M. and Suriñach, J. (2002) 'Demand segmentation in urban tourism: Empirical evidence for the city of Barcelona', in K. Wober (ed.) *City Tourism 2002*. Vienna: Springer Verlag.

Shaw, G. and Williams, A.M. (1994) *Critical Issues in Tourism: A Geographical Perspectives*. Oxford: Blackwell.

Van der Borg, J. (1992) 'Tourism and urban development: The case of Venice, Italy', *Tourism Recreation Research*, 17 (2): 45–56.

Van der Borg, J. (2004) 'Tourism management and carrying capacity in heritage cities and sites', in H. Coccossis and A. Mexa (eds) *The Challenge of Carrying Capacity Assessment*. Basingstoke: Ashgate.

Van der Borg, J., Costa, P. and Gotti, G. (1996) 'Tourism in European heritage cities', *Annals of Tourism Research*, 23 (2): 306–21.

Walmsley, D.J. and Jenkins, J. (1992) 'Tourism cognitive mapping of unfamiliar environments', *Annals of Tourism Research*, 19 (3): 268–86.

Walmsley, D.J. and Lewis, G.J. (1993) *People and Environment: Behavioural Approaches in Human Geography, Second Edition*. London: Longman.

Weston, L. and Handy, S. (2004) 'Mental maps', in D. Hensher, K. Button, K. Haynes and P. Stopher (eds) *Handbook of Transport Geography and Spatial Systems 5*. Oxford: Elsevier.

Further reading

Page, S.J. and Hall, C.M. (2002) *Managing Urban Tourism*. Harlow: Prentice Hall.

22 Rural Tourism

Learning outcomes

After reading this chapter and answering the questions, you should be able to:

- understand the context of rural tourism and the nature of rural areas

- identify the impacts of rural tourism

- understand the need for rural tourism management and issues affecting the future development of tourism in rural areas.

Overview

For many tourists, the countryside is an attractive choice of destination. The relationship between tourism and the environment is particularly marked in rural areas. Rural areas can be sensitive to change through tourism. Changes in the environment, effects on the social fabric and economic well-being require careful monitoring. With this in mind, recognizing the impacts and planning sensitive approaches to rural tourism is a challenge for the twenty-first century. This chapter explores the concept of rural tourism and highlights some of the issues relating to different types of tourism in the countryside setting. Issues associated with the management of rural tourism, including the principles for tourism in the countryside are examined to illustrate how public agencies approach this issue.

Introduction

Rural areas have featured prominently in the development of tourism and leisure and many of the seminal works in rural studies (e.g. Clout 1972; Davidson and Wibberley 1977) recognized and developed these themes as areas for investigation. These early studies noted both the historical evolution of tourism and leisure in these environments and the continuity and changes in tourism and leisure activity which have transformed the rural landscape. In contemporary times, the countryside continues to form an important tourist destination in its own right although the links with urban areas as centres of demand continues to be a powerful force shaping these areas. The appeal of the countryside as a holiday destination is complex, linked to opportunities for a variety of sports and activities, peace and quiet, space, nature and traditional ways of life. It might be argued that the countryside symbolizes a lost 'golden age'; that it contains everything that urban areas lack. Indeed, the countryside is seen as special and deserving of protection across the world, demonstrated, for example, by the designation of National Parks. The relationship between tourism and the environment is particularly close in rural areas, which necessitates sensitive planning and management of both the resource base and tourism activity. Tourism can result in positive and negative impacts on the rural economy, environment and society.

Policy and research directions on rural tourism worldwide tend to focus on one of two emphases. First, many rural areas attract large numbers of tourists, for example National Parks in the USA which receive over 250 million visits a year. The emphasis in these areas is on visitor management. Visitor management is a management focus that aims to balance the protection of the environment with visitor experience and provision of appropriate services. The second type of rural area includes those where tourism is viewed as a mechanism for rejuvenating a declining or stimulating a poor economy and community. Many peripheral regions fit into this category as Hall and Boyd (2005) show, such as Lake Plastiras, central Greece (Koutsouris 1998), and Oberschwaben-Allgau, southern Germany (Oppermann 1997). These areas may not receive many visitors but the potential for organizing tourism services to generate more visitors and create vital income and employment is the motivating force. Keane and Quinn's landmark study (1990) recognized the significance of tourism in rural economic development and the value for local communities.

Simply defined, rural tourism is 'tourism which takes place in the countryside' (Lane 1994). This term, however, is problematic. Before we even begin to think about rural tourism as a concept, the complexity of the terms 'tourism' and 'rural' add further complications. The meaning of tourism has bean dealt with already in Chapter 1 but how should we approach the definition of the term 'rural'?

The nature and scope of rurality

Defining **rurality** has taken much space in geographical and rural sociology texts but there is little consensus on what constitutes the phenomenen termed 'rural' (Robinson 1990; Ilbery 1997). There are three recognizable perspectives on defining rurality:

1 *Anything non-urban.* Glyptis (1991) terms this 'land beyond the urban edge'. This is known as a negative approach to defining rurality as it implies the rural environment has few special features and transfers the onus of definition to urban commentators.

2 *Attempts to outline the elements of the countryside or the functions of rural space.* This is known as a positive perspective as the distinguishing features are identified, such as a low-density population, visual components and forms of settlement and land use.

3 *Perception and/or user-based definitions.* The definitions are based on how individuals experience and define rurality (i.e. what people think it is). The distinction lies in the eye of the beholder. Halfacree (1995) explores the dimensions of rurality and makes the point that what one person sees in a rural area might be seen in a contrasting way by another. For example, we tend to think of the countryside as a relaxing environment, but for those who live and work there, for instance, in farming, the environment is stressful and hard work.

In 1977, Cloke published initial work on indices of rurality. Using 16 indicators, an index of rurality was constructed (see Figure 22.1). From this work, two main types of rural areas were identified. The first is the *remote rural area*, typified by remoteness from urban areas; declining, static or modestly increasing population; an ageing population; declining employment opportunities; low female activity rates and high per capita service provision cost. The second is the *accessible rural area*, defined by relative proximity to urban areas, rapidly increasing population, high levels of commuting, youthful population structure and high levels of car ownership. A key feature of accessible rural areas is relative economic buoyancy, with lower rates of unemployment than remoter rural areas and urban areas and growth in employment opportunities.

Moving from the more geographical approach to rurality, it is worth noting alternative perspectives on the countryside. For instance, Halfacree (1993) identifies four approaches to defining rural areas:

1 *descriptive* – which describes the countryside using empirical data and measures, such as a census of population

2 *sociocultural* – which draws associations between social and spatial attributes, i.e. population density affects behaviour and attitudes

3 *rural as a locality* – whose defining characteristics are what makes areas 'rural' – i.e. their distinctive qualities

4 *rural as a social representation* – how rural is perceived and relates to the social construction of the countryside by individuals and groups.

Finally, Murdoch and Marsden (1994) present an interesting framework for thinking about the contemporary countryside and the possible outcomes as a result of change:

1 *The Preserved Countryside* – accessible rural areas, characterized by anti-development and preservationist attitudes.

2 *The Contested Countryside* – lies outside the main commuter zones. Farmers and developers have dominant interests and push proposals through.

3 *The Paternalistic Countryside* – large estates and tenant farms dominate. Development is controlled by local landowners with a traditional and long-term view.

4 *The Clientelist Countryside* – in remote rural areas where agriculture dominates but is dependent on state subsidy. Policies are geared towards local community and employment.

The concept of the countryside can be defined in many different ways. It is multifaceted, complex and dynamic. Halfacree (1993) states that a single, all-embracing definition of 'rural' is not really feasible. Yet the term 'rural' is an important distinction because behaviour and decision-making are influenced by perceptions of rurality (Halfacree 1995). It appears that there are two main ways of thinking about the definition of rurality. First, as there is no unambiguous way of defining rural areas, there is no point in trying to define it. One might ask whether definitions are significant to those who live and work in rural areas. The distinction between rural and urban is deeply rooted in planning matters; therefore the definition is crucial. With the development of policy and funding for rural development, there is an increasing need to think about the parameters of rural areas.

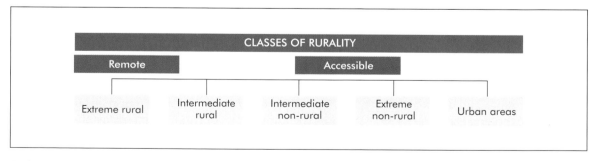

FIGURE 22.1   Index of rurality

Conceptualizing rural tourism

While rural areas are dynamic environments and change is implicit, more radical change has been witnessed in the post-war period than any other time before, relating to social, environmental, political, economic and technological elements of the countryside. Changes in agricultural practice and policy (intensification and modernization) through time, particularly since the end of the Second World War, have created unemployment, falling agricultural incomes and economic marginalization of smaller farms. Jenkins, Hall and Troughton (1998: 50) term the changes in agriculture as 'industrialization' and state that in many countries and regions, farm numbers have been dramatically reduced and, of those remaining, a minority contribute the majority of farm production (in both volume and value terms). With a lack of employment opportunities, out-migration to urban areas in search of work has occurred. Lower numbers of rural residents and the subsequent reduced demand for services has partly resulted in their withdrawal. A decline in rural services has been particularly marked in rural England. The Rural Development Commission (1994) illustrates the level of service provision in rural parishes (Table 22.1). The situation is generally more marked in remoter areas.

In some areas, there has been a repopulation of the countryside. This is as a result of a reverse migration trend of urban dwellers moving to the countryside, particularly in the accessible rural areas. In some areas, tourism and recreation have spearheaded this change, as second home owners, retirees and countryside converts move to rural residences. The issue of second homes in the countryside has caused much debate, particularly in Finland and Canada, where a large majority of rural, lakeside and coastal homes are purchased for weekend and holiday use only. These part-time dwellers may exacerbate the problem of service provision, as the permanence of the community declines. Having explored the context of rural areas, it is evident that rural tourism and recreation have evolved partly due to an increase in supply of opportunities created by the need for a more diverse rural economy. This process is broadly summarized in Figure 22.2, which conceptualizes the problems of rural areas. Generally, this typifies the trans-European position but has wider applicability across the globe.

It is clear that it is not an easy task to accurately define 'rural tourism'. It is often described as a form of tourism that takes place in the countryside but this is ambiguous and on further reflection points to a broad variation of types of countryside and activities. A further complication is in trying to separate what is meant by rural tourism as opposed to countryside leisure. Curry (1994) clarifies this by expressing the components of countryside leisure in seven categories of which rural tourism is just one part. The danger of this is thinking purely about rural tourism in terms of overnight stays. It is essential to consider the activities which tourists engage in during their stay to generate a more complete analysis. Bramwell (1994) questions whether the special characteristics of rural areas shape the pattern of tourism, creating a specific form of 'rural' tourism. In addition, the commodification of rural space which has taken place in recent years intimates rural

TABLE 22.1 Rural services in 1994 and 2000

Rural service	% of parishes without the service in 1994 (2000 in brackets)
Village hall/community centre	29
Permanent shop	41 (43)
Post Office	43 (46)
Primary school	52 (48)
Daily bus service	71
General practitioner	83
Bank/building society	94
Day care for elderly	92

Source: Adapted from Rural Development Commission (1994); Countryside Agency (2000)

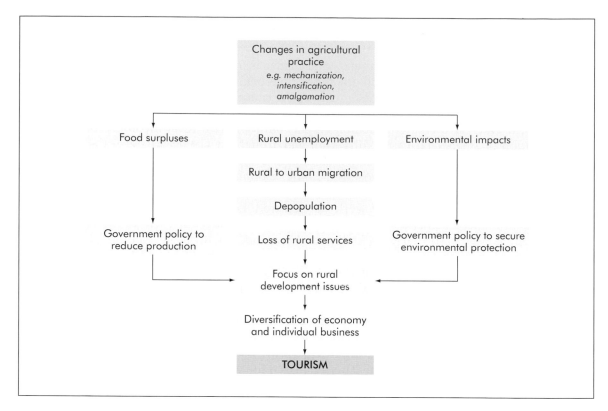

FIGURE 22.2   The context of rural tourism

tourism has moved into a new era, away from more simple forms of farm-based tourism to a more commercial use of the countryside (Cloke 1992). Some studies such as Fleischer and Tchetchik (2005) argue that we no longer need working farms to develop **farm tourism**, as it is the setting which is important. Commercialization and formalization of countryside experiences is evident in the range of tourist products available in rural areas. In Malaysia, the development of what Turner, Davies and Ahmad (1996) call rural awareness tourism is apparent. An 'agro-forestry park' was opened in 1988 in Selangor State which is now one of Malaysia's top attractions. The initiative provides the visitor with experiences linked with agricultural development and recreational opportunities, for example an area set aside for padi cultivation, with 12 sections illustrating the range of cultivation practices used through time that can be seen from a boardwalk. There is also an animal park, several areas specializing in horticulture, a four seasons temperate house based on the climate of New Zealand, nature trails and fishing lakes. This contrasts with the form of tourism associated with wilderness areas, where the will of the individual to experience what he/she wants guides the visit. It is clear that rural tourism can vary greatly in what it purports to be. It can range from the very informal to the greatly organized product, which can represented by constructing a spectrum of rural tourism activity and experience (see Figure 22.3). So, what are the parameters of rural tourism?

Lane (1994) outlines the special features of rural tourism. These features assist in distinguishing a more specific form of rural tourism. First, it is located in rural areas. Second, it is functionally rural; that is, based on small-scale and traditional activities and enterprises, environmental aspects and heritage. Third, it is rural in scale, relating to small-scale buildings and settlements. Fourth, it relies on the traditional qualities of the countryside and develops slowly under the control of local people. Last, it is non-uniform; that is, it reflects the complexity of the rural environment and has several forms.

The characteristics of the rural tourism experience that create special appeal and explain why people enjoy the countryside are:

- remoteness and solitude
- peace and quiet, relaxing environment

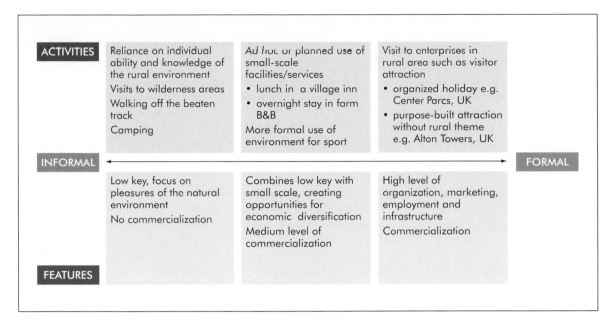

ACTIVITIES	Reliance on individual ability and knowledge of the rural environment Visits to wilderness areas Walking off the beaten track Camping	Ad hoc or planned use of small-scale facilities/services • lunch in a village inn • overnight stay in farm B&B More formal use of environment for sport	Visit to enterprises in rural area such as visitor attraction • organized holiday e.g. Center Parcs, UK • purpose-built attraction without rural theme e.g. Alton Towers, UK
INFORMAL	←	→	FORMAL
FEATURES	Low key, focus on pleasures of the natural environment No commercialization	Combines low key with small scale, creating opportunities for economic diversification Medium level of commercialization	High level of organization, marketing, employment and infrastructure Commercialization

FIGURE 22.3 The rural tourism spectrum

- adventure and challenge, opportunity to pursue sport or hobby
- health and fitness concerns, fresh air
- wildlife and landscapes, interests in the environment
- experience of rural communities, culture and lifestyles
- pleasant backcloth for being with friends and family
- a change from everyday urban life
- take part in rural activities such as conservation work
- explore historic identities, interests in heritage. (after Page and Getz 1997; Countryside Commission 1992).

Hall and Jenkins (1998: 28) suggest that the expansion of tourist flows in rural areas is designed to achieve one or more of the following goals:

- to sustain and create local incomes, employment and growth (Image 22.1)
- to contribute to the costs of providing economic and social infrastructure
- to encourage the development of other industrial sectors
- to contribute to local resident amenities and services
- to contribute to the conservation of environmental and cultural resources.

Sharpley and Sharpley (1997: 20) provide a neat overview of the meaning of rural tourism: 'rural tourism' may be defined both conceptually, as a state of mind, and technically, according to activities, destinations and other measurable, tangible characteristics'. Overall, Sharpley and Sharpley believe rural tourism to be an economic activity which both depends on and exploits the countryside.

Image 22.1: Visitor attractions, such as this thermal park with geysers and mud pools in Orakei Korako Geserland, Rotorua, New Zealand is located in a rural environment which provides an idyllic setting for visitors and an unusual and memorable experience based on the natural environment. Source © S.J. Page

The growth of rural tourism

According to Sharpley and Sharpley (1997), rural tourism emerged as an identifiable activity in Europe during the latter half of the eighteenth century, although it can be traced back through history. Wild, mountainous regions such as the Canadian Rockies, the Swiss Alps and the English Lake District began to attract aristocrats initially, then middle-class tourists. Thomas Cook directed the first package tour to rural Switzerland in 1863 which marked the beginning of a rapid growth in the industry in this area based on health and mountain sports. For the working classes, the countryside was viewed as a workplace until the time of industrialization and urbanization in the nineteenth century – therefore, class distinctions can be identified in the temporally uneven demand for rural tourism. Despite previous developments, it was not until the twentieth century that rural tourism became a more widely enjoyed activity when evidence demonstrates a rapid growth in demand for and supply of rural activities. As Chapter 2 observed, new forms of technology and state promotion of tourism such as in California led to the development of rural tourism. As Figure 22.4 shows, in the 1870s companies such as Thomas Cook and the Boston-based company Raymond and Whitcomb had begun tours, and rural hinterlands such as Yosemite and other inland areas were accessed by a combination of rail and stagecoach.

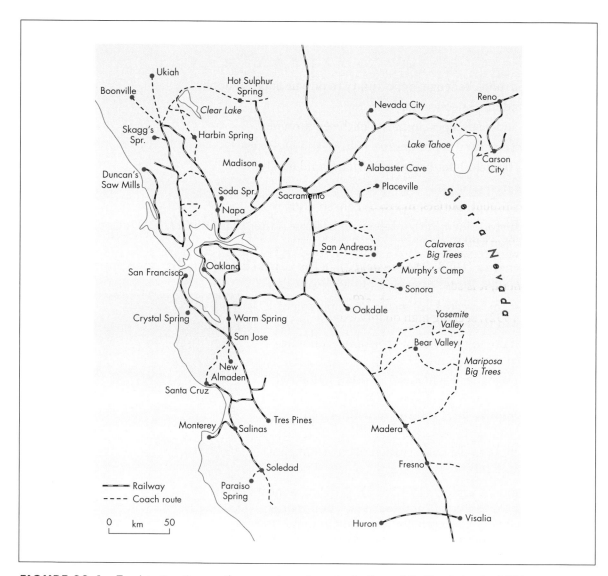

FIGURE 22.4 Tourist attractions, railways and coach routes in Central California by the 1870s.
Source: *An Historical Geography of Recreation and Tourism in the Western World 1540–1940*, Towner, copyright (1996) John Wiley and Sons. This material is used by permission of John Wiley and Sons Ltd

Walking and cycling became increasingly popular during the inter-war years in England, especially in the Pennine hills close to the major industrial centres of the north. Declining prosperity meant that there was a demand for inexpensive pursuits and membership of outdoor pursuit organizations, such as the Cyclists Touring Club and the Youth Hostel Association. Elsewhere, increases in rural tourism participation increased along with urban migration and a desire to return to the countryside for holidays, particularly in parts of southern and northern Europe. Since the 1950s, rural leisure generally has been subject to increased participation along with the growth in other forms of tourism. Improved mobility (Image 22.2) and increased disposable income and free time, along with an increase in supply of opportunities, have partially explained some of this increase. Other factors include a rise in environmental concern and the need to be close to nature from time to time to balance the needs of urban societies ('urban' here should be viewed in locational and psychological terms). There are also links to societal change in the form of post-modernism which rejects modernity and reflects positively on traditional ways of life.

In some European countries, especially in southern Europe, the traditional perspective on tourism in rural areas is that rural holidays are a cheap alternative to resort holidays. For example, rural tourism in Portugal has been traditionally associated with staying on farms with the farming family. In other areas, such as Germany and Austria, rural tourism has always been linked with the more affluent. There is evidence that the traditional perspective of rural holidays as a poor relation to other forms of tourism is waning. This was reinforced by Perales (2002) in Spain where a new modern domestic rural tourist aged 25–44 years of age has developed an interest in consuming the rural environment. This confirmed the higher levels of education and affluence of these new groups of middle classes, based in urban areas, as Cánoves *et al.* (2004) also noted in Spain. They traced the evolution of farm-based tourism as an inexpensive option for the domestic population in the 1960s to a more commodified product in the 1990s for these new rural tourism consumers. Cánoves *et al.* (2004) noted that this was reflected in the growth of supply of farm-based accommodation in Spain from 1074 units in 1994 to 4987 in 2001 and 6534 in 2003. Even so, this still only accounts for 1.6 per cent of farms operating in this market, which is influenced by the urban demand from Madrid and Barcelona reflected in the geographical concentration in the regions of Castilla-León, Catalonia and Aragón. In Portugal, for example, the Alto Minho region in the far west of the country is being promoted as a rural tourism destination based on sustainable principles and is attractive to educated and affluent tourists. In France, a wide range of rural tourism products are available, such as the famous **Gîtes** and *chambres d'hote*. The rural tourism product and experience has been developed and promoted on a global scale throughout the 1990s. Much of this development has become synonymous with ecotourism or specialist interest tourism that takes place in a rural environment. However, there is an inherent danger in assuming that, because rural tourism relies on the countryside environment, it is somehow more environmentally friendly than resort-based tourism.

Rural tourists tend to be more affluent and better-educated tourists (see Countryside Commission 1992), seeking high quality experiences and products. However, the range of products that comprise rural tourism and the associated range of experiences are far too great to generalize. Page and Getz (1997: 17) state that identification and segmentation of the market is not well researched. Looking at an overall picture of one country, the Great Britain 2002–2003 Day Visits Survey indicates that 24 per cent of all leisure trips are taken in the countryside, which equates to almost 1.3 billion visits per year. Since the 1980s, there has been a levelling off in growth but an increase in the diversity of activities and types of rural tourism. Active sports participation is increasing. New activities such as snow sports, mountain biking, climbing, air and water sports are witnessing large gains in popularity, a theme developed in Chapter 4 and returned to again in Chapter 26. New technology has assisted this, by bringing cheaper yet effective materials and equipment to a larger audience. Other trends such as health promotion, the appeal of the great outdoor life, interest in the environment and increased marketing of activities all partly explain this increase.

Image 22.2: Major natural visitor attractions such as this 51m high 1000 year old kauri tree in northern New Zealand (Tane Mahuta, 'Lord of the Forest') have a spiritual meaning for the indigenous population (Maori) but excessive visitation in a rural location has led to the extreme measure of introducing man-made visitor management tools to protect the tree and its environment through the use of a boardwalk.
Source © S.J. Page

Impacts of rural tourism

The aim of tourism development in rural areas is, in general terms, to provide opportunities for economic and social development. In some areas, tourism provides the main source of income and employment, as well as providing social and environmental benefits. Inevitably, negative aspects of rural tourism development are evident also. There is a substantial literature on the impacts of tourism in rural areas (PA Cambridge Economic Consultants 1987; Gannon 1994; Healy 1994). Much of the early tourism impact research focuses on rural areas, arguably because the relationship between tourism and the environment in the countryside is more pronounced. The positive and negative impacts of rural tourism are summarised in Table 22.2.

In England, the Rural Development Commission carried out research on a sample of English rural settlements to evaluate the impact of tourism (Rural Development Commission 1996). The research found that tourism results in several benefits, the magnitude of which vary according to settlement/community characteristics and the nature and scale of tourism activity. The benefits in general are that tourism:

- increases the range and viability of local businesses (food and non-food shops, hotels, pubs and cafés, garages, indirect spending to other non-tourist businesses)
- contributes to social and community life (encourages new businesses, provides employment, supports fund-raising and community events, makes a greater choice of recreational opportunities available to local people)
- helps to maintain or improve services (health services, entertainment, banks, public transport)
- brings about environmental and/or infrastructural improvements (pride generated, revenue pays for environmental improvements, larger car parks, interpretation, enhanced visual amenity).

Several negative impacts were reported. Rising house prices, traffic congestion, parking problems, disturbance and litter were the most common aspects reported. The success of rural tourism

TABLE 22.2 A summary of the positive and negative impacts of rural tourism

Impact	Positive	Negative
Economic	Assists viability of existing tourism and non-tourism businesses Creates new employment Attracts inward investment Encourages pluriactivity, helping to stabilize economic base	Encourages dependence on industry prone to uncontrollable change Creates part-time, seasonal or low-grade employment Incurs development costs and public service costs Leads to local land and house price inflation
Sociocultural	Assists in viability of local services Creates sense of pride Revitalizes local cultural traditions, events and crafts Leads to opportunities for social and cultural exchange	Creates feeling of invasion by tourists; overcrowding and traffic Increases crime Reduction in local services, e.g. food shops replaced by gift shops Import of new cultural ideas –challenges existing way of life
Environmental	Leads to environmental improvements in settlements Provides income for conservation of buildings and natural environment Fosters awareness of conservation as worthwhile activity	Increases wear and tear on landscape features Creates need for new developments which may not be in keeping with local area Increases pollution (noise, visual, air, water, litter) Affects local biodiversity

depends on maintaining a balance between the needs of a working, living community and an intrinsically valuable environment. It is with this in mind that a more sustainable approach to rural tourism has been advocated.

Sustainable rural tourism

One of the inherent dangers in thinking about rural tourism is to make it synonymous with sustainable tourism. As Clarke (1998: 130) states, 'they are not, decisively *not*, one and the same'. Lane (1994) outlines why a sustainable approach to rural tourism is required. Visitors to the countryside are increasingly mobile and are able to penetrate more remote areas than just a few years ago. Advances in modes of transport have assisted this coupled with the increasingly sophisticated marketing of new destinations. An unknown footpath can become an overused one almost overnight as a result of an editorial in a special-interest publication or promotional literature. A threat from badly managed tourism is posed. Rural tourism may be managed by outsiders who have little understanding of the people, culture and heritage of that area. Undermanagement of environmental resources could lead to their ultimate degradation. Tension between conservation and rural development interests commonly exist. While one realizes there is a need to stimulate some rural economies, reliance on tourism may lead to an unbalanced economy. A sustainable approach takes a more holistic perspective towards rural development. Page and Getz (1997) state that rurality and all of its components must be preserved and nurtured because they are, in essence, the selling point of the countryside and can be used in planning and marketing strategies. Rural tourism ideally should be included as part of an integrated rural development strategy. A sustainable approach to rural tourism should be based on a multifaceted view of sustainability to achieve balanced development. Consideration of the needs of the community, the viability of the economy and the conservation of the environment should receive appropriate consideration.

The planning and management of rural tourism

On an international scale, there are a number of different strategies that can be adopted to manage rural tourism. To some extent, rural tourism is comparable to tourism in any area but there are some distinct features or other aspects exacerbated in rural locations which need to be recognized:

Issues in rural tourism management

- *The lack of statistical base.* It is difficult to establish volume and value of rural tourism as a specific market sector in a nation, and is even harder on an international scale. Many countries have different definitions of 'rural' and will therefore collect different data. Data on rural as a specific form of tourism are not easily obtainable.

- *Rural communities.* These tend to be non-uniform, for example remote versus accessible rural areas contain very different types of settlement, employment opportunities, socio-demographic characteristics. Different community structures will have diverse responses to tourism.

- *Tourism development strategies may not benefit all rural areas.* Where there is an inadequate supply of attractions and/or accommodation, tourism cannot flourish, however good the marketing strategies to attract visitors may be. Likewise, development of tourism provision by local people may not be feasible in a depressed rural economy.

- *Tourism in rural areas is highly dependent on an attractive natural and culturally interesting environment.* This highlights the need to ensure that sustainable approaches to tourism management are adhered to. This may conflict with the desire to attract greater volumes of visitors to the countryside and requires sensitive consideration.

Providers of rural tourism – farm tourism

One of the important issues in rural tourism is that many providers are involved in tourism part-time. For example, the main business of a farm is in managing land, stock, machinery and the land. Running bed and breakfast accommodation may be an ancillary business which provides supplementary income. As the enterprise may not be the main thrust of a business, there may be a lack of skills in managing a tourism business. Many farmers are isolated with a lack of knowledge, expertise and training in tourism and government agencies can advise on these issues. Many farm tourism providers belong to the Farm Holiday Bureau, which assists in marketing, while others choose to use other channels, such as guide books, adverts in tourist information centres or agencies. In France, a centralized system exists, supported by the public sector, to coordinate rural accommodation bookings for over 40 000 gîtes. The Ministry of Agriculture initiated the gîtes scheme, in the 1950s, giving financial assistance to farmers to restore old farm buildings as tourist accommodation. Private sector companies, such as Gites de France, assist in promoting accommodation and travel packages to consumers. Gites de France have been commended for their performance in providing an environmentally responsible product by **Tourism for Tomorrow** Awards sponsored by British Airways.

There appears to be much debate in the literature regarding farm tourism. It is certainly clear that many farms have diversified into providing accommodation. A survey by Evans and Ilbery (1992) indicates about 6000 farm businesses with accommodation in England exist, mainly in the south-west and uplands areas. Both large and small farms have done this, contrary to the opinion that it is only small, less economically viable units which diversify into tourism. Family labour tends to be the main source of assistance in farm tourism enterprises. Successful farm tourism development requires substantive capital input, marketing, reliance on external advice and finance. Farmers face constraints from planning legislation and farm tourism is not necessarily a panacea in terms of solving critical problems of low farm incomes or failing businesses. Jenkins *et al.* (1998) state that the returns for small farms are limited.

Criteria for success in rural tourism

According to a study undertaken by PA Cambridge Economic Consultants (1987), rural tourism can be a significant part of local economic activity. This reiterates many of the findings of the earlier studies of rural environments (e.g. Clout 1972) but in this case, the report by consultants was used for public policy purposes. The economic rationale for rural tourism also assumes a significant role when one consider the extent of resources which a public body such as the Countryside Agency manages (Figure 22.5) and its role as possible shaper and funder of rural tourism initiatives to promote economic development. However, total economic contribution from rural tourism depends on:

- the extent of direct and indirect benefits retained in the area
- the provision of accommodation in the area
- the existence of facilities to support tourism in the area

thereby expanding upon some of the issues raised in Chapter 17 on the economic impacts of tourism.

In individual businesses, criteria for success in rural tourism generally depends on a combination of a number of factors. Briefly, this includes the commitment of the proprietor; the provision of additional facilities, for which visitors are willing to pay a higher price; generating visitor satisfaction and therefore recommendations and repeat visiting; ability to promote off-peak visits, thus reducing the effects of seasonality; understanding the needs and characteristics of customers and potential customers; existence of attractive natural environment and cultural/historic features of interest. Recent discussions of the suitability of branding the rural tourism product has led to various attempts to identify certain products: for example, in UK, the Farm Holiday Bureau, a cooperative, membership-owned body consisting of over 1000 farm accommodation providers market their own products; a similar body exists in New Zealand (the New Zealand Association of Farm Home Holidays). A new project in south west England called Cartwheel, which aims to assist farmers in branding and marketing tourism, has recently been established – the results will

FIGURE 22.5 The countryside designated and defined interests, reproduced with permission from the Countryside Agency

provide evidence of whether or not this is a successful approach. The aim of branding is to help identify rural tourism destinations and communicate the benefits, such as quality (Clarke 1998).

One of the foci of rural tourism strategy in general is to encourage a higher number of overnight stays and day trips. But rural areas need significant visitor spend to support employment. Attractions are particularly well suited to drawing in visitor numbers but accommodation is needed to encourage these visitors to spend more time in that area and subsequently, more money. PA Cambridge Economic Consultants (1987: 63) state: 'The major issue for rural areas is the creation of a critical mass of tourism facilities, both accommodation and attraction projects, which can succeed in making visitors additional to the region.'

Community involvement is an important aspect of rural tourism development. Common patterns indicate that residents need to feel tangible benefits from tourism and a degree of control over development and promotion. In the absence of perceived benefits, opposition is likely to increase (Page and Getz 1997). A 'bottom-up' approach where initiatives stem from the community is likely to lead to much less antagonism from local residents as opposed to a 'top-down' approach where an outside agency imposes a particular policy of tourism development on a community. Many of the sustainable rural tourism projects around the world have been developed in a bottom-up way because there is a recognition that tourism is a way for local people to generate income and employment. For example, the Otago Peninsula Trust (southern New Zealand) is a voluntary organization which has taken a lead in establishing many facilities which are for the benefit of locals, the environment and visitors. So rather than a tool of blatant commercialism, this approach recognizes the wider developmental role which tourism can play. Such a balanced approach can be seen to characterize the work of government agencies such as the Countryside Agency; this organization seeks to add value to rural tourism while meeting statutory obligations for planning, management and the wider public interest as shown in its range of current research and initiatives it supports on tourism (Table 22.3).

Management issues

Visitor management, discussed in more detail in Chapter 20, is a key part of managing tourism in rural areas. National government may provide the overall policy framework for tourism development as Insight 22.1 on Namibia shows.

At regional and local levels, more precisely defined policies for visitor management can be identified. In England, the Countryside Commission (1995) has developed a wide range of different projects aimed at achieving sustainable rural tourism utilising various visitor management practices. Many rural tourism initiatives have arisen through organizations and groups working in collaboration, mainly public and private sector partnerships. Visitor management may be aimed at encouraging certain types of desirable behaviour or limiting undesired behaviour. **Demarketing**, a policy of discouraging visitors, might well be part of the strategy. The Quantock hills in Somerset, UK, are not promoted by South West Tourism (the regional tourist board) to help protect the area from further visits. Principles for tourism in rural areas also assist in the translation of policy to practice. The Countryside Commission, English Tourist Board and Rural Development Commission published guidelines in 1989, displayed in Table 22.4. As rural tourism is in a constant state of flux, new research agendas are developing to which attention now turns.

TABLE 22.3 Focus of the Countryside Agency research activity in rural tourism

- Links between rural tourism and countryside capital research study
- *Working for the Countryside: A Strategy for Rural Tourism in England 2001–2005* in partnership with VisitBritain
- Development of a computer model, 'Leaky Luggage Model' to track local visitor spending and to identify ways of reducing economic leakage
- *Tourism and Market Towns Guide* to show the importance of tourism in these settings and to identify ways to enhance visitor spending through improved research
- *Integrated Quality Management* trialled by Exmoor National Park to improve the quality of the visitor experience
- Green Audit Kit as a self-help tool for small businesses to identify environmental improvements and their value to adding value to the tourism product and business performance

Source: Adapted from the Countryside Agency, www.countryside.gov.uk, accessed 10 March 2005

Rural tourism in Namibia

Namibia, a large country in south west Africa with a population of 1.8 million, is a country of unspoilt landscapes and significant populations of wildlife, from the Big Five to unusual insects and plantlife and is among the world's driest countries. The world's largest cheetah population lives here. Some 15 per cent of the country is covered by National Park designations. Since the country gained independence in 1990, tourism has been viewed as an important source of economic support. Tourism is the country's third most important industry and foreign exchange earner, after mining and fishing. Between 1993 and 1997, tourist numbers increased by 18 per cent to 500 000. In 2002, numbers had slipped to 430 000 which dropped further in 2003 to 300 000. One result has been promotion in key markets (e.g. Germany and the UK) with a campaign in 2005 to target high-spending visitors given that the sector employs 23 000 directly and 32 000 people indirectly. The objectives of Namibia's Development Plan are to revive and sustain national growth; create employment; reduce inequalities in income distribution; and eradicate poverty (Jenkins 2000). The government is committed to developing tourism based on sustainable development which must support the objectives of the Plan. The draft tourism policy was published in January 1999 and subsequently revised for the period 2001–2010 (www.namibweb.com) by the Ministry of the Environment and Tourism. The national mission statement for tourism development is: 'To develop the tourism industry in a sustainable and responsible manner to significantly contribute to the economic development of Namibia and the quality of life of all her people.'

A significant amount of accommodation is available on farms as farmers seek methods of economic diversification. These enterprises are generally working farms, often extensive ranches, and offer the visitor the chance to experience life in rural Namibia. Some offer activities and excursions while others emphasize the opportunity to relax and enjoy what the local area has to offer. Guest farms are viewed as a way of generating economic benefits in harmony with the environment. However, there is some concern that tourism is less labour intensive than ranching, and that jobs are being lost as a result of tourism (Shackley 1993).

Four important guide principles guide the implementation of the tourism policy. These are:

Management of the industry

The future success of Namibia's tourism sector requires appropriate marketing and management at an international level. Government intervention is needed to enhance Namibia's ability to compete in the international tourism market. The government controls about one third of accommodation in the National Parks under its Wildlife Resorts initiative (for example, self-catering camps in Etosha National Park) and is based on low-volume/high-spending tourists. This has been facilitated by the world of NGOs such as the World Wildlife Fund for Nature and the US aid organization, US Aid (www.USaid.org) to bring local economic benefits.

Local participation

The benefits of tourism will be most effectively translated at the local level if there are opportunities for local participation and equity. Local people will be encouraged to take ownership and control of tourism and its management.

Environment

The protection of biodiveristy and the natural resource base is crucial: this includes environment, wildlife and culture. Natural resources must be used in a sustainable way to create employment and income.

Government's role

The government's role in tourism development should be that of a facilitator and not an operator. It should guide and facilitate the direction of tourism and provide an enabling environment for small-scale operators and the informal sector. This will lead to the achievement of sustainable and socially desirable tourism in Namibia. Recent government legislation, designed to actively encourage communities to establish conservancies, gives to communities the right to earn revenue from tourism on communal land. The Himba nomadic people living in Puros, north west Namibia, are a good example of an indigenous community which has developed a wildlife tourism initiative. While retaining their traditional herding practices, the local community has initiated game-monitoring and protected wildlife from poachers, devised guidelines for appropriate tourist behaviour and started a camp site. Local people act as guides, tourists are charged a daily levy which goes directly into the local community and local crafts are sold to tourists. While, almost inevitably, some sociocultural effects have arisen as a result of this initiative, this example demonstrates that local people can create the type of development that suits their needs without destroying the natural resource base.

(Sources: Namibia Ministry of Environment and Tourism 1999; Shackley 1993; Gehrels 1997; Jenkins 2000)

TABLE 22.4 Principles for tourism in the countryside

Enjoyment	The promotion of the tourist's enjoyment of the countryside should be primarily aimed at those activities which draw on the special character of the countryside itself, its beauty, culture, history and wildlife
Development	Tourism development in the countryside should assist the purposes of conservation and recreation, such as bringing new life to redundant buildings, supplementing farm incomes, aiding derelict land reclamation and opening up new access opportunities
Design	The planning, design, siting and management of new tourism developments should be in keeping with the landscape and wherever possible should seek to enhance it
Rural economy	Investment in tourism should support the rural economy, but should seek a wider geographical spread and more off-peak visiting both to avoid congestion and damage to the resource through erosion and over-use, and to spread the economic and other benefits
Conservation	Those who benefit from tourism in the countryside should contribute to the conservation and enhancement of its most valuable asset – the countryside, through political and practical support for conservation and recreation policies and programmes
Marketing	Publicity, information and marketing initiatives of the tourism industry should endeavour to deepen people's understanding of and concern for the countryside leading to fuller appreciation and enjoyment

Contemporary issues in rural tourism

In recent years, one new concept that has come into vogue to seek to understand the holistic nature of rural tourism is that of 'countryside capital', championed by bodies such as the Countryside Agency. The concept identifies the different components of the countryside as different forms of capital including:

- physical capital (the environmental features)
- natural capital (the built environment)
- social capital (the language, culture, people, lifestyles and food).

This highlights how the tourism product of rural areas can be created through the wider process of production (i.e. assembling its constituent parts) so as to show where investment in the different forms of capital will help add value to the tourism experience. This approach is gaining a great deal of credence. An example is the use of farmers' markets and festivals to develop a local differentiation of the rural experience, thereby adding value to the tourism sector but also indirectly to local food producers and the wider image of the area through the use of locally sourced products. A key element here is understanding the tourism supply chain in rural areas and the wider interdependencies which exist, which a crisis such as foot and mouth abundantly highlighted, where the countryside capital is intertwined and interrelated to such an extent that a negative impact in one area can devastate its entire supply of rural tourism. Conversely, the countryside may be a potential beneficiary in other crises. If the potential flu pandemic affects countries worldwide and urban-based attractions and gatherings are not permitted so that the spread and contagion rates can be managed, the countryside, with its high degree of open space, dispersed resources and environments capable of absorbing visitors without allowing close contact and proximity, may see a temporary growth in demand (Page, Walker and Connell 2005). Recognizing these many interdependencies is a growing area of research interest as Table 22.3 earlier showed where the example of research on rural market towns by The Countryside Agency highlighted the need to understand many of these fundamental links and how crises and changes in demand and consumer tastes may impact upon the countryside and service centres such as market towns. Seeking to quantify these relationships and impacts, allows us to see the value of tourism and leisure to rural societies and economies.

Conclusion: The Future Development of Rural Tourism

It is clear that rural areas are an integral part of the modern tourism experience. However, rural areas need to be understood to ensure that appropriate forms of tourism are developed which assist in achieving the goals for national, regional and/or local rural development objectives. There is an inherent responsibility to appreciate long-term effects of tourism in rural areas, recognizing both the benefits and costs related to development. The relationship between tourism and the environment is particularly strong in rural areas. There is also an imperative to understand to what extent tourism achieves the desired economic effects in rural areas and the criteria for successful business strategy needs careful examination. Butler and Clark (1992) recognize that tourism is not necessarily the key to rural development, highlighting concerns about income leakage, multipliers, local labour, wages, limited number of entrepreneurs. 'The least favoured circumstance in which to promote tourism is when the rural economy is already weak, since tourism will create highly unbalanced income and employment distributions' (Butler and Clark 1992: 175). The final point must be to emphasize the need to embed tourism within a diverse rural economy to enable stable rural communities to exist.

Discussion questions

1 Explain why 'rural tourism' is a difficult term to define.

2 'The aim of rural tourism is to aid economic development'. Discuss.

3 Discuss the reasons why tourism may have a negative impact on a rural area.

4 Suggest reasons why tourism is more successful in some rural areas than others.

References

Bramwell, B. (1994) 'Rural tourism and sustainable tourism', *Journal of Sustainable Tourism*, 2 (1 and 2): 1–16.

Butler, R. and Clark, G. (1992) 'Tourism in rural areas: Canada and the UK', in I., Bowler, C. Bryant, M. and Nellis (eds) *Contemporary Rural Systems in Transition. Volume 2: Economy and Society*. Wallingford, Oxon: CAB International.

Cánoves, G., Villarno, M., Priestley, G. and Blanco, A. (2004) 'Rural tourism in Spain: An analysis of evolution', *Geoforum*, 35: 755–69.

Clarke, J. (1998) 'Marketing rural tourism: Problems, practice and branding in the context of sustainability', in D. Hall, and L. O'Hanlon (eds) *Rural Tourism Management: Sustainable Options. Conference Proceedings 9–12 September 1998*. Ayr: SAC Auchincruive.

Cloke, P. (1977) 'An index of rurality for England and Wales', *Regional Studies*, 2 (1): 31–46.

Cloke, P. (1992) 'The countryside as commodity: New spaces for rural leisure', in: S. Glyptis (ed.) (1992) *Leisure and the Environment. Essays in Honour of J.A. Patmore*. London: Belhaven.

Clout, H. (1972) *Rural Geography: An Introductory Survey*. Oxford: Pergamon.

Countryside Agency (2000) *Rural Services in 2000*. Cheltenham: Countryside Agency.

Countryside Commission (1992) *Enjoying the Countryside: Policies for People*. Cheltenham: Countryside Commission.

Countryside Commission (1995) *Sustainable Rural Tourism. A Guide to Local Opportunities*. Cheltenham: Countryside Commission.

Curry, N. (1994) *Countryside Recreation: Access and Land Use Planning*. London: E&FN Spon.

Davidson, J. and Wibberley, G. (1977) *Planning and the Rural Environment*, Oxford: Pergamon.

Evans, N.J and Ilbery, B.W. (1992) 'The distribution of farm-based accommodation in England and Wales', *Journal of the Royal Agricultural Society*, 153: 67–80.

Fleischer, A. and Tchetchik, A. (2005) 'Does rural tourism matter? *Tourism Management*, 26 (4): 493–501.

Gannon, A. (1994) 'Rural tourism as a factor in rural community economic development for economies in transition', *Journal of Sustainable Tourism*, 1 (1&2): 51–60.

Gehrels, B. (1997) 'Namibia: Rhetoric or reality?' *In Focus*, 23: 15–16. London: Tourism Concern.

Glyptis, S. (1991) *Countryside Recreation*. Harlow: Longman.

Halfacree, K. (1993) 'Locality and social representation: Space, discourse, and alternative definitions of the rural', *Journal of Rural Studies*, 9 (1): 23–37.

Halfacree, K. (1995) 'Talking about rurality: Social representations of the rural as expressed by residents of six english parishes', *Journal of Rural Studies*, 11 (1): 1–20.

Hall, C.M. and Boyd, S. (eds) (2005) *Nature Based Tourism in Peripheral Areas*. Clevedon: Channel View.

Hall, C.M. and Jenkins, J. (1998) 'The policy dimensions of rural tourism and recreation', in R. Butler, C.M. Hall, and J. Jenkins (eds) *Tourism and Recreation in Rural Areas*. Chichester: John Wiley and Sons.

Healy, R. (1994) 'The common pool problem in tourism landscapes', *Annals of Tourism Research*, 21 (3): 596–611.

Ilbery, B.W. (1997) *The Geography of Rural Change*. Harlow: Longman.

Jenkins, C. (2000) 'The development of tourism in Namibia', in P. Dieke (ed.) *The Political Economy of Tourism in Africa*. New York: Cognizant.

Jenkins, J., Hall, C.M. and Troughton, M. (1998) 'The restructuring of rural economies: Rural tourism and recreation as a government response', in R. Butler, C.M. Hall, and J. Jenkins, (eds) *Tourism and Recreation in Rural Areas*. Chichester: John Wiley and Sons.

Keane, M. and Quinn, J. (1990) *Rural Development and Rural Tourism*. Galway: SSRC, University College.

Koutsouris, A. (1998) 'The quest for a sustainable future: Alternative tourism as the lever of development', in: D. Hall, and L. O'Hanlon (eds) (1998) *Rural Tourism Management: Sustainable Options*. Conference Proceedings 9–12 September 1998, Ayr: Scottish Agricultural College, Auchincruive.

Lane, B. (1994) 'What is rural tourism?' *Journal of Sustainable Tourism*, 2 (1&2): 7–21.

Murdoch, J. and Marsden, T. (1994) *Reconstituting Rurality*. London: University College London Press.

Nambia Ministry of Environment (1999) Draft tourism policy, www.iwwn.com.na/namtour/namtour.html

Oppermann, M. (1997) 'Rural tourism in Germany: Farm and rural tourism operators', in S.J. Page, and D. Getz (1997) *The Business of Rural Tourism. International Perspectives*. London: International Thomson Business Press.

PA Cambridge Economic Consultants (1987) *A Study of Rural Tourism*. London: English Tourist Board and Rural Development Commission.

Page, S.J. and Getz, D. (eds) (1997) *The Business of Rural Tourism. International Perspectives*. London: International Thomson Business Press.

Page, S.J., Walker, L. and Connell, J. (2005) *Avian Flu: A Pandemic Waiting to Happen*. Report for VisitScotland. Stirling: Department of Marketing, University of Stirling, June.

Perales, R. (2002) 'Rural tourism in Spain', *Annals of Tourism Research*, 29 (4): 1101–1110.

Robinson, G.M. (1990) *Conflict and Change in the Countryside*. London: Belhaven.

Rural Development Commission (1994) *Survey of Rural Services*. London: Rural Development Commission.

Rural Development Commission (1996) *The Impact of Tourism on Rural Settlements*. London: Rural Development Commission.

Shackley, M. (1993) 'Guest farms in Namibia: An emerging accommodation sector in Africa's hottest destination', *International Journal of Hospitality Management*, 12 (3): 253–65.

Sharpley, R. (1996) *Tourism and Leisure in the Countryside*. Huntingdon: ELM.

Sharpley, R. and Sharpley, J. (1997) *Rural Tourism. An Introduction*. London: International Thomson Business Press.

Turner, J.C., Davies, W.P. and Ahmad, Z. (1996) 'Challenges for sustainable rural tourism development in Malaysia', conference paper at Sustainable Tourism Conference, University of Central Lancashire, Newton Rigg, Penrith, 17–19 April.

Further reading

Butler, R., Hall, C.M. and Jenkins, J. (1998) *Tourism and Recreation in Rural Areas*. Chichester: John Wiley and Sons.

23

Coastal and Resort Tourism

Learning outcomes

After reading this chapter and answering the questions, you should be able to:

● understand the importance of tourism in coastal areas

● recognize the impacts of coastal and resort tourism

● identify issues relating to the development and management of tourism in coastal areas.

Overview

Coastal areas offer some of the most desirable resources for tourism on the globe. Sun, sand and sea (the 3 Ss) remains one of the most significant types of holiday in the world. However, new forms of coastal and marine recreation are emerging and increasing in popularity. This has broadened the coastal tourism product in recent years beyond resort holidays. While coastal tourism provides an important commercial sector of the tourism industry, tourism-related activities have been seen to cause negative environmental impacts. This chapter considers the importance of coastal areas for tourism, the nature of the coastal environment and the challenges for future management.

Introduction

The relationship between coastal areas and tourism is as old as tourism itself. Early tourists favoured seaside locations and made journeys to fashionable resorts to bathe in sea water to take advantage of its alleged curative powers. This was a major departure in the eighteenth century from a time when the sea and coast were revered as places and even feared. This is illustrated by Lenček and Bosker (1999: xx) who state that 'the beach...historically speaking, [is] a recent phenomenon. In fact, it took hundreds of years for the seashore to be colonised as the pre-eminent site for human recreation'. The coast continues to be one of the most important environments for tourism in contemporary times building on its established heritage. As Hall and Page (2005: 291) observe

> The coastal environment is a magnet for tourists ... although its role in leisure activities has changed in time and space, as coastal destinations have developed, waned, been reimaged and redeveloped in the twentieth century. The coastal environment is a complex system which is utilised by the recreationist for day trips, while juxtaposed to these visits are those made by the domestic and international tourist.

Today, for some regions, **coastal tourism** is the main type of tourism activity and is epitomised by the '3 Ss' – sun, sand and sea. The beaches of the Mediterranean remain the most popular destination for European tourists, accounting for around 30 per cent of all tourist arrivals in Europe, although other regions of the world have highly developed forms of coastal tourism. Arguably, the coast remains the most dominant image of holiday brochures and travel programmes worldwide, epitomized by the romantic images of the South Pacific islands with their golden beaches and palm trees in the background. In the EU alone, there is 90 643km of coastline which is a valuable resource for tourism, with 12 991km in Greece, 11 930 in Sweden and 17 457 in the UK.

Coastal areas are usually defined as those regions influenced by the proximity of the sea. However, other terms are in frequent use which have more specific meanings:

- the 'coastline' refers to the boundary between the land and the sea
- the 'coastal strip' is a narrow piece of land up to 1km which borders the sea
- the 'coastal zone', a term which is often used in a management context, includes land and sea up to a width of 50km – this takes in the coastal area through to the open sea.

Other definitions to consider are 'coastal tourism' and '**marine tourism**'.

- 'coastal tourism' usually refers to the type of tourism which takes place at the seaside – so resorts figure highly here
- 'marine tourism' usually denotes activity that takes place in the water – such as scuba diving, sailing and jet-skiing (Orams 1998).

Tourism at the coast

The coastal zone is of great environmental and economic significance. The meeting of land and sea creates biologically and geologically diverse environments as well as attractive and unique landscapes which may form the basis for tourism. The surface of the earth is made up of 70 per cent ocean. Coastal tourism is growing at a faster rate than most other forms of tourism and this growth presents special management challenges as the EU (2005) coastal zone management report highlights (www.europa.int), where 20 per cent of the coastline is suffering from severe impacts due to erosion. However, coastal areas across the globe face intense pressures, not just from tourism. The Organization for Economic Cooperation and Development (OECD) (1993) cite the main pressures as:

- rapid urbanization and settlement
- pollution

- tourism development
- haphazard development

which led the EU (2005) to highlight the importance of Strategic Environmental Assessment so that coastal issues are considered more fully in planning decisions, given the erosion problems.

Population is often concentrated in coastal areas. At a global scale, coastal zones account for 15 per cent of the earth's surface but contain around 60 per cent of the world's population, and around 86 per cent of such environments are suffering from unsustainable use in Europe. In the USA, the average population density of coastal counties is five times greater than that of non-coastal counties. California has a large network of beaches stretching along 264 miles, shown in Figure 23.1, and serving a resident population of 35 million with an additional visitor population. The top three state beaches in 2003 were Santa Monica (7.8 million visits), Lighthouse Field (7.3 million visits) and Dockweiler (3.8 million visits) which generate US$75.4 million in travel and tourism expenditure for the Californian economy, supporting up to 1 million jobs and generate a further US$4.8 million in tax revenue. In New Zealand, Japan and UK, no-one

FIGURE 23.1   Californian beaches. Source: copyright S.J. Page

lives more than two hours' travelling distance from the sea and 17 million people live within Italy's coastal zone. In Denmark, 70 per cent of the population live in coastal zones, with 51 per cent in Ireland, 44 per cent in Portugal and 50 per cent in Sweden. Coastal populations in retirement resorts are growing disproportionately as the population ages in the **coastal resorts** of the south of England which are popular migration destinations for retirees, a trend being mirrored in many other developed countries. Increasing population usually results in pressure for development for both residential and business uses. Traditionally, tourism has led to development in coastal areas. People who may have spent their annual holidays in a certain resort may choose to retire to that place, creating a need for more housing. More significantly, resort tourism requires infrastructure in order to support the industry and this results in construction of new buildings, placing pressure on green-field sites.

The economic significance of marine-related industry must not be forgotten. Fishing is an important commercial element in many regions, such as Canada and Scandinavia but raises questions of over-exploitation and indirect effects on marine ecology. The main issue raised by inadequate controls over coastal management is the international scale of the problems – pollution is a transnational issue and one country cannot alleviate the problem alone. The European Environment Agency (1998) for instance notes that water quality, fresh water supply, fisheries, tourism, pollution and habitat deterioration transcend political boundaries and require strategic planning, and the EU has been leading initiatives on bathing water quality since 1976. Mismanagement of these issues results in what is known as 'the tragedy of the commons'.

The attraction of the coast

A variety of factors combine to form the attraction of the coast for tourism and recreation. These may be summarized as follows:

- *Natural*: The landscape of cliffs, beaches, open sea, estuaries and the sky
- *Structural*: The townscape, architecture and tourist-related features (piers, promenades, gardens and lighthouses) (see Insight 23.1)
- *Psychological*: The meanings and values attached to the natural and built environments which gives a sense of place.

Visitors to a coastal area or resort will be attracted by the combined elements contributing to the sense of place and the imagery associated with the area. They will be keen to seek out desired experiences from the holiday – which might range from the need to escape urban life (the unspoilt coastline), such as holidays to Bonaire, the Caribbean, to the need to integrate with others in a social setting (the resort), typified by clubbing holidays to San Antonio, Ibiza.

The evolution of coastal tourism

The coast has received much attention in the tourism literature and three excellent surveys of the development of resorts by Towner (1996) and Walton (1983, 2000) are reviewed in Chapter 2. Researchers have studied different facets of coastal tourism including:

- the historical dimension, including sociological analyses by Lenček and Bosker (1999) and the construction of place identities (Andrews and Kearns 2005)
- the evolution of resorts (e.g. Gilbert 1939; Naylon 1967)
- tourist travel to the beach and tourist behaviour at the beach (e.g. Tunstall and Penning-Rowsell 1998)
- the physical and environmental aspects of coastlines as resources to be managed for tourism (e.g. Wong 1998; Jennings 2004)
- models of resort development (e.g. Pigram 1977).

Attractions and the coast: Heritage resources

With the historical development of coastal areas for tourism, a wide range of built facilities and attractions have been developed to cater for tourist needs, such as promenades and piers (see www.piers.co.uk) with Southport in Lancashire developing the first iron pier in the UK in 1861. The same resort also opened its Bathing Rooms in 1871 and the Winter Gardens and Concert Pavilion in 1874, during its Victorian heyday. Many of these features have become icons of the coastal tourism product, where they have been saved from dereliction, destruction and redundancy, since they often have high maintenance costs. This highlights the need for ongoing investment in coastal tourism attractions to retain competitive and to attract visitors. For example, Hastings in the UK has undergone a £6 million regeneration funded by the public sector. Yet the built environment that pre-dates mass tourism development also has a major role to play as an attraction for coastal tourism. For example, the following historic castles in prominent and commanding positions on the UK coastline are an integral part of the tourism attraction system: Bamburgh Castle, Northumberland; Conwy Castle, Wales; Lindisfarne Castle, Northumberland; Tintagel Castle, Cornwall; Dover Castle, Kent; St Michael's Mount, Cornwall. A further element of the built landscape that pre-dates mass coastal tourism around the world and that is proving to be a popular attraction is the lighthouse.

Lighthouses have a long history in coastal locations to protect shipping from dangerous physical features, but their current form as permanent structures with a distinctive architectural style (Image 23.1) date to the eighteenth and nineteenth century, with the influential work of Trinity House. At a global scale, there are still over 8300 worldwide in coastal locations, despite the newer global satellite technology that has reduced their critical role in ship navigation. As Williams (2004) observes, their conservation and conversion to tourism-related uses (e.g. heritage centres, visitor centres, novel accommodation units and working museums) has become a popular coastal attraction worldwide. In the USA around 40 per cent are open to the public, with Cape Orway in Victoria, Australia, overlooking the Bass Straits, receiving over 70 000 visitors a year. In fact lighthouse visiting has a long history dating back to the Victorian period when Trinity House issued guidelines to lighthouse keepers on this function. In the UK, some 12 of the 72 remaining lighthouses are open to the public and steps to retain them as part of our coastal heritage is reflected in the work of bodies such as the World Lighthouse Society, National Trust and Trinity House in the UK. In New South Wales, Australia, lighthouses are used as a key promotional tool in attracting visitors to coastal locations: (www.lighthouses.net.au).

Image 23.1: Lighthouses are not only a relic feature in the coastal landscape but also provide a visitor attraction in their own right

Thus it is clear that this subject has been studied for many years. As Hall and Page (2005: 292) note:

> The beach developed as the activity space for … tourism, with distinct cultural and social forms emerging in relation to fashions, tastes and innovations in resort form. The development of piers, jetties and promenades as formal spaces for organized recreational and tourism activities led to new ways of experiencing the sea. The coastal environment, resort and the beach have been an enduring resource for tourism and recreation since the 1750s in western consciousness, with its meaning, value to society and role in leisure time remaining a significant activity space.

Yet seeking to understand how this evolution has occurred and generated resort development has led several researchers to seek to explain the essential features of coastal resort development.

Coastal resort development

Miossec's model of tourism development (1976 cited in Pearce 1995: 15) illustrates the temporal and spatial growth of a tourist region. Smith (1991, 1992) applied this model to Pattaya in Thailand and developed a tentative beach resort model, where development is observed from no development to full resort development. Figure 23.2 illustrates the model of resort development in time and space.

Aside from these evolutionary models, common structural features may be observed in coastal resorts as indicated by Pearce (1995). The seafront, linear in form, usually consists of the beach, a promenade, a road and a line of beachfront buildings. These buildings tend to incorporate the most expensive and luxurious accommodation and restaurants, as well as some tourism retailing. Behind this first line of buildings can be found, on a graded scale of price, density and height, smaller hotels, guest houses and bed-and-breakfast establishments, which gradually merge with residential and town centre functions. Many of the well-known coastal resorts reflect this simple pattern of development – see Figure 23.3. Additionally, in many English resorts, a classic 'T' pattern of development exists, with the 'T' being formed by the road from the railway station meeting with the promenade, which constitutes the basic structure.

In the Mediterranean, Swarbrooke (1999: 155) argued that Spanish coastal resorts 'symbolize the worst aspects of coastal resort development in tourism'. The reasons for this are broadly:

- inappropriate development, bearing little or no resemblance to local conditions, such as scale, style, materials
- impact on habitats and species, especially dune areas
- water pollution, most markedly sewage pollution of coastal waters
- effects on the local economy (inflation, higher land prices and in-migration of workers) and society (changes in cultural traditions, rapid changes in social composition, employment opportunities limited to lower paid work).

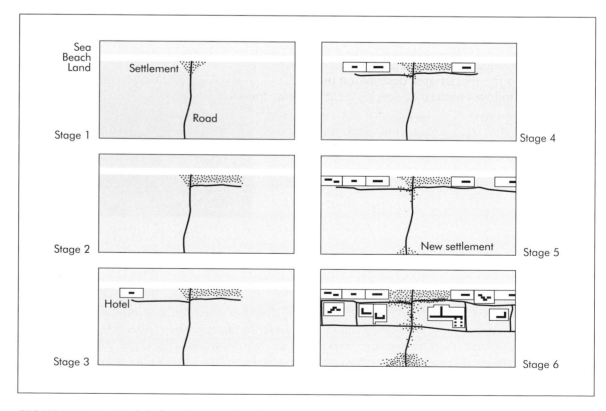

FIGURE 23.2 Model of tourist resort development. Source: Reprinted from *Landscape and Urban Planning*, vol.21, Smith, 'Beach resorts: A model of development evolution', 189–210, copyright (1991), with permisssion from Elsevier

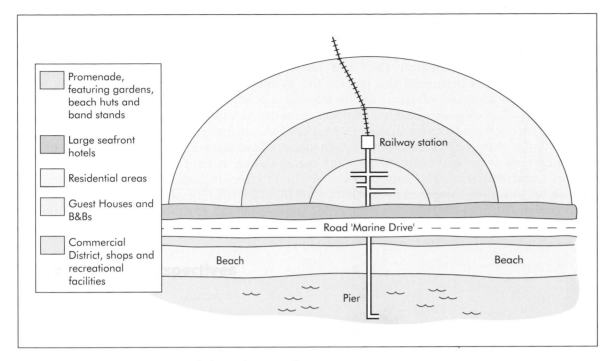

FIGURE 23.3 The basic morphology of a coastal resort. Source: Adapted from Pearce (1995)

Torremolinos is a good example of a large-scale resort which has grown because of the rate of tourism development since the 1950s. From its origins as a small fishing village to the elite resort of the mid-part of the twentieth-century to the mass-market resort of today (Image 23.2) comprising over 50000 bed spaces, Torremolinos has witnessed extensive environmental, economic and sociocultural change. However, Torremolinos, like many other similar resorts on the Costa del Sol, Costa Brava and Costa Blanca, began to lose their tourist appeal due to the deterioration in environmental quality. Less desirable tourists began to visit as prices were reduced. Some tourism development models assist in the explanation of resort growth and decline.

According to the tourist-area destination lifecycle devised originally by Butler (1980), destinations seem to follow a pattern of development. This model is similar to the concept of the product lifecycle used ostensibly in marketing and is illustrated in Chapter 2. The model has gained general acceptance and has proved to be reasonably effective in empirical trials. The model suggests that a newly emerging destination will gradually become known by tourists so initially only a small number will visit. As the destination becomes more well known, tourists will visit in larger numbers and tourism providers will increase their operations – the original tourists are probably less likely to want to return by this point. Eventually, the destination becomes a mass-market resort with the inherent problems of environmental degradation, resulting in some tourists being motivated to find an alternative resort which is less spoiled for their next holiday. This leads to a decline in tourist numbers and affects the level of business in the resort. Strategies to rejuvenate the area may be required at this point to maintain or improve on the required numbers and types of visitors. Many English seaside resorts display

Image 23.2: Resort hotels are able to provide large integrated facilities for tourists

the decline stage of the destination lifecycle, as discussed above in the case of Hastings, where public sector intervention has set about regenerating the resort. Other local authorities, in an attempt to remain competitive and entice visitors to stay, have also launched rejuvenation strategies, for example Bridlington, Rhyl and Torbay. Many of the Mediterranean resorts, like Torremolinos, have experienced this process too, as they were built haphazardly, without planning controls or adequate infrastructure. In Majorca, a policy of demolishing outdated hotels and shabby tourist buildings has enabled the local authority to improve the physical environment of the resort through landscaping. Insight 23.2 explores this in more detail.

Despite the example of Calvià, other commentators have argued that in many mature resorts, redevelopment is generally superficial – for example, new street furniture, landscaping, new facades – and that while this improves the aesthetic value, it does not tackle the underlying problem of sustaining appropriate levels of growth and attracting new markets. Often, resort development is hampered by highly fragmented land ownership, existing infrastructure, utilities, development and traffic congestion. In many cases, a holistic approach to resort regeneration, while desirable, remains expensive and is often impractical.

INSIGHT 23.2

Calvià – an ageing resort with new hope for the future

The municipality of Calvià is one of the largest tourism-receiving areas on the island of Mallorca, accounting for about one third of the total flow of tourists to the Balearic Islands. It is a municipality of 143km^2 with a 60km coastline, 50 000 inhabitants, 120 000 bedspaces and 1.6 million visitors a year (Aguiló, Algere and Sard 2005).

Tourism development in Calvià boomed in the 1960s and has been based on short-term economic gain. As Aguiló et al. (2005) note, it was one of the first municipalities to experience the negative effects of mass tourism. Lack of planning regulations resulted in urban sprawl and lack of environmental regard, similar to many Mediterranean resorts. Water quality, deforestation, alien building styles and the density of development were among the main issues. Towards the end of the 1980s, the effect of this development strategy began to demonstrate negative consequences. The environment was degraded and tourists began to look elsewhere for higher quality resorts. Lower-spending tourists were attracted to the poor quality hotels and bars and a pattern of inappropriate behaviour based on the European 'lager lout' image set in. Calvià City Council, concerned at the problems of managing an 'ageing' tourist destination, proposed a series of policies and actions to assist the sustainable development of tourism in the resort. The strategy was published in 1995 and based on the framework of Local Agenda 21. The mission statement is: 'To develop a philosophy, strategy and programme of actions for the tourism sector based on sustainable development.'

The objectives are as follows:

• to develop a possible framework for the implementation of sustainable tourism policy which could be applied to Mediterranean resorts with similar characteristics

• to identify key subject areas applicable to resorts

• to identify a framework for involving a wide range of bodies including residents in sustainable tourism projects in Calvià.

The long-term aim of the project is to achieve a modern coastal tourism destination offering high quality and a more appropriate bed-space capacity and this was incorporated into the Local Development Planning Regulations. The underlying basis of future development will be based on the principles of sustainability with the environment and local community at the core. Already, much work has been initiated. Sea-water quality is monitored on a weekly basis, obsolete hotels have been demolished reducing bed-space capacity and removing ugly buildings, and a proposed large-scale development has been halted. Environmental management in hotels and other buildings has been encouraged – waste recycling, reduced electricity consumption, purchase of more environmentally sound products. A wide acceptance of the principles of Agenda 21 has been established through broad community consultation and participation. A significant spin-off to the Calvià initiative is the transferability of the concept of environmental management and improvement to similar resorts. Indeed, Aguiló et al. (2005) found that prices of holidays in Calvià were now higher than other areas of the Balearic Islands as it enters a restructuring phase using the principles of sustainability, whilst meeting the needs of visitors and repositioning the destination. Sharing good practice and integrating the principles of Agenda 21 in plans for sustainable development are seen as the way forward for the local authorities in Mediterranean resorts.

Source: www.calvia.com; Aguiló et al. (2005)

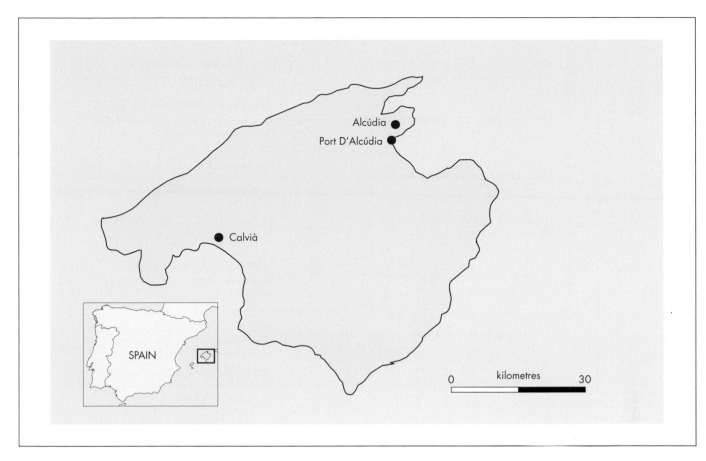

FIGURE 23.4   Location of Calvià, Mallorca

More recent attempts to understand resort developments (Image 23.3) are by Weaver (2000) and Prideaux (2000). Weaver states that after 20 years of debate, it is generally agreed that Butler's model typifies just one sequence of possible events in the evolution of a destination. Weaver proposes a broad context model which includes four types of tourism:

- circumstantial alternative tourism (CAT)
- deliberate alternative tourism (DAT)
- sustainable mass tourism (SMT)
- unsustainable mass tourism (UMT).

Seven possible scenarios are drawn up using the four tourism types. These are illustrated in Figure 23.5.

Butler's model fits the movement from CAT to UMT. The model can be used to categorize the status of tourism at a resort at the current time. Once this is done, it is then the responsibility of resort managers to consider all possible future scenarios. Desirable scenarios can then be pinpointed and worked towards. Weaver applied the model to Australia's Gold Coast, typified by high-density urban resorts, as discussed in Chapter 10. The broad context model categorizes the Gold Coast as UMT. A desired state of SMT must be worked towards with appropriate management strategies.

Image 23.3: Resort development follows a set pattern, as models of development indicate

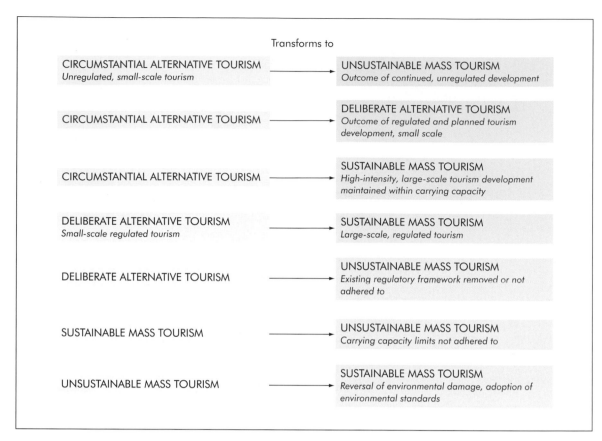

FIGURE 23.5 Scenarios of destination development. Source: Adapted from Weaver (2000)

Prideaux (2000) proposes another new model, termed the **resort development spectrum**. This model identifies five phases of growth:

- Phase 1 – local tourism
- Phase 2 – regional tourism
- Phase 3 – national tourism
- Phase 4 – international tourism
- decline/stagnation/rejuvenation.

Prideaux states that development is not necessarily sequential or that growth is automatic. Another element to the model is the inclusion of market factors. As growth occurs, new market sectors are added, which affects accommodation types, promotion, tourism infrastructure and transport modes. The move from local to international resort reflects a greater professionalisation, higher investment, great diversity of attractions and availability of top quality services.

The impacts of coastal tourism

Conflict between coastal tourism and the natural environment arises in a number of areas and concern has been expressed about the implications of continued growth. Effects may be observed in a social, environmental and economic context. The main environmental issue is that the marine environment is of greater ecological diversity than land environments, with the most biologically significant areas being close to shore – such as coral reefs, estuaries and wetlands. Coral reefs, for example, are said to contain a higher biodiversity than tropical rainforests. With increasing levels of recreational use, coastal impacts are likely to remain a significant issue, especially in view of the potential effects of global warming as discussed in Chapter 19.

Environmental issues

Goodhead and Johnson (1996) cite some of the environmental concerns in relation to nature conservation in the marine environment. The loss of habitat is the main threat and this may arise through short- and long-term disturbance. Developments such as marinas, jetties, promenades and car parks entail loss of coastal land. There is much concern about habitat destruction and disturbance of fauna. In Norway, the building of leisure cabins and the popularity of outdoor pursuits such as boating place pressures on the coastal environment. In Finland, second home lodge developments cause similar concerns and create opportunity costs. Intertidal and coastal land habitats may be affected by recreational activities taking place on the beach. The effects of trampling on sand dunes is, for example, well documented. On the Spanish coast, the disappearance of large stretches of dune system as a result of tourism development has resulted in an unstable coastline (Organization for Economic Co-operation and Development 1993).

In some cases, environmental changes are necessary to sustain tourism. In Florida, demand for development has exceeded land available so additional island waterfront has been created by infilling marshes and building finger-like extensions into the water, as at Boca Ciega Bay. Some of the barrier islands on the eastern coast of the USA are very popular tourism destinations. Barrier islands are long, thin barriers of sand separated from the shoreline by a lagoon or marsh area. Some 2000 miles of coast from New York to Texas contain such islands. Before 1939, 10 per cent of the barrier islands were developed – now a large proportion is covered with resorts, houses, apartments, hotels and other services. By the early 1980s, the development rate of barrier islands took in about 6000 acres per year. This was slowed dramatically by Congress legislation which covered small areas of undeveloped land. Erosion and coastal flooding are severe problems in this environment, often exacerbated by groynes and sea walls in place to protect buildings but with a longer-term deleterious effect on beach stability. Erosion necessitates beach replenishment if developments are to be protected. The value of the tourism industry in most cases justifies spending. Miami Beach is a barrier island 10 miles in length (and containing US$6 billion of real estate), naturally consisting of fine coral, shells and coarse grains of sand. Some US$60 million was spent on replenishing the beach, making a more compact surface – better for tourists and more able to withstand coastal erosion (Ackerman 1997).

Hall and Page (1996) discuss the effects of tourism on the coastal environment of the Pacific Islands. While similar impacts are found to exist elsewhere, impacts in the Pacific are more problematic because tourism is concentrated on or near ecologically and geomorphologically dynamic coastal environment. The main environmental impacts occur as a result of damage to mangroves and coral reefs as shown in Table 23.1, and this is pronounced where resort development occurs as:

Resorts have interfered with the hydrological cycle by changing groundwater patterns, altering stream life, and engaging in excessive groundwater extraction. Coastal reefs, lagoons, anchialine ponds, wastewater marshes, mangroves, have been destroyed by resort construction and by excessive visitations and activities with the consequent loss of marine life and destruction of ecosystems. Beach walking, snorkelling, recreational fishing, boat tours and anchoring have damaged coral reefs and grasses and have disturbed near shore aquatic life ... (Minerbi 1992: 69)

In the case of Fiji, where the construction of a resort complex on Denarau Island was built in drained mangrove swamps, necessitating extensive coastal protection. Effects on coral are widespread. In the Maldives, for example, an airport has been constructed on a re-formed coral island, and coral is damaged by waste water from beachside hotels contaminated by chemicals found in shampoos and bathing products. As environmental impact assessments are not yet required in many less developed countries, there is less control over damaging types of development.

Wildlife issues

Effects on wildlife are notable. Shackley's (1992) study of **manatee**-related tourism in Florida (Image 23.4) is particularly noteworthy. Manatees are appealing to tourists because they are known to interact voluntarily with humans and are often attracted to marinas and harbours for

TABLE 23.1   Environmental and ecological impacts of tourism on the Pacific Islands

Environmental degradation and pollution

- Degradation and pollution of the environment due to golf courses
- Pollution by littering

Destruction of habitats and damage to ecosystems

- Poorly managed tourism may result in the destruction of high quality natural environments
- Unmanaged human interference of specific species of fauna and flora
- Dynamite blasting and overfishing

Loss of coastal and marine resources

- Interference with inland and coastal natural processes excessive groundwater extraction by large resorts induces salt-water intrusion and deterioration of water quality and recharge of the aquifer
- Coastal ecosystem damage and destruction through tourism development
- Terrestrial run-off and dredging on coastal areas damage to coral reef and marine resources caused by the construction of tourist infrastructure such as runways, marinas, harbours, parking areas and roads, and use of coral limestone in hotels and resort developments
- Destruction by tourist activities
- Destruction of coral reefs, lagoons, mangroves, salt-water marshes and wetlands due to excessive visitation and/or unmanaged exploitation of those resources
- Disturbance to near shore aquatic life due to thrill crafts and boat tours
- Introduced exotic species
- Increased sea and air inter-island traffic creates the danger of accidental importation of exotic species, which can be very destructive to indigenous flora and fauna
- Tourism enterprises alter the integrity of the environment and encroach on local lifestyles with imported exotic species for safari hunting
- Damage to sand-cay ecosystems
- Damage to mangrove ecosystems
- Damage to coastal rainforest ecosystems
- Loss of sandy beaches and shoreline erosion
- Loss of sandy beaches due to onshore development and construction of seawalls

Coastal pollution

- Waste water discharge and sewage pollution
- Coastal water pollution and siltation due to near shore resort construction and run-off from resort areas results in the destruction of natural habitat, coral and feeding grounds for fish
- Marine and harbour pollution
- Coastal oil pollution due to motorized vehicles and ships

Surface water and ground water diversion

- Diversion of streams and water sources from local use to resort use, with resulting decline in water availability for domestic and other productive uses and farming, particularly taro cultivation

Source: Hall and Page (1996: 70)

food. Divers have been observed following and touching manatees and boat operators circling around the creatures in the water, both practices exacerbated by the docility of manatees. This occurs despite legal protection and published codes of conduct for visitors wishing to see a manatee. Shackley states that 'anyone who wants to ensure the survival of the species would be well advised to avoid visiting them.' The manatee, like other slow-moving marine mammals, is threatened by the use of personal watercraft. Many are hit each year by jet-skis which can operate in shallow waters, mangrove swamps and estuaries. Manatees are also subject to proportionately high levels of mortality from being struck by boats, particularly in areas where higher speeds are permitted. Birds are driven away by the noise of these machines thus affecting feeding and behaviour patterns. A popular pursuit which has developed recently is that of whale and dolphin watching (see Insight 19.2).

Image 23.4: The Manatee interact with humans but are very vunerable to careless tourist activities such as jet-skiing in shallow waters

Socio-economic issues

In terms of the sociocultural impacts of coastal tourism, many of the issues cited in the earlier chapters on sociocultural and economic impacts apply. A specific example of where there has been a negative effect is when local people in some areas have been prohibited from using the beaches. Some beaches in, for example, Antigua and the Gambia have become preserved for the use of exclusive beach resorts. St Thomas, an island in the Caribbean, originally contained 50 beaches but after tourism resort development, only two were left for public use. However, the economy in coastal areas may be stimulated by tourism, creating employment and encouraging investment. The whale watching boom at Kaikoura on South Island, New Zealand, assisted in the regeneration of a declining area, reducing unemployment and raising average household incomes with the creation of new enterprises in accommodation, catering and retailing and is a good example of how indigenous people have managed to develop a world-class tourism attraction (www.whalewatch.co.nz).

Protection of the coastal environment

The coast has been recognized as an environment which requires protection and sensitive management. As far back as 1972, countries such as the United States created legislation introducing the notion of **coastal zone management**, ideas which were soon adopted in Sweden, Australia and later more widely. This was acknowledged as a central issue at the Earth Summit in 1992 and is reflected in the Oceans Chapter of Agenda 21. Internationally, it has been agreed that coastal nations must 'commit themselves to integrated management and sustainable development of coastal areas and the marine environment...' (EU 2005). The main objectives of coastal zone management are to:

- encourage sustainable use of the environment
- identify and resolve conflicts
- balance economic and environmental objectives
- adopt strategic planning function

and these are reiterated in the EU (2005) Coastal Zone Management Strategy. Many attempts have been made to assist in managing the impacts of tourism on coastal land and in coastal waters. Conservation in coastal areas is often approached through designations. **Marine park**s and nature reserves have been designated on an international scale covering areas as diverse as the Great Barrier Reef, Australia, to Lundy Island, off the coast of north Devon, UK.

Moves to help conserve the coastal areas of Europe have generated the idea of the European Coastal Code, first proposed by the European Union for Coastal Conservation in 1993. The aim of the code is to provide guidance to those who are responsible for coastal management as well as users to ensure ecologically sustainable development. The code, formally adopted in 1995, is integral to the Pan-European Biological and Landscape Diversity Strategy which in turn is part of the European implementation of the Convention on Biological Diversity agreed at the Earth Summit in Rio in 1992. The code is an attempt to bring together other codes, guidelines and action plans to form a practical set of guidelines with the aim of striking a balance between the environment and the economy.

The future of the coast

Herman Melville, author of *Moby Dick* wrote: 'Strange! Nothing will content them but the extremest limit of the land' which indicates that it is highly likely that pleasure-seekers will continue to visit coastal areas in the future and Kay and Alder (1999) highlight that sustainability has emerged as the dominant **paradigm** in coastal planning and management, as reflected in the range of planning manuals now in vogue. This raises three issues:

- *the role of economic factors*: local communities need to earn a living wage and businesses may prioritize financial gain over the environment
- *the role of environmental factors*: the environment is the attraction in many cases, therefore it needs to be conserved
- *the role of social and cultural factors*: local people should be involved in the decision-making.

What is clear is that the market for coastal tourism is increasing, and in the USA around 85 per cent of all tourist-related revenue comes from coastal states. It is arguably the USA's leading destination product, being accessible to the large urban populations, a historical and contemporary feature in USA and many other societies. The coast has a special place in many of the lives of urban populations globally, as a dynamic ecosystem that accommodates a diverse range of uses. The range of products on offer is expanding and has reached far beyond the traditional sun, sea and sand experience. The emergence of marine tourism poses new threats and challenges in diverse environments: whale watching in Africa, Australasia, Iceland; diving in the Seychelles, Borneo, the Red Sea; action sports such as sea-canoeing, yachting and personal watercraft use. As noted in Chapter 10, there are even underwater hotels being built. These activities are increasing in popularity, and, if not managed carefully, will have enormously detrimental effects on the natural environment as the example of Pacific Islands and resort development has indicated. The rejuvenation of resorts illustrates a desire to maintain quality and to adapt to new circumstances, demonstrating a commitment to sustainable ideals. These ideals need to be embraced more fully so that sustainable management of tourism at the coast ensures that future generations can enjoy the same environments as much as the tourists of the past and today.

Discussion questions

1 Explain why coastal tourism is the most popular form of tourism today.
2 Why is a sustainable approach to coastal and resort tourism development desirable?
3 What is coastal zone management and how is it relevant to tourism?
4 Explain the evolution of coastal resorts using relevant theoretical models.

References

Ackerman, J. (1997) 'Islands at the edge', *National Geographic,* 192 (2): 2–31.

Aguiló, E., Algere, J. and Sard, M. (2005) 'The persistence of the sun and sand tourism model', *Tourism Management,* 26 (2): 219–31.

Andrews, G. and Kearns, R. (2005) 'Everyday health histories and the making of place: The case of an English coastal town', *Social Science and Medicine,* 60 (12): 2697–713.

Butler, R.W. (1980) The concept of the tourist area cycle of evolution: Implications for management of resources', *Canadian Geographer,* 24 (1): 5–12.

European Environment Agency (1998) *Europe's Environment: The Second Assessment.* Oxford: Office for Official Publications of the European Communities, Luxembourg, and Elsevier Science.

EU (European Union) (2005) *Coastal Zone Management.* Brussels: EU, www.europa.int, accessed 14.03.05.

Gilbert, E.W. (1939) 'The growth of inland and seaside health resorts in England', *Scottish Geographical Magazine,* 55 (1): 16–35.

Goodhead, T. and Johnson, D. (eds) (1996) *Coastal Recreation Management: The Sustainable Development of Maritime Leisure.* London: Spon.

Hall, C.M. and Page, S.J. (eds) (1996) *Tourism in the Pacific: Issues and Cases.* London: Thomson.

Hall, C.M. and Page, S.J. (2005) *The Geography of Tourism and Recreation, Third Edition.* London: Routledge.

Jennings, S. (2004) 'Coastal tourism and shoreline management', *Annals of Tourism Research,* 31 (4): 899–922.

Kay, R. and Alder, J. (1999) *Coastal Planning and Management.* London: E &FN Spon.

Lenček, L. and Bosker, G. (1999) *The Beach: Paradise on Earth.* London: Pimlico.

Minerbi, L. (1992) *Impacts of Tourism Development in Pacific Islands.* San Francisco: Greenpeace Pacific Campaign.

Naylon, J. (1967) 'Tourism – Spain's most important industry', *Geography,* 52 (1): 23–40.

Orams, M. (1998) *Marine Tourism.* London: Routledge.

Organization for Economic Cooperation and Development (1993) *Coastal Zone Management. Integrated Policies.* Paris: OECD.

Pearce, D. (1995) *Tourism Today. A Geographical Analysis, Second Edition.* Harlow: Longman.

Pigram, J.J. (1977) 'Beach resort morphology', *Habitat International,* 2 (5–6): 525–41.

Prideaux, B. (2000) 'The resort development spectrum – a new approach to modeling resort development', *Tourism Management,* 21(3): 225–40.

Shackley, M. (1992) 'Manatees and tourism in Southern Florida: Opportunity or threat?' *Journal of Environmental Management,* 34 (4): 257–65.

Smith, R.A. (1991) 'Beach resorts: A model of development evolution', *Landscape and Urban Planning,* 21 (3): 189–210.

Smith, R.A. (1992) 'Beach resort evolution. Implications for planning', *Annals of Tourism Research,* 19 (2): 304–22.

Swarbrooke, J. (1999) *Sustainable Tourism Management.* Wallingford, Oxon: CAB International.

Towner, J. (1996) *An Historical Geography of Recreation and Tourism in the Western World 1540–1940.* Chichester: John Wiley and Sons.

Tunstall, S. and Penning-Rowsell, E. (1998) 'The English beach: Experience and values', *Geographical Journal,* 164 (3): 319–32.

Walton, J. (1983) *The English Seaside Resort: A Social History, 1750–1914.* Leicester: Leicester University Press.

Walton, J. (2000) *The British Seaside.* Manchester: Manchester University Press.

Weaver, D.B. (2000) 'A broad context model of destination development scenarios', *Tourism Management,* 21 (3): 217–34.

Williams, P. (2004) *Beacon on the Rock: The Dramatic History of Lighthouses from Ancient Greece to Present Day.* Edinburgh: Birlinn.

Wong, P. (1998) 'Coastal tourism development in Southeast Asia: Relevance and lessons for coastal zone management', *Oceans and Coastal Management,* 38 (2): 89–109.

Further reading

Boissevain, J. and Selwyn, T. (eds) (2004) *Contesting the Foreshore: Tourism, Society and Politics on the Coast.* Amsterdam: Amsterdam University Press.

24

Tourism in the Less Developed World

Learning outcomes

After reading this chapter and answering the questions, you should be able to:

- understand the role of tourism in less developed countries

- outline the problems which less developed countries face in tourism development

- recognize the impacts of tourism in less developed countries

- identify types of tourism which may assist communities in less developed countries.

Overview

For many developing countries, tourism is a favoured choice of economic activity. The lure of generating foreign exchange from a country's natural attractions has led many nations into tourism. Some countries are now well-established providers of tourism such as Turkey, Malaysia and Mexico but other such as Bhutan and Belize are more recent entrants. While most of the world's tourism activity occurs in the developed world, some less developed countries are high-volume tourist destinations with accompanying impacts and effects.

Introduction

Tourism offers an alternative economic activity to primary and secondary industries, especially if there is a lack of development choices for a less developed country. For the tourist, less developed countries offer a taste of the exotic, an opportunity to encounter different cultures and to experience an unspoiled environment. While most tourism movements take place between developed countries, an exploration of global tourism arrivals over time indicates that an increasing number of people are selecting holidays in less developed countries. New destinations are appearing on the world market catering for a range of tourists seeking alternative holiday experiences. At a global scale, around 1:5 international tourist trips are to less developed countries and their climate, culture and environment combine to form a tourism product for the 'new' tourist. Generally speaking, less developed countries are geographically located in central and South America, Africa, South Asia and the South Pacific (Hall 1992) and Figure 24.1 illustrates the range of destinations by volume (where data is available), although other large areas of the world, such as the South Pacific and small islands, also feature prominently in tourism to less developed countries (LDCs). A number of recent and more dated studies examine the nature of tourism in LDCs ranging from texts such as Oppermann and Chon (1997) and Scheyvens (2002) to the more geographically specific, regional studies including:

- Africa (Dieke 2000)
- Latin America (Lumsdon and Swift 2001)
- the Caribbean (Wilkinson 1997; Duval 2004)
- the Pacific Islands (Hall and Page 1996; Harrison 2003)
- South and South East Asia (Hall and Page 2000)
- the Middle East (Kester and Carvao 2004; Mansfeld and Winkler 2004).

Whilst many of these studies examine a wide range of issues associated with tourism in LDCs, much concern has been expressed regarding the impact of tourism on such nations, with the focus on the inequality between the tourist (usually Western) and the host.

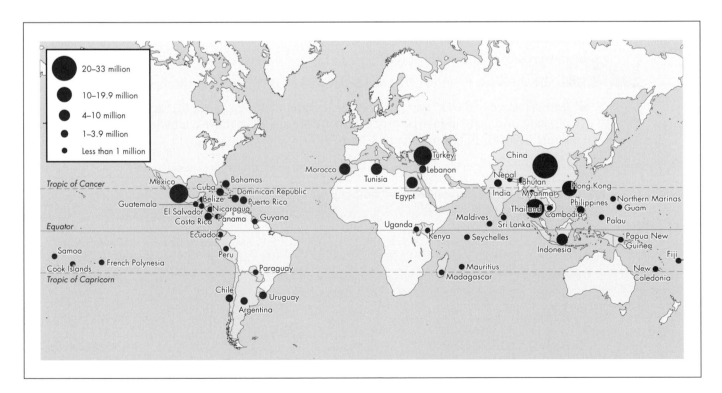

FIGURE 24.1   Tourist arrivals in less developed countries in 2004. Source: Based on WTO data, copyright S.J. Page

The concept of development and the emergence of tourism in less developed countries

Webster (1990) defines 'development' as the replacement of traditional values with modern ones. It is a process of change and aims to achieve improvement. Theories of **modernity** emerged in the 1950s and early 1960s prompted by the decline of the old colonial empires. Later, in the 1970s, thoughts turned towards a theory based on the notion of dependency, which focused on the unbalanced relationship between developed and less developed countries that has evolved in **post-colonial** times (see Hall and Page 2000).

Less developed countries – types and characteristics

Various labels exist to define less LDCs. Up until recently, the First, Second and Third World categories were used widely but following the demise of Communism across eastern Europe and the closing wealth gap between the First and Second Worlds, the differentiation no longer seems appropriate. The 'Fourth World' is a term used to define the least developed countries. Other definitions to consider are the East/West and North/South divides and core/periphery. These labels are used more extensively in contemporary times to distinguish development status. Table 24.1 outlines a range of these descriptions that are commonly used.

Some of the characteristics of LDCs include:

- high birth rates and population pressures
- fast rate of urbanization
- limited economic base
- high unemployment
- low literacy rates
- low levels of industrial production
- high rates of national debt, highlighted by the G8 meeting in Gleneagles, Scotland in 2005 to discuss mechanisms to reduce debt through aid
- dependence upon overseas aid and international finance for development, with a range of donors listed in Table 24.2
- low gross national product (GNP).

There are different types of LDCs and Swarbrooke (1999) outlines these as:

- *least developed countries*: average incomes less than $355 per year, literacy rates of less than 20 per cent and little industrial production. There are 42 of these countries, often termed 'the Fourth World' (Oppermann and Chon 1997)

TABLE 24.1 Terminology commonly used to describe development status

Label[1]	Description	North/South	Development
First World	Westernized countries, with capitalist political and economic structures	North	Developed
Second World	Less wealthy, Communist countries	North	Transitional
Third World	Poor countries	South	Less developed/developing

[1] Used less extensively now, due to changes in eastern bloc countries (Second World) and fall of Iron Curtain.

TABLE 24.2 Selected donor organizations from developed nations assisting LDCs with tourism development

Asian Development Bank
Australian International Development Assistance Bureau
Canadian International Development Agency
Commonwealth Development Corporation
Danish International Development Assistance
European Commission
European Investment Bank
Food and Agricultural Organization
Finnish International Development Agency
Global Environment Facility
Inter-American Development Bank
International Finance Corporation
Irish Aid
Japan International Co-operation
Ministry of Foreign Affairs, New Zealand
Multilateral Investment Fund
Netherlands Development Assistance
Norwegian Agency for Development Corporation
Swedish International Development Agency
United Nations Development Programme
US Agency for International Development
World Bank

- *developing countries*, beyond the level of least developed but still relatively poor and non-industrialized
- *newly industrialized countries* (NICs): these countries share characteristics of both less developed and developed worlds.

It should also be noted that within each category of country, there are disparities in wealth in the population, i.e. there are some very wealthy people and many poor people.

Traditionally, development has been measured in terms of economic measures such as GNP, economic growth rate and employment structure – measures of the economic wealth of a country. As understanding of the development process changed, it was realized that this measure was insufficient to show all aspects of development. The United Nations Development Programme uses the **Human Development Index** (HDI) which integrates welfare and economic aspects to produce a more holistic picture of a nation's status (www.undp.org). The World Bank, however, uses economic measures only and identifies three types of country: low income, middle income and high income.

Tourism development

Agel (1993 cited in Oppermann and Chon 1997) suggests that three stages can be identified in tourism research which typify the changing perspectives on tourism development in LDCs since the late 1950s. The first stage, from the late 1950s to 1970, was the time of great expansion and hope for future economic benefits. Tourism was considered as a tool for economic development and a generator of foreign exchange. The second stage, from 1970 to 1985, is termed by Agel as the 'disenchantment period', when the value of economic benefits was brought into question and a more critical approach to tourism development ensued. This was because many of the great hopes for tourism had not been fulfilled. The third stage covers the period from 1985 and is termed the 'differentiation period'. This distinguishing feature of this stage is the emergence of alternative forms of tourism, such as ecotourism, with an emphasis on planning for a better future. The features are developed in more detail in Table 24.3 which identifies some of the different studies which resulted and their perspectives on tourism and LDCs.

TABLE 24.3 The evolution of tourism thought and approaches to the less developed world

1950s and 1960s	• Dominated by economic growth theory, with a Western orientation arguing that tourism was a good thing to achieve • Governments in LDCs highlighted the benefits to the economy of tourism, foreign direct investment and participation in the international economy, reinforced by aid donors • Resort-style development encouraged by planners and governments • The dominant academic viewpoint is economics.
1970s and 1980s	• Emergence of criticisms of the economic development arguments (e.g. Bryden 1973) as the outcome of uncontrolled economic growth and resort enclaves emerge • Growing criticism of how tourism development debates are devoid of people, as anthropologists (e.g. de Kadt 1979; Smith 1977 question the economic perspective • Geographers (e.g. Britton 1980, 1982) enter the debate highlighting the neo-colonial patterns of tourism development in LDCs after independence • New areas of thinking on tourism, designed to be more people- and environmentally- compatible, enter the debate in the 1980s, as the alternative tourism and sustainability movements gather momentum
Mid-1980s to late 1990s	• Governments in LDCs are faced with a growing debt crisis, as identified in the 1980s by Brandt (1980). Governments use tourism as one mechanism to pay off foreign debts • Growing concern over the rise of very undesirable forms of tourism in some LDCs (e.g. sex tourism and exploitation of women and children by organizations) by ECPAT and Tourism Concern • Sustainable tourism and more niche products like ecotourism are developed in LDCs such as Belize • Some LDCs take policy decisions to move to low-volume/high-value tourism (e.g. Botswana), while others exhibit growing dependence on First World tour operators for tourists • A number of financial crises illustrate how volatile the tourist market to LDCs is, such as the Asian economic crisis • There is increasing interest in the political economy perspectives of tourism in LDCs
2000 to date	• Growing criticisms over the use of labels such as 'ecotourism' (e.g. Page and Dowling 2002) and its reformulation into different market segments which can damage LDC environmental resources if not controlled • New labels, such as 'responsible tourism' are also questioned, given the lack of planning and management of tourists in LDCs, so as not to detract from the images marketed to Western tourists • Lobby groups point to the need for tour operators, multinational companies and investors to assume a greater degree of corporate responsibility for the impact that their forms of tourism induce on LDCs • New trends emerge, such as a growing middle class in LDCs who wish to travel and thus the impacts within countries from domestic tourism are expanded • A much higher level of debate amongst tourism organizations emerges over the need for more ethical and environmental forms of tourism in LDCs. • Greater roles are required for NGOs to promote more responsible forms of tourism and activity, to monitor programmes of change and to lobby for change amongst governments, tourism industry and communities (e.g. ECPAT's campaign on sex tourism contributed to legislation in many countries to eradicate child sex tourism)
Future?	• There will be a greater advocacy role for academics and students in critically examining the effect and impact of existing models of tourism on LDCs • Innovation will occur amongst communities in LDCs as they build knowledge and capacity to harness more positive benefits locally and an ability to manage tourism • More attention will be given to low-volume and high-volume tourism and limiting numbers on small islands

Source: Developed from Pearce (1990); Page and Dowling (2002); Scheyvens (2002)

Table 24.3 shows that the role of tourism in the development process of LDCs is subject to many debates, some of which are dealt with in this chapter. For example, one justification for tourism development is the potential benefits that may accrue to a country to assist with its development, in terms of, for instance, poverty reduction and employment growth. If tourism is viewed as a political tool, then tourism can transform an economy as:

- a way of obtaining hard currency and improving balance of payments/indebtedness through admitting large numbers of Western tourists
- a catalyst of social change, with closer contact between the indigenous community and the tourist
- a symbol of freedom, allowing citizens to travel freely within and outside their own country (in the case of eastern Europe)
- a mechanism for improving local infrastructure to cater for tourist need, thereby benefiting local people
- an integral part of economic restructuring through privatization, exposure to national and international market forces and transnational corporations
- a complement to commercial development through growth of business tourism market as well as through encouraging small-scale entrepreneurial activity, as the discussion of South Africa in Chapter 12 highlighted (developed from Hall 1992).

In many cases, the negative impacts are less tangible than the anticipated economic effects and often receive less attention.

The nature of tourism in less developed countries

Many studies of tourism in LDCs give the impression that the evolution of individual countries' international tourism markets is a comparatively recent phenomenon, given the relatively high rates of growth in the 1990s. However, studies of tourism in the South Pacific (e.g. Hall and Page 1996) and the Caribbean (e.g. Duval 2004) concur that the images of a tourist paradise are a literary creation by European and North American writers from the nineteenth and twentieth century, which have continued to shape the promotion of idealized images of a tourist paradise (Image 24.1). As Table 24.4 shows, tourism in the South Pacific has been conditioned by the process of colonization and it is only in recent history that the independence of many island states has been achieved.

Despite the strong colonial imprint on the development process in many LDCs, many countries have managed to develop a diversified product base for tourism in line with many of the changes outlined in thinking in Table 24.3. For example, the products include:

Image 24.1: Tour operators often create idyllic images of the less developed world as this Thomson Holiday's brochure suggests

- resort-based tourism, especially in small-island and coastal areas
- business and conference-based tourism
- ecotourism and wildlife tourism, especially in Africa
- cultural tourism, directed to more community-based initiatives
- VFR tourism, as migrants return to see their families and relatives, such as the Europe to Indian subcontinent flows

and many other niche products exist for international and domestic visitors.

Oppermann and Chon (1997) state that tourism is least important in peripheral regions of LDCs while the core economic and political centres gain an above-average share. Enclave and all-inclusive resorts lead to the spatial concentration of tourism and its benefits, which may be minimal for the host area in the case of all-inclusive resorts. Britton's (1982) work in the South Pacific illustrates that tourism perpetuates existing inequalities in LDCs. This is explained by four factors:

TABLE 24.4 Characteristics of Pacific territories

	Status	Date of Independence/ Free Association	Former Colonial Power	Capital	Land Area (sq km)
Australia	Independent State		United Kingdom	Canberra	7,682,300
American Samoa	Unincorporated US territory		United States	Pago Pago	197
Cook Islands	Self-governing in free association with New Zealand	1965	United Kingdom/ New Zealand	Avarua	240
Easter Island	Province of Chile	Annexed 1888	Chile	Hanga Roa	180
Federated States of Micronesia	Self-governing in free association with the US	1979	United States	Palikir	702
Fiji	Independent Republic	1970	United Kingdom	Suva	18,376
French Polynesia	Overseas territory of France	Annexed 1847	France	Papeete	3,521
Guam	Unincorporated US territory	Annexed 1898	Spain/ United States	Agana	549
Hawai'i	State of the US	1959	United Kingdom/ United States	Honolulu	16,641
Irian Jaya	Indonesian province	1950	Netherlands	Jayapura	410,660
Kiribati	Independent republic	1979	United States	Tatawa	726
Marshall Islands	Self-governing republic in free association with the US	1979	United States	Majuro	720
Nauru	Independent republic	1968	United Kingdom	Yaren	21.2
New Caledonia	Overseas territory of France	Annexed 1853	France	Noumea	19,103
New Zealand	Independent state		United Kingdom	Wellington	270,500
Niue	Self-governing in free association with New Zealand	1974	United Kingdom/ New Zealand	Alofi	258
Norfolk Island	Australian Territory	Annexed 1788	United Kingdom	Kingston	34.5
Northern Mariana Islands	Commonwealth of the US	1976	United States	Saipan	475
Palau (Belau)	Self-governing republic in free association with the US	1981	United States	Koror	500
Papa New Guinea	Independent state	1975	Germany/Great Britian/Australia	Port Moresby	461,690
Pitcairn Island	Dependency of Britain	(1)	United Kingdom	Adamstown	4.5
Solomon Islands	Independent state	1978	United Kingdom	Honiara	29,785
Tokelau	Dependency of New Zealand	(2)	United Kingdom/ New Zealand		12.1
Tonga	Independent monarchy	1970	United Kingdom	Nuku'alofa	696,71
Tuvalu	Independent state	1978	United Kingdom	Funatuti	25.9
Vanuatu	Independent republic	1980	France/ United Kingdom	Port Vila	12,189
Wallis and Futuna	Overseas territory of France	1961	France	Mata Utu	124
Western Samoa	Independent state	1962	United Kingdom	Apia	2,934

Notes:

(1) In 1970, Pitcairn and its dependencies were transferred to the control of the British High Commission in New Zealand who is also the Governor of Pitcairn.

(2) In 1877, the British High Commission for the Western Pacific was given jurisdiction of the Islands. In 1948, the Islands were included in the territorial boundaries of New Zeland.

Source: Hall and Page (1996)

- power and influence, with tourism often controlled by foreign companies
- foreign tourist demands often not met by local service provision, exacerbating a perceived need to build luxury facilites
- general conditions of underdevelopment, such as structural disadvantages, influence the direction of tourism growth and development
- it is difficult for host communities to take control of tourism supply

and Insight 24.1 highlights these problems in the case of Africa.

The outcome of enclave tourism is that host nations are often unable to break out of the poverty trap and the benefits of tourism do not filter through to those in need, even where luxury tourism is developed. The link between tourism and poverty is apparent from the fact that, in LDCs, tourism is a dominant feature in the poorest hundred countries and, in many countries which are recipients of aid, tourism is a dominant feature. In fact in some of the major LDC tourism destinations many of the population subsist on less than a dollar (around 75p) a day. In many LDCs, tourism is also viewed as a long-term contributor to reducing unemployment and underemployment as a economic development option. This is one reason why current thinking and strategies to alleviate poverty through tourism (see the discussion of pro-poor tourism later) have begun to dominate the potential agendas of lobby groups and NGOs. Governments can directly influence the direction of tourism development but often decide not to invest in tourism infrastructure. Instead, governments often give financial incentives such as tax breaks, easing of rules on foreign labour and subsidies, to foreign investors to develop facilities. Government policy tends to be centralized with little involvement of local communities. The

INSIGHT 24.1

Enclave tourism in Africa

There has been a long tradition since the 1970s of research on **enclave tourism** in LDCs (e.g. see Shaw and Shaw 1999). These studies question the economic development benefits of such forms of tourism, since visitors arrive in the main urban centre and are then transported to resorts/complexes, organized and managed by large organizations. Often these resorts are in remote areas and do not take account of local community needs, thus few benefits accrue to these areas. This is because of leakage, due to control of tourism spending by the highly organized form of tourism in the resort, a concept pioneered by all-inclusives such as Club Med. In LDCs, the disparities become even more profound due to the need to import luxury goods to meet the needs of enclave tourists, often equated with five-star tourism. This form of tourism is often controlled by a local elite or MNCs.

In Botswana, this model of development has occurred in the Okavango Delta (Figure 24.2) which has a number of transport links via one gateway airport (Maun International Airport). Visitors enter or depart from this gateway and are then transported by air or road to the delta to see wildlife. As Mbaiwa (2005) found, tourism has grown from a standing start in 1996 to the second most important economic activity in Bostwana, with over a million visitors going to the Delta by 2002. An upmarket tourism product has been developed. Yet foreign ownership of the tourism plant (e.g. lodges and transport) as well as concessions to view wildlife has led to an enclave style of development. Low levels of local involvement in the running of tourism enterprises and limited capital have effectively isolated many indigenous people from becoming entrepreneurs.

Much of the revenue from tourism is repatriated from the hotel and transport sector since it is paid for outside Botswana, especially with the international airlines which compete with Air Botswana (e.g. South African Airlines, KLM, Luftshansa and British Airways). The cost of importing food for tourist and payment of expatriate staff simply adds to leakage of revenue. A lack of taxation, with some companies not liable for local tax, reduces the benefits for the local economy. Weak linkages in the local economy are not assisting in locally beneficial tourism development. Many of the people employed locally experience the low pay and conditions of LDCs. Thus tourism has not been a major catalyst to eradicate poverty. Indeed, Mbaiwa (2005) points out that while there has been economic growth in tourism in the 1990s, rural poverty in the Delta has increased. Much of the effects have occurred because government tourism policy since 1990 to attract low-volume, high-spending visitors has detracted from encouraging casual budget travellers and campers who would add more value to the local economy.

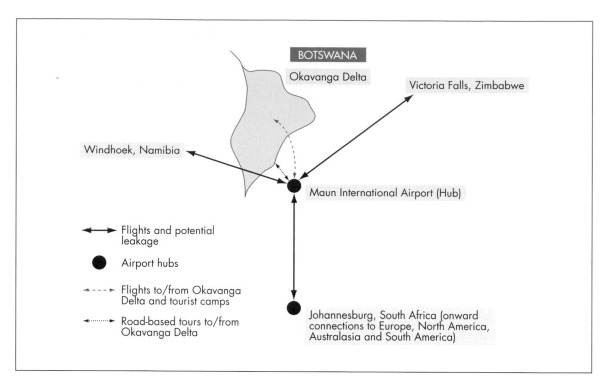

FIGURE 24.2 Okavanga Delta and tourism linkages in Botswana

focus tends to be on encouraging large foreign tour operators and developers to pursue tourism at the expense of indigenous operations. Traditional views on tourism can be interpreted as concentration on how much money can be generated rather than how it can be distributed to eliminate poverty in the wider population. Swarbrooke (1999) points out one of the problems with tourism in current times is the rapid growth in low-priced package holidays to LDCs. The plight of poor countries is often ignored by tourists in search of a cheap holiday. It is one form of economic imperialism emerging in the post-colonial era as the dependency relationship with the developed world has been replicated in the tourism arena.

Conceptualizing the nature of tourism in less developed countries

Mowforth and Munt (2003) provide a framework to outline the major processes which underlie the development of new forms of tourism in LDCs. The framework consists of four elements which are outlined below:

- *Intervention and commodification*: natural and cultural resources are transformed into products for consumption by tourists. For example, visitors to Thailand can purchase T-shirts imprinted with an image of a Padaung woman wearing brass neck rings (these neck rings damage skeletal growth but the value as a tourist attraction dictates that women continue to wear them in some areas). This example links to all the points below

- *Subservience (domination and control)*: communities and individuals in LDCs may assume subordinate roles in order to satisfy tourists and tourism development. They may have to accept low rates of pay and menial tasks in order to take enough money home to ensure survival

- *Fetishism*: tourists remain unaware of life of those who serve them on holiday as commodities hide social realities

- *Aetheticization*: objects, feelings and experiences are turned into objects of beauty and desire. Tourists may wish to experience scenes of real poverty or dangerous situations. For example, some tours take visitors to workplaces to see local crafts being made.

Development patterns

In many LDCs, an 'uncritical faith', as Marfurt (1983) states, has led to unrestrained development and expenditure on tourism facilities. Governments often strive towards the prestige of luxury tourism developments and the associated economic statistics. LDCs which create expansive tourism industries often create problems for their country which do not provide long-term solutions to social and economic problems. However, not all LDCs follow this path of development. Others adhere to a stricter policy of protecting culture, the environment and the local economy. Insight 24.2 outlines one of the best examples of alternative development paths – Bhutan.

Impacts of tourism in less developed countries

While a wide ranging discussion of the economic, sociocultural and environmental impacts of tourism can be found in Chapters 17–19, the impacts on LDCs warrant further attention. The main debates focus around the wide gap between the host and guest as well as power relations. Burns and Holden (1995) summarize the problems relating to tourism in LDCs as follows:

INSIGHT 24.2

Bhutan – an alternative approach to tourism development

For centuries, the kingdom of Bhutan (www.kingdomofbhutan.com), located in the eastern Himalayas, was little touched by outside influences. The population of Bhutan (600 000) is thinly scattered across the country which covers an area of over 46 000 square kilometres. The country is mainly mountainous and borders Tibet and India. Many habitats and species make up the well-protected ecosystem, some of which are rare and endangered, such as the red panda and the snow leopard. The people of Bhutan follow a Buddhist way of life. As one of the poorest countries in Asia, there has been a move towards economic growth through tourism since 1974 when visitors were first permitted entry to the country. Numbers of visitors have grown from 287 in 1974 to over 7000 a year (www.tourism.gov.bt). It now accounts for up to 15–20 per cent of Bhutan's exports (Dorji 2001). However, under the direction of the monarch, King Jigme Singye Wangchuck, and in tandem with the underlying cultural beliefs, Bhutan has been steered in the direction of sustainable growth rather than the 'boom and bust' or 'modernization at any cost' pattern of many other LDCs. A planned process of growth has been in place since the early 1960s. For example, under Bhutanese law, the extensive forests, which have been subject to logging, will be protected to ensure that forest cover is not depleted to less than 60 per cent of the land cover (it currently forms 72 per cent).

Tourism, now one of Bhutan's major economic sectors (Dorji 2001), has evolved in a stringently controlled way, with an emphasis on environmental and cultural protection and economic self-reliance. Tourism is recognized as a means of achieving socioeconomic development but only acceptable within the confines of the conservation ethic which is deeply embedded in the Buddhist faith. The Royal Government sees the opportunity to maintain biodiversity rather than destroy it through tourism development. Contrary to popular belief, the limit is not on annual tourist arrivals but to minimize impacts. However, a policy of attracting low-volume but high-value tourism along with a strictly enforced set of regulations (the 'tourist tariff') covering tourism management ensures effective translation of sustainable principles to practice. A brief summary of the regulations are given below:

- visitors must travel on a pre-booked package holiday – no independent travel allowed
- all visitors, irrespective of accommodation and choice of tour, must pay US$200 per person per day, which includes accommodation, food, travel itinerary, transportation, guides
- all bookings must be made through one of 33 companies licensed to operate in Bhutan
- not all areas of the country are open access to visitors, partly to ensure that religious life can continue unimpeded and partly for safety and environmental reasons, such as heavy snow
- all accommodation must be government approved and guides must be licensed.

- development of 'islands of affluence' in a poor society
- use of scarce national resources for tourist enjoyment
- the consequences of the demonstration effect (see Chapter 18)
- unreliable means of measuring the true economic benefit
- commercialization of culture and lifestyle
- beneficiaries likely to be foreign companies or already wealthy local people
- external control – tourism often in the hands of transnational corporations.

Economic perspectives

As Table 24.3 indicated, a distinct philosophy was promoted in the 1960s among LDCs and the World Bank, a major source of finance for LDCs encourage them to invest in mass tourism. Between 1969 and 1979, the World Bank loaned about $450 million to governments in 18 LDCs. This included large-scale resorts in Thailand, Mexico and the Caribbean. But by the early 1970s (see e.g. Turner and Ash 1975) it was recognized that tourism resulted in negative as well as positive impacts and that it could not be viewed as a panacea for LDCs seeking economic expansion. The virtues of tourism development were originally extolled in many LDCs based on the idea that it is a **smokeless industry**, using the natural resources of a country in a non-polluting way and providing employment, increased gross national product and improvements to the economy. But it soon became clear that a large proportion of tourist revenue did not remain in the host nation or benefit local communities. Employment tended to be low paid and poor quality, perpetuating the poverty experienced by many of the working population, while managerial-grade jobs were given to expatriate staff. Tourism is often an activity which can be developed relatively quickly, as in the case of the Dominican Republic (Pattullo 1996). Some countries demonstrate an overdependence on tourism to the extent that traditional industries have been abandoned in favour of a more lucrative tourism-connected trade. This makes countries vulnerable to changing markets and the vagaries of international currency. It also means that LDCs continue to depend on developed countries for their economic survival, perpetuating colonial trends of the past.

Leakage

Foreign exchange generated by tourism in LDCs does not remain there in sufficient volume to justify the benefits it is supposed to yield. It may go to tour companies, travel providers and accommodation providers based in industrialized nations. Many of the LDCs cannot afford the investment required to attract high-spending Western tourists and so wealthy multinational corporations grasp opportunities. The percentage of income derived from tourism returning to wealthy nations is termed 'leakage'. More discussion of leakage can be found in Chapter 17. For example, Worldwatch Institute (www.worldwatchinstitute.org) estimated that half of the revenue from international tourism in LDCs leaks out to foreign-owned companies, in part through the import of goods and labour. This obscured the much wider concerns in certain destinations, such as Kenyan coastal resorts where rates of up to 70 per cent leakage occur and, similarly, in Thailand rates of 60 per cent are reported.

Social and cultural perspectives

The demonstration effect is clearly evident in LDCs. Daniel (1998) reports an example of a Thai hill village where tourism has caused community conflict and is viewed by some as cultural invasion. The younger members of the community prefer the style of clothing that tourists wear and now children wear T-shirts and baseball caps in an attempt to be like the foreigners. Young people aspire to the material standards and values of tourists but are unable to achieve them. Young males have committed suicide because they could not see a way out of their lifestyle. Cultural imperialism is evident in tourists from developed countries visiting less developed countries. **Sex tourism** might be termed a form of leisure imperialism – sex tourism in Thailand and the Philippines as a form of military aggression. In the case of the Gambia in the 1990s, beach boys were performing a sexual service for female travellers: this highlights the diversity of sex tourism forms (i.e. romance, casual encounters, prostitution, sex slavery and mail order brides) (Clift and Carter 2000). Traditional patterns of life and kinship are disrupted by tourism as reported by Sallah (1998): in the Gambia, relationships between parents and children have degenerated as a result of loss of land and employment when land was taken for tourism development. Local people are often driven to begging because their means of self-support have been removed through insensitive development, lack of respect for traditional land and property rights and exogenous control of tourism businesses.

Katya Mira recounts the experience of backpacking in Mexico and the issue of beggars in Oaxaca city. As a tourist, she was constantly asked for money. On telling an old lady that she had no more money the rebuke came swiftly. 'You come all this way over here. You stay in hotels. You eat in restaurants. I live in a hut with no hot water and have no potatoes to feed my family. Look. Look at the holes in my skirt! You have no money? You don't know what "No money" means' (Mira 1999).

Power and tourism: Colonialism and neo-colonialism

Power relationships can be identified at various levels with regard to tourism. At a macro level, the unequal nature of the relationship between developed and less developed countries is illustrated by the volume, wealth and mobility of tourists from developed countries and also the ability of developed countries to control and gain from tourism located in LDCs (Britton 1992). At a micro level, unequal relationships clearly exist within LDCs, with a powerful minority of wealthy elite with power over poor local communities. Taking the macro issue first, this may be viewed in terms of theories of underdevelopment. As Western culture has become the dominant culture in the world, issues of power have been raised. The relationship between industrialized and non-industrialized nations are typified by a failure to recognize and respect differences (Hall 1992). The concept of development tends to assume that Western culture is applied as a standard to others nations. Colonialism from the 1850s proved to be a valuable political instrument for controlling overseas territories with the purpose of improving the capitalist economies of the West, particularly Great Britain and France, as shown in Table 24.4. Countries subject to colonizing powers provided cheap resources such as labour and land. From the 1960s, a new force of colonialism began to emerge. This has been termed **neo-colonialism** and is based on the growing power of multinational corporations. Tourism has been described as a force of neo-colonialism as it may take the form of exogenous development, controlled by overseas interests with a large proportion of income leaking overseas rather than benefiting the host nation. It might be said that tourists have superseded the armies of the colonial powers. Britton (1982) argues that Fiji is a neo-colonial economy and illustrates this with comparisons to pre-independence and a reinforcement of associated economic patterns.

As various studies of tourism planning in LDCs have shown, much of the work on plan preparation has been from aid donor countries, often on an ad hoc basis, and with Western-based philosophies towards tourism. Concepts such as sustainable tourism have only recently begun to feature in the language of tourism plans for LDC, particularly in relation to tourism and small islands.

Tourism, less developed countries and small islands

Hall and Page (1996) examined the problems facing tourism in small islands which pose particular development challenges in LDCs including:

- accessibility
- attracting investment
- the colonial legacy and economic system
- the limited resource base to support intensive tourism

and other studies have expanded these constraints including:

- no advantages from economies of scale
- a limited range of resources
- a narrowly specialized economy, based on agricultural commodities
- small, open economies with minimal ability to influence terms of trade or to manage and control their own economies
- limited ability to adjust to changes in the international economic environment
- a narrow range of local skills and problems of matching local skills and jobs (often exacerbated by a brain and skill drain)
- high transport, infrastructure and administration costs
- cultural domination by metropolitan countries
- vulnerability to natural hazards (Duval 2004 based on Connell 1988 and Wilkinson 1997).

Added to these problems are the loss of indigenous labour through outmigration, a dependence upon remittances and aid and an outdated bureaucracy, derived from colonial legacies. These problems led to the use of an acronym, **MIRAB** (migration, remittances, aid and bureacracy) to depict the range of issues. Not surprisingly, many of these problems are outlined in island Master Plans, such as the *Maldives Tourism Master Plan 1996–2005* (www.maldivestourism.govt.md). Among the problems highlighted are:

- lack of hospitality and managerial skills
- geographical polarization of resorts from the community and concentration of ownership in a few companies
- the rapid growth of the expatriate labour force
- high economic leakages
- homegeneity within products
- dependence on a single geographical market segment
- problems related to direct foreign investments and multinational corporations
- requirement to adhere to international ethical standards in production
- deteriorating identity of Maldivian tourism products and diminishing visual quality of seascapes.

Yet the island has around 500 000 visitor arrivals a year, and the Master Plan recognizes the social and cultural effect of this on Maldivian culture, environmental pressures and long-term problems related to climate change and the rises in sea level that could eventually engulf the island. It is widely recognized by charitable bodies that a large proportion of the population live on around US$1 a day despite a very successful tourism sector. This raises many ethical issues for tourists who visit the island (see Smith and Duffy 2003).

Host community issues

One of the worst **human rights** contraventions linked with tourism in recent times is that of Myanmar in Burma. This particular example highlights the stance which tour operators may take in relation to corporate social responsibility. In 1996, the pro-democracy leader, Daw Aung San Suu Kyi, who opposed the military junta, SLORC (State Law and Order Council) called on tourists not to visit the country. This was an attempt to stop foreign exchange flowing into the country and ultimately to the government. 'Visit Myanmar Year' in 1996 was SLORC's attempt to bring in hard currency through a projected 500 000 tourists (from a base of 100 000 in 1995). From 1990, SLORC tried to attract foreign investors in hotel and tourism developments, offering ten-year tax breaks and full repatriation of profits (Mahr and Sutcliffe 1996). After the grand launch was over-taken by an uprising of 50 000 student protestors and subsequent high profile media coverage (for example, John Pilger's TV documentary *Inside Burma: Land of Fear*), tourists mainly stayed away. It was reported that local communities had been forcibly moved from their homes to make way for new tourism infrastructure, such as luxury hotels and new roads. Mahr and Sutcliffe (1996) report that people were forced without pay to restore the moat around Mandalay Palace. Examples of 'picturesque' ethnic peoples have been relocated to special villages where tourists can visit – an example of zooification. Despite the high-profile reporting of the human rights violation and the link with tourism in Myanmar, many tour companies continue to promote the destination, highlighting the superb natural and cultural aspects but ignoring contemporary social and political issues. Ongoing opposition to such issues led to the public awareness campaign in the UK, with the Prime Minister and celebrities highlighting the use of slave and child labour in the 'I'm not going' campaign in 2005.

Environmental perspectives

As discussed in Chapter 19, tourism activity results in environmental damage. LDCs often contain areas of high biodiversity and environmental fragility; ecological disturbance can result in habitat damage and even species extinction (Doggart and Doggart 1996). Damage, for example, to the islands and coral reefs off the west coast of Thailand (famously cited in Alex Garland's novel *The Beach*) has led to limits on day trips. On a positive note, tourism can be a force of positive change in LDCs, where tourism provides a more suitable alternative land use to intensive, commercial or environmentally damaging activities, such as intensive agriculture, logging or hunting. For

Image 24.2: Underdeveloped areas such as Machu Picchu in Peru are controversial as they are highly contested due to the impact of tourism

example, in the forests of Thailand, elephant keepers have turned to tourism since the logging ban left them unemployed in 1989. Tourism can also provide income for conservation purposes. The Peruvian Government barred independent trekkers from the Inca Trail from 1 April 2000 in an attempt to prevent further damage to the National Park area around Machu Picchu. Access is now restricted to those on organized treks and numbers are capped at 20 000.

One of the major growth areas of tourism that directly affects LDCs is ecotourism (see the case studies in Weaver 1998). This form of tourism is growing at 30 per cent compared with mainstream tourism, at about 4 per cent per annum and thus poses a significant challenge (Page and Dowling 2002). According to Honey (1999), nearly every non-industrialized country was promoting ecotourism as part of its development strategy by the early 1990s. Ecotourism overtook primary production as the largest foreign exchange earner in some countries, e.g. bananas in Costa Rica, coffee in Kenya and textiles in India. There has been much debate about how ecotourism should operate and distinctions between nature-based tourism (which may not be at all sustainable) and ecotourism which, by definition, includes benefits to local communities and protection of the environment need to be made.

Issues of equality in tourism in less developed countries

Fair trade

One of the main questions posed is how can tourism become more equitable to those in less developed receiving countries? Tourism ought to benefit the people who live in destination areas but often does not. **Fair trade** is an issue that has gained momentum in recent years. A range of products are now widely available for purchase which have been 'fairly traded', such as tea, coffee, chocolate and bananas. 'Fair trade' means that the workers involved in the production of these goods have been given a fair wage and have not been subject to dangerous working conditions (for example, exposure of grape pickers to insecticides) or exploitation. Now, tourism faces a similar challenge. Organizations such as Voluntary Services Overseas (VSO) (www.vso.org.uk) have actively campaigned to promote awareness of fair trade in tourism.

One example of where fair trade is working effectively is in St Lucia. The Sunshine Harvest Fruit and Vegetable Farmers' Cooperative consists of 66 farmers. The cooperative coordinates production and marketing of produce to hotels on the island. An 'adopt-a-farmer' initiative is being trialled, where hotels agree to buy produce from a specific farmer at an agreed price before planting. Smallholders are being encouraged to diversify their cropping to produce a wide range of fruit and vegetables, not just bananas. Farmers have access to favourable loan rates from local banks to help them buy seed and fertilizers. This scheme has the potential to assist in greater retention of tourism revenue on the island. The integration of fair trade philosophies into tourism may be achieved in several ways via the International Network on Fair Trade in Tourism and a very good international example is Fair Trade in Tourism in South Africa (www.fairtourismsa.org.za).

Community-based tourism is an expanding concept in LDCs and provides a mechanism for ensuring as much economic benefit as possible remains in the host community. It also means that the community is able to control the direction and form of tourism. Many schemes are managed communally and profits are shared. Some communities work with tour operators or other organizations to promote their initiatives. Some communities operate 'village stays', where visitors stay with local families and engage in holiday activities such as bush walking, fishing, snorkelling and caving. There are many examples across the developing world, such as the Solomon Islands and Taquila on Lake Titicaca in Peru (see Mann 2000).

The International Porter Protection Group (IPPG) (www.ippg.net) fosters the well-being of porters. Working with the trekking industry, governments, and NGOs, the IPPG promotes the safety and protection of porters and collects data on deaths, accidents and injuries. Guidelines on adequate protective clothing, medical care and financial protection in relation to rescue and medical treatment have been developed to raise awareness at grassroots level.

There is still much more development work and monitoring of community-based initiatives needed before any conclusions can be drawn. This is still a minority aspect of tourism provision and is seen at present as a niche market rather than a philosophy which underpins tourism management, although there are signs that a number of new perspectives are being developed in this area.

New agendas for addressing poverty and inequality through tourism

There are new ideas emerging on how to harness tourism to reduce poverty in LDCs, notably **pro-poor tourism** (see Goodwin 1998). As the pro-poor website suggests (www.propoortourism.org.uk), it is an approach to tourism development designed to enhance the links between poor people and tourism to reduce poverty. As a concept, pro-poor tourism seeks to develop strategies which increase local employment for the poor in destination areas (including the expansion of employment opportunities for the poor). This area of thought might be seen as one dimension of **responsible tourism** (www.responsibletourismpartnership.org) as well as the growing emphasis on corporate social responsibility (CSR) for tour operators. For example, one NGO, Tearfund (www.tearfund.org), is a relief and development agency which acts in partnership with Christian agencies and churches worldwide to tackle poverty. The NGO has produced various reports and spearheaded different initiatives on responsible tourism, including its seminal report in 2002, *Worlds Apart: A Call to Responsible Global Tourism* with its emphasis on the need for the tour operator sector to become more socially responsible. It has also worked in partnership with ABTA to formulate the Tour Operator Initiative, to develop a more sustainable approach to tourism via CSR with a greater focus on ethical behaviour. But other studies have pointed to the intransigence in some sectors of the tour operator industry, citing small profit margins and a limited role in destination areas compared to hotel chains. These ambitions and visionary studies such as that by Scheyvens (2002), developing concepts like justice tourism, gender sensitive tourism and a more critical role for NGOs, the tourism industry and governments in LDCs, certainly is a refreshing, thoughtful and an alternative model for tourism development whereby communities are empowered.

Conclusion

Burns (1999) states that most societies have a desire for material wealth and social improvement; it is thus inevitable that impacts will occur and sacrifices will be made. Tourism ideas produced by consultants for government planners tend to follow either a normative set of values, based on the traditional economic growth of Western ideas, or a patronizing 'no growth' model. Burns suggests that until community ownership is established as a proactive policy in tourism planning, local people will continue to be poorly served by the promises of social and economic progress. The Department for International Development (DFID) (1998) suggest that nature tourism is well placed to offer a viable income for local communities in LDCs. However, the problem is in ensuring that the benefits of tourism are distributed fairly. For example, DfID reseach shows that out of US$300 spent by a tourist for a two-night trip to Bali or Lombok to see Komodo's dragons,

only 70 cents is received by the National Park. Transparency is required to inform stakeholders where money is going.

The future of tourism in LDCs is beset with challenges. It seems likely that the volume of tourism will continue to increase as tourists from developed countries venture further afield and those in the newly industrialized countries participate more in tourism activity. Changes need to be made if tourism is to become more sustainable across the developing world. While tourism has great appeal as a mechanism for achieving economic development, appropriate policies are needed to retain sufficient tourism revenue in the host country and fair distribution within the economy. Tourism in LDCs raises complex issues and problems which have no easy solutions; it also raises many issues about the nature of the tourist experience in LDCs and future planning issues, to which we now turn in Part VI.

Discussion questions

1 Discuss the rationale for tourism as a tool for development.
2 Explain why fair trade is advocated a way ahead for tourism in less developed countries.
3 Why is tourism described as 'neo-colonialism'?
4 How realistic is the implementation of pro-poor tourism as a development strategy for tourism destinations in LDCs?

References

Brandt, W. (1980) *North–South: A Programme for Survival*. London: Pan.

Britton, S. (1980) 'The spatial organization of tourism in a neo-colonial economy: A Pacific case study', *Pacific Viewpoint*, 21 (2): 144–65.

Britton, S. (1982) 'The political economy of tourism in the Third World', *Annals of Tourism Research*, 9 (3): 331–58.

Bryden, J. (1973) *Tourism and Development: A Case Study of the Commonwealth Caribbean*. Cambridge: Cambridge University Press.

Burns, P. (1999) 'Paradoxes in planning. Tourism elitism or brutalism?' *Annals of Tourism Research*, 26 (2): 329–48.

Burns, P. and Holden, A. (1995) *Tourism: A New Perspective*. Hemel Hempstead: Prentice Hall.

Clift, S. and Carter, S. (eds) (2000) *Tourism and Sex: Culture, Commerce and Coercion*. London: Pinter.

Connell, J. (1988) *Sovereignty and Survival: Island Microstates in the Third World*. Research Monograph No 3. Sydney: Department of Geography, University of Sydney.

David, E. (1998) 'Spirits in the village', *Orbit*, VSO, second quarter: 8–9.

de Kadt, E. (1979) *Tourism: Passport to Development*. New York: Oxford University Press.

Department for International Development (1999) *Changing the Nature of Tourism. Developing an Agenda for Action*. London: DFID.

Dieke, P. (ed.) (2000) *Tourism in Africa*. New York: Cognizant.

Doggart, C. and Doggart, D. (1996) 'Environmental impacts of tourism in developing countries', *Travel and Tourism Analyst*, 2: 71–86.

Dorji, T. (2001) 'Sustainability of tourism in Bhutan', *The Journal of Bhutan Studies*, 3 (1): 84–104.

Duval, T. (ed.) (2004) *Tourism in the Caribbean: Trends, Development, Prospects*. London: Routledge.

Goodwin, H. (1998) 'Sustainable tourism and poverty elimination', discussion paper, DFID/DETR Workshop on Sustainable Tourism and Poverty, London, 13 October; www.tourismpoverty.com, accessed 05.02.05.

Hall, C.M. (1992) *Tourism and Politics: Policy, Power and Place*. Chichester: John Wiley and Sons.

Hall, C.M. and Page, S.J. (eds) (1996) *Tourism in the Pacific: Issues and Cases*. London: Thomson.

Hall, C.M. and Page, S.J. (eds) (2000) *Tourism in South and South East Asia: Issues and Cases*. Oxford: Butterworth-Heinemann.

Harrison, D. (ed.) (2003) *Pacific Island Tourism*. New York: Cognizant.

Honey, M. (1999) *Ecotourism and Sustainable Development. Who Owns Paradise?* Washington, DC: Island Press.

Kester, J. and Carvao, S. (2004) 'International tourism in the Middle East, and outbound tourism from Saudi Arabia', *Tourism Economics*, 10 (2): 220–40.

Lumsdon, L. and Swift, J. (2001) *Tourism in Latin America*. London: Continuum.

Mahr, J. and Sutcliffe, S. (1996) 'Come to Burma', *New Internationalist*, 280: 28–30.

Mann, M. (2000) *The Community Tourism Guide*. London: Earthscan.

Mansfeld, Y. and Winckler, O. (2004) 'Options for viable economic development through tourism among the non-oil Arab countries: The Egyptian case', *Tourism Economics*, 10 (4): 365–88.

Marfurt, E. (1983) 'Tourism and the Third World: Dream or nightmare?', in L. France (1997) *The Earthscan Reader in Sustainable Tourism*. London: Earthscan, 172–75.

Mbaiwa, J. (2005) 'Enclave tourism and its socio-economic impacts in the Okavango Delta, Botswana', *Tourism Management*, 26 (2): 157–72.

Mira, K. (1999) 'Postcard from Mexico', *In Focus*, 33: 20.

Mowforth, M. and Munt, I. (2003) *Tourism and Sustainability. New Tourism in the Third World, Second Edition*. London: Routledge.

Oppermann, M. and Chon, K. (1997) *Tourism in Developing Countries*. London: International Thomson Business Press.

Page, S.J. and Dowling, R. (2002) *Ecotourism*. Harlow: Prentice Hall.

Pattullo, P. (1996) *Last Resorts. The Cost of Tourism in the Caribbean*. London: Cassell.

Pearce, D.G. (1990) *Tourist Development, Second Edition*. Harrow: Longman.

Sallah, H. (1998) 'Faulty towers', *Orbit*, Second quarter: 12–13.

Scheyvens, R. (2002) *Tourism for Development*. Harlow: Prentice Hall.

Shaw, B. and Shaw, G. (1999) 'Sun, sand and sales: Enclave tourism and local entrepreneurship in Indonesia', *Current Issues in Tourism*, 2 (1): 68–81.

Simpson, K. (2004) 'Doing development: The Gap Year, volunteer tourists and a popular practice of development', *Journal of International Development*, 16 (5): 681–92.

Smith, N. and Duffy, R. (2003) *The Ethics of Tourism Development*. London: Routledge.

Smith, V. (ed.) (1977) *Hosts and Guests: The Anthropology of Tourism*. Philadelphia: University of Pennsylvannia Press.

Swarbrooke, J. (1999) *Sustainable Tourism*. Wallingford, Oxon: CABI.

Turner, L. and Ash, J. (1975) *The Golden Hordes: International Tourism and the Pleasure Periphery*. London: Constable.

Weaver, D. (ed.) (1998) *Ecotourism in the Less Developed World*. Wallingford, Oxon: CABI publishing.

Webster, A. (1990) *Introduction to the Sociology of Development*. London: Macmillan.

Wilkinson, P. (1997) *Tourism Policy and Planning: Case Studies from the Caribbean*. New York, Cognizant.

Further reading

Mowforth, M. and Munt, I. (2003) *Tourism and Sustainability. Development and New Tourism in the Third World, Second Edition*. London: Routledge.

Many of the challenging concepts developed in this chapter can be explored further in this book.

VI

Managing Tourist Activities

In Part V, the focus was on how supply and demand in specific locations culminated in different forms of tourism. At these locations, tourists would have experienced different types of products and services, and formed an overall image and perception of the locality. In Part VI of the book, the emphasis is on that perception and evaluation of tourism, the tourism experience and how the public sector may develop plans and measures to develop the potential of tourism. It focuses on current and future issues which may impact upon that experience, notably tourist safety and security and future trends which are emerging. Chapter 25 discusses the nature of the 'tourism experience', exploring many of the concepts and techniques used to assess how tourists rate and perceive their experience of tourism. This is a culmination of the interactions between all the chapters discussed throughout the book, where specific relationships exist that can condition and affect the way the tourist rates their holiday experience, visit to an attraction or destination. A starting point for Chapter 25 is how the public and private sector seek to manage this experience through macro techniques such as planning for tourism and micro techniques by businesses at the individual visitor level. This theme is then expanded in Chapter 26, examining some of the highly visible factors which impact upon the visitor experience – tourist health and safety. It is widely acknowledged that these factors are now assuming a global significance as tourism enters an age of greater turbulence. This is followed in the last chapter of the book, Chapter 27, by a detailed analysis of the future of tourism. This highlights many of the management challenges facing the tourism industry and likely changes which will occur in tourism activity in the new millennium. Specific issues such as forecasting changes in tourism are discussed together with issues facing consumers and specific examples.

25

Planning and Managing the Tourist Experience

Learning outcomes

After reading this chapter and answering the questions, you should be able to:

- identify the importance of tourism planning

- outline the tourism planning process

- indicate the key factors which interact to shape the tourist experience

- understand the importance of service quality issues in shaping the tourist experience.

Overview

The nature of the tourist as a consumer has received considerable attention in the analysis of tourism impacts and the need for planning to control and manage it. One consequence of tourism planning and management is the need to integrate tourist needs and satisfaction to understand how tourism can achieve a sustainable future and sustainable experiences for visitors. Many of the principles of management discussed in Chapter 5 are considered in this chapter to illustrate how the tourist experience needs to be managed so as to ensure that tourists' needs and the resource base are balanced with the commercial needs of the tourism sector.

Introduction

There is a growing interest within the tourism sector on the development of concepts and mechanisms by which to understand how destinations and businesses can plan for the growth and sustainable evolution of tourism. One of the fundamental building blocks to any such strategy at a destination or business level is the need to plan for the development of tourism. This chapter examines some of the tools and approaches which the public sector use to evaluate the best route to control and develop tourism at a destination level. Some localities have used visitor management tools to control sites and areas. What is needed is an integrated planning process which brings together different stakeholders and interests groups. These issues then have to be developed in the business plans and activities of individual tourism businesses if tourism is to pursue a direction which stakeholders wish to endorse; although reaching agreement, as Chapter 14 has shown, is far from a straightforward process. For this reason, the chapter examines the need for **tourism planning**, how it is progressed as a process and some of the features of tourism plans which set the direction for tourism planning. This is followed by a discussion of the concept of the 'tourist experience', as one objective of tourism planning is to ensure that visitors are attracted, and are satisfied (if not delighted) by the experience they encounter at the destination. This should be seen as part of the process of developing value in the experience of being a tourist, as discussed in Chapter 15, through the marketing process to meet consumer expectations.

The management and planning of the tourist experience

Planning is normally one task which is subsumed under the heading of management as discussed in Chapter 5 and this noted that the principal activities are:

- planning
- organizing
- leading
- controlling.

These four tasks are important for tourism destinations in coordinating the private and public sector interests (i.e. the **stakeholders** who include the residents) in relation to the tourist experience. This is where a managing agency with a view of the 'tourist experience' can be important in ensuring that some of the potential interactions evident in Figure 25.1 are managed. This shows that planning is normally a macro-level issue which is undertaken at different geographical scales, and yet frequently fails to move beyond a broad strategy and series of objectives at the local level (although exceptions exist in resorts and highly developed destinations). However, as Figure 25.2 shows, a potential mismatch exists between the scale at which tourism planning normally occurs and, conversely, at the scale at which the tourist experience is important. It is important to emphasize that it is businesses which deal with the tourist experience whereas, in planning terms, it is the public sector which address wider tourism planning issues and rarely do the two functions get integrated. So the two are optimized. Therefore, as Figures 25.1 and 25.2 suggest, there are a number of stakeholders in any given destination who can impact upon the tourism industry, ranging from the different businesses producing the supply of services and goods, the tourist (i.e. demand) and the residents. Achieving a balance between each of their needs and the viable development of the local tourism industry is a challenge and a fundamental reason for planning.

Planning: What is it and does it exist in tourism?

According to Chadwick (1971: 24) 'planning is a process, a process of human thought and action based upon that thought – in point of fact for the future – nothing more or less than this is planning, which is a general human activity'. What this means is that change and the need to accommodate

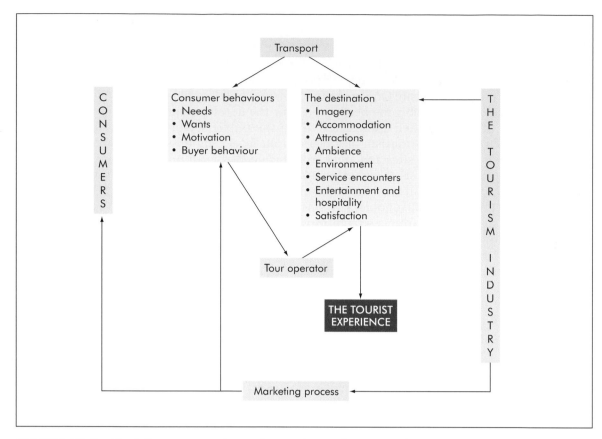

FIGURE 25.1   The influences upon the tourist experience of tourism at destinations

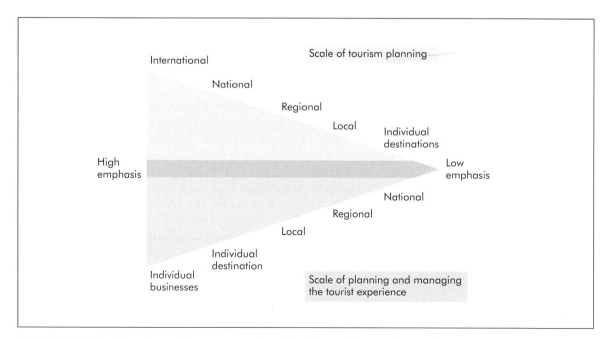

FIGURE 25.2   The mismatch between tourism planning and the tourist experience

change in the future requires a process whereby a set of decisions are prepared for future action. Hall (1999: 10) argues that

> *Demands for tourism planning and government intervention in the development process are typically a response to the unwanted effects of tourism development at the local level. The rapid pace of tourism growth and development, the nature of tourism itself and the corresponding absence of single agency responsibility for tourism related development has often meant that public sector responses to the impacts of tourism on destinations has often been ad hoc, rather than predetermined strategies oriented towards development objectives.*

Planning is therefore a process which aims to *anticipate, regulate* and *monitor change* to contribute to the wider sustainability of the destination, and thereby enhance the tourist experience of the destination or place. What Hall (1999) and other commentators recognize, is that while tourism planning has followed trends in urban and regional planning, tourism is not always seen as a core focus of the planning process at the local level.

Getz (1987) observed that there are four traditions to tourism planning: **boosterism**, an **economic-industry approach**, a **physical-spatial approach** and a **community-oriented approach** while Hall (1999) has recognized that a fifth approach now exists – 'sustainable tourism planning', which is 'a concern for the long-term future of resources, the effects of economic development on the environment, and its ability to meet present and future needs' (Page and Thorn 1997: 60). As Page and Thorn (1997: 61) suggest: 'In most countries, tourism planning exists as a component of public sector planning, and its evolution as a specialist activity has been well documented (Gunn 1988; Inskeep 1991)' which is shown in Table 25.1 for Spain and the changing emphasis 1959 to 2004. As a component of public sector planning, tourism planning (where it exists as a discrete activity or is subsumed within wider economic planning processes) aims to optimize the balance of private sector interests which are profit driven. In some cases this may prove problematic in getting the balance right as Insight 25.1 suggests.

TABLE 25.1 Phases of tourism planning in Spain	
1959–74: Indicative planning in a centralized state	Integration of tourism into state-indicative planning. Lack of regional- and local-scale planning. The growth of supply is favoured despite serious infrastructure deficits and high environmental costs. Land use and town planning are subordinated to tourism growth (boosterism approach)
1975–82: Guiding plans in the transition towards a decentralized system	An unsuccessful attempt is made to link land use and tourism planning. Non-compulsory tourism planning. Guiding plans contained recommendations not implemented. Provincial-scale plans are prepared that can be methodologically attributed to the physical approach, but without a real application
1982–89: State's withdrawal and first regional plans	Central administration-promoted plans are replaced with specific studies (statistics, marketing etc.). White Books are developed in Catalonia and the Balearics that help design the first regional tourist policy. Urban growth under local control thanks to municipal autonomy laws
1989–93: Reaction plans and structural adjustment policies	Reactive plans in which the loss of competitiveness drives the strategic plans with a sectorial approach. The legal basis to link tourism and territorial planning in the regional scale is created but not implemented. Start of planning within the European regional policy (1989–93 EU Support Framework)
From 1994: Regional planning formalized in autonomous tourism laws	Regional and subregional planning instruments are regulated in tourism laws, but their elaboration takes considerably longer. Tourism plans are differently linked to land use and town planning depending on the autonomous communities, but few planning initiatives have been developed. Rise in value of the local scale with interadministrative cooperation (Excellence and Dynamization Plans). On the theoretical level, reinterpretation of the physical approach with the incorporation of sustainable development principles

Source: Reprinted from *Annals of Tourism Research*, 31, Baidal 'Tourism planning in Spain', 313–33, copyright (2004), with permission from Elsevier

Planning and small islands: Resort enclave development in Zanzibar – local community issues

Zanzibar, off the east coast of Tanzania (Figure 25.3) is an archipelago comprising one main island (Zanzibar Island) and a series of smaller islands with a population of one million people. Tourism developed during the 1980s as a development option and the Tourism Commission of Zanzibar (www.zanzibartourism.net, accessed 7 March 2005) states that:

Zanzibar discourages any tourism that does not conserve and improve the welfare of local people. The policy emphasizes ... responsible tourism, which has far reaching implications for the development and promotion of tourism. The objective behind the Zanzibar tourism development policy is to elaborate, taking into account Zanzibar's own reality and vision 2020, a framework of reference which will permit the establishment of the country's future tourism development, sustainability, quality and diversification as the most important factors.

Among the development problems facing the tourism sector, according to the Zanzibar Tourism Commission, is the fact that:

Tourism in Zanzibar has grown at an estimated 16 per cent per annum over the last 10 years. However, much of the food consumed by the tourists – including about 80 per cent of fresh vegetables, 20 per cent of fresh fruits and 40 per cent of herbs and spices – is imported from mainland Tanzania, Kenya, South Africa or even further afield in Europe. The Zanzibar Tourism Commission is anxious to reverse this trend, both to reduce costs to the tourist hotels and restaurants, to bring economic benefits to local farmers, and hence to improve relations between the tourists and the surrounding communities. (Ministry of Trade, Industry, Marketing and Tourism 2002, Integrated Tourism Development Project, Zanzibar)

This illustrates one of the problems facing planners – how to address leakage from the local economy. A report by Action Aid in 2004 criticized the tourism sector in Zanzibar for 'creating enclaves of wealth' as few local people had benefited from tourism and foreign investors were the main beneficiaries. Many of the local population survive on US$1 a day on an island receiving in excess of 90 000 overseas visitors a year in a destination promoted as an island paradise. Tourism has now replaced the country's former dependence upon spices.

One illustration of the impact of foreign investment is apparent from plans in 2000 for Nungwi, on the northern peninsular of Zanzibar. It is just is one example of where the interests of corporations and foreign investment have been put before the interests and feelings of local people.

The government of Zanzibar leased 57 square kilometres (at US$1 per year for 49 years) to the British-based East African Development Company (EADC) for a US$4 billion tourist enclave. It was planning to create the biggest tourism development in East Africa: 14 luxury hotels, several hundred villas, three golf courses, a country club, an airport, swimming pools, a marina and a trade centre.

The main concerns are that:

- there has been no consultation and local people have not been kept informed of plans
- 20 000 people live on the peninsula. They have not been informed whether they will have to move and if so, whether they will receive compensation
- Nungwi is a fishing and farming community, with a few small hotels and guest houses. The opportunites for a local mixed economy which would benefit the local community are likely to be lost if this development goes ahead, since Action Aid were already pointing to the problems fishermen were facing in accessing the coastline due to tourism development
- people fear the loss of fertile agricultural land and access to beaches as a result of the enclave.
- water supply is an existing problem in the area, with a lack of supply and poor distribution
- no social or environmental impact studies have been carried out.

At the present time, lobbying from the local community and NGOs has halted the development but once the potential of an area has been identified, it is not likely to be long before another similar proposal, albeit of a smaller scale, will be pursued. This poses many ethical dilemmas for planners who seek to grow tourism as a development option and yet have policies which clearly state responsible tourism is to be pursued.

Source: Tourism Concern website 2000; Zanzibar Tourism Commission website

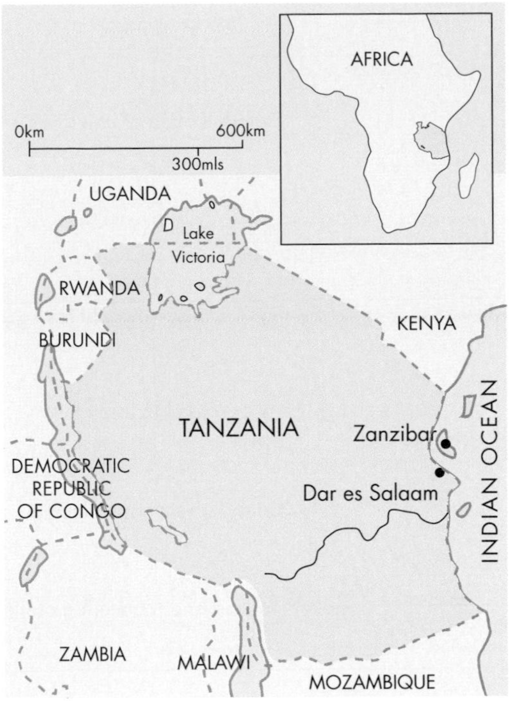

FIGURE 25.3 Location of Zanzibar

According to Inskeep (1994: 6) the effective management of tourism requires certain 'organizational elements'. The most important of these in a planning context are organizational structures, which include government agencies and private sector interests groups as well as the involvement of local and regional government bodies to plan for tourism activity, and tourism-related legislation and regulations as discussed in Chapter 14. One also has to have appropriate marketing and promotional programmes together with sources of capital and finance. When a government agency engages in tourism planning, a set process is usually followed which involves a series of steps.

The tourism planning process

As Figure 25.4 shows, the tourism planning process typically comprises:

1. *Study preparation*: the planning authority within the local or regional government (it may be one national agency on small islands that do not have a complex planning structure) decides to proceed with the development of a tourism plan. Heeley (1981) observed that while a number of agencies may be actively involved in tourism, it is normally a statutory body which undertakes the plan although quite often where a local and regional agency both develop a tourism plan, it is important that they dovetail and are integrated to ensure a unified structure to tourism. This was a problem in London in the 1990s, when the 33 London boroughs each had unified development plans but pursued different approaches to tourism (i.e. some councils promoted tourism development while others positively discouraged it) despite the efforts of the London Tourist Board, which sought to coordinate their activities in tourism.
2. *Determination of objectives*: the main purpose of the plan is identified (i.e. is it pursuing a sustainable strategy to development? Is it being undertaken in response to a crisis such as saturation tourism to identify managerial measures to reduce the social, cultural and environmental impacts?).

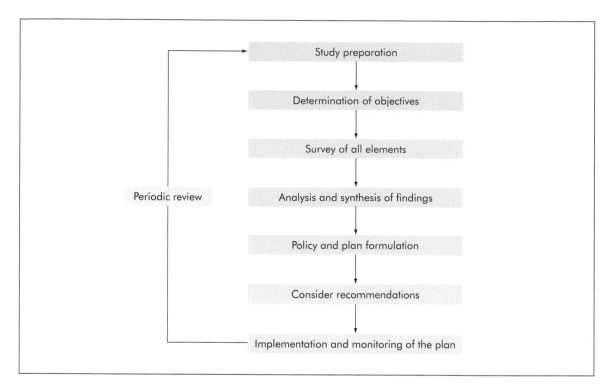

FIGURE 25.4   The planning process

3   *Survey of all elements*: an inventory of all the existing tourism resources and facilities are surveyed together with the state of development which are illustrated in Figure 25.5. This will require the collection of data on the supply and demand for tourism, the structure of the local tourism economy, investment and finance available for future development. It will also involve identifying the range of other private and public sector interests in tourism within the destination or locality.

4   *Analysis and synthesis of findings*: the information and data collected in the previous stage are analysed and incorporated as data when formulating the plan. As Cooper *et al.* (1998) argue, four principal techniques are frequently used here: asset evaluation, market analysis, development planning and impact analysis (especially economic impact analysis such as input–output analysis, multiplier analysis and tourism forecasting).

5   *Policy and plan formulation*: the data gathered in the previous stage are used to establish the various options or development scenarios available for tourism. This frequently involves the drafting of a development plan with tourism policy options, with certain goals identified. Acernaza (1985) argued that there are three main elements evident in most tourism policies that are germane to the tourist experience: *visitor satisfaction, environmental protection* and *ensuring adequate rewards exist for developers* and *investors*. By developing a range of policy options at this stage of the planning process, the future direction can be considered.

6   *Consideration of recommendations*: the full tourism plan is then prepared and forwarded to the planning committee of the public agency responsible for the process. A period of public consultation is normally undertaken in most Western industrialized countries. The draft plan is then available for public consultation so that both the general public and tourism interests can read and comment on it. A number of public hearings may also be provided to gauge the strength of local feeling towards the plan. Once this procedure is completed, the plan will then be approved by the planning authority and the final plan is then produced.

7   *The implementation and monitoring of the tourism plan*: the plan is put into action; this is normally seen as an ongoing process by the planning team. In some instances, legislation may be required to control certain aspects of development (e.g. the height of buildings and developments) which will need to be implemented as part of the plan. The political

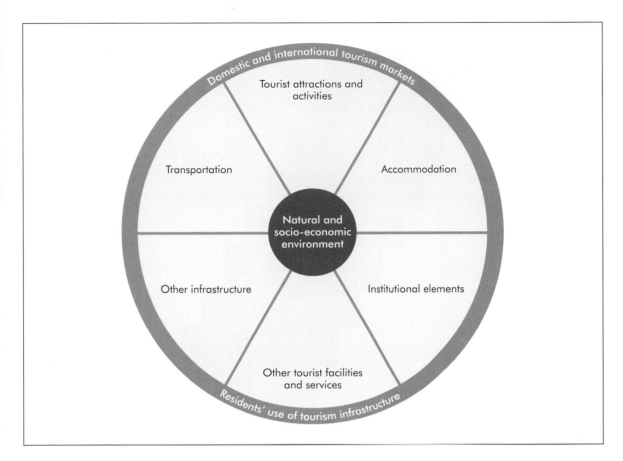

FIGURE 25.5   The elements of a tourism plan

complexity of implementing the plan should not be underestimated (see Hall and Jenkins 1995 for more detail). Often, the political complexion of the elected representatives on the statutory planning authority may change and cause the priorities to change although, if an Action Plan is produced alongside the plan, it will allow for some degree of choice in what is implemented and actioned in a set period of time. At the same time as the plan is implemented, it will also need to be monitored. This is an ongoing process where the planning agency assess if the objectives of the plan are being met. The operational time frame for a tourism plan is normally five years after which time it is reviewed.

8   *The periodic review*: the process of reporting back on the progress once the plan has run its course and been implemented. Some of the reasons for the failure of the plan to achieve its stated objectives may relate to a change of political complexion amongst the elected members of the planning authority (e.g. where an anti-tourism lobby dominates the local authority when the plan was commissioned by a pro-tourism council), a failure to achieve a degree of consensus between the private and public sector on how to address 'bottlenecks' in the supply of services and facilities for tourists; inadequate transport and infrastructure provision; and public opposition to tourism from a misunderstanding of residents' attitudes.

This planning process is not dissimilar to that outlined by Godfrey and Clarke (2000: vii) in Figure 25.6, which shows that marketing also needs to be incorporated into the planning process especially at the local or destination level.

Yet, as Page and Thorn (1997, 2002) show in relation to the development of sustainable tourism planning in New Zealand, while some local authorities may have plans for tourism, an absence of a regional or national plan for tourism to spread and distribute its benefits highlights the need for integration of planning between the three levels at which it commonly occurs: the *national* (i.e. the country level), *regional* (e.g. the county or state level in the USA) and the *local level*

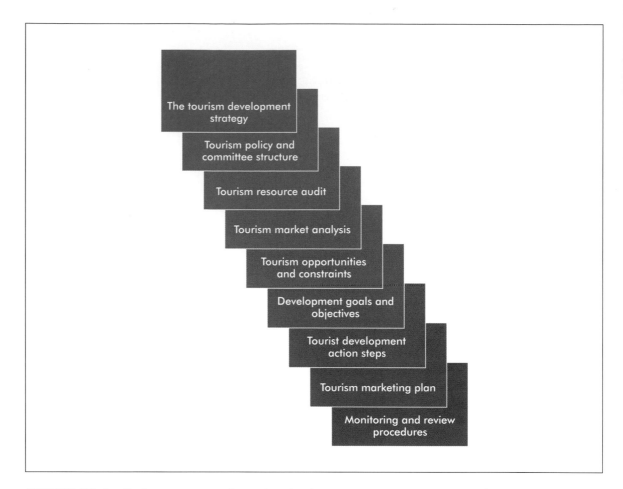

FIGURE 25.6 Basic components of a tourism development strategy. Source: Adapted from Godfrey and Clarke (2000: vii)

(i.e. the specific city, district or locality. At each level strategic vision is important, as Chapter 14 illustrated, as planning is more than simple notions of the land-use planning that has remained a permanent feature of urban and regional planning, with the local and global processes of tourism development often overlooked.

In the real world, 'planning for tourism' is a more apt description of the way tourism is treated by the public sector, since it is frequently incorporated in wider planning considerations which influence tourism development. Whatever form of management or planning which is developed for tourism in a given locality, a strategic view will need to satisfy the long-term provision of tourist experiences that are compatible with the locality, environment and resources available to planners and managers of the tourism. Therefore, with these issues in mind regarding the planning process, attention now turns to the issue of the tourist experience.

The tourist experience: Concepts and issues for planning and management

Hall and Page (1999: 164) note that 'there is a growing literature on tourist satisfaction ... and what constitutes the experiential aspects of a tourist visit to a locality' as reiterated by Uriely (2005). One way of starting to try and understand the tourist experience, is to consider the following observations by Ryan (1997) in relation to holidays:

- it has an important emotional involvement for the tourist

- there is a strong motivation for successful and satisfactory outcomes on the part of the tourist
- there is a significantly long period of interaction between the tourist on the one hand and, on the other, the place and people in the holiday destination – a period wherein the tourist can manipulate his or her surroundings to achieve the desired outcomes
- manipulative processes are part of the holiday experience and a source of satisfaction
- a number of holiday services exist, so that the tourist can select among alternatives
- holidays have a structure, whereby the tourist can play several different roles – each role may have separate determinants of satisfaction and each role may have unequal contributions to total holiday satisfaction
- a temporal significance not found in many service situations – it resides in the memory as a preparation for the future and is a resource for ego-sustainment during non-holiday periods.

In other words, the 'tourist experience' is a complex combination of objective, but predominantly subjective factors that shape the tourist's feelings and attitude towards his or her visit (Image 25.1). Yet it is almost impossible to predict tourist responses to individual situations, as a series of interrelated impacts may affect the tourist experience which itself is a dynamic entity, constantly subject to change. Pearce (1988) suggests that the sources of satisfaction differ between more and less experienced tourists at the same location – with greater levels of satisfaction likely to be gained by the more experienced tourist. Regardless of experience, there are many factors that contribute to tourist satisfaction, some of which are beyond the tourist's control (e.g. climate, traffic, noise and pollution). Many of these issues are important at the micro level (i.e. the individual tourist, place and service being consumed).

Yet the tourist experience is not just specific to holiday travel, since other types of tourists make decisions and evaluate their experiences as business travellers for example, where certain attributes are ranked importantly in the service they consume. One way to understand the issues associated with the visitor experience is to focus on one sector of the tourism sector, which is shown in Insight 25.2 with regard to visitor attractions.

Modelling the tourist experience

What Insight 25.2 illustrates is the need to develop some conceptual framework which can be used to model the tourist experience. Ryan (1997) offers one such framework as a two-stage process which is largely drawn from perspectives in marketing. In the first stage, Ryan (1997) points to the importance of the tourist decision-making and the determination of the destination choice. Once the choice to purchase a product for that destination occurs, Ryan (1997) points to the booking and creation of an anticipated event – the holiday. This is followed by the travel experience as well as the tourist's ability to also adapt to disappointments and problems which in themselves may not directly cause dissatisfaction: tourists may overcome any such problems and carry on with the holiday, since problems are also experiences which form the basis of the holiday, as shown in Figure 25.8. But there are many difficulties associated with researching the tourist experience.

Image 25.1: Crowding is not always detrimental to the visitor experience as indicated by attendees at the Glastonbury Festival, UK

INSIGHT 25.2

Factors influencing the tourist experience at visitor attractions – key studies and issues

Clawson and Knetsch (1966: 170) in their seminal work on outdoor recreation point out that 'the quality of the recreation experience is affected by the design, the investment and the management of outdoor recreation areas'. Likewise Heeley (1989) recognized that design issues, such as signposting and seating provision, present an image of the attraction to the visitor, which may or may not be favourable. Coupled with the physical management of the site is the importance of customer care, acknowledging the crucial relationship between the staff, the service and the needs of the visitor. Laws (1998) observed that each element is important and a lack of care – whether it is in the signage, car parking, quality of catering or cleanliness of the toilets – can destroy the overall visitor experience (Image 25.2). Indeed, Schouten (1995: 260) states that the attitude typified by 'visitors: who cares about them, they come anyway, so why bother?' is beginning to change at more professionally run and managed attractions. But as Schouten (1995) argued, in many cases there is still a gap between the product and visitor perception, which will be returned to later under service quality issues. Interestingly, Graefe and Vaske (1987) emphasized the influence of other visitors within the tourist site or destination. Visitors respond to perceived levels of crowding and this impacts on the resource base and can lead to dissatisfaction with the site or, indeed, displacement of the visitor.

In reality, the tourist experience is likely to be affected by a wide range of factors, some of which are inevitably not linked with the destination per se, but which hinge on the mood and personal circumstance of the visitor. Page (1995: 24) notes that the tourist experience may be affected 'by individual, environmental, situational and personality-related factors as well as the degree of communication with other people'. The experience is also likely to be affected by the expectations and preconceived ideas that the visitor may possess prior to a visit, as well as the cultural origin of the visitor and prior socialization. The recognition of these individual factors reflects the modelling of consumer-based experience when previous product experience or expectations influence the satisfaction/dissatisfaction process. Ryan (1997) highlights the overall importance of a closer understanding of social factors and individual motivations to more precisely identify the range of factors which impact upon the tourist experience in terms of how tourist expectations are shaped and the outcome as satisfaction or dissatisfaction (shown in Figure 25.7). This is a vital starting point in any conceptualization of the visitor experience, so we can better understand how individuals reach these perceptual decisions on the overall experience of tourism.

Image 25.2: Cleanliness and upkeep of destinations is important in promoting positive tourist experiences, such as in the Botanic Gardens in Singapore

Difficulties in researching the tourist experience

There are several inherent difficulties associated with researching tourist experiences which are associated with the concept of satisfaction. A visitor might be content with the core product but not with specific service elements; this emphasizes the **flow** of experiences notion conveyed by Beeho and Prentice (1997). Tourism operators and organizations are generally only concerned with the quality of the products that they are offering and thus approaches to quality are limited to specific components of a visitor's total experience. It is impossible to control all the factors relating to the visit experience and it should be recognized that, while a visitor may be completely satisfied with the core product and the tangible service elements, an external factor, such as the weather or transport infrastructure, might spoil the experience. Another factor to recognize is that satisfaction is not absolute and depends on individual needs, wants, expectations and experience. In addition, satisfaction thresholds inevitably change over time, as visitors gain more experience and industry standards advance.

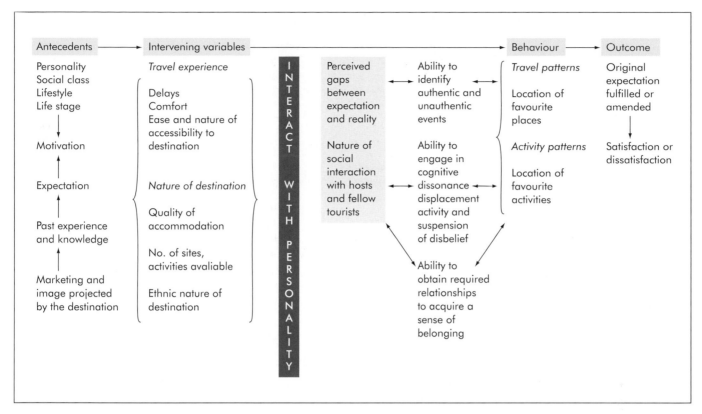

FIGURE 25.7   The link between expectation and satisfaction. Source: Ryan (1997: 50)

According to Swarbrooke and Horner (2001), two main factors underpin the need to ensure customers are satisfied with their visit experience. First, tourist satisfaction can encourage regular and repeat visitation, which is more cost effective for operators and organizations than seeking new visitors. Second, positive word of mouth recommendations work in the favour of attraction operators since minimal marketing input is required to attract new visitors. Word of mouth can work inversely too and the communication of bad experiences to friends and family is likely to negatively influence visit decision-making. Consequently, managing the tourist experience is a vital although complex requirement to sustain visitor satisfaction and, inevitably, numbers. Understanding the tourist experience is a key factor in determining the success of any tourist operation and has wider implications for the public perception of destinations, which requires appropriate tools and approaches to evaluate the tourist experience.

Evaluating the tourist experience

Despite being a key research issue in recent years (e.g. Vitterso *et al.* 2000), the study of the tourist experience remains one of the least understood fields in tourism research. Beeho and Prentice (1997) note that the experiential aspects of tourism are often omitted from visitor survey research in favour of sociodemographic data collection and more easily identifiable issues, such as mode of transport used to access a recreation site. One of the major reasons for this neglect is that measuring the tourist experience is beset with conceptual and methodological problems, not the least of which is agreeing on the way in which the experience is framed and measured. Ryan (1997) recognized that the complexity of researching the tourist experience is due to its highly subjective nature, based on perception and cognitive views of the environment, as well as the products that tourists consume. Otto and Ritchie (2000: 404) concur and state that in tourism, 'emotional reactions and decisions prevail'. Beeho and Prentice (1997: 75) recognize that 'visiting a tourist attraction is likely to involve a *flow* of experiences', which

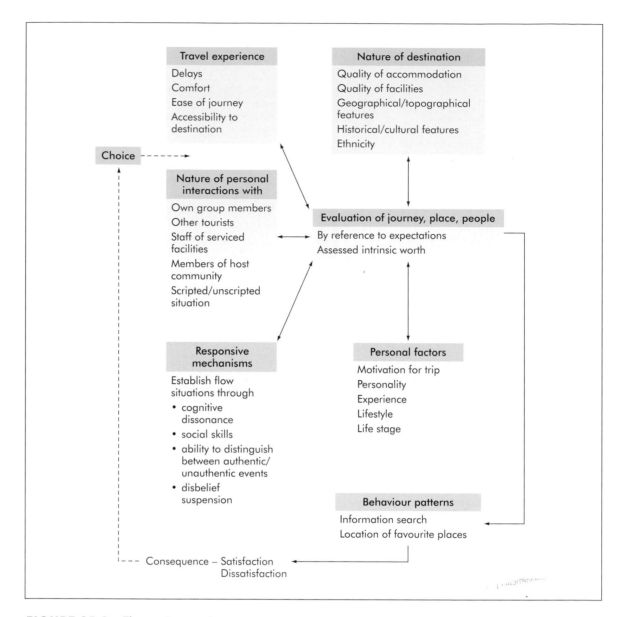

FIGURE 25.8 The tourist experience. Source: Ryan (1997: 54)

further complicates its study since there is likely to be a series of experiences rather than one focus, as tourists encounter different feelings and respond in different ways to each experiential element.

Research has focused on the tourist experience at heritage sites, presumably because, as Richards (1999) points out, 'heritage' alone is no longer sufficient in attracting visitors, and an understanding of visitors is a crucial aspect of ensuring future enterprise viability. Beeho and Prentice (1997) developed the use of the ASEB (activities, settings, experiences, benefits) grid analysis, a refinement of SWOT analysis (strengths, weaknesses, opportunities, threats), to gain insights into tourist experiences at the New Lanark World Heritage Village in Scotland. Experiences were found to be emotional; visitors found the village thought-provoking and overall an enjoyable educational experience. Having used the ASEB technique at the Black Country Museum (Beeho and Prentice 1996), Beeho and Prentice (1997) suggest that the grid analysis method allows the experiential components of tourism to be studied. It can provide qualitative consumer insights into tourism experiences and how they might be improved at a site or destination level. The ASEB approach appears to be a feasible methodology for on-site examination of tourist experiences but would be impractical to use on a wider scale because of its open-ended nature.

Service quality and the tourist experience

Service delivery and quality is a well-established field of inquiry in the marketing and consumer behaviour literature. Tourism and recreation researchers have applied the notion of service quality in varied contexts, including outdoor recreation, hospitality, travel services and the airline industry. A number of models have been developed to evaluate quality and customer satisfaction in business operations, the most notable of which is **SERVQUAL** (Parasuraman, Zeithmal and Berry 1985). Considered as a seminal study in consumer behaviour, the basis of this evaluative framework is the difference between consumer expectation and perception of service, based on five generic service quality dimensions necessary for customer satisfaction (see Table 25.2).

Further development of the model has led to the emergence of a range of allied quality assessment frameworks, such as HOLSAT to evaluate holiday experiences (Tribe and Smith 1998) and HISTOQUAL to evaluate the quality provided in historic houses (Frochot and Hughes 2000). HOLSAT is designed to increase holiday satisfaction through the use of expectations/performance analysis. Key attributes of the destination are first identified and addressed, and then tourists' attitudes to these attributes are analysed to produce a measure of satisfaction/dissatisfaction.

The HOLSAT method views satisfaction as the relationship between the performance of the holiday attributes against the expectation of the performance of these attributes as declared by tourists. Dissatisfaction is considered to have been experienced when expectations exceed the actual performance. Yet the five generic dimensions of service quality in Table 25.2 are a useful starting place for researching the tourist experience in relation to services. While Parasuraman *et al.* (1985) identified five gaps between service providers and consumers, later work suggested that another gap existed, that between the customer and the provider perception of the experience.

Gilbert and Joshi (1992) present an excellent review of the literature, including many of the concepts associated with the service quality. In tourism, it is the practical management of the 'gap' between the expected and the perceived service that requires attention by managers and the tourism industry. In reviewing Parasuraman *et al.*'s (1985) service quality model, Gilbert and Joshi (1992: 155) identify five gaps which exist between:

1 The expected service and the management's perceptions of the consumer experience (i.e. what they think the tourist wants) **(Gap 1)**

2 The management's perception of the tourist needs and the translation of those needs into service quality specifications **(Gap 2)**

3 The quality specifications and the actual delivery of the service **(Gap 3)**

4 The service delivery stage and the organization/provider's communication with the consumer **(Gap 4)**

5 The consumer's perception of the service they received and experienced, and their initial expectations of the service **(Gap 5)**.

TABLE 25.2 Dimensions of service quality based on the SERVQUAL principle

Reliability	Ability to perform services dependably
Responsiveness	Willingness to assist customers and provide prompt service
Assurance	Courtesy, trustworthiness and knowledge of staff
Empathy	Display of caring attitude to customers
Tangibles	Presentation of physical facilities

Gilbert and Joshi (1992) argue that the effective utilization of market research techniques could help to bridge some of the gaps. For:

Gap 1 – providers should be encouraged to elicit detailed information from consumers on what they require

Gap 2 – the management's ability to specify the service provided needs to be realistic and guided by clear quality standards

Gap 3 – the ability of employees to deliver the service according to the specification needs to be closely monitored and staff training and development is essential: a service is only as good as the staff it employs

Gap 4 – the promises made by service providers in their marketing and promotional messages need to reflect the actual quality offered. Therefore, if a city's promotional literature promises a warm welcome, human resource managers responsible for employees in front-line establishments need to ensure that this message is conveyed to its customers

Gap 5 – the major gap between the perceived service and delivered service should be reduced over time through progressive improvements in the appropriate image which is marketed to visitors and in the private sector's ability to deliver the expected service in an efficient and professional manner.

Such an approach to service quality emphasizes the importance of the marketing process in communicating and dealing with tourists. To obtain a better understanding of the service quality issues associated with the tourist's experience, Haywood and Muller (1988) identified a methodology for evaluating the quality of the tourist experience in an urban tourism setting.

Haywood and Muller's tourist experience framework

This framework involves collecting data on visitors' expectations prior to and after their city visit by examining a range of variables. It may be costly to operationalize, but it does provide a better appreciation of the visitation process and Haywood and Muller argue that cameras may also provide the day-to-day monitoring of city experiences. Haywood and Muller (1988) outline the factors to consider in evaluating the urban tourism experience (Table 25.3). These variables were selected as a result of a review of the literature on criteria for tourist attractiveness (Image 25.3), city liveability measures and other experiential attributes. Table 25.3 indicates that there are a number of general factors which can be applied to any tourism environment which functions as a destination. It highlights the diversity of components that may contribute to the overall level of satisfaction. It is clear that some factors are less easy to control than others and also that subjective factors can affect the experience.

Although Haywood and Muller's (1988) framework relates very specifically to urban areas, it is a relatively straightforward task to rework these factors to apply to alternative tourism locations. Most of the factors listed in Table 25.3 are generic to most visitor destinations, merely requiring some rewording to make them appropriate to a particular setting. Connell (2002) adapted this framework for the visitor experience of garden visiting (Table 25.4) and modelled different elements of that experience (Connell and Meyer 2004).

What Connell (2005) acknowledges is that knowing what the customer expects is the first step in delivering quality service. Despite several

Image 25.3: Public art, sculpture and other cultural features add interest to destinations and enhance the tourist experience

TABLE 25.3 Factors to consider in evaluating the urban tourism experience

- Unpleasantness of the city's weather during the visit
- Adequacy of standards in hotel accommodation
- Cleanliness and upkeep of the city
- The city's setting and scenic beauty
- Safety from crime
- Ease of finding and reaching places in the city
- Whether the city makes a visitor feel like a stranger
- Choice of artistic and cultural amenities
- Pleasurability of walking or strolling about the city
- Amount of crowding and congestion
- Choice of nightlife and entertainment
- Choice of good restaurants
- Pleasurability of shopping in the city
- Attractiveness of price levels
- Friendliness and helpfulness of citizens
- Adequacy of health care in case of emergency

Source: Adapted from Haywood and Muller (1988: 456) based on Connell (2002)

TABLE 25.4 Factors to consider in evaluating the garden visitor experience

- The weather conditions at the time of the visit
- The standard and quality of the garden and its features
- The tidiness and upkeep of the garden and cleanliness of facilities
- The setting and aesthetic value of the garden
- Health and safety considerations
- Accessibility of and ease of transport to the garden
- Access for disabled and less mobile visitors to the garden
- Warm and hospitable welcome extended to visitors
- Provision of information for international visitors
- The ambience of the garden as a place to walk around
- The level of crowding and congestion
- Range of events held in the garden
- Provision of a good quality tea-room
- The opportunity and pleasurability of plant purchasing and other retail opportunities
- The price of entry to the garden and prices of other goods and services
- Staff helpfulness in responding to visitor enquiries

Source: Connell (2002)

attempts to delineate the features of the tourist experience, there is no specific theory or model that provides an overarching view. In many evaluations of tourist experiences of products and services, the dominant element of dissatisfaction is often related to the staff–tourist encounter, and given the high human contact nature of tourism consumption, it is pertinent briefly to consider this feature.

Human resource issues and the tourist experience

Employee performance is crucial in tourism, given the dependence upon staff to deliver many elements of the tourist experience, to add value and to delight the consumer. Since businesses are usually responsible for the tourist encounter at the micro level, these issues assume great significance for such businesses: staff can make or break the tourist experience as already discussed. Positive interactions with staff can transform a negative experience and there should be a constant focus on training personnel in interaction skills as discussed in Chapter 11. Such programmes as **Welcome Host**, originally devised by the English Tourist Board, and company schemes are useful to educate staff to provide quality service.

The success of such programmes can be monitored through the analysis of customer comments and market research. This is part of how tourism businesses develop quality systems to ensure consistency and satisfaction with the services and products they supply. Foley, Lennon and Maxwell (1997) argue that systems of quality control need to be created to ensure that quality service delivery is taking place. Methods of monitoring and gaining feedback on quality include 'critical incident analysis'. This involves a detailed tracing back of service failures to discover what customers found to be unsatisfactory and how this can be avoided in the future. As Chung and Hoffman (1998: 66) state 'since the customer's perception of reality is the key factor, the analysis of service failures from the customer's point of view allows managers to minimize the occurrence of service failures through adjustments in operations and human-resource procedures'. Another useful management tool in this context is the 'zero defect'. Everybody has a level of tolerance before deciding to make a complaint. Here the goal for the firm is to identify those tolerance levels and achieve 'zero defect', i.e. no complaints.

Quality marks also offer opportunities for guiding and forming quality expectations. National and international standards such as BS (British Standard) and ISO (International Organization for Standardization) can help businesses to design and implement quality management systems, the awarding of which can provide assurances to customers. The introduction of such standards may lead to a reduction in complaints, improved management and lessened need for third-party intervention. An important dimension in managing the tourist experience, in the context of the tourism firm, is the consideration of aspect of service quality. To achieve this firms need the three 'Ss', strategy, staff and systems. Businesses need a strategy to better understand the expectations and satisfactions of their customers and need to their communicate service standards to their staff and provide them with adequate training. Systems of quality may be assured through ISO standards being achieved.

Graefe and Vaske (1987) argue that the development of a management strategy is necessary to:

- deal with problem conditions which may impact on the tourist experience
- identify causes of such problems
- select appropriate management strategies to deal with problems

and that how businesses handle customers is a key element of such strategies.

Godfrey and Clarke (2000) offer a great deal of practical advice for looking after the tourist, particularly customer care in terms of adding value to the experience (Image 25.4), increasing the length of stay, generating positive word of mouth recommendation, encouraging repeat visits from satisfied visitors and differentiating the destination from competitors. They point to five interrelated themes for retaining tourists:

- a tourist-focused organization and industry

Image 25.4: Memorable visitor experiences can be created through unplanned moments over which the tourism industry has little control

- authenticity in the experience
- provision of quality experiences and a commitment to quality by businesses
- integration in the tourism sector by cooperation to get strategic advantages over competitors
- innovation, with creative thinking and product/service development which can often be achieved by making small, incremental changes to make a difference.

In setting up a service quality standard, Godfrey and Clarke (2000) point to the importance of introducing:

- *hard standards*, where definable standards can be measured to assess progress and outcomes
- *soft standards*, where measures such as staff friendliness, courtesy and ability can be assessed.

One of the most important features here, which tourists are quick to judge, is the ability of businesses in complaint handling. As a result, destinations need to empower staff to address complaints in a systematic and professional manner as discussed in Chapter 11. Godfrey and Clarke (2000) outline a number of practical tips for staff handling complaints (Table 25.5) to ensure dissatisfied customers can have their grievance resolved.

TABLE 25.5 Practical tips for staff handling complaints

- ✓ DO dress professionally as this sends positive signals
- ✓ DO remain calm and confident
- ✗ DON'T argue with the tourist
- ✓ DO use positive body language
- ✓ DO establish and maintain eye contact
- ✗ DON'T raise your voice or shout
- ✓ DO observe and listen carefully – allow the tourist to speak
- ✓ DO apologize that the situation has happened and thank the tourist for raising the matter with you
- ✗ DON'T blame colleagues in front of the tourist
- ✓ DO take responsibility for solving the problem
- ✓ DO ask questions to find out more information
- ✗ DON'T be aggressive
- ✓ DO summarize information to check mutual understanding
- ✓ DO analyse the information regarding cause and behaviour
- ✗ DON'T personalize the situation
- ✓ DO present alternative solutions, any explanations and then agree on a solution
- ✓ DO carry out the agreed solution or check that it is carried out
- ✗ DON'T offer excuses
- ✓ DO check that the tourist is satisfied with the final outcome
- ✗ DON'T reach conclusions before you have sufficient information

IN SOME INSTANCES

- ✓ DO walk and talk to the tourist at the same time maintaining eye contact – useful for removing the complainer from a public area
- ✓ DO refer the problem to management if necessary or the tourist insists
- ✓ DO take notes on incidents as a precautionary measure immediately afterwards
- ✓ DO coax the tourist to tell you about a problem if you think they are reluctant to speak to you

Source: Godfrey and Clarke (2000: 178)

Conclusion

Evaluating the tourist experience is a complex process which involves modelling the factors that may affect the experience and then measuring the tourists' views and attitudes, often against a scale or list of factors. This is both a time-consuming and a costly process and yet its value to the tourism industry should not be underestimated. The motivating factors (i.e. the tourist's perception of what makes them choose a particular destination); their actual activities and the extent to which their expectations are matched by reality all feed into how satisfying the experience of being a tourist may be. The highly personal nature of tourist expectations and satisfaction is highly subjective and changeable, making it hard for the tourism industry to create products that will guarantee satisfaction. But this is vital to the future viability and sustainability of tourism destinations, and it is not surprising that many tourism destinations are concerned with ways in which they can manage the tourist and the tourist experience to improve the overall experience.

The management of the tourist experience is an absolutely vital, but complex requirement. Tourism planning is part of a wider planning process, however, where the needs of other industries as well as the local population are considered, and the tourist experience is often overlooked. Therefore, there is a need for national policies to integrate with tourism policies at the regional or local level with clear guidelines on what the tourist experience is deemed to be and how to add value to it. To be successful the wider tourism industry need to have a strategy for understanding their customers, employ well-trained staff and have an appropriate system of quality assurance as a prerequisite for achieving a prosperous tourism sector.

Discussion questions

1 Why is tourism planning needed in tourism?

2 Who is responsible for the tourism planning process, and what are the stages involved in developing a tourism plan?

3 What is the tourist experience?

4 How would you go about developing a plan to assess the tourist experience of tourism for a specific destination?

References

Acernaza, M. (1985) 'Planificación estratégica del turismo: Esquesma metológico' *Estudiios Turisticos*, 85: 45–70.

Baidal, J.A.I. (2004) 'Regional tourism planning in Spain: Evolution and perspectives', *Annals of Tourism Research*, 31 (2): 313–33.

Beeho, A. and Prentice, R. (1996) 'ASEB grid analysis and the Black Country Museum in the West Midlands of England: Understanding visitor experiences as a basis for product development', in L. Harrison and W. Husbands (eds) *Practicing Responsible Tourism: International Case Studies in Tourism Planning, Policy and Development*. New York: Wiley.

Beeho, A. and Prentice, R. (1997) 'Conceptualizing the experiences of heritage tourists: A case study of New Lanark World Heritage Village', *Tourism Management*, 18 (2): 75–87.

Chadwick, G. (1971) *A Systems View of Planning*. Oxford: Pergamon Press.

Chung, B. and Hoffman, K.D. (1998) 'Critical incidents: Service failures that matter most', *Cornell Hotel and Restaurant Administration Quarterly*, June: 54–70.

Clawson, M. and Knetsch, J. (1966) *Economics of Outdoor Recreation*. Baltimore, MD: Johns Hopkins University Press.

Connell, J. (2002) 'A critical analysis of gardens as a resource for tourism and recreation in Great Britain', unpublished Ph.D. thesis, Department of Geographical Sciences, University of Plymouth.

Connell, J. (2005) 'Toddler, tourism and Tobermory: Destination marketing issues and television-induced tourism', *Tourism Management*, 26 (5): 763–76.

Connell, J. and Meyer, D. (2004) 'Modelling the visitor experience in the gardens of Great Britain', *Current Issues in Tourism*, 7 (3): 183–217.

Cooper, C.P., Fletcher, J., Gilbert, D.G. and Wanhill S. (1998) *Tourism: Principles and Practice*. Harlow: Addison Wesley Longman.

Foley, M., Lennon, J.J. and Maxwell, G.A. (1997) *Hospitality, Tourism and Leisure Management: Issues in Strategy and Culture*. London: Cassell.

Frochot, I. and Hughes, H. (2000) 'HISTOQUAL: The development of a historic houses assessment scale', *Tourism Management*, 21 (2): 157–67.

Getz, D. (1987) 'Tourism planning and research: Traditions, models and futures', Paper presented at the Australian Travel Research Workshop, Bunbury, Western Australia, 5–6 November.

Gilbert, D. and Joshi, I. (1992) 'Quality management and the tourism and hospitality industry', in C. Cooper and A. Lockwood (eds) *Progress in Tourism, Recreation and Hospitality Management, Vol. 4*. London: Belhaven.

Godfrey, K. and Clarke, J. (2000) *The Tourism Development Handbook: A Practical Approach to Planning and Marketing*. London: Cassell.

Graefe, A. and Vaske, J. (1987) 'A framework for managing quality in the tourist experience', *Annals of Tourism Research*, 14 (3): 389–404.

Gunn, C. (1988) *Tourism Planning, Second Edition*. London: Taylor and Francis.

Hall, C.M. (1999) *Tourism Planning: Policies, Processes and Relationships*. Harlow: Addison Wesley Longman.

Hall, C.M. and Jenkins, J. (1995) *Tourism and Public Policy*. London: Routledge.

Hall, C.M. and Page, S.J. (1999) *The Geography of Tourism and Recreation: Environment, Place and Space, First Edition*. London: Routledge.

Haywood, K. and Muller, T. (1988) 'The urban tourist experience: Evaluating satisfaction', *Hospitality Education and Research Journal*, 453–9.

Heeley, J. (1981) 'Planning for tourism in Britain', *Town Planning Review*, 52 (1): 61–79.

Heeley, J. (1989) 'Visitor attractions and the commercial sector', *Insights*, D1–13.

Inskeep, E. (1991) *Tourism Planning: An Integrated and Sustainable Development Approach*. New York: Van Nostrand Reinhold.

Inskeep, E. (1994) *National and Regional Tourism Planning: Methodologies and Case Studies*. London: Routledge.

Laws, E. (1998) 'Conceptualizing visitor satisfaction management in heritage settings: An exploratory blueprinting analysis of Leeds Castle, Kent', *Tourism Management*, 19 (6): 545–54.

Otto, J.E. and Ritchie, J.R. (2000) 'The service experience in tourism', in Ryan, C. and Page, S.J. (eds) *Tourism Management Towards the New Millennium*. Oxford: Pergamon.

Page, S.J. (1995) *Urban Tourism*. London: Routledge.

Page, S.J. and Thorn, K. (1997) 'Towards sustainable tourism planning in New Zealand: Public sector planning responses', *Journal of Sustainable Tourism*, 5 (1): 59–77.

Page, S.J. and Thorn, K. (2002) 'Towards sustainable tourism planning in New Zealand: Public sector planning responses revisited', *Journal of Sustainable Tourism*, 10 (3): 222–39.

Parasuraman, A., Zeithaml, V. and Berry, L. (1985) 'A conceptual model of service quality and its implications for future research', *Journal of Marketing*, 49 (4): 41–50.

Pearce, D. (1988) *Tourist Development, Second Edition*. Harlow: Longman.

Richards, G. (1999) 'Heritage visitor attractions in Europe: A visitor profile', *Interpretation*, 4 (3): 9–13.

Ryan, C. (ed) (1997) The Tourist Experience: A New Introduction, Cassell: London.

Schouten, F. (1995) 'Improving visitor care in heritage attractions', *Tourism Management*, 16 (4): 259–61.

Swarbrooke, J. and Horner, S. (2001) 'Researching tourist satisfaction', *Insights*, A161–9.

Tribe, J. and Smith, T. (1998) 'From SERQUAL to HOLSAT: Holiday satisfaction in Varadero, Cuba', *Tourism Management*, 19 (1): 25–34.

Uriely, N. (2005) 'The tourist experience: Conceptual developments', *Annals of Tourism Research*, 32 (1): 199–216.

Vitterso, J., Vorkinn, M., Vistad, O. and Vaagland, J. (2000) 'Tourist experiences and attractions', *Annals of Tourism Research*, 27 (2): 432–50.

Further reading

Connell, J. and Meyer, D. (2004) 'Modelling the visitor experience in the gardens of Great Britain', *Current Issues in Tourism*, 7 (3): 183–217.

Ryan, C. (ed.) (2002) *The Tourist Experience, Second Edition*. London: Thomson Learning.

26 Tourist Health and Safety: Global Challenges for Tourism

Learning outcomes

After reading this chapter and answering the questions, you should be able to:

- understand the significance of health and safety issues in the operation and management of tourism

- identify the range of issues which may impact upon the tourist and the destination in terms of tourist well-being

- outline some of the main links between tourism and health, tourism and crime and the role which public sector agencies play in managing these issues

- explain how a tourism crisis can impact upon a destination.

Overview

Tourist health and safety is now a global theme associated with tourist travel as a wide range of threats, risks and potential hazards affect travellers. This chapter provides an overview of these threats and risks, together with a framework for conceptualizing and analysing these issues. There is growing evidence that tourist safety, especially the role or threat of terrorism is now one of the top ten most important world tourism issues for both travellers and the tourism sector. For this reason, tourist travel is increasingly being affected by global issues which may affect our propensity to travel, and the tourism industry in different destinations.

Introduction

Throughout the history of travel, visitors have faced the tourist-related phenomenon of leaving their home environment to visit one which they may find unfamiliar, and has associated risks and hazards inherent in their lack of knowledge associated with that environment, illustrated by the tourists stranded in the USA following Hurricanes Katrina and Rita in 2005. This highlights two interrelated themes which combine to make tourist travel unique: the pursuit of enjoyment, rest, relaxation and the use of leisure time in unfamiliar surroundings to improve one's sense of well-being (Gilbert and Abdullah 2004) with the associated environmental and behavioural-related risks. The underlying risks, potential hazards and safety issues which travellers face is predominantly a function of the knowledge of the individual or group travelling, and their willingness and ability to understand the information available to adapt their behaviour to reduce the potential risks. However, certain forms of tourism (e.g. adventure tourism – see Insight 4.1) are based upon the notion of risk to generate an experience of being a tourist that is memorable, involving significant personal or group risk. This may be to seek the enjoyment of a personal challenge posed by **environmental risk** (e.g. mountaineering, white-water rafting and potholing) although making such generalizations are questionable when examining the different motivations and segments in niche markets such as adventure tourism. This chapter seeks to provide a wide-ranging understanding of the scope and extent of the issues associated with tourist health and safety, together with a discussion of concepts essential to understand how the notion of tourist safety and well-being are integral to tourist enjoyment and the tourist experience (see Chapter 27).

When things go wrong, a growing culture of **litigation** in travel and tourism can often have dire financial consequences for businesses and can tarnish the image of a destination or product. This has led to the growth of interest in practical measures to address major problems, especially crises like the Bali bombing, **biosecurity** risks associated with the importation of microrganisms by visitors that can harm the agriculture sector (Hall 2005), the 9/11 terrorist attack and the 2004 **tsunami** in the Indian Ocean. Such events can lead to major impacts on the tourism economy, environment and resident population as shown in Table 26.1, when over 250 000 people died and the WTTC estimated that the cost to tourism would be £3 billion (but 9/11 was estimated to have cost 37.5 times that amount). The World Tourism Organization (2003a) have devised practical advice for destinations to address such issues with a crisis recovery strategy, arguing that action needs to be taken:

- before the crisis, with the active preparation of a crisis management plan
- during the crisis, so as to minimize damage as the 9/11 insight will show later in the chapter
- after the crisis, with a recovery strategy to boost visitor confidence and active strategies to boost tourist numbers by promotion campaigns.

But these events are comparatively rare compared to the wider issues which prevail in relation to tourist health and safety and therefore, throughout the chapter, appropriate examples and insights illustrate the significance of tourist health and safety as a growing area of research in tourism studies, as shown by the rapid expansion in articles and books in this area (e.g. Clift and Page 1996, Wilks and Page 2003, Wilks, Prendergast and Leggatt 2005). These issues have growing significance for both the tourist and the tourism industry. Indeed, the World Tourism Organization (2003b) produces a tourist safety and security handbook which provides practical advice for the tourism sector on this area. Yet, given the complexity of tourist health and safety, it is useful to examine some of the ways this can be understood.

Conceptualizing tourist health and safety

The media is a powerful force in modern-day society and the imagery, headlines and reporting of global events have portrayed the immediacy of threats posed by terrorist groups and **natural disasters** (e.g. hurricanes and floods) to tourist destinations. This increasingly heightens the

TABLE 26.1   The impact of the Indian Ocean tsunami 2004 on tourism : Selected implications

Category of impact	Implications for tourism
Environmental	• Destruction of coastal tourism resources • Destruction of tourism infrastructure and resort areas • Pollution of groundwater/sanitation of drinking water, aquifers and wells • Post-tsunami disease risks (cholera and diarrhoea) • Destruction of sea defences and walls • Destruction of agriculture and sanitation on small islands
Economic	• Interruption to tourism industry and direct effect on GDP, foreign exchange earnings and visitor arrivals • Destruction/interruption to tourism-related enterprises • Direct losses from uninsured property • Loss of entrepreneurs and local tourism business structures and networks • Repatriation of existing tourists/evacuation of existing visitors by inbound tour operators • Increased dependence upon foreign aid to rebuild tourism infrastructure and international businesses to reconstruct hotels/infrastructure and loss of local control • Over-dependence upon tourism in specific localities (e.g. coastal areas and island destinations such as the Maldives) means there are few existing alternatives for immediate economic diversification • Loss of tourism labour force, trained employees and human resource capital • Cost of reconstruction and clean-up to national governments aid agencies/UN • Cost of tsunami warning system for tourist destinations • 30 per cent loss of GDP in the Maldives, equivalent to US$55 million
Political	• Major pressure on foreign embassies, tour representatives and operators working in a crisis management role within emergency political situation • Humanitarian efforts and aid efforts assume a high priority to address human catastrophe on a vast scale and tourism revitalization is a low priority • Media imagery and international coverage of resorts devastated will deter visitors in the short to medium term, requiring a major advertising campaign to rebuild the visitor base • Dependence upon international aid/investment to rebuild the tourism sector and political complexity of tourism internationalization versus local capital and employment • Leadership and knowledge crises at the local level due to key decision-makers in the public sector lost in the tsunami and loss of local knowledge • Re-evaluation by politicians and decision-makers on the role of tourism recovery and its role in economic redevelopment, with the need to secure foreign exchange and tourist income to rebuild local economies, especially on small islands
Social	• Loss of communities, families and kinship groups leading to temporary social disintegration and a focus on human survival • Pressure on shelter and surviving tourist infrastructure locally/regionally in the evacuation of survivors • Greater visitor–host interaction in a disaster setting, with displaced residents and tourists in different roles • Overseas humanitarian aid effort targeted at residents with varying motives that will cast visitors in a different light (i.e. the aid donor–recipient relationship, see Hall and Page 1996) • New tourist–resident relationships built in extreme situations • Loss of local communities' feelings of control of the tourism development process, as post-tsunami reconstruction may be due to the influence of non-local decision-makers or politicians with no local knowledge • Residents' fear of residing in coastal areas

traveller's awareness of potential risks but this alone will not ensure their safety and well-being, since the risk-taking behaviour of the tourist is also crucial to understanding why some individuals avoid risk whilst others seek risk. This was discussed in Chapter 4 in relation to tourist typologies. Tourist behaviour will directly influence the willingness of the tourist to listen to health education promotions, safety advice and the messages from the media on specific destinations and activities. Therefore, the complexity of tourists' behaviour and actions needs to be understood in some organizing framework which outlines the basic assumptions and features of tourist health and safety – well-being.

Tourist well-being

Tourist well-being is beginning to be accepted by researchers and the tourism industry as an important concept in relation to tourist satisfaction (Gilbert and Abdullah 2004), which will shape purchase behaviour and recommendations as well as in relation to the tourist experience. A dissatisfied visitor is the worst publicity for a destination or product as word of mouth dissemination of the experience can damage the credibility and image of the product and destination. Yet, as previous chapters have shown, tourist satisfaction is a measure of the satisfaction/dissatisfaction with the product and overall experience. But this in itself does not broach the fundamental issue associated with visitor safety: who is responsible for the well-being of the tourist? Walker and Page (2003) discussed this issue, identifying a wide range of agencies and bodies who interact with tourists and who collectively have a responsibility for the tourist, as shown in Figure 26.1. This is not to suggest that the tourist should not be responsible for their own actions, but the unfamiliarity with a destination means that the various agencies and bodies who interact with the tourist should also have a responsibility for their well-being (Unter-Jones 2000), and thereby the resulting satisfaction/dissatisfaction with the destination and product. As the tourist experience is such a complex and multifarious phenomenon, there are a wide range of factors which can impact upon the resulting perception and satisfaction. But

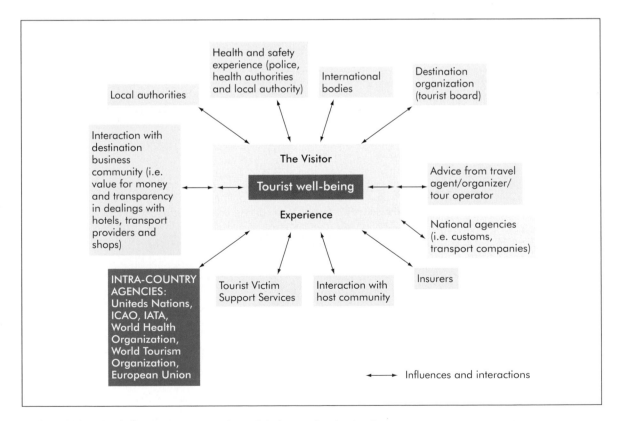

FIGURE 26.1   Influences upon tourist well-being at the destination

it is certainly the case that safety and the well-being of the visitor are core elements in the experience. As Figure 26.1 confirms, tourist health and safety are essentially bound up in the wider tourist experience of the destination but few studies have explicitly discussed the roles and responsibilities for the visitor. In a growing age of litigation when things go wrong, this debate is becoming more critical, over and above directives such as the EU's (1993) Package Holiday Directive which set out who is responsible for the commercial transaction. Tourist well-being is a complex topic because it is value laden, meaning that to some observers the tourist's experience and well-being assume a high-profile role but to others the public policy approach means that these are not issues to consider. Therefore, those destinations which treat tourist well-being seriously coordinate many of the issues outlined in Figure 26.1 and are able to deal with incidents quickly and efficiently. Therefore, positive notions of well-being in the destination can become a potential competitive advantage. Here, if the tourist feels safe and well looked-after, and their stay is as problem-free as possible, then word of mouth on the destination acts as positive recommendations.

The overall notion of well-being, where the reason for taking a holiday is a positive experience during leisure time, highlights the importance of understanding how important health and safety issues are. One way of illustrating the potential scope and scale of such issues is shown in Figure 26.2. This shows that there are many high-risk–high-volume health and safety issues which impact upon tourist travel and the tourist experience which may be preventable if appropriate advice and action are offered prior to the visit and during the visit. This highlights the importance of:

- pre-travel planning
- the trip from origin to destination
- personal safety and tourist health at the destination
- tourist health on the return to the origin area or subsequent areas they pass through, especially in the case of SARS which was transmitted by travellers moving across borders and by air travel.

There is a considerable variability in the accuracy of information and advice offered by travel professionals in the pre-travel stage. For example, in a study of New Zealand travel agents' advice to outbound travellers to the Pacific Islands, Lawton and Page (1997) identified significant omissions

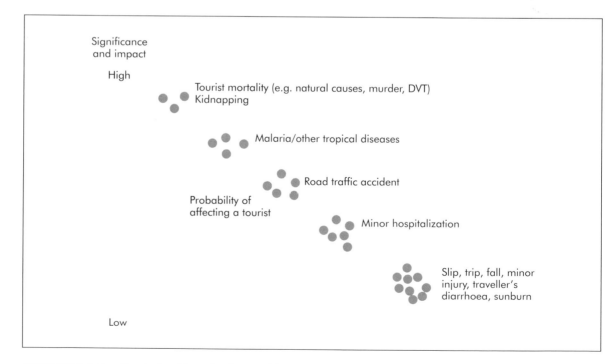

FIGURE 26.2 Tourist health and safety problems: Scale and incidence

and oversights. They concluded that guide books such as the **Lonely Planet** offered more robust and reliable information although this was not as up to date as information on health risks and inoculations needed from GPs and practice nurses. In the UK, travel clinics and online travel advice make extensive use of global surveillance sources from the World Health Organization and the Centre for Disease Control, Atlanta, USA, and the equivalent UK body. The significance of these bodies was illustrated during the SARS outbreak (Page 2005) and they assumed a critical surveillance role in advising visitors on travel plans, travel behaviour and risk factors, highlighting the inter-connections between tourism and health inferred in Figure 26.1 between the destination and inter-country agencies.

Figure 26.2 also shows that other high-risk events such as kidnapping and crime can be advised upon by information from government surveillance websites such as the CIA and the Foreign and Commonwealth in London, as discussed later in the chapter. Low-risk events like traveller's diarrhoea (see Cartwright 1996), which can affect high proportions of visitors during a package holiday depending upon the destination visited, can be treated by appropriate drugs. In 2004, there were 36 outbreaks of the highly infectious and hard to kill norovirus, which causes acute gastroenteritis, on board cruise ships calling at US ports. Outbreaks affected between 4.4 per cent and 21 per cent of passengers. The severity of this virus has led some cruise firms to waive the cancellation penalties rather than have passengers who are vulnerable to illness travelling and contracting the virus. Indeed, the extent of travel health issues is reflected in the specialist publications like the *Journal of Travel Medicine* which has highlighted that over 50 per cent of travellers returning to Australia after visiting LDCs reported health problems. More worrying is the recent mutation of animal viruses which have jumped across to humans like avian flu. In 2004, this killed 44 in South East Asian countries and over 60 in 2005, and poses many problems similar to those posed by SARS. Numerous studies exist in the *Journal of Travel Medicine* on the possible causes and risk factors associated with commonly reported travel health problems (e.g. motion sickness, car accidents, injuries and accidents) as well as less common events such as tourist mortality, commonly associated with cardiovascular problems and Insight 26.1 focuses on these issues in adventure tourism.

The studies of travellers' health published in the *Journal of Travel Medicine* reveals the correlation of specific tourist groups (e.g. kidnapping of backpackers in South America) and market segments (youth travellers) in terms of car accidents as well as certain risk factors that make specific groups more likely to incur injury. The travel insurance industry is fully cognizant of these issues, and they are reflected in their premiums for specific destinations, exclusions for specific activities and the application of excesses for commonly reported health and safety issues.

As any form of human activity will involve risk (Page and Meyer 1996), then injuries, accidents and safety issues will occur. For the tourism industry and the wide range of agencies who interact in this area to provide advice and information, their responsibility is to point the visitor to necessary advice. However, if they choose not to take that advice or heed the warnings, the tourism sector has fulfilled its obligations (Image 26.1). In these cases, insurance provision can often be invalidated where the 'small print' requires advice to be followed. However, there is a global recognition among insurers of the importance of risk assessment by destination and activities to be undertaken and one area of growing concern among the travel sector and the travelling public is air travel and the problems this may pose. This is discussed in Insight 26.2.

Image 26.1: Capital cities, like London, are considered a terrorist target but visitors are not deterred by such perceived threats

INSIGHT 26.1

Accidents and injuries in adventure tourism

In a study of the adventure tourism sector, Bentley, Page and Laird (2001) also pointed to the problems which contributed to accidents and injuries. This led them to construct a model (see Figure 26.3) which attributed the risks of participating in adventure tourism to a series of interconnecting factors which combined the:

- problems of clients participating (i.e. human failures in communicating levels of risk and experience levels)
- environmental factors (i.e. the unpredictability of the terrain, natural environment and hazards)
- equipment-related problems, such as failures of safety equipment
- significance of factors outside the control of businesses (i.e. weather and forecasting)
- management and organizational failures, including a lack of experience amongst employees and failure to brief clients properly and to undertake safety audits and risk assessment of activities, as well as cultural problems in seeking to save money by taking short cuts amongst some businesses.

More recent research in Scotland by Page, Bentley and Walker (2005) and in New Zealand reinforced the applicability of such a model in adventure activities along with the problem of safety issues for predominantly small operators (i.e. employing fewer than five staff) in this sector. One consequence of research by Page et al. (2005) is that one

can begin to construct a distinct geography of injury/accident risk by tourist board region (Figure 26.4) according to:

- the number of clients and type (i.e. day visitor, domestic or international visitor and adult/child)
- activity type (land-, air- or water-based or mixed)
- number of participation hours which are expressed in Figure 26.4 in terms of injuries per million participation hours (IPMPH) so that the risk can be standardized in terms of the risks faced in terms of how long each activity lasts.

As Figure 26.4 shows, certain regions with a highly developed adventure tourism sector (e.g. Perthshire) have a high concentration of injuries reflecting the prominent nature of these activities in this region of Scotland.

The consequences of such research reinforce the importance of regulatory bodies and codes of practice to improve client safety as well as a need to raise standards to the levels of best practice that exist within the tourism industry. Research undertaken by the authors for organizations such as the New Zealand government and Perthshire Tourist Board recognize the importance of the tourism sector improving its own industry without government legislation to intervene and regulate it more fully, which could stifle innovation and creativity. However, as the legal case history research in New Zealand shows (Callander and Page 2003), there is a trend towards litigation when adventure tourism accidents cause personal injury and loss, despite the provisions of the country's unique No Faults, No Suing accident compensation legislation (Page and Meyer 1996). What this insight shows above all is that accidents and injuries attract litigation against a global growth in the participation of adventure tourism. Visitor risk may be understood more fully if the hazards are understood, the behaviour of visitors is appropriate in the adventure setting, effective precautions are taken and warnings on possible hazards are given by adventure operators (Image 26.2).

Image 26.2: White-water rafting provides a major adrenaline rush for adventure tourists

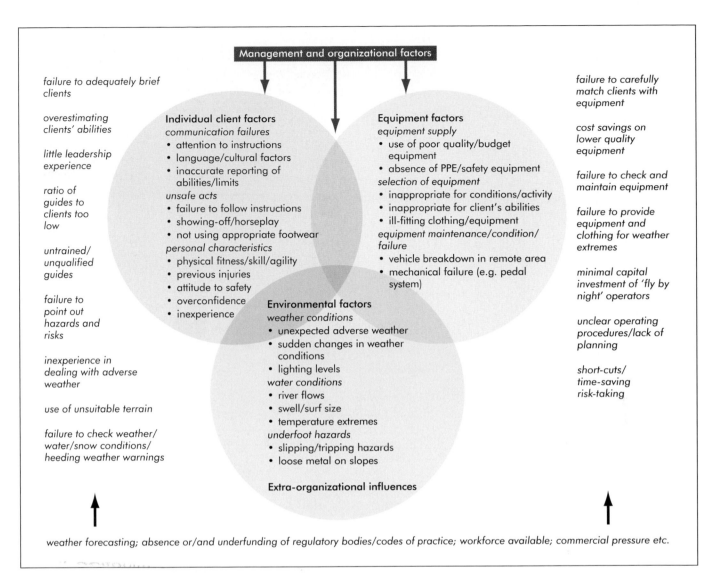

FIGURE 26.3 Conceptual model of risk factors for accidents in adventure tourism. Source: Reprinted from Safety Science 38, Bentley, Page and Laird, 'Accidents in the New Zealand Adventure Tourism Industry', 31–38.

Tourist health and safety problems and destinations

The most cited and seminal study by Cossar *et al.* (1990) examined the problems among over 14 000 returning Scottish holiday-makers to understand the problems they faced in the destination and the common issues they faced on their return. Thirty-six per cent of travellers reported some element of illness including diarrhoea and vomiting (18 per cent), alimentary problems (10 per cent) and respiratory problems (2 per cent) along with accidents and injuries. These figures are consistent with many of the in-house studies undertaken by tour operators on the return journey although these remain confidential to the operator. Nevertheless, subsequent studies of tourist health by Clift and Page (1996), Clift and Grabowski (1998) and Wilks and Page (2003) highlight the range and scope of problems which impact upon the tourist experience in the destination. In most extreme cases, tourist mortality may be a media issue, particularly where it is associated with crime or road accidents.

Tourist road accidents (RTAs) in the destination are a common non-fatal but serious health and safety issue, after more personal health issues that can be avoided by careful precautions on the food and water which is consumed, often following advice: 'Don't eat or drink it, if it has not been boiled, cooked or washed.' However, in the case of RTAs, these commonly result from:

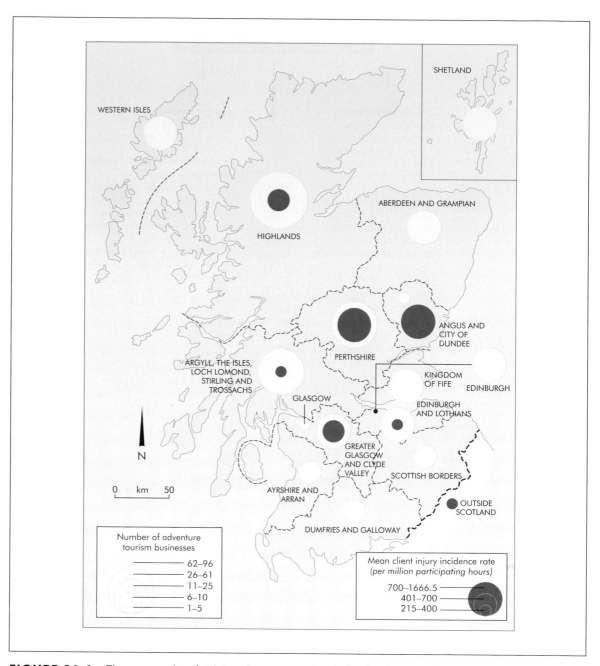

FIGURE 26.4   The geography of risk in adventure tourism in Scotland, copyright S.J. Page

- tourists being unfamiliar with local road conditions
- tourists driving too fast
- tourists being under the influence of drugs or alcohol
- tourists lacking experience of driving in other countries or on different terrains
- tourists failing to give way to other vehicles and to pedestrians
- driver fatigue and falling asleep at the wheel
- defects with vehicles
- poor visibility or experience of overtaking on unfamiliar roads and following too close to other vehicles
- sudden braking or swerving
- poor weather conditions.

Tourist health problems and air travel

In the pre-travel, travel and post-travel phases of tourism, air travel now plays a major role in the movement of would-be holiday-makers from origin to destination. At each stage, tourist health can actually be adversely affected (temporarily or in extreme cases permanently) rather than improved through travel. Take, for example, the journey from home to the airport and the perceived and actual stress of check-in, waiting around in crowded departure lounges, delays, and the impact upon a population with increased levels of high blood pressure. This can not only raise anxiety levels, which are high for infrequent fliers, but also may contribute towards and compound existing medical conditions.

Among the common problems associated with air travel are motion sickness, which is potentially caused (though research evidence is not conclusive) by the stress of travel (up to 60 per cent of travellers have a fear of flying) and imbalance in the ear which causes nausea and vomiting. Yet two of the more controversial issues affecting travellers involves the onset of **deep vein thrombosis** (DVT) and the poor quality of cabin air.

DVT was in the world media in recent years after a number of people developed the condition following a lack of mobility and cramped seating on board aircraft on long-haul flights, resulting in death or an embolism. Whilst research is still in its infancy on the topic, high-profile court actions and media attention have led some airlines to improve the pitch of seating (the distance between the seats) to make long-haul more comfortable. Precautions for those most at risk include increased mobility of the passenger in-flight, medical DVT-preventing socks and exercises. Although the number of reported cases has been relatively low, where data exist, they have highlighted an additional problem with mass air travel. Yet this problem is much less widespread than the effect of jet-lag, where long-haul travel crossing different time zones causes the body's circadian rhythms to be affected. Many remedies exist for jet-lag and these are listed on popular travel websites.

The second prominent problem which has also hit the media headlines is the quality of cabin air. As the cost of providing air in flight, particularly fresh air requires additional fuel, the quality is highly variable (see www.sia.com for a useful diagram explaining this issue). As a result, the cockpit and first/business-class passengers enjoy better standards of air, leading to less dehydration, while dry eyes, throat and noses result from poorer air which is recirculated. The use of hepa filters is recommended to improve air quality but it depends upon the budgeting for this by airline companies. Recent research by the UK government (UK Government Select Committee on Science and Technology on Air Travel and Health (www.publications.parliament.uk) in November 2000 indicated the need for airlines to improve on-board air quality to help address the well-being issues for passengers, mirroring the lobbying by groups in the USA such as the American Cabin Crew Associations. The UK government also highlighted the need for better monitoring of these issues and to improve travel advice via the available leaflets and online advice.

In many cases, a combination of factors contribute to accidents and injuries. Fortunately, most accidents are not serious and where hospitalization occurs it may be fewer than ten days. In Bermuda, for example, tourist RTAs had an incidence of 1.57 accidents per thousand visitors, while among US tourist deaths abroad, 28 per cent were the result of car accidents. In contrast, these were the most common cause of death for international visitors to the USA. In Scotland, research by Connell (2005) in the new Loch Lomond and Trossachs National Park highlighted the geographical patterns of tourist accidents, which concentrated at specific blackspots where visibility was poor or speed combined with rapidly changing road conditions, caused serious RTAs and fatalities. Yet the most problematic issue for the national park was the volume of weekend leisure and domestic motorcyclists who rode at excessive speeds and took big risks in overtaking, leading to numerous fatalities on certain stretches of road. Whilst many of these safety issues are a direct result of risky tourist behaviour in the destination area, the other notable issue for destinations is tourist crime and safety.

Tourist crime and safety in destination areas

An extensive tourism and **criminology** literature has been developed around the theme of tourism and crime. Despite the development of many key studies in this area (e.g. Pizam and Mansfeld 2005), there is no clear evidence to support the notion that the development of tourism in destination areas leads to crime. Nevertheless, a wide range of case studies of destinations exist which highlight two important themes:

- the perceived risks of visiting a destination due to the images, perceived safety and likelihood of a safe visit
- the actual occurrence of incidents affected by crime such as robbery, assault, terrorism, murder, kidnapping and **victimization**.

The scope of tourist-related crime is largely undocumented in many destinations, and the less frequent occurrence of tourists victimizing local residents (e.g. including hedonistic behaviour by football hooligans travelling as sports tourists to other countries) remains even less documented despite media attention when it occurs. One example illustrates the problem of understanding the scope and scale of the problem: in Ireland, the Irish police force, the Garda, estimate that of six million visits a year, 3200–3400 tourists become victims of crime. In contrast, estimates for Europe by the organization Victim Support suggest up to eight million tourists are the victims of crime each year, which occurs almost entirely in the destination area. If one considers the following quotation it highlights many of the consequences of tourist crime:

> *International tourist crime is a chronic and growing problem, increasingly causing economic decline, deterring investment, and threatening quality of life in all countries all over the world. Tourists who become victims of crime often face unique issues such as isolation and culture shock, lack of familiar social support, travel stress, and language barriers. In addition most tourists are not familiar with the laws of the country they are visiting, or the criminal justice, social services, health and mental health systems they must interact with after their victimization (New Rights for Victims of Crime in Europe 2004: 4).*

This highlights a common set of behavioural issues for travellers: they tend to be less safety conscious when travelling, engage in more deliberate or indirect forms of risk behaviour (i.e. visiting areas of destinations they do not perceive to be no-go or crime hot spots) and these make them much more liable to be victims of crime.

Tourists also exhibit many visible elements which make them targets for crime including racial differences, cultural differences such as clothing type and the existence of expensive portable items such as cameras or video cameras. This combines with behavioural traits such as more hedonistic activity associated with the enjoyment of alcohol. As a result, tourists aged 15–24 years of age are most likely to be the victims of crime on holiday.

In common with other forms of criminology, **predatory tourist-related crime** tends to geographically cluster in areas which police identify as hot spots, notably in tourist shopping areas, resort areas and where tourists congregate (i.e. at attractions). Existing studies of tourist crime which compare rates of victimization among visitors and residents show that visitors are much more likely to be victims than local residents. This is not surprising given the behaviour of criminals who are often opportunistic or work in organized gangs to target unsuspecting tourists. Among the common problems which tourists in Europe reported were:

- car theft or break-in (27 per cent)
- handbag theft (23 per cent)
- fraud on money exchange (20 per cent)
- theft of cash, credit cards, cheques (15 per cent)
- other problems (15 per cent) (Source: European Travel Monitor 1997).

The impact on the visitor's image of the destination is severely skewed towards negative associations with the visit where criminal victimization occurs. But simple precautions which police advise visitors to take may reduce the likelihood of victimization if they take heed. However, a distinction needs to be made between the more random, unfortunate victimization and petty crime such as handbag snatching and the more serious criminal activity associated with binge drinking and **hedonism** among the youth travellers (i.e. those under 20 years of age). For example, the Torbay area and its night-club district in Devon reported numerous tourist-related criminality issues associated with alcohol, culminating in a tourist murder in September 2004 which severely tarnished the area's image. In European mass tourists resorts such as Falaraki, Greece, alcohol consumption and hedonism were associated with the predatory behaviour of a number of young females who were raped, which led to a massive police crackdown on binge drinking and organized pub crawls. These severe criminal events damaged the resort image and public attention highlighted many of the risk factors associated with youth hedonistic behaviour. But tourism and crime are probably of less significance in terms of media coverage than the impact of **terrorism** on tourism.

Tourism, terrorism and political instability

Tourism is a highly volatile activity which is extremely sensitive to the impact of safety and security issues. Yet, surprisingly, the study of tourism and political instability has really only become a major issue for research in the 1990s, despite the seminal study by Richter (1989) and subsequent studies by C.M. Hall (1994) and the collection of papers in Pizam and Mansfeld (1996). Political instability is 'a situation in which conditions and mechanisms of governance and rule are challenged as to their political legitimacy by elements operating from outside of the normal operations of the political system' (Hall and O'Sullivan 1996: 106). Many facets of political instability exist and Hall and O'Sullivan (1996) summarized them into:

- international wars
- civil wars
- coups
- terrorism
- riots/political protests/social unrest
- strikes.

In each case, the impact upon tourism can be direct, in terms of the negative images it conveys to prospective visitors via the media, word of mouth or visible government policies (i.e. civil rights abuses). One of the most clear examples of this relationship was the effect of the Chinese government crackdown on Tiananmen Square protests in 1989 which led to a temporary downturn in tourism, as negative images directly caused tourists to change their travel behaviour. Yet, perhaps the most media worthy area of attention is terrorism.

Tourism and terrorism: Critical relationships

Terrorism can take many forms, from simple hijackings, skyjackings, kidnapping, bombing of transport systems and resorts through to the new concerns over bio-terrorism using undetectable germs. Among the direct effects of terrorism on tourism are:

- reduced tourism activity
- relocation of tourism to other areas
- damage to public images of tourist destinations
- economic damage to the tourism industry.

Figure 26.5 provides a broad typology of some of the examples where tourism and terrorism interact and Table 26.2 explores some of the issues in more detail for specific countries. A consequence of the continued effect of terrorism in many countries is a depressed tourism industry. However, probably of greater concern for the tourism sector is the impact of a catastrophic event in countries with a low level of terrorist activity, which can devastate the tourism industry, visitor confidence and public perception (Image 26.3), such as the case of 9/11. Indeed, public health disasters such as the 2001 **foot and mouth** epidemic in the UK (see Sharpley and Craven 2001 for

Image 26.3: Security screening, now a key feature of tourist travel, Changi Airport, Singapore.

Source: Copyright, Civil Aviation Authority of Singapore

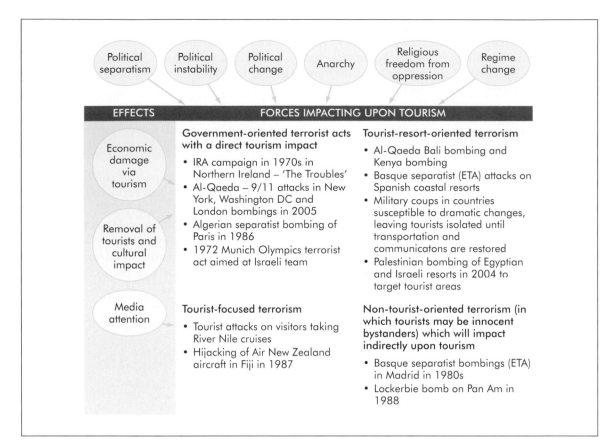

FIGURE 26.5 Terrorism and tourism: A typology with selected examples

---

TABLE 26.2 Examples of countries where tourism has been affected by terrorism or political unrest

CHINA: With the world as witness, Chinese authorities cracked down on student protests in Beijing's Tiananmen Square on 4 June 1989. Prime-time news coverage of army tanks and chaos coincided with a period when the People's Republic of China had officially opened itself to international tourism. World view of the government turned very negative. As a result of the conflict, hotel occupancy rates in Beijing dipped below 30 per cent, 300 groups (approximately 11 500 individuals) cancelled their travel plans and tourism earnings declined by US$430 million in 1989.

EGYPT: Al-Gama'at al-Islamiyya (The Islamic Group), an indigenous Egyptian Islamic extremist group interested in replacing President Hosni Mubarek's government with an Islamic state, became active in the late 1970s. The group has specifically targeted and launched attacks against Egypt's tourism industry since 1992. Over 120 attacks were systematically carried out against tourists between 1992 and 1995, causing the death of 13 tourists. Egypt experienced a 22 per cent drop in international visitors, a 30 per cent drop in tourist nights and a 43 per cent decrease in tourism receipts. The crisis caused Egypt to be removed from programmes of international tour operators. The last terrorist attack against tourists took place in April 1996: 18 Greek tourists were killed in Cairo.

FIJI: Two military coups occurred in Fiji within months (14 May and 28 September) in 1987, following the election of a mainly non-Fijian government. Sensational media coverage was followed by travel advisories issued by Australia and New Zealand. The first coup was followed by a hijack attempt of an Air New Zealand Boeing 747 at Fiji's Nadi Airport.

ISRAEL: Since Israeli's establishment in 1948, both Israelis and Palestinians living in the occupied territories have experienced continuous turmoil. In 1987 the Palestinian uprising (*Intifada*) intensified and the Islamic Resistance Movement (HAMAS) formed from the Palestinian branch of the Muslim Brotherhood to establish an Islamic Palestinian state in place of Israel. Attacks initiated by both Israelis and Palestinians have resulted in heavy death tolls and casualties. Tourist arrivals between 1970 and 1994 have climbed steadily with sharp declines in numbers after negative events.

TABLE 26.2 continued

MEXICO: When the North American Free Trade Agreement (NAFTA) went into effect on 1 January 1994, the Ejercito Zapatista de Liberacion Nacional (EZLN) initiated an armed rebellion against the Mexican government. The first 12 days of the uprising resulted in 145 to 500 deaths (depending on the source). Military troops established road blocks and searched vehicles in Chiapas (south-eastern Mexico). The March 1994 assassination of Luis Donaldo Colosia, a favoured presidential candidate, created further agitation in Mexico. San Cristobal in Chiapas, the largest town held by the Zapatistas where the uprising occurred and also where negotiations occurred, experienced sharp declines in international and domestic tourism. As a result 1994 visitation dropped by 70 per cent in January and 70 per cent in February, compared with the same period of the previous year.

NORTHERN IRELAND: The Provisional Irish Republican Army (PIRA) formed in 1969 as the covert armed wing of Sinn Fein (legal political movement with the goal of removing British jurisdiction over Northern Ireland and unifying it with the Republic of Ireland). Targets have included senior British government officials, British military and police in Northern Ireland. Terrorist activity and retaliation by British troops have impeded tourist activity. Visitor arrivals fell from the 1967 peak of 1 080 000 to 321 000 in 1976 as a result of an image of risk and danger. The ceasefire which began on 31 August 1994 was observed until 9 February 1996 when a bomb exploded in London killing two bystanders and injuring 43. During the 18-month ceasefire, the Northern Ireland Tourist Board recorded a 59 per cent increase (from the previous year) in inquiries, 11 per cent increase in hotel occupancy, 18 per cent increase in out-of-state visitors and 68 per cent increase in holiday visitors. More recently, a hotel near Belfast was bombed in July 1996; however, a second ceasefire was ordered to begin 20 July 1997.

PERU: The Sendero Luminoso (Shining Path), a Maoist terrorist group, formed in the late 1960s to replace existing Peruvian institutions with a peasant revolutionary regime and free Peru of foreign influences. Attacks caused a steep decline in tourism from 350 000 international visitors in 1989 to 33 000 in 1991. On 17 December 1996 a rival terrorist group, Tupac Amaru Revolutionary Movement (MRTA) – demanding the release of imprisoned rebels – raided the Japanese embassy and took 500 people hostage. The stand-off between the rebels and the Peruvian military force lasted for 126 days, during which time small groups of hostages were released periodically. On 24 April 1997 the final 72 hostages were released after the military organized a successful rescue.

SLOVENIA: The Yugoslav Army attacked Slovenia in June 1991. Slovenia's war continued for ten days before fighting moved to Croatia in 1991 and Bosnia-Herzegovina in 1992. Specialized tour operators for Yugoslavia lost over one million booked tourists in 1991 as a result. Even two years after the ten-day war, the figures for Slovenian tourism were still far behind the pre-war figures. The number of total nights in 1993 was 32 per cent lower than in 1990.

SPAIN: The Basque Fatherland and Liberty (ETA) was founded in 1959 to create an independent homeland in Spain's Basque region. Politicians and members of the military and government have been traditional targets; however, ETA specifically targeted Spain's tourism industry between 1984 and 1987. Tourist hotels and travel agencies were bombed. Over 200 letters were mailed by ETA to foreign embassies, travel agencies and foreign media in Spain stating intentions to terrorize tourists (Enders and Sandler 1991). ETA's 1996 'summer campaign' included six bombing attacks in early July. At Reus Airport near Barcelona, 35 were injured and hotels along Spain's Costa Dorada were bombed. Downward trends in tourism activity have been recorded.

TIBET: Nationalist unrest which began in 1987 was punctuated by the declaration of martial law in March 1989, in Lhasa. In 1990 three foreigners were shot at and one was killed in Kathmandu, as they tried to photograph pro-democracy demonstrations. Tibet's tourism industry suffered a serious blow as a result. In 1988, 22 000 visitors were recorded, but in the first six months of 1989, 1092 tourists arrived in Tibet (down from 5 000 visitors during the same period in 1988). Only 3.1 per cent of the visitation projected by the government was recorded and a loss of 4.52 million yuan was reported by tourism businesses.

THE GAMBIA: This small West African developing country enjoyed political stability following its independence from Britain in 1965. In the summer of 1994, a bloodless coup occurred. The Travel Advice Unit of the British Foreign and Commonwealth Office (FCO) issued several subsequent and stringent travel warnings against the Gambia. As a result, first British then Scandinavian tour operators pulled out, virtually crippling the country's tourism industry. Arrivals fell from 5 000 to 300; over 2 000 jobs directly and indirectly linked to tourism were lost, eight hotels closed and the country's economic and social conditions quickly deteriorated.

TABLE 26.2 continued

TURKEY: The Kurdistan Worker's Party (PKK), a Marxist-Leninist insurgent group interested in establishing an independent Marxist state in south-eastern Turkey, was established in 1974. PKK primarily targeted Turkish government forces and civilians until recently. Since 1993, PKK has become more active in western Europe against Turkish targets and has specifically targeted Turkey's tourism industry since 1991. The PKK has emulated ETA's letter campaign warning foreign companies against sending tourists to Turkey, bombed tourism sites and hotels, and kidnapped foreign tourists. Foreign visitor arrivals dropped 8 per cent from 1992–1993. After a self-imposed ceasefire by the PKK, international arrivals reached record levels (9.5 million) in 1996.

ZAMBIA and ZIMBABWE: Zimbabwe's (previously South Rhodesia) Unilateral Declaration of Independence (UDI) in 1965 was followed by a 15-year liberation war which lasted until 1990. As a result, tourism to the immediate area (including neighbouring Zambia) was seriously impeded. Teye (1986) compared Kenya's tourist arrivals, which increased from 250 400 in 1964–6 to 3 524 000 in 1970–8, to Zambia's arrivals which only increased incrementally from 429 700 to 466 800 for the same period. During the 1967–9 period, Zambia was unable to record any tourist arrivals because of the war.

Source: Reprinted from *Annals of Tourism Research*, vol.25, Sonmez, 'Tourism, terrorism and political instability', 416–56 (1998), with permission from Elsevier

more detail) can have equally dramatic effects on the tourism industry, in much the same way natural disasters such as earthquakes, floods and volcanic eruptions do (see Wilks and Page 2003 for some examples). Consequently, the sudden impact of a crisis such as terrorism underlines the need for crisis planning and contingency tourism planning, in much the same way that hospitals have major trauma plans in the event of major disasters such as an aircraft crash. For this reason, it is useful to briefly examine the case of 9/11 and its effect on the USA's tourism industry in Insight 26.3.

Managing tourist health and safety issues

Where destinations acknowledge that **tourist safety** issues are important for the wider sustainability of the tourism product, practical measures and guidelines can be offered to tourists without sounding alarmist. Where governments feel that risks need to be alerted to prospective outbound travellers, websites such as the Foreign and Commonwealth's (www.fco.gov.uk) can provide targeted information, and Figure 26.6 provides a global illustration of the advice it gave in 2005 to British citizens in terms of areas to avoid travel to. However, destination advice needs to be supplemented by good advice from many of the agencies listed in Figure 26.7 as well as visiting a **GP** for health advice as prevention is better than cure. But it needs to be emphasized that responsibility has to be placed with the tourist to take the advice available.

In destination areas, being prepared for a highly mobile and changing tourist population requires medical and police services to be adequately resourced. Some large tourist resorts have dedicated tourist police and natural disaster plans where the resort is in an area liable to flooding, earthquakes and disease. But at a more operational level, crime prevention in hot spots, including **CCTV** and a visible police presence, may be necessary. Yet tourists cannot be nursemaided so they have to be well informed of any risks they may encounter.

To assist in improving the experience of visitors who are victims of crime, initiatives such as Tourist Victim Services in Ireland provides a model which many destinations could follow with its offering of help with:

- replacing travel and identity documents
- contacting insurers for claims and liaising with banks, embassies and airlines
- offering advice on legal support.

It is a voluntary agency to help redress the negative experience.

The impact of 9/11 on the USA tourism industry

9/11 occurred at a time when the global tourism sector was facing an economic downturn and slow growth. One consequence of 9/11 was that it sped up many of the current problems facing specific sectors of the tourism industry, such as the US airline industry, and made it face major financial and operational issues. However, the immediate impact of 9/11 on the global tourism industry was a 10 per cent drop in the number of tourists travelling; a 10 per cent drop in worldwide flights; a 16 per cent drop in US domestic flights; the cancelling of business travel, events and conferences and a sharp fall in hotel-room occupancy in the USA. Theme parks were left empty. Blake and Sinclair (2003) noted the economic effects of 9/11 on income from tourist spending and loss of jobs by reducing domestic and international tourism together with the impact of no state intervention. However, the most immediate federal government response was to pass the Air Transportation Safety and System Stabilization Act which did provide federal US$10 billion credit to airlines, plus US$5 billion to airlines facing increased insurance premiums and limiting their liability arising from terrorist attack. The Act also provided US$3 billion for aviation safety. This all reiterates the economic significance of taking action, since Table 26.3 depicts the real expected effects if no intervention occurred. The Travel Industry Recovery Coalition, advocated a six-point plan to assist tourism recovery:

- federal government should provide a US$500 tax credit for domestic travel
- expand loan facilities to small businesses
- provide a tax credit for employment in tourism
- subsidize marketing campaigns
- increase tax allowances to allow businesses to offset 9/11 induced losses against future earnings
- increase business entertaining expenses from 50 per cent to 100 per cent, which emphasizes the problems facing non-aviation businesses.

Blake and Sinclair (2003) observed the effectiveness of targeted subsidies for the airline sector rather than for more general tourism subsidies. Thus, the federal government crisis response sought to intervene to address the immediate downsizing announced by airlines post-9/11 as documented by Goodrich (2002) in Table 26.4. Blake and Sinclair point to the US$30 billion loss of GDP which would have occurred through the tourism sector without the state intervention in the airline industry, which probably staved off up to 500 000 job losses. This illustrates the sudden impact of an event of the magnitude of 9/11, which not only hit business and consumer confidence but also tourism demand. Yet Goodrich (2002) also outlined the US government's travel advice warning its citizens to avoid a wide range of countries (Table 26.5) post-9/11 due to the terrorist threat posed by Al-Qaeda. Many European destinations with a traditional US market were also affected. Yet the most severe effects on tourism were felt in cities such as New York with a drop of visitors in 2001 of five million and a drop of US$2 billion in visitor spending which was reflected in falling hotel occupancy rates (Image 26.4).

What is notable about New York was the influential leadership of its mayor, Rudy Giuliani, in setting up a recovery programme which involved a media campaign to target New York visitors, day visitors and nearby leisure trippers, with an emotional and patriotic *Stronger Than Ever* campaign which was strengthened by its winter promotion – *Paint the Town Red, White and Blue*, with special offers, discounts and incentives to build the business back up again.

What the 9/11 Insight illustrates is that clear leadership is needed to redevelop tourism through a crisis management strategy, which needs to be quick, timely and highly visible, preferably with a very charismatic leader able to counter the negative connotations after a terrorist event. Above all, a coordinated approach across the tourism sector, with government funding as the US federal government provided, helps to reduce some of the short- to medium-term effects of a collapse in the tourism sector. This is in direct contrast to what happened in many of the countries which were affected by the SARS outbreak in 2002–2003, where the tourism industry's inability to formulate rapid responses, combined with media hype and misinformation, created a devastating impact on the Asian airline industry and in many destinations, as Page (2005) discusses in detail.

Image 26.4: 9/11 had a substantial impact on the New York tourism industry

TABLE 26.3 Effects of reductions in tourism demand following September 11

Type of effects	Effects of September 11, without policy responses	Effects of reduced demand by international tourists	Effects of reduced demand for domestic air travel and tourism
Total change in tourist spending (US$bn)	−50.69	−15.89	−40.88
Constant dollar GDP (US$bn change from base)	−27.27	−10.54	−17.97
Net effect on government budget (US$bn change from base)	−7.27	−2.60	−4.94
Constant dollar factor adjustment (US$bn)	30.93	12.88	21.44
Relative factor adjustment (%)	0.75	0.32	0.49
Constant dollar employment (US$bn)	−13.57	−5.96	−7.85
FTE employment ('000)	−383	−155	−248
FTE jobs lost ('000)	559	198	414
FTE jobs lost in airlines ('000)	203	42	160
FTE jobs lost in hotels and other accommodation establishments ('000)	174	42	146

Note: Columns two and three do not sum to column one because of increased demand for domestic travel and tourism by non-air transport
FTE= Full Time Equivalent

Source: Reprinted from *Annals of Tourism Research*, vol.30, Blake and Sinclair, 'Tourism crisis management: US response to September 11', 813–52 (2003), with permission from Elsevier

TABLE 26.4 Proposed layoffs by airlines

American Airlines	20 000
United Airlines	20 000
Continental Airlines	13 000
Delta Airlines	13 000
Northwest Airlines	10 000
British Airways	5 000

Source : Reprinted from *Tourism Management*, vol.23, Goodrich, 'September 11, 2001 attack on America: A record of immediate impacts and reactions in the USA', 573–80, copyright (2002), with permission from Elsevier

TABLE 26.5 US citizens to avoid travel to these countries

Afghanistan	Israel, the West Bank and Gaza
Albania	Liberia
Algeria	Lebanon
Angola	Libya
Burundi	Macedonia
Bosnia and Herzegovina	Nigeria
Central African Republic	Pakistan
Colombia	Sierra Leone
Democratic Republic of Congo	Solomon Islands
Federal Republic of Yugoslavia	Somalia
Guinea–Bissau	Sri Lanka
Indonesia	Sudan
Iran	Tajikstan
Iraq	Yemen

Source: Reprinted from *Tourism Management*, vol.23, Goodrich, 'September 11, 2001 attack on America: A record of immediate impacts and reactions in the USA', 573–80, copyright (2002), with permission from Elsevier

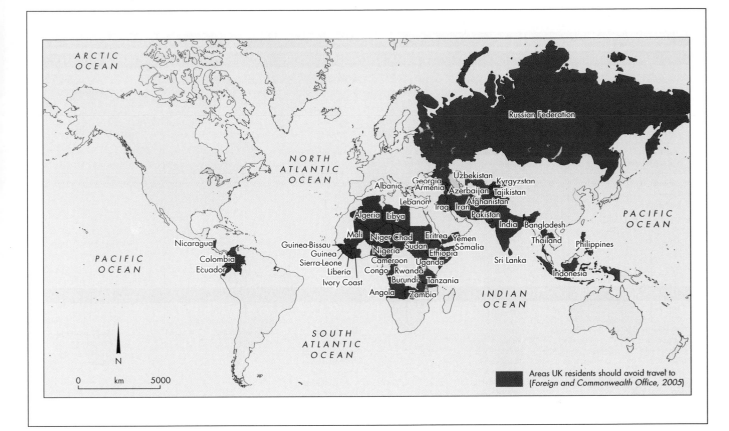

FIGURE 26.6 Areas to which British citizens were advised not to travel to in 2005. Source: Copyright S.J. Page

The tourism industry has to have a proactive approach to these issues and be committed to reducing health and safety problems, or at least in warning clients of risks. After all, if tourism is an experience, and if inadequate advice is given or safety precautions are not taken, then the business may not be meeting its legal obligation of duty of care to its clients. This is becoming an increasingly contentious area of tourism, as lawyers specializing in litigation associated with such issues now feature prominently when things go wrong. Yet there is no substitute for tourists following some of the very practical advice from guide books and websites concerning unknown environments:

- stay in touch with friends and relatives
- consult guide books
- avoid dark and unlit streets and short cuts
- avoid carrying valuables around and carry a minimum of cash
- never put up a struggle against violent theft
- if hitchhiking, do so in pairs
- never tell strangers where you are staying
- always use registered taxis and official means of transport
- beware of pickpockets
- take advice from holiday reps in destinations
- do not engage in arguments and chastising of locals in public which may lead to trouble
- always defuse difficult situations by walking away

although in the case of terrorism, it may be best to avoid areas targeted by known terror groups, which is where government websites may be most helpful.

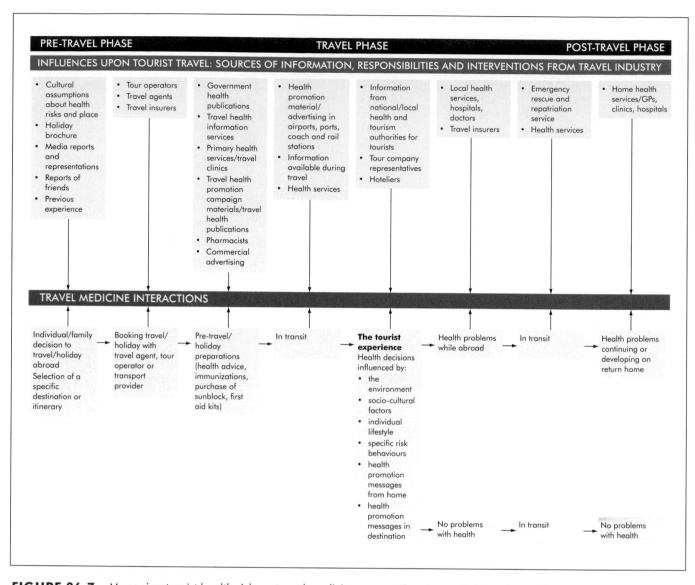

FIGURE 26.7 Managing tourist health risks: a travel medicine perspective. Source: Redrawn from Clift and Page (1996) with modifications

Conclusion

There is little doubt that global travel has been adversely affected by terrorism, albeit in the short-term; as Hall (2005) points to the quick recovery times for many destinations affected, adverse events have a short-term impact on travel. This is evident from the experiences of 9/11 and SARS on global travel and it is widely argued by travel medicine researchers that it is the everyday concerns which tourists need to be aware of, such as the risks of AIDS, DVT and diseases which can be inoculated against such as hepatitis A and B. However, the global media impact of crises such as 9/11 tend to attract the bulk of attention in the media and the resources to formulate travel policy such as the new biometrics scanning of travellers in the USA after The 9/11 Commission Report (2003). The creation of the US Department of Homeland Security illustrates how serious the terrorist threat is to USA travellers and for travel to the USA. But one has to put these events in perspective: it is the scale, reality and media hype that need to be disentangled to understand how significant such events are to tourist travel, compared to the health and safety issues which tourists face every day. Even so, studies such as the Worldwatch Institute (2005) highlight that security issues are one of the most pressing issues at a global scale and they are underpinned by wider problems relating to the global economy, poverty and inequality, environmental problems and other social and political pressures.

The conceptualization of tourist health and safety is complex, as many disciplines study it including researchers in medicine, safety science and tourism, and each approaches the subject with different perspectives and insights. The case of SARS illustrates how disease can easily be spread by global travel and natural disasters are also receiving attention following the Indian Ocean tsunami in 2004. But underlying all these issues is the concept of risk – what risks the traveller takes when they go on holiday, what precautions they take to reduce risks and how their behaviour, knowledge and understanding of tourism, health and safety interact to produce incidents and events which can spoil the tourist experience. Above all, global travel means that many of these issues affect all parts of the world, although climatic and environmental factors make some risks greater in certain parts of the world, such as the risk of AIDS and catching other diseases. Tourist health and safety are now central issues in the operation of tourism, especially given the media interest in negative events. From the tourist perspective, their behaviour is a central element determining what places and destinations visitors travel to, and media images play a critical role in shaping this behaviour. Not surprisingly, many destinations are beginning to grasp this issue, or facets of it (e.g. tourist crime) as they wish to enhance rather than damage the image and perception of the locality.

Discussion questions

1 Why has tourist safety and security become such a critical issue for travellers in the new millennium?
2 Outline the range of issues and problems associated with the management of tourist health.
3 What are the underlying causes of tourist accidents and injuries, and how can the tourism industry reduce them?
4 What sources of advice exist to advise tourists which destinations to avoid or to take special precautions when travelling in?

References

Bentley, T., Page, S.J. and Laird, I. (2001) 'Accidents in the New Zealand adventure tourism industry', *Safety Science*, 38 (1): 31–48.
Blake, A. and Sinclair, M. (2003) 'Tourism crisis management: US response to September 11', *Annals of Tourism Research*, 30 (4): 813–52.
Callander, M. and Page, S.J. (2003) 'Managing risk in adventure tourism operations in New Zealand: A review of the legal case history and potential for litigation', *Tourism Management*, 24 (1): 13–23.
Cartwright, R. (1996) 'Travellers diarrhoea', in S. Clift and S.J. Page (eds) *Health and the International Tourist*. London: Routledge.

Clift, S. and Grabowski, P. (eds) (1998) *Tourism and Health: Risks, Research and Responses.* London: Cassell.

Clift, S. and Page, S.J. (eds) (1996) *Health and the International Tourist.* London: Routledge.

Connell, J. (2005) 'Case study: Analysing coach tourism in Scotland: Trends and patterns', in S.J. Page (2005) *Transport and Tourism: Global Perspectives.* Harlow: Prentice Hall.

Cossar, J., Reid, D., Fallon, R., Bell, E., Riding, M., Follett, F., Dow, B., Mitchell, S. and Grist, N. (1990) 'Accumulative review of studies of travellers, their experience of illness and the implications of these findings', *Journal of Infection*, 21(1): 27–42.

Enders, W. and Sandler, T. (1991) 'Causality between transnational terrorism and tourism: the case of Spain', *Terrorism* 14 (1) 49–58.

European Travel Monitor (1997) *European Travel Monitor.* Munich: IPK.

Gilbert, D. and Abdullah, J. (2004) 'Holiday taking and the sense of well-being', *Annals of Tourism Research*, 31 (1): 103–21.

Goodrich, J. (2002), 'September 11, 2001 attack on America: A record of immediate impacts and reactions in the USA', *Tourism Management*, 23 (6): 573–80.

Hall, C.M. (1994) *Tourism and Politics: Policy, Power and Place.* Chichester: John Wiley and Sons.

Hall, C.M. (2005) 'Biosecurity and wine tourism', *Tourism Management* 26 (6): 931–8.

Hall, C.M. and O'Sullivan, V. (1996) 'Tourism, political stability and violence', in A. Pizam and Y. Mansfeld (eds) *Tourism, Crime and International Security Issues.* Chichester: John Wiley and Sons.

Hall, C.M. and Page, S.J. (eds) (1996) *Tourism in the Pacific: Issues and Cases.* London: Thomson.

Lawton, G. and Page, S.J. (1997) 'Evaluating travel agents' provision of health advice to travellers', *Tourism Management*, 18 (2): 89–104.

Page, S.J. (2005) *Transport and Tourism: Global Perspectives.* Harlow: Prentice Hall.

Page, S.J., Bentley, T. and Walker, L. (2005) 'Scoping the nature and extent of adventure tourism operations in Scotland: How safe are they?' *Tourism Management*, 26 (3): 381–97.

Page, S.J. and Meyer, D. (1996) 'Tourist accidents: An exploratory analysis', *Annals of Tourism Research*, 23 (3): 666–90.

Pizam, A. and Mansfeld, Y. (eds) (1996) *Tourism, Crime and International Security Issues.* Chichester: John Wiley and Sons.

Richter, L. (1989) *The Politics of Tourism in Asia.* Honolulu: University of Hawaii Press.

Sharpley, R. and Craven, B. (2001) 'The 2001 foot and mouth crisis – rural economy and tourism policy implications: A comment', *Current Issues in Tourism*, 4 (6): 527–37.

Sönmez, S. (1998) 'Tourism, terrorism and political instability', *Annals of Tourism Research*, 25 (2): 416–56.

Teye, V. (1986) 'Liberation Wars and tourism development in Africa: the case of Zambia', *Annals of Tourism Research* 13 (4): 589–608.

The 9/11 Commission Report (2003) *Final Report of the National Commission on Terrorist Attacks upon the United States.* New York: Norton and Company.

Unter-Jones, J. (2000) 'Identifying the responsibility for risk at tourism destinations: The UK experience', *Tourism Economics*, 6 (2): 187–98.

Walker, L. and Page, S.J. (2003) 'Risks, rights, responsibilities' in 'Tourist well-being: Who should manage visitor well-being at the destination?' in J. Wilks and S.J. Page (eds) *Managing Tourist Health and Safety.* Oxford: Elsevier.

Wilks, J. and Page, S.J. (eds) (2003) *Managing Tourist Health and Safety.* Oxford: Elsevier.

Wilks, J., Pendergast, D. and Leggat, P. (eds) (2005) *Tourism in Turbulent Times.* Oxford: Elsevier.

World Tourism Organization (2003a) *Crisis Guidelines for the Tourism Industry.* Madrid: World Tourism Organization.

World Tourism Organization (2003b) *Safety and Security in Tourism: Partnerships and Practical Guidelines for Destinations.* Madrid: World Tourism Organization.

Worldwatch Institute (2005) *State of the World 2005.* Washington, DC: Worldwatch Institute.

Further reading

Page, S.J. (2002) 'Tourist health and safety', *Travel and Tourism Analyst*, 5.

Mansfield, Y. and Pizam, A. (eds) (2005) *Tourism, Security and Safety: From Theory to Practice.* Oxford: Butterworth-Heinemann.

Wilks, J., Pendergast, D. and Leggat, P. (eds) (2005) *Tourism in Turbulent Times.* Oxford: Elsevier.

Wilks, J. and Page, S.J. (eds) (2003) *Managing Tourist Health and Safety.* Oxford: Elsevier.

27

The Future of Tourism

Learning outcomes

After reading this chapter and answering the questions, you should be able to understand:

- the role and application of tourism forecasting and its importance for tourism businesses

- the methods which can be used to understand the potential impact of factors affecting changes in tourism, including demographic and political factors

- the importance of demand and supply issues on future tourism provision.

Overview

Tourism is constantly evolving, and to understand what may affect tourism trends in the future, planners and managers need to understand techniques such as forecasting, and the range of factors likely to influence tourism in the next decade. The future evolution of tourism is uncertain and attempting to plan for future growth scenarios poses many challenges for an industry where change is the only constant feature. A wide range of factors impact upon the future of tourism as demographic, political, economic and technological changes shape the nature, trends and participation in tourism. For governments and the tourism sector, such changes need to be recognised, understood and managed to ensure the long-term sustainability of tourism in different countries and destinations.

515

Introduction

Understanding how tourism can be developed, improved and be more in tune with the environmental resources it consumes is a global challenge as shown in Chapter 20. In 2003, the World Travel and Tourism Council (WTTC) launched its strategic vision for the future global tourism industry entitled, *Blueprint for New Tourism*. This ambitious leadership role which WTTC has taken outlined three fundamental conditions for tourism (see Table 27.1). It recognizes that all stakeholders involved in tourism (tourists, destination communities and the natural, social and

---

TABLE 27.1 The WTTC's *Blueprint for New Tourism*

In order to meet the challenges ahead and achieve the vision, the *Blueprint* establishes three fundamental conditions:

1. Governments must recognize travel and tourism as a top priority
2. Business must balance economics with people, culture and environment
3. All parties must share the pursuit of long-term growth and prosperity

1. Governments must recognize travel and tourism as a top priority
   To meet the first condition, governments must:
   - Elevate travel and tourism as an issue to the top level of policy-making
   - Create a competitive business environment
   - Ensure that quality statistics and data feed into policy and decision-making
   - Invest in developing the appropriate human capital
   - Liberalize trade, transport, communications and investment
   - Build confidence in safety and security
   - Promote product diversification that spreads demand
   - Plan for sustainable tourism growth, in keeping with cultures and character
   - Invest in new technology, such as satellite navigation systems

2. Business must balance economics with people, culture and environment
   To meet the second condition, the industry must:
   - Expand markets while protecting natural resources, local heritage and lifestyles
   - Develop people to narrow the gap between the 'haves' and 'have-nots'
   - Provide traditional tourism products sensitively
   - Reduce seasonality and increase yields with imaginative new products
   - Improve quality, value and choice
   - Agree and implement quality standards at all levels
   - Transfer skills and best practice throughout the industry
   - Increase the sophistication of information, to make better business decisions
   - Communicate more broadly and more effectively

3. All parties must share the pursuit of long-term growth and prosperity
   To meet the third condition, all the main stakeholders must:
   - Ally best practice in tourism with government policy
   - Prepare sustainable master plans for entire destinations
   - Create locally driven processes for continuous stakeholder consultation
   - Restructure national tourism boards
   - Set environmental policy goals that can be met
   - Develop and deploy skills effectively
   - Collaborate on information requirements
   - Collaborate on security
   - Develop confidence on all sides

Source: WTTC (2003) www.wttc.org, accessed 28.1.2005

cultural environments affected in the destination) need to look beyond the short-term 'benefits' that have characterized tourism growth and development throughout history: a new more sustainable approach to tourism is needed. But how do we begin to understand how this sustainable approach can be developed, if this involves considering future change in tourism? One starting point is to consider **forecasting** in tourism.

Forecasting change in tourism

According to Jefferson and Lickorish (1991: 101), forecasting the demand for tourism is essential for commercial operators, 'whether in the public or private sector... [as they]... will seek to maximize revenue and profits in moving towards maximum efficiency in [their] use of resources'. Archer (1987) argues that:

> no manager can avoid the need for some form of forecasting: a manager must plan for the future in order to minimize the risk of failure or, more optimistically, to maximize the possibilities of success. In order to plan, he must use forecasts. Forecasts will always be made, whether by guesswork, teamwork or the use of complex models, and the accuracy of the forecasts will affect the quality of the management decision (Archer 1987: 77).

Reliable forecasts are essential for managers and decision-makers involved in service provision to try and ensure adequate supply is available to meet demand, while ensuring oversupply does not result, since this can erode the profitability of their operation. In essence, 'forecasts of tourism demand are essential for efficient planning by airlines, shipping companies, railways, coach operators, hoteliers, tour operators...' (Witt, Brooke and Buckley 1991: 52). Forecasting is the process associated with an assessment of future changes in the demand for tourism. It must be stressed that 'forecasting is not an exact science' (Jefferson and Lickorish 1991: 102), as it attempts to make estimations of future traffic potential and a range of possible scenarios, which provide an indication of the likely scale of change in demand. Consequently, forecasting is a technique used to suggest the future pattern of demand.

According to Jefferson and Lickorish (1991: 102) the principal methods of forecasting are:

- 'the projection by extrapolation, of historic trends' (i.e. how the previous performance of demand may shape future patterns)
- pextrapolation, subject to the application of ... [statistical analysis using] ... weights or variables'.

While additional methods may include structured group discussions among a panel of tourism experts to assess factors determining future tourism forecasts ('The Delphi Method') more qualitative scenario planning exercises can be used to depict future development situations (Page et al 2005). The quantitative forecasting methods used in econometrics are reviewed in Song and Witt (2000). Bull (1991: 127) notes that the most common variables used in these models are:

- number of tourist trips
- total tourist expenditure and expenditure per capita
- market shares of tourism
- the tourism sector's share of GDP.

Depending on the complexity of the methodology employed, the forecasting model may examine one dependent variable (e.g. tourist trips) and how other independent variables (e.g. the state of the national and international economy, leisure time, levels of disposable income, inflation and foreign exchange rates) affect the demand for tourist trips.

Ultimately, forecasting attempts to establish how consumer demand for tourism has shaped previous trends and how these may change in the future, often over a five- to ten-year period. At a world scale, WTO (2001) forecasts predict that international tourist arrivals will grow to 1.5 billion by 2020. Domestic tourism, however, is expected to grow at a slower rate, and so be more constrained by the availability of leisure time.

Although forecasting will never be an exact science, it is one of the bases upon which decision-makers plan for the future changes to be accommodated in tourism and one of the best ways to understand its significance is to look at how it has been used in one country (see Case Study 21.1W).

The discussion of forecasting also raises a wider discussion of the factors which are likely to influence the demand for tourism in the new millennium and the most influential factors are now discussed.

Factors affecting the future shape of tourism trends

Within the tourism and marketing literature there is a recognition that tourism trends are influenced by a wide range of factors which are external to tourism and beyond its control (exogenous or external factors) while a range of tourism-related factors have a bearing on future trends and for this reason which are outlined in Figure 27.1. This shows that there are two broad considerations according to Cooper *et al.* (2005):

- exogenous and factors within our control
- factors outside of our control.

These two forces also impact on the tourist experience and specific 'tourism processes of change' exist as shown in Figure 27.2. To outline some of these broad processes of change, Table 27.2 lists some of the main features which can be grouped under the following headings:

Demographic factors

Changing tastes are affecting consumer behaviour as noted in Chapter 4, with the emergence of what Poon (1989) described as the new consumer who rejects the regimented, traditional packaged sun, sea and sand holidays in favour of more flexible holidays which are different from the mass tourism of the past. Combined with these consumer changes is a wide range of underlying demographic changes in the developed world, especially the ageing of the population, more

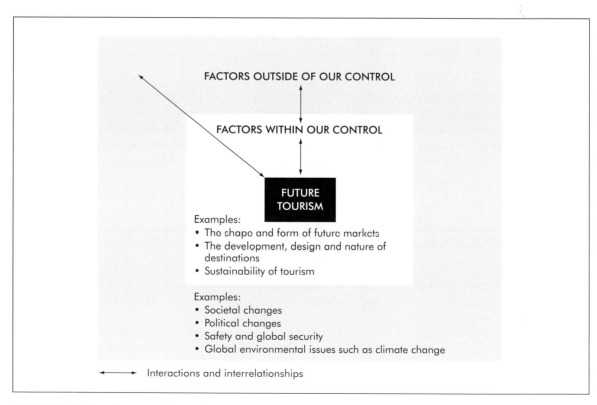

FIGURE 27.1 Factors within and outside of our control in tourism

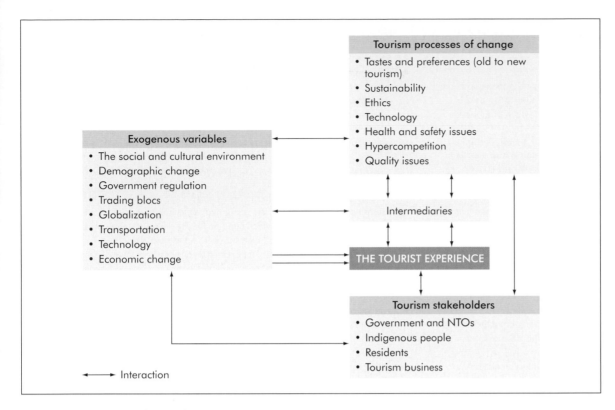

FIGURE 27.2 The future of tourism

flexible work practices, early retirement, the trend towards special interest holidays and a greater concern with the social and environmental consequences of tourism. One of the most significant changes is the growth of the **senior market** as shown in Insight 27.1.

Aside from the immediate demographic changes there are also more profound global processes at work which are shaping future tourism trends. One such trend can best be explained as the relationship of tourism to migration: tourism can generate permanent immigration, and in turn, permanent immigration can generate a demand for tourism, particularly for the purpose of visiting friends and relatives (hereafter VFR). Many forms of migration generate tourism flows, in particular through the geographical extension of friendship and kinship networks. The migrants themselves may travel back to their country of origin for VFR or other purposes. Moreover, the migrants to a new country may be followed by their friends and relatives who choose to visit them in their new country. In the case of Vietnam, Page (2004) outlined the major expansion plans of Vietnam Airlines to grow international arrivals, especially the VFR market, given the global distribution of many family members who fled the country in the 1970s and who are now established overseas.

Such changes can also be related to changing lifestyles in both developed and undeveloped countries. For example, there are greater levels of prosperity among a wider range of the population and new social trends such as later marriage, couples deferring having children, the greater role of women in travel and role of the senior travellers. All of these factors directly affect patterns of tourism combined with the greater levels of discretionary spending among these groups on tourism.

Political change

Governments directly affect the pattern of travel, and can constrain and facilitate travel depending on the policies, activities and climate they promote for their citizens and visitors. In the 1990s the opening up of eastern Europe dramatically altered the pattern of travel in Europe, especially the demand for cultural tourism in eastern European destinations as improved infrastructure and opportunities for travel have created a host of new urban tourist destinations. Many of the fast-expanding destinations in the new millennium in Europe are located in these areas, as low-cost

TABLE 27.2 Demographic, economic and societal changes which will impact upon the future of tourism and travel

- **Demographic changes**
  - In the next 20 years, the over-50 age group is likely to become larger than the under-50s group, especially in Western nations which are major drivers of tourism demand
  - The growing segmentation of the senior market, where reaching 60 years of age is now viewed in Western countries as the 'new 40 years old', seeking multiple travel experiences, dominating luxury travel with increased disposable income. In the UK, one in five over-60-year-olds take over three holidays a year
  - Increasingly experienced over-60s travellers, with facilities and services (e.g. medical services) to support their travel needs
  - Increasing trend towards single-parent families and double-income households
  - Older parenting and smaller family size
  - Single people comprise 32 per cent of the US market, and 29 per cent of the UK market, comprising key characteristics – ICT savvy, time poor, independent with individual needs but lucrative spenders
  - Declining amount of annual holiday leave time taken by managerial groups (e.g. only 50 per cent take the full amount of leave in the USA)
  - Rise of well-being and stress management holiday trips (e.g. revitalization of spa and treatments)
  - Hedonistic behaviour, with occasional large purchases in search of quality, memorable experiences
  - Increasing life expectancy which is set to rise to over 80 years of age in the next 20 years and rise of 'second homes', 'multiple careers' and importance of an ongoing workforce

- **Economic changes**
  - Growing household affluence, with rich elite (the new upper class) rising and growing middle class driving outbound tourism in many developing countries
  - Global inequality between the consumer society which the Worldwatch Institute (www.worldwatch.org) estimate comprises 1.7 billion people, half of which live in the developing world. One illustration of consumption by these groups is that over 531 million cars exist worldwide and this is growing by 11 million a year and US$14 billion is spent on cruising each year which would virtually eliminate world hunger and malnutrition
  - The Worldwatch Institute State of the World (2005) report highlights the disparity between rich and poor in the global economy and the misallocation of resources to consumerism, including tourism

- **Environmental challenges**
  - A growing debate on sustainability, the interdependence of man and nature and the impact of excessive consumerism on resource consumption
  - According to Mastyn (2001) the issues of global inequalities are replicated in patterns of tourism consumption: 80 per cent of international tourists originate from Europe and the Americas and only 3.5 per cent of the world's population travels internationally, though the World Tourism Organisation expect this to rise to 7 per cent by 2020. However, international travel will still remain an elite form of travel
  - The globalization of tourism activity by large companies has seen the sustainable benefits of tourism dissipated, especially in many African countries while generating impacts which threaten the long-term resource base. This results in tourists cocooning themselves from their own impacts
  - Environmental issues remain important for consumers, in spite of their limited understanding of their own impact. Global warming, climate change and pollution are key issues and will gather momentum in the next decade

- **Patterns of travel**
  - According to Frechtling (2002), changes to outbound long-haul travel in 1998–2010 will see developing nations such as Taiwan and South Korea generating compound annual rates of growth of over 10 per cent per annum, though slower rates of long-haul travel after 2020
  - Frechtling (2002) notes the continued importance of US travellers in long-haul travel, followed by Japan, the UK and France. The retirement market will continue to hold significant growth potential
  - Müller (2002) outlined ten future holiday models based on a study of the future of tourism which may encompass:
    - a growth in adventure-seeking holiday behaviour
    - a rise in independent travellers seeking flexible holiday products
    - the demand for more sophisticated travel products
    - forms of relaxation, wellness and well-being enhanced tourism and recreation
    - a growth in second home ownership
    - the pursuit of winter sun holiday destinations
    - cheaper travel products, promoted by online booking
    - more frequent and shorter trips
    - greater spontaneity in travel decisions
    - more mobile travel patterns, including multiple-destination trips

- **Challenges for the tourism industry**
  - Improving the quality of tourism and making it a greener product
  - Widening participation to tourism via greater access
  - Being technologically sophisticated using ICTs to meet the needs of the online consumer and changing patterns of consumer behaviour
  - Managing a more diverse industry, with a number of trends occurring simultaneously (e.g. mass tourism, elite tourism, domestic and international tourism, business and leisure travel and full service and no-frills service) and a greater disintermediation brought about by new technology
  - Increased competition between destinations seeking to lure the tourist dollar whilst still aiming to be unique, different and customer focused
  - Changing demographic and economic trends which are challenging existing concepts of tourist motivation, leisure, lifestyle and the meaning of travel and tourism

Sources: Various

INSIGHT 27.1

The senior market: A market opportunity for the global tourism industry?

The senior market is invariably defined as those travellers in middle age (55 years and over). Smith and Jenner (1997) suggested that international arrivals by this group would accounting for over 1:6 of global trips. This 'greying' of the population base of many Western nations are often people who possess significant disposable income and an expectation of increased mobility reflected in greater international travel habits, as life expectancy rises. As Jang and Wu (2006) show, previous studies of the senior market have identified the various travel motivations of this group in terms of:

- rest and relaxation
- social interaction
- physical exercise
- learning
- nostalgia
- excitement
- visiting friends and relatives

and different segments have been identified including passive visitors, enthusiastic go-getters and culture hounds (You and O'Leary 1999).

This reflects a growing activeness of the over-50s, with around one in three taking a holiday in the UK, combined with increasing affluence once the family members have 'fled the nest'. New images of the over-50s age group are epitomized by **SAGA**'s current advertising campaign (Image 27.1) which embodies many of these ideas that life now begins at 50. Indeed, SAGA's innovative advertising to this growing market illustrates how one organization is catering to the needs of a lucrative market. One element of the work of such organizations is to facilitate self-fulfilment among this group, including their desire to be treated as individuals. Their participation in short breaks and long-haul trips as

well as in adventurous holidays certainly questions many of the existing stereotypes of this market. On average the senior population comprise 25 per cent of the population in most countries, with Germany, Italy, France, the UK and Spain having the largest population in this age group in the EU with the following patterns:

- In Germany, 16 per cent of the population is aged 65 or more and by 2014 this will be 20 per cent of the population.
- In France, 16 per cent of the population is over 60 and by 2020 this will be 20 per cent.
- In the UK, 16 per cent of the population is aged over 65 and this will rise to 20 per cent by 2024.

One consequence for the tourism industry is the potential for more tailored, specialist or niche products. Even the US hotel chain, Hilton, has acknowledged the significance of this market in filling leisure capacity at preferential rates, with a Senior Discounts Scheme for over-60s.

"If we have one regret, it's not sending for the brochures sooner."

SAGA
THINK AGAIN

Image 27.1: One of the UK's most prominent tour operators for the over-50 age group is SAGA which has run a very successful media campaign based on the Think Again campaign that has highlighted the active role of this group in international travel. Source: SAGA

airlines, low-cost accommodation and an undeveloped tourism environment offers competition to many established west European destinations. One case in point is the rapid growth of Prague in the Czech Republic as a major urban destination. Coastal destinations like Montenegro also offer an attraction for the adventurous traveller. No one in the early 1980s could have forecast these changes and it illustrates how rapid change can be in tourism where political forces change. Conversely, destinations emerging from political turmoil such as Vietnam after the Doi Moi reforms of 1986 and move to market socialism and current industrial expansion, the rise of the 'new' South Africa and Cambodia can also provide new opportunities for tourism.

The impact of trading blocs such as the EU and NAFTA (the North American Free Trade Agreement) may contribute to a greater harmonization of travel regulations to ease the flow of travel in these new free trade areas. One also needs to recognize that the state is an agent of economic development in many countries where the secondary sector (e.g. traditional manufacturing activities) declined and a greater emphasis was placed on the facilitation of tourism. Among some of the future issues which will impact upon the political acceptability of tourism in different destinations are:

- *community attitudes,* acceptance or non-compliance with a tourism-led strategy for economic development
- *human rights issues,* including labour rights, political oppression and the ongoing civil disturbances and war. Examples are Ethiopia and Sri Lanka where insurgence has compounded the opinion of tourism needing a stable political environment
- *political stability of governments,* notably the ability to plan for tourism and maintain political support for its development, as political ideologies change
- *the role of international tourism companies* and their ability to generate local benefits which make tourism a viable economic proposition rather than simply expropriating all profits from the host country (i.e. investing in the human capital of the destination)
- *the role of the nation state versus the new trading blocs* like the EU, as more members are added and political cooperation challenges existing models of European tourism
- *the role of conflict between nation states* (e.g. the Arab–Israeli conflict) and the wider public perception of instability and tourism
- *newly emerging countries and regions,* such as the 48 states in Latin America, some of which have begun to develop inbound tourism, and their significance in establishing a new image for their countries via tourism development. In this instance, democracy will be a key issue in public acceptability of tourism
- *the significance of political fragmentation* and movements for alternative states within countries and public perception of the role of tourism in adding legitimacy to their claims
- *global politics and international relations* will pose a major challenge to achieving greater political harmony and agreement between countries to ease travel and access which will be counter-balanced by the need to address terrorist threats.

Technological change

Technology and virtual reality have brought major changes to tourism, by potentially replacing the pursuit of the authentic tourism experience with entertainment-based experiences. While there are varied arguments about whether it will have an impact, with the increasing role of technology in the everyday lives of people, it is unlikely to remove the pursuit of 'getting away' to relax in different environments and places. In terms of technology, one of the principal changes occurring globally is the continued growth of artificial environments for tourism and leisure activity. This is reflected in the global theme park industry which has grown to a US$11 billion. a year business, with an estimated 119 major theme parks spread across the world.

In the tourism industry, ICTs have revolutionized the organization, management and day-to-day running of businesses. ICTs have helped to reduce some of the costs of business operations. They have assisted in the globalization of tourism business activity and the impact of the internet is all-embracing. The use of technology in this way will certainly continue as tourism suppliers increasingly target the online booker, providing the flexibility of booking in your own home. Yet according to Ma, Buhalis and Song (2003) in China, there have been numerous obstacles to the growth of e-tourism which is a long way behind the adoption levels in the USA and Europe. Network security, a lack of trust and a different culture in doing business are obstacles to adoption. Watson *et al.* (2004) highlight one of the major constraints in the field of tourism ICTs: they are a highly fragmented series of information systems, generating vast amounts of tourist information that has to be sifted through by the consumer. There is also a lack of technology to support tourists while they are touring. In addition, there is no easy framework whereby tourists can share experiences gained during touring. Watson *et al.* (2004) propose a more interconnected form of technology to meet the tourists needs – *u-commerce*.

U-commerce is defined by Watson *et al.* (2004: 317) as 'the use of ubiquitous networks to support personalized and uninterrupted communications and transactions between an organization and its various stakeholders to provide a level of value over, above and beyond traditional commerce'. This means that the technological solution they propose has four elements beginning with U:

- *ubiquitous*, such as the ubiquity of mobile-phone ownership which reaches a much wider audience than the internet
- *universal*, such as the internet which can be accessed in many ways without a certain type of hardware that universally works on all networks
- *unique*, so it can easily be customized to the needs of each user
- *unison*, where electronic information can be synchronized across a range of devices.

If these features are incorporated into a system, they may help to generate a flow of personalized and useful information for tourists. This may herald the next era of tourism technology to make tourists better informed and able to maximize their time and enjoyment in a destination.

In the transport sector, technological innovations in the way aviation is organized and managed in the future will see cooperation, collaboration and mergers pursued as a key element to reduce costs. One area where this has been achieved in the construction of new aircraft, such as the Airbus 380 which is the focus of Insight 27.2.

Probably one of the most exciting developments in technology is the potential development of **space tourism** (SP). SP has been a widely debated topic since the first moon landing in the 1960s and the Space Tourism Society (www.spacetourismsociety.org) defines the nature of SP as:

- Earth orbit and suborbital experiences
- beyond-Earth orbit experiences (to Mars, for example)
- Earth-based simulations (i.e. Sim Experiences), tourism and entertainment-based experiences such as the NASA centres
- cyberspace tourism experiences.

The concept of SP received a major boost in 2001 when a US businessman, Denis Tito, joined a one-week voyage to an international space station moving the issue from fantasy to fact. Despite the multi-million dollar cost of the experience, a number of SP companies were subsequently founded by multi-billionaires (e.g. Paul Allen, co-founder of Microsoft, and Sir Richard Branson, founder of Virgin Airlines). Their ideas range from building orbital access vehicles, lunar cruise ships to orbital superyachts to reach a much wider market. Much of this is discussed in Spencer (2004), which depicts future scenarios for space tourism.

Changing business practices

What will continue to characterize the tourism industry is the pace and scale of change, with globalization and increased competition the buzz words of the new millennium. The growing trend towards increased efficiency in the tourism industry worldwide has led to the continued expansion of multinational chains providing services in many countries. The hotel industry is a good example of this. The many advantages of such concentration in the different tourism sectors are associated with economies of scale, the ability to resource promotional campaigns and a greater brand awareness using modern marketing techniques such as television, direct mailing and billboards. One of the most profound changes in the business environment, as Page (2005) observed, is the concept of **hypercompetition**, particularly in the international airline industry.

INSIGHT 27.2

Future changes in air travel: The role of technology – the A380

Many forecasts of changes in global air travel recognize that annual growth rates in excess of 5 per cent per annum may pose a significant challenge for airlines and airports in accommodating the level of expected growth. One solution mooted by carriers is the move towards larger aircraft which are currently under development by one leading aircraft manufacturer, the Airbus Industries consortium in Europe. Whilst Boeing examined the viability of such a project, it has focused on aircraft production to meet the medium- to long-haul market, considering that there would only be demand for 400 aircraft larger than a jumbo jet in the next two decades. Its focus is on long-range medium sized aircraft like the new 787 'Dreamliner' to be launched in 2009, with 250 seats and a cost of £60 million. In January 2005 Airbus Industries unveiled the Airbus A380 (Image 27.2) outlining the potential changes that may occur in air travel over the next decade. The A380 is a £10 billion project which will initially be a jet aircraft capable of seating between 555 passengers (with larger versions planned) which compares with the 400–500 seating capacity of Boeing 747 (the 'jumbo jet'). The A380 will have wingspan of 262 foot, a tail fin seven storeys high and, at a cost of £150 million per plane, 50 per cent more space on board than a 747. With a top speed of 565 miles per hour (equivalent to the top speed of a Boeing 747), speed has not had to be sacrificed for size, while the range of the aircraft will be 9000 miles (5 per cent further than a Boeing 747). It also offers fuel savings of 12 per cent over the 747, consuming three litres of fuel per passenger per 100km.

In March 2000, the UK government provided a loan package to Airbus Industries of £530 million to assist in the implementation of the A380 project. One of the major challenges of increased aircraft size is that they will need to fit

into the existing infrastructure (e.g. airport aprons and slots) and the A380 is intended to fit within a 80 × 80m horizontal box so that airports can accommodate the new aircraft without massive redevelopment work. Airbus Industries expect that the A380 will be able to use the existing runways, taxiways and gates although it will place additional pressure on ground-handling facilities, with increased numbers of passengers at check-in gates and in holding areas. The gate-handling facilities will certainly need expanding to accommodate the increased numbers at the gates and ground-handling facilities (e.g. luggage transfer) will have additional pressures placed upon them. Some airport authorities are also concerned about the complementary infrastructure required to serve the needs of passengers to get to and from terminals, where existing airports are already facing growing pains from additional increases in passenger use. In 2005 British Airports Authority was spending £450m to modify Heathrow airport to accommodate the aircraft, since it is only expected to operate on global trunk routes between the world's top 60 airports.

There are varying forecasts on the likely demand for larger aircraft like the A380. Airbus hopes to be able to produce and sell 750 A380s and this is based on the assumption that in the period 1999–2018, world airports will be able to accommodate a 95 per cent increase in daily departures. In terms of the usage of aircraft, the top 25 world airports are expected to absorb 30 per cent of all world air traffic by 2018 and half the aircraft will be used on flights from the top 60 airports, which will be located in North America, Europe and Asia Pacific. In January 2005, some 149 A380s had been ordered, but the aircraft manufacturer needs to have orders for over 250 to cover its research and development costs: over £5.6 billion has already been spent and this could rise even further. One of the largest orders was by Emirates, which signed up in 2000 for 45 A380s. For global airline operators, the A380 is set to revolutionize long-haul travel with the first truly double-decker aircraft, with a lower breakeven point for profitable operation (i.e. 58 per cent load factor compared to 70 per cent for the 747) which increases the potential profit margins for airlines able to fill the seats. Above all, lower operating costs, typically 15–20 per cent below the 747, are expected to give airlines more flexibility on the configuration of seats/on-board facilities as well as the pricing of air travel.

Image 27.2: The new Airbus A380, launched in January 2005. Source: Airbus Industries

Hypercompetition

Within the global marketplace, tourism providers are constantly striving to improve their business performance. This has to be set in the context of wider changes in the operating environment of sectors such as the airline industry, which has confronted a deregulated environment, with state controls lifted to encourage competition. This has seen the role of traditional state airlines, which previously had an oligopolistic position, challenged by new entrants and competitors. D'Aveni (1998) characterized hypercompetition in this sector of the tourism industry in terms of:

- rapid product innovation
- aggressive competition
- shorter product lifecycles
- businesses experimenting with meeting customers' needs
- the rising importance of business alliances
- the destruction of norms and rules of national oligopolies.

The principal changes which hypercompetition induce are related to the way the competitors enter the marketplace and how they disrupt the existing business. They do this in a number of ways:

- by redefining the product market
- by shifting the benchmark on quality
- by offering more at a lower price
- by modifying the industry's purpose and focus by bundling and splitting industries. This can be seen in BA's response to easyJet: establishing a low-cost airline – Go – with a lower cost of operation from London Stansted airport. However, easyJet eventually purchased the company during BA's repositioning and restructuring
- by disrupting the supply chain by redefining the knowledge and know-how needed to deliver the product to the customer, such as exploiting new forms of technology and distribution channels
- by harnessing global resources from alliances and partners to compete with non-aligned business. This is very evident in the international airline industry now that the major global alliances have a greater degree of control over service provision

although running parallel to such trends are global concerns about tourist safety and security, as discussed in Chapter 26.

Global security and safety

The 9/11 Commission Report published in 2003 acknowledged that global terrorism has now made the world a much less safe place for international travel. These security concerns have had a profound effect on the volatility of international tourism demand, as the 9/11 event, the Bali bombing and the consequences of the 2004 tsunami are broadcast by the global media. According to WTTC's (2002) *Travel and Tourism Security Action Plan*, to counter the threat of terrorism on global tourism there needs to be:

- *coordination of policy, actions and communications* so security and safety permeates the entire organization and leads to cooperation among employees and stakeholders. For travel advisers (e.g. travel agents), an informed decision on risks and areas to avoid is necessary rather than blanket negative images
- *measures to ensure a secure operating environment*, including the deployment of biometric measures to defeat terrorism. New technology is vital to implement security requirements
- *measures to deny terrorists the freedom of action*, so communities do not make it easy for terrorists to work within them; employees' grievances in enterprises and community antagonisms should all be addressed

- *access to and work with the best intelligence,* from staff and the public sector and communication to employees. Intelligence needs to flow in all directions, as Figure 27.3 shows (downwards, sideways and upwards).

These four principles highlight how a more vigilant tourism sector can help to reduce the global threat of terrorism.

Issues of concern to tourists

Ethical and moral issues

There is also a growing concern with ethical business practices in tourism which is reflected in the WTO's (1999) development of a *Global Code of Ethics for Tourism,* which is wide ranging as Table 27.3 shows. This is a wider recognition of the understanding and complexity for tourism as an activity which has wide-ranging implications for the tourist, the tourism employee, countries and the natural environment. Linked to these concerns are the legal and moral concerns with the spread of sex tourism and the impact on children, as reflected in the excellent advocacy work of the agency End Child Prostitution and Trafficking (ECPAT).

Sustainability and the environment

The continued interest in tourism and sustainability continues to attract a great deal of interest among tourists, government and the tourism industry. Yet implementing strategies for sustainable tourism and monitoring their effectiveness remains a fundamental stumbling block which the tourism industry has to overcome. For example, consider the reality of countries in South Asia where rapid population growth, images of rural poverty and urbanization exist alongside the government's pursuit of tourism development to gain much-needed foreign currency to assist with development objectives. Whilst existing regional surveys of the area and the respective countries such as India, Pakistan and Bangladesh highlight the range of development problems facing the governments and the policies adopted to deal with them, urbanization is a major problem

'Downwards' – correctly disseminated information and direction must cascade from strategic or global policy-makers at the top, through regional to local levels, and from them to those responsible for security protecting each individual enterprise

'Sideways' – from the industry to its customers, who may well be first to detect a threat, engendering a two-way exchange of information at every level; across the public–private interface, both through formal channels and via 'informal' personal contacts, which must be assiduously cultivated by industry employees at every opportunity; and through close liaison across the industry, which is vital to reduce misunderstanding, eradicating the negative impact of competition and creating a culture of shared common practice

'Upwards' – because employees and customers at the local level will often be the first to pick up the signs that a threat is about to escalate the passage of information from grass roots upwards is of paramount importance. Senior managers must be open to comments and suggestion from below, and must ensure that information they receive is efficiently and rapidly disseminated

FIGURE 27.3   The flow of intelligence in the tourism sector to defeat terrorism. Source: WTTC (2002)

TABLE 27.3 *A Global Code of Ethics for Tourism*

The World Tourism Organization developed a code of ethics for tourism in conjunction with its members, following their initiative to draft a code in 1997. This is a recognition of the need to enshrine many of the principles of global action on the environment and the rights of tourists and workers, considering global legislation from other bodies and outcomes such as Agenda 21.

The basic principles inherent in the code are:

- Tourism's contribution to mutual understanding and respect between peoples and societies
- Tourism as a vehicle for individual and collective fulfilment
- Tourism as a factor of sustainable development
- Tourism as a user of the cultural heritage of mankind and contributor to its enhancement
- Tourism as a beneficial activity for host countries and communities
- Obligations of stakeholders in tourism development
- Rights to tourism
- Liberty of tourist movements
- Rights of the workers and entrepreneurs in the tourism industry
- Implementation of the principles of the *Global Code of Ethics for Tourism*

Source: Adapted from WTO (1999)

associated with each country and poses major concerns for the sustainability of tourism in these environments. The region contains five of the world's 25 largest cities: Bombay (15.1 million population); Calcutta (11.7 million population); Dehli (9.9 million population); Karachi (9.9 million population) and Dhaka (7.8 million population) and rapid urbanization is adding a new series of development problems for South Asia that also impact upon tourism (Image 27.3).

The essential feature of sustainable tourism development identified by the WTTC *et al.* (2002: 11) was

> *The challenge for stakeholders involved in all industries is to find a balance between sustenance, prosperity and people's desire to improve their financial/ material well-being, with the underlying need for identity, community, religion, home and family. Travel and tourism can play a vital role in balancing these forces. It not only provides the livelihoods for both rural and urban communities, but has the capacity, when planned, developed and managed properly, to enhance community relations and build bridges of understanding and peace between nations.*

WTTC *et al.* (2002) suggested governments should:

- *develop a more cooperative approach* among government departments, NTOs, trade associations and the tourism industry
- *integrate tourism policy with environmental policies* to achieve sustainable goals
- *create incentives* for the tourism industry to embark on sustainable initiatives
- *be committed to controlling tourism expansion* and apply environmental taxes fairly
- *encourage policies to promote corporate social responsibility,* so businesses are more rooted in the communities they operate in and have a meaningful relationship with them.

Image 27.3: Urbanization in Asia is creating global cities which will face congestion and pollution problems

WTTC *et al.* (2002) saw the need for tools to monitor and measure progress with achieving sustainability goals. More specifically, individual tourism businesses need to:

- put sustainable development as a core principle of tourism management
- develop and apply more widely certification schemes, such as eco-labelling
- introduce innovative new technology and improve the environmental training and education of staff.

Without more concerted action at government and public–private partnership level and within individual countries, tourism will continue to gain an image as a resource consumer and destroyer.

Managing change in tourism

Managing change in a fast-moving business sector such as tourism will continue to pose enormous challenges for tourism businesses in the twenty-first century. In a practical business setting, management occurs in the context of a formal environment – the organization. But the future shape and nature of global tourism organizations is changing. These organizations are becoming more fluid, moving from being place specific to being more global as ICTs and virtual locations provide opportunities to develop less hierarchical and more interwoven series of webs. The recent restructuring of tourism agencies in Scotland in 2005, removing area tourist boards and unifying the bodies under VisitScotland, has begun that process. Many functions in the VisitScotland network are no longer managed at a regional level, but nationally, regardless of the managerial team's location.

What is critical is the tourism manager's ability to be adaptable and flexible to change as new organizational models develop, particularly, in fast-moving areas like tourism. Change is a modern-day feature of management and any manager needs to be aware of, and able to respond to, changes in the organizational environment. For example, general changes in society such as the decision of a new ruling political party to deregulate the economy, have a bearing on the operation of organizations. More specific factors can also influence the organizational environment including:

- *sociocultural factors*, which include the behaviour, beliefs and norms of the population in a specific area
- *demographic factors*, which are related to the changing composition of the population (e.g. birth rates, mortality rates and the growing burden of dependency in consequence of the increasingly ageing population will have to be supported by a declining number of economically active people in the workforce)
- *economic factors*, which include the type of capitalism at work in a given country and the degree of state control of business. The economic system is also important since it may have a bearing on the level of prosperity and factors which influence the system's ability to produce, distribute and consume wealth
- *political and legal factors* that are the framework in which organizations must work (e.g. laws and practices)
- *technological factors*, where advances in technology can be used to create products more efficiently. The use of information technology and its application to business practices is a case in point
- *competitive factors*, which illustrate that businesses operate in markets and other producers may seek to offer superior services or products at a lower price. Businesses also compete for finance, sources of labour and other resources
- *international factors*, where businesses operate in a global environment and factors operating in other countries may impact on the local business environment.

Change and uncertainty are unpredictable in free market economies, and managers have to ensure that organizations can adapt while ensuring that survival and prosperity is ensured. Change may be vital for organizations to adapt and grow in new environments and the introduction of information technology is one example where initial resistance within businesses had to be overcome. Increasingly, tourism managers are not only having to undertake the role of managing, but also the dynamic role of 'change agent'. Tourism managers have to understand how systems and organizations work and function to create desirable outcomes, often without the experience of how change will affect them. Two illustrations of this are how to develop new niche products and how to foster innovation.

According to Hall (2003: 18) niche tourism concerns:

- identifying and stimulating demand, segmenting consumers into identifiable groups for targeting purposes
- providing and promoting supply, by differentiating products and services from those of competitors.

One example of this has been the development of media-induced tourism, particularly film and television programme locations which can increase visitor numbers by a third in the first year. This may assist with the advertising and promotion of an area using a new image. Yet even this highlights the challenge for tourism managers, where undesired effects may arise from overcrowding, congestion, excessive merchandising, local price inflation and other impacts on local communities. Conversely, the nature of tourism development is such that the ability of other areas/destinations to imitate or copy successful models of development, will limit the lifecycle of new products and innovations. As a result, constant innovation is needed if niche products are to be developed and, ultimately, the niche product of today may end up being the mass product of tomorrow.

Conclusion

This chapter has highlighted a range of issues which are relevant for the tourist and the tourism sector in the new millennium since the pace of change and development in tourism is fast. In contrast, planning and developing new areas for tourist activity is a slower process, with the provision of infrastructure such as an airport expansion taking five to ten years before the benefits are realized. This illustrates the need for tourism managers to be realistic about the ability of resorts and destinations to accommodate visitors, with a view to assessing the appropriate carrying capacity. There are no simple solutions to developing tourism in new areas and in redeveloping tourism in areas that are flagging or have lost their sparkle. Understanding global processes of tourism combined with the individual processes affecting tourism in a given area or location is no substitute for planning. Understanding the consumer is essential and monitoring their needs and what they feel about their tourist experience remains a vital element in the tourism industry understanding

its consumers. What is now being regarded as tourism is constantly expanding as new ideas and new trends develop. What we call and define as 'tourism' is forever changing, and businesses and planners need to have an open mind.

Above all else, anyone working and managing in the tourism industry will need to appreciate the need to implement new human resource policies, and ensure employees are well trained and educated as well as able to cope with change. The tourism industry is an exciting sector to work in, even though some of the glamour and glitz associated with images of working on a tropical island may not always be met in reality. For anyone seeking a challenge and a career in a sector changing rapidly, the tourism industry offers a great deal of interesting and varied work. For the industry, promoting this image and creating a positive image of long-term career structures in both the tourism and hospitality sectors is vital to continue to attract high-calibre staff at all levels.

Discussion questions

1 What are the prospects for developing space tourism?

2 How would you set about forecasting the future market for, and changes in, tourism in a specific destination?

3 Is the future growth of tourism going to be constrained by political events and concerns over safety?

4 Will the tourist of the future be one who is environmentally responsible?

References

Archer, B.H. (1987) 'Demand forecasting and estimation', in J.R.B. Ritchie and C.R. Goeldner (eds) *Travel, Tourism and Hospitality Research*. New York: Wiley.

Bull, A. (1991) *The Economics of Travel and Tourism*. London: Pitman.

Cooper, C., Fletcher, J., Fyall, A., Gilbert, D. and Wanhill, S. (2005) *Tourism, Principles and Practice*. Harlow: Prentice Hall.

D'Aveni, R. (1998) 'Hypercompetition closes in', *Financial Times*, 4 February (global business section).

Frechtling, D. (2002) 'World population and standard of living: Implications for international tourism', in A. Lockwood and R. Medlik (eds) *Tourism and Hospitality in the Twenty First Century*. Oxford: Butterworth-Heinemann.

Hall, D.R. (2003) 'Niche tourism in question: Keynote', in D. Macleod (ed.) *Niche Tourism in Question – Interdisciplinary Perspectives on Problems and Possibilities*. Dumfries: University of Glasgow Crichton Publications.

Jang, S. and Wu, C. (2006) 'Senior's travel motivation and the influential factors: An examination of Taiwanese seniors', *Tourism Management*, 27.

Jefferson, A. and Lickorish, L. (1991) *Marketing Tourism: A Practical Guide*. Harlow: Longman.

Ma, J., Buhalis, D. and Song, H. (2003) 'ICTs and internet adoption in China's tourism industry', *International Journal of Information Management*, 23 (6): 451–67.

Mastyn, L. (2001) *Travelling Light: New Paths for International Tourism*. Washington, DC: Worldwatch.

Müller, H. (2002) 'Tourism and hospitality in the twenty-first century', in A. Lockwood and R. Medlik (eds) *Tourism and Hospitality in the Twenty First Century*. Oxford: Butterworth-Heinemann.

Page, S.J. (2004) 'Airtravel in Asia', *Travel and Tourism Analyst*, May.

Page, S.J. (2005) *Transport and Tourism: Global Perspectives*. Harlow: Prentice Hall.

Page, S. J., Walker, L. and Connell, J. (2005) *Avian Flu: A Pandemic Waiting to Happen*, Report for VisitScotland. Stirling: Dept. of Marketing, University of Stirling.

Poon, A. (1989) 'Competitive strategies for a new tourism', in C.P. Cooper (ed.) *Progress in Tourism, Recreation and Hospitality Management Volume 4*. London: Belhaven.

Smith, C. and Jenner, P. (1997) 'The seniors travel market', *Travel and Tourism Analyst*, 5: 43–62.

Song, H. and Witt, S. (2000) *Tourism Demand Modelling and Forecasting: Modern Econometric Techniques*. Oxford: Pergamon.

Spencer, T. (2004) *Space Tourism: Do You Want To Go?* Burlington, ON: Apogee Books.

Tourism Research Council of New Zealand (2004) *International Visitor Arrival Forecasts 2004–2010*, www.trcnz.govt.nz, accessed 27.1.05.

Watson, R., Akselsen, S., Monod, E. and Pitt, L. (2004) 'The open tourism consortium: Laying the foundations for the future of tourism', *European Management Journal*, 22 (3): 315–26.

Witt, S.F., Brooke, M.Z. and Buckley, P.J. (1991) *The International Management of Tourism*. London: Unwin Hyman.

WTO (World Tourism Organization) (1999) *Global Code of Ethics for Tourism*. Madrid: World Tourism Organization.

WTO (World Tourism Organization) (2001) *Forecasts to 2010*. Madrid: World Tourism Organization.

WTTC (World Travel and Tourism Council) (2002) *Travel and Tourism Security Action Plan*, www.wttc.org, accessed 28.1.05.

WTTC (World Tourism and Travel Council) (2003) *Blueprint for New Tourism*. London: WTTC.

WTTC (World Travel and Tourism Council), International Federation of Tour Operators, International Hotel and Restaurant Association and International Council of Cruise Lines (2002) *Industry as a Partner for Sustainable Development*. London: United Nations Environment Programme/WTTC.

You, X. and O'Leary, J. (1999) 'Destination behaviour of older UK travellers', *Tourism Recreation Research*, 24 (1): 23–34.

Further reading

Lockwood, A. and Medlik, R. (eds) (2002) *Tourism and Hospitality in the Twenty First Century*. Oxford: Butterworth-Heinemann.

Index